James STIRLING

James STIRLING

ADMIRAL AND FOUNDING GOVERNOR
OF WESTERN AUSTRALIA

PAMELA STATHAM-DREW

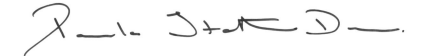

UNIVERSITY OF WESTERN AUSTRALIA PRESS

First published in 2003 by
University of Western Australia Press
Crawley, Western Australia 6009
www.uwapress.uwa.edu.au

Publication of this work was assisted by generous funding from the Western Australian
Department of the Premier and Cabinet. The publisher also gratefully acknowledges
substantial financial support from the Statham-Drews and the UWA Business School, as well
as a grant from the Charles and Joy Staples South West Region Publications Fund to assist
with the cost of cartography.

National Library of Australia
Cataloguing-in-Publication entry:

Statham-Drew, Pamela, 1944– .
    James Stirling: admiral and founding governor of Western Australia.

    Bibliography.
    Includes index.
    ISBN 1 876268 94 8.

    1. Stirling, James, Sir, 1791–1865. 2. Governors—Western Australia—Biography.
    3. Great Britain. Royal Navy—Officers—Biography. 4. Admirals—Great Britain—
    Biography. I. Title.

994.102092

Produced by Benchmark Publications Pty Ltd, Melbourne
Consultant editor: Ross Haig, Perth
Cartography by Camille Cooper and Natalie Ladner, Perth
Index by Anne Batt, Perth
Designed by Sandra Nobes, Tou-Can Design Pty Ltd, Melbourne
Typeset in 11pt Adobe Garamond by Lasertype, Perth
Printed by BPA Print Group

Foreword

Prior to the publication of this biography, Sir James Stirling was the only Founding Governor in Australian history without a full academic biography. As such, this important work fills a void in our understanding of one of this State's most influential forefathers. Pamela Statham-Drew provides a compelling and valuable insight into the man who played a pivotal role in the British Government's decision to colonise the Swan River area, and in shaping that colony.

Stirling's hand is far-reaching, and continues to touch us all today: his decision to split the capital and port, his naming of many prominent landscape features and his laying of the groundwork for Western Australia's early institutions.

Dr Statham-Drew's insight into her subject's formative influences and later achievements—based on official records and the extensive correspondence he wrote and received—allows us to view Stirling's entrepreneurial activities in the broader context of his family, naval and political background.

James Stirling: Admiral and Founding Governor of Western Australia offers a thorough and intriguing account of the character and accomplishments of this key figure in Western Australian history. From this perspective, the author's comprehensive and insightful publication deepens our understanding of the State's defining early years.

And by placing his Swan River Colony years in the context of a long and far-reaching naval career, we can more fully see Stirling's broader contribution in service of the British Empire.

It is my pleasure to congratulate Dr Statham-Drew on her dedicated and enthusiastic research, so clearly evident throughout this outstanding publication on the life of Sir James Stirling.

DR GEOFF GALLOP MLA
PREMIER

This book is dedicated to my father,

Francis West Statham, OBE,

who as Director of the Commonwealth Department of Housing

and Construction 1965–81 brought to fruition Stirling's dream of

a Naval Base in Cockburn Sound

Contents

List of Illustrations

Colour plates

between pages 80 and 81 (sequentially):

Mount Eliza; view from Fraser's Point; bivouac on the Swan;
    Swan River at start of fresh water; red bank on the Swan; preparing to
    encamp for the night; near the river's head; encampment at the head
    of the river; view across coastal plain; view from Mount Eliza,
    setting camp at Clause's lagoon; King George's Sound

between pages 448 and 449 (sequentially):

Belmont House, painted in 1882, and map of estate; Ellen Stirling c. 1840;
    Mary Mangles; Anne and Andrew Stirling and sons Walter, John, Charles,
    William and James; Stirling's presentation sword and scabbard, and
    commemorative snuff box

Maps

Acknowledgments

THIS BOOK HAS taken many years to complete and has involved a large number of people—and to all of them I owe heartfelt thanks and beg to be excused any omissions. First and foremost, I would like to thank the Stirling relatives who have given so much of their time, records and photos. The book could never have been as revealing without their support—particularly direct descendants, the Hon. Lavinia Fleming and her daughter Charlotte, and Edward Buckley, who really instigated this project. From brother John's line (source of most of the records) I owe a huge debt to Margaret Lenfestey, who allowed us to use their filing cabinet full of handwritten letters before depositing them safely in St Andrews University Library, and to her husband Richard, who spent hundreds of hours preparing the draft index. Marion Leeper, another descendant from the same line, together with her husband Finian and brother Frank Stirling, have helped in many ways, particularly with photographs and portraits.

For early research I am deeply appreciative of the unstinting assistance of Dr Pennie Pemberton, who still reads Stirling's handwriting better than I do, while for later help I am grateful for the prompt and detailed responses provided by Public Records Office researcher Tim Hughes at Kew, London. For help in Western Australia I am indebted to Gillian O'Mara—particularly in untangling Stirling's land grants. In Britain John Pile generously allowed us to use his research into the Belmont Estate, while John Squires did the same for Henley Park. Lyn Clark gave us access to her research into Woodbridge, as well as proofreading the entire volume with the help of her companion, Nig Thomas, and sister, Alwin Clark. Walter and Jo Wilcox have been a tower of strength in Guildford locating material, proofreading, operating as post office, and providing a long-distance computer help line.

Throughout the entire project I have been wonderfully supported by the Economics Department at The University of Western Australia. Although biography is somewhat off the Economic History agenda, the book stemmed from my Ph.D. research and successive heads of department, especially Professors Reg Appleyard, Paul Miller and Ken Clements, have strongly encouraged me—and approved travel and study leave grants. The department also provided generous financial assistance ($8,000) towards publication costs—which was matched by the Dean of the Business School, Professor Paul McLeod. I am also very grateful for the help and encouragement of Economics Department secretary Helen Reidy, who has done a lot of typing and copying, and Administrative secretary Glenys Walter, who helped me sort out accounts.

Clearly the staff of many institutions and libraries have been involved, and to all I extend heartfelt thanks. For assistance in the complex realm of illustrations I am particularly grateful to Belinda Corrigan of Heytesbury Gallery; Julie Martin at Battye Library and Jessica Morris of State Records Office of Western Australia; Jenny Moroney at the Western Australian Museum; Melanie Morgan at the Art Gallery of Western Australia; Jennifer Broomhead at Mitchell Library, New South Wales; Sylvia Carr at the National Library; Julian Pooley and Mary Mackay at the Surrey History Centre; Chris Rich at the National Maritime Museum; Christopher James of Torosay Castle, Mull; and Mrs Stirling Aird of Kippenross, Dunblane, Scotland. For first-class photography of items and portraits I am also very grateful for the help of Murray Glover and Simon Jauncey (UK) and Victor France (WA).

To our State Governor, His Excellency Lieutenant General John Sanderson AC, I owe a huge debt. From the moment he saw the huge initial manuscript he has done everything possible to assist its publication—even approaching the Premier on my behalf. The $25,000 grant to University of Western Australia Press from the State Government made publication of this large book possible, and I am deeply grateful.

I would also like to acknowledge a grant from the Charles and Joy Staples South West Region Publications Fund of $1,000 towards mapping costs. Charlie Staples was a good friend and encouraged me to write this book, and I have benefited from his early detailed research into the history of south west Australia.

UWA Press has done a magnificent job in publishing the book and I would especially like to thank Sam Wilson for her anchor role. To Natalie Ladner and Camille Cooper, who have drawn most of the maps for this book, my warmest commendation. They have done a superb job (in between final exams) and cheerfully undertook dozens of requests for change. I must also thank my editor, Ross Haig, who, like my husband, has eaten and slept with Stirling for months as well as grappling with me, ever so politely, over wording.

Finally, I must thank my husband, Nick Drew, who has been part of the project since our wedding day. Without his constant support, encouragement and calm commonsense this book might never have seen the light of day.

PAMELA STATHAM-DREW
April 2003

Conversion Table

REFERENCES TO WEIGHTS and measures are given in the way in which they were expressed at the time, in imperial units. Conversions to the metric system are as follows:

1 acre	0.405 hectare
1 square mile	2.59 square kilometres
1 inch	25.4 millimetres
1 foot	30.5 centimetres
1 yard	0.914 metre
1 mile	1.61 kilometres
1 fathom (6 feet)	1.8 metres
1 ounce	28.3 grams
1 pound	454 grams
1 ton	1.02 tonnes
1 gallon	4.55 litres

CURRENCY

Australian currency changed from pounds, shillings and pence to dollars and cents in 1966. Because of variations in currency values over time, actual conversions are difficult. At the time of the currency changeover, the following conversions applied:

1 penny (1d)	1 cent
1 shilling (1s)	10 cents
10 shillings (10s)	1 dollar
1 pound (£1)	2 dollars
1 guinea	2 dollars and 10 cents

I

The Formative Years

1791–1805

JAMES STIRLING, FUTURE Admiral, Knight and founding Governor of Western Australia, was born on 28 January 1791 at Drumpellier, a beautiful estate in Lanarkshire, near Glasgow in Scotland. He was the fifth son of Andrew and Anne Stirling, who were second cousins of the same surname, so he was a Stirling through and through. From his mother's side he inherited a strong naval tradition and a link with America through his Philadelphia-born grandmother. From his father's side came a vested interest in all aspects of the textile trade, a staunch Whig tradition, an enviable Scottish pedigree and enormous family pride.[1] Andrew often reminded his children they were descendants of one of the oldest untitled families in Europe[2] who could trace their ancestry from Willielmus de Strivelyn, named in the early twelfth century *Chartulary of Glasgow* as the rightful owner of lands in the county of Lanark.[3] Over generations these lands had been lost, but it was a matter of great pride that Andrew had been able to purchase Drumpellier, near the heart of this Lanark land, in 1779.[4]

James knew neither of his grandfathers, but he definitely heard stories about both of them. His maternal grandfather, Sir Walter Stirling, had been a dashing naval officer who had wooed and won the daughter of a wealthy Philadelphian merchant, Charles Willing. Somewhat against the family's wishes he brought his Dorothea back to live in London, where she charmed his peers. He had a distinguished career, having been made 'The Regulating Captain of the Impress at the Tower',[5] knighted for naval pursuits against the Dutch, and then appointed Commander-in-Chief at the Nore.[6] James' mother liked to tell the story of how her father had lost the chance to be Governor of Halifax because he had been visiting her in Scotland when that offer came in.[7] Her young sons, however, were more impressed with the story of how Grandfather had persuaded the reluctant Nelson family to allow young Horatio to enter the navy.[8]

It was also a matter of pride that King George III, after reviewing Sir Walter's ships at the Nore, was so impressed that he had offered to make him a baronet— which he declined. It was subsequently claimed, and taken up, by his eldest son, also Walter, who thereby became the first Baronet of Faskine. Walter turned to banking and therefore did not have the spirited stories to tell his nephews that their mother's other brother, Charles, could spin. Charles had followed his father into the navy and was a favourite with all Anne's children—who referred to him as 'the Admiral' long before he attained that status.

Anne (James' maternal grandmother) Family Tree *(surviving children only)*

Sir Walter STIRLING (1718–86) m Dorothea Willing (1735–82)

Walter (1758–1832)	**Charles** (1760–1833)	**ANNE** (1762–1830)
Banker & MP, 1st Baronet of Faskine	Admiral, Sir	m 1778
m 1794	m 1789	**ANDREW**
Susannah Goodenough	Charlotte Grote	**STIRLING**

Stories from father Andrew's side of the family were just as interesting.

Andrew (James' paternal grandfather) Family Tree *(surviving children only)*

William STIRLING (1717–77) m Mary Buchanan (172?–1806)
21st Baron of Cadder

Marion	**ANDREW**	John	Elizabeth	James	Agnes
b 1750	b 1751	b 1752	b 1758	b 1760	b 1763
m	d 1823	d 1811		d 1822	
Robert	m **ANNE**	m Janet	m Will'm	m Marg't	m Dug'ld
Mackay	**STIRLING**	Bogle	Hamilton	Murdoch	Bannatyne

Grandfather William had served in Bonnie Prince Charlie's army in 1745 and fought at Culloden,[9] but he had then returned to Glasgow where he founded the first large-scale textile bleaching and printing works. His company, William Stirling & Sons, had prospered, trading printed textiles widely in the United Kingdom and overseas.[10] At one stage he had been ranked among the 'Young Virginians', so known for founding the 'mercantile greatness of Glasgow' by trading textiles for tobacco from the southern American plantations.[11] William had then married the daughter of another of the Virginians, Andrew Buchanan, and in so doing had restored his family's connection to the Lanark lands. Andrew Buchanan purchased the Drumpellier estate in 1730 and, when he died in 1759, the estate passed to his eldest son, James Buchanan, one-time Lord Provost of Glasgow and William Stirling's brother-in-law. Together these two wealthy and influential men managed to break the coal monopoly that was impoverishing Glasgow in the 1760s. They achieved it

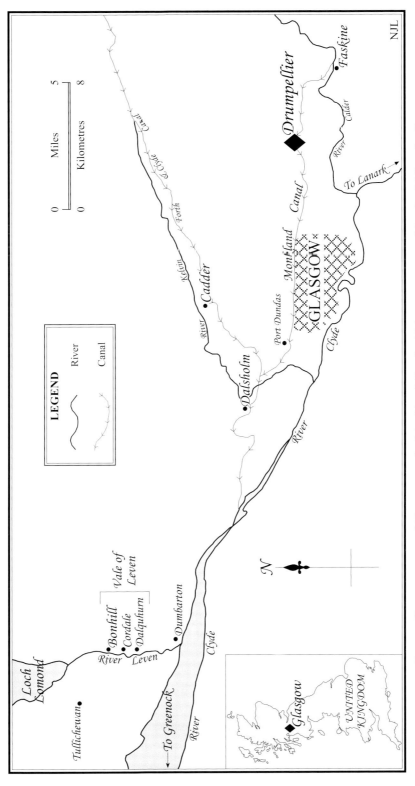

Drumpellier estate, east of Glasgow on the Monkland Canal which was part-owned by the Stirling family

by forming a share-based company, given Royal Assent in 1770, to build the Monkland Canal to introduce coal from another source.[12]

Designed by famous inventor James Watt just before his steam discoveries,[13] the Monkland Canal ran through the Drumpellier estate, for which Buchanan was handsomely compensated.[14] But in 1777 Buchanan was brought to the brink of bankruptcy by the loss of his Virginian plantations during the American War. When forced to sell Drumpellier he had turned to the Stirlings, but as grandfather William had died in May of that year it was his eldest son Andrew, James' father, who had agreed to the purchase over a period of three years. Father Andrew was then living with his mother and sisters at Bonhill, near the family's new printing works on the River Leven, while his younger brothers John and James managed the older works at Dalsholm on the Kelvin River. Andrew at this time was also contemplating marriage, having fallen in love with his youthful cousin Anne, whom he had met when escorting his sister to London the previous year.

From all accounts a beautiful and captivating young woman, Anne was just 15 when she married Andrew, 12 years her senior, in June 1778. Andrew would later advise all his sons to marry very young women, considering them more natural, and unspoiled by society. His 'Lovely Nan' was, nonetheless, well educated, with a knowledge of languages, enough mathematics to keep track of the family finances, and a fluent writing style. Whenever parted, she wrote to her husband regularly and throughout her life kept in touch with all twelve of her children who survived to adulthood, though they scattered widely. Through her correspondence and warm personality, Anne created strong family bonds and a sense of mutual obligation, but she also fostered gaiety and wit. As a young adult James was to comment that 'Our family is so different to the rest of the World, and a person feels so open and so much interest when with them that the change on leaving it is too great, it is like a move from Italy to Russia covered in snow'.[15]

Anne's first two children came quickly. The eldest, William, was born at her parents' home in London on 18 March 1779, while Walter was born on 20 November 1780 in an apartment Andrew had taken in Glasgow. Financial problems associated with the Monkland Canal had made it difficult for Andrew to meet the last payments due on Drumpellier. With help from Anne's father the deal was completed,[16] and plans were made for refurbishing the stone mansion-house. 'Drumpellier House' had been built in 1741 by Andrew Buchanan, who had transformed the entire estate into 'a landscaped pleasure ground, parklike in the manner of Capability Brown, [with] a loch and a Swanhouse'.[17] The family had moved in by April 1782 when Anne's third child and first daughter, Dorothea, was born. Grandmother travelled from London to visit her namesake as soon as the weather improved, but Anne was shocked to find her mother suffering a 'gradual decay of the nervous system'.[18] There had apparently been an estrangement between Dorothea and her Philadelphia relatives which so depressed her that she lost the will to live, and died at Drumpellier in September 1782, aged only 45.[19]

Stone-built 'Drumpellier House' and (inset) parents Anne and Andrew Stirling

Courtesy Clayton Zeidler (house); Margaret Lenfestey and Marion Leeper (portraits c. 1790s)

This loss seemed to trigger a period of bad luck for the Drumpellier family. The Monkland Canal Company was in debt and badly needed more capital. It was decided to sell more shares and William Stirling & Sons, who were already large shareholders, purchased the majority of those on offer.[20] The brothers pushed ahead with spirit, injecting enough capital over the next two years to extend the canal east to the Calder and, in conjunction with the Great Canal Company, west to Port Dundas.[21] Its principal trade was to take coal to the city from the collieries at Faskine, near Drumpellier. Andrew seems to have been the prime mover in canal affairs while his younger brothers, John (later of Tillichewan)[22] and James (later of Stair),[23] continued to manage the textile businesses. But split responsibilities put a strain on the relationship between the brothers.

Between 1783 and 1785 Anne gave birth to two more daughters, neither of whom survived.[24] John, the third son, was born at Drumpellier on 7 October 1786 and christened in Old Monklands Church, but parental celebration was cut short by the news that Anne's father, Sir Walter, had died in London aged 68. A year later, in October 1787, there was another tragedy when 5-year-old Dorothea died of a fatal head injury, possibly due to a fall from a horse, as father Andrew insisted that all the children were taught to ride at an early age. Early in 1788 Andrew took the still grieving and again pregnant Anne to London, renting a house at Greenwich.

Another daughter was born mid-year, but died soon afterwards in Greenwich hospital. The following year things began to look up.

At Drumpellier, on 30 September 1789, Anne gave birth to her fourth son, Charles, who thrived. Father Andrew's previously stretched finances began to improve and he was able to purchase the 280-acre coal-rich Faskine estate in 1790, raising some of the money by selling 80 acres back to the canal company.[25] So it was into a far more financially secure world that James was born early in 1791.

An entry in the Family Bible records the event thus: 'at 11 o'clock at night on Friday the 28th of January 1791 our son James was born at Drumpellier'.

James was Andrew and Anne's fifth son and ninth child, but to this time only males had survived. None of these boys were given a second name. William was by this stage 12, Walter 11, John 5, and Charles only 2. The older pair were no doubt present in October that year when their father's dream of joining the Monkland Canal to the Clyde and Forth was finally realised.[26] The canal ran right through the Drumpellier property, providing constant fascination for the small boys and probably extending their maritime interests—already stimulated by the seafarers in their mother's family.

James was the baby of the family for only eighteen months, as Anne gave birth to another daughter, Anna Hamilton,[27] at Drumpellier on 2 September 1792. This daughter proved healthy. With canal business apparently sorted out and his Faskine coal fields producing well, father Andrew was becoming restless, eager for new challenges. In October 1792 he withdrew from William Stirling & Sons to form, in partnership with a John Hunter, an extensive commission house in London designed to sell Scottish goods, predominantly textiles.[28] The firm was registered as Stirling, Hunter & Co. and operated from premises at Bow Church Yard, the centre of the London textile trade.[29] Andrew was also becoming more interested in Whig politics, receiving a thankyou letter in December from the Saltmarket Society 'for obtaining a more equal representation in Parliament' and so championing their cause.[30]

With business interests now in London and Scotland, Andrew moved frequently between Drumpellier and Bow Church Yard—quite a feat given the transport difficulties of the day—whereas Anne remained most of the time at Drumpellier with 'the infantry', as she wryly called her growing brood.[31] She was pregnant almost every year, having another daughter on 28 December 1793. This child was named Dorothea Willing in memory of her American Mama. A year later, on 19 January 1795, she gave birth to a sixth son, Andrew, while the seventh son, Robert Mackie, arrived on 9 April 1796. So James grew up in a noisy, cheerful nursery with a great deal of freedom. By the time he was 5 his two eldest brothers had completed their schooling and been sent to join their father in London. Anne kept in constant touch with her separated family, writing almost weekly with typical motherly concern. When John, aged 10, went to join Walter in London she was concerned that they must surely need new coats. She wrote '…we can't afford to be fine but must all go clean and whole for credit's sake', ending with the endearment 'Jimmy [James], Dorothea, Andrew and the little one [Robert] in Status Quo'.[32]

James' Immediate Family

(surviving children only)

ANDREW m ANNE 1778

William	Walter	John	Charles	**JAMES**	Anna
b 1779	b 1780	b 1786	b 1789	b 1791	b 1792
d 1850	d 1864	m Eliz.	m Ch'lotte	m **ELLEN**	m Sir J
		Willing	Stirling	**MANGLES**	Home
		d 1853	d 1867	d 1865	d 1866
Dorothea	Andrew	Robert	Edward	Mary Noel	Agnes
b 1793	b 1795	b 1796	b 1797	b 1798	b 1799
d 1841	d 1816	d 1829	d 1873	m Henry	d 1873
				Halsey	
				d 1834	

Each of the Stirling boys received a sound education. At Drumpellier their early lessons, under the watchful eye of Miss Wallis, the governess, included an introduction to French which Anne felt was important for all her children. But the boys were pushed further in schools chosen for academic excellence. The oldest went to schools in Glasgow, and all were sent in turn, through the influence of Uncle Charles, for a period of training on board one of Britain's warships. This was a recognised way of introducing young boys of good family to a naval career. The boys, usually aged between 9 and 13, were known as 'young gentlemen' and served in uniform as cabin and messenger boys for the Captain. They were made to practise their writing and were taught practical skills such as navigation, calculation of speed and distance, the use of various sails and knots, and keen observation. James' brother John had been sent for a stint as a 'young gentleman' with his Uncle Charles, then Captain of the *Jason,* in January 1797. In a candid letter to brother Walter, the 11-year-old remarked that 'I was something like a fresh water sailor at first, but soon got the better of it…'[33]

Uncle Charles had an enormous influence on all the boys—and James in particular. They were told stories of famous naval battles, with graphic details of red-hot lead shot, broken rigging, ship battle lines and clever strategy. Of them all, his account of the 'Glorious First of June' 1794, when Admiral Lord Howe had bested the French fleet in the first decisive naval battle of the French Wars,[34] was indelibly imprinted on their minds.

While John was still at sea, there had been another addition to the Drumpellier nursery. Anne and Andrew's eighth son, Edward, was born on 8 May 1797. Young James was not totally bereft of his older brothers' company at this time

'Uncle Charles', Admiral Charles Stirling, James' uncle and mentor

Courtesy Marion Leeper

as William, the eldest, had returned to Glasgow to attend university and often
visited the family. Occasionally, too, Anne took the entire family to London,
staying either at a house in Surrey Street, taken as a base for the older boys, or at
Greenwich, which Andrew felt was more beneficial for his wife's health and where
the family spent the Easter of 1798. Anne was pleased to have everyone together,
and for the younger children it was an ideal time for play and bonding. Walter, she
observed, favoured his 7-year-old brother James, although 'Jimmy' in turn did not
always pay the desired 'profound attention' to her second eldest son's commands
that he desired.[35]

When Anne returned with the little ones to Scotland a month later, she left
Charles and James behind in London under the watchful eye of Mrs Rogers, the
housekeeper, to experience life in the Bow Church Yard agency business with their
father. The business primarily handled the sale and export of textiles printed by the
Glasgow Stirlings, but it also purchased raw textiles for the company and acted as a
clearing house for other Scottish goods. The boys would have seen the bolts of
material stacked in the warehouses and listened as their father and older brothers
arranged shipments to various ports in Europe and America. They would also have
heard of the increasing competition that Scottish linens were receiving from cotton,
which was then being produced in greater quantities in Lancashire.

James was not to see London again until 1799, by which time his mother had given birth to her fifteenth child, Mary Noel, on 27 August 1798. The second London visit was occasioned by trouble in the Bow Church Yard business, for the increasing worries of her husband and older sons caused Anne to move quickly to provide support. A sudden fall in produce prices early in 1799 had meant merchants in the West Indian trade could not pay the £95,000 they owed Stirling, Hunter & Co.[36] When Andrew's partner, John Hunter, decided to leave the business in October 1799, it was teetering on the brink of bankruptcy. In addition, the company owed £50,000 to the bankers Hodsall and Stirling, whose namesake, Anne's brother Walter, was not prepared to grant favours.

To a large extent this financial crisis washed over James and the younger children as they continued school lessons at the Surrey Street house.[37] They missed the freedom of Drumpellier, and especially their favourite dogs and horses.[38] They seldom saw their older brothers, for William and Walter lived above the Bow Church Yard business, John remained at Newland College, Glasgow, and Charles had become a 'young gentleman' with Uncle Charles. It was an exciting time to join the navy, for word had just come through of Lord Nelson's famous victory at the Battle of the Nile in August 1798, and, as Uncle Charles knew many of the officers involved, his nephews would have heard all the details.

As the old century drew to completion, so did the Stirling family. Anne, now 36 and pregnant for the last time, gave birth to her sixteenth child, a daughter named Agnes, on 8 November 1799. James now had four older and three younger brothers, and four younger sisters with whom he would remain in frequent contact all his life. Family solidarity was strong, even though they were seldom together, and each member appears to have been given a feeling of self-worth. All were brought up as Anglicans, though church was more a familiar background than a formative influence. Anne and Uncle Charles encouraged all of them to write well and fluently, to value education and travel, to aim for independence of thought, and to be optimistic in outlook. They also taught them to strive to be amusing, as it was thought to be good for the spirit and eased social tensions. Father Andrew, on the other hand, emphasised honour and duty, and the need to be worthy of the family name. He insisted on social correctness, but believed also that they had a responsibility to society. As he spent less time with his younger sons, Andrew possibly had less influence on James than Uncle Charles, but the latter held similar beliefs. What father Andrew did pass on was a tall, strong physique, black eyes and a restless energy and enthusiasm for life. Financial problems were to beleaguer the family over the next few years, and shape the fortunes of all the younger boys. But the pride, security and peace that life at Drumpellier gave them in their childhood was to help them all weather the coming storms.

By 1800 father Andrew was earning a reasonable income from the coal on his Faskine estates, shipping some 50,000 carts down the Monkland Canal per annum.[39] But the coal mines were a constant source of friction between Andrew and his brothers, who were the other canal shareholders. All had poured considerable sums into the venture, but it was yet to show a dividend. Andrew's brothers felt that toll charges for using the canal should be raised to clear a profit, something that Andrew, as a major user, stoutly resisted, and the argument escalated into litigation. As a distraction Andrew turned to politics, putting himself forward (unsuccessfully) as a candidate for Dumbarton in Scotland.[40] It was possibly this interest in politics that led Andrew to enrol James at Westminster school,[41] the first English school chosen by the Stirlings for their sons, and which then had some 300 boys.

Westminster was known for its scholastic traditions and also, at this stage, for its Whig leanings.[42] James was first enrolled in 1801, the last year presided over by the headmaster, Dr William Vincent, who had held the post since 1788. The amply cassocked Vincent was known as a flogger, but admired by his boys for the sonorous sentences he delivered while pacing up and down 'like a captain on his quarter deck'.[43] To enter the school, 10-year-old James would have had to satisfy a panel of scholars that he was literate and knew 'by heart the 8 parts of speech'.[44] The curriculum at this time contained only Latin, Greek and religious exercises—there was no French, writing or arithmetic, except as 'extras on half days'. Dressed in knee breeches, stockings and a full-length monastic-style gown, the boys underwent about nine hours of study six days a week, watched closely by senior boys acting as monitors. Daily lessons included

> the testing of grammar, repetition of passages from memory, translation, prose and verse composition both from given passages and on set themes…and the extraction by the boys of expressions, phrases, terms of speech, antitheses, epithets, synonyms, proverbs, likeness, comparisons, narratives, descriptions of time, place and persons, fables, bon mots, schemes and apothegms. The weariness of this routine was recognised: boys could formally request permission to 'dor'—drop his head on his hand for sleep. All proceedings in the schoolroom had to be in Latin, and speaking English there was punishable.[45]

Relief came with meals at 8 and 11 a.m. and 6 p.m., although during lunch and dinner there were readings in Latin from Old and New Testaments. The firm grounding in Latin was highlighted every year in the 'Latin Play', a reference point in the calendar of fashionable London life. Every play was introduced with a prologue by the headmaster, elegantly reviewing the year, and ended with an epilogue, written generally by an old boy and consisting of satirical comment upon topical events, spoken by the cast, 'and…presented in a Roman perspective'.[46]

Being a new boy, James would have been accountable to all senior boys, as well as being linked with one as a personal fag. At the end of their first year, students were required to write doggerel verses about the seniors they had served in preceding months, and recite them before the rest of the scholars. 'Though the event was a rowdy ordeal, performed by candlelight on top of a pyramid of furniture with the audience trying to put out the candles with missiles, it was accepted the junior had complete liberty to express his views of his senior and the senior was bound to accept them without reprisal',[47] which provided some guarantee of a curb on a senior's conduct.

The most harrowing event of the school year was 'the Challenge', six to eight weeks of oral examinations which determined each student's academic rank. Except for the top form, boys examined one another and immediately replaced the one above if the slightest mistake was detected in reciting Latin and Greek passages. It was an excellent training in memory which was to serve James, and his classmates, very well. Amongst those at Westminster with James was the future Bishop of Adelaide, Augustus Short, and the future Colonial Office Secretary and Prime Minister, Lord John Russell, while the renowned colonial reformer, Edward Gibbon Wakefield, and the Earl of Stradbroke's son, Henry Rous (who would become a particular navy friend), were to join the school before James left.[48]

Even in his first year James would have been exposed to the fighting that was part of school life in the very early years of the nineteenth century. But it was good training. By the time a boy left 'he was invariably handy with his fists and a good judge of pugilistic form in others'.[49] This no doubt assisted James when he left the

Typical uniform as worn at Westminster school in early 1800s

From John Field, The King's Nurseries

school at the end of 1801 for his turn as a 'young gentleman' in the Royal Navy, under the watchful eye of Uncle Charles. He returned to Westminster in May 1803 with his older brother Charles[50] to face his final 'Challenge', which he apparently passed well enough to leave the school at the end of 1803.

By this stage James had acquired sufficient grounding in Latin, Greek and French to form the basis for a facility in foreign languages that he was known for in later life. Moreover, between the age of 10 and 13 he had been trained to be adaptable, having been moved from the countrified life of Drumpellier to the hustle and bustle of central London, the elite academic regime at Westminster and, briefly in between, to the regimental discipline of the navy.

Whether James had any aspirations in other career directions when he left school is unknown. Straitened family financial circumstances constrained his choices. Owing some £140,000, father Andrew had withdrawn from the London agency, leaving it to his eldest sons, William (now 25) and Walter (24) to trade as Stirling Brothers & Co. His financial affairs were then placed under inspectors,[51] and he returned to Scotland. All the boys now had to earn their keep and help the family, and for James the navy was the only profession in which all-important family connections could help advance his prospects. Unfortunately, Uncle Charles was not in a position to provide immediate assistance as he had been appointed Resident Commissioner of Jamaica in the middle of 1802 and was still there. However, he had arranged for James to be taken on as a 'young gentleman' under Captain John Ayscough, and on 16 July 1803 (in the school summer break) James was entered on the books of the HMS *Camel*, aged 13, as a 'No Bounty Volunteer' (i.e. unpaid).[52]

Captain Ayscough thought enough of his young volunteer to offer him a place when he left school. On 14 January 1804 James entered the navy as a First Class Volunteer on the storeship *Camel*, bound luckily enough for the West Indies.[53] His uncle's Jamaican post gave James opportunities not normally offered to such a junior officer, but his background stood him in good stead and he seems to have been well accepted and liked by his ship's company. Whilst based in Jamaica James also served on *L'Hercule* under the flag of Sir John Duckworth, one of the heroes of the 'Glorious First of June', but it was on the *Camel* that he did his training for Midshipman.

On 20 January 1805, just eight days before his 14th birthday, James passed his midshipman tests and ended his days as a volunteer.[54] Now he would be paid.

2

Naval Training: an Eye for Detail

Soon after passing his midshipman tests, James was posted to the HMS *Prince George,* joining the ship on 1 March 1805. Uncle Charles had been recalled to England late in 1804 to resume active duty, but had assured his nephew that when he received a new command he would request his transfer. On reporting to the Admiralty, Uncle Charles found he had been promoted to Rear Admiral and given command of the HMS *Glory 98,* flagship of the Rochefort squadron, and one of the famous ships involved in the First of June 1794 action.[1] At the Admiral's request James was transferred to the *Glory,* joining as Midshipman on 27 June 1805,[2] just in time to witness some exciting action.

On 15 July Admiral Sir Robert Calder had joined the squadron and ordered the *Glory,* with some nineteen other ships of the line, to take on the combined French and Spanish Fleet returning from the West Indies. This action, for which Calder was subsequently court-martialled, took place just off Cape Finisterre (the extreme north-west tip of Spain) on 22 July. Bad weather and poor positioning made it an indecisive clash (which was refought and won by Nelson at Trafalgar three months later), but it was a first battle experience for James.[3] Despite being kept behind the action, he heard the roar of the cannons and saw and smelt their acrid smoke, finding himself more excited than afraid. The squadron thereafter returned to England with two captured Spanish vessels,[4] soon heading out again on a course that the young Midshipman later described to his brother John as confusing. 'No one I believe in the ship but the Admiral knows where we are bound', he wrote, adding 'I know nothing of any of the family and consequently I must hope you will not be offended if you do not receive a letter for a long time'.[5]

Perhaps it was just as well that James had had no family news for some time, as their financial worries had, if anything, intensified.[6] Almost all Andrew's property except the Faskine coal land and the Drumpellier home farm had been sold. The farm was rented, but for how long was uncertain—it too might have to go. But by the time James heard this, it paled against the glorious news of the fleet's victory at Trafalgar on 21 October 1805. Every detail of the battle, and of Nelson's brave words

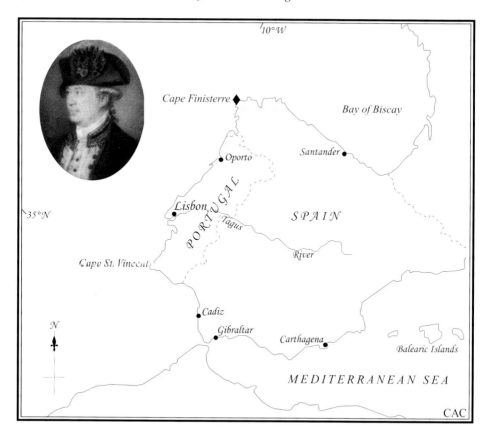

Cape Finisterre, where young Midshipman Stirling first saw battle action.
(Inset) Admiral Charles Stirling

and untimely death, would have been discussed and acclaimed by the young officers, to whom he was a hero. The victory at Trafalgar quieted naval activities for a time, but ships of war were still occupied in surveillance and checking any suspected supply runs. When a non-allied ship was captured and brought into a British port, the navy paid 'prize money' to the captain responsible, and this was generally shared out among the crew on a coded scale, providing a very welcome addition to their somewhat meagre pay.[7] Throughout the remainder of the war years James was to able to save a quite considerable sum from such sources.

In July 1806 Rear Admiral Charles Stirling had been given a new commission and a new ship, and James was again transferred with him, leaving HMS *Glory* on 17 July and next day joining the 64-gun HMS *Sampson*, where he was to serve as Midshipman for just over five months.[8] Uncle Charles' new orders were to proceed with a convoy to Buenos Aires, where Admiral Sir Home Popham had come unstuck. Popham had captured Cape Town from the Dutch half a year earlier (in January 1806), but then following intelligence that the people of Montevideo and Buenos Aires were discontented under Spanish rule, and anticipating trade benefits, he planned to seize those cities. In so doing he set in motion events that would result in his court martial 'for embroiling his country in a war of his own making'.[9]

In April Popham had taken his fleet—and some 1,200 soldiers of the 71st Regiment under the command of Brigadier-General W. C. Beresford,[10] from Cape Town to Buenos Aires, which they captured after a reasonably easy surprise attack. Popham had then sent home a glowing account of 'Britain's new possession' which delighted the British public (and some ministers), as South America was still associated with untold riches. Arrangements were immediately made to reinforce Britain's presence in the area. General Auchmuty was ordered to take army troops out to reinforce Beresford, and Rear Admiral Charles Stirling was ordered to take out a convoy of troop ships, transports and naval men-of-war to replace Popham, who was to return home.

Leaving England on 28 August 1806, Stirling's convoy ran into bad weather, and within a fortnight the Admiral's log showed a mounting concern with illness among his men.[11] The first death on the *Sampson* occurred on 27 September and sixty-four other crew were under the surgeon.[12] By 15 October the Admiral noted that 'most scratches turn to ulcers', and bilious complaints were getting worse.[13] How 15-year-old James fared is unknown. It was not until 10 November that the surgeon decided the problem was caused by poor drinking water. By this time the *Sampson* had intercepted a Portuguese brig bearing the news that Buenos Aires had been retaken by the Spanish on 12 August, which reduced the urgency of arriving with reinforcements and allowed the Admiral to make a detour in search of fresh water. On 13 November he went into Rio de Janeiro and negotiated with the Portuguese for water from their single source of supply, a fountain fed by an aqueduct.[14] While waiting for it to be loaded, the Admiral made a thorough investigation of the potential and defence capabilities of the land around Rio de Janeiro before leaving on 19 November.

Just before Christmas 1806 the *Sampson* reached the River Plate and anchored off Montevideo.[15] But instead of a smooth transition of power from a disgruntled Popham, Admiral Stirling actually had to order his predecessor to leave. He then transferred his flag from the *Sampson* to Popham's ship, HMS *Diadem,* once more taking James with him.[16] As soon as he had taken stock of the situation, Admiral Stirling decided any naval effort against Montevideo or Buenos Aires would be futile, as the shallow River Plate would not allow ships to get near enough to use their guns. Accordingly, he ordered some of his ships on guard to prevent escapes from the harbour, and gave his whole attention to providing everything required by General Auchmuty for a successful military attack. Landing guns, ammunition, stores, provisions and hundreds of men from the ships proved extremely difficult, given the distance of the ships from shore and the almost constant high winds and swell. But early in the morning of 6 February 1807 Auchmuty successfully stormed the city of Montevideo, though he lost 600 men, one eighth of his whole army.[17]

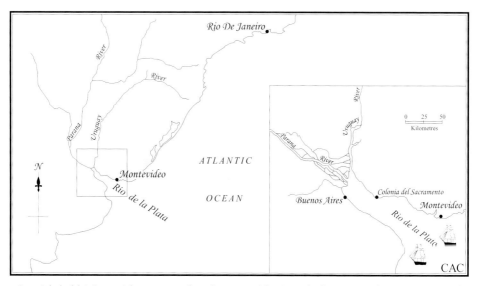

Spanish-held Montevideo, stormed and captured by British forces in February 1807, and
Rio de Janeiro, where Stirling wrote his first long report on territory

As soon as Montevideo had been breached, Stirling's squadron took possession of the battery on an island in the harbour and as many vessels as possible.
Though a few boats were set on fire by their crews, most of the other vessels in the
harbour were saved by the exertion of British seamen. Their total prizes amounted
to twenty-five armed warships, two Indiamen of 650 tons each, and upwards of
10,000 tons of merchant shipping. The loss sustained by the squadron during the
assault amounted to no more than six killed, twenty-eight wounded and four
missing. Admiral Stirling's good judgement and diligence in the capture of
Montevideo were later the subject of praise in both Houses of Parliament and in
the British Press.[18]

The family at home read of the Admiral's exploits in *The Times* of 14 April
1807; but more detail concerning any part James may have taken had to wait receipt
of letters. One, written to brother John from Montevideo in June 1807, is
interesting for two reasons: first, it shows him clearly champing at the bit to be
involved in real action, for he complained that the 'Admiral would not allow me to
go though I wished and tried hard enough', and second, it reveals a view about the
army that he would never lose. 'The manner of warfare in the Army is not
gentlemanlike as ours, we only fight men or something in the shape of them, they
distress all manner of beings.' The Admiral's postscript to this letter showed the sort
of familial warmth and choice of words that endeared him to the whole family:

> Our James has just left me room to ask you to remember me most kindly to your
> father & mother, the grown up men and the men growing, with my love to the
> girls and you, I assure you I am, Your most affc. Uncle, C Stirling.[19]

As it happened, the Stirlings took no further part in the recovery of Buenos Aires, for new orders had been given to reinforce the existing parties and relieve the leaders. Admiral Murray had been sent to relieve Uncle Charles (much to his displeasure) and Auchmuty had been replaced by Lieutenant-General Whitelocke.[20] These two new commanders planned a combined naval and military attack on Buenos Aires, which they carried out on 5 July 1807, but it failed miserably. Some 2,200 men were killed or wounded and the British were forced to surrender.[21] During this disastrous campaign, Admiral Stirling was ordered by Murray to remain at anchor off Montevideo. Afterwards he was given Admiralty orders to proceed to the Cape of Good Hope, to take Popham's previous place as Naval Commander-in-Chief.

So in August 1807 James crossed the South Atlantic bound for the Cape for a stay of some four to five months, until Uncle Charles and the *Diadem* were recalled to London. It was the first of many visits he would make to Cape Town, and the striking view of Table Mountain as they entered Simon's Bay no doubt stirred him as much as it did others arriving for the first time. After the flurry of action he had just seen, port duty probably seemed rather dull to James, but trips into town accompanying Uncle Charles would have been a welcome diversion.

While James was at the Cape he heard that the family had finally had to sell Drumpellier, to David Buchanan. The sentiments held by his brother John would have struck a chord with the homesick young Midshipman:

> …so long have I been accustomed to consider [Drumpellier] my father's and so intimately are the pleasantest scenes of my life connected with it that, like losing an intimate friend, I cannot but still imagine it belongs to him.[22]

Although the property had reverted to the Buchanans, from whom father Andrew had bought it, the Seignory (or Superiority)—part of title that went with the land—was to remain with Andrew and his heirs, who continued to refer to themselves as 'of Drumpellier'.[23]

The same letter that brought this distressing news would have informed James that his younger sister Anna had been sent to a school in Bath, where Uncle Charles' family was based.[24] It was to prove a lucky move, as the lady who ran the school, Mrs Twiss, had a son named Horace who, at a later date, was to help James establish the colony of Western Australia. No further letters from home would have reached James before the *Diadem* left Cape Town to return to England. Once more he crossed the Atlantic, and by the end of February 1808 was again in Rio de Janeiro. While the ship was watered, James took the opportunity offered by a few days' shore leave to explore his surroundings, and afterwards wrote comprehensively on what he had seen. The account is quite remarkable for a 16-year-old, bearing all the hallmarks of the eye for detail and reporting ability that would later gain for Stirling the reputation of being a colony-builder. It also reveals the romantic in James and a tendency to see things through rose-coloured glasses.

The report describes how James, accompanied by a Dr MacLeod and two French officers from the corvette *L'Esperance*, set out from Rio de Janeiro on 12 March 1808 to visit Calcavados, a mountain some 7 or 8 miles from the city.

> …the road we took led us past the Aqueduct and we had an opportunity of seeing that fine public work. Aqueducts…are in my opinion the most bieutiful [sic] subjects for the display of Architecture. The endless succession of arches uniting the opposite sides of a valley, or the banks of a wild and picturesque river, arrest the attention too forcibly to be passed by without exciting admiration…
>
> The wooded hills that embosom this Sylvan retreat are beautifully diversified with flowers and shrubs, the blue rhododendra (a species of Rectia) and the yellow mimosa abound everywhere and give a remarkably gay appearance to the scene… On quitting this valley the road became steeper and more winding, and we ascended with difficulty…Three or four twisting turns brought us in sight of the Emperor's Summer-House…and another effort placed us on top of the Calcavados!
>
> …Surrounded by lofty granite peaks bearing the imprints of their primitive origin we looked down on Oceans, rivers, mountains and plains, cities and forests spread out in wild confusion, glowing in infinite beauty under the rays of meridian sunbeams…
>
> Turning to the southward where the 'roaring main ever toils beneath,' the deep cerulean blue was enlivened by the white sails of vessels bearing the traffic of all quarters of the globe, and it caused our hearts to exult in seeing the British flag floating over many of these ships proclaiming from whence they came…Here Captain Cook in one of his voyages concealed his ships—Recollections of the early enterprise of our own Navy may thus be indulged…a ride home in the evening completed our day's work…[25]

After leaving port the next day, the *Diadem* reached England in April and, as the Admiral planned to take leave, James was posted to the third-rated *Warspite 76* under Captain Henry Blackwood. He joined the ship on 28 April 1808, a day earlier than the rest of the 'young gentlemen' volunteers.[26] Among this intake was 13-year-old Mark Currie, who was to become a lifelong friend. James clearly enjoyed the posting, and commemorated his time with Captain Blackwood some twenty years later when he named a river in Western Australia after him. But by September he was contemplating a move from the *Warspite* to a 'gun brig'—more, as it transpired, from wounded pride than sound planning. James had received a stinging rebuke from Uncle Charles which cast aspersions on his seamanship, and his response showed just how he was smarting. The gun brig, he explained to his older brother in penitential tone, would be 'the best place to study Seamanship especially in winter and on the North Sea Station'. In the absence of fires, he would be unable to write many letters or long ones, for 'a fine day would be the only chance of thawing the Ink'.[27] Both the Admiral and James' mother were sceptical of the move, which never eventuated. As plans to visit the Baltic with Captain Blackwood also came to nothing, signs of bored frustration were beginning to show in James' letters towards the end of the year. While others were experiencing all the excitement of action, he was still 'sine Battle sine prizes', he told John,

> nor do we intend to attempt anything till the Winter is over…I had a letter from the Admiral today…I hear from him Walter intends to winter in Philadelphia and to come home in the Spring. If it had been at all in my way I should have liked to have accompanied him on his American jaunt. I either am or I fancy myself very fond of change.

While James was yearning for change, there were unsettling developments back home. His mother was in the midst of packing up the Carleton Place, Glasgow apartment ready for a move, but was as yet uncertain where they would live. Meanwhile the Admiral had decided to sell the parental home in Grosvenor Street and live permanently in Bath, a decision which clearly upset Anne, who confided to son John that she felt 'half choked [to] think I shall never be in Grosvenor House again. Had I been told so when I left it…I believe I shd. have wished to have been knocked on the head.'[28]

Concerned with the family upheaval and frustrated by the lack of action on the *Warspite*, James went absent without leave for ten days in late November to visit the family. He returned to the ship in some trepidation but, as he told brother John, had managed to get away with it:

> As soon as I got into the coach when I parted from you I began to consider what I have been about and was not a little afraid of the consequences. By the time we reached Deal I had so unmercifully tormented myself that I expected to find a Sergeant of the Marine and party on shore in search of me but I got on board on Sunday afternoon sine attendants and all the questions I was asked by the First Lieutenant were to dine in Wardroom and how I have been amused…[29]

James continued to serve officially as Midshipman on the HMS *Warspite 76* in the first half of 1809, but Captain Blackwood also arranged for his aspiring young charge to have short stints as Acting Lieutenant on various other vessels in the Channel Fleet. Thus James became acquainted with the HMS *Lynx* in late January and HMS *Prometheus* in May. Throughout this time he was preparing for his examination to become a full Lieutenant, and there appears to have been little shore leave. News from the family would have been reassuring however, for letters in February informed him the Grosvenor Street house had not yet been sold and his father's rearrangement of affairs was nearing completion.[30]

As to his studies, by now James would have been well schooled in navigation, known how to handle all types of sails, to describe and predict weather patterns and plan appropriate responses, been well versed in all flag instructions, warnings and salutes, able to recognise most types of ships at a distance, able to manage all sized guns and cannons and run gunnery drills, and also known how to command large groups of men. Nevertheless, without the support of Uncle Charles it would have been a nervous James who presented with other young officers for examination at Somerset House on 1 August 1809.[31] The presence of Mama and his sisters in town would at least have ensured his clothes were immaculate for the verbal ordeal, and they would surely have celebrated with him when news was posted that he had passed. On 12 August James rejoined the *Warspite* as full Lieutenant, and his heart would have skipped a beat as the pipers acknowledged his promotion.

By this time father Andrew had finally cleared his debt with his Scottish trustees, both principal and interest. Ultimately, all his creditors were satisfied 'so that though impoverished as a consequence of unmerited misfortune, his integrity was vindicated and his honour remained unsullied'.[32] He had stayed in Scotland when the family went south, but kept in constant touch and was most concerned with news that the Admiral had decided to retire. 'Dreaming away his time with his family is a most dreadful waste of time', he wrote, and hoped that he would 'soon hoist his flag again'.[33]

James remained on the *Warspite* until 1 April 1810 when he was transferred to the larger HMS *Hibernia*, under Captain R. D. Drum. For six months they were engaged in home service on Channel duties, so he could keep in regular touch with the family. It also meant that he probably attended the celebrations surrounding the announcement, on the last day of July, that Uncle Charles had at last been made Vice Admiral and granted Freedom of the City of London.[34]

Some months later James had the choice of remaining with the *Hibernia* for overseas duty under a new captain, or staying with Captain Drum, who had been assigned to a smaller ship, the *Armide 38*. He chose the latter course, joining the *Armide* on 20 November for continued duties in the Channel.[35] His decision could well have been influenced by the fact that the agency business in London was in serious financial difficulty. A letter from father Andrew in Glasgow, dated 2 December 1810, urged his two eldest sons to raise £20,000 in Exchequer Bills to get Stirling Brothers & Co. out of debt and to create a new and smaller company.

There was a degree of urgency in Andrew's tone (he hoped to effect the change by the end of the month), interspersed with typical optimism. His coal interests were doing well and were 'a prop to the family…I trust 6 months will put us in a very independent & lucrative situation'. Touchingly, he asked his sons to 'Tell Mama it is doing no good to take any part of the load on her shoulders'.[36]

The end-of-year target was not met, but in 1811 the old business was wound up and a new firm, simply called Stirling & Co., was formed.[37] Brother John was now out of the partnership, due to a bad bout of rheumatic fever, and had decided to visit his mother's relations, the Willing family, in America. It was no doubt hoped that he might be able to foster links between their highly successful mercantile business and the Stirling enterprises.[38]

After a year's service with Drum in the *Armide*, Lieutenant Stirling took a brief period of leave before assuming a new appointment. Uncle Charles had come out of retirement to take the position of Commander-in-Chief of the Jamaica Station,[39] and he had asked the Admiralty for his nephew to join him as Flag Lieutenant—a major promotion. The Admiral's flagship was the *Arethusa 38*, which James joined on 20 November 1811. He was to serve in the *Arethusa* for nearly two months before transferring, as First Lieutenant, to the small *Shark 10* for another month, acting as messenger to the fleet.[40]

It appears that during the Jamaica posting Uncle Charles had pledged to find James his own ship, a promise realised on 3 March 1812. At the age of 21 years and 1 month Lieutenant James Stirling was appointed Acting Commander of the 18-gun sloop *Moselle*. Now, for the first time, he would be called 'Captain Stirling'. He must have done a creditable job, and his uncle must have recommended him very strongly to the Admiralty Board, for just three months later, on 19 June 1812, he was officially made Commander.[41] Now all the years of training would pay off—he would have his own ship.

3

First Command: HMS *Brazen*

1812–1818

SIX DAYS AFTER his promotion, Stirling took command of the HMS *Brazen,* on which he was to serve for six years.[1] She was a sixth-rated, 28-gun ship built in 1808 at Portsmouth, and some 110 ft long and 30 ft wide.[2] On Monday 29 June 1812, in Port Royal harbour, Jamaica, the ship's log entry noted: 'am. light airs and clear W…joined the ship Capt. Jas. Stirling and read his Commiss'n. pm strong breezes and cloudy'.[3]

For the next week the ship was readied for sea, provisions and fresh water were loaded, rigging checked, etc. Stirling was pleased with all he saw but was also impatient to leave the harbour and see the *Brazen* in action. On his first Sunday in full command he took Divine Service and read the Articles of War, as was usual, but it gave the entire ship's company a chance to see their new captain. The Articles of War set out in graphic detail the punishments a captain could impose upon anyone who flouted naval discipline, and were a timely reminder of his authority. On 11 July, with fresh afternoon breezes, *Brazen* finally 'weighed and dropt into the fairway'. The pilot left at 7 a.m. and the ship was on its way to undertake Stirling's first official mission, to harass and assail American ports and American shipping in the Gulf of Mexico.

War between Britain and America had been declared on 18 June 1812, basically over Britain's insistence on the right of search of ships belonging to non-combatants, and to seize and impress any former British subjects (whether they had been granted American citizenship or not). This mightily offended the Americans, who were neutral carriers between France and Britain during the Napoleonic wars, and they threatened blockades. As this would seriously jeopardise Britain's valuable trans-atlantic trade, it had to be resisted. Additional naval forces were summoned to Bermuda to launch from there an attack on America's east coast ports, to destroy their ships and stores. Stirling's role, together with the other ships at the Jamaica Station, was to operate similarly but lower down in the Gulf of Mexico. His first attack was aimed at New Orleans and the Mississippi Delta, but a hurricane so severely damaged the *Brazen* that Stirling was forced to seek shelter at Pensacola, then held by the Spanish, where he was able to carry out mast repairs. All was not lost, however, for he was able to survey the territory and capture an American ship, the *Warren,* on its way from Havana to New Orleans, which he took back to Jamaica as a prize. Another prize, the *Maria,* had been found 'in a sinking condition', so its cargo had been removed and the ship abandoned.[4] The Admiral, who was entitled to a share of any prize brought into his station, could thus be well pleased with his nephew when the *Brazen* returned on 20 November 1812.

On his arrival James submitted a lengthy formal report on the expedition which, although formally addressed to 'Charles Stirling Esq., Vice Admiral of the White, &c, Jamaica', was clearly intended to be forwarded to the Admiralty Board. It was to be a significant report for two reasons. First, James had been able to become thoroughly acquainted with the Spanish-held Florida coastline, which was to prove invaluable three years later in a rescue of British troops after a failed attack on New Orleans. Second, making the report honed his skills in evaluating and communicating his views on the economic and strategic importance of a territory, skills which were to be of enormous importance in persuading the British Government to establish a colony in Western Australia. There were even similarities

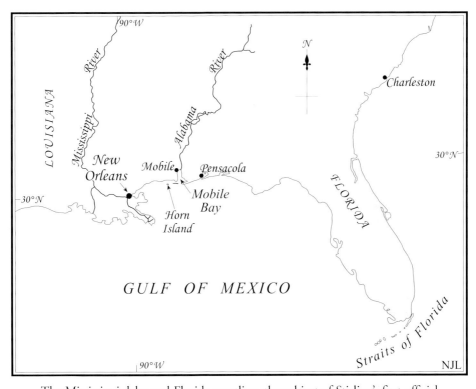

The Mississippi delta and Florida coastline, the subject of Stirling's first official
naval reconnaissance, and Mobile Bay, where Stirling rescued British troops
in the last action of the 1812 War

in terrain for, like the Swan River, the Mississippi also suffered from a restricting bar at its mouth, although with ramifications of a vastly different nature. Stirling noted that

> The Navigation of the Mississippi is of the highest importance, since five of the United States and four Territories depend upon it for the exportation of their Produce…and should the Mississippi therefore be well blockaded, or possession taken of New Orleans (an undertaking not very difficult) the distress which the interior States would be subject to, would be extreme, and it would increase the number of those in America who sigh for peace with England…

He was appalled by the conditions he saw in Florida, remarking that 'Although the Country is capable of improvement, it has not advanced a Single Step towards it, under the Government of Spain'. He predicted that the whole territory could be taken from the Spanish, especially if 'less regular means' were adopted for its capture. His irregular suggestion was to 'engage the Indians of the Creek Nation in the Contest'. This is the first time he is known to have referred to indigenous peoples, and whether his subsequent comments were from first-hand experience is doubtful. He continued:

> They have still the highest attachment to the English, and the greatest hatred to the American name, the Government of which Country has lately circumvented them in the purchase of Lands. They do not, it is true, exceed 10,000 Warriors but as the Americans will come down through the Woods, Indians would be useful Allies, and as they Scalp at this time all the straggling Americans who fall into their hands, the fear of such treatment would, probably, tend to thin the ranks of the American Arm…[5]

His youthful enthusiasm for action was to be denied, however, as word had come through from the Admiralty that the *Brazen* was due to return to England for a maintenance survey. Uncle Charles, meanwhile, had been told he was to proceed to Bermuda and there join forces with Admiral Sir J. B. Warren and work with Sir George Cockburn, who had been sent out especially by the Admiralty, to plan further action against the Americans. Stirling was part of the squadron which accompanied his uncle to Bermuda, and before he left had met Admiral Cockburn and was party to the main thrust of the group's plans. Cockburn was to lead a squadron to the north, where he engineered a series of highly successful coastal attacks,[6] while Admiral Charles Stirling was to concentrate his squadron in the south.[7]

It would thus have been with some reluctance that Stirling ordered the *Brazen* to weigh anchor for the return trip on 19 December 1812. As the days passed, however, his desire to see his family again overcame his disappointment with the lost chance for action, and he welcomed the sight of the Scilly Isles and finally the Lizard. On 9 February 1813 the *Brazen* moored at Spithead, before proceeding to Sheerness for survey. From there he wrote to his family advising that his share of prize money (or 'stuff', as he called it) would be at the Bullion Office within the week, and he wished them 'to fight it out for me that the charge of carriage may not fall upon my shoulders …'[8]

From family correspondence it seems that James did not finally reach London until early March, and as an eligible young bachelor was undoubtedly caught up in a social whirl, for grand parties, card games, opera and plays were in full swing. But more sobering was news of his father's ill-health and the family's continuing financial problems. His mother and father had not yet reached a decision about selling the Faskine coal lands, and they were so strapped for funds that Mother had suggested selling her carriage to economise. Son William had pleaded that this was unnecessary, especially as he had just 'taken the bull by the horns' to relieve some of the pressure by arranging with Uncle Walter Stirling, the banker, for his father's private £5,000 debt to be settled by a mortgage over the houses and land at Bow Church Yard.[9]

After a month of hectic shore leave, Stirling returned to the *Brazen* in dock at Sheerness (which he called 'the most uncomfortable hole in England'). He confided to his mother[10] that he felt as useless as 'a fifth wheel would be to a carriage', and lonely 'were it not that the Commissioner here has a mind to marry me to one of his daughters…' Like many a young blade of his time, Stirling was wary, and watchful: '…the fish shall not bite at the hidden hook and although I enjoy the game I shall take care not to enter into it…' He also broached financial matters with Anne, offering to pay her £200 a year for board and lodging, 'commencing on Midsummer's Day next'.

> My freight account is not settled yet but I calculate I shall be worth about £3,000
> —I think it had better remain in my brother's hands since it may be of use to
> them also…I trust my dear Mother you will not be hurt by my making this offer
> but consider it as arising from a desire on my part to have no property or interest
> separate from that of my family…believe me your dutiful & affectionate son,
> James.[11]

For a 22-year-old, James was doing extremely well. The £200 per year he offered his mother was the equivalent of a middle-ranking government official's salary at that time, and £3,000 was a small fortune. That he offered it to his brothers, presumably for the ailing Bow Church Yard business, shows the strength of the family bonds.

As the *Brazen* did not sail until 4 June 1813 James had a couple of months to catch up with his scattered family. William was back at Bow Church Yard with Walter, after his electioneering stint, and John had returned from America to join his brothers in London. Charles had left the navy and become a merchant seaman, making several dangerous crossings to Santander in Spain with goods from the Stirling agency.[12] Andrew was to return with him as a 'young gentleman' on the *Brazen*, Robert had left college and was about to enlist in the army, while Edward (Ned) was still at school. The girls were with their mother in the new home at York Hill, on the outskirts of Glasgow, where father Andrew was apparently still unwell with 'rheumatism in one arm and his Leg again inflamed'.

But family concerns soon had to be cast aside, for Stirling's new orders were to take the *Brazen* to Hudson Bay in North America, as naval escort for a convoy of ships bearing settlers and stores to Churchill, a small trading post at the base of the Bay. It was to be Stirling's first close encounter with colonisation, for this was part of Lord Selkirk's attempts to establish a colony in upper Canada, in the area now known as Winnipeg. Stirling could well have heard of the venture before becoming involved, for Selkirk recruited many of his immigrants from Glasgow. A first party had gone out in 1811 and suffered considerable hardship before reaching their destination.[13] This was the second group, consisting of Scots, English and Irish, who were to travel in a convoy of merchantmen and Hudson Bay Company ships.[14] With Stirling and the *Brazen* in the lead, they left Sheerness harbour on 4 June 1813. Taking a northerly route, they reached the Orkneys by the 25th where they took on supplies and water. By 10 July they were 185 miles off the tip of Greenland, and on the 29th entered Hudson Strait and encountered bad weather.

On 6 August they were still bearing towards Salisbury Island at the top of the Bay when a foreign sail was sighted, and Stirling ordered the *Brazen* to give chase. The ship was the *Beaver,* an American privateer, which they successfully captured, to the joy of all on board. Stirling sent an officer and five men to take charge and return their prize to port, then rejoined the convoy. Nearer Salisbury Island the *Brazen* had to grapple with ice, but got through it to cross the Bay and anchor off Churchill on 19 August 1813.[15]

Although there is no written evidence of Stirling's impressions of the settlement, he remained at Churchill for four weeks, in which time he met the new Governor of the region, and the Hudson Bay Company personnel in charge of the trading post. Indeed, Governor MacDonnell[16] had greeted the convoy and announced to the settlers that each head of family would be allotted 100 acres of land, an Indian pony and a musket, bayonet and ammunition which they were told to use to resist aggressors, French and Indians.[17]

During his stay Stirling would have had plenty of time to observe the Indians who brought their furs into the trading post, and to learn how relations between the company and the natives had been managed. Company representatives told him they had learned that strong character and shrewd judgement were essential qualities in all dealings with the natives. Relations depended on whether the tribes were by nature friendly or warlike, and they differed considerably from the peaceable Inuits to the warlike Algonquin. None of the tribes had permanent

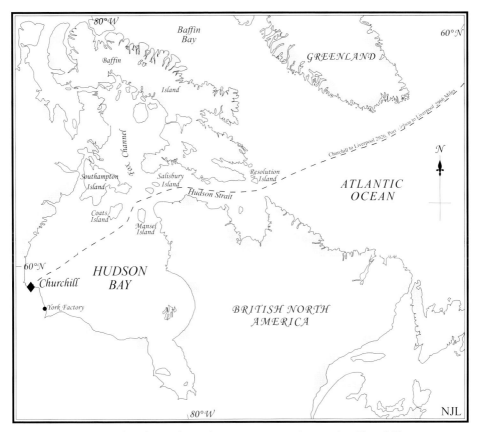

Route taken by Stirling when escorting settlers to the Churchill
outpost in Hudson Bay

leaders, and the chiefs made decisions as a group, which made agreements difficult.
He was told that their culture demanded a life for a life, but in revenge for any
killing they did not necessarily seek out the perpetrator—any relatives, however
distant, would suffice. So if a white man killed an Indian, any white man could be
slain in response. Stirling was warned to show no fear in any encounter, for want of
courage was an invitation to attack whilst fearlessness was greatly admired.[18]

Leaving Churchill on 20 September 1813, Stirling took the *Brazen,* again in
convoy, back to the Orkneys where they dropped anchor on 26 October.[19] For a
week or two the *Brazen* was on guard duty, sighting and chasing a couple of foreign
vessels, but without capture. On 17 November the convoy got under way and
reached the Downs (an offshore naval anchorage at the top of the Strait of Dover)
for decommissioning on the 25th. There was little time for shore leave, however, as
Stirling then received confidential orders to take the Duke of Brunswick, the Prince
Regent's brother-in-law, to Wyk in Holland. It seems likely that the Duke was being
sent as an emissary to Holland to ensure its continued resistance to the French, and
it was thus an important mission for young Stirling. The crew of the *Brazen* fired a

full 21-gun salute when the Duke boarded on 9 December for the five-day crossing. Once he had safely delivered his passenger to a party of horsemen waiting outside Noordyk church,[20] Stirling weighed anchor and made for the Downs where the *Brazen* was to be stationed over the New Year.

During this time, the welfare of Uncle Charles was causing family concern. The Admiral had earlier returned from Jamaica to be told of his impending court martial on charges of accepting payment for protecting foreign seamen. He had been 'almost overwhelmed with the storm which has burst over him', his nephew reported, and, as he firmly maintained his innocence, he wanted the case to be heard quickly so he could clear his name.[21] But it would be many anxious months before the hearing.

The festive season at the end of 1813 gave the family a chance to catch up, and James would have heard that his brother Robert had been made an Ensign in the 78th foot Highland Regiment in September,[22] and Edward accepted at Haileybury, the school for those intending to enter the East India Service.[23] He would also have heard of the changes to the Bow Church Yard business, for the partnership had changed again, this time to include John. But it was a short family reunion, as James was back on the *Brazen* on 7 January 1814.

Early in March he received orders to take the *Brazen* on patrol up and down the Irish Sea and around the Outer Hebrides in search of French or American vessels. As his base for this mission was to be Greenock, the port for Glasgow, he would be very near his parents, and so welcomed the task. In what must have been a very chilly trip (it had been a particularly severe winter[24]), Stirling manoeuvred the *Brazen* out to the small isolated island of St Kilda in the Northern Atlantic, then around the Butt of Lewis at the top of the Outer Hebrides through the Minch to the Skerry Isles, and back to anchor and reprovisioning at Greenock. It seems to have been a time of particular personal contentment, and he wrote to brother John that he meant '"en verite" to enjoy the summer coming whatever Buonaparte may think', and that he was happy 'indeed almost too much so for I have hardly anything left to wish for'. The degree of freedom which the patrols afforded evidently were agreeable, and he indulged in some brotherly fantasy:

> …I think in the purpose of establishing your health that you should come and take a month's run with me about here. We will take Dr Johnson for our guide no further than to direct us to the best houses and I have not a doubt of us eclipsing the Doctor. Do we not dance better, are we not landowners and above all are we not good tempered? Who need fear, we may if we please carry off a Miss Mac somebody or other with half a dozen islands for her portion. Come then to me now or any time before July and we will give these Islanders a treat. We will carry with us all the laughing good humour of the age…My Father is downright mad for a sail and he shall have it when the weather becomes fine. I was never more agreeably surprised than in seeing him so much better than I expected…[25]

For the next two months he continued to cruise around the beautiful islands of the Hebrides and in the Irish Sea, buoyed by the chance to see family members at regular stops for water and supplies. But one such meeting took a sombre turn for, as sister Anna later noted, she had to break the news to her brother in Greenock of their uncle's sentence, which she feared would 'greatly sink his spirits'.[26] The results of Uncle Charles' court martial, held aboard the *Gladiator* at Portsmouth[27] early in May, were now public. The verdict was that 'the charge had been in part proven'.[28] Although the court cleared him of some of the charges, it had decided that the evidence pointed towards the Admiral having accepted payment, at least once, for protecting foreign seamen in Jamaica. Justifiable on humanitarian grounds, this nevertheless was against navy regulations, and breached the Navigation Laws, and as a result he was placed on half-pay and barred from further promotion.[29] It was a bitter blow for the family, especially James who lost his patron and was thereafter sceptical about courts martial.

But this was not the only bad news Anna had to convey to James. Brother Charles had had a disastrous trading voyage to Spain, losing his entire cargo, which further stretched the finances of the Bow Church Yard business on which the family depended.[30] James wanted to help, and with dwindling chances of capturing prizes in the northern seas he would have been happy to receive notice of a new posting. The Admiralty wanted him to take the *Brazen* to Barbados to rejoin the West Indies Station and, although the sticky climate did not appeal, it was a welcome chance for action and reward.

Leaving Portsmouth harbour on 29 December 1814, James set sail for the West Indies, where Admiral Duckworth was now Commander-in-Chief. James knew of and liked Duckworth, having served briefly under him on *L'Hercule* in 1804.[31] Arriving in Barbados early in February, he presented his compliments to the Admiral, and was welcomed back by many of those he had met during his earlier posting with Uncle Charles. There were now two major West Indies naval stations: one at Kingstown for the Jamaica Station, and the other at Bridgetown in Barbados, headquarters of the Leeward Islands Station. Each had an Admiral, but the Commander-in-Chief was at Barbados. There was frequent communication between the two Admirals as they attempted between them to contain the piracy that plagued the Spanish Main with resources depleted by the American War.

It was on a reporting mission of this kind to Jamaica that Stirling was introduced to Simon Bolivar, the leader of the South American revolutionaries. Bolivar has been described as presenting 'one of history's most colossal personal canvases of adventure and tragedy, glory and defeat'.[32] Known as the 'Liberator' after several successful campaigns against the Spanish Royalists in 1813, he had been badly defeated in September 1814 and gone into exile in Jamaica.[33] He was at this time composing the famous 'Jamaica letter', published in September 1815,[34] in which he outlined his vision for South America. After eliminating the Spanish colonial presence, Bolivar wanted to create constitutional republics, based on the British parliamentary system, but with a president elected for life. James would have been intrigued by this well-educated and charismatic man, especially as Bolivar's revolutionary ideas ran counter to his own Royalist loyalties. But what James had previously seen in Florida tied in with Bolivar's descriptions of the ill-effects of the feudal Spanish colonial system in South America. He would therefore have been comfortable with the somewhat ambiguous official line Britain had taken when Bolivar had requested assistance in 1810. Britain would not recognise the Revolutionaries' claim for independence, but would act as mediator in settling differences with Spain and provide naval support in the event of a French attack.[35] The meeting between James and Simon at this time was significant, for just two years later James was to be employed on a secret mission to help Bolivar in his struggle for South American independence.

Only a few days after James' arrival in the West Indies hostilities against the United States ceased, a treaty being signed at night on 17 February 1815. A week later Stirling was ordered to take the *Brazen* to effect the rescue of British troops caught up in the last action of the war, the failed attack on New Orleans. The vanquished British soldiers had had to find a way of escape, and under the command of Lieutenant Harry Smith they had made their way over the bare Gulf territory towards Mobile Bay, which Stirling had reconnoitred in 1812. To reach the ships waiting to aid their escape, the troops first had to capture Fort Bower, which Smith did by bluffing its commander into surrender. Stirling and the *Brazen* arrived just in time with evidence that peace negotiations actually had begun. The weary troops were conveyed in relays on the *Brazen* to an island at the entrance to Mobile Bay.[36] On 5 March proof that peace had been declared was brought by additional ships, and all the troops were embarked. Smith, and as many of the wounded as possible, were to return to England on the *Brazen* after sailing first to Havana for fresh provisions.

Though six years older, Smith took a great liking to Stirling. The two found they had much in common: both, for example, had been present at the storming of Montevideo, and both enjoyed cigars.[37] Stirling was not above showing off to his new friend on the return journey. When the *Brazen* was caught in a terrific gale in the Gulf of Florida, Smith was initially bedridden but Stirling roused him to 'see how I manage my craft'. Smith was impressed:

> He was and is a noble seaman, all animation, and he was so clear and decided in his orders! Sail was made amid waves mountains high, and the *Brazen*, as impudent a craft as ever spurned the mighty billows, so beautifully was she managed and steered, rode over or evaded seas apparently overwhelming; and Stirling, in the pride of his sailor's heart, says, 'There, now, what would you give to be a sailor?'[38]

Smith remained a long-standing friend and was later to influence several potential Swan River migrants (particularly the Molloys) by recommending Stirling as a man whose judgement and leadership was to be trusted.[39]

In London Stirling would have heard of further changes to the Bow Church Yard business. William and Walter had admitted Sir James Home of Blackadder as a one-third partner for an injection of £15,000. Mother Anne was not impressed, writing to John from Bath: 'If Sir James married a lady with fortune it will make him much more respectable as a partner'.[40] (In fact, Sir James was to marry her daughter Anna some years later.) John was not mentioned in the partnership at this stage as he was about to pay another visit, successful as it turned out, to the Willings in Philadelphia. There he won the heart of Elizabeth Willing, who would bring her not inconsiderable portion into the Stirling family. It was some time before they returned, however, and in the interim the family had moved to Lord Halsey's large country estate, Henley Park, near Guildford, Surrey, on which they had taken a seven-year lease. The property had beauty and certain attractions, like good shooting and a lake for fishing, and it was not long before Stirling paid a brief visit and formed an immediate attachment to both house and grounds. As sister Mary noted in a letter to John, although the *Brazen* was to be paid off early in September, it was scheduled to be recommissioned, and the three-month refit meant that James could 'bless us with his pleasant company between whiles'.[41]

A new appointment, instead of postwar retrenchment, was a great relief for James. The Admiralty was bent on downscaling: at the beginning of 1816 there were over 5,800 commissioned officers in the navy (about 4,000 of them naval lieutenants), but after the war only about 542 were needed afloat at any time.[42] This meant drastic pruning was necessary, and James was still among the junior and more vulnerable officers. But his facility with languages, and particularly Spanish, had not gone unnoticed and led the Admiralty Lords to select him for peacetime

Henley Park in 1911. Loved by James when leased by the Stirlings from 1815

Courtesy Normandy Historical Society

employment back in the West Indies, where trouble was escalating along the Spanish Main.

So on 5 September 1815 Stirling again raised his flag on the *Brazen*. With orders for her manning and outfit left in the hands of his senior men,[43] he was free to pursue other interests—of a romantic kind. At about this time 24-year-old James was involved with a young lady to whom he became engaged. Her name and background are unknown, and it seems to have been a short romance which could not withstand the prospect of a long separation. Soon after the refitted *Brazen* ultimately left Gravesend, on 2 December 1815, Mother Anne wryly commented that the engagement was 'put to sleep by the lady herself…and heartily glad I am'.[44] Whether James was glad or hurt is not known, but having had his fingers burned once, it would be a very long time before he would chance his heart again.

Apart from James' reappointment, 1816 was a momentous year for his parents. In January the first of their children married, and in June the first of those surviving to adulthood died. On 4 January John married Elizabeth, eldest daughter of Thomas Mayne Willing, in a grand ceremony in Philadelphia. And following in the footsteps of her great-aunt, John's grandmother, Elizabeth, consented to live in England. But the joy brought by this addition to the family was dashed just months later with news that midshipman Andrew, aged just 21, had died of fever on 5 June 1816 aboard HMS *Inconstant* off the coast of Africa.[45]

James by then had reached Barbados, where duties for the fleet stationed there included cruising to keep the peace and prevent contraband trade. Affairs in the Spanish Main had concerned British consuls in the West Indies for some time. There had been moves for independence among the Spanish-held provinces in South America, and the insurgent 'Patriots' were proving a magnet for runaway slaves. Although Britain was officially pro-Spain (an ally in the late war), her diplomats were also wary of offending the Spanish-American Patriots in case it risked the valuable South American trade. At the same time Britain was anxious to recover as many of the runaway slaves as possible.

One of Stirling's first tasks, at the behest of his Commander-in-Chief, Admiral John Harvey, was to take the Harbour Master from Barbados to Guyria, opposite Trinidad, to gain intelligence about the strength of the revolutionaries' forces. They left on 20 July 1816 and returned to report that this small town was in the hands of the insurgents, but its defence was weak. Stirling then resumed anti-smuggling cruising duties, but in the process made an unfortunate decision, one that would keep coming back to haunt him over many years.

On 27 September 1816 the *Brazen* apprehended, and took as prize, the *Hercules,* a South American ship commanded by William Brown, an ex-British sailor who had been made an Admiral of the Patriots Fleet.[46] Brown had called in at Barbados, very low on rations, after the *Hercules* had been damaged from a collision with an iceberg near the Falklands. The Governor of Barbados, following the official line of not offending the Spaniards, had refused Brown permission to repair his vessel. On leaving Barbados the *Hercules* was seized by Captain Stirling and the *Brazen*, but subsequently released on the Governor's orders. Brown maintained that Stirling had then 'treacherously suggested' that the two ships should sail in company to Antigua where 'he was sure I would obtain permission to repair the *Hercules* in an English harbour'.[47] Once clear of Barbados, Stirling had given orders for the *Brazen*'s men to again board the *Hercules* and take her to Antigua as a prize.[48] The Vice Admiralty Court was convened there on 18 October, when 'the ship and property was proceeded against for a breach of some or one of the laws of trade and navigation'. This immediately initiated complaints from the Patriots, and long consultations ensued between diplomats. Stirling was called to give his testimony on 13 November, strongly supported by his Admiral, and the court brought in a verdict in his favour. The *Hercules* was ordered to be condemned and her property sold by public auction 'at a great sacrifice'.[49] Brown later returned to England to press his claims and was initially successful in having the original verdict reversed. But he then found his claim to the proceeds had to be divided between himself, the agents of the King of Spain, and the local government in South America. Stirling was called to account on many occasions and told to pay some of the costs, although he denied having benefited from the proceeds. He was eventually exonerated in January 1819, the judge declaring that 'no man could have acted better than Captain Stirling did'.[50] Despite this verdict, Stirling continued to receive demands for payment of damages related to the *Hercules* until the mid-1820s.

In November 1816 Stirling was asked to undertake another South American surveillance task—a secret mission, because officially Britain opposed intervention in the affairs of Spanish America by any nation outside Spain which held it by conquest.[51] Nevertheless, in British eyes Spanish America was still the Eldorado and 'now, thanks to the Patriots, within reach of any hand bold enough to fight its way in'. Informally, therefore, there was increasing pressure to recognise the independence of South America, and particularly Venezuela, the country nearest to British West Indies' interests. But independence could only be recognised if the Patriots possessed a sufficiently organised government 'with forces and resources capable of enforcing respect for their liberties'.[52] This is what Stirling was asked to establish. He was selected partly because of his knowledge of the area, partly because he spoke Spanish fluently, and partly because he had already met Bolivar, the leader of the Patriots and the key to relevant intelligence.[53]

During December 1816 and January 1817 Stirling carried out a detailed inspection of conditions in and around the Captain-Generalship of Caracas (the capital), which constituted the eastern half of the north coast of Venezuela. On 2 February he signed a detailed report, which he submitted to Admiral Harvey for forwarding to the Foreign Office. The report outlined how he had first revisited Guyria in the eastern extremity, where the insurgents were still in control, and then sailed west to examine conditions in Caracas and its port, La Guaira. Here Spanish Royalists troops occupied a garrison, but were lazy, ill-disciplined and outnumbered by another 400 European troops in the town who favoured the Patriots. The city was run down, with barely a new house built since the earthquake of 1812. Stirling had then returned eastward, noting that the interior of the country had been devastated, 'Houses in ruins, Plantations over-run with bushes, the roads destroyed and lost'.

Stirling laid some of the blame for this deteriorating situation on the 'ancient colonial system' which had been imposed by Spain. A small number of large plantation owners employed and exploited large numbers of native people and slaves, while small free communities had been ground down by debt, and there had been endemic corruption. The Royalists wished to restore the system, the benefit of which, Stirling commented, was not for him to determine. But it was clear to the people 'in the rigour with which it is enforced, in the exactions of officers, and in the re-establishment of the Inquisition, that nothing liberal is to be looked for in the conduct of the Mother Country'.[54]

Stirling was careful to disclaim any personal judgement,[55] but he did believe that Spain would eventually withdraw. In concluding remarks he noted that the Royalists did not have the means 'to restore the authority of the King' and themselves anticipated the country's collapse within two years. The Insurgents, on the other hand, were optimistic about overthrowing the Government, but doubtful that they could 'avert the storm which they themselves have raised by arming the blacks'. Both parties, Stirling observed, wanted Great Britain to intervene.[56]

Stirling submitted this report to Admiral Harvey at a very appropriate time, for Cortes Madariaga, Bolivar's agent, was then visiting the two British Admirals soliciting aid and protection. Madariaga recorded that these meetings had assured him that the British Government was contemplating recognition of the independence of South America, including Venezuela, once they had written assurances that it possessed 'organized governments'.[57] Stirling was asked to transport Madariaga back to Bolivar's headquarters on Margarita Island and collect such written assurance. Bolivar, however, was not there—he had gone to the mainland—and Stirling's further attempts to find the revolutionary leader were at that stage to no avail.

Madariaga nevertheless managed to round up enough support to hold a Congress on 8 May 1817 which appointed an Executive Committee to draft a constitution for the Republic of Venezuela.[58] A Proclamation of Six Articles, including trade policy, was subsequently passed and a copy given to Stirling for forwarding to England as evidence of an 'organized government'. But as Bolivar had not signed the document, it did not surprise Stirling when he contemptuously dismissed the new Government a month or so later. Bolivar by then had established his headquarters at Angostura, 'a little town lost in a tropical forest and washed by the crocodile infested waters of the Orinoco river',[59] and given himself the title of 'Supreme Chief of the Republic of Venezuela'. He used it in a widely distributed open letter written on 27 August which declared the independence of the Republic

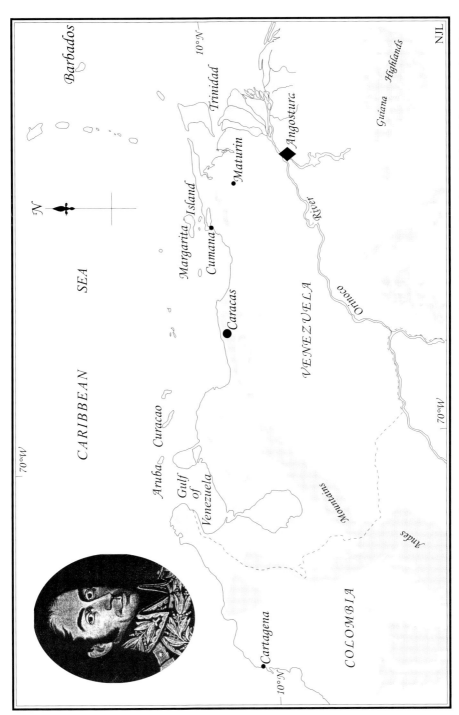

The South American coastal area of insurgent activity, examined in secret by Stirling. (Inset) Bolivar, leader of the revolutionaries

and his intention to favourably receive the vessels of *all* nations for trade.[60] This displeased British officials, as they wanted preferential treatment in trade. Appeasing Bolivar was essential, but it had to be done in secret.

Although the granting of independence in South America was discussed in the British Parliament in 1817, it was also a period of intense diplomatic negotiation over the Quintuple Alliance. Finalised the following year, this Alliance established the European Congress of Continental Powers comprising Russia, Austria, Prussia, Britain and France. As Britain's Royalist allies were committed to supporting Spanish efforts to recover and control her South American colonies, the Foreign Office was told to back-pedal on the South American issue. But 'that most discreet of all military engines, the Royal Navy' could and did unofficially intervene.[61] A British man-of-war was detailed to bring one of Bolivar's principal agents and advisers from Gibraltar, and a meeting was arranged with him and Bolivar, and British envoys, to discuss terms. The British Government's terms to assist Bolivar's War of Independence were a secret supply of gold in return for preferential trading rights over the Dutch, French and Americans—terms which were apparently agreed to just off the Venezuelan coast aboard Stirling's *Brazen*.[62] Secrecy was paramount— all traces of the *Brazen*'s log for the period 1 January to 30 June 1817 have been removed from Admiralty files. Bolivar went on to fight the Spaniards and claim Venezuela and Columbia in 1819, although Britain did not actually recognise South American independence until 1824.

Other problems confronted Admiral Harvey in July 1817. The Governor of Trinidad and the Mayor of Kingston, among others, were beseeching him to provide protection for merchants at British ports by controlling piracy.[63] In view of his brothers' business interests, Stirling was only too happy to carry out orders to seize and detain any suspect vessels,[64] and the *Brazen* was involved in a number of interventions. This period of adventure in Stirling's life drew to a close when, on 15 June 1818, Harvey advised the Admiralty the ship was badly in need of repair, and would be sent back to England.[65] Her young captain's efforts had not gone unrecognised, for accompanying James was a glowing letter of commendation from his Commander-in-Chief. The zeal and alacrity of 'this intelligent and excellent officer' were above praise, wrote Harvey, and

> it is to his acquaintance with foreign languages, his thorough knowledge of the station, particularly the Spanish Main, and his gentleman like and conciliatory manners, that I am so much indebted for assisting me in the preservation of a friendly intercourse with the foreign colonies in this command…it will be as gratifying for your Lordships to hear as it is for me make so honourable a report of this intelligent and excellent officer, whom I detach from my command with considerable regret; but I feel at the same time a very sincere pleasure in thus recommending him to the notice of your Lordships.[66]

The *Brazen* was paid off on 11 August 1818 and taken out of commission. Though looking forward to seeing the family, it no doubt saddened Stirling to leave his first ship and his shipmates behind him. Reporting his return to the Admiralty, Stirling was given the news he dreaded. Like so many other aspiring young officers, he was to be placed on half-pay, a redundancy measure that kept them waiting on the lists until another active post became available. It is possible one of the Admiralty Lords hinted that his service had been of value and promotion was likely, but it was not until 7 December 1818 that anything was heard. On that day James was finally promoted to Post Captain, which meant a higher salary and the right to command larger ships. It also meant he was now in line for automatic promotion, through to Admiral, on the basis of seniority, though in December 1818 James Stirling was 675th on the Seniority List.[67] Nevertheless, his half-pay pension was over £220 per annum, so he could look forward to an enjoyable leave.

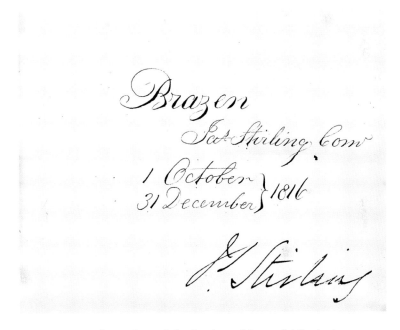

Front page of HMS *Brazen*'s log book, and James Stirling's signature

4

Mangles, Marriage and a New Challenge

ONCE HIS LEAVE had been arranged, James caught up with his family at Henley Park. During the latter part of 1817 and early 1818, the whole family had been involved in a battle to establish father Andrew's right to bear the Arms and claim descent from the ancient Stirlings of Cadder. Proving that he was the legitimate male heir was of utmost importance to family-minded Andrew, but as he was now 67 and in 'precarious health',[1] it was his eldest son William who collected most of the documentary evidence to fight the claims of other Stirlings (particularly the Stirlings of Keir). The case was heard in the Court of Lord Lyon, and rested 'on the identity of their ancestor, Robert Stirling of Lettyr with the umquhile Robert Striveling whose bairns were in 1541 declared next in the Cadder succession to Janet Stirling, the last of the old line of Stirling of Cadder'.[2] It was a long, drawn-out hearing involving many lawyers, but Andrew of Drumpellier eventually emerged victorious as the 21st Baron of Cadder.

During the remainder of 1818 and in the following year, James travelled widely. He visited a cousin, W. G. Stirling, who lived on the Isle of Wight, staying for a while with him at Borthwood Farm (inland from Sandown on the east coast),[3] becoming quite attached to what the locals called their 'Garden Isle'.[4] He then toured the Continent, possibly undertaking some diplomatic work for the Foreign Office.[5] While in France Stirling met James Mangles, cousin of his future bride. James Mangles was six years older than James Stirling, had entered the navy as a boy, and served under Captain Ross Donnelly during the French Wars. He had seen service at the Cape and South America, though never at the same time as Stirling, been made Lieutenant in 1806 (three years before Stirling) and given his first command in 1814. The following year he had been promoted to Captain and placed on half-pay.[6] From 1816 he and a friend, Charles Irby, had toured Egypt, Syria and Asia Minor, reaching the hidden city of Petra early in 1818, where only two Europeans had ever been seen before, and returning via Constantinople, Cyprus and then by French ship to Marseilles.[7] Their descriptive letters home formed the basis for a book titled *Travels in Egypt, Nubia, Syria and Asia Minor in 1817–1818,*

Stirling Crest. Motto Castrum et Nemus Strivilense means the camp
and woodlands of Stirling

Courtesy Margaret Lenfestey

published in 1823.[8] Many of the letters had been sent to James Mangles' 56-year-old
uncle of the same name, who lived with his large family at Woodbridge, near
Guildford. Mangles senior had made a small fortune in banking and owned a
merchant shipping company whose ships traded to India and conveyed convicts to
New South Wales.[9] He was a pillar of county society, having held the position of
both Mayor of Guildford and High Sheriff of Surrey,[10] and it is almost certain that
Andrew and Anne Stirling, living only 10 miles from Guildford at Henley Park,
would have met him some time after their arrival in 1815.

The younger Mangles (cousin James) was known for his passion for botany,
and in 1819 had been asked to join the well-known gardeners of the day, John and
Jane Louden, on a tour of the great gardens of Britain and Europe. Knowledge
gained at this time undoubtedly helped his future studies and identification of West
Australian flora (particularly the Kangaroo Paw *Anigozanthos manglesii*). When
cousin James returned from this trip in 1820, he invited James Stirling to meet his
relatives at Woodbridge. Family lore holds that when Stirling drove his horse and
carriage from the gates to the house for this first meeting, he had to swerve to avoid
hitting a small girl riding two donkeys, one foot on the back of each.[11] This was
James' introduction to 13-year-old Ellen, his future bride.

While James was touring abroad and meeting those who called on his parents and sisters at Henley Park,[12] changes had occurred in the Bow Church Yard business. Father Andrew now had nothing to do with the firm, which was run by his older sons. However on 22 July 1819 the eldest son, William, had sold out his interest in the family firm to Sir James Home, already an investor.[13] This left Walter to actually run the business, for Home returned to India, John was still in America, and Charles was pursuing his own interests. William had correctly forecast the change in demand from linens to cotton and had entered a partnership with Joseph Beckton of Manchester to invest in the cotton spinning industry.[14] Trading as Stirling & Beckton from May 1821, the partners built and operated a cotton mill in Lower Mosley Street, Manchester, using all the new technology of the age.

During 1821 brother John returned from America with Elizabeth and their two children, Jane and Andrew.[15] This little boy, who was dearly loved by the whole family, was destined to follow his uncle James to Western Australia and die there while still quite a young man. John was not very interested in the family business and was keen to take his family back to Scotland, where he eventually settled at St Andrews. James' youngest brother Edward was now employed as a Collector for the East India Company at Nursingpore, having left Haileybury College with high recommendations in 1816. Brother Robert had left with his regiment for a tour of duty in New South Wales, while his sisters Dorothea, Anna, Mary Noel and Agnes were still unmarried, living with their parents but spending time in frequent visits to relatives. The only cloud on the horizon was the Admiralty Board's refusal to readmit Uncle Charles to active service, despite his appeal in July,[16] though he was restored to Flag Officer status and once more addressed as Senior Vice Admiral of the White.[17]

The year 1822 was a more significant one for the Stirling clan. The Bow Church Yard business was keeping its head above water, even though Sir James Home pulled out of the partnership in October.[18] In Manchester the mill was prospering and William was contemplating opening a new factory.[19] And two more of the family married. Brother Charles wed the Admiral's only daughter, Charlotte Dorothea Stirling, whilst James' second youngest sister, Mary Noel, pulled off a coup by marrying her parents' landlord, Henry William Richard Westgarth Halsey, owner of Henley Park. James was at home at the time of the engagement, and thus involved in the search for alternative accommodation for his parents and sisters. Fortunately, a suitable lease was found just a few miles away, at Pirbright Lodge, Pirbright, which became the family base for the rest of their parents' lives.

For James, Mary's wedding day was a special occasion for more reasons than one. That very morning, 26 November 1822, he approached James and Mary Mangles for permission to marry their second youngest daughter, Ellen, with whom he had fallen hopelessly in love. She was everything he wanted: adventurous, not yet introduced to the simpering ways of high society, well educated, amusing and attractive. Her extreme youth was no concern for, after all, his mother had married at 15 and had had no regrets. Mary Mangles' account of this formal meeting, so much a convention of the day, is refreshing in its candour and revelation of its emotional nature. She told her brother, General Sir John Hughes, how Stirling had 'for some time past, nay, for these two years, been exceedingly attached to my daughter Ellen', and had been gathering resolve since spring to make a proposal. Mary was hard pressed to disguise her delight, describing James as

> deservedly a great favorite with both of us, high in his profession, having been a post Captain for, I believe, from four or five years (and I have known him for four), his character unimpeachable for honour and integrity, joined to an intelligent mind and a handsome face and figure…very domestic, prudent, and steady…and really a most gentlemanly, elegant young man.[20]

Could the 15-year-old Ellen (who was not present at the meeting) object? Mary described her as 'juvenile even for her years', preferring 'riding on horseback, swinging, driving the donkey chaise, and rowing the boat, to dancing or conversing sentimentally with the Beaux'. Just 'yesterday she said she did not like any gentlemen much, but doubtless in this respect her taste will alter'. She was concerned her daughter might see Stirling as 'not desirable', 'being double her age and not weigh'd down with riches'. His 'want of fortune' was a drawback, she confided to her brother,

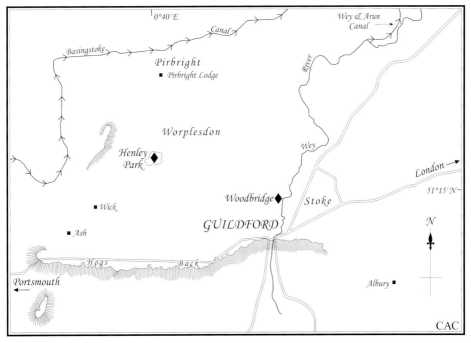

County Surrey, showing the location of Henley Park, Pirbright (the later home of James' parents) and Woodbridge, the Mangles' estate

'but in every connection of this sort there is always something one would wish otherwise, and, as he is high in his profession for his age, money may be acquired in after life, but ability to acquire it never can'.

It was agreed that Ellen not be told of the proposal until she finished her schooling in two years' time, and that in the meantime James would be invited to travel around with the Mangles family, who were expecting their son Charles home in a few months' time. Charles was seven years James' junior, but the two young men had become great friends and were likely to be an asset together in social situations.

Over the winter members of the two families spent a lot of time together, even ice-skating on the frozen River Wey which ran in front of Woodbridge House.[21] The Stirling girls liked Ellen very much, and in the carefree environment any objections Ellen might have felt about a man twice her age totally evaporated. James also found that he sympathised with many of the views expressed by his larger-than-life future

Ellen as a young girl
Courtesy Battye Library 1324B

father-in-law. Politics, the Empire and colonisation were all subjects upon which Mangles senior had definite and somewhat reformist ideas, and he thoroughly enjoyed debating them with James. He also impressed on his daughter's suitor the need to cultivate powerful friends if he wanted to make his way in the world—a far cry from proud Andrew, who never advised his sons to seek favours.

At this very time James' father's health was deteriorating rapidly. Long conversations were a thing of the past, and it was painful for all the family to see the man they loved waste away to a shadow. After what the Family Bible recorded as 'an illness of many years continuance which he endured with the most gentle patience and the humblest resignation to the Divine Will', Andrew died on 29 March 1823 aged 73, and was interred in Pirbright Church.

Whilst expected, Andrew's death was still a shock for the family, who gathered from various quarters to support their mother and to acknowledge William as the

James' father, Andrew Stirling

Courtesy Mrs Stirling Aird/Simon Jauncey

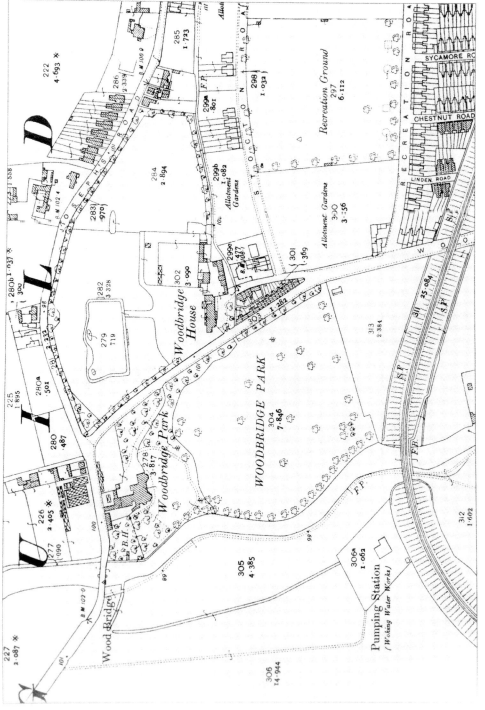

The Woodbridge estate near Guildford in 1912. The Mangles' home was Woodbridge Park. *Courtesy Guildford Museum and Lyn Clark*

Ellen's family home at Woodbridge

Courtesy Surrey Record Office, Woking ref. PX/136/11 (sketch); Guildford Museum and Lyn Clark (photo)

new head of the family, 22nd Baron of Cadder and holder of the Drumpellier Superiority. All felt a keen sense of loss, and it was perhaps James' sadness at this time that led Ellen's parents to release him from his promise to wait two years, and allow the pair to marry on Ellen's 16th birthday. This fell on 4 September, time enough for the Stirling family to end their mourning, and time also to plan a splendid occasion, for James Mangles never did anything by halves. With loud voice and bulbous nose (he was known as 'Old Potato Face'[22]), he had at one time owned 'a yellow coach with coachman and footman in livery of yellow & buff and his crest and coat of arms displayed on the coach sides'. As the coat of arms consisted of two black crosses separated by a diagonal blue and white band, and with two leopards and three fleurs-de-lis,[23] it could hardly be missed.

His wife Mary was in many ways his opposite. She was a beautiful and deeply religious woman, the daughter of John Charles Hughes, of Middleton Hall, Northumberland, and known for her taste and good works. James and Mary had twelve children, the ten surviving to adulthood all becoming significant members of James Stirling's extended family, especially the brothers Charles and Ross Donnelly.

'Old potato face' James Mangles, banker, ship owner and MP

Courtesy Guildford Museum

Both brothers were then in the service of the East India Company: Ross as a Collector and Charles as a Lieutenant on one of the company's ships. Charles had just returned from a round voyage to Bengal on the *Marchioness of Ely,* a ship he would eventually command, but Ross was still in India and Stirling would not meet him for some time.

The Mangles Family Tree

(surviving children only)

James Mangles   m   Mary Hughes

(1762–1838)   1790   (1773–1852)

Caroline	Frederick	Pilgrim	Charles E.	Emily	Ross Donnelly
1792–??	1794–1869	1795–1828	1798–1874	1799–1826	1801–77
m 1815	m		m	m 1825	m 1830
1. Arthur	Marion		Rose	Henry	Harriet
Onslow	Scott		Newcomb	Waitby	Newcomb
Jane		**ELLEN**	(Rev) Albert	Hamilla	
1803–24		1807–74	1809–65	1812-??	
		m 1823	m 1833	m 1833	
		James	Georgina	William	
		STIRLING	Scott	Preston	

The day before his wedding on 4 September 1823, James wrote to the Admiralty requesting six months' leave of absence. It was standard procedure for half-pay officers to advise the Admiralty of a change of address, and James cheekily informed them 'it is my intention to reside at Geneva, and my object is amusement'.[24] His further object would have been to introduce his very young bride to married life, and consolidate their relationship, far away from her childhood home.

The wedding, at Stoke Church, Guildford, was officiated by the Reverend Arthur Onslow who, being married to Ellen's eldest sister, thereby became Stirling's brother-in-law. The witnesses were both Admirals: Uncle Charles Stirling came down from Bath to stand for James, while an old friend of the bride's father, from East Indies trading days, Admiral Ross Donnelly, stood for Ellen.[25] Uncle Charles, Vice Admiral of the White, and Donnelly, Rear Admiral of the Red, knew each other, having both seen action at Montevideo in 1807. Now in their 60s, the two would have had plenty to reminisce about at the grand reception at Woodbridge, the property looking as handsome as any country gentleman's seat, with its manicured lawns leading down to the river. Old James may well have over-imbibed, for he inadvertently inscribed the wedding date as one day earlier in the Family Bible.[26]

James and Ellen spent some nine months on honeymoon in Europe, including a Grand Tour, before returning home to Woodbridge, where Mangles senior had had extensions made to accommodate them.[27] Being away for so long probably sweetened the homecoming, for James commented on being 'ever grateful for the invention of steam and steamboats' following the 12-hour Calais–Dover crossing, and of 'the gratification of finding myself at home'.[28] The couple returned in June, somewhat short of funds, which led James to write to the Admiralty asking for reinstatement of his half-pay pension.[29] While in France James had been involved in tracking down some missing papers to support William's retention of the Cadder title against another challenge lodged by the Keir Stirlings. Apparently the papers were found, for the family's right to the Cadder title was re-established by the end of 1824.[30]

Stoke Church, Guildford, in the 1820s
Courtesy Surrey Record Office, Woking, PX/136/2/1

Ellen had arrived home in an advanced state of pregnancy, and their first child, Andrew, was born at Woodbridge on 24 October 1824. The year had brought mixed blessings for the family—Ellen's older sister Jane had died earlier, aged just 21, and her sister-in-law, Mary Halsey, had given birth to a daughter, Anna, in February. In the midst of all these family milestones, James had busied himself writing a proposal to the Board of Longitude, originally formed to co-ordinate efforts to determine longitude but now offering a prize for the first person to suggest a practical means of establishing declinations of the compass at sea. Stirling's suggestion, that it could be calculated from variations in the earth's gravity, was read by the Board on 4 November 1824[31] but considered too impractical for prize-winner short-listing. It was, nevertheless, a clever move as the First Lord of the Admiralty, Lord Melville, was known to be keenly interested in polar exploration and magnetic variation.[32] A few months later Stirling was on another tack, writing directly to John Barrow, Secretary of the Admiralty, respectfully submitting 'a Plan and Model of a new mode of arranging the Stowage of Ships of War', adding:

> This Plan has already been submitted to the inspection of several Naval Officers and I feel authorised to believe by the opinions expressed by them that its adoption in His Majesty's Navy, would be found highly beneficial.[33]

These were two of a number of ideas Stirling put forward in his efforts to gain preferment in a return to active service. It was a highly competitive business, as the Admiralty was flooded with proposals and letters from hundreds of similarly ambitious young officers on the half-pay lists, and many had better connections than James. But by December 1825 he was becoming desperate, all the more so because he had 'been brought into a situation of great hardship'. Stirling's nemesis, the *Hercules* indemnity case, had returned to haunt him. During that year the case was reheard, the previous verdict overturned, and Stirling found himself £363 out of pocket, as he had to pay the balance of the prosecution expenses after getting some support from the Treasury. The case still left a bitter taste for, as he pointed out, he had 'seized the *Hercules* in obedience to my Instructions…proceeded against her by the advice of the Crown Lawyers [and] had the approbation of my Admiral as to my Conduct'.[34]

This brief trough in Stirling's affairs was not to last. On the other side of the world, events were unfolding that would influence his future career. Following a decision by senior policy makers to strengthen Britain's position in the Eastern trade, and complement the Singapore base recently ceded to them by the Dutch,[35] a British outpost had been established on Melville Island, at the northern tip of Australia, on 26 September 1824.[36] Captain Bremer, who had chosen the site on directions from the Admiralty, oversaw the construction of Fort Dundas and a garrison to house the troops and convicts before he left on 12 November. His report on the mission reached the Admiralty on 25 April 1825. John Barrow, Secretary of the Admiralty, was delighted with its content and informed his counterpart in the Colonial Office, Wilmot Horton, that

> there never was so promising a spot in a naval coml. & agricultural point of view, as the islands of Melville & Bathurst & the intervening strait…I have no doubt that…it will become another Singapore. If I am right, would it not be eminently advisable to colonise it at once either by Government or an Association of Individuals?[37]

But their jubilation was short-lived. By January 1825 the small, isolated settlement had become low on food and fresh water, and scurvy had broken out. This news, plus further discrediting comments about the usefulness of the site, finally reached the Colonial Office early in March 1826,[38] and by April orders had been given for the relief of the outpost.[39] The job was assigned to HMS *Success*, under the command of the recently recommissioned Captain Stirling.

It has been thought in the past that Stirling's commission was tied in with the deteriorating situation on Melville Island, but his commission was dated 23 January 1826[40] (five days before his 35th birthday), and thus *pre-dated* the orders to relieve Melville Island. It would appear, in this age of patronage, that someone had pulled strings behind the scenes to have his name put ahead of the hundreds of other officers desperate for recall—but who?

While the Melville Island situation was thought to be linked to Stirling's command of the *Success*, many supposed James Mangles to have been the string-puller.[41] As the East India Company had been consulted over the plan to settle Melville Island,[42] it was thought that James Mangles, with his trade and shipping interests, may have held sufficient sway to have suggested his son-in-law for the relief mission. But Mangles was only a shareholder, not a director of the East India Company, and so lacked major influence.[43] Unquestionably, he would have helped had the opportunity arisen; the dealings of his shipping company had furnished a wide range of contacts and a vast collection of literature. His library held works on many topics, but he was particularly interested in New South Wales and had books and records of parliamentary proceedings covering everything from Cook's first discoveries to the recently submitted Bigge report. When Stirling learned through contacts[44] of the Admiralty Board's interest in Australia, he used these library resources extensively to advance his knowledge of the region. Three of the Mangles' ships had constantly plied the route from London to New South Wales. The *Guildford* and the *Mangles* between them had carried out fourteen convict voyages, and the *Surrey* eleven, including a nightmare trip in 1814 when all on board went down with typhus, leaving no one to navigate until another ship supplied a volunteer to get her into port.[45]

Both the first Viscount Melville, Henry Dundas (First Lord of the Admiralty 1804–05), and the second Viscount, Robert Dundas (First Lord of the Admiralty

1812–27), had been concerned with reports from returning Mangles' convict transport ships,[46] and their owner could well have capitalised on the connection to bring his son-in-law to this powerful family's notice. (Stirling had referred to 'My Lord Melville' in some of his very early letters and clearly admired both men, but no direct connection has been found.)

The most likely source of influence behind Stirling's appointment to HMS *Success*, however, was Tory MP and Third Lord of the Admiralty, 52-year-old Vice Admiral Sir George Cockburn, whose name James later gave to the sheltered sound south of Fremantle.

Cockburn's links with the Stirling family can be traced over a long period, beginning in the 1790s when he was stationed for nine years in the West Indies (marrying there), and where he would have known, or known of, Uncle Charles, the Resident Commissioner from 1803 to 1811. In 1811 Cockburn had been appointed Commissioner in 'an attempted mediation between Spain and her South American Colonies',[47] and as he evidently was well versed in Bolivar's revolutionary cause, his advice in all likelihood was sought by the Admiralty before Stirling's secret mission in 1817. Cockburn had by then met James, for he had been sent, as a Rear Admiral of the Blue, to Bermuda in 1812 to plan actions against the Americans in conjunction with Admiral Warren and Admiral Charles Stirling (who had been accompanied by James).[48] Cockburn had subsequently undertaken a series of highly successful coastal attacks which brought him Admiralty praise and elevation.[49]

After the war Cockburn became MP for Portsmouth and, in April 1818, a Junior Lord of the Admiralty.[50] He was thus on the Board when Stirling made his report at the end of his *Brazen* command in August 1818. Three years later, when Uncle Charles was submitting his appeal for remission of his court martial sentence, Cockburn was Vice Admiral of the Blue and Fourth Naval Lord. The appeal was refused, but Cockburn's influence perhaps can be seen in the Lords' decision to restore Charles Stirling to Flag Officer status.

In February 1824, when James was seeking a return to active service, Cockburn was Third Lord of the Admiralty and in a clear position to influence preferment. James' record of diplomatic work in South America, combined with his growing interest in, and knowledge about, Australia, cast him as an ideal candidate for any Australian mission the Admiralty Board was contemplating—and there were more significant issues than little Melville Island.

For quite some time both the Foreign Office and the Admiralty had been concerned about Australia's western third, then known as New Holland. They were worried that France might lay a claim if the Dutch, who by discovery had prior claim, were not prepared to act. Indeed, the Admiralty had sent Lieutenant Phillip Parker King to New Holland in 1817 to complete without delay the exploration and coastal survey work begun by Matthew Flinders. King had returned in poor health in 1823 with reports which had switched attention from southern New Holland to the northern end. His discoveries, together with the push from East India Company traders, had resulted in the establishment of the Melville Island outpost in 1824. This allayed Admiralty anxieties for a while, although they knew that the French ship *Coquille* (under Captain Duperry) had been given explicit instructions in 1822 to investigate the western coast of New Holland.[51]

When the Admiralty Lords met early in January 1826, information had been received that the French were again taking a close interest in New Holland. The French *chargé d'affaires* in London had issued a memorandum that His Most Christian Majesty had despatched the corvette *L'Astrolabe* on a voyage of discovery, and requested British officials in Australia to afford every facility to its Captain, Dumont D'Urville.[52] This was disturbing enough, but within days fresh news came in that the young French surveyor, Jules Blosseville, who had accompanied Duperry on the *Coquille* and returned with her in March 1825, was preparing detailed reports and recommending south-western Australia as a site for a French penal colony.[53] Blosseville's first report was published in January 1826, and the second in March (which appears to have triggered the letters sent by the Secretary of the Admiralty, John Barrow, in March 1826 to Governor Darling in New South Wales, ordering the establishment of additional outposts).

The possibility of being forestalled by the French in occupation of Australia's Western Third seriously alarmed the Admiralty Lords. There was clearly a need to ascertain the extent of French interest in New Holland without arousing international concern. Here Cockburn could have recommended James for his past diplomatic skills. The HMS *Success* had been readied to join the Eastern Station at Trincomalee (responsible for the western Pacific and Indian Ocean region) and if Stirling was given its command, he could from there, in secret, help to ascertain the extent of French interest in New Holland. This would explain his appointment before the news arrived in March that the beleaguered Melville Island outpost required relief.[54] That news, in fact, provided a heaven-sent smokescreen for a direct voyage to Australia, as also did a request from Treasury for a vessel to convey specie to New South Wales, which was acutely short of legal tender.[55] The official confirmation that the *Success* could undertake this request was dated 23 May 1826,[56] although the *Success* log recorded that eighty-three cases of money had been loaded on board almost a month earlier, on 30 April.[57]

On 12 February, possibly in company of family members, Stirling was piped on board to take official command of the *Success*.[58] She was a brand new ship, having been built at Pembroke dock in 1825 as a model of the newer, smaller ships needed for peacetime deployment. At 114 ft long and 32 ft wide, she was a 6th-rated ship with 28 guns, 20 of them 32-pounders.[59] Her complement of 171 sailors and marines was mostly raised from other ships, some from HMS *Britannia.* The ship's company would have been impressed with their new captain, for he was tall and slim with an unmistakable air of authority. Some had heard on the grapevine that he had a reputation for fairness, with high expectations of his crew. When he spoke his voice carried well, and he enunciated his words slowly and clearly. He had a full head of

HMS *Success* hove-to off Carnac Island —1827. *Contemporary watercolour painting by Ross Shardlow*

dark hair and black eyes that missed nothing and were usually alight with
enthusiasm. On the other hand, Stirling was pleased with the senior officers he had
been assigned. His First Lieutenant was Edmund Yonge, who came with high recommendations; Second Lieutenant was John Carnac who, like himself had seen action
in the 1812 War, and whose father was an Acting Governor in India; and Third
Lieutenant was William Preston, an Admiral's son whose family home was not far
from Guildford.[60] (Preston would later become Stirling's brother-in-law.) The Master
was R. W. Millroy from the Navy Board, the Surgeon F. R. Clause, and Purser
Thomas Woodman, an Admiralty appointment.[61]

There was much to be done readying the ship for sea, and time passed quickly.
But Stirling's eager anticipation was suddenly crushed by receipt of news on or
before 19 February that the family's Bow Church Yard business had failed.[62] A
shocked James replied in subdued tone immediately to Walter, unable to 'offer any
ideas for your consideration that can in any way lighten your distress'. But he
counselled his brother:

> You must take for comfort your own conscious rectitude, in patient resignation to
> the Divine Will, and under his permission, trust to the long exercised fortitude of
> your spirit for power to bear up under this great affliction…I am aware how little
> comfort there is in such general views, but my dear Walter, look forward still with
> hope; we have many solid sources of gratification, and many circumstances may
> arise, in the hope and expectation of which we may find comfort.[63]

Many small joint-stock companies failed in the recession of 1825, but to the
family the collapse of the Bow Church Yard business was more than just a financial
disaster. James' mother Anne, for example, lamented the social stigma that came
with the debacle. But as one long-time friend noted, there was at least 'one subject
for congratulation…the success of Captain James Stirling'.[64]

The said Captain must have felt keenly the need to capitalise on his present
commission in order to restore the family fortunes. He would most certainly have
spent time in London during March and April 1826 at the Admiralty's hydrography
room, pouring over maps of his coming route into seas he had never before
encountered. And the Admiralty had a wealth of maps from the voyages of Cook,
Flinders and recently King, as well as the Dutch maps of the 1600s, and French maps
from the 1790s. It is probable that Stirling met for talks with Lieutenant King[65] in
London at this time, as King was finalising sketches and charts for his book *Narrative
of a survey of the intertropical and Western Coasts of Australia 1818–1822* which was
published in 1826.[66] From King, Stirling would have learned that the only part of the
coast he had not surveyed minutely, because of illness among the crew, was that
between King George's Sound and Shark's Bay.[67] However, on King's third voyage he
had anchored off Rottnest Island (where he had been unable to find water) and noted
both the dangerous offshore reefs and the entrance to a river which, he accepted from

previous reports, held nothing of importance.[68] Meeting King would have given Stirling a chance not only to obtain copies of his charts, but also to learn first hand about tidal variations, wind patterns and safe anchorages in the regions he would sail.

As Stirling readied the *Success* for departure, he just had time to meet his brother Robert, who had returned from New South Wales on the *Mary Hope* with Governor Brisbane, to whom he had been aide-de-camp.[69] Arriving at Milford Haven on 27 May, Robert caught up with James some days later and had much to tell. He had been quickly accepted into New South Wales society and had dined many times at Government House, even with the 'Governor's Noble Guest'— Hyacinthe de Bougainville, commander of the French ships *La Thetis* and *L'Esperance*.[70] Bougainville had arrived in Sydney in July 1825 and stayed three months, ostensibly on a voyage of scientific discovery, but Robert (along with the Governor and many others) had doubts. The French ships had spent time surveying the south coast with a suspiciously close interest. This information James was able to pass on to the Admiralty before they received the official Colonial Office report, for the returning Governor Brisbane took a few days' leave in Scotland before visiting Downing Street. Robert was able to pass on other information about conditions in eastern Australia, both environmental and socio-political, and advice about the acquisition and value of a land grant. He had been part of Surveyor Oxley's expedition to Moreton Bay in 1823, and commended for his service,[71] for which he had been allocated a grant of land in the Hunter Valley. This he wanted James to see, and hopefully build on. There was very little time for further chat, for after a final inspection and the issue of two months' advance pay on 6 June,[72] the *Success* was cleared for departure.

On 9 June 1826 she finally sailed, but without Ellen who had been persuaded, despite her wishes, to remain behind with 2-year-old Andrew at her parents' home in Guildford.

5

Second Command: HMS *Success*

1826–1828

DESPITE THE BRIEF reunion with Robert, James left England with a heavy heart. Brother Walter's bankruptcy case had yet to be heard, and his mother was sick with worry. Although missing Ellen, James was pleased she and little Andrew could provide some comfort for her in what would be a very stressful period. Somehow his present commission had to be turned to advantage to restore financial security for his mother and sisters, for William's Manchester business was now carrying the entire burden and the textile trade was still depressed. But just how he could make more than his regular pay was perplexing; there were no longer the prizes of wartime. His official orders were explicit: to proceed directly to New South Wales, where he was to deliver specie to the Governor, General Ralph Darling, and check the latest news about Melville Island. He was then to head north to determine a more acceptable location for that trading post, preferably closer to Croker Island, east of the present base, and with at least more fresh water.[1] When his mission was complete, he was to report to the Commander-in-Chief of the Eastern Station, Admiral William H. Gage, to serve out the rest of his commission (normally three years).

The voyage went well, although the ship was becalmed for a day before crossing the Equator on 16 July 1826. They arrived at the Cape of Good Hope on 2 September and remained there until the 20th, taking on fresh provisions.[2] Immediately on arrival, James reported to the Naval Commander-in-Chief, Commodore H. H. Christian, taking with him Admiral Sir James Saumarez, the Napoleonic War hero who had been a passenger from London.[3] Some days later he paid an official visit to the Acting Governor, Richard Bourke (who would later govern Victoria). A similar protocol took place at Mauritius (then called Isle de France), which *Success* reached on 19 October. During a two-day stay[4] Stirling paid his respects to its Governor, Sir Charles Colville, before giving the order to weigh anchor for the last and most challenging leg of his journey.

Bearing directly east and taking advantage of the westerly winds, *Success* rounded Cape Leeuwin, the southern tip of Western Australia, just twelve days later, on 4 November. Stirling was deeply impressed by the constancy of the winds across the southern Indian Ocean, and it was probably around this time that his plans to explore the west coast above Cape Leeuwin finally took definite shape.

From his naval colleagues and the Mangles family, Stirling knew that British naval and merchant ships engaged in the valuable India trade were constantly at risk during the voyage between the Cape of Good Hope and the British bases in Bombay, Madras and Trincomalee. Ships had to tack along the east coast of Africa, often against the winds or with no wind at all, and cross the northern Indian Ocean exposed to attack by pirates or French or Dutch ships from their respective East Indies bases. It was a serious and costly problem, but Stirling believed he could see a solution. With a British outpost on the western coast of New Holland, India-bound ships could instead take advantage of the 'roaring forties' (the westerly winds across the southern Indian Ocean), so staying well clear of attack, and then bear north up the west coast of New Holland with the aid of winds from the land. A base of some kind would be necessary to secure the route and provide food, water and shipping supplies, as the rapid southerly passage could be very damaging. The deep harbour at King George's Sound had been used several times for repairs and watering since being discovered and named by Britain's George Vancouver in 1791.[5] But the south-facing sound could not provide the command of the Indian Ocean necessary to secure a supply base. Stirling well realised that foreign powers would only recognise a west-facing base as presenting any danger to their ships.

From charts at his disposal Stirling judged the most promising area on the west coast for this purpose to be that surrounding the Swan River, so named by the Dutchman Vlamingh in 1696 after the numbers of black swans he observed. Vlamingh had been in search of trade items for the Dutch East India Company and signs of previously wrecked Dutch vessels, and, finding neither, had left the area convinced it held nothing of importance.[6] He did, however, name 'Isle Rottenest' (later Rottnest) after the many rat-like animals (now known as the marsupial quokka) seen on that island which he, like King after him, condemned for its lack of fresh water. Nevertheless, the Swan River region was well south of the arid areas scorned by the Dutch and by Britain's William Dampier in 1699, and, as far as Stirling could tell, it had never been thoroughly examined by a British officer, for neither King nor Flinders had entered the river.

To Stirling's trained eye, the region held promise as a possible trade or naval base. The presence of islands off the river mouth suggested the possibility of secure anchorages and, being on the same latitude as Sydney, it should be temperate. Most importantly, it faced west and could command a large area of coastline. If he could get permission to explore the Swan River and surrounding country, it would provide an unparalleled opportunity to get his name on the map as explorer, impress the Admiralty, and possibly improve his and his family's fortunes. So, well before the *Success* entered Sydney heads, on 28 November 1826 (after a record thirty-seven day passage from Isle de France[7]), Stirling had made up his mind to explore the Swan River area. He had also thought through all the arguments he would need to persuade the authorities that it was in their interests to allow him to do so, before or after his Melville Island mission.

The day after his arrival, Stirling supervised the unloading of the thirty-three cases of specie containing £20,000 for the colony's privy chest,[8] then, donning dress uniform, he reported to the Senior Naval Officer in port, Sir James Brisbane, whose health was declining.[9] Brisbane was Commander of HMS *Warspite 74*, the largest naval vessel to visit Sydney harbour. He had arrived at Port Jackson from Trincomalee on 18 October, accompanied by HMS *Volage 28* under Captain Dundas,[10] with orders to show the flag before proceeding to South America.[11] When HMS *Success 28* arrived as well, it was the first time Sydney had seen three sizeable British warships in harbour at one time. Their crews boosted Sydney's population by some seven hundred men, and caused much rejoicing. The captains and their respective lieutenants were invited as honoured guests to celebrate St Andrew's Day (30 November) at Cumming's Hotel, in Sydney Town. Led by Captain Piper, one of the wealthiest residents, the fifty-five gentlemen present at the dinner made a series of toasts, including one to 'Captain Stirling and HMS *Success*'.[12] It was noted at this time that there was a close resemblance between Captain James Stirling and his younger brother, Lieutenant Robert Stirling, who had been known to many of those present. The following day Stirling made an appointment to see Governor Darling.

Darling had been expecting him and was well aware of the Admiralty's fears of French intent. Indeed, on 9 October he had informed Colonial Office officials that

> it will not be easy to satisfy the French, if they are desirous of establishing themselves here, that there is any valid objection to their doing so on the Western Coast.[13]

The Secretary of State for War and the Colonies, Lord Bathurst, had been less concerned with the West Coast when he had written to Darling on 1 and 11 March 1826. In the first of these dispatches, Bathurst had instructed that immediate possession be taken of Western Port (east of Port Phillip Bay in modern Victoria), for

> if the French have any designs on any part of New South Wales, it would be *there*, because in the first place it commands the Strait directly opposite Van Diemen's Land; and in the second, they have claimed the discovery [sic] (which is not true however) of that part of the Coast.[14]

But he also ordered a survey to be made of Shark's Bay on the West Coast, which he changed in his second dispatch to King George's Sound, because Shark's Bay 'is understood to be for the most part barren and devoid of all circumstances which could invite a Settlement'.[15] Darling had responded immediately to these instructions, sending out two parties on 4 November. He reported his actions to Bathurst on 24 November, just four days before Stirling's arrival, stating:

New South Wales Governor, Major-General Ralph Darling

Cygnet Swan River booklets

> I have the honor…to transmit to Your Lordship, a copy of the 'Secret Instructions' with which Major Lockyer and Captain Wright were furnished, the former proceeding as Commandant of King George's Sound, and the latter of Western Port.[16]

Darling's orders to Lockyer—to establish a settlement, with a party of convicts, at King George's Sound[17]—had certainly overstepped his official instructions for a survey only. It would have come as a surprise to Stirling, and a possible obstacle to his plans for Swan River. The explanation Darling later gave for amending his instructions was that he wished to forestall the French. He had heard, and reported, that French discovery ships were bound for the West Coast, though he had no actual evidence of fresh French interest at the time he was writing. Darling may also have had other motives—for example, to establish another isolated place of confinement for the worst convicts, or to divert official attention from the storm brewing in internal New South Wales politics.[18] But there is little doubt that his concern regarding French intentions increased with the visit of a French 'vessel of Discovery' commanded by Captain D'Urville, which reached Port Jackson on 2 December 1826.[19]

On the day of its arrival, and in the company of Captain Dundas of the *Volage*, Stirling made an official visit to the corvette *L'Astrolabe*. They exchanged pleasantries with D'Urville, who found them both to be 'well bred officers who enjoy a high reputation'.[20] Before he left on 20 December, D'Urville dined several times with Stirling, providing an opportunity to discuss the Melville Island mission and a chance for James to examine D'Urville's charts, for he knew the French had very detailed maps of parts of the Australian coast. But the sight of one particular map gave Stirling a shock; it was a copy of a detailed map of the Swan River that had been completed in June 1801.[21] Stirling knew, of course, about the Baudin expedition of 1801–02 in the ships *Geographe* and *Naturaliste*, for journals had been published in English in 1807, and again in 1817, and even reviewed in the influential *Quarterly Review*.[22] But such reports had provided very few maps and little detail of an interlude at Swan River when the *Naturaliste* had become separated from Baudin in the *Geographe*. The *Naturaliste*'s Captain Hamelin and Lieutenant Freycinet had waited for the *Geographe* for some three weeks, anchored off Rottnest Island, and in the interim had sent out exploring parties. They had mapped the offshore islands, noting dangerous reefs, and bestowed names on various prominent features. Simultaneously, the draftsman Heirisson was sent with another party to map the river. Crossing the bar at the river mouth, they travelled a considerable way inland, past the islands in the river that still bear his name. However, Heirisson and Freycinet had not been impressed, noting that the Swan 'was difficult to enter and one had to travel a great distance up river before finding fresh water'. When all this was relayed to Baudin at Shark Bay, the expedition leader decided not to return, for the place 'was not worth the trouble of stopping there' because

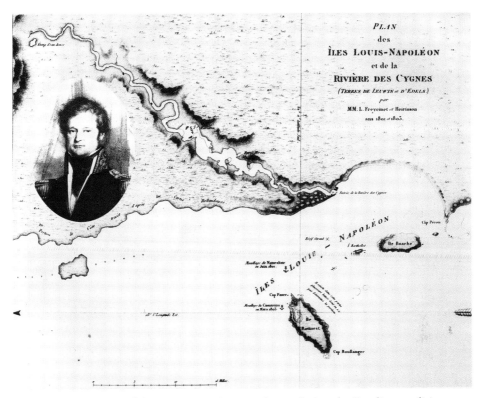

The French map of the Swan River in 1801, drawn during the Baudin expedition.
(Inset) Captain Dumont D'Urville

Reproduced from Leslie Marchant's France Australe*, with kind permission of the author*

the anchorage is very bad, insecure and open to the winds from South-west to North-west, and that at such times as they are blowing, the sea is very heavy there. The Swan River, which was explored for 18 to 20 leagues, offers no resources at all. Here and there some fresh water was found in the streams that enter into it, but they are very small.[23]

Baudin died before reaching France, and the journals that were subsequently published provided nothing to alter prevailing and unfavourable official opinions in England about the west coast of New Holland. The English versions of the journals certainly contained no maps or information to alert the Admiralty, or King before his 1821–22 voyages, of the fact that the Swan River ran a considerable distance inland and was worth investigating.

When Stirling first saw the 1801 Swan River map in D'Urville's chart room, it dashed his hopes of gaining fame as the region's first explorer. But his optimism soon resurfaced as he realised the French had not pursued their initial survey, nor had they traced the river to its source.[24] Moreover, D'Urville was very insistent that the French were no longer interested in the West Coast as their attention was now directed to New Zealand. His brief stay at King George's Sound the previous October (which had worried Darling) had simply been an unscheduled stopover to restore his crew.[25]

While Stirling dwelt on these issues, Governor Darling had had unexpected news. On the very same day that D'Urville anchored in Sydney Harbour (2 December), another much smaller ship had arrived—the *Isobella*, returning from Melville Island. Instead of confirming the dire circumstances of the island depot, she brought reassuring news in dispatches from the new Commandant, Major Campbell. Links had been established with Timor, scurvy was under control, and the settlement, despite initial difficulties, was now progressing most satisfactorily.[26] Governor Darling lost no time in passing on the good news to London, writing to Bathurst on 4 December. In this dispatch he also noted that he had spoken to Captain Stirling about his northern mission, and (whether at Stirling's instigation or his own) had advised that 'the season is not favourable for his proceeding at present'. Moreover, he added, the latest news 'may possibly prove that Melville Island is not altogether so unfavourable for the purpose intended, as has been represented'. The last issue Darling raised in this dispatch concerned the arrival of D'Urville, who had admitted spending six days at both King George's Sound and Western Port. Accepting D'Urville's assurances that he had come on a scientific voyage, a wary Darling nevertheless concluded:

> It is perhaps a fortunate event that he has found His Majesty's Ships lying here…as he may in Consequence have been more circumspect in his proceedings than he otherwise would have been.[27]

Stirling must have spoken to his Senior Naval Officer about his discussion with Darling for, although weak from dysentery, Brisbane wrote to London on 5 December to report that 'Captain Stirling is concerting with His Excellency the Governor for the speedy accomplishment of the important Service with which he is charged'.[28] But Stirling's mind was not wholly focused on his Melville Island mission. In a letter to Darling three days later, confirming an earlier discussion, he gave reasons for postponing the northern mission, and concluded by recommending 'that in the mean time the prosecution of His Lordship's wishes, relative to a New Settlement on the Western Coast, be forthwith adopted'.[29]

It would appear he had already persuaded Darling that a base at King George's Sound was insufficient protection from the French, and that British interests required another settlement on the West Coast.

Stirling's next submission to Darling on 14 December—carefully worded, well argued and politically adept—summarised his plans to explore the Swan River area. It was a crucial letter, for he needed Darling's support to justify so deploying a British warship without prior Admiralty approval. The arguments, indeed the very words Stirling used in this initial approach, before he had even seen Swan River, were to be repeated constantly in the lead-up to the establishment of the Colony. The letter began:

> Your Excellency having decided upon delaying the removal of the Establishment from Melville Island to Croker's Island until the termination of the Rainy Season in that Quarter, I have, in consequence, been led to consider in what way His Majesty's Ship, under my command, may in the meantime be most beneficially employed in furtherance of My Lord Bathurst's wishes. In the prosecution of these considerations, certain Ideas have been presented to me by Professional observation, relative to the necessity of immediately Seizing upon a position on the Western Coast of this Island near Swan River, in the 32nd Degree of Latitude. The various advantages, resulting from a Settlement in that Situation, and the reasons for occupying it, I now beg leave to submit to Your Excellency's notice.[30]

In eloquent, quite lengthy prose he put forward essentially four arguments to support his belief in the importance of the Swan River site:

1. *Navigational and strategic value* The Swan River lay at the pivot of 'two strong opposing wind forces' that would give ships stationed there control over the whole Indian Ocean. An enemy fleet aiming to attack the India Station, for example, could be quickly routed by ships, and refreshed men, from a Swan River base.

2. *Trade potential* The temperate climate of 32° latitude would allow production of many commodities that could be traded with tropical neighbours such as India, the islands of Malay and Mauritius.

3. *Cost advantages* Supplies for Swan River would provide an outward cargo for ships engaged in the China trade, which could also refurbish there before continuing their long journey.

4. *Re-victualling and convalescent potential for the Indian Establishments* Madras would only be three weeks away instead of three months (to England). As well as shortening essential supply lines, it would be a huge advantage for personnel whose health was often undermined by service in the tropics, as they could benefit from the healthy and bracing climate of nearby Swan River.[31]

The strategic location of the Swan River site clearly made it important, and Stirling urged Darling to take immediate action 'to prevent Britain being anticipated in the occupation of a position of such value'. As Darling had been sufficiently worried about the unclaimed Western Third to suggest to the Colonial Office on 9 October 1826 that his commission be altered to encompass the whole of Australia[32] (rather than just to the 129th parallel as it then stood), it is not surprising that he gave the proposed exploratory venture his conditional blessing. His dispatch to the Colonial Office on 18 December explained:

> I avail myself of this opportunity of forwarding for Your Lordship's consideration Copy of a Report which Captain Stirling has given in, pointing out the advantages which the local situation of Swan River holds out for the formation of a Settlement. The advantages, as stated, appear numerous and important, but I have no means of forming an opinion of the correctness of the data on which they are estimated; as he, however, is confident and sanguine, he cannot, that I am aware of, be better employed, until he proceeds to Melville island, than in ascertaining whether Swan River is as eligible for a settlement as he has been led to suppose; and I have accordingly acquiesced in his proceeding, as it is of great importance that so advantageous a position should not be taken possession of by the French…But I shall suspend my opinion until he returns.[33]

Once he had Darling's approval for the expedition, Stirling was eager to leave, but preparations had to be put on hold following the death of Sir James Brisbane on 19 December 1826.[34] His illness had taken a marked downturn during the month, and, as Stirling noted in a formal report to the Admiralty, 'the contest between his Constitution and his Complaint has terminated fatally'.[35]

With Brisbane's death Stirling became, by rank and length of service, the Senior Naval Officer of the British fleet at Port Jackson. This meant he was responsible for making the necessary adjustments to officer positions on all the naval vessels in port, as well as dealing with Sir James' funeral, his grieving family (who needed immediate assistance as well as arrangements to return home), and all the accumulated paperwork on Brisbane's desk.

Much later Stirling was to inform the Admiralty that certain papers he had found among Brisbane's effects had led to his decision to explore the Swan River area, viz:

> Among the papers which came into my possession by the Commodore's decease there was an Order from the Admiralty directed to the Senior Naval Officer… Having consulted with His Excellency General Darling on the subject to which that Order pertained it was decided advisable and expedient that it should forthwith be acted upon, and as the *Success* could not proceed to the Northward before April, that the intermediate time should be given to an exploration of the Western Coast of New Holland in furtherance of the wishes and view of His Majesty's Government.[36]

Dispatches to Brisbane undoubtedly had mentioned the problem of the unoccupied West Coast, but Stirling's plans had been laid long before Brisbane's death. However, the close coincidence of the timing of his submission, Darling's approval and Brisbane's death did allow for a little sequential blurring, in a report written eight months later. Moreover, both Darling and Brisbane had been convinced that it was in Britain's strategic interests to prevent any foreign claim to the West Coast, and both men would have understood Stirling's argument that the outpost at King George's Sound was an insufficient deterrent to occupation of the coast facing the Indian Ocean. There were no doubts that the exploratory investigation was warranted.

Stirling then threw considerable effort into arranging a suitable naval funeral for Brisbane, and Governor Darling gave every assistance. As a result the funeral, on Thursday 24 December, was a full ceremonial occasion, on a scale never before seen in Sydney. The procession consisted of

> the Band of the 57th Regiment; 101 rank and file from the Buffs; the Marines marching with guns for the firing party; Archdeacons and Chaplains, 8 pallbearers [including Stirling]; 24 coffin bearers; 200 seamen marching 4 deep followed by similarly lined midshipmen and warrant officers; members of the NSW Legislative Council; Private gentlemen and carriages.[37]

Sydney came to a standstill and 'every house in George Street thronged with Spectators, anxious to catch a glimpse at the noble though melancholy scene'. The *Sydney Gazette*, which carried a long description in its Saturday issue, noted that 'Captain Dundas, of the HMS *Volage* was much affected and seemed to mourn as a son while Captain Stirling, too, feelingly sympathised in the public loss'.

Under naval protocol, Stirling should have replaced Sir James Brisbane and taken command of *Warspite* until instructions were received from London. But doing this would have destroyed his chance to explore Swan River, and negated all his dreams. Instead, Stirling announced that Captain Dundas would be given command of the vessel, and be entrusted with taking Brisbane's family back to England. His own First Lieutenant, Mr Yonge, was to replace Dundas as commander of the *Volage*, while a midshipman from the *Volage*, Mr Belches, was promoted to Third Lieutenant on the *Success*.[38] These decisions were not popular, for Stirling had passed over the First Lieutenants of both the *Warspite* and the *Volage* and given their respective commands to younger men, and had also promoted Belches over a fellow midshipman of over seventeen years' service.[39] Grumbles reached the *Sydney Gazette*, though its editor refused to comment, 'particularly as we are willing to suppose Captain Stirling was influenced by impartiality'.[40] Apart from rewarding friendship and loyalty, the major influence over Stirling's decision to appoint younger men who he knew would get on with the job in hand, was more likely to have been impatience. He was aware that Major Lockyer was already on his way in the *Amity* to King George's Sound and could well steal a march on him at Swan River. He was yet to learn that the *Amity* had already arrived, dropping anchor off present-day Albany on Christmas Day.

On 6 January 1827 the *Warspite* and *Volage* sailed from Sydney harbour according to previous instructions.[41] This left Stirling free to ready the *Success* for the voyage of exploration. Not only were the normal stores and water put aboard for the complement of 160 men and eleven boys, the *Sydney Gazette* reported on 15 January that

> *Success* takes to Rottnest Island 2 cows and a bull, a sheep and a ram, 2 goats and 2 pigs for the purpose of leaving them to increase. This island is about 10 miles from the entrance of the Swan River; and from the circumstances of the natives never having visited it, there is no doubt but these animals will increase rapidly…All sorts of culinary seeds will be sent with the expedition for the purpose of benefiting future colonists.

Success was to be accompanied by the colonial schooner *Currency Lass* which was to take additional stores and survey equipment. Loaded aboard the *Success* were several smaller boats: a cutter, a pinnace, and two gigs for rapid transit.[42] Stirling also had two passengers, for Governor Darling wanted skilled observers to accompany the expedition. First was the New South Wales Colonial Botanist, Charles Frazer, and second, the highly regarded landscape artist Frederick Garling. Both men boarded the *Success* at Point Piper on 15 January 1827.

Charles Frazer had arrived in the colony with the 46th regiment in April 1816, but his botanical talents had been quickly recognised by fellow Scot, Governor Macquarie, who made him ex-officio Colonial Botanist. In following years he had accompanied expeditions to northern New South Wales, Moreton Bay, Van Diemen's Land and Norfolk Island. In 1821, when formally discharged from the army, he was officially appointed Colonial Botanist. From the new Botanic Gardens he raised numbers of useful plants for new settlements—including Melville Island. He clearly had an extensive knowledge of the eastern Australian landscape and its capabilities, and was an obvious choice to join Stirling.[43]

The artist Frederick Garling had arrived in Sydney with his parents in 1815. Far less is known of his background, but Garling was a self-taught and quick painter, working mostly in watercolour and rarely signing his pictures. He was called Sydney's 'first marine artist', as he painted almost every ship that entered Port Jackson in the 1820s, mostly with landscape backgrounds. His ability to sketch and paint realistic representations made him admirably suited for the Swan River expedition.[44]

On 17 January 1827 Stirling's longed-for adventure began when he took the *Success*, with *Currency Lass* following, out of Sydney harbour bound first for Hobart Town in Van Diemen's Land to deliver seventeen boxes of specie, before finally heading west. After a slow eleven-day passage, the two vessels arrived in Hobart and anchored off Sullivans Cove, the following day unloading and delivering the boxes of specie. Van Diemen's Land's Governor, Sir George Arthur, was delighted to see

Van Dieman's Land Governor, Sir George Arthur

From A. G. L. Shaw, Sir George Arthur 1784–1854

them and entertained Stirling, his officers and passengers right royally. The favours were returned, for it appears that Stirling did some maritime survey work whilst in Hobart, as the *Success* log records several otherwise inexplicable movements up and down the Derwent River during their ten-day stay.[45] Stirling continued to correspond with Arthur for many years and commemorated his warm hospitality when he named the highest bank at the mouth of the Swan River, 'Arthur's Head'.

On 4 February Stirling was joined by Captain H. J. Rous, his friend from schooldays, who arrived on the HMS *Rainbow* from Trincomalee. Son of the Earl of Stradbroke, Rous was described as 'a fine, tall good natured fellow, and…a great Sporting character'.[46] His name was given to many Australian landmarks, not least the north bank of the Swan River, opposite Arthur's Head, bestowed by Stirling. Rous would have brought news from the Commander-in-Chief of the Eastern Station, Admiral Gage which, together with their own plans, would have given the pair a lot to discuss. Hobart society also opened its doors to the two handsome young officers, one lady reporting:

> There has been a good deal of gaiety here lately some of it in Compliment to the Men of War that have been stationed here. The *Success* commanded by Captain Stirling, a nephew of Sir Walter's, has just left to the regret of his numerous Friends here.[47]

By 7 February, with farewells said, the *Success* and *Currency Lass* left Hobart bound, according to the local Press, for 'Rottnest Island, Swan River, on Discovery'.[48] Just off the south-west corner of Van Diemen's Land, however, the *Currency Lass* ran into difficulties in big seas. As Stirling put it in his later report to the Admiralty, 'the Vessel alluded to, after being torn to pieces by bad weather and having lost her rudder to the stroke of the Sea',[49] required help from the *Success* to return to the Derwent River. At this stage, and despite clear Admiralty orders against exploration by solitary vessels, Stirling decided to take the *Success* westward alone.[50]

The voyage from Hobart to Cape Leeuwin, the south-western tip of Australia named by the Dutch, took twenty-three days. Stirling used the time to closely peruse all the maps he had of the south-west coastline, but especially the copies his draftsmen had made from D'Urville's folio of French maps.

6

—

Swan River Explored

MAKING VERY GOOD time up the coast after rounding Cape Leeuwin, *Success* came in sight of Rottnest Island on 5 March 1827 and, after an unsuccessful attempt to find an anchorage nearer the mainland, spent the night just outside Thomson Bay, on the north-east side of that island. Stirling was to write two quite separate reports on this exploratory visit: one to Darling, dated 21 April 1827, which was forwarded to the Colonial Office,[1] and the other, dated 31 August 1827, directed to the Admiralty.[2] The report to Darling was in two sections: first, a day-to-day 'Narrative of Operations',[3] and second, 'Observations on the Territory' plus its 'Capabilities' which included a letter from Surgeon Clause on the healthiness of the climate.[4] Enclosed separately was the report from Frazer, the botanist.

The report to the Admiralty was shorter[5] and more organised, with information presented under headings similar to those Stirling had used in his South American report. The major difference between the two is that the long 'Narrative' of daily activities contained in Darling's report was cut to an outline in the Admiralty report. And, as might be expected, the latter placed more emphasis on anchorages and strategic value. As a more immediate document, the 'Narrative' is a good guide to James' experience of the region and, as this vitally affected the establishment of the new colony in Western Australia, it will be dealt with in some detail. Unless otherwise specified, all quotes are from the report to Darling. Seen as a whole, the joint reports were the most thorough ever to precede British colonial settlement in Australia, and far more detailed than Banks' observations about Botany Bay.

The *Success* log records that the day after arrival, the anchor was weighed at 5 a.m. and the ship made its way towards the mouth of the Swan River, with the gig going ahead to sound depths. It was an anxious time, for Stirling noted areas of discolouration on the sea floor, which looked like rocks but proved to be seaweed. He had reason to be cautious, for *Success* had a draft of some 18 feet (5.5 metres), whereas the depth over two extensive sand banks between the islands and the mainland is often less than 4 metres. Eventually they anchored in 12 fathoms (a fathom is nearly 2 metres) about a mile south-west of the river's south head to observe the coastline in more detail. Stirling then sent the ship's Master, Millroy, to look for a channel, hoping to find a suitable landing place. Meanwhile, in his own words, 'the Neighbourhood of the River tempted me to reconnoitre it and taking Mr. Frazer with me, I proceeded in the Gig for that purpose; we crossed the bar and ascended the Stream for 5 or Six Miles'.

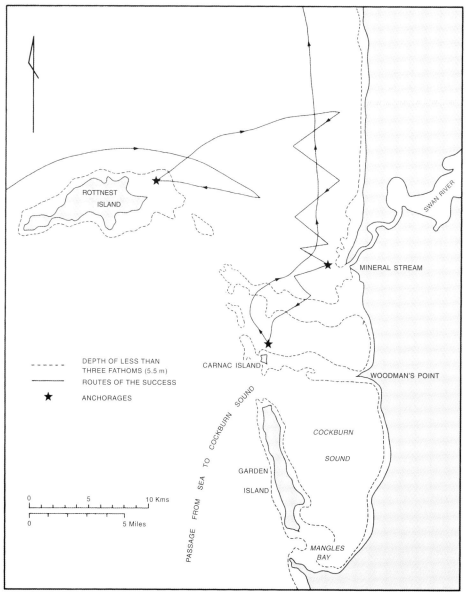

Stirling's 1827 survey of the approach to Swan River and Cockburn Sound

With kind permission from James Cameron, Ambition's Fire

This first expedition into the Swan River began about 2 p.m. and took them past the heads along a broad reach and around a corner into a bay lined with high cliffs and limestone caves. Another long picturesque reach followed, until the river turned, becoming a broad expanse of water almost crossed at the turn by a sandy spit. He named this expanse Melville Water (after the First Lord of the Admiralty) before turning back. Generally, Stirling did not mention bestowing names in his 'Narrative'—they just appear on the map. Two other points on the river were named on this first expedition: one, opposite modern Rocky Bay, after Lieutenant Preston, and the other, the high ground above the turn in the river and the long spit, after his favourite older brother Walter. During the seven-hour expedition Stirling 'had the good fortune to kill three of those magnificent Birds, which give a Name to the Stream we were embarked upon'.

Back on the *Success* Millroy reported that the ship was surrounded by sandbanks and shoals, but that he had found a channel of about 3½ fathoms into deep water. At daybreak on 7 March the party headed out gingerly towards the channel, but overnight tidal fluctuations and winds had changed the soundings, so for a time they were in extremely shallow water. Realising what had happened, Stirling felt there was no reason 'to censure the Master for the discrepancy'.

Along the line of islands, then called Bauche, Berthelot and Rottenest, and between them there are rocky outcrops, making a safe entry into the water separating the islands and mainland extremely perilous. 'Rocks, Breakers or Land were visible in every point of the Compass', Stirling noted, but found a safe anchorage not far from Isle Berthelot (dubbed such by the French in 1801). This small island he renamed Pulo Carnac Island after his First Lieutenant, John Rivett Carnac. Pulo was the Malay word for island, and why he added this prefix is unknown—it was soon dropped. Stirling also changed the French name of the other island, Isle Bauche, to Garden Island. It has been thought this was because his men planted a garden there before leaving, but this is unlikely as he used the name well before they did any planting. It was not the *land* on Garden Island that caused Stirling to so name it, but rather the shelter it provided for shipping—in much the same manner as the Isle of Wight, known locally as the 'Garden Isle', sheltered the waters off Portsmouth at Spithead.[6]

A visit to this island and an 'examination into the soundings and Bays on its Eastern side' had revealed 'a Magnificent Sound between that Island and the Main possessing great attractions for a Sailor in search of a Port'. Stirling noted that 'altho' we could not find an entrance into it, I saw the value of the position too strongly not to resolve upon its exploration as soon as circumstances would admit'. As previously mentioned, Stirling gave Lord Cockburn's name to this stretch of water, which he considered to be one of the most valuable assets of the Swan River site. Leaving Lieutenants Carnac and Preston in charge on the *Success*, with instructions to find a safe entrance into the sound, Stirling began preparations for a week of inland exploration.

At noon on 8 March the eighteen-member party, split between cutter and gig, crossed the river bar to reach the entrance. Stirling was accompanied by Lieutenant Belches, the surgeon, Mr Frederick Rushbrook Clause, botanist Charles Frazer, artist Frederick Garling, ship's clerk Augustus Gilbert, midshipman, Mr Heathcote, seven seamen and four marines. Stores included two suits of clothes, a blanket and hammock for each man, a tent and 'Arms sufficient to repel any attack that might befall us'. With some excitement, the party set off to the mouth of the river.

The 'Remarks Book' which accompanied the log of the *Success* stated that 'The Black Swan River has a ledge of rocks across the mouth with not more than 7 feet of water'.[7] It was an impediment to shipping that lasted until the 1890s, but Stirling does not seem to have realised its seriousness, suggesting later it could be easily removed. His narrative then named both heads, after Rous and Arthur, and went on to make a point that he considered most important:

> I must protest here against the term 'River' as applied to the Estuary in which were now entering. It is a misnomer which leads to confusion of Ideas; and I shall therefore designate the various ramifications of the Sea within the two heads just mentioned by the general name Melville Water, limiting the use of the name Swan River to that Stream, which joining the Sea at the Islands below Frazer's Point [Heirisson Islands at the top of Perth Water] concludes its career as a River. For the extent and direction of the various Arms of Melville Water, I refer to the Chart.

It is interesting that Stirling made no distinction at this stage between Perth Water and Melville Water, and indeed used the latter name to describe all the water from the river entrance to the present site of Perth. Yet at a point now known as 'the Narrows', which Stirling named Point Belches, Melville Water is nearly closed by land. Here a narrow channel leads into a second very large expanse of water, now called Perth Water, which extends east to the small islands in the river named 'Isles Heirisson' by the French in 1801. Stirling actually made very few comments, in either of his 1827 reports, about the 12 miles of extremely scenic riverscape between Heirisson Islands and the sea. His observations were mainly confined to utilitarian features, such as fresh water and geology, with none of the euphoric comment that he gave to the largely unexplored upper river reaches. It would appear he felt a detailed description of what he called 'the estuary' was unnecessary, as the French had already been this far and recorded their impressions. He wished instead to concentrate on the largely unexplored river beyond, which is perhaps why all the Garling paintings relate to this area.

Aided by a sea-breeze, the cutter and gig sailed smoothly to Point Belches, where they were grounded, and attempts to find a channel failed. Stirling's 'Narrative' records: 'The only alternative left was to drag the Boats over the Banks which was practised for a distance of two Miles, until night overtook us'. This

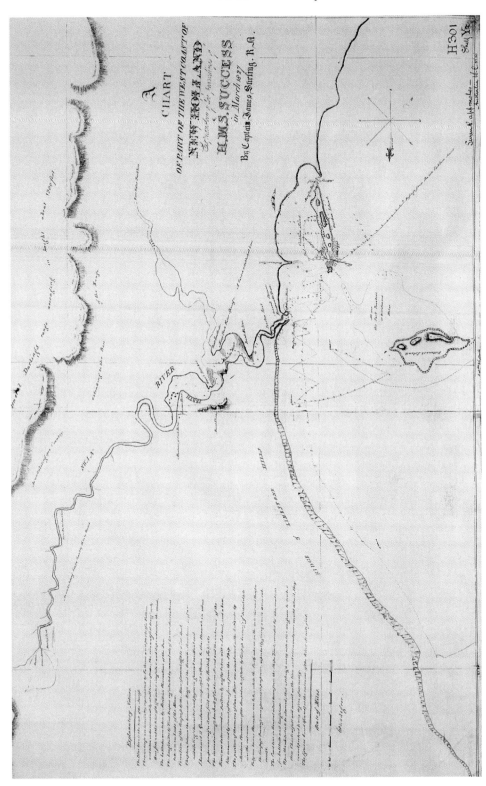

Stirling's 1827 chart of the Swan River area
Courtesy Taunton Hydrographic Office

distance would have traversed the shallow Perth Water—even today only navigable through constantly dredged channels—up to the Heirisson Islands, where again the land closes in, creating a fordable crossing that was used by Aborigines as their major route across the river.

Whilst his men were struggling with the boats, from which everything had been unloaded, Stirling, Frazer and Garling climbed a nearby high hill for a magnificent view over both river basins. Stirling named this vantage point Mount Eliza in honour of Governor Darling's wife, who had entertained him several times during his stay in Sydney. Garling sketched his 'View from Mount Eliza' at this point, clearly showing the extent of the two waters, and the entrance to a river on the far side—though when painting it later he 'misread the indentation of bays on the southern Shoreline as islands'.[8] The river opposite Mount Eliza had been named by the French 'Entrée Moreau', as they believed it to be an 'arm of the sea'. Stirling subsequently named it the Canning River, after George Canning, the then British Prime Minister. The blue hills visible in the distance he named 'General Darling's Range' to give recognition to the man who had encouraged his venture, while the whole area between the coast and the hills he later called the 'Great Plain of Quartania'.

Dragging the boats through the shallows meant, for the seamen, 'unremitting exertions above their middle in Mud and Water', starting at 5 a.m. and continuing to nightfall, when they changed into dry 'blanket suits' for dinner. During this two-day struggle there would have been ample time for Stirling and his officers to explore the area around Mount Eliza, where the city of Perth now stands. Point Frazer was their likely camp site but the need for fresh water led to a search for new supplies. Stirling was cheered when Frazer discovered 'an extensive lagoon of Fresh Water' one mile north-east of Point Frazer 'sufficient to supply all our wants'. The party moved camp and named the creek and lagoon Clausebrook (now Claisebrook, East Perth) after their surgeon. Clause later completed a large oil painting of the camp at Clause's Lagoon which was etched and lithographed by his friend, the marine artist John Huggins.[9] It is believed that this painting is based on a Garling sketch, and there are a number of versions of it in existence—all taking a degree of artistic licence. As the Garling paintings remained in official hands, this was the only portrayal of the Swan River that was published prior to settlement.

While in this area the group first saw some of the native inhabitants, 'three Armed Natives [who] seemed angry at our invasion of their Territory…by their violent gestures [but] they eventually retired'. In referring to 'their territory', Stirling acknowledged that the land belonged to others, and it is pertinent that he later used the word 'invasion' even for his exploring party. But his experience in South America had taught him that invasion led to ownership, and that ownership by Britain was an enviable position. This he never queried.

Above Heirisson Islands the going became easier, though the river was still shallow as it wound in large loops across the plain. Not much distance was gained after a late start on 10 March, and at nightfall the boats pulled to the left shore, the men tired after the hard day's work. Stirling recorded that

> in a few Minutes a blazing fire, with roasting Swans before it, shed cheerfulness on our resting place; our dominion here however was not undisputed for of all places I have ever visited I think it contained the greatest number of Musquitoes [sic]…we had taken up our Quarters on a narrow ridge between the River and a Swamp.

Stirling evidently thought it necessary to bring some shipboard routine into their activities, for his report reveals a crisp daily schedule—breakfast at 4 a.m., start at 5 and row or sail till 11, rest from then till 3 p.m., and then proceed further till 6 in the evening. On 11 March, the fourth day out, he described 'a bieutiful [sic] reach of the River' and some level country 'covered with brazen grass and studded by a few green trees'. After around three hours on the water, the party entered a long, narrow stretch (through today's Belmont-Bayswater-Redcliffe), from where they could see the distant range and 'the smoke from many fires'.

Further upstream, on a rising left bank, his men also found a spring of fresh water at what is now 'Success Park'. Around this area Frederick Garling painted his 'Red bank—30 miles up', and at their camp site for that night, his 'Swan River, preparing to encamp, 35 miles up', which, with their now muted colours do not completely do justice to this extremely picturesque area of the river.

It was in this area that Stirling recorded his first real meeting with Aborigines, and the policy he intended to adopt in such contact. He believed the best means of preventing hostilities was 'neither to seek nor avoid an interview'. Initiating the first approach could prompt an Aboriginal to strike the first blow out of fear, he reasoned, whereas to retreat might tempt him 'to make conquest of Enemies [exhibiting] symptoms of weakness and fear'. Using knowledge gained in North America, he 'decided in the present case to let our new acquaintances seek or shun us as they best pleased'. Gesturing violently, the natives noisily followed the boats along the narrow river for quite a distance, and Stirling wondered whether 'we should shortly have a shower of spears', for the tribe was on higher ground. The situation improved as the bank levelled out, and led to expressions of goodwill on both sides. Stirling noted:

> they had assumed more confidence and began to mimic our various expressions of 'how do you do'; and at last we held up a Swan, which seemed to amuse them, and, having cast it to them, they testified the greatest delight at the present.

By this stage they were near the confluence of the Swan and what was later called the Helena River, land which Stirling described as 'a rich and romantic Country…generally of an undulating character'. He noted occasional sections of high ground, viz. 'steep red, brown and yellow Cliffs, of one or two hundred feet high'—somewhat of an exaggeration as the river banks today are only a quarter that height. His next comments indicate that Stirling was already thinking of the needs of an agricultural colony, and assessing soil suitability, density of timber, and ease of access. He refers, for instance, to the 'Iron Stone grit' base overlaid by good red loam and, on the lower grounds, 'a deep dark coloured loam devoid of clay or sand' where the high grass, 'turned yellow by the Sun', resembled fields of grain.

Stirling estimated they had travelled 15 miles that day—a mistake, for the whole distance from Heirisson Islands to their final stopping place at Ellen Brook is only 22 miles (36 kilometres). But 5 miles of winding river could well have felt like

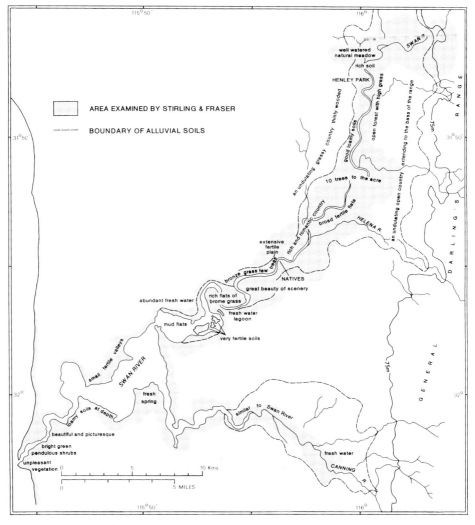

Map showing Stirling's observations on the territory examined
around the Swan River in 1827

With kind permission from James Cameron, Ambition's Fire

15 miles, so perhaps he can be excused. They camped that night in the rich Swan Valley wine growing country. Stirling was delighted at this 'first commodious sleeping place we had encountered', for 'we had delicious Weather and abundance of every thing, including cheerfulness'. However, next morning (13 March) the cutter was holed an hour after departure by a submerged tree, and had to be quickly patched with lead and fearnought (a thick flannel-like material). Obstructions continued along the ever-narrowing river, and at eleven o'clock, after several halts, they reached a confluence where the Swan River veered east just above a 'considerable creek' on the left side. Past this point, Stirling observed, were 'unsurmountable obstructions to our further progress, in fact we had reached the termination; for beyond this there was the Bed of a torrent, but no longer a River'. From here the Swan winds through a succession of rapids, where rocks stir up white water, interspersed with pools. Today intrepid canoeists and white water specialists use the stretch in winter, but Stirling's more cumbersome boats, even with their modest draft, were blocked.

The creek at this furthest navigable spot Stirling called Ellen Brook, the only feature he named after his wife. Fate and geography thus placed the final turnaround camp in one of the most fertile places in Western Australia, the site now marked by a plaque in the Upper Swan churchyard. Stirling's and Frazer's observations from this camp regarding the fertility of the soil were, therefore, quite accurate. It was the generalisations that later flowed from their examination of the surrounding land that were to prove misleading. Stirling lauded the beauty of the area, stating

> the richness of the Soil, the bright foliage of the Shrubs, the majesty of the surrounding Trees, the abrupt and red coloured banks of the River occasionally seen, and the view of the blue summits of the Mountains, from which we not far distant, made the scenery around this Spot as bieutiful [sic] as anything of the kind I had ever witnessed.

Garling's paintings of this area, 'Evening—near the head of the river' and 'Encampment at the head of the river, 70 miles up', tie in well with Stirling's description, but again the colours are muted.

The men spent the rest of the very warm March day setting up camp, exploring and 'observing the latitude'. When it cooled a little, Stirling set off with a party for the hills, but evidently misjudged the distance, so that it was sunset when they 'reached the summit'. Garling's 'View across the coastal plain' suggests that they had gone up Greenmount on the Darling escarpment, an area that even today impresses visitors with its views. It certainly captivated Stirling, who described it eloquently: 'As far as the eye could carry Northward, Southward, and Westward lay extended an immense plain covered in general with Forest and varied by occasional eminences and glimpses of the River winding through it'. The 7-mile return march was in darkness and the men lost their way, but Frazer 'very kindly and considerately sent out Scouts', and they reached camp about nine o'clock.

The following day Stirling decided to split his officers into several parties and send them in different directions to obtain as much information about the surrounding country as possible. Frazer went east, Belches and Heathcote north, while Stirling and Surgeon Clause headed west, soon to discover 'a Fresh Water Lagoon and a bieutful [sic] running brook watering several hundred Acres of natural Meadow, covered…with rich green herbaceous grass' (possibly Bennett Brook). No Aborigines were encountered, but there were signs of deserted huts (which Stirling called 'ajaupa', possibly an American Indian term). That night the group established a rough garden in rich soil between the river and creek, planting some potatoes, peach trees and other plants. Stirling was so impressed with the country he saw around this junction that he named it Henley Park after the home he had loved in Surrey. Unlike other explorers, he was fairly reticent in giving his own, or his family's name, to places he discovered, for among the names on his 1827 map only the tiny Ellen Brook, Henley Park, Mangles Bay in Cockburn Sound, and Point Walter can be linked directly to his family. Some of the names he bestowed were clearly for political reasons, but most simply honoured his fellow explorers, like Points Belches, Frazer and Heathcote.

The return journey, begun on 15 March, was much quicker than that upstream. Landfall for the night was at Point Garling, no longer identified on maps but probably today's Burswood Peninsula. The distance covered in five days on the upward journey had been covered in just one day on the return, obviously helped by strong easterly winds. The 'Narrative' continued:

> On the Morning of the 16th we were at Point Frazer very early and understanding now the nature of the Shoals we had both the Boats below them and reladen by Noon. We then proceeded to Point Heathcote [at the entrance to the Canning River], which I had fixed upon for a resting place on our route.

Stirling had seen earlier from Mt Eliza the branch of the river named 'Entrée Moreau' by the French, and he now despatched Belches to explore it. After two days Belches reported it to be a fresh water river, 'similar in every respect to the one we had just descended'. Meanwhile Stirling and the others returned to the *Success*, anchored off Carnac Island, at 9.30 p.m. on the 16th.[10] While he was away his men had made considerable progress in sounding the surrounding waters, but had been unable to find a safe channel into Cockburn Sound. In consequence, Stirling decided to devote the next few days to surveying the surrounding islands and banks, and the approaches to the river. These efforts bore fruit, for Stirling was able to report to Darling the discovery of a channel 'not less than 5 fathoms' into Cockburn Sound, and another of 3.5 fathoms from *Success*'s anchorage into Gage's Roads. A survey was made of the entrance to Melville Water, and fresh water discovered near

Arthur's Head and at Point Heathcote, where a garden was established. On Bauche (Garden) Island another larger garden was planted[11] with the seeds brought from Sydney, and a cow, two pregnant ewes and three goats were also left 'to benefit from the abundance of grass…and a large Pool of Water, which we had prepared for their use'. When Stirling returned in 1829, there was no evidence of either garden or animals, and it is likely that in the sandy soil any water collected would have dried out fairly quickly.

Exploration of this area was now all but complete, so on 21 March at 1 p.m. the *Success* weighed anchor and made sail into Gage's Roads, where they anchored for the night. This relatively safe area, just outside the mouth of the river, Stirling had named after his future Commander-in-Chief, Rear Admiral William Gage, of the East Indies Station. Next morning *Success* bore into the sea-breeze and ran north along the coast, travelling some 35 miles before nightfall. As nothing was seen to warrant a closer look, Stirling gave the order to turn south, setting course for Cape Leeuwin.

As already mentioned, Stirling's report to the Admiralty was shorter than Darling's, and was systematically organised under eight headings. After an introductory outline, Stirling strategically placed his 'Hydrographical Observations' first. Here he gave the Admiralty what he knew they wanted to hear: his assessment of the various anchorages available in the area. These included Thomson Bay, on Rottnest Island's north-east, which he thought 'a good temporary anchorage'; Gage's Roads, 'much superior in security to Table Bay as well as in its closeness to shore'; the small, shallow bay south of Arthur's Head (now Fisherman's Harbour) which he classed 'for small vessels only'; 'Port Success', possibly in the Rockingham area, which he classified as secure but inconvenient due to the distance from Arthur's Head; and then Cockburn Sound, between Garden Island and the mainland. This latter area he proudly claimed was 'perfectly secure and available for vessels of the greatest dimensions as well as for any number of them'. Its value, he stressed, was 'not to be established solely by its own merits', but because

> no other [port] is known to exist on the whole of the Western Coast except Shark's Bay where the heat of the climate and sterility of the Soil forbid the formation of a Settlement.

Of all the possibilities he examined, Cockburn Sound offered by far the best anchorage, having good holding ground and, once clear of the banks, soundings of over 15 fathoms quite close to shore, conditions the Admiralty then looked for in a safe harbour. The main entrance from the sea to this sound, Stirling reported, was through a 5-fathom channel between Garden and Carnac islands. Unfortunately for Stirling, this channel is in an area highly subject to wind and tide variations, so in balmy March weather he did not fully appreciate how very narrow and rocky it was, or how dangerous the surrounding waters. In Stirling's view, Cockburn Sound's only limitation as a major port site was

its inconvenience for Merchant Vessels who have Cargoes to deliver in Swan River
6 or 7 miles away. But they need only use Cockburn Sound when north-west gales
were expected; at other times Gage's Roads will be both safe and convenient.

He then went on to mention a sixth possible anchorage, inside the river, which was
inaccessible at that time due to the bar across the mouth of the Swan. He suggested
to Darling that the 'magnificent basin' surrounded by a 'succession of natural cliffs
or wharves' about a mile inside the heads would be 'the finest Harbour in the World
if it had an entrance'. And in the Admiralty report he intimated that such an
entrance could be gained either by dredging a channel over the bar or by 'cutting
through the Isthmus in Gage's Bay', which consisted of about 450 yards of limestone
rock. Neither, he thought, would be 'difficult or expensive'.[12] He was mistaken, for
despite many plans and efforts it would be more than half a century before the bar
was successfully removed. The reference to Melville Water as a potentially fine
harbour can be misunderstood, for Stirling used that name to refer to all the water
inside the heads, including deep Rocky Bay, whereas today it relates only to the
fairly shallow waters opening out after the sandy spit at Point Walter. It is,
nevertheless, true that some of the problems that Stirling had experienced with sand
and mud banks in the river appear to have been minimised in the reports.

Stirling was clearly convinced that Swan River should become another British
colony, and to persuade the Admiralty and the Colonial Office he included in both
reports a table showing the number of days' sail required to reach Cockburn Sound
from various places, viz. Sydney 20 days, Madras 25 days, the Cape 35 days, and
London 100 days. He admitted, however, that these estimates assumed favourable
weather. His next section on 'Climate and Weather' not only gave the average
temperature during his March visit as a mild 72°F (22°C), with extremes of
84°–59°F, but particularly noted the regularity of the afternoon sea-breeze which
gave way to land breezes around midnight. This is the first written reference to the
now famous 'Fremantle Doctor', the cool wind which Perth people eagerly
anticipate every hot summer's day. He included here Surgeon Clause's opinion on
climate and health (enclosed separately in the report to Darling) which drew
attention to the fact that, despite exposure of *Success's* expeditionary group to
'fatigue, to night air in the neighbourhood of marshy grounds and to the causes
usually productive of sickness, he had not a case upon his sick list except for slight
complaints unconnected with the climate'.

The fourth section of the Admiralty report, 'General Structure and aspect of
the country', contained geological observations illustrating Stirling's familiarity with
different rock forms. In summary, he noted: 'First, The Limestone edge of an
average breadth of three Miles on the Sea Shore, then the plain, an undulating
Valley of an average breadth of thirty Miles, and lastly the Mountain Range rising
abruptly from the plain to the height of 1,200 feet and extending North and South
on a line parallel with the Coast and apparently co-extensive with it'.

Frederick Garling. *Mount Eliza, 15 miles from the entrance of Swan River, Western Australia* 1827.
Watercolour, pen, ink and pencil. 22.2 × 33.2 cm. Collection, Art Gallery of Western Australia.
Acquired with funds from the Geoffrey William Robinson Bequest Fund, 1990

Frederick Garling. *Swan River – View from Fraser's Point* 1827. Watercolour and pencil.
23.7 × 32.8 cm. Collection, Art Gallery of Western Australia

Frederick Garling. *Bivouac on the banks of Swan River; preparing for supper* 1827. Pencil and watercolour. 24.5 × 33.3 cm. Collection, Art Gallery of Western Australia

Frederick Garling. *View of Swan River, taken at the commencement of the fresh Water* 1827. Pen and ink and watercolour and pencil. 22.5 × 32.8 cm. Collection, Art Gallery of Western Australia

Frederick Garling. *Red bank – 30 miles up the Swan* 1827. Pen and ink and watercolour. 22.2 × 32.9 cm. Collection, Art Gallery of Western Australia

Frederick Garling. *Swan River, preparing to encamp for the night, 35 miles up* 1827. Pen and ink and watercolour. 21.9 × 33.1 cm. Collection, Art Gallery of Western Australia

Frederick Garling. *Evening – near the head of the river* 1827. Pencil and watercolour. 23.5 × 33.4cm.
Collection Art Gallery of Western Australia

Frederick Garling. *Encampment at the head of the river, 70 miles up* 1827. Watercolour and pencil.
21.3 × 33.3cm. Collection, Art Gallery of Western Australia

Frederick Garling, *View across the coastal plain* 1827. Watercolour. 13.1 × 37.5 cm. Collection, Art Gallery of Western Australia

Frederick Garling. *View from Mount Eliza* 1827. The Holmes à Court Collection, Heytesbury

F. R. Clause (after Garling). *Setting Camp of the naval survey expedition at Clause's lagoon, Western Australia 1828.* The Holmes à Court Collection, Heytesbury

Major Lockyer's sketch of King George's Sound in 1827.

This led into his observations on 'Mineral Productions'. He stated that 'in our hasty inspection' a wide variety of minerals had been discovered, including quartz, granite and limestone, pitch, copper ore and lead ore with arsenic. Ten minerals were named in the Darling report, but this was extended to forty-four in the report to the Admiralty. In both he included the comment that 'Coal was not found, simply I believe because it was not particularly sought for', a statement that was later ridiculed as indicative of his extreme optimism. But coal does exist in the south-west, and it has been pointed out that in reaching this conclusion Stirling had mistakenly, but understandably, equated the West Australian coastal limestone (of Pleistocene age) for the mountain limestone of northern England (of Carboniferous age), which did have coal.[13]

Moving from minerals to 'Vegetable Productions' in the Admiralty document, Stirling inserted the report of the Colonial Botanist, Charles Frazer (which he appended separately in the report to Darling). Frazer's assessment was, in fact, far more euphoric than Stirling's, and his conclusions, cited below, went further than Stirling's more qualified observations.

> In giving my opinion of the Land seen on the Banks of Swan River, I hesitate not in pronouncing it superior to any I ever saw in New South Wales east of the Blue Mountains, not only in its local character but in the many existing advantages, which it holds out to Settlers; these advantages I consider to be:
>
> First—The evident superiority of the Soil.
>
> Secondly—The facility with which a Settler can bring his Farm into a state of immediate culture, resting upon the open state of the Country; a state which allows not a greater average than 10 trees to an Acre.
>
> Thirdly—The general abundance of Springs producing water of the best quality, and the consequent permanent humidity of the Soil, two advantages not existing on the Eastern Coast, and
>
> Fourthly—The advantage of Water carriage to his Door, and the non-existence of impediments to land carriage.

The last sections of the Admiralty report, titled 'Animal Productions' and 'Concluding Remarks', included material relating to Geographe Bay, and will be dealt with later.

It is clear that both Stirling and Frazer were delighted with the region they had explored. For Stirling it was a dream come true. He had hypothesised that the Swan River would be suitable for settlement, and had found every indication that it would be even more advantageous to Britain than New South Wales. But, as indicated earlier, although their observations were accurate, some of the generalisations made on the basis of what they had seen were erroneous. Both Stirling and Frazer were misled by criteria for soil evaluation that applied to Britain and Europe, but not the Antipodes. They believed that the height of trees indicated soil fertility and that similar vegetation meant similar soils,[14] and when they found tall trees and similar plants as far as the eye could see, they deduced that the whole 'Plain of Quartania' was as fertile as the land they had closely examined on the banks of the Upper Swan. In fact, the rich alluvial soil that Stirling found in the Swan Valley only extends in a narrow band along the river, and quickly gives way to sand and swamp land.[15] As they had done very little over-land exploration, except in the fertile Swan Valley, they had no idea that similar vegetation hid impoverished sandy soils, or that the tall trees they observed over an immense area were jarrah eucalypts, which prefer sandy soils. Even today Perth residents wanting to grow native plants are urged not to use fertiliser.

The other factor to influence Stirling's and Frazer's impressions was the weather. The visit was in March, a month usually benignly hovering between the scorching century-plus temperatures of January and February and the rains which begin in May. The alternate land and sea winds are also less extreme than at other times of the year, so the dangers of the shoals and rock protuberances in the surrounding seas were largely disguised. Constant sunlight meant the sea and the river reflected the blue sky, and also brought out various shades of green in surrounding foliage, which tend to merge to a similar grey-green under cloud or in rain. This was important, as colour variation, especially in long vistas, was also an accepted criterion in the evaluation of landscape. The balmy weather therefore turned the whole exploratory venture into what one writer has called a 'picnic episode'.[16]

After leaving Swan River, *Success* reached 'Port Leschenault' near Geographe Bay on the morning of 24 March. Governor Darling believed (and had undoubtedly told Stirling) that the French were 'supposed to have some claim to Geographe Bay',[17] so Stirling had been asked to examine it. This comprises the last part of his day-to-day 'Narrative of Operations'. From the head of the bay the ship took a course within sight of the shore, and at 8 a.m. was in the vicinity of Vasse River (named by the French). An hour later, near 'a small opening into a Lagoon', some Aborigines appeared on the beach and began to track the boat's course for several hours, without any signs of hostile gestures, until one

> …who seemed the General, left his Spears behind and, advancing upon a projecting rock, stripped himself of his only garment a kangaroo Skin to show he had no concealed Arms; he seemed so vehemently desirous of an interview that the Boat backed in and gave him a knife and two or three little presents.

A little later, this same 'General' was mentioned again. Stirling had made a sketch of him, and then pocketed his notebook—or so he thought! He wrote, 'No London adept could have removed it more adroitly from thence than the Man we called the

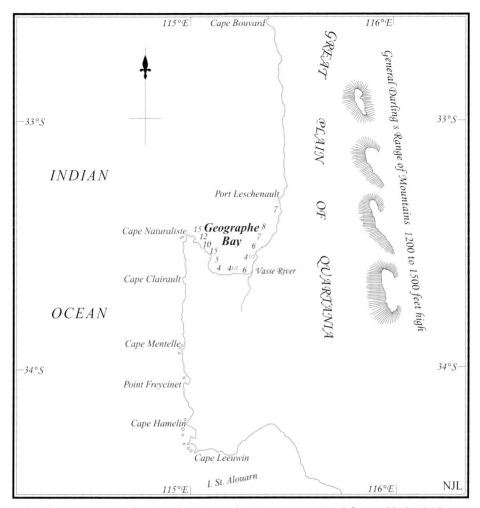

South western coast showing the Geographe Bay area examined favourably by Stirling

General did, and I should not have recovered it had not my Coxswain perceived it under his Cloak'.

Bad weather set in the following day, and while *Success* sheltered in Geographe Bay, Stirling and Frazer continued their exploration on land. Stirling's report noted the undulating country extending east to 'General Darling's range…covered with large Timber, and [displaying] the rich and lovely verdure of a Country frequently Watered by Showers'. Mindful of its potential value for shipping, he noted:

> Wood is here abundant for the use of Ships, and whenever we sought we found Water…At the same time, although there is abundance of fresh water I am not at Liberty to call it at present a convenient water place, although I do not doubt that it may be so.

His party again met the indigenous inhabitants, who turned out to be 'harmless, lively and extremely inquisitive into the fact of our white complexions; it was not until after repeated trials by rubbing and washing that they would be persuaded that our white colour was not a deception'.

Botanist Frazer also included observations of this area in his report, and was particularly impressed with the limestone caves near Cape Naturaliste. He described their interior as 'covered with beautiful Stalactytes of great magnitude and exceedingly brilliant…The Sea makes a breach into each of the lower range over blocks of Granite; the Scene is then truly grand…' Although impressed by the whole Geographe Bay area, Frazer did not believe it compared with the promise of Swan River as a site for settlement. Stirling agreed, as Geographe Bay did not have the access to water transport offered by the Swan. But he was well aware of its strategic value (lying between the Swan and King George's Sound), and he loved the hills in the background, as they reminded him of Scotland.

Stirling's encounter with Aborigines at Geographe Bay had refined impressions gained at Swan River, which he included, somewhat inappropriately, under the heading of 'Animal Productions' in his report to the Admiralty. Physically, he considered they resembled their counterparts in New South Wales, with

> large Heads, spare Trunks, long and disproportionate limbs. They are active and hardy in habit, and seem to possess the qualities usually springing from such habits; Bravery, Vivacity, and Quickness, and a Temper alternating between kindness and ferocity.

He adopted the same non-confrontational policy as at Swan River, 'avoiding by every possible means a quarrel', and concluded, 'I am happy to say that…after many communications with them, we departed without any misunderstanding, and indeed on terms of amity with several Tribes'. He made no estimate of the native population, but did remark that 'numbers are considerable when it is remembered that the sources which supply Food are so precarious'. He was surprised to find they only fished in shoal areas, having 'no idea of navigation, not even of a raft'. He was also surprised to hear them use words he recognised, viz.

> the terms 'Kangaroo' where we touched their Cloaks, 'Wallebie' 'Walle Walle' and 'Wollamia' when we shewed them a particular kind of Fish; these are all Port Jackson terms.

Of the actual fauna observed, Stirling reported having actually seen kangaroo, possum, tortoise, lizards and 'guanas', and a solitary snake, whereas 'the Native Dog we heard occasionally at night but did not see'. Among birds he noted emus, many swans, duck, black and white cockatoos, pigeons, quails, parakeets and 'some Birds of very melodious Note, which again were heard but not seen'. Seals were spotted on nearby islands, and whale carcasses along the beaches of Geographe Bay. Sharks were 'enormous and numerous', and there was an abundance of fish—sufficient 'to look forward to the time when a valuable fishery may be established on these Shores…'

Stirling's 'Concluding Remarks' differ in the two reports, the Admiralty version being more specific and succinct. Stirling was at his persuasive best here, using every point that his experience indicated would appeal to the Admiralty Lords:

> Compared with New South Wales the Southern portion of the West Coast of New Holland is not inferior in natural attractions. Under the same management, therefore the same success, the same astonishing prosperity would probably attend its occupation. But in Soil, Climate, and spontaneous products, it is not only not inferior it is much superior…I do not believe that a more eligible spot could be found in any part of the World.

He extolled the commercial potential of the Swan River area for trade in various areas: the nearby Malay markets, hitherto neglected, could be 'fed and fostered' by 'convoys of small vessels…under the protection of a Vessel of War'; empty China-bound vessels could profit by off-loading freight in New Holland, and then loading local produce such as trepang, whale oil, sealskins, salted fish and timber for Asian markets; other ships bound for New South Wales or Van Diemen's Land could benefit by stopping at Cockburn Sound, as could those plying the new India-South America route; and there was potential also to trade with Isle de France.

But to Stirling, one of the most important advantages of the Swan River site was its proximity to the jewel in Britain's crown, India, and he played this card well:

> The mildness of the Climate, the shortness of the distance from India…make a Settlement on this Coast an object of the greatest interest and importance to the India Company…With a pleasing country so near at hand, a bracing Climate and a great variety of Mineral waters, voyages to England and long leave of absence would no longer be necessary. It is not to the Company alone that the place has this recommendation. His Majesty's Naval and Military Forces on the Indian Establishment might occasionally be reinvigorated and restored, and kept in condition for Service which long residence in Tropical Climates is able to render them unfit for.

Aside from trade, Stirling pressed the strategic advantage of the Swan River site, which could become 'an important Naval and Military Post [from where] Troops and Ships may be conveyed speedily to New South Wales, Van Diemen's Land, the China Seas or South America'. And, well aware of the Admiralty's drive to reduce costs, he hastened to add that settlement could be accomplished with minimal expense:

Convalescent Troops and Ships from India or such Forces kept there for other purposes would form the Guard necessary for the protection of the place. The expenses of the Civil Establishment would be supported by the sale of lands, and beyond this, there would scarcely be any demands upon the Public Purse except it were made a Penal Settlement…The visits of wealthy Invalids from India would furnish sufficient capital for circulation; and for the encouragement of all necessary speculation.

After pointing out all the benefits of the site, Stirling concluded with a warning:

In proportion as the possession of that Country would be as valuable to Great Britain, so would its occupation by any Foreign Power be injurious and ruinous. The Dutch and French have already visited those Shores, the latter might obtain millions of Slaves among the Malay Islands and in a future War might pour out swarms of Privateers upon some of the most important channels of our Trade in its neighbourhood.

Stressing again that Cockburn Sound should be secured at the earliest opportunity, Stirling concluded that he had not taken formal possession 'because I was not ordered to do so'. Nevertheless, 'by the formation of Gardens and by leaving Stock' he had performed 'Acts of Occupation upon which at any time a just claim to the Territory might be founded and maintained'. Stirling was well aware that occupation, more than proclamation, was the key to possession.

The *Success* finally left Geographe Bay on 27 March for King George's Sound, where Darling had asked him to collect Major Lockyer. Six days later they anchored just off the small settlement which had been established by Lockyer on Christmas Day 1826. They found it in dire need of provisions, so Stirling sent ashore all the stores he could spare, retaining just enough for the fourteen-day 1,900-mile voyage back to Sydney.[18] Leaving on 3 April, Stirling would have seen little of the area now known as Albany, but probably heard much from Lockyer. As both men had to submit reports to Darling on their return, the two doubtless spent most of the fortnight's voyage writing up their notes. The atmosphere, though polite, was possibly chilly, for both men were keen for their respective sites to be chosen as the location for a future British settlement. Moreover, Lockyer had heard unfavourable reports about Swan River from some abandoned sealers who had subsequently been brought into the tiny settlement. They had told him that the anchorages at Swan River were dangerous, the bar at the mouth of the river insurmountable, and the native inhabitants hostile. All this Lockyer relayed in his report to Darling as a counterfoil to his arguments in support of King George's Sound—its large, safe harbour, its favoured position for ships on the London to Sydney or Hobart route, the variety of its marine life, and ample fresh water supplies.[19]

None of this would have pleased Stirling, who had already decided to ask for the position of Governor of the Colony he hoped would be established at Swan River. Much would depend on Governor Darling. It would therefore have been with some trepidation that Stirling anchored off Sydney Cove on 16 April 1827.[20]

Major Edmund Lockyer, in charge of the
garrison at King George's Sound 1826–27
Courtesy Battye Library 605P/148B

7

Melville Island and Home

On 18 April 1827 Stirling penned a covering note to Darling and packaged up his report for hand delivery to Government House. His letter apologised for any shortcomings which he felt could arise 'from the very short time I could devote to this Service', as well as from 'the want of experience in Surveying on my own part and that of the Officers of His Majesty's Ship under my Command'. But he also paid tribute to those who had accompanied him, noting that it was due to their 'cordial and zealous co-operation that I have been enabled to collect the details on which this report is formed'.[1]

As mentioned, the report submitted to Darling was differently crafted from the more ordered version sent later to the Admiralty. It was a far more enthusiastic, immediate document, as the following often cited extract indicates:

> This Country…is more valuable for that which it might produce, than for its actual productions. Situated in a Climate which admits of Labour, possessing great varieties of excellent Soil, well Watered by Springs, Creeks and refreshing Showers…it appears to hold out every attraction that a Country in a State of nature can possess.[2]

Stirling also uses more international comparisons in this report, his past experience proving useful. For instance, he noted: 'Its resemblance in all material points…to the States of America, situated to the South of New York, will sufficiently explain its agricultural resources'.

Having spent time with Darling before the expedition, Stirling deliberately played upon the Governor's fear of foreign, particularly French, annexation of Australian territory, and he also put forward his belief that profitable private enterprise was the only way to ensure long-term colonial survival. He was well aware of the British Government's reluctance to incur expense and suggested various ingenious ways in which a new settlement could be administered with minimal cost. The last paragraph of this report also contains the name that Stirling chose for the lands he had discovered, the only time this appears. As a starting point, he stressed the trade advantages of the site:

The Shortness of the Voyage between this Country and the Cape of Good Hope, the Mauritius, the Indian Peninsula, and the Indian Archipelago, would afford an easy and profitable interchange of productions between these Countries...The China Ships outward bound through the Eastern passages might here find not only refreshments, but many Articles to make up a Cargo...Ships from England bound to New South Wales might also touch here and perhaps find commodities suited to the wants of the Eastern Coast.

Then came the argument regarding its advantages for those stationed in India:

Considered with reference to its becoming a convalescent Station...its Situation offers great and important attractions. It is not distant from those Shores; the passage between Short and easily made; its Climate cool, temperate and healthy, and among the various mineral Springs which it contains, perhaps some may be discovered favourable to the removal of Indian Complaints...

He pointed to its strategic importance

as a valuable Naval and Military Station. The excellent Anchorage for Ships of War afforded by Cockburn Sound...superior in convenience and more than equal in safety to Spithead, is another recommendation...and it has this further quality that Troops or Ships, while recovering there from the effects of Service in India, would at the same time form the Guard necessary for its protection.

And then concluded:

It now only remains to state that, from Cape Leeuwin to Shark's Bay, the neighbourhood of Swan River is the only part where a Port is known to exist. The Port therefore has a value far beyond that which it might have in other circumstances, for it is the Key of the whole intervening Coast.

I am therefore of opinion that it ought to be immediately retained for the French Nation have the shadow of a right founded on discovery to a portion of that Coast, which cannot be too speedily extinguished by British occupation, particularly as it will be impossible now to prevent the attractions of that Country from being known.

It is also important to occupy Geographe Bay, its mineral wealth and fertile Territory as well as its convenient Summer Anchorage render it too attractive to be left unguarded.

These two places, with a Settlement on their Northern flank at or near Shark's Bay would probably be sufficient to exclude all foreign intrusion. I also take the liberty to recommend the adoption of a general name for the Western Coast of New Holland. The Name of 'Hesperia' indicating a Country looking towards the Setting Sun, would be descriptive of the Situation of the Country in question; it would not interfere with any Name previously given, nor would it be subject to the imputation of Nationality. James Stirling, Captain, R.N.[3]

Stirling had studied Virgil at Westminster school and well knew that 'Hesperia' not only meant a land looking west to the evening star, but was also the land sought by Aeneas after the fall of Troy, directed by a sense of duty to his family and his gods.[4] And James undoubtedly felt similarly driven.

Governor Darling was impressed. He obviously read the report with care, as his reservations reveal, but he was as eager as Stirling that the newly discovered territory be claimed quickly for the Crown, and so lost no time in forwarding it to the Colonial Office. On 21 April he appended a letter which, after initial pleasantries, quickly adopted a supportive tone.

Assuming that the Calculation of the periods necessary to make the respective Voyage to and from India, and other parts are correctly stated, Swan River would appear to hold out advantages highly deserving attention…[here he cites the convalescent station argument].

The Establishment, however, if to any extent, must be effected directly from England or India, totally independent of this Colony, Swan River being too remote and the Voyage too uncertain to admit of its depending on this place [New South Wales] for its supplies.

It will be seen by the Report that Captain Stirling considers that Swan River possesses all the advantages with reference to the Trade with the Eastern Islands, which attach to Melville Island or any other part of the North West Coast of this Territory. Among the natural advantages of Swan River, it will be observed that good Water is abundant. The Country is besides favourable for Cultivation, the Soil in general being excellent, some Specimens of which I do myself the honour to forward to Your Lordship by this opportunity. And the Scenery is represented as at once grand and picturesque.

It is much to be regretted that the Water at the entrance of Swan River is not of a great depth, there being only six feet for a Mile above its Mouth… Nautical Men can, however, best determine whether the advantages of the external Anchorages of Gage's Roads and Cockburn's Sound are likely to compensate for the inconvenient nature of the River.

As Captain Stirling's visit to Swan River may attract attention and the report find its way into the French papers, it appears, should His Majesty's Government entertain any intention of forming a Settlement at that place, that no time should be lost in taking the necessary Steps.

I cannot close this communication without pointing out the Zeal and Ability with which Captain Stirling undertook and has completed this Voluntary Service; and I beg to be permitted to mention him as an Officer highly deserving Your Lordship's approbation and the confidence of His Majesty's Government.[5]

Together with Stirling's report, and Frazer's 'Observations', Darling enclosed Stirling's earlier letter requesting permission to explore the area, plus charts of the Swan River region and samples of soil and minerals. Garling's paintings were not included in this submission to the Colonial Office, possibly because they had not been completed by the time the ship left with Darling's dispatches (it is known he did some of the paintings in his Sydney studio). They were eventually sent to England in August, with Stirling's Report to the Admiralty,[6] but the earlier omission was most unfortunate, for the paintings never saw the light of day, simply remaining in official Admiralty files. Only versions of Clause's painting were made available to the public and both the number, and the greater realism, of Garling's representations could have influenced many decisions if they had been available from the outset.

Even Sydney did not see Garling's work (though doubtless Governor Darling did). On 18 April the *Sydney Gazette* ran a long article on the recent 'Expedition to Swan River', but without illustrations. Informed by 'a gentleman who accompanied the expedition' (from the wording, probably Frazer), this was the first of many Press reports which were to turn the reasonably objective 'Observations' of the report into a description of paradise. For example, the two occasions on which Stirling noted, with some amazement, finding fresh water within inches of the shoreline were magnified in the Sydney Press, to wit:

> The beaches all along the river were found, upon examination, every where to contain fresh water in great abundance, so much so that scratching with the finger within two inches of the salt water it was found to be plentiful and of the best quality.[7]

Swan River was doubtless a major topic of conversation at the grand ball and supper which His Excellency and Mrs Darling gave for 200 invitees on 24 April in honour of the King's Birthday. Captain Stirling was invited together with his friend Captain Rous, who had arrived on HMS *Rainbow* from New Zealand a few days before. The ball was described in the *Sydney Gazette*:

> At nine o'clock the company poured in with rapidity; and about half past nine, quadrilles commenced, which were maintained with unusual animation until midnight, when the sound of the music summoned the company to the supper room…The tables, it is needless to observe, groaned beneath the substantial varieties which the illustrious Host and Hostess had munificently prepared for the entertainment of their Guests. The Governor having impressively given, as a toast, His Majesty, retired from the supper table, and anew, escorted the Ladies to the ball room, where the excellent Band of the 57th Regt. was still in attendance to prolong the festivity.

The next day, the 25th, a grand regatta was held off Sydney Cove. Stirling and Rous, with their officers and crews, not only ran the event but contributed the prize monies in Spanish dollars. Once again the 57th Regiment band was there, this time on board the *Success*, which was flagship for the day. As the *Gazette* reported, 'the Ladies, during the interval of the Races, were engaged by the Gentlemen to while away the lingering moments on the light fantastic toe'.

There were three races, all called from the *Success*—a rowing match, won by *Mercury* belonging to Captain Rous, whose victory was greeted with cheers from the yards, followed by a sailing match and another rowing contest. As the *Gazette* concluded:

> Captains Stirling and Rous, as well as their Officers, did all in their power to contribute to the happiness of their guests…Dawes' Point and Macquarie Fort were crowded with spectators of all ranks and denominations. The Harbour was thickly strewn with floating vehicles of all shapes, dimensions, and colours. In fact it does not come within our recollection that such another gratifying exhibition presented itself to the view of the Australian Public since the day that venerated Macquarie for ever bid adieu to the rising Empire of Australia…[8]

With the King's Birthday festivities behind him, Stirling turned to more serious matters. The ship had to be readied for the voyage to Melville Island, and various strategic matters had to be discussed with Governor Darling. Their discussions would have been somewhat delicate, as neither was accustomed to ask favours. Both were proud men from very different service traditions, yet both needed something from the other. Darling had heard private reports about land 125 miles south around Bateman's Bay, but had no resources to investigate and confirm them. *Success* could perform such a service at no cost to his government. Stirling, on the other hand, badly wanted Darling's support for his application for the 'Superintendence and Governance' of any settlement to be formed at Swan River, and also a land grant in New South Wales, similar to the one issued to his brother Robert for services rendered. In gentlemanly fashion, an understanding was reached.

The exact purpose of the mission to Bateman's Bay is unknown, though the *Sydney Gazette* reported that 'Inspection of the coast, harbour and capabilities for a Settlement are the ostensible objects of the tour'. Given Darling's stated antipathy to outlying settlements, the objective was probably to validate reports from private individuals concerning a river issuing into that bay, backed by plentiful pasturage and groves of valuable cedar trees.[9] On 7 May the Surveyor-General, J. Oxley, the Colonial Secretary, Mr McLeay, and the Colonial Engineer, Colonel Dumaresq, boarded *Success* which left Sydney Cove very early the next morning. She anchored off Snapper Island just outside Bateman's Bay on 10 May and was there for two days before returning to Sydney three days later.[10]

Darling, meanwhile, had read Lockyer's report on King George's Sound and was a worried man. He realised occupation was essential to prevent annexation of territory by another power, but was also convinced that numbers of small settlements could not be serviced from Sydney. He was having considerable trouble supplying and keeping in touch with those already in existence at Launceston, Hobart, Western Port, Newcastle, Port Macquarie, Moreton Bay, Norfolk Island, Melville Island and now King George's Sound. As he stated to the Colonial Under-Secretary on 14 May:

> Having pointed out the inconvenience and Expense, which must attend the maintenance of so many Settlements, I would beg to submit to my Lord Bathurst, whether any of them can consistently with the views of Government, be dispensed with. If it be intended to shut out the French from establishing themselves on the Coast of New Holland, which I conceive is an object of some importance, I am not aware that King George's Sound can be abandoned.[11]

The following day Stirling wrote a short letter of application to Lord Bathurst at the Colonial Office:

> The Mail will convey, through the medium of His Excellency General Darling's report, some important and interesting information relative to the western coast of New Holland. The Part which the performance of my duty induced me to take in the Exploration of those Shores, and the successful result of the investigation these effected, emboldens me to apply to your Lordship and to solicit, in the Event of an Establishment being formed on that Territory, the honour of its Superintendence and Government.
>
> In making this application, I feel that I have but little Claim upon Your Lordship's notice. I possess, however, some knowledge of the Country, to which I allude; and I pledge myself, should your Lordship be pleased to consider that knowledge as a recommendation for the Employment I solicit, to promote with zeal and industry the Wishes and Views of His Majesty's Government.[12]

Darling, who was writing to the Colonial Office on the same day, supported Stirling's application, recommending him as 'a very Zealous Officer…well qualified for the Situation he is desirous of obtaining'. The Governor's letter dealt generally with affairs of the colony, in particular the problem of absentee land holders, which he felt arose principally from the habit of granting land to serving naval officers.[13] So it seemed strange in this context that Darling disclosed he had authorised the grant to Stirling of '2,560 acres on condition of its being Stocked and improved in the course of 18 Months'. Explaining his decision, the Governor pointed out that Stirling had

> already exerted himself in the Service of the Colony, and is proceeding to establish a Settlement on the Northern Coast, and has evinced his intention of employing some considerable capital here by applying to purchase some 9,600 acres, to which I have also acceded.[14]

The land Stirling was granted was near his brother Robert's grant in the Hunter Valley.[15] Darling's reference to a further large land purchase implies that James was looking at alternative future opportunities in case his Swan River dream came to nothing.

Four days later, on 19 May, HMS *Success* left Sydney for Melville Island, accompanied by the 80-ton colonial-built brig *Mary Elizabeth* under the command of Lieutenant Hicks. On board were provisions and other supplies for an 'establishment' force which included an assistant surgeon, thirty rank and file members of the 39th Regiment joined by fourteen Royal Marines from *Success*, and twenty convict mechanics and labourers.[16]

Darling had selected Captain Smyth, 'a person particularly well qualified for the Situation', as Commandant of the new settlement and had urged Stirling to remain with him until it was established. This meant delaying his return to the Eastern Station, but Darling pointed out that a small warship would

> prove the best means of…protecting Traders and keeping the Malays in check, until they should by experience be made sensible of the advantages they would derive from intercourse with our Settlements.[17]

Supplies of small trade items had been sent with the expedition in the hope they could be traded with the Malays for trepang (or *bêche-de-mer*) which, when dried, was prized as a gastronomic delicacy in China. Darling told the Colonial Office that he could not yet say where the settlement would be established, but that Stirling would 'proceed in the first instance, as instructed, to Croker's Island'.[18]

The instruction to head for Croker Island rather than Melville Island, where the Commandant, Major Campbell, had been anxiously awaiting Stirling for several months, was odd. Croker Island, to the east of the Coberg Peninsula and some distance from Melville Island, had been mentioned in London as a possible alternative settlement site—but that was before news had been received that the Melville Island settlement was progressing. Darling himself had raised the prospect that the depot might not need moving. An initial rendezvous would have been a sensible move, but this was not ordered. Stirling therefore stuck to the letter of his original instructions to find an alternative site and this, together with his desire to finish the mission and return to pressing his Swan River claims, initiated an unfortunate train of events.

Stirling's impatience comes through clearly when, in a repeat of the *Currency Lass* episode, he became separated from his escort, the smaller *Mary Elizabeth*, on the second night out of Sydney.[19] Instead of waiting or searching for her, Stirling pressed straight on, anchoring in Palm Bay on the western side of Croker Island on 15 June after a passage of only twenty-eight days from Port Jackson.[20] On the *Mary Elizabeth* Lieutenant Hicks was left with 'no instructions where to proceed', and totally inadequate charts to negotiate the Barrier Reef and Torres Strait. He was lucky to reach Melville Island early in July. Because Stirling did not visit Melville Island before beginning his search for a suitable site, he was unaware that Major Campbell was already convinced that Port Essington would be the best location for a mainland settlement. Port Essington had a good anchorage, ample fresh water and appeared to be the hub of the Macassan trepang fishery. Lieutenant King had come to the same conclusion in his exploration of the northern coastline in 1818. But Stirling instead chose Raffles Bay, further east, for the settlement, selecting a site on its eastern side near the entrance.

It was a very hurried choice. The day *Success* arrived off Croker Island, Stirling had established that it was unsuitable for settlement, and on 16 June had 'despatched a boat to the opposite coast of the Main Land for the purpose of exploring Raffles Bay'.[21] Reports proving satisfactory, he looked no further, jubilantly claiming that the Raffles Bay site offered 'abundance and goodness of Fresh water', security of anchorage and 'all the minor advantages of soil, shade, timber, grass and fishing'. It also 'had the further recommendation of being known to be the Resort of the Malays', he reported, as he had found several of their wooden curing frames.[22] It is interesting that, in the *Success*'s Remarks Book, Stirling praised the accuracy of the charts of the area drawn by Lieutenant John Septimus Roe, who had accompanied King, as Roe was to be the future Surveyor-General at Swan River.[23]

At 4 p.m. on 18 June Stirling and his officers went ashore to take possession of Raffles Bay and surrounding territory in His Majesty's Name. They hoisted the flag and fired a 21-gun salute, which was returned with a *feu de joie* from the marines and men of the 39th Regiment. Next day the artificers, marines, soldiers and stores were landed and construction of a stockade begun. Stirling named the settlement 'Fort Wellington', as he had taken possession of the area on the anniversary of the Battle of Waterloo. He described the fort, constructed under the direction of Lieutenant Belches, as follows:

> The Fort is an hexagonal Stockade, formed of solid timber…having at four of the angles, 18 pd Carronades mounted on platforms to fire over the Stockade. In the middle of the enclosed space…there is a Cavalier or Tower twenty feet square and twenty feet high, built of solid Logs and impervious to Musketry…Over the solid part of this building, there is raised a house for the Commandant, the under apartments containing in Safety almost all the Stores of the Settlement. Around this Fort, at proper distances…are four Houses or Barracks for the Troops, Marines and prisoners…Surrounding the whole Camp there is a rough paling to prevent any body of men from rushing in on the Centinels [sic].[24]

It was a fairly typical British fort, but in the absence of Malays or other foreigners the security was aimed at warding off the local natives, whom King and Roe had reported as hostile.[25] In ensuing weeks several incidents of theft occurred 'without

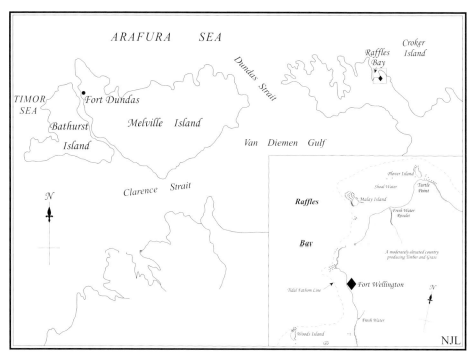

Melville Island and the outpost Stirling founded at Raffles Bay in June;
the location of Fort Wellington (inset)

alarming the sentries, and certainly without any provocation on our part', which
reinforced Stirling's opinion of the 'cunning, boldness and mischievous disposition'
of the Aborigines. He reported:

> They scarcely allowed a night to pass without displaying something new, bold and
> ingenious in their mode of attack…until the precautions taken made it impossible
> for them to succeed…They are similar in person to the Native of New South
> Wales, but they very far exceed these latter in intelligence, activity and love of
> mischief. During our stay in Raffles Bay, I do not think there were seen more than
> fifty Individuals, all of whom were middle aged men, their families to all
> appearance having been removed to a distance.[26]

On 23 July, thirty-seven days after the party's arrival, the fort was complete, together
with accommodation and pens for livestock. A garden had been established, with
peas, carrots, cabbages, pumpkins, bananas and orange trees, and was well advanced
by the time Stirling left. He felt he could at last bid farewell to Commandant
Smyth, who wrote a warm letter of thanks, concluding:

> I beg leave to embrace this opportunity of conveying to you the high sense I
> entertain of the very liberal and kind assistance affording to us on all occasions by

the Officers and Crew of HM Ship the *Success*, under your able direction, in which both public zeal and private friendship have been so truly manifest.[27]

Stirling forwarded this as an enclosure to his own report titled 'Proceedings while forming a new Settlement on the North Coast of New Holland', which he added to the report on Swan River for the Admiralty and signed on 27 August.

Success set sail for Melville Island on 23 July, its Captain believing all was well. But by October the little settlement at Raffles Bay was in real trouble. Scurvy decimated the numbers able to work and there was no lime or other antiscorbutics to treat the sick. The settlement's medical officer repeatedly attempted suicide before dying of fever. Provisions were dangerously low, and the small brig left for their use was too unsafe to send to Timor for supplies. Moreover, the anticipated intercourse with the Malay traders and fishermen had not eventuated. Relief was eventually sent from Melville Island, which also suffered from illness. This outpost was disbanded in November 1828 and the little Raffles Bay settlement struggled on until it was finally broken up in July 1829, most of its personnel being transferred to King George's Sound.[28]

Dispatches from the commandants at Raffles Bay and Melville Island, and from Darling, concerning the northern settlements were to reach the Colonial Office at the same time as Stirling's report on Swan River. And they continued to arrive throughout the whole time the question of a new colony on the West Coast was under consideration. As these dispatches continually pleaded for more supplies and more expenditure, they were not a positive influence.

Of all this Stirling was completely unaware. Anchoring off Fort Dundas, Melville Island on 25 July, he met Campbell, the Commandant, and reported establishing the settlement at Raffles Bay—probably to the latter's surprise, given King's preference (and Campbell's) for Port Essington.[29]

The two northern settlements were very isolated when *Success* departed, for the *Mermaid*, the little colonial vessel Campbell had been given to maintain supply lines, was declared unseaworthy by Stirling himself, as was the *Mary Elizabeth*. Even after temporary repairs had been effected, neither vessel was in a position to handle bad weather or any extended time at sea. So Stirling must have realised that communication between Melville Island and Raffles Bay would be precarious and infrequent, leaving each settlement isolated and in danger of starvation. And instances did occur when food supplies were destroyed overnight by freak winds, and medicines ran short to treat outbreaks of illness. But Stirling's impatience to leave blinded him to such risks. Instead of remaining to ensure a supply link, which the tenor of Darling's instructions would have suggested was his duty, he set sail on 29 July to report to his immediate superior, Admiral Gage, Commander of the Eastern Station.

In Stirling's defence it should be pointed out that during his month-long stay several ships had called in (the *Caledonia* and the *Marquis of Lansdowne*, bound for

Batavia, and the *Amity*, bound for King George's Sound), so he probably believed relief would be available from passing ships. After all, in official eyes before he left England, the northern Australian settlements were destined to become a second Singapore, a hub for trade in the region—an enthusiastic projection by his superiors that James would have been unlikely to question.

Success reached Java on 11 August and, after reprovisioning, sailed for Madras on the 15th. Throughout this voyage Stirling would have been drafting his report to the Admiralty, which he signed on 27 August 1827 'at anchor in Madras Roads'. To his disappointment Admiral Gage was not there, having sailed for Penang. So after four days on shore and collecting his mail, he set sail again. Before leaving, Stirling forwarded duplicates of his report to the Admiralty by one of the ships in harbour,[30] but he kept the original, the charts and the ten Garling representations to deliver to Gage personally. The duplicates were received by the Admiralty in March 1828, but were held over until a covering letter was received from Gage.[31] Stirling caught up with Gage in Penang in late September 1827,[32] and the Admiral forwarded the originals with a letter dated 1 October that was not received until August 1828, well after Stirling's negotiations with the Colonial Office had begun.

Success appears to have been based in Penang for two months,[33] and during this time sickness hit the crew. Lieutenant Carnac was so ill that a specially convened 'Survey', or medical investigation, was held on 1 November, releasing him from service to return home on half-pay.[34] On 2 December *Success* set sail for Madras, arriving on 15 December.[35] With Christmas just ahead, a time when everyone thinks of family, James must have yearned to see his wife and small son, as well as his mother and siblings. On New Year's Day 1828 Stirling left Madras under orders to base *Success* in Trincomalee harbour, Ceylon (now Sri Lanka) which he reached on 4 January. It was here that Stirling also succumbed to illness, an 'intestinal inflammation with a great derangement in the functions of the liver & bowels'.[36]

Stirling later told his brother John that he was afraid he would die if he remained in the tropics, and so was forced to apply for suspension from active service. But he also admitted 'how far my own wishes and views, or wife-sickness, might have of themselves caused me to give up my ship I need not say'.[37] Nevertheless, the official 'Survey' on 21 February 1828, by the surgeons from three Royal Navy vessels, certified that he was ill and in a considerably 'reduced state',[38] requiring his immediate return to England. Gage was sympathetic, quickly organising a replacement captain for the *Success* and permitting Stirling to travel home by merchant vessel, rather than waiting for a ship-of-war.[39] James left the *Success* with mixed feelings, making a speech to the men and recommending his successor, Captain Stoddart. To the sound of cheers he was conveyed by the ship's gig to the waiting *Henry Porcher*, a large East Indiaman.

The voyage was uneventful and Stirling reached England on 7 July 1828,[40] quickly making his way home to Pirbright and a reunion with his 'agreeably surprised' family. There was evidently a sense of urgency, for his mother Anne records seeing her son only for about quarter of an hour, when he 'carried off his sisters to Woodbridge to see his wife and boy'. James may have been somewhat nervous; he had left a child bride and would now meet a young woman, and he possibly thought his sisters' company would break any awkwardness in their first meeting. His mother was very concerned about her son's debilitated condition, observing he had been 'obliged to fly from Trincomalee as a matter of life or death; his medical attendant considering the danger extreme if he remained ten days longer in the country. He is still far from well and I hope will go at once to London and consult the best physician there.'[41]

During James' absence, Ellen had lived with her family at Woodbridge, some 2 to 3 miles away. When the excitement of reunion subsided, she wanted to hear every detail of the journey and enthusiastically supported all James' plans. On learning that he would have to spend some time in London after reporting to his employers, in order to see officials regarding Swan River, she was determined to join him. They moved into leased premises at 22 Norfolk Street, London, before the end of the month.

8

Assault on Downing Street

On 28 July 1828 Stirling wrote to the Admiralty informing them that 'in consequence of a dangerous sickness arising from the effects of Climate & exposure on service, I was under the necessity of quitting the Indian Station and returning to England for the preservation of my life'.[1] He enclosed the relevant medical certificates and applied also for recompense of his passage monies. With official permission to retire on half-pay, he could turn his attention to Swan River.

To this time James had received no official response to his report on Swan River, and he was in a fervour of impatience. He apparently did not know that a decision had already been made: to take no action. On 24 December the new Colonial Secretary, the Rt Hon. William Huskisson, had sent a memorandum to his Under-Secretary, Robert Hay:-

> I have read with attention Captn Stirling's Report…[and] I am decidedly of opinion that it would be inexpedient on the score of expence [sic], and that it is unnecessary with a view to any urgent interest, to attempt any further settlement at present…the Settlement if formed, must be in fact not a dependence on the present Colony, but an entirely new one, with all the Machinery of a separate Govt.
>
> If the East India Company think it worth their while to form a Settlement for any purpose at Swan River, I should have no objection, and would afford them every proper facility, but I am not aware of any sufficient motive to induce them to embark in such a Project.[2]

Indeed, a negative reply to Stirling's application for 'Governance' of the new settlement had already gone out, on 29 November 1827, advising

> as it is not the intention of His Majesty's Government to form an Establishment on Swan River, it is not in his power to comply with your wishes in the manner to which you allude.[3]

But Stirling had missed it. The same message was conveyed to Darling in a dispatch dated 28 January 1828.[4] It would have come as a complete surprise to Darling, for at that very time he was thinking of transferring the outpost at King George's Sound to Swan River in readiness for future action.[5] The Colonial Office did send a letter to the East India Company directors, but even before Stirling reached England they had decided against any such move.[6]

It is doubtful that James knew of any of these missives when he arrived home, but he was certainly well aware that the Government disliked new expenditures and that persuading them to found a new settlement would be difficult. He therefore began what has been called his 'assault on Downing Street'[7] with a visit to the Colonial Office to try to convince the authorities that the area was worth claiming. He was introduced to Under-Secretary Robert Hay on this first visit, which must have taken place on 28 or 29 July, and apparently told to put his ideas on paper. Consequently on the 30th, while staying with his brother Walter at 18 Upper Baker Street, he wrote to Hay with the first of several suggestions to effect settlement at minimum cost, viz:

> The Report, which I had the honour to make last year to His Majesty's Government, differs so widely from that of the preceding Dutch and French Navigators, that it will scarcely be believed they undertake to describe the same Country, for, while they report it as Sterile, forbidding and Inhospitable, I represent it as a Land which, of all that I have seen in various quarters of the World, possesses the greatest natural attractions.

After summarising these attractions, he used a veiled threat as an inducement to action. The territory was, he claimed

> …a spot so eligible for Settlement, that it cannot long remain unoccupied. It is not inferior in any natural essential quality to the Plain of Lombardy, and, as by its position it commands facilities for carrying on Trade with India and the Malay Archipelago, as well as with China, and as it is moreover favourably circumstanced for the Equipment of Cruizers for the annoyance of Trade in those Seas, Some foreign Power may see the Advantage of taking possession, should his Majesty's Government leave it unappropriated.

He even tackled head-on the difficult question of expense:

> With reference to the plan I took the liberty of mentioning to you, as a cheap and simple Mode of forming a Settlement in that country by the Employment of a Vessel of War there, and by placing every Individual Settler for a certain time under the control of naval discipline, I beg to state that many of the inconveniences attending the early stage of all settlements would thereby be obviated…

And, in case a dim view had been taken of his earlier application, he added: 'I beg leave to disclaim any indirect view of my own Employment in such Service'.[8]

At this stage Stirling seems to have had in mind a settlement very like New South Wales, where wealthier free settlers employed convict labour under the umbrella of government ordinance, which in this instance he suggested could be supplied by the navy, or, as he had raised in an earlier letter to Darling, by troops and officials on recuperative leave from India. The Indian connection had been brought home to Stirling by both his brother Edward, who had been a Collector for the East India Company since 1816,[9] and brother-in-law Ross Donnelly Mangles, who had been similarly employed since 1820.[10] Both had stressed the need for a place closer than England for company employees to regain their health when sapped by working in the tropics. Both also had friends in India who would be very interested in a new British colony.

During these first few days in London Stirling also sought an audience with Sir John Barrow, Secretary of the Admiralty and the recognised expert in matters Antipodean. Barrow's initial reaction to Stirling's report on Swan River[11] had not been enthusiastic. In a private letter written on 15 October 1827, he did not dispute the claims made by Stirling and botanist Frazer regarding Swan River's attractions for settlement, viz. 'a safe and extensive anchorage…a luxuriance of vegetation superior to any on the Eastern Coast…abundance of fine fresh water, with a climate similar if not superior to that of Sydney…' But here, to him, the matter ended. 'Captain Stirling's anticipations of a commercial intercourse with India, with the Malays &c are quite fallacious…the Western Coast, even that part of it in question, is full of danger, and ships bound to India will avoid rather than seek it.' Then there was the question of whether 'Indian Gentlemen would even think of repairing to a penal Settlement on the Western Coast of New Holland to recruit their health, as Captain Stirling has vainly imagined'.[12] However, he added, if the settlement at King George's Sound was to be continued, he would support another at Swan River to form, through expansion, 'an extensive and valuable settlement'.[13]

But after a meeting with Stirling, Barrow changed his tune. In a memo to the Colonial Office dated 2 August, he strongly recommended transferring the establishment at King George's Sound to Swan River:

> and perhaps the sooner the better, as the publication of the Chart containing so fine an anchorage (entirely overlooked by the French navigators) may induce that Nation, or the Americans who are prowling about for some detached Settlement, to assume possession of the only spot on the Western Coast of New Holland that is at all inviting for such a purpose…[14]

This memorandum was actually addressed to Horace Twiss, son of the schoolmistress who had boarded James' sister in Bath. James had met the flamboyant Twiss on several occasions, and his recent transfer from the Admiralty to the Colonial Office as second Under-Secretary gave Stirling an entrée to their thinking. And at this stage, as far as settling Swan River was concerned, they were still apprehensive of expense. Nevertheless, the question of occupying the area was a major topic of conversation in late July at the Colonial Office and the Admiralty, where it was heard by a young naval Lieutenant who was interested in the area because he had been with Phillip Parker King surveying the north-west coast in 1820-22. This was John Septimus Roe, whose charts Stirling had admired at Raffles Bay. On 4 August 1828 Roe wrote to his brother:

> There is now great talk of their being about to take possession of the Western Coast of Australia and to form a settlement at the entrance of Swan River (opposite to Rottnest island of the charts) where a fine Sound has recently been discovered and is said to be in the neighbourhood of very good land…As there is said to be much want of some person there to effect a close examination of the coasts and country, I should have no objection to being sent upon that service, though there appears not much likelihood of them taking me off from my present work which is not yet half finished.[15]

A few months later Roe was to be taken from his unfinished work for the very purpose mentioned in his letter, but only because Stirling's persistence in pressing his plans on government officials eventually won the day.

At this stage the Colonial Office was still briefing its new Secretary for War and the Colonies, Sir George Murray, who had taken over from Huskisson at the end of May 1828. Murray, the member for Perth in Scotland, had been the Duke of Wellington's Quartermaster, and when the latter became Prime Minister, he did not forget loyal officers. But Murray found the complexities of administering colonies round the globe a very different kettle of fish from organising and maintaining army stores, so increasing the work of his Under-Secretaries Hay and Twiss.

By the end of July Stirling had moved his family to Southampton, though he frequently commuted to London. He was in Southampton on 4 August when he wrote to his brother John at St Andrews, confessing that he had been 'distracted by a variety of ideas out of business since my return'. His plans for the future were

> in the greatest obscurity as I cannot tell whether I may pass my next Christmas in peace here or be on my way to govern a new colony on the West Coast of New Holland. Last week was taken up in endeavouring to convince the Colonial Administrators to settle that Coast at once and I believe I left them on Saturday last resolved to set about it immediately.

Almost as an afterthought, he added that he had done 'pretty well' since being abroad, 'besides which I have an estate in New South Wales which it is true does not

Sir George Murray, Secretary for War and the Colonies 1828–29

Courtesy The West Australian

pay me a great rent but keeps me in hopes'. He told John that he had had 'famous fun' whilst in New South Wales and 'had I not been troubled with a constant inclination to wend homeward I could have been happy to remain there for years'.[16]

It was at this stage that Stirling heard, no doubt from Twiss, that the East India Company 'did not deem it expedient' to form any settlement at the 'spot lately discovered in New Holland'.[17] His hopes of government action were diminishing. As he told brother John:

> About 3 weeks ago I persuaded the Colonial Office People into the necessity of immediately occupying the Territory and I left town convinced that they would set about it immediately. I returned there last week but found them trembling at the thoughts of increased expenditure and nothing yet done in the business.[18]

But, he reported, he had just met 'a certain Major Moody' who he thought might help. Major Thomas Moody was an ex-West Indian Plantation owner who had been an adviser to the Colonial Office on matters concerning slavery, and particularly the welfare of freed slaves. He had been appointed by Lord Bathurst in 1824, but recently relieved. His experience, advice and contacts would have immediately attracted a rather despondent Stirling.

Moody had approached Hay as early as 6 August seeking an audience 'on the subject of the occupation of the Swan River, & adjoining district, in Australia by Great Britain without incurring any expense on the part of Government'.[19] He apparently met Stirling the following week, for James told John in a letter written on 23 August that the pair had seen the Under-Secretaries and 'prepared their minds for a general application which we subsequently made by letter and which is still subjudice'.[20]

That letter from Stirling and Moody, dated two days earlier, contained a proposal for settling Swan River. Assuming the British Government annexed the land, they asked whether

> any objection would be made to the unsupported employment of Private Capital and Enterprise in the occupation and improvement of that territory; and whether we may be permitted to form an Association, with a view to obtaining a proprietary Charter, upon principles similar to those formerly adopted in the settlement of Pennsylvania and Georgia.
>
> From our personal experience in matter connected with Colonies, and from the local knowledge which one of us possesses relative to the Country in question…we respectfully recommend our present applications to the notice of His Majesty's Secretary of State for War and Colonies.[21]

Moody had apparently persuaded Stirling that he could get a number of individuals interested in settling the Swan River area under the umbrella of a private company. But Moody had other ideas as well, which he set out in a letter to his friend and mentor Wilmot Horton (previous political Under-Secretary at the Colonial Office). This reiterated the idea of an association based on the Pennsylvania model, but contained more detail on how Moody proposed to set up three classes of settlement—one for convicts on what he termed 'the Dutch system', a second 'for the profits of the Association, conducted by the parish paupers & persons of that class in Ireland', and a third 'for the encouragement of half castes from India, Chines and others who may be induced to settle in the northern climates of the Colony to raise cotton &c'.[22]

Whether Moody fully explained these ideas to Stirling is unknown, but seems unlikely. Stirling's ideas were modelled on the large properties he had seen in New South Wales, not the small agricultural allotments of the Dutch model referred to by Moody.[23] James' letter to John had given no inkling of such detailed plans. Rather, Stirling believed that 'the Purpose of the Application was for leave to occupy…by means of an Association the Country in question, engaging…to meet all [the Government's] views without subjecting them to any expense'. And he added:

> If I succeed in getting leave to form such an Association I hope to make it beneficial to us all and…meet most agreeably with our views & wishes. Until then you will perceive that it is useless to speculate in the matter and we have only to wait quietly until we know what the Answer of the Government will be. No doubt they will take some time to come to a conclusion particularly as it is an idle season of the year.

You will see from what I have said that your view of a Swan River Company
is in a fair way to be realised…Under such advantages [that Swan River possesses]
the success of the Company will probably be equal to that of the Australian
Company whose shares have borne and still bear a high premium.[24]

Stirling's reference to the Australian Agricultural Company is a little misguided, for
the latter was not a colonisation company. It was formed in 1824 to raise sheep in
New South Wales and export fine wool, and though its share prices remained high
the company showed no dividend for its first ten years.[25] It is clear from this letter,
however, that the brothers had conversed at length about the proposed colony and
had even envisaged forming a family company to facilitate settlement, but all would
depend on the Government deciding to claim and occupy the area.

It was now mid-summer and most government officials were leaving town
to escape the London heat. Stirling realised he could do little more, and he needed
a break, having been busy meeting people and writing letters ever since arriving
back, despite the tiring after-effects of his illness.[26] He decided to take the family
to the Channel Islands, not just because of its healthy air but as a nostalgic
return to a place he and Ellen had loved early in their married life. The trip to
Jersey would give him time to talk to Ellen about his plans, for at this stage
she did not wish to emigrate. James had told brother John that 'nothing but
a most important consideration would induce me to press her to do so'.[27] But
he *could* tell her his hopes. He was not interested in emigrating to New South
Wales, despite its advantages, but would hold out for the Governorship of a new
settlement at the Swan. Such a position could well be the 'important consideration' that might change Ellen's mind. He needed time, too, to get to know his
son, for Andrew was now 4 years old and stretching Ellen's ingenuity with his
love of mischief.

The party Stirling took to Jersey included not only his own immediate family,
but also his mother-in-law (who had been staying with them at Southampton while
Woodbridge was painted), brother-in-law Charles Mangles with his intended bride,
and all their servants. Everyone thoroughly enjoyed the time away, so much so that
Stirling decided to extend the holiday, crossing to St Malo in France for a tour of
Brittany, and spending ten days in Paris before returning to Woodbridge on 1
October.[28]

Ten days later he and Ellen were at Henley Park, where his sister Mary Halsey
was waiting the arrival of her fourth child.[29] James realised he could not take things
further until his Colonial Office contacts 'had concluded their autumnal vacations'.
He described his activities in a chatty letter to brother John with a colourful turn of
phrase: '…as the weather is very fine I enjoy myself exceedingly among the living
Pheasants in the day time and over the dead when the dinner bell calls us to the last
great action of the day'. But the lack of a clear way ahead was frustrating, and his
musings in this same letter had a prophetic ring:

I believe it would be most beneficial to myself and my heirs that we live in London, but I doubt my ability to keep even the smallest house over my head upon £700 a year, while on the other hand to live in the country is in part to retire from my trade and to give up the game of life altogether. Mr Mangles wishes to build us a small house in this neighbourhood but a country life loses much of its attraction when contemplated as a permanent course of existence, unless one has an interest in the place where he lives and can hope by attention and improvement to enhance the value of the property either for business or for his children. To have the latter object is the only state in which I should like to engage in a country life. Altogether I am full of doubt and difficulty and cannot as yet decide which course I shall pursue.[30]

The eventual reply to his and Moody's application was not favourable. Sir George Murray noted (at a later date) that 'it was deemed desirable to exercise a more immediate control over the settlement by government, than by such an arrangement it would possess'.[31] His views were discussed privately with Stirling early in October, when it was probably also intimated that the Moody connection was not helping his cause, for thereafter Stirling allowed their brief acquaintance to lapse.[32] He was also advised that, while the Colonial Office was not keen on the idea of a private chartered company controlling a British settlement, they would like to see evidence of private interest in investing in Swan River.

The truth was that Colonial Office objections to the new settlement had begun to melt. Apart from a little personal influence on Sir George Murray, which Anne Stirling was not above exerting through her Scottish kinsfolk, there had been a barrage of dispatches from Darling complaining of the cost and difficulty of supplying the many Australian outposts from Sydney. So Hay wrote to Barrow on 3 October:

The only point to be settled is whether we should colonise Swan River, to which there is no other objection than the expense of the undertaking…My own opinion is that we ought to abandon all our Possessions on the North Coast of New Holland & transfer [them]…to Swan River.[33]

Barrow replied the following day: 'The French having turned their eyes towards that quarter makes it absolutely incumbent on us [to] take possession of Swan River, Geographe Bay & King George's Sound'.[34]

Unaware of Barrow's support, and believing that by recruiting private investors he could lessen the expense to Government and pressure them into immediate action, Stirling began to publicise his discoveries as widely as possible. To this time his report had been a confidential government document, seen by very few, so only those whom he had spoken to personally knew of its contents. Now that he had been given the go-ahead to attract private interest, he could go to the Press. He chose the *Hampshire Telegraph*, published in Portsmouth and known for its naval reporting, to carry the first long article on Swan River, which it ran on 18 October. This article was quickly picked up by the London papers, and appeared in summarised form in *The Times* and the *Sun* on 20 October. It generated such interest that letters of enquiry immediately began to arrive at the Colonial Office.[35] They all were answered with a brief note to the effect that the Government was not at that time contemplating a settlement at Swan River.[36]

Through his family and in the clubs and coffee houses, Stirling continued to woo wealthy individuals who might invest in his dream. It was at this time, late in October 1828, that he appears to have met Thomas Peel, cousin to the then Home Secretary, Sir Robert Peel. Thomas had moved from Scotland to London earlier that year, with his wife and baby daughter, to make further enquiries about emigrating to New South Wales, an idea that his father had encouraged by offering part of his future inheritance.[37] Taking a house near Regent's Park, Peel joined the recently established Windham Club in Pall Mall. It was an era of clubs and this one, in the former home of the Rt Hon. William Windham, had been founded by Lord Nugent for gentlemen connected with each other by a common bond of literary or personal acquaintance.[38] Stirling, a member of the Travellers' and the United Services clubs,[39] was taken to the Windham Club by associates and there introduced to the bluff, hearty Peel, who was enraptured by Stirling's enthusiastic descriptions of the Swan and excited by the prospect of leaving a mark on a new colony. Stirling would have been well pleased that such a wealthy and potentially influential person was interested in settling at Swan River. But Thomas Peel was a talker rather than a doer, and Stirling would live to regret having met him.

Peel excitedly discussed his change of thinking with wealthy friends and fellow club members, Colonel Thomas Potter MacQueen, Sir Francis Vincent and Edward Schenley Esq. They had not met Stirling but had read the piece in *The Times* and were also interested in Swan River, seeing opportunities for commercial gain. Together the four came up with a plan. They would form an Association and pool funds in order to send labour and capital assets to the Swan where food, livestock and raw materials of all kinds would be produced on land converted from its virgin state, and exported to bring them a return. To secure their investment, however, they needed title to the land that would be involved, which meant the British Government would first have to claim the territory. Guided by MacQueen, who had had experience in New South Wales,[40] they decided to ask for the proportion of land to invested capital that had applied in the case of the Australian Agricultural Company, viz. 1 acre for every 1s 6d invested.[41] The group estimated they could meet the costs of sending out 10,000 persons with all that they would need to start production, and, after a juggle of figures costing their passage and assets, believed they were entitled to apply for 4 million acres of land.[42]

Officially, the Peel Association's proposal was not submitted to the Colonial Office until 14 November, but well before this Peel was talking to Twiss and others of their plans.[43] Stirling was not involved in any of the Association's planning, but

Thomas Peel in a contemporary caricature—there is no known portrait

there is little doubt that Twiss kept him informed. Their ideas excited him, for at last it suggested a way of settling Swan River at minimal government cost. All that would be required would be for the Government to annex the land, send a minimal civil establishment to administer its distribution and uphold the legal system, and a small military detachment for its protection.

On 5 November Sir George Murray sent an official request to the Admiralty Commissioners to despatch a ship-of-war 'to proceed to the Western Coast of New Holland and take possession of the whole territory in His majesty's name'.[44] Whether James was told about this order at the time is not known, and if he was told, would he have judged it as capitulation to his scheme, or purely a preventative measure? J. S. Battye, in his authoritative *A History of Western Australia*, concluded that 'although this action set at rest the question of actual possession, there does not appear to have been at that time a definite decision to establish a colony forthwith'.[45] But that is difficult to sustain in the light of another order given on 12 November for the Admiralty to ready a ship to transport a small detachment of military troops to Swan River.[46] (Orders to the army for the selection of men, particularly those with skills, had been sent earlier.[47]) As ships-of-war carried marines, who were capable of fighting off potential invaders, ordering additional troops would have been unwarranted unless they were to guard a settlement. Furthermore, a note had been sent on 13 November from Barrow (Admiralty) to Twiss (Colonial Office) informing him that they had 'ordered the *Sulphur* Bomb vessel at Chatham to be brought forward with all dispatch for the service of conveying settlers to the Western Coast of New Holland'.[48] So the Colonial Office decision to settle the territory was made *before* the Peel group officially submitted their proposal on 14 November.

The Government's change of heart has to be attributed in the main to the fact that the Peel group's verbal proposal had convinced authorities that a system of land grants, which had been used for years to encourage settlement in established colonies, could be adapted to form a low-cost way of establishing a new colony. And it was not only the Peel group that was interested. The department had had a stream of enquiries ever since *The Times* had run its article on the Swan River.[49] Large-scale private investment would certainly lower government expenses, but it would not obviate them entirely. The trigger for their acceptance of the necessity for some 'minimal' expense seems to have been word from a British envoy that the French Government were again taking a serious interest in Western New Holland.[50] The *Morning Chronicle* had reported on 10 November, under 'news from Portsmouth':

> There was a rumour current that the French Government have recently applied for permission to establish a colony on some part of the West Coast of New South of Wales in which the latter have refused to acquiesce; and that such refusal being communicated, a confession was made by the Ministry of France, that the means to colonise had already left a French port.[51]

The rumour proved untrue, but it was just the catalyst needed to force the issue. It was used subsequently by Colonial Office staff to justify their actions,[52] and there is little doubt that Stirling played it for all it was worth, for the French threat had figured in all his arguments for immediate settlement.

There was no time for Stirling to glory in the achievement of his dream, for once the Colonial Office's wheels were in motion there was no stopping them. Stirling was in constant demand to answer queries about the territory, the voyage, the prospects and a host of other matters. The Colonial Office even procured him an office in Cannon Row, near Downing Street, in order to facilitate the process.

On 1 December, a Monday, he was invited by Peel to dinner at the Windham Club to meet Vincent and MacQueen. The Association had already laid out some £20,000 on an 800-ton vessel they had named the *Lady Nugent*, as well as on various supplies and recruiting. For undertaking this expense, and so 'paving the way for those who follow',[53] the members expected priority treatment, and Peel had been assured by Twiss that they should have it. But at the dinner Stirling told them bluntly that they would be treated in the same way as other settlers, and 'certainly not as patrons and proprietors of the whole settlement'.[54] The assumption by the wealthy group that their investment automatically gave them the right to choose the best of the land he had discovered, touched a raw nerve in Stirling. But the somewhat flippant and drama-loving Twiss[55] had said different things to each person regarding priority of choice. Fortunately, Stirling had been the last to see him, talking for four hours on Sunday 30 November, but the Monday night dinner party ended uncomfortably. Early the following morning Peel sent a note to Twiss, holding him to his word and claiming: 'It is surely asking nothing unfair when we solicit superior advantages to the public as a boon for the very arduous and first attempt at colonisation'.[56] But Stirling actually visited Twiss later that Tuesday, and in consequence it was agreed to call everyone together for a second dinner at nine o'clock that night. They met at 8 James Street and, as Stirling related to his brother John:

> There were present Peel, MacQueen, Twiss and myself. It was one of the most amusing scenes I ever witnessed, for they attempted to fasten a promise upon him [Twiss] that they should have the extent of ground above mentioned [4 million acres] and that they should have the first choice. He conducted himself to my great admiration, and showed such a Temper, Spirit, Firmness and Talent as I did not think he possessed. The conclusion was that he beat them hollow and cut them down to the rank which alone they ought to occupy, namely, that of private Settlers. We consented to give them 500,000 acres upon the same conditions as the others and with no priority, if they should carry out property corresponding within the first year, but not one acre beyond.
>
> He told them that they might go or not, it was quite immaterial to the Government, but if they would go, they should be viewed as other Individuals and not as Patrons of the Settlement, which did not please them, and MacQueen canted a great deal about the purity and disinterestedness of his views, and lost my esteem.
>
> Peel, on the contrary, rose much in my estimation for he closed at once with Twiss's offer and said Mr MacQueen might do as he liked but that he would go with Captain Stirling under any circumstances. Twiss said before then that Sir George [Murray] had authorised him to say that the first choice of land even before leaving England if I liked, to the extent of 100,000 acres, was to be given to me as a compensation for my services, and my Family would afterwards be considered as having a good claim to the extent of their investments as others.[57]

The Peel Association's claim for 4 million acres was hardly likely to have been approved, for in English eyes land carried so much value and political power that granting such a large quantity to four men was unthinkable. So the reduction in acreage alone would not have upset the worldly MacQueen; rather it was Twiss's intransigence on the issue of priority and expected indulgences that led to his outburst. MacQueen parted with Peel after this, even though the Association did not receive the Colonial Office's formal reply to their proposal until 6 December.

Between the 2nd and 6th the land regulations for the new settlement and the terms to be offered to the Association were hammered out, far too quickly as time would show. Twiss had forced the department's hand, and as he was sent to Paris (possibly deliberately), Hay signed the formal offer to the Peel Association.[58] The Government agreed in principle with their scheme, but limited the amount of land to be granted to 1 million acres. Half would be made available when assets and at least 400 persons of both sexes had been landed in the colony, and the balance when the first grant had been 'covered by investments in accordance with the enclosed terms'. The rest would be 'allotted by degrees as fresh imports of settlers and capital shall be made'. But the Association was not to have priority of choice or exclusive settlement rights. It was made quite clear that priority of choice 'to the extent of 100,000 acres' would be given to Captain Stirling, acknowledging the fact that his 'Surveys and Reports of the Coast have led to the Formation of the Settlement'.[59]

Enclosed with this reply was a broadsheet dated 5 December 1828 which set out 'Regulations for the Guidance of those who may prepare to embark as settlers for the new settlement on the West Coast of New Holland'. They began with the emphatic statement that 'the Government did not intend to incur any expense in conveying settlers or supplying them with necessaries after their arrival'; would-be settlers emigrated entirely at their own risk. The terms upon which land would be granted were set out in some detail, the extent of the grant being dependent on the value of articles introduced and the numbers of persons whose passages had been funded, in the proportion of 1 acre for every 1s 6d so invested. Title to the land granted would only be issued when it had been improved, for which a time limit was imposed:

> Any Land thus granted, which shall not have been brought into Cultivation, or otherwise improved or reclaimed from its wild State, to the Satisfaction of Government, within Twenty-one Years, from the Date of the Grant, shall, at the End of the Twenty-one Years, revert absolutely to the Crown.[60]

This was to become the most controversial of the regulations. The 21-year improvement period was reduced to 10 years in January 1829, and to 7 years in the final issue of the regulations on 3 February 1829. The conditions ended with the statement that it was not intended that 'any convicts or other description of prisoners be sent to this new settlement', which would be administered by Captain Stirling of the Royal Navy as 'Civil Superintendent'.

No one was pleased with this announcement. The Association was profoundly disturbed, for they felt their huge investment could be profitless without priority of choice. They needed at least assurance of river access to reduce transport costs in a roadless country. On 18 December they wrote to Hay[61] and followed up with personal representations to Sir George Murray.[62] As a result it was agreed that they could select land before departure, once Stirling had made his choice. Both Stirling and Peel, in that order, were asked to call at the Colonial Office and point out on the map the particular quarter in which they wished to select their grants. Copies of this map, when marked up and approved by Murray, were then to be given to each party. This satisfied Peel for the time being. He chose a large area on the southern side of the Swan River, and encompassing the Canning River, which would be reserved for him until his arrival. Stirling, on the other hand, deliberately chose lands away from the Swan River.

In a note to the Colonial Office dated 26 December, Stirling outlined his land choice as comprising Garden Island, together with the stock he left on it in 1827,

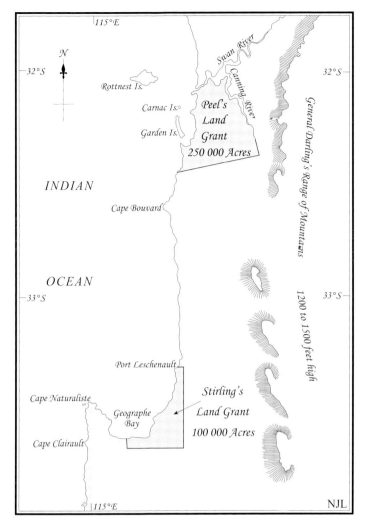

The original land grant choices made by Stirling
and Peel in December 1828

and 'The remainder of the hundred thousand acres…those which are situated close
to Cape Naturaliste in Geographe Bay'. But he requested that, 'as the latter portion
must remain for a considerable time unprotected', he be excused improvements
'until after a protecting force be stationed in that area'.[63] His choice was sanctioned
by Sir George Murray, with one proviso, as Hay informed Stirling on 1 January 1829:

> I am directed by Sir George Murray to acquaint you in answer that he will have
> no objection to allow the Bauche [Garden] Island to be considered as part of the
> grant to which you will be entitled in conformity with the original understanding
> but that it will be necessary to reserve for the use of the Crown…any point of land
> which should appear adapted to the erections of defence at some future period…[64]

Stirling's choice for the main part of his grant to be so far away from the Swan River has puzzled many, but is not difficult to understand in context. James believed his 100,000-acre grant was in compensation for his past services in exploring the area and agreeing to lead the first settlement. He also believed he could obtain more land in the future on the same basis as other settlers, i.e. in return for assets and labour introduced. This view had been stated clearly to John on 5 December 1828 when he said that

> 100,000 acres was to be given to me as a compensation for my services, and my Family would afterwards be considered as having as good a claim to the extent of their investment as others.[65]

So in selecting his 100,000-acre grant, Stirling could let other factors influence his choice. First, at a purely personal level, he had liked the appearance of the Geographe Bay area, particularly the background southern hills which reminded him of Scotland. Second, and a canny reason for his choice, the grant would save him money, being so far south it would 'remain for a considerable time unprotected' and hence delay the need to pay for improvements. Third, choosing land more than 100 miles from the Swan River would prevent this area being occupied by another power. Stirling had seen enough of the world to realise that if the Swan River area alone was settled, there was a vast area of land between the Swan and King George's Sound over which another power could claim territorial rights. He knew Geographe Bay had been visited by Dutch and French ships and that, outside the Swan River area, it was the only other relatively sheltered anchorage on the south-west coast. In British interests, it needed to be visibly claimed. Finally, Stirling seems to have chosen the Geographe Bay area because he believed that he would provide a lead to other large investors. He had seen in New South Wales that small settlers needed to be near the main towns and required river frontage for transport, while larger investors, who were able to provide their own means of transport, could hold land at greater distances from the capital. Peel's choice had already limited the land that would be available along the Swan for small settlers, so large investors in the new settlement would have to be persuaded to take their grants further away. And his experience convinced him that if he, as Commander-in-Chief, took a lead others would inevitably follow.

But there were still some outstanding issues. So far Stirling had only been given the title of Civil Superintendent, not Commander-in-Chief or Governor of the new colony. This rankled, especially as the family were already calling him 'the Governor'. He also disagreed strongly with the decision that the new settlement was not to have the full status of a colony, but be attached to New South Wales in the same way that had applied initially to Van Diemen's Land. And he wanted to get around a new navy regulation by which officers (such as himself) holding a civil appointment could lose their half-pay unless the position was ratified by the last day of the year.

So, on Boxing Day he wrote again to Under-Secretary Hay, effectively applying some gentle pressure by reminding him of the impending change and seeking confirmation, before 31 December, of his own appointment, and also those of an old friend, Captain Mark Currie, and Lieutenant John Morgan (a connection of Hay's).

At some length he also begged 'you will reconsider the point of placing the new Settlement in the Situation of a Dependency of New South Wales', listing four objections to the two colonies 'being incorporated under one Government'. First, he cited their dissimilarity in population and commercial position; second, their great distance from each other which renders communication slow and uncertain, and puts mutual assistance and protection out of the question; third, the favourable anticipations which have been entertained of the new Settlement, because of its independence from penal New South Wales; and fourth, because its remote distance would necessitate it 'being independent and responsible only to His Majesty's Minister for the Colonies'.

Towards the end of his letter, he drew attention to the matter of his title. He hoped Hay would 'pardon his presumption', but he felt the matter important and begged to suggest,

> if it is not finally decided on that I am to be styled 'Civil Superintendent', that my influence would be much increased in the opinion of those around me by altering that Style and naming me 'Governor'. There is a precedent in the case of Capt Phillip, who formed the Settlement on the other shore; and I should be much gratified by the alteration independent of the persuasion I entertain that my hands would be thereby strengthened.[66]

By this time most of the appointments to the Civil Establishment had been made, and kept to an absolute minimum. Morgan had been appointed Storekeeper on 4 December and John Septimus Roe as Surveyor-General on the 5th. By that time Peter Brown had also been appointed as Colonial Secretary. Stirling had nominated Mark Currie for the position of Harbour Master, which had been confirmed before Christmas, while the Scot James Drummond was appointed Government Naturalist on the 27th. The Surgeon, Charles Simmons, Assistant Surveyor, Henry Sutherland, and several clerks were appointed in the New Year. Interestingly, the Colonial Office did not consider an engineer or person skilled in public works necessary among initial appointments, although it may have been hoped that such expertise could come from the accompanying soldiers. These were 100 men from the 63rd Regiment, under the Command of Captain F. C. Irwin, who were then readying at Chatham for duty at Swan River.[67] In addition to HMS *Sulphur*, which was to convey the troops, the Colonial Office had decided to engage another vessel, the 443-ton *Parmelia*, to take the civil officers, their families and stores to the new colony.[68]

At this stage Stirling was clearly expecting John to join the venture, praising his brother's wife Elizabeth 'for her resolution and self-denial…allowing you to go out and prepare her reception'.[69] Other family members and their close connections were also involved in the venture. Sister Anna's husband, Sir James Home, had been contacted in India and was interested in participating in the venture, as were two of Ross Donnelly Mangles' friends, Lowis and Yule. All the Mangles family, as well as Stirling's own, were supportive and busy spreading the word about the new colony to as many friends and connections as possible.

On the very last day of 1828, Stirling finally received his official letter of appointment. The major clauses in his commission were as follows:

> It having been determined by His Majesty's Government to occupy the post of the western coast of New Holland, at the mouth of the river called 'Swan River', with the adjacent territory, for the purpose of forming a settlement there, His Majesty has been pleased to approve the selection of yourself to have the command of the expedition appointed for that service, and the superintendence of the proposed settlement.
>
> You will accordingly repair, with all practicable dispatch, to the place of your destination, on board the vessel which has been provided for the purpose…As Swan River and the adjacent territory are not within the limits of any existing colony, difficulties may easily be anticipated in the course of your proceedings…from the absence of all civil institutions, legislative, judicial, or financial. Until provision can be made…the difficulties to which I refer must be combated, and will, I trust, be overcome by your own firmness and discretion.
>
> You will assume the title of Lieutenant-Governor, and in that character will correspond with this department respecting your proceedings and the wants and prospects of the settlement you are to form.
>
> Amongst your earliest duties will be that of determining the most convenient site for a town to be erected as the future seat of government. You will be called upon to weigh maturely the advantages which may arise from placing it on so secure a situation as may be afforded on various points of the Swan River, against those which may follow from establishing it on so fine a port for the reception of shipping as Cockburn Sound is represented to be…You will cause it to be understood that His Majesty has granted you the power of making all necessary locations of land. For your guidance in this respect, ample instructions will at a future period be prepared. In the meantime I enclose a copy of the instructions of the Governor of New South Wales on this subject, to which you will adhere as closely as circumstances will admit…
>
> I think it necessary also to caution you that you must be careful not to grant more than a due proportion of sea or river frontage to any settler. The great advantage to be derived from an easy water communication will of course not escape your consideration…
>
> In regard to the surveys and explorations of the country…it is perhaps premature to give you any instructions…[but] I should be inclined to think that

it will be expedient to make the country south of Swan River the scene of your labours, rather than the tract of country north of that stream, and that you will do well to invite the settlers to locate themselves according to this suggestion…

You will recommend, by your counsels and example, the habitual observance of Sunday as a day of rest and public worship…With these few and general instructions for your guidance, assisted by the oral and written communications which have taken place between yourself and this department, you will, I trust, be able to surmount the difficulties to which you may be exposed at the outset, enhanced though they may be, by the want of any regular commission for administering the government. An instrument of that nature, accompanied with all the requisite instructions, will be transmitted to you as soon as the indispensable forms of proceeding in such cases will allow. I am etc G. Murray.[70]

After reading this once or twice, and conveying the news to Ellen, Stirling sat down to write two letters that were to seal his fate for the next few years. The first was addressed to John Wilson Croker at the Admiralty:

Dear Sir I have the honour to inform you that I have this day received a Communication from Secretary The Right Honble Sir George Murray acquainting me that I have been appointed to conduct a New Settlement proposed to be established in Western Australia with the Title of Lieut. Governor.

In laying this representation before My Lords Commissioner of the Admiralty, I request you will be please to move My Lords Commissioners of the Admiralty to grant me leave of absence to enable me to fulfil the duties of the Station to which I am appointed, and I respectfully solicit their Lordships' assurance that my temporary employment in this Branch of His Majesty's Service may not militate against my return at any future time to the active duties of my Profession.[71]

The second letter, addressed to Under-Secretary Hay, was short but sweet in the writing:

I have the honour to acknowledge the Receipt of your letter of the 30th Inst. acquainting me that I have been appointed to conduct the new Settlement about to be established in Western Australia with the Title of Lt. Governor. I beg leave to inform you in reply thereto that I gratefully accept the nomination conferred on me, and that I shall endeavour to discharge the duties of the Office with Zeal and Fidelity.[72]

On that same day, 31 December, Hay wrote to inform Treasury of the venture.

…intimation having been received that the French Government intend to colonize some part of the West Coast of New Holland, & especially that position adjoining to the River lately explored by Captain Stirling, the Sec. of State has thought it expedient to send out that officer to form a small settlement in that quarter, to which such persons may advantageously resort as may be desirous of establishing themselves in a climate as favourable as New South Wales & a soil as promising without the disadvantages which attach to a Penal Colony...It is proposed that Captain Stirling, the superintendent, should bear the King's Commission as Lt. Governor of the Settlement and that a Bill should be brought in Parliament during the ensuing session for granting a Charter to this New Colony.

Being fully aware of the necessity of adhering to the strictest economy...Sir G. Murray has provided that the Expedition which is preparing should be on the least expensive scale...it has been thought proper to send out a detachment of 60 men, with a proportionate number of officers, from one of the Regt's which in the routine of service are destined for India & to attach to this duty one of the small ships of war employed under the orders of the Officer Commanding HM Naval Forces in the Indian Seas. The number of the Civil Establishment to be employed has been fixed as follows.[73]

Lieut Governor	Captn Stirling	no salary
Secretary	Mr Peter Brown	£400
Clerk to ditto	Mr W Shilton	no salary
Storekeeper	Mr J Morgan	£200
Surveyor	Mr Roe	£300
Assistant do	Mr Sutherland	£200
Surgeon	Dr Simmons	15/- per diem
Harbour master	Captn Currie	no salary
Naturalist	Mr Drummond	no salary

It has not been considered feasible to place their salaries at a lower rate. In those cases where no salary is stated it is not intended that any should be given at least until the duties should appear to be such as to require compensation. They will be entitled however to a free passage, which is also given to all those who go out on the public account.

As in the outset of this colony no funds can be derived from it for its support...the Sec. of State feels his inability to prepare in the outset any Estimate of the Expenditure which may be required but he does not doubt that before the Expiration of the year he will have in his power to submit a calculation to the Lords Commissioners which may answer their Lordships purpose in making the necessary application to Parliament.[74]

With this official request for the finance to underpin the venture, the Swan River Colony was no longer a dream.

9

Preparations and the *Parmelia*

OVER THE 1829 New Year period James had persuaded Ellen, then six months pregnant with their second child, to leave with him for Western Australia. His brother John's wife Elizabeth was to stay in St Andrews with their children until things were more settled, but John seemed determined to go with them. They were an adventurous family, for word had come through from the Persian Gulf that brother Edward had taken leave from the East India Company to go exploring in what is now north Afghanistan, and later claimed to have been the first white person to return from there alive, though half blinded.[1] James' youngest brother Robert was also leaving to join his regiment in India, so mother Anne faced saying goodbye to almost all her younger sons. But far from regret or sentimentality, her main concern was their advancement, as can be seen in her letter to John on 5 January 1829:

> My Dear John…I was hardly prepared to hear that yourself and the Governor were to move off so quickly. I fervently hope however it is for the best, and that every good thing may attend you both. It appears at first sight to be unfortunate that Mr Twiss shd. have stayed so long at Paris which has prevented his settling all matters with Mr Peel in a way most desirable for Jamie. From all we have known of him he appears an artful clever man that will take every advantage for his own interest that he can catch at—and of course a dangerous man to have to do with…
>
> I hope James may have fixed upon the land most likely to be useful to him in the end…Is he to have money allowed for building the Government House or is Government to do so?…should Jamie do it at his own expense, so that he might retain it, or dispose of it hereafter, any new Governor might take it into his head to remove the seat of Government far from Jamie's possessions, which would hurt his estate…

Anne knew the family's financial resources were still slim, except perhaps for John who had the benefit of his wife's fortune. Proud as well as practical, Anne did not fully approve of this arrangement, and was delighted that John was to accompany James to Swan River. She advised him not to 'hurry away from Western Australia till you have time to thoroughly investigate matters in every way', in particular urging her third son to guard against 'wife-sickness'. She cited as examples her own father, and also Uncle Charles, who had on different occasions hurried home too soon for that reason. After advising John to 'leave nothing undone that may secure your independence', Anne's letter concluded with remarkable presentiment on James' future:

> The game is only begun to be played and though all is sunshine at the present moment one cannot help feel nervous as to the result, with every confidence in Jamie's talents and good intentions…The fortune he may make in my estimation is comparatively speaking, but as dirt below his feet—great as he tells me he expects it to be in the course of ten years. If he succeeds in his wish in founding this new settlement—the credit he must acquire from it cannot fail of helping him forward in his professional career…[2]

Five days later, on 10 January, John wrote to the Colonial Office explaining his plans to introduce to Swan River Colony a steam engine for cutting timber and grinding corn, and in return asked for a reserved grant of land next to his brother's at Geographe Bay.[3] He was disappointed when the request was rejected, on the grounds that to accede

> would open a door to similar applications from other persons, who upon the ground of intended investments…would occupy some of the most desirable Tracts of Land, to the injury of those who may be in a condition to render their Capital available immediately.[4]

In between this request and the Colonial Office reply four days later, new and more specific 'Regulations for the guidance of those who may propose to embark, as settlers, for the new Settlement on the Western Coast of New Holland' had been released.[5] Dated 13 January 1829, they differed from those of December 1828 in several important respects:

1. They stipulated that grants would be allocated with occupation rights only, full title being dependent on 'improving' the whole area to the value of 1s 6d an acre;
2. They cut the time limit for improvement of land grants from 21 to 10 years, after which grants would be resumed by the Crown, and added penalties for slow performance (a fine of 6d per acre for land not improved after 3 years);
3. They stipulated land grants would be allocated to settlers in order of arrival, so cutting out absentees and reservations; and

4.   They limited the land allowance of 200 acres per person introduced to the colony at the settler's expense, only to those over 10 years of age. (This was amended in the final 3 February regulations when a sliding scale was introduced awarding land according to the age of children.)

John must have known of the first two changes when he applied for his grant, but possibly not the others. He had definitely not realised that all property had to be landed before a grant could be made. Things were changing quickly, and James was busy running around the country recruiting people, arranging purchases and other business—even an extraordinary licence for his future Surveyor-General, John Septimus Roe, to marry his childhood sweetheart, Matilda Bennett, on 8 January.[6] So it is not surprising that John, who had moved to Duke Street, London in the New Year, was unaware of the Colonial Office's increasing stringency. The grant setback, however, checked his enthusiasm and this, together with news that his wife Elizabeth was ill, caused him to postpone his departure and return to Scotland. He had not yet totally abandoned his plans to emigrate, for he wrote to Hay again on 24 January suggesting that, if he provided a bond to cover his future investment, he be granted some 100,000 acres next to his brother's land.[7] But the Colonial Office was wary, insisting that all investment property had to be landed in the Colony by the end of 1829.[8] It was the last proposition John put forward.

James was worried about his own financial situation. As early as 11 December Treasury had approved a payment of £600 'to defray the expenses of his passage and other charges'.[9] But the appointment of other civil staff on the promise of a free passage meant that some of his expenditures had been unnecessary, and he was running short of funds. He put his concerns to Twiss on 16 January 1829:

> At a time when I understood that the question as to the undertaking of the Enterprise would be decided on reference to the attendant Expenses, I did not hesitate in offering to conduct and manage it without salary, earnest as I was from public as well as private motive that it should not be abandoned. From that proposal I feel no inclination to withdraw, and as I consider that the payment of my outfit would be in fact salary in disguise I feel disinclined to propose it. I must therefore be content to support the expenses of my station from my private Funds, and I shall not ask for remuneration for my services until Sir George Murray, whose Liberality I entirely concede, shall think fit to remember that I am an unpaid Governor.

The issue he next raised was to become contentious in the future:

> As you seemed to think yesterday that the sum of £600 which I have received is an allowance for my outfit, I take the liberty to say that is barely sufficient to meet the expense of my passage; and as I am on the subject of my private affairs I hope

you will pardon me for saying that the Grant of 100,000 acres, most liberal as a complimentary acknowledgment of the part I have played connected with these transactions, has neither reference nor value as a recompense for future exertions, in as much as I hold it subject to the 'same conditions as ordinary Settlers as to outlay, Cultivation &c &c'. I shall be sorry if you believe from these notions that I am not content and most happy in the liberal reception I have met. My only view is that when I am remote from the power of personal explanations I may neither understand nor be understood, and that before I quit England I may know precisely the terms on which I go.[10]

Here again Stirling was restating his belief that the 100,000-acre grant was for past services, and that he held expectations of further entitlements.

That same day, the new regulations for Swan River appeared in the *Morning Chronicle*, and again in *The Times* along with an editorial about the venture.[11] Together they created a ferment of interest among would-be investors, and Stirling was rushed off his feet with queries, as were Colonial Office staff. One group not pleased at the more stringent regulations was the Peel Association, whose members felt their large investment entitled them to different treatment. They met Under-Secretary Twiss on 20 January, when it was made clear that the only concessions the Association would receive were the already promised 21-year improvement period and their prior choice of 250,000 acres. Otherwise all the new regulations would apply to them as well.[12]

This proved mortal for the Association. An angry Peel, complaining of the Government's 'want of candour', advised Twiss the following day that Sir Francis Vincent had withdrawn from the Association. Another founding member, Colonel MacQueen, had previously quit, and in Peel's view, 'were he now to view our condition I am satisfied he would consider us little better than lunatics to attempt further to proceed'.[13] On the 23rd Edward Schenley too resigned.[14] One of the last straws prompting his resignation was the about-turn the Colonial Office took on his request for three passages on the *Parmelia*, the merchant vessel which had been chartered to take the civil establishment out to Swan River. At first Hay had agreed to provide passages for one member of the Peel Association, plus a surveyor and manservant, on condition that restitution in kind be made for any rations drawn.[15] But less than a week later, on 11 January, he wrote to say that the *Parmelia* was 'fully occupied' by civil officers and their families and regretfully could not accommodate the three persons.[16]

With the departure of three of its four members, the Peel Association seemed to have expired. But on 28 January Peel informed Twiss that he was prepared to carry on alone, on the same terms that had been offered to the Association.[17] He had acquired the help of a most persuasive Jewish emancipist from New South Wales, Solomon Levey, who took over organising Peel's venture as a silent co-partner.[18] The delay, however, meant that their group would not be ready to leave England with

Stirling, so Peel asked for additional time to land his first consignment of people
and goods to claim his priority grant. The Colonial Office agreed to allow him until
1 November 1829,[19] but both Peel and Stirling were told that, if he failed to arrive by
that date, his right to his chosen land would lapse, leaving him on the same footing
as other settlers. Thus the matter stood when Stirling left England.

Peel was by no means the only large investor communicating with the
Colonial Office about Swan River. On 29 January 1829 the department had
acknowledged an official application from Colonel Peter Augustus Latour for
100,000 acres in the new colony.[20] Latour had opened verbal negotiations the
previous November, but had now applied in writing. Son of a wealthy merchant,
Latour had joined the army in 1804 and served at Waterloo before being placed on
half-pay in 1817. He had then become interested in investment opportunities in
Australia, possibly through old army friends. In 1825 he had been a major investor
in the 'Van Diemen's Land Company' which, modelled on the Australian
Agricultural Company, was intended to be an agricultural and horse-breeding
enterprise on lands granted on the basis of introduced capital assets. Latour sent out
an agent to act on his behalf and remained in England where, at the age of 38, he
married the society beauty Una Barclay Innes. The Van Diemen's Land Company
did not succeed, but Latour was unaware of this when he heard of the proposed new
colony in Western Australia from Peel Association members in November 1828.[21] He
had then applied to the Colonial Office for a grant in return for a considerable
investment. The official reply at the end of January had simply cited the regulations
governing settlement, and stressed that land would only be allocated when assets
and labour were actually landed in the colony. Undaunted, Latour set out to acquire
the necessary assets and people, including an overseer, Richard Wells, and arrange
for their transportation. In all, he spent some £30,000 in preparation, and some of
his property was on board the first merchant ship to follow the *Parmelia* out to
Swan River.[22] But of all this Stirling remained unaware. There is no evidence that he
met Latour before departure, and he was definitely on the high seas when Latour
demanded the same 21-year improvement period that had been allowed to Peel and
Stirling. The subsequent fate of Latour, and Peel, was to loom large in Stirling's
future.

When the Colonial Office replied to Latour's application, the *Parmelia* had
already left London Docks on her way to Spithead.[23] Such was the rush of departure.
By Stirling's birthday, on 28 January, the *Parmelia* was fully loaded and apparently
in 'a sad state of confusion'.[24] On board were half her passengers, their baggage,
livestock and government stores and, as additional passengers and cargo were
expected to be loaded in Portsmouth, the crew could not organise stowage. The
Navy Office had already contacted Stirling on 15 January asking for some of the
stores to be left behind,[25] but Stirling was loath to see anything deleted. Indeed, he
requested additional stores, tents and waterproof canvas on 21 January, and two days
later asked the Navy Office to provide a 27 ft whaleboat for use in the shallows.[26]

Piloted by a steam vessel, the *Meteor*,[27] the *Parmelia* had 'a tedious voyage' down the Thames and 'grounded upon a shoal while passing through the Needles Passage',[28] so delaying her arrival in Portsmouth. This was another vexation for Captain Dance, commander of the troop ship HMS *Sulphur*, which had now been waiting for some days.[29] The *Sulphur* was also very overcrowded. She not only carried the 100-strong military guard with their commander, Captain Irwin, a bachelor, but also the ten women who had won the ballot for accompanying wives (the number allowed per regiment), together with their children, servants and luggage. Then there was three years' worth of army stores: tents and poles, guns and ammunition, provisions including livestock, summer and winter clothes and bedding, musical instruments, etc. In addition she was carrying 10,000 bricks, ordered by Captain Stirling, which were stacked on deck where they impeded normal activities.[30] The *Sulphur* also carried the new Colony's Treasury or Public Chest: sixteen boxes containing £200 in copper coin, £200 in silver Spanish dollars, and £600 in English silver coinage[31]—a total £1,000 to meet all the expenses of government, which Dance was to deliver to Stirling on arrival.

Although a little larger than the *Sulphur*, the *Parmelia* was just as crowded. Contrary to the belief of many old Western Australian families, the *Parmelia* carried only government employees and their families and servants, as well as mountains of government stores, plants, luggage, building materials, etc. Stirling himself had personally ordered some household goods and chattels to the value of £123 15s.[32] His own party included the very pregnant Ellen and 4-year-old Andrew, two married couples as servants (Thomas and Sarah Blakey and John and Elizabeth Kelly), James' cousin William Stirling (from the Scottish side of the family), who was eight years younger than James and was to act as his private secretary, and George Mangles, who was Ellen's young cousin and whom Stirling had made Director of Stock. Also in his party was 11-year-old George Elliot, the recently orphaned nephew by marriage of James' sister Mary Halsey, who had been engaged as a junior clerk.

The men chosen to form his civil establishment also had families and servants. In order of precedence they were the Colonial Secretary, Mr Peter Brown (later Broun), who emigrated with his wife Caroline, their 2-year-old son McBride and baby Ann, plus three servants (Richard Evans, Margaret MacLeod and Mary Ann Smith); next was the Surveyor-General, John Septimus Roe, with his 'dearest rib' Matilda and one manservant (Charles Wright); the Harbour Master, Captain Mark Currie, with his wife Jane and three servants (Frederick and Matilda Ludlow and Jane Fruin); then the Storekeeper or Commissary, John Morgan with his wife Rebecca and daughter of the same name with their servant (Ann Skipsey.) The Naturalist, or Superintendent of Gardens, James Drummond,[33] brought his wife Sarah and six children, ranging from the 18-year-old Thomas to 3-year-old Euphemia, as well as one servant (Elizabeth Gamble); and then there was the Colonial Surgeon, Charles Simmons, a Yorkshireman and bachelor, the Assistant Surveyor, Henry Sutherland, who emigrated with his wife Ann, and the Clerk to the Colonial Secretary, young Mr William Shelton.[34] Also on board *Parmelia* was the Assistant Surgeon to the 63rd Regiment, Dr Daly, whose large family (wife and eight children) could not be accommodated on board the *Sulphur*.

The remainder of the *Parmelia*'s passengers were government-appointed tradespeople (or artificers, as they were called): the cooper, builder, boat builder and blacksmith together with their wives and families, about twenty people in all. Most of the tradespeople had been recruited from the Portsmouth dock area and employed on an indenture contract, i.e. they had signed an agreement to work for keep, but little or no wages, for an agreed number of years, to offset passage fares paid on their behalf. Common in apprenticeship agreements, the indenture system was used by many intending settlers to ensure that the labour they transported to the new land stayed around long enough to work that land, and so undertake the improvements necessary for their masters to gain title to their grants. The Government needed the same assurance for the completion of public works.

Although appointed on no pay, James Drummond had his work cut out from the moment he boarded the *Parmelia*, for the Horticultural Society had kindly made a gift of nine boxes of plants and cuttings. These contained dozens of flora varieties, from fruit trees to strawberries as well as bulbs and seeds, which all had to be cared for during the different climatic conditions of the long voyage. But space on board for plants was scarce. Each family had brought not only personal and household belongings to last one to three years, but also as many land-qualifying assets as possible, including animals. Part of the deck, as well as the hold and individual cabins, was piled high with boxes, trunks, parcels, etc. And then there were government stores of all descriptions, as well as the victualling needs of the voyage—dried rations, water and rum barrels, and livestock to boost dried rations on the voyage out. Just before departure from London, Stirling had requisitioned a number of books 'for the use of the Colony', which would also have taken up space and needed careful packing to guard against damp. The titles and subjects he chose are interesting, as they show some forethought into the reference needs of a new settlement. They included a set of *Encyclopaedia Britannica*, works on natural history, common architecture, planting and raising fruit trees, vines, grasses and grains, Cobbett's *Cottage Economy* and *American Farmer*, three books on geology and mineralogy, Burr's *Justice*, the East India Commercial Dictionary and a work on the Law of Customs, one ordinary dictionary (Jacobs), three sets of Bibles and Prayer Books, and four presents of glass beads. Finally, his own interests in exploration were covered by the request for Baudin's *Voyage by Peron & Freycinet*, Crawford's *Malay Archipelago* and Flinders' *Terra Australis*.[35]

The book selection, too, may have been a bit of resourceful insurance, for so hastily had the expedition come together that Stirling had yet to be briefed on some key issues. If there were gaps left unanswered, suitable reference books would be invaluable in the new colony.

On the day that the *Parmelia* left London Docks, 24 January, Stirling wrote to Twiss asking for Colonial Office guidance on a number of matters:

In the case of Persons having fulfilled the Conditions as to Outlay &
Improvement of Land, am I to give Full Title to the Land as stated in the
Regulations and what Form is to be observed in such proceeding? Is it proper to
direct that all Correspondence with the Colonial Department shall be submitted
to the Office of the Lieut. Governor as in other Colonies? Are foreigners to be
entitled to Land and admitted to Title? Is the Settlement to be considered a Free
Port open to all Nations without payment of duty? May Vessels be built and
registered? Have I authority to licence the Importations and retail of Spirituous
Liquors, or may I restrain them? [36]

He was also still uncertain whether the 21-year improvement period offered to Peel
applied to his own grant, or whether it was subject to the new 10-year regulations.
This was clarified in a note from Twiss;

I am directed by Sir George Murray to acquaint you that you may consider Mr
Hay's letter of the 1st of this month as the authority to occupy the lands therein
designated…the term of 21 years has been allowed to you as well as to Mr Peel
because your engagements with the Government were entered into, as were his,
before the making of the New Boundaries which reduced the period of 21 to 10
years for all subsequent settlers. [37]

Stirling was given his final instructions on 28 January, and the following day
the *Morning Chronicle*, citing the Court Circular, reported:

Captain Stirling, the commander of the expedition proceeding to form a new
settlement on the Swan River…received his final Instructions yesterday at the
Colonial Office, and afterwards left town for Portsmouth; which port Captain
Stirling, with the two vessels containing the settlers, &c, it is expected, leaves this
day, for the purpose of proceeding on the voyage. [38]

But there was still nothing on paper to answer any of his major queries. In fact,
Stirling was to have no real guidance until his commission arrived belatedly at the
end of 1831. The only practical help available was a copy of the instructions given to
Governor Darling in 1825, when he had been appointed Governor of the convict
colony in New South Wales, and now enclosed with Stirling's letter of appointment. [39] Indeed, the haste and casual nature of the pre-departure arrangements made
it extremely difficult in future years for anyone, even Colonial Office officials, to
rule on the fine details of this colonisation experiment.

James, Ellen and young Andrew boarded the *Parmelia* at Spithead on
3 February 1829. [40] This must have been quite an effort for Ellen, as she gave birth
to their second son, Frederick Henry, only six weeks later. Mother Anne had
evidently stayed behind at Pirbright. It must have been difficult for her to say

goodbye, knowing the risks of the undertaking and the long time that they would be away.

On board the *Parmelia* no one was comfortable, for although well appointed the ship was seriously overcrowded and the weather abysmal. Twiss and the Treasury wanted a full account of all those on board, including the ages of all children, and after calling a muster, Stirling sent the required information on the 5th.[41] He was irked, however, to find that the number of tradespeople he had requested had not been found, despite last-minute recruiting.[42] So, while being buffeted by winds too contrary to permit departure he wrote to request that the remaining seven he had been promised be sent out on the *Calista*, the first of the passenger vessels readying for the Swan. He pleaded that these men

> will be indispensable in forming Buildings &c for the reception of Stores, Troops, Sick Persons and Houses for the Officers. If you approve this suggestion I recommend that 5 out of the 7 be house carpenters and the remainder masons.[43]

For several days the ship lay off Portsmouth, waiting for the bad weather to improve. Already it was aggravating seasickness and restricting the restowage of luggage, making accommodation very cramped. For the women and children those first few days would have been particularly unpleasant. But by Sunday 8 February, in company with the *Sulphur*, they were sailing towards the Lizard light and under way at last.[44]

Beginning his adventure on a ship commanded by another man must have seemed strange to Stirling, though Captain Luscombe was judged 'a very superior man in his station'.[45] He was, nevertheless, pleased that the Navy Office had given orders to Luscombe that on board ship Stirling was to be the Commanding Officer.[46] Soon after departure, Luscombe had the ship restowed to provide a little more space for his passengers, and a regular routine was established. Stirling had much to do. At last he could peruse the detailed general instructions that he had received with his appointment. Although not specific for Swan River, they did set out regulations for the division of territory, the granting of land, provision of land for churches, cemeteries and public works, public spaces, townships, etc. These were to supplement his own orders, which were to determine the site for the major town and seat of government, and to explore, survey and map the territory. During the voyage he spent many hours with his new officials and clerks, planning courses of action and drafting regulations to cover most of the eventualities he could foresee. What he could *not* have anticipated, however, was the mounting frenzy of interest in Swan River in London and the provinces, as his initial report was blown up by the Press to represent a southern paradise.

The final land regulations had been released to the Press in London on 3 February 1829, just as the *Parmelia* arrived at Spithead. This began what was subsequently dubbed a period of 'Swan River Mania'.[47] In the volatile economic conditions of the late 1820s many British people were finding 'former channels of procuring what our habits of life rendered familiar to us, being closed by the progress of change', and emigration was viewed as a relief.[48] For such people the regulations governing settlement at Swan River Colony had enormous appeal. To the wealthy, like Peel and his associates, investing in a new colony was a chance to leave a mark for posterity; to officers on half-pay and soldiers on pensions, who were offered the prospect of land in lieu of their pensions, the venture held enormous promise; for tenant farmers, unable to afford land of their own in Britain, the regulations meant they could obtain land by simply transporting their existing farming equipment and animals to the Swan. Opportunities were also open to the poor, who normally could never afford to emigrate, as potential employers were advertising for labour. Several Poor Houses even directed their inhabitants to recruiting agents. Shipowners were delighted, seeing large profits, and even before Stirling left, several vessels were advertising to take passengers to the Swan.[49] Enquiries to the Colonial Office reached an all-time high in February, and their replies to queries began a process of misinformation.

Possibly to relieve the pressure of such enquiries, Sir John Barrow of the Admiralty published anonymously an article based closely on Stirling's official, and till now confidential, report on Swan River. He sent it to the *Quarterly Review*, a major middle-class monthly journal of the day, and it appeared in the April 1829 edition. Accepted as quasi-official, the *Quarterly Review* article had a huge impact. It revealed detailed information hitherto not publicly available, and although fairly true to Stirling's report, it nevertheless exaggerated the positive features and tended to whitewash the negatives. For example, Barrow summarised Stirling's day-to-day narrative as follows:

> We found the country in general rich and romantic, gained the summit of the first range of Mountains and had a birds eye view of an immense plain, which extended as far as the eye could reach to the northward, southward, and westward. After ten days absence we returned to the ship; we encountered no difficulty that was not easily removable; we were furnished with abundance of fresh provisions by our guns, and met with no obstructions from the natives.[50]

Highlights from the *Quarterly Review* article were quickly picked up by the London papers and later by the provincial Press. The Stirling family's friend John Cross even used it to publish a pamphlet titled *Hints on Emigration to the New Settlement on the Swan and Canning Rivers* in June 1829. Inevitably further distortions occurred, and features such as the amount of fertile land and fresh water were magnified many times.[51] The rosy picture painted by the Press attracted many who were totally unsuited for emigration, and encouraged very unrealistic expectations of what would be found on arrival. But initial excitement was intense, and by late February there was 'an extraordinary rush of people'[52] anxious to depart in order to have the best choice of land. Within a few months thirteen ships had left London for the Swan (combined tonnage 5,000) carrying some 1,370 passengers.

Stirling and the *Parmelia*, meanwhile, had reached the Cape of Good Hope. En route, and unmentioned in the ship's log, Ellen had given birth to her second son, Frederick Henry, who arrived safely on 26 March.[53] It must have been a traumatic event for her, in a tiny cabin, with the ship rolling in the swell and without the mother who until recently had been her constant companion. When they passed the Equator on 9 March,[54] the heat was less troublesome; however, fresh water supplies were limited and becoming smelly.

Unbeknown to Stirling, a sad incident had occurred on the final southward leg to Cape Town. His brother Robert, bound for Bengal on the *Admiral Benbow*, had been killed in a brutal attack by a pirate vessel. Stirling would not learn details of the tragedy for a further six months, but *The Times* reported details of the 11 April attack, describing how the pirates killed and injured crew members, and seized charts, compasses, books and livestock. 'Captain Stirling of the 3rd Buffs, a passenger, jumped overboard, but was picked up again: he destroyed himself rather than stay with the pirates.'[55] Family reaction back in England was one of shock. Walter, who investigated the matter in London, commented: 'Had it been in the field, we should have had no reason to complain, it would have been the fate of war…but to be sent out of the world by the hands of a set of rascally pirates is hard indeed!'.[56] In a strange coincidence, it appears Stirling encountered the very same pirate vessel, family letters stating:

> by a letter from Jimmy from the Cape, written about the 25th April, he mentions having been hailed by a Pirate of much the same description & most probably the identical one, nearly about the same latitude and in all probability would have shared the same fate, if they had not spoken of the near vicinity of the *Sulphur*, which they said was only a few leagues away, which seemed to alarm the scoundrels who then made off very quickly.[57]

A lucky escape, for the *Sulphur* was *not* 'in the vicinity'. Around the time of Frederick's birth, the *Sulphur* had dropped behind the *Parmelia*. A leak had been discovered in the carpenter's store and required constant pumping.

The *Parmelia* thus entered Simon's Bay at the Cape alone and in the midst of a fierce squall on 16 April 1829. This was almost a portent of a tragic event towards the end of their thirteen-day stay. On 25 April Surgeon Daly of the 63rd Regiment and his 10-year-old daughter were drowned when their boat overturned while returning from the shore to the ship.[58] Daly's body was recovered, though his daughter's was never found, and he was buried ashore. The funeral was attended by members of his regiment who had arrived on the *Sulphur* on the 26th. Mrs Daly decided to continue on to Swan River, while another military medical man in Cape Town, Surgeon William Milligan, also attached to the 63rd Regiment, was asked to take Daly's place.

The presence of the vessels in Cape Town, and their purpose, would have sparked much local interest, for Stirling observed that many were 'quite convinced to the benefits which the Cape can derive from the New Settlement'. He himself was more circumspect, writing to John that he thought Swan River could well 'injure the Cape both in the supply of the Isle de France and in attracting Indians [who] have caught eagerly at the prospect…'[59] In this letter he also mentioned that the animals he had brought out from England for his own farm use (two Alderney cows, a calf and some English hogs and poultry), had all survived the journey, and that he intended purchasing at the Cape '2 rams, some goats, some sows and a good stock of Poultry for myself besides Plants and Seeds and also some draught oxen &c for Government'.

Caulking and repairs to the *Sulphur* took time, and Stirling was anxious to depart. On 29 April he sent Captain Dance a note to that effect, to which Dance replied that departure before at least 2 May was impossible.[60] Dance also complained of having to take on board some of the cattle Stirling had purchased for the new settlement. James had spent some £41 and had drawn a Bill on Treasury to cover it, but in a private letter to Twiss asked him to 'have the goodness to recommend me to the notice of the Treasury that all knowledge of me may not be denied there when my Bills come to be presented'.[61] He also sought instructions as to how to proceed in drawing future Bills, for even that crucial matter had been omitted in the Colonial Office's rush to have him beat the French.

From the outset Stirling had been concerned that he lacked an engineer. Whilst at the Cape he managed to persuade a civil engineer, Henry Reveley, to take on the position. The extent of Stirling's persuasive power is well illustrated by the fact that Reveley and his wife had packed up and were ready to join the *Parmelia* when it left on 30 April. To find Reveley in the first place Stirling needed contacts, and he had many at the Cape. His old friend Harry Smith, for example, was serving at the Cape as Quartermaster-General,[62] and this was no doubt a huge help for Stirling in ordering provisions. With Ellen, James made official calls to both the Governor of Cape Colony, Sir Galbraith Lowry Cole, and the Naval Commander-in-Chief, Charles Schomberg, as well as other key figures both ashore and on ships in port. Cementing contacts for possible future use was part of Stirling's make-up and, as another boat was preparing to head eastward across the Indian Ocean, he took the opportunity of sending a letter to Governor Arthur in Van Diemen's Land. Stirling offered the latest parliamentary news from England, but mainly spoke of his own concerns for the new colony:

> Our new Settlement on the West Coast of New Holland had excited some sensation and…several vessels with free Settlers were preparing to follow us, and I confidently hope that we shall have a considerable number of persons in the Settlement before the expiration of this year…I do not anticipate such rapid prosperity as took place in New South Wales and Van Diemen's Land but there are

many classes who will find their interests suited by coming to us, and no class so much as the Emancipists of the older Australian colonies.[63]

This last is an interesting observation, for nowhere else does Stirling express his lack of opposition to freed convicts, and it ran counter to the sentiments of many intending immigrants who were attracted to the new colony by the express condition that it would receive no convicts or other type of prisoners.

One piece of news at the Cape which would have perturbed Stirling was the rumour that the French had actually taken possession of the western coast of Australia the previous January.[64] Offsetting this was the knowledge that Captain Fremantle of HMS *Challenger* had left the Cape for Western Australia on 20 March[65] with orders to annex the territory for the Crown.[66] Fremantle had marines on board, and the *Challenger* was capable of taking on a single French vessel, but it would be a different story if the French had established a settlement.

James would have been dancing with impatience to leave and find out for himself, but his escort the *Sulphur* was still not ready. However, he'd left escorts behind before so, after informing Twiss he intended pressing on alone,[67] Stirling gave the order for the *Parmelia* to set her sails for Swan River. Once at sea again, he devoted time to writing up regulations for the guidance of his civil officers and, as they crossed the Indian Ocean, long discussions were held so that all would know their duties upon arrival.[68]

At noon on 31 May 1829 the western coast of Australia was sighted, and by nightfall the *Parmelia* was anchored off the west side of Garden Island. Strong emotions would have stirred James that evening—his land of promise lay just ahead and he would step ashore on the 'Glorious First of June', an auspicious day for Stirling who held naval traditions dear. But the day did not unfold as planned. At daybreak the *Parmelia* weighed anchor to commence the narrow entry into Cockburn Sound, but a heavy swell made the task very dangerous. After a number of unsuccessful attempts, and in the face of rising winds, she was taken northwards to anchor off Rottnest Island for the night of the 1st.[69] Luckily her sails had been seen by men from HMS *Challenger*, which had arrived on 27 April and was then anchored on the shore side of Garden Island, so they could place their ship to assist if necessary. Captain Fremantle had also had difficulties with the area when he had first arrived, and for four days had been prevented by boisterous weather from reaching the mainland. Landing at the river mouth on 2 May with twenty-five seamen and marines, Fremantle had ordered a flagpole to be erected, raised the Union Jack and toasted the King, and began to establish a 'redoubt', or small fort, to command the entrance to the river. The rest of the *Challenger*'s crew waited anxiously for the sight of a sail.[70] Fremantle's instructions had been not only to occupy the territory, but also to assist Captain Stirling establish the settlement, and nothing further could be done until his arrival.

Captain Charles Fremantle, Commander of HMS *Challenger*
Courtesy Battye Library 1321B

Early on 2 June, Fremantle boarded the *Parmelia* and she again made for Cockburn Sound. What happened next is perhaps best described in Stirling's own words. In a letter to his brother Walter he admitted:

> We found the *Challenger* in the Sound but unfortunately in approaching the Anchorage, the *Parmelia*, under my over confident pilotage took the ground and, the night becoming stormy and a heavy swell setting in, our situation became highly perilous. You may easily imagine what a night it was to me. I expected the ship to go to pieces and saw in that prospect my own total ruin, but, after eighteen hours of beating, at daylight she floated off and was brought into an anchorage inside of the Island.[71]

In a later letter to a naval friend, he again admitted the mistake and the consequent danger:

> The *Parmelia* Transport in which I was embarqued made her passage from land to land in 28 days, & on the 1st of June we reached the neighbourhood. By my over confident pilotage however, the ship took ground in coming into the back-haven Sound & she thumped about on the bank for 18 hours notwithstanding Charles

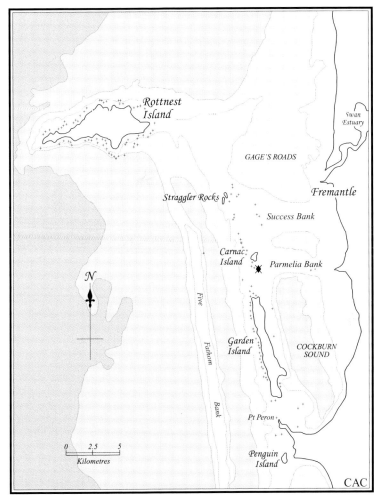

The rock hazards and sandbanks which confronted the *Parmelia*'s
approach to Cockburn Sound; ✳ indicates the site of the accident

Fremantle's exertions & our own to get her off. You will easily imagine how
dangerous to the fate of our infant Colony such an accident was, but it ended
without much serious injury to us...[72]

Fremantle's official account leaves out the fact that Stirling was at the helm, but his
description is still quite graphic:

In running into Cockburn Sound she [the *Parmelia*] grounded on the Bank
between Pulo Carnac and Woodman's Point on the Main, and it was not until the
next morning with all the exertions of this Ship's crew and boats that she was
extricated from her perilous situation after she had received much damage; she was
subsequently brought near the *Challenger*, and secured in Cockburn Sound.[73]

Fremantle recorded in his private diary that he had taken Mrs Stirling and the other women and children on board the *Challenger* during the danger, and that when it was over he had found his 'Cabin a complete pig sty, full of Women & children squalling and making dirt'.[74] All except Mrs Stirling and Mrs Currie (the two naval wives) were sent back to the *Parmelia*, the two exempted ladies joining their menfolk for dinner on board *Challenger* that evening. His official account continued:

> His Excellency the Lieutenant Governor having determined to make his first landing on Garden Island…the weather being generally boisterous rainy and unsettled and the communication with the Main Land very uncertain, he requested that I would render him all the assistance of the *Challenger*'s crew in building houses for himself and the rest of the colonists…I immediately employed every means in my power to forward his wishes.[75]

Fremantle privately thought the decision to build on Garden Island was unwise, noting in his diary that 'he must eventually move to the main & everything that will be done on the island consequently be thrown away'.[76] It is possible to attribute a mercenary motive behind Stirling's instructions to build on Garden Island, as it was part of his own land grant—but he really had no other choice. Gale winds prevailed from the 4th to the 6th, and the *Parmelia*'s hull had been considerably damaged in the incident, requiring her cargo to be offloaded somewhere close. On Garden Island Stirling also expected to find augmented groups of the animals he had left in 1827, to supply fresh meat and milk for the passengers. He must have been distinctly disappointed when informed by Fremantle's men of their total disappearance. In fact, Fremantle recorded in his diary on 9 June that the name Garden Island was 'a misnomer, the soil in my opinion being generally very sandy, and only a few spots capable of producing even the commonest vegetables'.

Following orders, Fremantle's artificers and seamen began work on Garden Island on 8 June, clearing ground and constructing shelters. Unfortunately, on the 10th one of the *Challenger*'s crew, William Parsons, was killed when a falling tree hit his temple. He was buried the following day on the outskirts of the settlement.[77] An anonymous sketch of the camp site on Garden Island shows a small group of huts clustered on a hillock and a number of service tents on shore, near the point where Stirling had originally found fresh water and Fremantle's men had dug a well and lined it with stone.[78] Cattle and cargo were landed from the *Parmelia* on 9 June, while on the 11th, in continuing wet and windy weather, the women and children were finally landed to take up residence on the island.

Both Stirling and Fremantle recorded the safe arrival in Cockburn Sound of HMS *Sulphur*, with the detachment of the 63rd Regiment, on 8 June.[79] Fremantle's private diary, however, reveals that he thought 'Captain Dance very rash in attempting to run for the coast during such tempestuous weather; we all thought he must have been wrecked'.[80] Some of the troops were immediately landed on Garden

Windswept Garden Island, where Stirling's first temporary Government House was a one-room hut

Artist unknown. *Garden Island in Western Australia, Seamen's Huts and Workshops, South View c. 183–*. Pencil, pen and ink and wash.

Collection, Art Gallery of Western Australia. Gift of a Descendant of Governor Stirling, London, 1924

Island to assist with the construction of huts and buildings, but Stirling wanted Captain Irwin and his troops to relieve the *Challenger*'s men at their post on the mainland as soon as possible. Continuing bad weather, however, meant that the *Sulphur* could not get near enough to disembark the troops until 17 June. And nor did Stirling. His 'Journal of Events' records that on the 17th Captain Irwin landed on the mainland and read a 'proclamation', prepared by Stirling, which conveyed His Majesty King George IV's approval of the appointment of Captain James Stirling as Lieutenant Governor.[81] It was read again on Garden Island, in Stirling's presence, the following day and is dated 18 June. Why Stirling remained on Garden Island is unclear, but possibly because all his civil establishment were there. Fremantle's diary made no mention of the event at all, except to note that bad weather had delayed the landing of Irwin's men.

The reading of this fairly lengthy Proclamation, and its content, was later justified by Stirling as follows:

> The absence of a Regular commission and charter establishing any system of law, as well as the apprehension I entertained that if no law were declared to be in force among Persons at such a distance from Authority, doubts might arise as to the power of punishment and offences be committed in consequence. I found myself compelled to declare by the Proclamation alluded to that, being in His Majesty's Possession, the Country became subject to the laws of the United Kingdom as far as they are applicable. How far this doctrine be strictly accordant to the Principles of Law, or consistent with your views, I submit to your consideration; and request Instructions as to the future enforcement of the rule…[82]

Essentially, Stirling used the Proclamation to legitimise his authority and to specify the type of behaviour he expected from colonists. He cautioned them

> to abstain from the commission of Offences against the King's Peace or the Laws of the realm upon pain of being arrested, prosecuted, convicted, and punished as is usual in similar offences committed in any other part or Parts of His Majesty's Dominions subject to British Law.

He commanded that 'due obedience and respect be shewn' to all persons he appointed to government positions, including those 'filling the Offices of High Constable, Constables, Bailiffs, and Surveyors of the High Ways'. He particularly stipulated that

> if any Person or Persons shall be convicted of behaving in a fraudulent, cruel or felonious Manner towards the Aborigines of the Country, such Person or Persons will be liable to be prosecuted and tried for the Offence, as if the same had been committed against any other of His Majesty's subjects.

First reading of Stirling's Proclamation, by Captain Irwin on the mainland near Fremantle
(after J. Allcott *The Proclamation*)

Courtesy The West Australian

He called for the formation of a militia force 'to assist His Majesty's regular troops in the defence of the laws and property', and announced that all intending grantees had first to see the Colonial Secretary and 'make application for Permission to reside in the Settlement', whilst anyone intending to depart had to provide a week's notice 'upon pain of being liable to be apprehended and detained'.

Stirling was clearly intent on imposing naval discipline on his settlement, but he was to find it difficult to sustain. His clear warning about any interference with Aborigines showed initiative, as it had not even been mentioned in his official instructions. On the mainland the Proclamation had been read on the 17th at what is now Fremantle, but Stirling had ended it, 'Given under my hand and seal at Perth this 18th day of June 1829. James Stirling Lieutenant Governor.' So he used the name 'Perth'—which he later bestowed on his capital—before he had determined its location. Clearly, he had decided on the name for his seat of Government before arrival.

Once Stirling had proclaimed his command, the soldiers of the 63rd Regiment officially took over from Captain Fremantle's marines, who had formed a permanent guard by the flagpole at the river mouth since 2 May. The fort built by the marines on Arthur's Head consisted of a trench 8ft deep and 11ft wide which circled the hill for 170ft, and had a mounted gun at its centre.[83] Its main purpose was to deter any foreign ships, but it also served to keep things secure from the incredibly curious natives, with whom amicable relations had been maintained despite frequent theft. The number of marines ashore at any one time had been fairly small, so their impact on the indigenous inhabitants had been minimal, but with the arrival of the Governor, settlers and soldiers, and the commencement of exploring parties, this was to change.

In London, much had occurred since Stirling's departure. Final estimates of the expense of sending out the expedition had been prepared by the Navy Office in May,[84] and to Sir George Murray's satisfaction they had come in at £124 15s less than the estimates prepared in March. The latter had allowed £4,400 for government freight and personnel conveyance on the *Parmelia*, *Marquis of Anglesea* and *Calista*, and £4,500 for wages—an exact total of £9,068 15s.[85] Joining the last two mentioned ships readying at Portsmouth, and others elsewhere, were many intending private settlers and their families. As the *Hampshire Telegraph* reported, 'Many highly respectable and indeed distinguished individuals, whose names we have learnt, are eagerly engaged in forming parties on a large scale to emigrate thither'.[86]

At the Colonial Office, Under-Secretary Hay had been besieged by people wanting information, appointments or letters of introduction. Following official practice at the time, each was dealt with in a separate letter to Stirling, so his first mail —when it eventually reached him—was huge. Hay specifically asked Stirling to comply with the Zoological Society's request for specimens and drawings of native fauna and flora,[87] and for attention and favour to certain individuals who had been highly recommended by peers of the realm, Members of Parliament or top civil servants. Among the first of these were Messrs Rivett Bland, Edward Waterton, John Kellam, Neil Talbot and James Woodward.[88] And many more were to follow. At almost the same time, Peel and Levey were advertising in the Press for settlers and labourers to join their forthcoming expedition. Peel's involvement was a boon for political satirists in London looking for ways to embarrass his powerful relation, the Home Secretary. In the very week that Stirling arrived in Western Australia they had launched a series of cartoons virtually accusing Sir Robert Peel of nepotism. 'Peel, Peel, Swan River Peel' and 'A country job for my country cousin' are the best known of several cartoons published at this time.[89] But their impact, and that of the *Quarterly Review* article and further Press reports, would not be known to Stirling until the following year.

IO

Swan River Colony:
First Six Months

WITH HIS PARTY safely ensconced on Garden Island, Stirling's first task was to select a site for his principal township. Fremantle noted that on 9 June, one of the less boisterous days, he and Stirling had examined a possible site on Mangles Bay[1] (near present Rockingham). In this, Stirling was obeying Sir George Murray's instructions to 'weigh maturely' the relative advantages of a site on Cockburn Sound versus a secure site on various points of the Swan River.[2] But there is little doubt that Stirling had decided, long before arriving, that he would place his capital inland. He had seen in North and South America the damage that naval cannon could wreak upon seaport towns, and was determined that his capital would be secure from such bombardment. And, as evident in his Proclamation, he had also determined its name. Captain Fremantle noted in his diary that the town of Perth was named 'according to the wishes of Sir George Murray',[3] so Stirling had agreed to the suggestion. Being a Scot himself, he would have had no objections to using the name of one of Scotland's oldest and proudest towns. But he disagreed with Murray on another matter. Of possible inland sites for the principal town, Murray had stated a decided preference for Point Heathcote, at the confluence of the Swan and the Canning. Stirling preferred the present site at the foot of Mount Eliza and, when later chastised for ignoring this advice, justified his choice as follows:

> On our arrival here with the expedition, the imperfect knowledge which I had of the country was, of course, soon extended and it was found in consequence that a Town at the mouth of the Estuary would be requisite for landing goods and as a Port town, while another sufficiently high on the river to afford easy communication between the agriculturalists on the Upper Swan and the commercial interest at the Port would tend much to the speedy occupation of that useful district. In selecting a site for the purpose, the present site of Perth seemed to be so decidedly preferable in building materials, streams of water, and facility of communication, that I was induced on these grounds to establish the Town there.[4]

It has been thought that Stirling invented this justification after the event, as this was written in 1832, but his reasoning is very close to that in a letter to Walter dated 7 September 1829 from Garden Island:

> I have however established two other towns, one called Fremantle at the Entrance of the river on the south side as a port or landing place, and the other on the north bank of the river about ten miles above Fremantle, just at the Islands. The latter is called Perth. It is the last point at which the boats can ascend until the navigation of the river is improved, and immediately above it commences the country which from the richness of its soil will be the first district put into tillage.[5]

His decision to place his capital away from the coast flew in the face of usual custom, as port and capital city were usually one and the same. It was also a decision that would have some unfortunate consequences. The first impressions that ships' captains and new arrivals would gain of the new colony would be based purely on

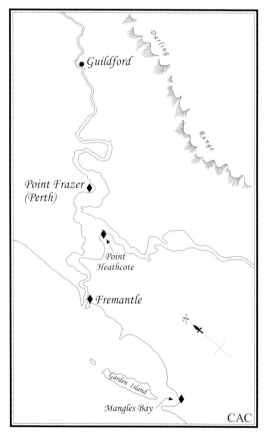

Coastal choices of a capital were at Mangles Bay or
Fremantle; inland, Point Heathcote or Point Frazer (Perth)

the commercial port, which in the early years would lack the public investment bestowed on the administrative, and more picturesque, capital.

Soon after the reading of the Proclamation Stirling led a small party of officials, soldiers and sailors straight up the river, past the shallows, to the area below Mount Eliza. They apparently landed near the present Supreme Court building,[6] way back from the current shoreline, which has been affected by years of infill. A camp was made on the higher ground, land cleared and tents erected to form a base for further exploration. Getting supplies to the camp site from ships still anchored at Garden Island was a long and tedious business. The bar at the river mouth meant everything had to be unloaded, and then reloaded into boats which themselves had to be half lifted over the bar. Progress upriver was further slowed by successive shallows, where heavily laden boats had to be dragged considerable distances.

There is little doubt that Stirling was disappointed when first overland expeditions showed that much of the land behind the alluvial river soils was sand and swamp. Dr Alexander Collie, assistant surgeon of the 63rd Regiment (under Milligan after Daly's death), participated in much of the early exploration and reported to his brother on 14 July that 'A few spots only afford a loam fit for grain or the majority of garden stuffs'. He noted, however, that much of the coastal plain, which extended 10 to 15 miles from the coast, and the 'range of rugged mountains' beyond were not yet explored.[7]

At this stage Collie was still living aboard the *Sulphur*, anchored near Garden Island. Most of the women and children from both vessels had been housed in tents on the island, and a small building had been erected on a lookout hill for the Governor and his family, but continued winds and rain made life very uncomfortable for all. At first, supplies had been kept aboard the *Parmelia*, but by 16 July Captain Luscombe begged Stirling to have them removed so that his damaged ship could be repaired. Only *Challenger's* men were capable of the undertaking, so Luscombe asked Stirling to gain Fremantle's help, arguing that as Stirling had been responsible for the damage, it should be repaired at His Majesty's cost.[8] Fremantle was not impressed, initially refusing the request because it came just as his ship was ready to depart.[9] But an appeal, to the effect that the *Parmelia* would have to be abandoned if the *Challenger's* assistance was withheld, led to his being 'requisitioned' (Fremantle's wording) to heave down and make good the defects of the *Parmelia*, a task which took his crew well over a month to complete.[10] The delay benefited the infant colony, however, in that Fremantle and his officers buoyed passages in the sound and explored and reported fully on the Canning River region, which Peter Belches had examined in 1827. This, they noted, 'was decidedly wrongly laid down on Captain Stirling's chart'.[11] Stirling was quick to acknowledge his debt to Captain Fremantle, writing not long afterwards, 'I cannot say how much I owe to his personal kindness, as well as to the zeal & alacrity he displayed in forwarding the service here'.[12]

Having decided on the optimal site for his capital, Stirling issued the following notice from Garden Island on 27 July:

On the 12th August, the anniversary of the day on which His Gracious Majesty [King George IV] was born, the first stone will be laid of a New Town to be called Perth, near the entrance to the estuary of the Swan River. After that date the Public Business in the several Departments of government will there be transacted, and all applications for land, or on other subjects, received.[13]

On the appointed day, a large party assembled in a clearing in the bush at the edge of the enlarged camp site. Captain Irwin had lined up the soldiers of the 63rd in ceremonial dress, Captain Fremantle and Captain Dance had brought contingents from HMS *Challenger* and HMS *Sulphur*, and most of the civil officials were there, as well as ship and regimental surgeons. It had taken several days for all of them to arrive from Garden Island. Only one woman had accompanied the party; all the others were either pregnant, busy with small children or not well. It was thus Mrs Helena Dance, and not Ellen Stirling, who entered history by cutting down a tree to mark the occasion, 'there being no stone contiguous to our purpose'.[14] But Ellen, who was unwell[15] (probably with the then prevalent diarrhoea), was not forgotten because wood from the felled tree was used to make her a beautifully crafted and suitably inscribed sewing box.[16] Once Mrs Dance had been helped to fell the tree, Stirling proudly proclaimed the birth of Perth: the soldiers fired a *feu de joie*, and all present gave three hearty British cheers.[17]

Not all were happy with the name of the new town. Back in London the father of one of the early settlers, William Leake, complained of Stirling's 'imprudence' to the Colonial Office. Had Perth been chosen, he asked, because

> Sir George Murray was born at this insignificant place, known only to reading men or to Geographers as an obscure place in Scotland? I have heard a vast number already declare against Swan River because they now consider it a place where Scotch interests will only prevail. There is Perth Town, Melville Water, Cockburn Sound…in fact nothing but Scotch names. Pray…give a friendly hint to Captain Stirling…he ought to endeavour to get the Colony established before he gave birth to his Scotch prejudices and feelings.[18]

But Perth it was to remain. There was little time for celebration on Foundation Day, for instead of a holiday all the officers were ordered to commence business that afternoon, in tents that had been erected as temporary government offices. Altogether there were twelve civil officials, four clerks and seven artisans to begin the task of exploring, surveying and charting the territory, laying out town sites and allotments, clearing roads, establishing experimental crops, preparing landing facilities and erecting buildings—especially storehouses and a barracks for the regiment. The soldiers, in turn, were busy laying out a parade ground at the top of present Barrack Street, planning fortifications and accompanying exploring parties as they set out in various directions.

George Pitt Morison's depiction of Mrs Dance
about to cut the tree to mark the birth of Perth
Courtesy The West Australian

Ellen Stirling was not present, but received
a memento in the form of a wooden
sewing box made from the fallen tree
Courtesy the Western Australian Museum CH76.236 (box)

Stirling's personal situation was becoming more settled. He told brother Walter on 7 September that although it had 'required some management to allay people's apprehensions' after their disastrous arrival, people were becoming more organised. He was sure Walter would be interested to know that:

My own farmyard contains 2 cows and a heifer, a share in a bull, 2 horses, 5 sows, 5 geese, 3 turkeys, 12 ducks, 17 fowls for breeding and 2 goats. My household comprises Mr and Mrs Kelly, Mr and Mrs Chilcott and their brother and 3 children for outdoor work, a black cook, a white servant, a steward, a woman to take care of the infant and a girl to keep Andrew out of mischief. I have a house on Garden Island and one at Perth, but houses here are not like houses in Grosvenor Square, being rather deficient in the article of defence against the wind and rain, the sun and cold. Ellen has resided heretofore on Garden Island where our largest depot of stores and provisions will be for some time, and in general the families of the civilians are still there.[19]

He admitted that on Garden Island

> Even in the Lieut. Governor's house I have been obliged to walk about with an umbrella in my hand to keep the candle burning, yet Ellen and my two boys have suffered no serious inconvenience although they have been glad to crouch over the fire every morning for the last four months.

But the Colony as a whole was doing well. Proudly he told his brother that

> We have at present here the *Sulphur, Parmelia* and three other merchant ships the *Calista, Anglesea* and *St Leonard*. About 200 private settlers have already arrived and we have in the Colony 35 horses, 17 cows, 3 bulls, 25 draught oxen and 10 calves, 200 sheep, 10 pigs and hogs, a large stock of poultry and some patches of garden ground already producing potatoes, peas, radishes, small salad and other little articles, vines, figs, pomegranates, quinces and other fruit trees are doing well and we have a good stock of them. Of the olives we have been able to bring out only one plant alive, but that and the New Zealand flax are doing very well as far as making an experiment on them is concerned.

In another letter to a naval friend, Stirling lauded the colony's progress by comparing it with New South Wales in its infancy—'we have already more stock than existed in New South Wales five years after its establishment, & more free settlers than were in that country until it had been settled 20 years…'[20]

The first shipload of private settlers had arrived on 5 August, even before the foundation of Perth. Nothing was ready for them. The women and children from the *Parmelia* were still on Garden Island, while the menfolk were either at Perth or out surveying and exploring. The weather had not improved, and the channels into Cockburn Sound had still not been properly buoyed. *Calista* was lucky and entered Gage's Roads without incident, anchoring off Arthur's Head, although she broke two anchors over the following days.[21] Her passengers with their luggage were landed in the small bay next to Arthur's Head, and forced to shelter and make do under canvas. The livestock they had brought with them were swum to shore but inadequately penned, causing constant chaos. The numbers of animals swelled quickly as the very next day the *St Leonard* arrived, bringing mainly livestock from the Cape, though they had lost many on the voyage from suffocation in bad weather. On 23 August the *Marquis of Anglesea* arrived, bringing eagerly awaited mail. But it also augmented the numbers on the beach at Fremantle, housed in tents and contending with rain, cold winds and blowing sand. Stirling must have felt desperate. No matter how hard he and his staff worked, it would take months before the increasing number of settlers could be assigned land, then moved on to their grants where they would have to start to build adequate shelter and plant crops to feed themselves. But little of this concern was evident in a private letter he sent to Under-Secretary Twiss as *Challenger* prepared to depart.[22] Progress in the first three months 'has been extremely prosperous', he wrote, 'and we have advanced as rapidly as the small extent of our means and the obstacles offered by the winter season could have allowed us to expect'. Stirling also noted the first real clash with Aborigines, stating:

> The Natives have kept very much aloof from our parties, and until within a few days such interviews as have taken place have terminated amicably. I regret, to say an Exception to this has lately occurred. A Soldier of the 63rd Regiment unfortunately quitted his party and lost himself for a week in the Woods. In the course of that time he met several parties of Natives and was attacked by one of them. In his own defence he was forced to fire, and I fear wounded a Man who had thrown a spear at him—they are not I believe disposed to be troublesome, nor have they the means to be seriously so—but under any circumstances I am most anxious to prevent hostilities. I therefore regret this commencement, for I believe they do not hesitate to resent any injury which they may receive whether they may have been aggressors or sufferers in the first instance.

Stirling admitted to Twiss that some of his expectations had been off the mark, but only narrowly:

> The Sound is not so easily approached in bad weather as I imagined it to be from my examination of it in the summer season, but it is now proved to be a better Port when in, than I then thought it. The quantity of very rich soil is not in such great proportions as I at first thought, but there is sufficient and the remainder of the land is better than I expected to find it…[but] I assure you with confidence there is every reason to believe that with moderately good management here, and the indulgence and protection of His Majesty's Government at home, it will speedily become a prosperous and valuable colony.[23]

But this hides his real concern, which came through clearly in his 7 September letter to Walter, when he said:

> it is a fearfully dangerous experiment to come so far to a country wholly unknown, and with habits formed in other modes of life as wide from this as Earth and Heaven.[24]

The onset of spring brought some capricious weather, for a violent storm on the night of 3 September wreaked havoc at Fremantle. Dr Collie recorded that the *Marquis of Anglesea* was driven onshore and filled with water, the *Calista* was damaged, tents were ripped from their stakes and belongings and stores were scattered and water-damaged.[25] Faced with storm damage and hungry settlers, Stirling had no option than to provide rations from government stores and, realising that extra supplies would be essential to meet future needs, he despatched the *Parmelia* to Java on 22 September 1829.

In the meantime, Surveyor-General Roe had begun the process of land alienation. A Government Notice had been issued on 28 August titled *General Regulations and Instructions relative to Crown Land*. These summarised the general instructions Stirling had been given, but also included regulations he had designed to meet the special needs of the colony. In brief, they stated that the territory would be progressively divided into counties, hundreds, townships and sections. Each section would contain one square mile or 640 acres, each township 25 sections, each hundred 4 townships, and each county 16 hundreds. In each county, 200 sections would be reserved for public purposes. Counties, hundreds and townships would be designated by names, and sections by numbers. All grants would be in complete sections of one square mile, no grant could have more than a quarter of its exterior boundary in river frontage, and no grant would be made to any indentured servant. Towns would be laid out in lots of nine-tenths of an acre, and these would be available on a 21-year lease. The town of Perth would comprise three square miles, and the future town of Fremantle would be laid down 'without delay'.

The regulations then went on to outline the steps settlers needed to take to obtain their land. Settlers were told to fill out a form titled 'Mode of Proceeding' 'available at the office of the Colonial Secretary', stating the value and description of all property they had imported, and the names and ages of their servants. This form was to be submitted to the Board of Audit, whose members would only accept property deemed 'applicable to the improvement and cultivation of land'. They would then estimate its worth according to 'such fair standard of reference as they may see fit to adopt', and calculate (on the basis of 1s 6d per acre, or 40 acres for every £3) the allowable grant acreage. This would be reported to the Lieutenant Governor, who would then accord 'permission to proceed to select land'. The settler's selection would then be submitted in writing to the Surveyor-General, who, 'if no prior claim existed', would allocate the grant to the applicant in 'the usual form of a primary conveyance', subject however to certain stated conditions.

These 'conditions,' or liabilities, were of two types: permanent and temporary. 'Permanent Liabilities' involved payments to County Offices for services, rights of resumption for road building, and charges for river navigation improvements, etc., while 'Temporary Liabilities' had to do with the specifics of the Land Grant Scheme. Here it was stipulated that grants conveyed only 'occupation' rights, and that neither the land granted, nor the property used in the claim for land, could be sold until full title had been gained through improvements (to the value of 1s 6d per acre). This had to be accomplished within ten years for most of the early arrivals; fines would be issued for slow improvement (a quarter was expected to be improved in three years), and land not fully improved at the end of ten years would be resumed.[26]

By 5 September Roe, with only two assistants, had surveyed the towns of Perth and Fremantle, pegged out roads, public spaces and building lots, and had surveyed

Cockburn Sound, though inadequately as he had been recalled by Stirling to begin land surveys before the sea approaches had been properly marked. In the township of Perth, Stirling selected part of the foreshore area to be reserved for Government House and gardens, where the naturalist James Drummond became busy. Once the town sites had been surveyed, Roe began the survey and allotment of rural grants, starting around the Upper Swan. Initially, he tried to abide by the direction that one quarter of the entire exterior boundary of a grant could be on the waterfront. But he was faced with two difficulties. First, settlers were entitled to very different-sized grants, and second, the river was not straight, but curved and looped back on itself. Stirling partially resolved the difficulty by limiting water frontage to half a mile—a practice used in other colonies. This meant settlers could quickly be allocated grants at half-mile intervals along the river, the extent of land running back from the river on any one grant being determined by the Board of Audit. The latter body (comprising Stirling's trusted cousin, William Stirling, friend Captain Mark Currie and Surveyor-General Roe) had delivered its first audit and assessment of land entitlements by 4 September,[27] but was faced with literally hundreds of claims to process.

On 10 September Stirling signed his first official dispatch to the Colonial Office from Swan River. Addressing Sir George Murray, he began:

> I have the honour to inform you that the Expedition entrusted to my care for the purpose of forming a Settlement on this Coast arrived at its destination in the month of June and that its progress in the execution of that service has since been almost uninterruptedly prosperous. Exposure to the Winds and Rains of a boisterous Winter has been the most serious Evil we have encountered, but that and the privations incident to such an undertaking have been borne with cheerfulness and overcome with proper spirit by all the Individuals forming the Civil and Military Establishment.
>
> Among the Settlers who have since arrived some disappointment has arisen in consequence of them being in general but little accustomed to encounter hardships and in all cases too sanguine in the expectations they have entertained respecting the Country. But as the Weather has improved they have been enabled to extend their explorations, and to attain more comfort, and I believe there is now existing among them a cheerful confidence in the qualities of the country and a general belief in its future prosperity.[28]

Attached to this dispatch were various enclosures including his 'Journal of Events', a copy of his Proclamation and the land regulations. With regard to the latter, his covering letter stated that he hoped they

> comprise all the points alluded to in the several Instructions I received before quitting England…If they meet with approval I believe I shall have no difficulty

in putting them in force…but if there be any point contained in them contrary to your wish I beg to be informed as early as possible that the errors may be rectified.

By 29 September almost all the land in the Upper Swan had been allocated, but to only seventeen grantees. Edward Barrett Lennard,[29] one of those involved, described how it had happened:

> The Governor is a very great pedestrian, and can undergo the greatest fatigue. We passed through lagoons up to our waist in water and, but for the kindness of our Colonial Secretary, Mr Brown, I must have been drowned, as I cannot swim and was grasping a tree for support when he most kindly came to my aid…The Governor himself was up to his middle in the water, and, when on the opposite side, encouraged me to cross
>
> After walking some distance, we arrived at the source of the river, called Ellen's Brook. Here the river is very narrow. The Governor next declared the land from this point for four miles down the river to be appropriated to Mr L— one of our party, who had a preference, in consequence of having proceeded a month previously to explore the country. The Governor then made other grants, distinguishing each by marking the trees.[30]

The 'Mr L—' who was allocated the first grant at the head of the river was Mr George Leake, who had arrived on the *Calista* with a naval officer known to Stirling, Lieutenant Henry Bull. (George Leake's brother Luke arrived with the rest of their family on the *Atwick* in October.)

According to Survey Department records, these first grants included one to Sir James Home (pronounced Hume), Stirling's brother-in-law who was not in the colony at the time. The Board of Audit had processed his perfectly legal claim on 22 August:

> Five mares, 3 of which are in foal, value of £200. (2,666 acres). I, William Stirling, do swear that the annexed schedule contains a true description of property imported by me from the ship *St Leonard*, and that the same is bona fide the property of Sir James Home Bart of whom I am the lawful attorney. Also that no previous grant of land has been made to the said Sir James Home in this settlement. Sworn at Perth before James Stirling, 21 Sep 1829.[31]

Home's grant was bounded on the south by Blackadder Creek, an allusion to his title as Sir James was the 14th Baronet of Blackadder. His grant, No. 15, was called Spring Park.

Stirling's name was not included amongst the first seventeen grantees, but an arrangement was made to reserve 4,000 acres at the bend in the river above Guildford for the Governor, and confirmed on the 30 September.[32] This grant, which Stirling named Woodbridge, is formally described as Swan Location 16, and was adjacent to

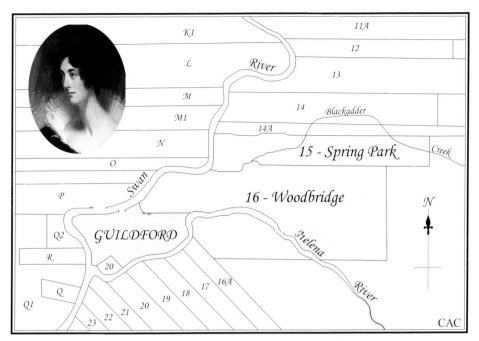

Location 16 was granted to Stirling, while 15 was granted to brother-in-law
Sir James Home (14th Baronet of Blackadder), who married sister Anna (inset)

Portrait courtesy Lady Hermione Malcolm

Home's grant. It is worth noting that the Woodbridge grant was smaller than those
Stirling granted to Captain Fremantle and Captain Dance. Both these men were
allocated 5,000 acres in the Swan River region on 29 September 1829, without
investment property to justify a claim.[33] Stirling had had no funds to pay them for
additional services, and so had used his power to grant land as recompense. This did
distort the original principles behind the grant scheme, but such grantees still had
to conform to the regulations and improve the land to gain title, or to appoint agents
to do so for them (e.g. Fremantle appointed William Stirling as agent before he left
the colony on 28 August[34]). Stirling knew that initial allocations were not absolute,
they were simply licences to occupy, and could be resumed if improvements were
not carried out. He was later charged with not having reserved land on the Swan for
later and perhaps less speculative immigrants,[35] but it is quite possible that he
sincerely believed some of the grants made to officers from the *Challenger* and
Sulphur would be resumed. He had, after all, stipulated in clause 4 of his own land
regulations of 28 August that 'failure of appearance of a legal claimant to an allotment
or his agent, within one year after due notice be issued by the Surveyor-General, the
same shall revert to the Crown, and resumed without further process'.

But by the end of September, far earlier than he had anticipated, it was
becoming painfully obvious that there was insufficient land for all incoming settlers
to take their full entitlements in the Swan River region. The south side of the lower

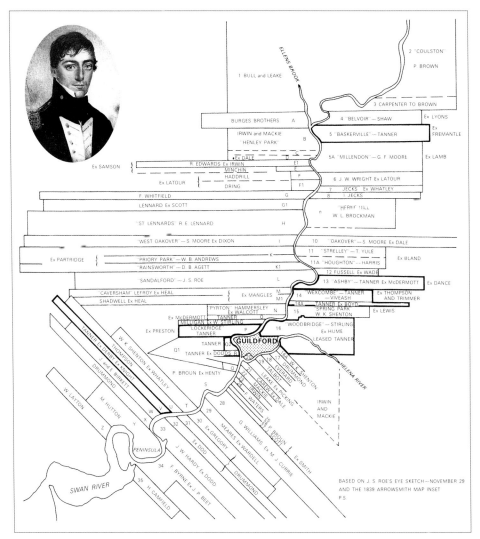

Redrawn eye sketch map made by Surveyor-General Roe showing original
grants along the Swan. (Inset) Roe as a young man

From P. Statham, The Tanner Letters

river and the Canning River was still reserved for Peel, and the amount of land
assigned to the early grantees had taken up most of the land in the Upper Swan,
leaving little for the dozens of clamouring settlers waiting at Fremantle. Had the
initial plan—of granting land in proportion to the value of productive assets and
labour introduced—been strictly adhered to, there is no doubt the land entitlements
of the early immigrants would have been smaller. For example, classification of lists
submitted to the Board of Audit by twenty-four settlers in September 1829 put the
total value of their livestock, seeds and implements at £5,025, and the value of
introduced labour at £753, making a total productive investment of £5,778. This

should have entitled them to occupy 77,040 acres of land. But the Colonial Office had directed that certain 'non-productive but applicable investments' should also be allowed, specifically arms and ammunition, the yearly value of a half-pay pension, provisions, and some miscellaneous goods (e.g. an iron bedstead was acceptable on the grounds that it could be melted down to make farm tools!). On this basis, the Audit Commissioners accepted a further £4,709 as 'investment', and as a result the first twenty-four grantees were permitted to select a total 139,826 acres of land.[36]

To ease the threatened land shortage, Stirling was forced to intervene. He sensibly decided to limit the amount of land any one settler could take in the Swan region to 1,000 acres, remaining entitlements to be taken either in the interior or to the south, where early exploratory missions had discovered more suitable land. In so doing, however, he fragmented grants, which would make it even more difficult for settlers to satisfy the improvement clauses. These had stipulated that *every acre* of a grant had to be improved, so heavy investment on one portion could not be averaged over the total. As early grantees would naturally concentrate investment on the portion of their grants near the Swan, they stood to pay heavy fines in the future or lose the rest. At the time, however, the 1,000-acre limit helped.

During October another ten ships arrived, including the first from the other Australian colonies which had learned of the 'Swan River Experiment' in their local Press. Several had been chartered as speculative ventures, bringing goods and livestock more suited to the Australian climate than those purchased in England.[37] This helped the colonists in one way, but also drained them of slender cash reserves. Stirling was besieged from all quarters. He had letters of introduction from new immigrants, shafts of paperwork to sign from his various departments, surveys and grant entitlements to approve and public works programs to authorise, especially water supplies and government buildings. Reveley, the civil engineer Stirling had hired at the Cape, was charged with establishing a water supply and complained bitterly on 7 October that the soldiers he had been assigned as labourers were performing poorly.[38] Stirling had to contact Irwin and request supervision and more discipline, which the soldiers undoubtedly resented, as common labour was not seen as part of their duties. Fortunately, among the early private immigrants Stirling found one with real building experience, Henry Trigg, who was contracted on 14 October to construct the first government office buildings.[39] Stirling also had to sort out quarrels between dissenting parties, for there was as yet no legal system for redressing such issues. And they were inevitable. For example, on 30 October William Stirling brought before him a matter concerning Peter Augustus Latour, whose first shipments had arrived in August on the *Calista* with Richard Wells, his agent. But subsequently, before the Board of Audit, Mr W. Shenton claimed he owned property that Wells had submitted as belonging to Latour.[40] This was the first of many confused dealings that Stirling was to have with Latour.[41]

Stirling was still under considerable pressure to find land for the new immigrants, who were arriving almost every week. He must, therefore, have been immensely relieved when the 1 November deadline for Peel's arrival passed with no sign of him. The very next day he threw Peel's reserved lands along the Canning open for selection,[42] on the limited acreage principle he had introduced a little too late on the Swan. He was soon able to report:

> In these districts, the first comers found suitable locations, and, acting under the impulse of novelty, there were many who at once established themselves on their lands, regardless of danger from the natives and of the difficulty they encountered in removing their goods from the coast. This adventurous and laudable spirit, which it was politic to encourage, I am happy in saying met with no check.[43]

Dr Alexander Collie's view of things on 9 November was not quite as sanguine. He and others were becoming concerned that there was little land remaining for new immigrants:

> A few farmers have embarked considerable capital for the Colony and are consequently entitled to large grants of land, but both the banks of the Swan and the Canning are already located and they do not seem disposed to take much of the sandy land behind these grants, and it is only on a few tributary streams that there is good land remaining to be granted. There is certainly another river that runs into the sea about 20 miles south from Cockburn Sound…where there may be a considerable quantity of good land.[44]

Collie was referring to the Murray River and its surrounds, which he and Lieutenant William Preston of the *Sulphur* had explored and named in September 1829, and where Stirling finally sent Thomas Peel.

Peel eventually arrived in the *Gilmore* on 15 December, furious and heartsick at the delays which had prevented him from reaching Swan River by the deadline. On a day when the mercury read over the old century mark, he was rowed upriver for an interview with Stirling who, though possibly sympathetic on hearing Peel's excuses for his late arrival, was impervious to his appeal not to be penalised. Peel claimed he had not been informed by the ship's captain, Geary, how long the voyage would take; Geary had not had the ship ready when requested; and the crew had mutinied against him before reaching Plymouth. This meant that Peel had had to get magistrates to enforce their terms of employment, again causing delay. Leaving at last on 10 August, the *Gilmore* had reached the Cape late in October, but instead of hurrying to reprovision and depart, Geary had obtained a special licence to marry one of his passengers, and took her ashore for a three-day honeymoon, adding to the delay and to Peel's anger.[45]

Stirling steadfastly refused to grant Peel his original choice of land (which had already been granted to others), and Peel blamed Captain Geary for his disappointment. Outraged, he at first demanded that Geary take himself and his immigrants in the *Gilmore* straight back to England, a plan that did not suit Geary, who felt 'insulted beyond endurance'. A violent argument ensued and there is some evidence that the two agreed to a duel.[46] As duels were illegal in Britain, and Peel was someone whose activities had already been widely publicised, the news would have seriously alarmed Stirling, who wanted 'his' colony to be seen in the best possible light. He quickly summoned Peel to further discussions regarding his grant, and offered the land recently discovered by Preston and Collie near the Murray River (after Sir George Murray of the Colonial Office). Peel, who was 'adept in the obligations of polite behaviour', and loved a little pomp and ceremony, was charmed when Stirling offered the services of the Surveyor-General, no less, to take him to see the land concerned. Moreover, the grant would include a portion of frontage to Cockburn Sound adjacent to Mangles Bay, which had been named for the Governor's wife's family, and Stirling would personally take Peel to see it. The Governor could be extremely persuasive when he wished; he even suggested names for a town site which were sure to appeal: Georgetown (after King George) or Clarence (for the heir apparent).[47]

Peel was mollified, and after inspecting the site on the south side of Woodman's Point, and agreeing to name his township Clarence, he ordered the *Gilmore* to anchor just south of Mangles Bay and discharge cargo and passengers on to the beach. Slowly tents and more solid shelters appeared and cargo littered the sand dunes. But neither Peel nor his party were happy. Although the children loved the seashore, their parents and other immigrants were appalled by the sandy land, the increasing heat, the lack of fresh water (all wells had only yielded brackish water), and the lack of longed for fresh food. They were some 7 miles from Fremantle without means of transport, and were still living on the salt pork they had brought out from England. Furthermore, flies were contaminating any opened barrel and mosquitoes were making life miserable for the women and children. When were they going to move to their promised grants? And what was going to be done about the food situation?

The Peel contingent's complaints were echoed by other free settlers who had flocked in from England and the eastern colonies to the end of December 1829.[48] Dr Collie colourfully assessed them as 'all sorts and sizes—half-pay officers chiefly of the army, speculators, stock-jobbers, Jews…lawyers, doctors, suitors, tailors, poachers, etc'.[49]

Most were still in tents at Fremantle, some drowning their disappointment in the grog tents, others filling in time until their claims were assessed and their grants assigned. But the queue moved slowly, as there were only two men to complete the necessary surveys, and one of them, Henry Sutherland, was having trouble with his sight. Stirling himself accompanied many of the exploring parties that had gone out searching for good land. At first he had seemed indefatigable, leading his companions at a spanking pace through the bush and even, at times,

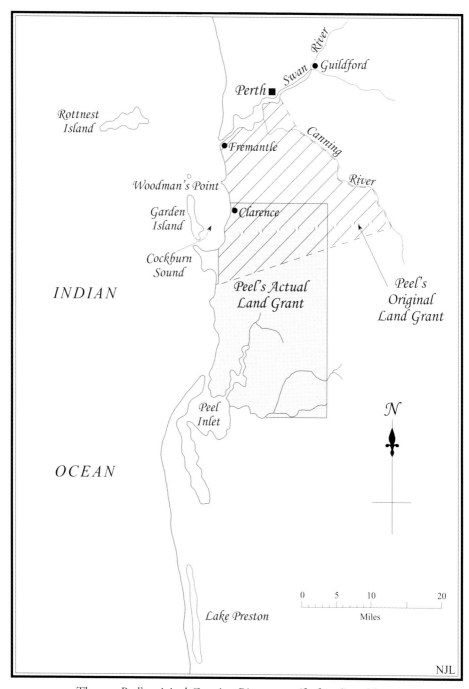

Thomas Peel's original Canning River grant (forfeited) and later
grant between Clarence and the Peel Inlet

forgetting their need for rest and sustenance.⁵⁰ But by early November his health was suffering, diagnosed as over-fatigue.⁵¹ He then curtailed his exploratory trips, but found rest impossible, given the never-ending stream of requests and complaints from the improvident and disappointed, as well as the bewildered 'Honest Johns'.

Dr T. B. Wilson, who visited the colony from New South Wales on the *Governor Phillip* in October-November 1829, gave an amusing account of the constant importuning that Stirling faced. Wilson was sitting on 'the brow of Arthur's Head' when he noticed the Governor approach at a brisk pace, but news of his presence having quickly spread,

> he was surrounded by many individuals; and as I had never before seen a levee held in the open air, I took up a favourable position in order to view the ceremony. I thought I could discern in the Governor's countenance some annoyance that he had been thus caught; but being so, he assumed an air of determination to be as civil and condescending as possible.
>
> Many passengers had arrived by the *Atwick*, who, it appeared, were now to be presented. The first was a gigantic, fierce looking gentleman, dressed, I suppose in the newest London fashion, who had been at some pains with his toilette; and it was very evident that he considered himself of no small importance. I thought at first, that he was ill adapted for the line of life into which he was about to enter; but on further consideration, I concluded, that if he took as much pains to cultivate the land as he appeared to have successfully bestowed on the culture of his whiskers, he might surpass those less careful in their attire; especially as his martial frown might tend to keep his servants in due obedience.⁵²

Others joined the throng to confront Stirling, continued Wilson—a dapper gentleman 'more at home behind the counter of a fashionable London repository... than wandering about the wilds of Australia'; a 'stout looking personage...whose jolly features...indicated a long acquaintance with beef and ale'; a 'modest-looking young man...with an expression on his face that seemed to say, "My fortune is made"... [and who] appeared confirmed in his opinion by the few civil words from His Excellency'; and many more. As Stirling 'could not bow his clients out of the drawing-room he was obliged to back astern', wrote Wilson, 'until he came to a spot of swampy ground...which he jumped over, bowed to the assembled throng, and walked away, as fast as decorum would permit' to the waiting boat, 'which as soon as he entered, was pulled with all speed towards Perth'.

It was becoming abundantly clear that many of the immigrants were unsuitable, and Stirling could not disguise his frustration at the many who were 'more or less disappointed on arrival, either with the state of things here or their own want of power to surmount the difficulties pressing around them'. In a dispatch to Murray, he noted that whilst:

Among the heads of families, there is a great majority of highly respectable and independent persons, in the working class there is a great variety; some masters have been careful in the selection of their servants and workmen, but the greater part have either engaged the outcasts of parishes, or have brought out men without reference to character; and the consequence is great inconvenience to such masters and endless trouble to the authorities established here.[53]

Establishing authorities to keep the peace had been difficult, as there was no legal expertise among the men originally appointed to the civil service. From past experience at the siege of Montevideo, and knowledge gained in New South Wales, Stirling was adamantly against military intervention in civilian affairs. He believed that peace-keeping was a civil responsibility, and so he decided to appoint a 'body of Constables' to assist 'Justices of the Peace' whom he had chosen from among the 'most reputable' of the settlers. The names of the thirteen constables were listed in a Government Notice dated 4 December 1829, so Stirling founded Western Australia's police force in the same year that Robert Peel created his 'Bobbies' in London. Later, Stirling added several Aborigines to the force, whose members were sworn in annually and received no salary, but fees for specific tasks.[54]

In the midst of all the anxiety and bustle of constant arrivals towards the end of the year, Stirling had one pleasant surprise. On 28 November his old ship HMS *Success* put into Gage's Roads, bringing his previous officer colleagues as well as a welcome clergyman, Archdeacon Thomas Hobbes Scott,[55] whom Stirling had last seen in New South Wales and who was returning to England. But a mishap occurred—perhaps fortunately for James—for, in coming in without a pilot, *Success* struck on rocks and was so badly damaged she needed to be hoved down for repair off Garden Island. Over the Christmas season Scott and the officers of *Success* were entertained by James and Ellen at Perth, in their recently completed 'commodious wooden house',[56] and their presence no doubt lightened the load on the shoulders of the beleaguered Governor.[57] On 30 January 1830 he was able to report to Murray:

> The erection of a decent place of worship, the regular performance of divine service, and the administration of the sacrament on Christmas-day were the last events of the year deserving of notice. To the zeal and energy of the venerable Archdeacon Scott, who is still here on his passage to England, I owe the furtherance of these great objects.[58]

Relations between the settlers and the native people, a matter of great concern to Stirling, had been relatively harmonious over the first six months. Only the men had ventured near the settlements; women and children had kept at a distance and only been seen by travellers. Some of the earliest grant occupiers, such as naturalist James Drummond, were befriended by tribesmen, who believed they were their own dead folk returned in white skins.[59] They brought gifts of game and fish to such families and taught their boys how to hunt. Other settlers repudiated even friendly gestures, equating the Aborigines with the feared American Indians. As some 669 Europeans had entered the Swan River region before the end of 1829,[60] already far more than the area's estimated 420 Aborigines,[61] there was little Stirling could do to prevent an inevitable clash of cultures.

Rush church (mid left) and Government House in central foreground

Artist unknown. *Perth, the seat of government on Swan River in Western Australia* c. 1830.

Pen Indian ink and green wash, pencil. 12.1 × 18.1 cm. Collection, Art Gallery of Western Australia.

Gift of a Descendant of Governor Stirling, London, 1924

11

Uncertain Prospects

1830

STIRLING SPENT MOST of the hot days of January 1830 closeted with his secretary, making out returns and writing voluminous letters to the Colonial Office. On the 17th he signed various returns and schedules accounting for every aspect of the colony's progress,[1] and on the 20th a long explanatory dispatch to accompany them. Parts of the latter have already been quoted, but Stirling added:

> In the course of October, November and December, some ships and many settlers came in. Their arrival before the country could be properly surveyed occasioned great inconvenience. Viewing no evil so great to the settler as delay in assigning him his land, I was accordingly forced to grant locations on unsurveyed lands, and to determine on the sites of towns without experience of their merits…
>
> Among the settlers who arrived, there were many indentured servants, who had been recommended to their employers by parish officers, and whose habits were of the loosest description. To control these and to protect their masters in their just rights, as well as to secure the safety of persons and property, I was obliged before the conclusion of the year to appoint a magistracy and a body of constables…To render the decisions of the magistrates more formal, I selected a gentleman bred to the law and of moderate temper to act as their chairman, and as adviser to the government in matters of law. Since these appointments, I am happy in saying there have been fewer irregularities.[2]

The 'gentleman bred to the law' was 30-year-old Cambridge graduate William Henry Mackie, a relation by marriage of Captain Irwin of the 63rd Regiment. Mackie had arrived on the *Caroline* in October 1829, and in partnership with Irwin took a land grant at Henley Park on the Upper Swan. He was apparently 'a very amusing, entertaining man' who read a great deal and had a retentive memory. Tolerance was his prime virtue, and 'as a lawyer he was neither profound nor academic, but as a Judge he was ideally suited to the conditions of the time'.[3] Stirling made him Chairman of Quarter Sessions and his chief law adviser on a salary of £200 in January 1830. It was an excellent choice.

William Mackie—the gentleman bred to the law
Courtesy Battye Library 816B/H7604

Apart from cases of drunkenness, Stirling needed help in enforcing his 'Masters and Servants Order' set out on 17 November 1829.[4] This order had summarised the law pertaining to master and servant obligations, and stressed that no servant under indenture could hold a grant of land or leave the colony without permission. At first the Colonial Secretary's Office had been the clearing house for complaints of absconding servants and insolvent masters, but in January 1830 Stirling formed the Magistracy with power to levy fines of up to £100 for breaking contracts. One of the first tasks Stirling asked of his magistrates was to draft regulations to govern rations, hours and conditions of employment for workers (not wages, as these were generally determined by individual indenture contracts). The regulations, which were published by Government Notice on 26 March 1830,[5] actually differed from the magistrates' proposals in that Stirling increased the scale of rations, adding vegetables, fish and fresh meat to the salt meat and bread they had proposed. Where they had recommended rum for men and tea and sugar for women, Stirling gave them both. He approved their suggestion for an eight-hour day in summer, and nine in winter, but refused to allow their proposal that masters could withhold indulgences for misconduct, and prevent servants from leaving their masters' premises without permission. The final regulations, which were in force for two years, were actually quite reformist for the time in that they gave workers a measure of security, and protected their rights in regard to hours of work and rations.[6]

In the first official dispatch of the year, Stirling provided the Colonial Office with a statistical summary of the colony's position after its first six months. With a certain amount of pride he recorded:[7]

Abstract from the Returns

Ships arrived from 1st July to present	25
Persons Resident	850
Persons not Resident	440
Amount of claims to land	£41,550
Lands allotted	525,000 acres
Locations actually effected	30
Cattle	204
Horses	57
Sheep	1,096
Hogs	106

The 'persons not resident' in his table were principally the crews of ships in port, including the HMS *Sulphur* and merchant ships, and 170-odd from HMS *Success*, still hove down at Garden Island. The 'persons resident' were the people that really concerned Stirling. He told Sir George Murray that

> …ten or twelve of the leading men of the Settlement having occupied their grounds, and having declared themselves fully satisfied with the quality of the soil and the condition of their cattle, I consider the undertaking is now safe from the effects of a general despondency, which at one time threatened to defeat the views of His Majesty's Government in this quarter.

After giving his own views on the condition of livestock and the nature of soils, he added: 'I am more anxious on this subject, because there have been opinions given by individuals, who have seen only the sea beach, and have stated broadly that there is no good soil'. He admitted, however, that the previous three months had been

> unfavourable to agriculture and gardening from the hard and dry state of the ground; but, the time for breaking it up being now arrived, I hope to see farming operations commence with vigour.

There really had been little time for agricultural pursuits, as settlers had been engaged in examining the country, selecting land, building houses and transporting goods from the shore to their allotments. The coming year, Stirling forecast, would see real progress in the two main branches of agriculture, tillage and pasturage.

In assessing the future prospects of various types of land use, Stirling was almost prophetic, stating at this early stage that 'I consider pasturage as the source whence the greatest returns will be made'—and he was speaking of sheep. He reported that the small flocks belonging to settlers James Henty and Arthur Trimmer were progressing satisfactorily, 'and to their increase and future profit I think we may look with confidence'. On the other hand, he believed that grain would be produced much more cheaply in other colonies, and it might be better to import. Fishing, he thought, would be profitable, both from the abundance of fish and the large numbers of whales visiting the coast between May and November. He hastened to add that these prospects only engaged the minds of those who had 'overcome the anxieties of their first establishment in a new land', warning Murray that not all settlers held such a favourable view. 'The greater part, incapable of succeeding in England, are not likely to prosper here to the extent of their groundless and inconsiderable expectations…' While he felt that Swan River might in the future absorb an 'immense migration of persons', he believed that if they were sent too soon, they would ruin the colony's prospects, and their own.

At the end of this January 1830 dispatch to Murray, Stirling presented a list of the 'most pressing wants of our settlement', one which showed considerable perspicacity. He had come to conclusions, and suggested remedies, that were almost identical to those put forward by the colonial reformers in London, where they had been shaped by a very efficient and experienced civil service. This is particularly true of his suggestions regarding the land regulations. He realised that the existing regulations would cease to apply at the end of 1830 and begged to know what would replace them, adding:

> If at this Distance I may take the Liberty to suggest another mode I should recommend the adoption of the American System by sale making the prices as low as may suit the Circumstances of the Country. If this should be adopted it must be taken in all its Details, as Grants made in such circumstances will destroy the selling price of Land.

The remainder of his 'pressing needs' were also itemised in a private letter to Twiss, written on 26 January, which was less formal and clearly revealed the stress that Stirling was experiencing. He began with a warning:

> In the infancy of a Colony there are difficulties to be overcome which all must meet & few can conquer; and therefore there is a natural tendency to complain. As long as this dissatisfaction is referable to the country or to the evils of the present moment it will do no harm & time will bring its cure; but if grounds of complaint shall be given by the non-fulfilment of any of the conditions held out,

the injury will be great, and dissatisfaction with the measures of Government will extend itself from those who are here or on their way, to their friends in England, & from them to those who are not friends to his Majesty's Government.[8]

Given that dire possibility, Stirling urged Twiss to help him achieve certain objectives that were beyond his control, 'but which demand immediate attention':

> In the first place it is necessary to decide on giving up this Settlement altogether on the part of Government, or to declare it to be in every respect a Royal Settlement. An intermediate course will ensure its ruin, & bring discredit on the measures of Government.

If it was to be 'considered a Royal Settlement', certain measures had to be taken urgently (here summarised):

- The Governor must have a regular Commission and Instructions.
- A Code of Laws and their administration must be established by authority.
- Land regulations must be laid down and acted on as may suit the views of Government.
- A Revenue system must be introduced and until the Income met the Expenditure the difference must be Bills on the Treasury.
- Adequate Salaries must be allotted to the those who are in Gov't. employment so that efficient and honest people may be induced to seek & prize them.
- Power must be given to the local Gov't. to warrant the Employment of persons whose services may be found necessary, and also the occasional Expenditure of Funds on objects requiring immediate attention, subject, of course, to the Approval of the Secretary of State.

Hammering home the need for these changes, Stirling said :

> I have no personal motive in these recommendations; for I may take the liberty of a friend to say, <u>I have no ambition to remain in this capacity</u> [sic] a day beyond the time when by the Establishment of a prosperous Settlement on this shore, I shall have justified the confidence reposed in me by Sir George Murray. The exertion and anxiety are too great and constant for my intellectual or physical Powers to make their continuance for a long time an object of desire.[9]

After this forthright appeal to Twiss, Stirling added that several events had occurred since he last wrote. First, five more vessels had arrived with passengers and stock, including the *Parmelia* bringing the stores he had ordered from Java. Second, HMS *Cruizer* had 'arrived here by direction from Sir Ed. Owen [then Commander-in-Chief, Eastern Station] to enquire if she could render any service to the Settlement'. Third, he announced Captain Bannister's discovery of a 'fine district of country in the vicinity of King George's Sound', which was 'so favourable that I shall extend the locations in that quarter'. And finally, he noted the late arrival of Thomas Peel who, 'having failed in his original agreement', was now to be treated as 'a common settler importing an equal quantity of Property'. The letter then became a little ingratiating, perhaps necessarily:

> It was not therefore a mistake when you viewed this Territory in a favourable point of view and decided on its occupation. I am convinced that it will prosper; and that most rapidly. I am satisfied that your measures with respect to it will be as judicious and liberal as the original determination to form it was wise. The only fear I entertain is that amid the hurry of other affairs and more general interests you may overlook us altogether…For my part I shall endeavour to go on as well as I can…

But then came a plea from the heart:

> I believe I am the first Governor who ever formed a Settlement without Commission, Laws, Institutions and Salary. You must not therefore be dissatisfied if I should sometimes step out of course.

He also asked Twiss to intercede with Murray 'on the subject of my pecuniary affairs'.

> At the time it was first decided on that an experiment should be made here…I proposed that the Governor should have no salary until the Settlement should be formed—and in thus foregoing my own remuneration, I afforded the best proof of my confidence in its success.
>
> The experiment is now made. I do not ask for remuneration but I take the liberty to state that I am under the necessity of keeping open house, that I must keep horses and servants not only for my private use but for furthering the business of my situation, that I am frequently absent from my house and have no time to manage my own affairs—& that under all three circumstances it is impossible to limit my expenditure to less than 12 or 1,300 pounds. This is nearly double my private income and as it must all be provided for out of my own Pocket…I think you will admit that I am supporting the Government at my expense rather too magnanimously…I cannot honestly undertake this expensive mode of life for too long a period. I beg to offer my best respects to Mr Hay & to assure you I am…[10]

The annotation on this last part of the letter, when received in London, was not sympathetic. It read:

> he doesn't propose that the whole expenditure shd be paid by the public. He is engaged in an extensive speculation in Land.

This Stirling would have been affronted to hear. He was almost at the end of his tether, as his comment about having 'no ambition to remain in this capacity' clearly indicated. The huge difference between being captain of a ship, where orders were immediately followed and every occupant knew their duty, and trying to run the colony without even the authority of a full Governor was telling. He was responsible for everything. And until mid-December he had been without even Ellen's support, for he had deemed it best that she, Andrew and the baby remain in the relative comfort of the cottage on Garden Island until a roof could be put over their heads at Perth.

In both this private letter and the official dispatch, Stirling had listed the administrative arrangements he considered absolutely necessary for the colony's survival, and which were currently lacking. The lists bring home sharply the difficulties he faced in the early months, and highlight also the haste of initial government planning whereby crucial administrative machinery had not been provided. In both dispatches Stirling had emphasised the unsuitability of many immigrants, his official account stating:

> Many of the settlers who have come should never have left a safe and tranquil state of life; and, if it be possible to discourage one set of people and encourage another, I would earnestly request that for a few years the helpless and inefficient may be kept from the Settlement, while, to the active, industrious and intelligent, they may be assured with confidence a fair reward for their labours.[11]

While privately to Twiss he said:

> In this particular current of Emigration there are more than a usual number of Men of Property & Family but at the same time it contains every description of persons and many who will be ruined by their own groundless expectations & helpless inefficiency.[12]

General progress, he reported, had been hard won. In the absence of roads, boats were the only way of moving property, so their construction had been a priority. This had made the services and advice of boat-builders crucial, and Stirling was fortunate in that he could call on the skills of crews from naval vessels in port, for the task would have been beyond the single government boat-builder. The latter, James Smith, had been recruited by Stirling from the Portsmouth dockyards and was invaluable, for very few private settlers had thought to include a boat or bring out a boat-builder. Peel was an exception, but his skilled boat-builder, Thomas Mews, did not arrive until the middle of 1830, and by then well over forty small boats had been constructed.[13]

Another dispatch Stirling prepared for the Secretary of State during the month of January raised matters which showed that he had been thinking not only of the colony's present needs, but also of its future.[14] First, he suggested that the military outpost established at King George's Sound by the New South Wales Government

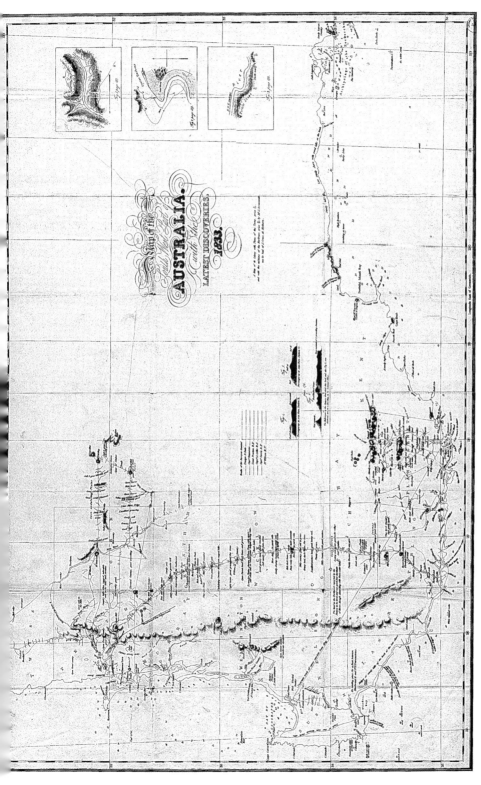

Roe's map of Bannister's trip south, revealing fine country near King George's Sound

Courtesy Battye Library 24/5/1

be withdrawn and replaced by some of Captain Irwin's soldiers, making the settlement part of Swan River Colony. This would open up the good land reported to lie in that vicinity to future settlers, and comply with his initial instructions to encourage settlement to the south. Second, he reported that Captain Colpoy of HMS *Cruizer* had visited the Cocos Islands, some 1,560 miles from Swan River, and discovered 'a Port which will be greatly valuable in trade or in any future War'. He recommended that Britain should establish whether it had been claimed and, if not, make it a dependency of Swan River Colony.

After these two major recommendations, Stirling threw in a number of routine items, such as approval for subsidised housing for the Colonial Secretary and Surveyor-General, ration allowances for soldiers and their dependants, a fodder allowance for Captain Irwin, and the need for better mathematical instruments. He next raised several other issues that he considered vital. One was the urgent need for additions to the staff of the Survey Department; then an increase in the Church Establishment, as one clergyman would find it impossible to attend to the needs of the present population 'spread as it is over an extended surface'; and finally, there was the matter of specie. Money was desperately short in the colony, his privy chest had been emptied in sending the *Parmelia* to Java for supplies, and as money was specifically *not* accepted as a basis for land grants, few immigrants had brought cash with them, each expecting to make money from the sale of the produce from their farms. But funds were needed to pay the troops and purchase provisions, which meant he had had to issue Treasury Bills at a discount. Ostensibly to 'prevent this depreciation in the market value of the Bills', but also to avoid the problems that had arisen in New South Wales with substitute currency, Stirling requested that ships-of-war taking specie to Sydney occasionally bring a portion to Swan River as well.[15]

It would be nearly a year before Stirling had official replies to his concerns, and six months before he learned that, despite all his efforts and those of the steadier settlers, 'disparaging, damaging rumours' about Swan River Colony were circulating in the British and colonial Press.[16] *Bell's Messenger* had trumpeted on 31 January 1830:

> Disastrous accounts respecting the colony on the Swan River have been obtained. It is stated that Captain Stirling, who went out from this country as Governor of the new settlement, having found it impracticable to carry the object of his mission into execution, has sailed for Mauritius…The settlers it was asserted, were in a state of starvation.[17]

Six days earlier the *Courier* and the *Globe* had carried reports of 'the total failure of the establishment', the news coming from the owner of the *Marquis of Anglesea* who had just heard from its captain about the wreck of his ship.[18] The Colonial Office heard the news about the same time through the good offices of Sir Francis Freeling, Secretary to the General Post Office, who had written on 26 January enclosing the following news from St Helena:

The ship *St Leonard* arrived at the Mauritius from Swan River two days before. She reports the total failure of that establishment and the loss of the ship *Marquis of Anglesea* in a Gale of wind while riding at Anchor secured by three anchors. The soil is not near so fertile as has been represented but is on the contrary of a light sandy nature, in consequence of which the heavy rains had washed away a great part of it, & the settlers were almost in a state of starvation.[19]

The source of this information was probably Captain Rutherford of the *St Leonard*, as he had been at Swan River from 6 August to 22 September, and thus witnessed the wreck and the general confusion prevailing at Fremantle in those early weeks. Used to situations where port and capital were one and the same, few of the early arriving merchant ship captains had ventured beyond Fremantle, and consequently did not see the progress being achieved 12 miles upriver around Perth. Instead, they took away impressions of the tent town at Fremantle and the discontent of those still waiting for the allocation of their grants. One such ship's officer, visiting in February 1830, recorded that:

Fremantle…consists at present of merely a few tents and marquees, with here and there a wooden house, but these are few and far between. There is one hut which is dignified with the name of a tavern…The liquors are so well watered that not even a temperance society could find fault with them…The people on shore gave very discouraging accounts of the land. The soil is all sandy, and as soon as their crops appear above the earth they wither away and not one had as yet been brought to perfection.[20]

Stirling was well aware of these opinions. But the damage was done, for the London daily papers were quick to seize on, and exaggerate, any unfavourable reports of a colony which only six months before had been represented as a land of milk and honey. Both the *Courier* and the *Globe* reported on Monday 25 January that a dangerous coastline, inclement weather, a barren landscape and a total absence of harbour facilities had created such difficulties that it was doubtful if Swan River Colony could survive. The colony had already been lampooned for having been given as 'a job lot' to a cousin of the famous Robert Peel, so the temptation for editors to denigrate now was irresistible. For example, the editor of the *Morning Journal* commented on 28 January with sanctimonious glee that:

When the Swan River Job came out…our readers will recollect we constantly warned the intended emigrants against the consequences of so wild and hazardous a project. But Uncle ROBERT spoke favourably of it in the house and Cousin THOMAS was 'a respectable young man', therefore the emigrating world took its own way, and embarked with their lame horses and blind goats for the finest harbour on the globe and the richest arable land on the face of the earth. We well knew it was all a piece of quackery, and we said so. We knew the poor people were imposed upon, and we said so—but on they went, paradise bound, and now we have the disastrous results lying before us.[21]

The *London Herald* and other papers followed suit, but on 27 January the *Courier*—one of the more esteemed papers—published a letter which gave a more accurate and favourable account of the colony. The letter was prefaced by the following editorial comment:

> We last night cautioned our readers against giving too implicit credit to the statements circulated of the disastrous condition of the Colony lately planted at the Swan River. We now furnish them with the contents of a letter from Captain Dance…received this day. Its contents abundantly prove the validity of the doubts we felt of the accuracy of the first intelligence.[22]

This, plus the content of the letter, which provided facts and praised Stirling's efforts to forward the settlement, stemmed the panic but did not remove doubts, as the *Bell's Messenger* excerpt published four days later showed.

Peel's agent, Solomon Levey, had been aghast when he first heard the unfavourable reports, as Peel's third ship, the *Rockingham*, was about to leave with 182 emigrants. On 26 January he wrote to the Colonial Office to establish the truth.[23] By this time Stirling's first dispatches had been received and Levey could be

The emblematic swan proved irresistible for newspaper cartoonists in Britain when lampooning the new colony. The caption refers to 'Captain Dick Demi-Solde on a Wild Goose Flight to the Swan River'

Courtesy Mitchell Library SV*/CART/10

reassured. The *Rockingham* then sailed, to eventually join other wrecks on the shores of Cockburn Sound. Because Stirling's dispatches were deemed 'official correspondence', they were not released to the Press, a fact that seriously annoyed one writer who accused the Colonial Office of

> a great dereliction of duty in not giving publicity to Captain Stirling's dispatch for the satisfaction of families who have sent to Swan River their Children in the hope of bettering their fortunes. You will tell me that you gave Captain Dance's report but I shall answer, however, until this report I have never heard of Captain Dance. It is from Captain Stirling we expected a Report.[24]

As more ships arrived with letters from settlers in the colony, more conflicting stories appeared in the Press. The following letter, dated Swan River 9 September 1829, was widely published in London papers between 27 January and 2 February 1830. The identity of its writer is unknown, and versions in the different papers varied slightly:

> We arrived here on the 5th [per *Calista*] there is no Harbour but a roadstead, and the spot where we were at anchor was much exposed to the NW winds. We were obliged to drop anchor about 2 miles from shore. This was the case with the *Parmelia*. We were told that there was a bar of six feet of water; now at times there is only a foot, and never more than 3. We experienced much trouble in getting the goods from the ship; the men worked like slaves, the distance from the beach to where the tents are pitched being a quarter of a mile, and up a hill. The weather has been very boisterous; you may suppose that our canvas habitations suffered much—mine keeps out the rain, but the wind affects it very much; a few nights ago one side was blown down, and I expected every moment to see the whole concern blow away. During these heavy gales the *Marquis of Anglesea* ran ashore, and must be sold here for the benefit of the underwriters. The *Calista* was expected to share the same fate, she lost 3 anchors.[25]

Such disparaging reports definitely put a dampener on emigration. Requests to the Colonial Office for information regarding settlement conditions, for example, fell from twenty-two in January 1830 to four in February, and the 'Shipping Intelligence' column of *The Times* contained notices of postponed departures for seven ships in February and March. James Mangles, Stirling's father-in-law, was among those concerned with reports of falling emigration. Expressing his wish 'to promote, in any way I may be consider'd able, this infant Colony', he asked Twiss to inform him of 'the Terms, and conditions, upon which government feel disposed, to encourage emigration, for which there is a strong disposition in this Neighbourhood, provided the means could be accomplished'.[26] But the decline in immigration in the second half of 1830 came at first as a boon for Stirling, who at the end of the year wrote:

The Progress of the Settlement during the present Year, although not unopposed by many adverse Circumstances, has been as rapid as could have been expected or desired…a greater Increase would have probably been disadvantageous to the Welfare of the Settlement while struggling in its Infancy.[27]

Some of the most disappointed immigrants were those in Peel's party. The first of his ships, the *Gilmore*, had arrived in mid-December 1829; its passengers had barely come to terms with the difficulties caused by lack of organisation, and their location on the sandy coast at Clarence, when Peel's second ship, the *Hooghly*, reached Cockburn Sound on 13 February 1830. It was an unsettling end to the long voyage, for, as Third Mate George Bayly recorded, 'when we came to the entrance it was truly horrible to see the rocks and reefs in all directions, the channel is not more than half a mile wide and only small beacons to direct us through'.[28]

Bayly went on to give a vivid word picture of the confusion and melancholy pervading at Clarence:

I left the Ship after breakfast. There was such a surf on the beach that it was impossible to get on shore without a soaking. Scarcely had I effected my escape from the briny fluid, all dripping as I was, when a sudden gust of wind sent a cloud of black sand all over me which stuck to my wet clothes and put me quite out of conceit with my white trousers. However…the people about the beach said it was an everyday occurrence…They said they had great difficulty in procuring fresh water that was fit to drink, their cooking was performed in the open air, and their victuals were generally liberally peppered with the black sand…

Mr Peel is at present living in the large box which was sent on board to hoist the horses out. It is about seven feet long, four feet high and three feet broad. Over the top he has an old sail spread by way of roof. There are only two passable houses in the settlement…The greater part of the settlers live in tents or marquees.[29]

Bayly was still in the colony when a party which had gone to investigate land around the Murray River returned early in March. He recorded that Peel himself had joined the expedition, and that they had found some good soil. They also had met several different tribes of friendly natives, and one incident in particular caught Bayly's attention. His journal notes that some of the natives had apparently

picked up a few words and spoke them very plain. A party was out one day with a gentleman named Waterton. He had strayed from the rest and in the meantime they fell in with a party of three or four natives. One of the gentlemen just then turning around said, 'Where's Waterton?' The sound seemed to tickle the fancy of one of the natives and he repeated them very plain. Two or three days afterwards the above-named gentleman was taking a solitary ramble in the woods when he met three natives one of whom startled him exceedingly by calling out as loud as he could, 'Where's Waterton?'[30]

By 12 March the *Hooghly* had discharged all its cargo and was preparing for departure by taking in sand for ballast. Bayly went to say farewell to his former passengers at Clarence and found

> most of the people quite in despair. A great many of the women and children were ill and there was no sort of nicety to be procured for them, not even a little oatmeal. The only provisions to be procured were salt beef and pork, musty flour and rice…[31]

In the absence of crops, the same situation was emerging in Fremantle. Stirling was becoming concerned about increasing reports of incidents of scurvy, though by now relief was available in the form of supplies introduced by incoming ships. The daily scale of rations for those in government employ, and the destitute, included vegetables and fresh meat, but Stirling had announced that when these were unobtainable they would be substituted with 'salt meat, pease and vinegar' or 'salt meat, flour and currants'.[32] He was clearly applying lessons learned in the navy about anti-scorbutics, and could maintain such rations as long as ships continued to arrive with new supplies. In fact, between 1 January and the end of March 1830 twenty-two ships arrived, nine large passenger ships from England, two from Bombay and many smaller vessels from the eastern colonies, together bringing hundreds of new immigrants.

Finding good new land which could be allocated to this stream of arrivals, and put into food production, was Stirling's most pressing problem. By early March he was telling new immigrants to go south, admitting that all the land in the Swan and Canning region had been allocated. This riled many of the newcomers, and the following letter by an unknown writer, published in the *Leicester Journal* on 24 September 1830, was typical of many sent home at the time. It was dated Swan River, Western Australia, 10 March 1830, and after describing his arrival went on to say of some fellow passengers:

> The following morning, [they] with some others, made the best of their way to the governor, for introduction and other purposes of business…after the lapse of two days the party returned to the vessel, with countenances blank, and sad disappointment on all their brows; we could glean very little from them—the governor told them there was no land to be given away on the Swan River! He would advise all that could, to go to the southward, where the land was much better than here!…
>
> The fact is simply this; all the land that is good for anything, and that is but little, a patch here and there, is kept as Government Reserves; and what land is given—is given to jews, stockbrokers, men of war's men and out of 1800 souls now in the colony…there are not a dozen, who know what to do, or where they are to go to!…The people here actually look horror-struck one at another in

absolute despair…more complete wretchedness you never beheld…His excellency the Governor was walking in his dressing gown in the garden, as it is called, (though not a green leaf in it) without shoes or stockings, when the party from our vessel waited upon him.[33]

On the very March day this letter was written, the said Governor was personally surveying land around Geographe Bay with a view to opening it up for settlement. He had hired the schooner *Eagle* for the purpose and taken a party with him, including his wife, Mr Roe (Surveyor-General), Lieutenant Preston, Dr Collie and a boat's crew from the *Sulphur*, Lieutenant Willis from the *Cruizer*, a detachment of the 63rd Regiment, and James Henty, a new arrival with extensive farming experience. The party had all the skills required to map and assess the area and, with so many fellow naval officers, was also congenial for Stirling. The main purpose of the trip was to investigate the land around the two rivers discovered earlier by Dr Collie and Lieutenant Preston, and which were now given their names. Henty reported to his father that he had been part of a group led by the Governor which had gone 9 miles up the Collie River and seen some very good land 'where a town was to be laid out'.[34]

Ellen had remained on board the *Eagle*, glad of the break from the children and the chance to take in the fresh sea air. Apart from her maid she was the only female on board, and the fact Stirling took her illustrates the strong bond between them. She would undoubtedly have been curious to see the land he had selected for their own grant. It is also highly likely that the sight of the sandy low shoreline of Leschenault Inlet proved very disappointing, especially after the lush, picturesque banks of the Swan near Guildford. Stirling's southern location had not yet been surveyed, although its position had been roughly drawn on the map in 1828 as extending along the inlet to near Cape Naturaliste. Sitting on deck, contemplating the shallow waters and varied bird life, Ellen must have realised that it would be many years before this area, so far from Perth and Fremantle, could be closely settled. Yet to restore the family fortunes, James needed to be able to sell his land at a profit.

All too soon Ellen was back in Perth, entertaining the wives and daughters of the Governor's small society. Perth at that time was described as lying so 'entirely in a Wood it is difficult at first to ascertain its position'.[35] It consisted of about twenty wood houses, including the Governor's, as well as marquees, tents and huts, amidst which social customs continued. The young Anne Leake took tea several times with Mrs Stirling, describing her as 'very affable and unaffected', while the very pregnant Georgiana Molloy, who had arrived a few days previously with her much older husband, Captain John Molloy, found her 'exceedingly amiable and pleasingly natural'.[36] Everyone was drawn to Ellen, for at a time when manners were formal and conventions rigid, she managed to combine ladylike manners with a simple and natural warmth. When Mary Morgan's children sickened with typhus fever, she sent

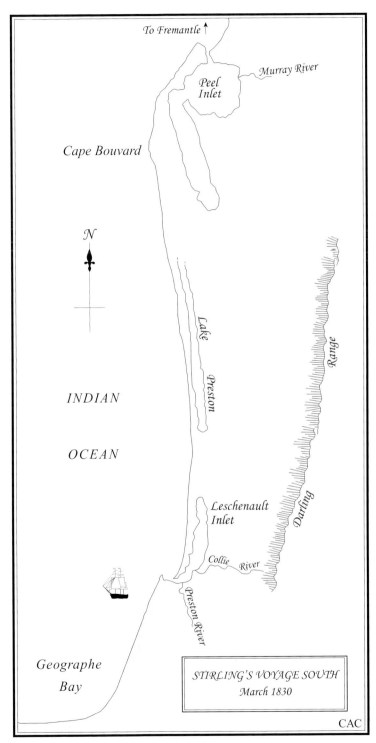

To Fremantle ↑

Murray River

Peel
Inlet

Cape Bouvard

N

INDIAN

Lake

Preston

OCEAN

Range

Leschenault
Inlet

Darling

Collie   River

Preston River

Geographe
Bay

STIRLING'S VOYAGE SOUTH
March 1830

CAC

Stirling's voyage south in March 1830. During this sortie,
favourable land was viewed in the Collie-Preston catchment area

her 'lady', Mrs Brown, to call on the family, and 'Wine, Porter, and every thing they wanted was sent in great abundance'.[37]

Apart from visiting the sick and bereaved (a number of men, including soldiers, drowned in these early months), Ellen tried to help the many settlers' wives who were acutely homesick. Recognising the shock many of them felt in being so far from all the social amenities taken for granted at home, she established, with the help of Matilda Roe, a Perth Literary Society, the two guinea subscription fee being used to acquire suitable headquarters.[38] Then just a few weeks later, on 23 April, she held a levee for sixty guests at Government House to mark the official King's Birthday.[39] It is not hard to imagine young Andrew Stirling, now 6, being allowed to stay up to see the glowing candles, the shiny instruments of the band of the 63rd Regiment, and the decorative flowers and greenery which he perhaps helped to collect for the occasion. Nor would the occasion have been lost on James   just two years earlier, in Sydney, he also had honoured the monarch's birthday by organising a spirited regatta.

But undertaking the 'Superintendence and Governance of the colony' was proving far more onerous than Stirling had ever imagined back then. Cut off by months from any assistance or advice, he was sole authority and expected to remedy all ills, though there were many beyond his power to repair. One of the saddest for him and Ellen was the drowning of a young boy about the same age as their Andrew, who got into difficulties while bathing in the river.[40] A month earlier, in March, another child had disappeared, a golden-haired and engaging 4-year-old boy named Bonny Dutton.[41] His parents raised the alarm and search parties scoured the bush around Perth, without success. Weeks went by, and it was feared he also had drowned, when suddenly he was restored, unharmed, to his family by natives who had 'borrowed' him to show to their wives and children.[42] Several diarists and letter writers at this time commented on the fact that Aboriginal women and children were kept away from the settled areas,[43] so one can imagine their curiosity about the newcomers, and especially the children.

In general, relations between the natives and settlers were amicable at this early stage, though, as Stirling reported to the Colonial Office in October, there were exceptions. In March it had been reported that natives had set fire to part of Perth, though it is more likely that some of the buildings on the outskirts of town caught fire as a result of sparks flying from fires the Aborigines lit to flush out animals and regenerate the bush. Now called 'fire farming',[44] this was a practice little understood by the newcomers, who spurned all 'bush tucker'. But the kangaroos and other wildlife which had sustained Aboriginal populations for hundreds of years were becoming scarce around settled areas—no match for the white man's guns. Hungry natives had naturally turned to spearing the settlers' livestock, including expensive imported bullocks. Captain Irwin and a party of soldiers were sent out to stop them. Anne Leake recorded that the soldiers fired to awe but not to kill, for 'under Capt. Irwin they were not likely to hurt the natives'. Like Stirling, Irwin believed that relations should be kept as harmonious as possible, and when two of the natives who had fled into the rushes were found wounded, they were taken to the colonial hospital marquee for medical attention. The marquee was opposite the gates of Government House and treatment, at Stirling's behest, was at government expense.[45]

After the levee, the civil officers and magistrates gave a large official dinner for the Governor, which went off to the satisfaction of all. Stirling referred to it in a subsequent report as 'the first public meeting in this colony…at which a most perfect unanimity prevailed'.[46] At the dinner there was earnest conversation between the Governor and three men of capital and standing who had arrived from London with their families and servants on the *Warrior* on 12 March. These were Captain John Molloy, James Turner and John Bussell. Stirling had already advised them to settle to the south of Perth, and they had entered into negotiations with the Captain of the *Emily Taylor* to take them and all their people and goods in that direction. Stirling had suggested an area below his own grant, between Cape Naturaliste and Cape Leeuwin, which had not yet been explored but which he believed would offer good quality land.[47] The Captain had agreed to take them for a sum of £200. No one had that sort of money available, and in despair the men turned to the Governor, who agreed to accompany them, making it an official visit at public expense.[48] A Government Notice on 1 May reported that the Governor would be accompanied by Captain Currie, the Harbour Master, Mr R. Dawson from the *Sulphur*, and Mr John Kellam, the Assistant Surveyor. The three grantees with their families and servants added another forty-five people to the party preparing to sail south, escorted by the *Sulphur*.

James Turner recorded that they landed on 2 May in Flinders Bay, near Cape Leeuwin, at the mouth of a river Stirling named the Blackwood. After exploring the territory for four days, the Governor and his party were 'well pleased with the area' and determined to form a settlement. Turner noted that 'a town is purposed to be built named Augusta, County of Sussex, in compliment to the Duke'.[49] Turner was by far the largest investor among the three grantees, bringing over £1,500 worth of assets, a family of eight, and twenty-one servants into the colony. But Stirling chose Molloy, a veteran of Waterloo, to be Government Resident in charge of the small settlement. Whether he felt for Molloy's young wife Georgiana, who in just a few days would see her baby born and die in a windswept tent,[50] is not recorded. Leaving the *Sulphur* and her crew, and a small detachment of soldiers, to help the settlers erect shelters and establish themselves, Stirling returned to Fremantle on the *Emily Taylor*. In later years he was blamed for advising this group to settle an area so far distant from Swan River that no assistance could be provided in any emergency. In Stirling's defence, it should be said that he had been told by the Colonial Office to encourage the move south, and in May 1830 he still had reason to believe that the Augusta settlers would be joined by other immigrants in the near future. He would also have been encouraged by the better quality land he had seen, but must have realised the tiny, isolated settlement would face difficulties in the short term.

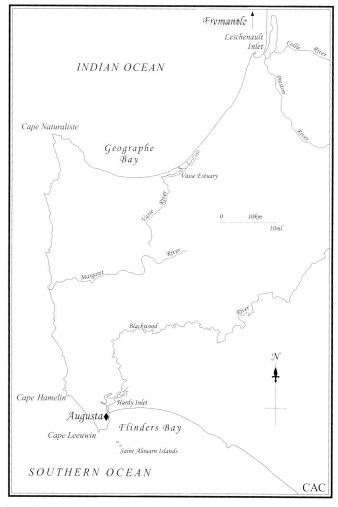

The isolated southern outpost of Augusta, settled in May 1830 by (top, left to right) John Bussell (*courtesy Battye Library 225084P*), Captain John Molloy (*courtesy Battye Library 1083B*) and wife Georgiana (*from A. Hasluck*, Portrait with Background)

By the time Stirling got back to Fremantle, arrangements had been completed for the Government to rent the refurbished wreck of the *Marquis of Anglesea*, partly as a Fremantle office for the Governor and his officials, and partly as a gaol for the many drunk and disorderly cases that were brought before the magistrates. Stirling had barely approved the expenditures involved, and been reunited with Ellen and his family, when he was confronted with two distressing incidents. The first was Captain Irwin's report that, during his absence, the natives had raided a settler's house and speared his poultry, and that soldiers had been called in to teach them a lesson. Irwin reported:

> The daring and hostile conduct of the natives induced me to seize the opportunity to make them sensible of our superiority; by shewing them how severely we could retaliate their aggression.

Shots and spears flew until one of the natives called from a tree, entreating an end as women and children were with them. Irwin continued:

> Considering the object I had in view as now fully accomplished, of impressing a salutary dread of our superiority and arms, while we shewed them we did not wish to injure them after having them and their families completely in our power, we left them at sunset, apparently on terms as friendly as usual.[51]

Stirling would not have been pleased with this incident, which crystallised his belief that native affairs were best handled by non-military means. Nevertheless, he shared Irwin's fear that the natives might take revenge by attacking the most isolated settlers. But things seemed to calm down after the brief affray, a considerable number of natives being seen to cross the river at Heirisson Islands the following morning, making for the hills.

Within days of this incident, news came of a very different crisis. The *Rockingham*, the last of Peel's ships, had arrived and anchored in Mangles Bay near Clarence, but been driven ashore during a gale on 14 May. Fortunately, no one had been harmed and the 182 passengers were got ashore with all their luggage, though continued driving rain created havoc among unprotected stores and made living conditions miserable for the new arrivals. Those already in temporary accommodation at Clarence did what they could for the newcomers, but it was all too much for Peel. Once again he quarrelled fiercely with the *Rockingham*'s Captain Halliburton, and his biographer believes that they also duelled.[52] Unlike his previous duel with Captain Geary, which had been harmless, Peel severely injured his right arm. According to the Colonial Storekeeper, who was still on Garden Island, 'nothing but the very excellent medical attention he received from the King's ships, saved his arm from amputation'.[53] Peel remained on Garden Island for many weeks,[54] on a small allotment Stirling had leased him, refusing to have anything to do with his people.

With the onset of winter, conditions at Clarence were going from bad to worse, and on 4 June Adam Elmslie, one of Peel's superintendents, asked Stirling for funds to pay his men which could later be reimbursed by Peel.[55] Stirling apparently acceded to this request, no doubt concerned with reports that had reached him of sickness and death at Clarence. He asked Dr Collie to investigate the situation immediately and report back, which he did on 25 July 1830. Of the 400-odd people landed at Clarence, Collie found one had died from a spearing and 28 of 'disease', including 11 children and 7 women. The predominant cause of death had been the still prevalent dysentery (124 cases) and scurvy (5). Collie reported that the cause of so much sickness was 'the want of antiscorbutic Diet, such as fresh meat, of Acids, as Lime juice and Vinegar, of Potatoes &c…'[56] He had visited the hospital and found it small and only used for single men, all other patients being treated in their own dwellings, which were only 'tolerably water-proof'. He concluded that health problems had been exacerbated by 'great irregularities of conduct' among men and women, by poor quality water towards the end of summer, and also, through inference, by Peel's mismanagement.

Stirling was appalled with Collie's findings, and anxious to assist. As Peel was unable to provide adequate or suitable food for his people, he had, in effect, broken the contracts he had entered into, and this was something which Stirling could act upon. In a private dispatch to the Colonial Office in October 1830, he stated:

> The gigantic schemes of Mr T Peel and Colonel Latour…have been broken up, and their servants discharged by their masters or by decision of the magistrates… Mr Peel's establishment, being much larger and less disposable, I have been obliged to interfere with for the prevention of famine, and have arranged with him that upon his consenting to liberate all but a very limited number of his people from their indentures, assistance shall be lent from the King's stores.[57]

Artisans quickly found work in Perth and Fremantle, but some of the families who had intended farming on Peel's land could not be accommodated so easily. They had insufficient assets for any regular grant, so Stirling requested the Surveyor-General to break up one of the government reserves that had been marked out near the recently opened town of Guildford, up the Swan River, into smaller 4 to 5-acre lots, and on them placed about twenty families.[58] Guildford, which Stirling had named after his wife's birthplace, was intended to become the hub of the agricultural region of the colony. The rich soils of the surrounding area would assist small farmers—although floods would also take their toll—and the larger grantees further up the river would be able to provide them with seasonal work.

Though most settlers were by this time finding their feet and feeling more positive, there were still some who remained disaffected. These included some of the discharged indentured servants who refused to work except in exchange for alcohol, and then became pugilistic. Such bad behaviour was slowly being curbed by the magistrates Stirling had put in place in April, and who handed out sentences of imprisonment for drunk and disorderly behaviour.[59] However, there was another group of disaffected immigrants, men from the eastern colonies who had read the glowing newspaper reports about the new colony, and chartered vessels to bring them to the new settlement. On arrival, many regretted their hasty action, comparing Swan River unfavourably with the places from which they had come. To return, however, required finance, so they were forced to sell up the assets they had introduced, and for most this meant selling livestock. So these short-stay immigrants did the new colony a favour by providing a larger livestock base than would otherwise have been the case, but their departure also meant that much of the colony's liquidity went with them. Another repercussion was that these disaffected colonial immigrants criticised Swan River vociferously on their return, providing another dimension to the 'disparaging damaging rumours'. On 24 July 1830 the *Sydney Gazette* carried the report of one such immigrant:

> I have seen quite enough and am convinced that broken down gentlemen and Cockney Corinthians are but indifferent subjects to colonize a wilderness…The wretchedness of the ruined and disappointed is unspeakable and in about fourteen months more a public subscription or a pawn broker will be wanting.[60]

Three days later the same paper carried the report of a suggestion to send provisions to Swan River and bring back labourers to work off their passage expenses for New South Wales masters, so there was also an element of profiteering!

With the onset of winter in 1830, Stirling had sent notices to all ships lying in Gage's Roads to warn them of possible gales and urge them to seek the safety of anchorage in Cockburn Sound. As he sadly wrote to the Colonial Office:

> This Warning being neglected on the first of June Three Vessels were driven in shore from that Anchorage, of which one has since been got off. Two others also were driven ashore from other anchorages one of which also has since been got off. Aware of the impression which these accidents make; and also of the regret you have expressed relative to the Losses thence arising, it is right that I inform you that these were occasioned principally from Neglect on the part of the Persons in charge.[61]

Three days after the gale, on 4 June, a ball was held at Government House, the planning of which would have taken a lot of Ellen's time. All the foremost settlers were invited to this first anniversary celebration, and the band of the 63rd Regiment once more called into service. Providing a suitable repast for supper taxed Ellen's ingenuity, for fresh fruit and vegetables were extremely scarce (she had even welcomed a gift of turnips from a settler,[62] a vegetable she would rarely have eaten at home). Potatoes had done reasonably well in the Government Gardens, and they undoubtedly featured on the table, but the *pièce de résistance* was probably a roasted pig, as hogs had done better than other livestock during the first year.[63]

Cattle and sheep did not seem to thrive on the coastal plain, and there had been several deaths from an unknown disease that made them stagger and walk in circles before expiring. It would be another ten years before the cause of this 'disease' was finally traced, by Colonial Naturalist James Drummond, to poisonous plants, especially the ubiquitous pea-flowered *Oxylobium*. As the long, hot summer gave way to winter rains, stock losses from poison plants gave way to stock drownings. Flash floods took many of the settlers by surprise. They had initially built near the river, as it was their main highway and also offered the most fertile soil, but with the solid rains of July the alluvial soils were flooded, causing extensive damage. Stirling, with Ellen beside him, visited afflicted settlers up and down the river offering what comfort they could. Many had to rebuild and, perhaps most upsetting for the Governor, start all over again sowing crops of wheat and vegetables.

During the floods the military was invaluable, rescuing small craft and stranded animals, as well as providing a line of communication for those farthest from the settlement. But the numbers Captain Irwin, their commander, could call into action in the Perth region had been considerably reduced. In all, sixty-seven soldiers had arrived with him in 1829, and five of these had died, mostly by drowning. A party of six had been left at Augusta, and the Murray River outpost, established in March 1830, had been augmented to eight in July after the mortal spearing of 19-year-old George McKenzie. His death seemed to have had no direct cause, though it was probably in retaliation for the intrusion by Peel's people into Murray tribal lands. It naturally exacerbated the fears of settlers and increased their agitation for military protection. But as soldiers also manned outposts in the Upper Swan, Guildford, Perth, Fremantle, Garden Island and Clarence, there simply were not the numbers to provide individual settlers with protection.[64] Stirling, nevertheless, was pleased with the efforts of the military and especially Irwin, his second-in-command and, as usual, hastened to say so in the right quarter.[65] Apart from their help in the floods, Stirling requested the military to assist the magistrates in registering the locations of the settlers. Since the end of May the number of ships arriving had slowed, only three passenger vessels had arrived in June, and as the confusion settled, it was time to take stock.

Dr Collie recorded in August 1830 that 'the colony musters about 3,000 souls'[66]—but this was a considerable exaggeration. Stirling had given the resident population at the end of 1829 as 850, with another 440 he classified as 'non-residents', making a total 1,290 civilians plus the military garrison of 67 men and officers, 18 females and 15 children. There was no further muster in 1830, but passenger lists suggest that the total population at the end of the year numbered about 1,520, with the military and their dependants bringing it to about 1,625. Some have thought that Collie's earlier figure was correct, and that large numbers subsequently left the colony disheartened or disappointed; in fact, Collie himself noted on 16 August 1830 that 'a number of persons are quitting and more will follow them'.[67] But in March 1831 Stirling estimated that only some seventy or eighty people had left the colony,[68] which is possible if he was excluding servants and children. A total of 287 people were actually named in passenger lists of vessels arriving at Hobart and Sydney from Swan River in 1830, though a number of these may not have been destined for Swan River anyway.[69] So there were just over 1,500 Europeans in the colony by the end of 1830, excluding the garrison at King George's Sound which had yet to be transferred from the New South Wales Government.

More accurate figures might have been obtained if Stirling's idea of placing a poll tax on arrivals to generate much needed revenue had succeeded, but the commotion that greeted its initial imposition led him to rescind it at once.[70] Until further instructions arrived, revenue could only be raised through a system of licences, especially covering the sale of alcohol. But funds so raised were totally insufficient to meet the constant demands on the public purse. One way of stemming the flood of appeals for government assistance was to place stricter controls on those leaving the colony, to prevent masters leaving debts and destitute servants behind them. From about February 1830 those intending to leave had to have the Governor's written permission, which meant proving themselves free of debt or other responsibilities.[71] This ruling was upheld by the Assistant Harbour Master, Daniel Scott, who inspected all ships for absconders before they left. With many drownings that winter, there were also a number of widows who wanted to go back to England with their children but lacked the means to do so, as their husbands' assets were completely tied up in unimproved, and hence untitled, land. Ann Whatley was one of these unfortunates when her husband, Dr Whatley, drowned in September.[72] Stirling generally managed to find a way to help, either directly through the pinched public purse, or by transferring the grant to a new immigrant and arranging a sale of assets.

So much occurred so quickly in this first year that not all was correctly documented. Stirling was called to account for this at a later date, but he often had no choice. For example, when he had marked locations at half-mile intervals up the river, to get settlers onto their land with as little delay as possible, he had left the exact grant entitlement and surveying to be ascertained at a later date. But the winding of the river made this a very difficult task and led to overlapping boundaries and squabbles between neighbours, which again Stirling was called upon to sort out.

The Governor's most pressing need was still land, good farming land, so that the remainder of settler entitlements could be allocated. The Board of Audit, assessing the value of each immigrant's introduced assets—human and physical— could only record their entitlement to a specific acreage (over and above their allowed 1,000 acres in the Swan region) 'to be taken in the interior'. Very few new arrivals were willing to follow the Molloy party and select land to the south. One

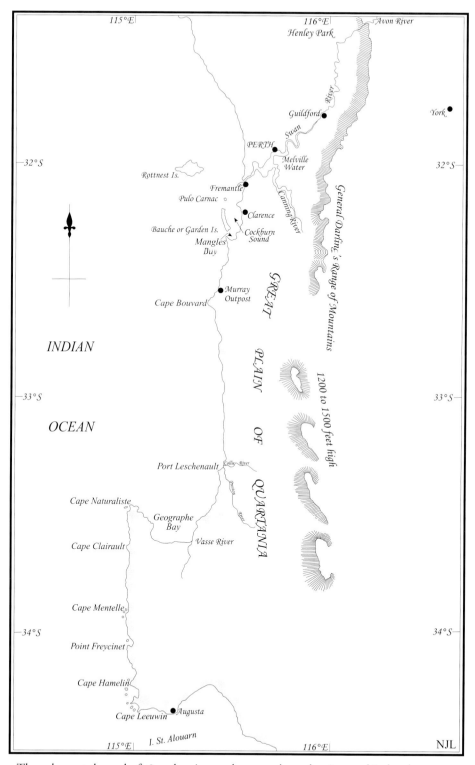

The colony at the end of 1830 showing settlements along the river and isolated outposts

possibility was the land over the Darling Ranges which Ensign Dale had explored with a small party in September. His report had been so favourable that Stirling was eager to see it for himself. Dr Collie was summoned to join him, as he told his brother on 3 October 1830:

> I am to leave the ship at daylight tomorrow morning to cross the mountains with the Governor to examine a new river with a great quantity of good soil on its banks, that has lately been discovered. The distance from the Swan is about 40 miles.[73]

The 'new' river, which they named the Avon, was actually an extension of the Swan, though that was not known for some time. The land they saw was all they were hoping for; fertile, well watered and not heavily covered in bush. The only obstacle was distance. Time and money would be needed to construct a track that could take the bullock wagons necessary for the transport of supplies, and even then the journey would take days. It was not an immediate solution, but did hold promise. Stirling told the Colonial Office in March 1831:

> …The effect [of this discovery] upon public opinion in the Settlement was very satisfactory, and from that period…there has been no longer any doubt entertained of the ultimate success of the Settlement.[74]

During this expedition he selected a town site and named it York, and the surrounding district Yorkshire after the county of that name in Britain 'which it was thought in some respects to resemble'. On his return he advised his cousin (and secretary) William Stirling to apply for land in that area, and also asked for some to be reserved for himself when it had been properly surveyed and declared open for selection.[75]

By October the first crops along the Swan were looking good, though just as the threat of flood subsided, another was emerging. Settlers were appalled to hear that Captain Irwin's recently completed house on the banks of the Upper Swan had burned down in a bushfire, the house, according to Collie, being worth 'upwards of £100'.[76] With only 100-odd acres actually under crop, and food still scarce, fires were a dreaded hazard and they could start so easily from open fires in the bush. The harvest eventually came in at just under 200 bushels, a disappointing yield, though its quality and weight were deemed excellent. Stirling also reported that vegetables and fresh meat were becoming available and that there were melons aplenty, which at last 'put an end to all apprehensions of scurvy'. This was a vast relief, as scurvy had attacked the settlement badly in the winter months. Indeed, food had been so scarce in July that he had sent to Van Diemen's Land for supplies of flour and grain, paying by Bills drawn on Treasury. Money was becoming a vexed question. Supplies for the settlement could be purchased with Bills, but there were a hundred and one things Stirling seemed to have to pay for himself, and he almost belligerently demanded restitution when forwarding his end of year accounts:

The first Entry in the Abstract is the sum of £900 paid to myself under the head of Lieutenant Governor's Contingent Expenses. That Amount is the Excess of my Expenditure over my private Income while filling the Office I hold here up to the end of the Year 1830. I might perhaps make out an Account of Horses, Servants, Table, and other Outlay unavoidable in the station I occupy but this I do not intend to do. I therefore represent this Amount for your consideration; & I beg leave to add that I shall not hold myself responsible for its repayment if so you shall decide.[77]

In this same report Stirling lamented that, due to lack of funds, no roads had been constructed except a bush track from Fremantle to Perth paid for by public subscription. As he hoped the King George's Sound outpost would soon be transferred to his Government, a road linking Swan River to that place, over the route recently established by Captain Bannister, would be a blessing. But at an estimated cost of £1,000 it could only be done if His Majesty's Treasury underwrote the expense. Nevertheless, as shipping was not always available and settlers were taking up land further to the south, some form of overland access was essential.

At the end of October, a person who was to have much to do with administrative decisions in the colony during its early years, George Fletcher Moore, arrived in Fremantle. Born on 10 December 1798 in County Tyrone, Ireland, Moore was a qualified lawyer, having graduated in 1820 at Trinity College, Dublin, and brought with him a personal letter of introduction to Stirling from the Colonial Secretary, Sir George Murray. Moore was an articulate man and a keen observer, and the diary he kept in the form of letters to his family provides a key insight into life in the colony during the first ten years of its existence.[78] Arriving on the *Cleopatra* on 30 October with four indentured servants from his father's farm, and sufficient assets to claim land, Moore lost no time in presenting his credentials. Stirling appeared relieved to meet him, for lawyers were still scarce.[79] Some weeks later Moore noted, in an unpublished letter,

I shall call soon on the Governor again. He is generally disliked as a governor though much liked as an individual.[80]

This was a comment that would be made many times and reflected the fact that, although Stirling was pleasant in all his personal dealings, his decisions favoured no one. The good of the colony was always more important than individual wants. His ideas on taxation and enforcement of penalties did not make him a popular Governor, while his quarter-deck background made him aloof even to his closest officers. Moore felt that 'he is sick of this place' already, but it was the position, more than the place, that was wearing Stirling down.

Although Moore had arrived when land on the Swan and Canning rivers had already been allocated, he did manage to acquire a grant on the Swan by agreeing to take half of the 8,000 acres assigned in October 1829 to William Lamb. Moore received his half (later called Millendon) on the understanding that he would carry out the improvement duties for the whole of Lamb's grant,[81] as Lamb had decided that he preferred trading at Fremantle to the life of a landowner. Such private negotiations, which were occurring constantly, made record-keeping by William Stirling (Registrar) and John Septimus Roe (Surveyor-General) almost impossible in this early period. And William was not well, for Stirling noted that his cousin's respiratory problems had not receded as far as had been hoped with the change of air.

In early December 1830 Stirling took William with him on the *Sulphur*, which was delivering supplies and a replacement detachment of soldiers to the tiny settlement at Augusta. Ellen, seven months pregnant, did not accompany them on this trip, though she knew Georgiana Molloy would be disappointed to miss the opportunity of chatting to someone of her own age and background. Stirling found all at Augusta well and reasonably contented with their condition and prospects, although Molloy complained about the high prices of provisions. Food had been scarce, and when promised supplies from an earlier trip by the *Sulphur* had not arrived, he had been forced to buy from the captain of the visiting *Eagle* at the prices demanded. Luckily, crops of grain and vegetables had prospered with the coming of warmer weather. James Turner, with his large family and retainers, had already built a comfortable home and outhouses, and had cleared and planted several acres. Molloy had made his wife's comfort a priority, and put his two servants to building, so as yet they had no crops in the ground. But the Bussell boys had managed to clear land and plant potatoes and vegetables, and even the soldiers had started a garden around their rough garrison.[82] Food shortages should not be as acute again, so Stirling could return with an easy mind.

As he was to note in his first report for 1831, building and its associated activities of brick making, sawing, quarrying and lime burning had taken up a great deal of the time and effort of most of the colony's labour supply during 1830. Fortunately, materials were abundant and there were now some very good houses in Perth and Fremantle. In December workmen had finished additions to the wooden Government House at Perth, its wide verandas offering Ellen and the children the prospect of shady summer afternoons. Next door the Government Gardens were progressing, and several fruit trees had taken root and also promised shade. As she prepared for their second upside-down Christmas, Ellen would have been pleased that the officers of HMS *Success*, which had been successfully righted on 28 November (a year to the day after being hoved down for repairs) would still be with them. Together with the *Sulphur*'s officers they made a merry crowd and helped her husband forget for a while the cares and responsibilities of his position. Stirling could afford briefly to relax. He had reported somewhat optimistically to Sir George Murray in October, 'the settlement is now securely established and its future prosperity no longer doubtful'.[83] He was, of course, quite correct. But conditions were to get a lot worse before his hopes could materialise.

12

A Dismal Year

1831

JAMES, ELLEN AND the children spent some of the hot days of January 1831 in the small brick house James had had built on their Woodbridge grant at Guildford. Later in the year a visitor from India, Colonel J. Hanson, described their retreat as 'a little cottage orné' built on an elevated and beautiful site

> at a turn of the river commanding a view along two extensive reaches and the land in front of it being all meadow land, very beautifully studded with forest trees, you may without much imagination conceive yourself placed in the midst of a gentleman's park at home.[1]

Hanson added that the Governor did not seem to spend much time there, being caught up with official business at Perth. An enormous amount of time and effort was certainly spent in drafting dispatches, with their numerous enclosures, private letters and reports which were always sent in duplicate on different vessels. On 10 January Stirling signed a letter to Rear Admiral Owen, Commander-in-Chief of the Eastern Station, expressing his gratitude for provisions sent by the *Comet*, and giving a report on progress. He briefly referred to the difficulties experienced by incoming ships and sent a plan of Cockburn Sound and its vicinity, adding that the *Comet*'s captain would provide him with 'a circumstantial account of its possibilities and defects as a port'. He knew that it had been deemed dangerous, and clearly hoped the verbal report would convince the Commander otherwise, but went on to say:

> This port appears to tell against the reputation of the Settlement but for my part I rejoice in it. There are always two description of persons who rush into such enterprises as these, of which one part is fitted to struggle with and surmount the difficulties and distress which they must meet, the other helpless and disabled…Of the first description we have enough to make the experiment, and of the last too many, but they are gradually leaving us and when we shall have

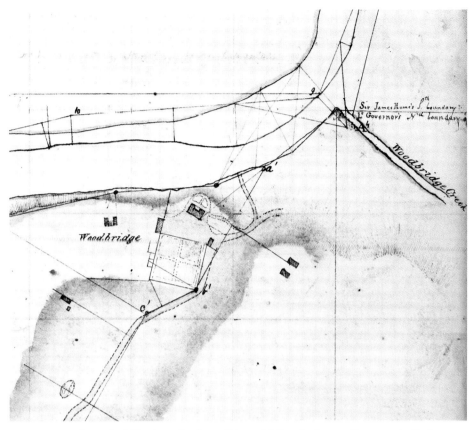

Upstream from Guildford on the Swan River, Stirling had a small cottage built from
bricks and fittings shipped out in 1829

Courtesy Department of Land Administration Hist. Plan 12

none but those who are doing well we shall probably take a fresh and more
vigorous spring.[2]

Stirling's views were echoed a month later in a letter to the Colonial Secretary
from a well-connected private settler, Robert Menli Lyon.[3] Arriving on the ill-fated
Marquis of Anglesea in August 1829, Lyon had had over a year to assess the territory,
and he fully supported Stirling's optimism.

Sir, The fate of a Colony, founded for the first time in British History by capital,
and left to find its way to maturity by the energies of the British people, must in
its infancy be a subject deeply interesting to the British Government especially to
the Secretary for the Colonies. You will therefore be probably not unwilling to
hear the sentiments of an early settler, respecting the prospects of this Colony.

Western Australia—I speak of the Quartania only…is a country capable
of producing almost everything that is produced within or without the tropics…

No doubt much has been said at home respecting the badness of the harbour. For nearly six months in the year, ships may lie…in as much safety as if they were anchored in a tub; & at the Garden Island side of Cockburn Sound, the proper place for ships of war, a navy may ride in perfect security…But what if, like the Baltic or the St Lawrence, the Port were to be entirely shut for one half of the year. Should that be a valid objection against belonging to one of the finest countries in the world?…The climate is very healthy. The only objections are that, to some, of whom I am one, it is too warm in the dry seasons, & in many parts the Musketoes [sic] are very troublesome for a few months of the year…

But I am not one of those who expected, the moment their feet touched the shore, to find Inns, turnpike roads, smiling orchards & cornfields, in a country untrod by civilised man since creation. However great the natural capabilities of the country may be, it will require both stock & labour to develop its riches & bring its products to perfection. But here is the great & only drawback. The want of money has already reduced many of the Settlers almost to a state of pauperism. Gentlemen who moved in the first circles of society at home, are here with the finest estates, destitute of the common necessaries of life…The capital of every settler with, perhaps, one or two exceptions, has been expended either in his outfit, or in carrying him to his location; & now he has no money to carry on agricultural operations, & no prospect of a market for his produce…Unless therefore, assistance comes from some quarter or another, the Colony must remain for many years to come an Aristocratical desert.[4]

George Fletcher Moore agreed, telling his father on 26 March 1831, 'Our greatest want at present is stock and the settlers have not funds…to bring stock in'.[5] Moore did not support Lyon's solution, which was to introduce convicts. Lyon's letter had concluded that such a move need not be seen as a breach of faith, given the initial condition of no convicts, because it was 'the only thing that will save most of them from utter ruin'. He had ended with a postscript:

Indentured servants are of no use. Almost every settler is obliged to dismiss his indentured servants for idleness, disobedience to orders & drunkenness; & so soon as they obtain their liberty they embark for either Hobart or Sidney [sic]. I have been ruined by laying out my money in the way recommended by Government in the published regulations.[6]

Whilst Lyon's views on convicts were not universally shared, his condemnation of indentured servants struck a common chord. Complaints of absconding or lazy servants still occupied much of the magistrates' time, and increasingly they were also handling requests from servants to be relieved of indenture to masters who were unable to provide the rations to which they were entitled.

During the summer months Stirling was involved in negotiations with Governor Darling concerning the transfer of responsibility for the King George's Sound settlement.[7] It ceased being an outpost of New South Wales and officially became part of Western Australia on 7 March 1831, and was then thrown open for selection by Swan River settlers.[8] The Commandant and his soldiers, as well as the convicts who had been stationed there, left for New South Wales on the colonial schooner *Isabella* a few days later (but not before several convicts had tried to escape, fearing far harsher treatment in the east[9]). They were replaced by Lieutenant Carew and twenty soldiers from the 63rd Regiment, who had been sent on the *Isabella* from Van Diemen's Land and took up their duties after reporting to Governor Stirling and Captain Irwin in Perth.

Shipping had been fairly quiet in early January, but the end of the month brought a flurry of activity as the *Isabella* was followed into Gage's Roads by the *Kate* from the Cape of Good Hope and the *Edward Loombe* from Timor on the 30th. This ship brought the last of the colony's appointed civil servants, the Colonial Chaplain, 40-year-old Reverend J. B. Wittenoom, who had been appointed by Sir George Murray a little too late to accompany the *Parmelia*. Next came the *Nerus* from Sydney on 1 February, while the 4th saw the arrival of the *Drummore* direct from London. It therefore provided good copy for the first issue of the *Western Australian Chronicle and Perth Gazette*, which was published in manuscript form on 11 February 1830. Along with various items of local news, the *Chronicle* announced that the *Drummore* had brought William Tanner, a young man with considerable capital, together with his family and thirty servants, as well as mail and the latest English papers. The mail brought two shocks for Stirling: first, that King George IV had died, and been succeeded by William IV and Adelaide, and second, that his own mother had died the previous June. In later correspondence with his brother John, he noted that

> A newspaper accidentally taken up had previously informed me of the event. To me as well as to all it must have been an unexpected affliction as there seemed no reason for doubting the probability of a long life.[10]

The family letters about the mournful event were not received until 5 March, when Stirling read Walter's account of her last hours:

> Written with a firm hand but bursting heart Mother died June 1. On our return from Church Sunday forenoon, found she had been very ill, and much apprehensive of an immediate termination but was then better & desired to see Walter & myself. We waited on her accordingly, and much interesting conversation took place, in which she repeatedly alluded to her Situation with much firmness…and expressed herself quite satisfied that in whatever might occur, we would, as we ever had done, implicitly follow what she herself would desire.[11]

These last words would have been of some comfort for James, who had loved and deeply respected his charming and determined Mama.

In his reply to John on 2 April, James also conveyed the news that Ellen had been safely delivered of another boy. The *Fremantle Observer* noted that the event took place at Government House on Sunday 27 February, but Stirling, in his April letter, was not as precise:

> Ellen has been brought to bed of a boy about the 1st of March and has made an excellent recovery. She has since however been dangerously ill with a complaint in the heart, but I trust she is now recovering…

The child was named William, in honour of Stirling's older brother but also as a tribute to cousin William Stirling, who had served James so well as Private Secretary throughout the vexed early months. James was still very worried about his cousin's health, confiding to John that he feared 'his constitution is such as to promise an early Death. He is fond of the country and has been a great comfort to me.' James' concern was well warranted, for William, aged only 32, died just a fortnight later, most probably of consumption (tuberculosis). The *Fremantle Observer* described how

> At an early hour on Saturday the 16th inst. the last sad duties to the remains of this highly respected individual were performed, the procession was attended by all the chief Officers of Government, and a long train of the most respectable inhabitants; several of whom were from Fremantle. On arrival at the place of interment the distance of a mile from Perth, the service was most impressively performed by the Rev J. B. Wittenoom.[12]

It was proving a dismal year for Stirling. William's death deprived him of a valued confidant, and there were so many matters where his best course of action was unclear. One bright spot early in March had been Captain Bannister's report on his epic overland journey from Perth to Albany, and the news that he had discovered considerable tracts of good land 'fit for the plough, sheep, or cattle, or indeed any cultivation...about 25 or 30 miles from King George's Sound'.[13] Another was the receipt of official mail by the *Eliza* on 5 March with dispatches which, as Dr Collie noted, showed that the Home Government was 'well disposed towards the Colony and the proceedings of our Lieutenant Governor'.[14] This gave both private and public satisfaction and raised spirits which had flagged over past weeks in consequence of the 'uncertainty of the light in which this rising settlement was viewed by the mother country'. The official mail praised Stirling for the efforts described in his two previous dispatches, reprimanded him for not writing more frequently, and urged him to keep expenses to an absolute minimum. But it did not bring the charter or the instructions he had been anticipating. A private letter from

Hay intimated that they were on their way,[15] but it would be almost a year before they reached the colony.

When Stirling signed his official report on 31 March, he was still hopeful the charter would arrive soon, stating in both the accompanying letter and his report that he felt he could not create institutions or enact laws until instructions arrived.[16] His dispatch contained a detailed summary of the past year and a report on existing agricultural and commercial progress. With regard to the latter, Stirling commented:

> Warehouses and Shop Keepers in the smaller Towns are becoming very common, & as it is not a laborious course of Life, and the Profits in it very high, a greater Number are drawn into it than it will support…Several cargoes have been brought…and the Necessity which the neighbouring Colonies labour to export their products has recently afforded us abundant supplies from all sides…[17]

He ended his report with a reference to the existing trade imbalance and a plea for investment in whaling, which he believed would 'tend in a great degree to the early prospects of the Colony'. It was a perspicacious comment, for whaling *did* provide one of the colony's first exports, but not until 1837.

Just two days after signing this long report, Stirling wrote to his brother concerning his mother's death. He also gave a description of the various parts of the infant colony:

> Fremantle is now a Town containing 400 people and 100 houses some of which are of two stories of white stone. Perth is not quite so large. Brick building is however begun. It is the home of the Government Officers. Guildford on the Swan contains about 100 persons, and is a flourishing little place. Augusta at Cape Leeuwin contains also about 100 and is a delightful place of residence. King George Sound is smaller than these but great prosperity awaits it and I am now taking measures to render it better known to ships passing on to N.S.W. & V.D.Land.

But he also told John that

> The first year of residence here was full of vexation and uncertainty. People came out expecting to find the Garden of Eden and some of the working class were astonished at finding hard work an indispensable preliminary to meat and drink…In the meantime the absence of an authority & proper instructions added to my troubles until at length the anxiety forced me to become the Ruler in earnest.

He felt depressed and homesick, telling John:

In the furtherance of [the Colony's] prosperity I have had but little share, it has been due principally to a succession of events which I have only had the negative merit of not obstructing. For me there now remains little to do and I begin to think that leave of absence…will be very agreeable before another year has passed.

His own situation was not as he had anticipated:

Of my own affairs I can say little that is agreeable to myself. The Colonial Office now seems disposed to consider my grant of land as sufficient pay. I have not yet selected more than 5,000 acres on the Swan where I have a good house, cows etc…Garden Island seems to be valuable but not so much as at first expected. These with the remainder of the land will probably have a great value when you and I have been forgotten, but scarcely till then.[18]

Ten days later, on 12 April, Stirling replied to a letter from Governor Arthur which had been delivered from Van Diemen's Land by the *Isabella* in January. Arthur had written with great concern, having read some of the disparaging reports about the colony still circulating in the British Press. Stirling commented:

…perhaps the uncertainty and doubts which have hung upon the undertaking from its commencement will still remain with it until Fact shall put an end of Opinion altogether…For my own part I have not time to speculate upon the future, but anxious that those who have ventured their Fortunes and Persons in this Country should not be disappointed I bestow upon its welfare all my industry and attention, and I hope for a favourable result.

If we shall surmount infancy there is scope enough for new future grants in the interior…but at present we have room enough upon the coast for all our wants.[19]

He had said much the same thing in his official 31 March report, but with more literary flair:

…progress has not been so rapid as might have been expected [for]…every Act in farming is an Experiment, as every Journey is an Exploration, and the result exhibited in produce appears to be wholly incommensurate with the Time, and Labor, bestowed on its attainment. But Lands once broken up will be available in future years.[20]

At the end of April 1831 both James and Ellen would have been overjoyed to welcome Ellen's cousin, Captain James Mangles, who arrived on the *Atwick*.[21] A keen botanist, James Mangles had come to Swan River to observe the native flora, and also to investigate trade potential for the Mangles family's shipping line. He

The Rev. J. B. Wittenoom who officiated at the funerals of
James' nephew William Stirling, and his baby son of the same name
Courtesy Battye Library 670P

would have brought all the news from home as well as letters and parcels, including no doubt new clothes for Ellen and the children, so his visit would have lifted the spirits of all. The Captain was to stay a couple of months, and was with the family when baby William died at the end of April. Never strong, William was said to have succumbed to a heart condition, rather than the dysentery and fever that took its annual toll on infants. Whether this was linked to the heart complaint that Stirling mentioned Ellen suffering after the birth is unknown, for there are no further references to this baby.

For both parents, the loss of baby William so soon after his namesake would have been difficult, but perhaps eased by the presence of the Reverend J. B. Wittenoom, who conducted the small private burial service on 2 May.[22] Wittenoom had been the Headmaster of Magnus College, Newark, before his appointment, and was more renowned for his input into education than for religious guidance and solace.[23] His parish was in any case so large, extending from the Upper Swan to Fremantle, that he would have had little time to comfort the bereaved mother. Stirling had his work and countless concerns to distract him, but for 23-year-old Ellen the loss would have been hard to cope with, especially as Matilda Roe, her closest confidante, had just been delivered of a healthy girl. Nevertheless, having her cousin James as a house guest through this period must have been a help, and one can imagine Stirling urging his young wife to forget her grief in arranging social events for his benefit. In fact, the diarist George Fletcher Moore recorded dining with the Governor and his lady, and Captain Mangles, on 21 June at Government House.

Moore had already been introduced to Mangles when the Governor and his party were inspecting a line of proposed road along the river between Guildford and Perth. But on Sunday the 21st Moore had joined the Governor's party for Mr Wittenoom's evening service in the rush church, later dining at Government House.[24] Ellen was the gracious hostess, interested in all the talk which would have centred around the land and its natural bounty, for Mangles was struck by the variety and uniqueness of the country's flora. The other guests, Moore, young George Elliot and Henry Ommanney, were also keen observers of nature. Elliot was still in Stirling's care, while Henry Mortlock Ommanney, who had arrived as a private settler the previous August, was the son of a baronet and related to the naval agent Stirling had used for many years. Just 20 years old, Henry was already a trained surveyor, so the Governor would have been doubly pleased to welcome him as the Survey Department was overloaded and desperately in need of help. Conversation around the dinner table that evening touched on Stirling's frustration over the continued absence of detailed instructions. As yet, even the geographical extent of the colony had not been delineated. And despite Hay's previous reassurance that steps were being taken to formalise government of the colony, Stirling had had no confirmation that either the settlement or his appointment had been recognised by the Crown. Even Moore commented that 'the Governor seems to be left here awkwardly placed with rather meagre instructions from home. No charter sent by the "Eliza" which was expected and no courts of law as yet established.'[25]

Stirling felt that his lack of instructions was impeding the colony's progress, and a note of desperation appeared in his June report to the Colonial Office:

> The Instructions which I had the honour to receive on quitting England were so few and general and so much better suited to the commencement of this Settlement than to its present circumstances that on almost every subject I am at a loss to know how to proceed.

He then added:

> I therefore cannot avoid wishing that I might be permitted...to absent myself sufficiently long from this Government to wait in person upon your Lordship...I am not aware whether it be customary to grant leave of absence in such cases or for such purposes, but I take leave to say that I cannot imagine any mode by which

Ellen's cousin, the botanist Captain James Mangles
Courtesy Battye Library 1306B

His Majesty's Service in this Settlement might be more effectively promoted than in personal communication as to its actual State and prospects.[26]

Stirling felt powerless. He could not establish courts without the permission of the Crown, for there were already enough men of substance in the colony to challenge his authority. He was also well aware of what had happened to other colonial governors who had acted without authority. Yet so many issues needed resolution, and he went on to list them to the new Colonial Secretary, Lord Goderich, stating that he needed to be 'more particularly…acquainted with the views of His Majesty's Government' on

the Amount and distribution of Expenditure; the Numbers, Duties, and Salaries of the persons comprising the Civil Establishment; the Amount of Funds to be appropriated to the subsistence and allowance of the Troops; the mode of keeping and transmitting Accounts; the amendments required in the general mode of granting Land; and the Extent to which the Aid of Government may be expected in hastening the progress of the Settlement by the Erection of Public Buildings and making of Roads.

George Fletcher Moore, diarist, lawyer and self-styled balladeer
Courtesy Battye Library 1090P

He had already exhausted the £380 borrowed from his father-in-law in the colony's service,[27] and drawn bills on Treasury, but was very conscious of the fact that if Treasury did not approve his expenditures, he would be held personally accountable. In his earlier private letter to Hay, Stirling had virtually begged for intercession if his actions did not meet with official approval.[28]

By early July Ellen was sufficiently recovered to attend public functions, though Moore reported that it was often under the eye of the Acting Colonial Surgeon, William Lane Milligan.[29] Milligan was actually the (replacement) Military Surgeon, but as the appointed Colonial Surgeon, Charles Simmons, was unwell (and died in October) Milligan was temporarily filling both roles.[30] Ellen's mourning had meant that the ball planned to mark the anniversary of the colony's foundation in early June had had to be postponed. Instead, a Government House ball was planned to coincide with a meeting of Perth's new Agricultural Society on 2 September, two days before Ellen's birthday. Even the urbane George Fletcher Moore was agreeably surprised at the jollity: 'I had no idea there would be so much society here, so much gaiety, so much dressiness. I thought I had bid farewell for ever to slight shoes, silk stockings, kid gloves, but I was wrong.'[31]

All the landed gentlemen of the colony who could attend came to Perth for this occasion. A grand dinner for fifty guests was followed by the ball where some 180 people danced till the early hours of the morning to tunes played by the regimental band. Half way through the evening James and Ellen would have been both amused and delighted when Moore tapped for attention and sang the following self-written ballad, titled 'Western Australia for me':

From the old Western world, we have come to explore
The wilds of this Western Australian shore;
In search of a country, we've ventured to roam
And now that we've found it, let's make it our home.
And what though the colony's new, Sirs.
And inhabitants yet may be few, Sirs,
We see them increasing here too, Sirs,
So Western Australia for me.

With care and experience, I'm sure 'twill be found
Two crops in the year we may get from the ground;
There's good wood and good water, good flesh and good fish,
Good soil and good clime, and what more could you wish.
Then let every one earnestly strive, Sirs,
Do his best, be alert and alive, Sirs,
We'll soon see our colony thrive, Sirs,
So Western Australia for me.

No lions or tigers we here dread to meet,
Our innocent quadrupeds hop on two feet;
No tithes and no taxes we now have to pay
And our geese are all Swans, as some witty folks say,
Then we live without trouble or stealth, Sirs,
Our currency's all sterling wealth, Sirs,
So here's to our Governor's health, Sirs,
And Western Australia for me.[32]

One of the settlers, reporting this event in a letter to his sister, commented:

Captain Stirling, the Governor, is a very good kind of man, and I believe has the welfare of every individual much at heart. Mrs Stirling is a very pretty agreeable woman and both of them very affable. They gave a very grand entertainment some time since at Perth, to which all persons in the Colony of a certain rank were invited. I did not go, not being inclined to have two days travelling for one evening's pleasure, but Mrs Scott and my daughter Elizabeth, who was on a visit to Fremantle, were there, and the former had the honour of dancing with the Governor.[33]

Two people unable to be present at the ball were Mrs Helena Dance (wife of the Captain of HMS *Sulphur*), who had cut down the tree to mark the foundation of Perth, and Dr Collie, originally *Sulphur*'s surgeon. The former had given birth to a son only nine days earlier on board the ship in Cockburn Sound, whereas the latter, who normally would have attended the birth, had been sent to Albany in April as Government Resident. Collie was impressed with this area and, in a letter to his brother dated 4 August, predicted that King George's Sound would eventually become the chief settlement of the Colony. He had heard, moreover, that

> The Governor with his lady and some other official persons are coming here to stop some months in September or October, and the Governor has ordered a house to be erected for his reception.[34]

The information was accurate but premature, for early September saw Stirling heading off in the opposite direction—towards the inland town of York. Moore noted that on Tuesday 6 September a party of twenty-one had assembled at the Governor's farm at Guildford to form

> the first expedition going to settle over the hills…The Governor himself was with us all first day's journey, and his presence infused a spirit of life and animation into the party. He led the van, then came the Governor's cart drawn by 5 horses, next Messrs Clarkson and Hardey's drawn by two horses, then Mr. Heales' cart drawn by two cows, then two or three horses carrying provisions and clothes in sacks, saddle-bags, and other contrivances, and numbers of footmen moving from place to place. We made 7 miles to the ascent of the hills, near a hill called Green Mount. The Governor on his return was greeted with 3 cheers.[35]

Much of the Governor's official time in 1831 was taken up with land grant matters, particularly applications for exchange, and he was desperate to find new good quality land. He had been able to reassign some of the early grants to service personnel along the Upper Swan, as they had failed to make the necessary improvements. Captain Fremantle's entitlement, for example, was granted to William Tanner,[36] Captain Dance's went to Marshall McDermott, who had arrived with his wife in June, and some of Colonel Latour's to J. W. Wright. A few early settlers had voluntarily quitted their grants and bestowed them on others, which is how William Shaw and his family acquired Belvoir, but there were still many outstanding claims.

James Henty, who had arrived with his brother in October 1829, had missed out on the first Swan grants, and yet had long farming experience. He had been assigned part of the land originally reserved for a government farm in April 1830,

The military surgeon, William Lane Milligan

Courtesy Dr John Brine

and part of one granted to Captain Bannister in June. But he had not been happy with his lot, and in a letter to Stirling in August 1830 had implied that grants had not been assigned impartially. Moreover he claimed that of his grant of 2,000 acres, only a tenth was good land, the rest being white sand or swamp.[37] He had ended with a veiled threat that his father and family, who were expected within a month or two, would not remain when they had seen the land and would go on to one of the other Australian colonies, 'where every encouragement has already been held out to him'.[38] Stirling's reaction to this was predictable. The icy correctness of his reply bore all the hallmarks of the naval commander. He stated that Henty's concerns

divide themselves under two heads: the first of which embraces strictures and allusions on the mode in which land has been assigned in this settlement, and the second an intimation that your family will not settle in it unless they meet with greater encouragement than has been experienced.

To the first of these, when they take the substantiated form of an accusation by competent authority, doubt not that I shall be able to reply. To the last, I shall only say that as long as your family remain in this settlement, it shall be admitted, in common with the rest of His Majesty's Subjects residing here, to a fair participation in the advantages the Colony may offer; but that I am not to be driven from this course of impartial dealing by the threatened secession of those who may expect greater encouragement in other Colonies.[39]

Stirling held by the principle of impartiality, though many felt that he had not always shown it. Several writers complained that the majority of grantees 'appear to consist principally of naval, military and civil officers'[40] who did not have the assets and labour to qualify under the regulations. But Stirling's instructions from the Colonial Office had been to allocate land 'in lieu of pensions from the Crown', which naturally applied to naval and military officers. Nathanial Ogle, writing in 1839, raised the issue of such grants, but felt the Governor should not be blamed for 'exercising his prerogative and serving his professional friends', as the Colonial Office had not given him enough instructions.[41] Neither he nor others appreciated the fact that Stirling *was* following instructions, the clause regarding pensions having been deliberately added to the initial regulations as a saving to the Crown. And it was a small step from there to using land grants as a means of payment for vital services, such as exploration, that the colony could not otherwise afford.

When Henty and his brothers finally decided to leave the colony, which they did in November 1831, they sold their Swan grant to the Colonial Secretary, Peter Brown, and asked that the remainder of their extensive grant entitlement be allocated in the vicinity of King George's Sound. James Henty had decided the family would be better off in Van Diemen's Land, but planned to leave his younger brother in charge of an establishment at the Sound, and begin a trade between the two with a small vessel he had acquired.[42] It must therefore have been a shock for his fiancée, Miss Charlotte Carter, who arrived on the *Atwick* on 25 April 1831 prepared to join James in a life by the Swan, to learn they were soon to move. But far from being faint-hearted, she adapted readily to change. Her wedding was hastily arranged and the Governor, perhaps mending bridges, offered to give her away but, as the family were informed:

> his infant child happening unfortunately to die on the very morning he was prevented by that circumstance from being present. He has since called and what is commonly termed 'done the civil' as well as many others.[43]

The couple did not actually leave till the end of November, so Charlotte had time to get to know the small society quite well. She would have shared their sense of isolation too, as month after month went by with no ship from England. Some news filtered through when small vessels arrived from the other colonies, but even these were few and far between. In total, only seven vessels arrived from April to November, including HMS *Zebra* from the Eastern Station.

With the decline in shipping, the problem of food scarcity rose again. Almost all the settlers were still basically on salt rations, lightened by home-grown vegetables.[44] Only 160 acres of land were planted with wheat, and stores of grain were diminishing rapidly. Native thefts from the stores were therefore viewed with alarm, settlers not realising their predicament as traditional sources of food disappeared. Moore told his family in a letter signed on 21 October 1831 that

> the natives have been making sad havoc among the flocks of sheep in this neighbourhood. They took eleven of Mr Brown's and speared his sow, and afterwards (having been fired at for this) they came stealthily and killed his shepherd. The next thing they did was to drive away no less than 67 sheep of Mr Bull and actually to slaughter 47 though pursued very soon after. These are wholesale doings and must be checked. [45]

In a dispatch written in November, Stirling informed the Colonial Office that although the settlement continued to advance, some 'annoyance' had been occasioned by

> the hostile conduct of certain Native Tribes inhabiting the District around Swan River. The pertinacious endeavours of these savages to commit depredations on property having called forth the determined resistance of the Settlers…they have in three or four instances succeeded in sacrificing the lives of white Persons to their fury…With the small Military Force at present in the Settlement, it has been found impossible to afford protection to every point.[46]

Stirling penned this report at King George's Sound, where he had taken Ellen and the children to avoid the heat of the summer. There she would have the care of Dr Collie, whom Stirling had made Magistrate (as well as Government Resident) of the area following his discharge from HMS *Sulphur*.[47] Collie informed his brother that, although part of the Governor's suite had arrived on the colonial schooner *Ellen* on 6 November, His Excellency and his family with the remainder of the party did not arrive until the 12th, the weather having been too inclement to permit the *Sulphur*'s entry.[48]

Knowing that *Sulphur*'s usual three-year term of duty was nearly over and that she would soon be recalled, Stirling had decided to acquire the *Ellen* as a replacement colonial vessel. The *Ellen* had belonged to a Captain Rae of the 20th Regiment, but had foundered on the beach in the storms of May 1830. Stirling had negotiated a purchase in repayment of a debt from its owner, and had her repaired by government workmen.[49] Although lacking cargo space, the *Ellen* was a 'very fine vessel of her class' and Stirling was pleased to be able to give its command to young William Preston, who was later to marry Ellen's younger sister Hamilla. Preston had been with him on the *Success* in 1827 and then made a Lieutenant on the *Sulphur*, where he had become friendly with Dr Collie. The two had explored the Murray and Leschenault area together in 1830, adding much to Stirling's knowledge of the territory.

The *Sulphur* was not to remain long at King George's Sound, for Stirling was worried about the scarcity of food in the Swan River settlement and had decided to send her to Van Diemen's Land to purchase supplies with £3,000 worth of bills which he had drawn on Treasury. But first *Sulphur* was needed as an accommodation base, for Stirling had brought down several families who wished to settle at the Sound,[50] along with Surveyor-General Roe and Ommanney (now officially Assistant Surveyor), who had been charged with laying out the town of Albany.

Major Lockyer, the first Commandant of the outpost at King George's Sound, had named his settlement 'Fredrickstown', in honour of the then Duke of York, but the name had never gained wide acceptance. Stirling changed it during this visit to Albany, another of the titles of the same Duke.[51] A certain amount of surveying of the future town had been done before Roe's arrival, radiating out from the parade ground of the original settlement. Roe then adopted the grid-line system he had used in Perth and Fremantle, though the high crags made this difficult, with allotments for private dwellings running east-west along the waterfront. It was here that Stirling and his family took up residence for the summer. Ellen was able to relax, and her husband was a different person. Away from the strains of constant importuning, and able to satisfy fully his love of exploring, James was gradually regaining his optimism and enthusiasm for life.[52] Day after day he set out, examining the coast and its inlets in small boats, and the inland on horseback. He was very impressed with the land he saw, and on 16 December wrote officially to Roe asking that certain areas be reserved for himself.[53] He wanted to exchange some of his Leschenault lands for land between Albany and Wilson's Inlet to the west, and land at the foot of what is now the Stirling Range. His descriptions, however, were so vague that Roe found them difficult to mark on the map. A month later, while still at Albany, he provided the Surveyor-General with a more precise description of the lands he wished to be reserved. They included 10,000 acres inland at Moorilup (later Plantagenet Location 12), 25,000 acres between White Island and Wilson's Inlet, and another 10,000 acres on the west side of the sound, extending to Torbay (later Plantagenet Location 33).[54] The first and last-mentioned grants became part of his final selection, as did his large harbour-facing town lot E1.

When news reached Perth that the Governor was selecting land so far south, it caused some disquiet, as it was feared that he was thinking of moving the capital from Perth to Albany. It is doubtful that Stirling ever seriously contemplated this, but as a naval man, and having now experienced the problems of the anchorages at Swan River, he undoubtedly saw the longer term importance of the harbour at King George's Sound. He was also trying to encourage more settlers to move into the recently acquired area, and selecting land himself would again provide a lead. It was also a place for the family to escape the summer heat which had proved so enervating the previous year.

Stirling's more cheerful attitude towards the future of the colony was amply repaid when, on 2 or 3 January 1832, his long-awaited Commission and the colony's

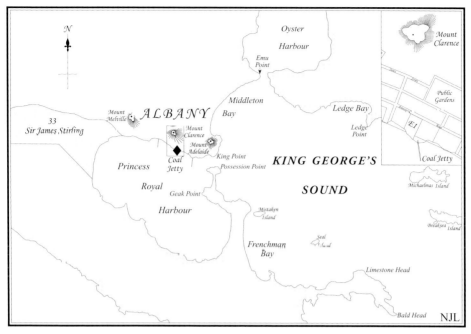

Stirling's early land choices in Albany

charter were placed in his hands. They had arrived at Fremantle direct from London with all the rest of the official and private mail, in the *Jolly Rambler* on 27 December, and then been sent on down to King George's Sound. How eagerly he would have scanned the large official documents and proudly read to Ellen the opening paragraph of his commission:

> William the Fourth, by the grace of God, of the United Kingdom of Great Britain and Ireland King, Defender of the faith, to our trusty and well-beloved JAMES STIRLING greeting. Know you that we, reposing especial trust and confidence in the prudence, courage and loyalty of you, the said JAMES STIRLING, of our especial grace…have thought fit to constitute and appoint you, the said JAMES STIRLING, to be our Governor and Commander-in-Chief in and over our territory called Western Australia, extending from Cape Londonderry in latitude 13° 44' from the Hartog's Island on the western coast in longitude 112° 52' to 129° degrees of east longitude, reckoning from the meridian of Greenwich; including all the islands adjacent in the Indian and southern oceans within the latitudes aforesaid, of 13° 44', and 35° 8' south, and between the longitudes aforesaid of 112° 52' to 129° east from the said meridian of Greenwich.[55]

The territory so designated exactly describes modern Western Australia, and although it excluded the Cocos Islands, which Stirling had hoped might be appended to his colony, it nevertheless encompassed a huge area. Swan River

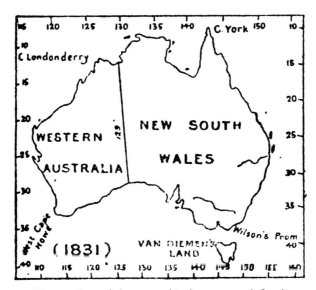

Western Australia's geographical extent, as defined
in Stirling's Commission received early January 1832

Colony to that time had just included lands south of the Swan—now Stirling was
responsible for Australia's entire western third.

His Commission not only conferred authority and delineated his powers as
Governor, it also authorised the appointment of councils to assist and advise him,
each of four persons with the quorum for decisions being set at himself plus two. An
Executive Council, authorised by the King, was to be in addition to a Legislative
Council empowered by Parliament through the Order-in-Council officially constituting the colony. The Legislative Council was to comprise the Governor, the Senior
Military Officer, the Colonial Secretary, the Surveyor-General and the Advocate-
General—exactly the same membership as the Executive Council. In an accompanying dispatch dated 28 April 1831, Lord Goderich took pains to explain the
distinction between the two councils. They were both necessary because 'the Royal
authority was not competent, without the aid of Parliament, to create a Legislature
except by popular representation, or to establish courts on lines that differed from
those of Westminster'.[56] But the Executive Council would convey assent, and do most
of the day-to-day business. Proceedings of both were to be kept separate.

Goderich's April dispatch also transmitted the change in the land regulations
which had been passed in England in March 1831. The whole land grant system,
which had been successively tightened since Stirling left England, had been
abandoned and replaced by the principle of sale. All Crown land was henceforth to
be sold at a minimum of 5 shillings per acre. The usual minimum acreage was to be
640 acres of rural land (though the Governor had discretion to allow smaller lots).
The only vestige of the grant system remaining was an allowance of £20 towards the
purchase of land for every married labourer introduced by settlers at their own

expense. All these changes were to be implemented immediately. Stirling was also told, at some length, that the additional civil servants he had appointed should be suspended, as they were not entitled to salary until such expenditure had been justified and approved in England. He was reminded to send more frequent dispatches, and to arrange as soon as possible for the return of the *Sulphur*, as the Admiralty had requested her recall.[57]

Stirling would have felt somewhat bemused by this avalanche of instructions after months of neglect. But on 5 January he began his replies, writing first a private letter to Hay in answer to his many questions. One of these had concerned the choice of the site of Perth, and it was in this letter that Stirling explained that he had chosen a site midway between the agricultural districts centred on Guildford and the commercial port at Fremantle. He then commented: 'It would be to assume the power of a Prophet to say at the commencement of a Colony where the Capital ought to be placed'.[58]

He went on to describe in detail the extent of the settlement, and concluded with his belief that the most desirable future course would be to increase settlement along the coast in order to encourage whaling, fishing, timber export and ship building. Nevertheless, he advised,

> it will still remain politick [sic] to afford every facility to those Capitalists who will invest money in Cattle, Horses and Stock, and as these can be kept nowhere to such advantage as in the Interior, I would recommend that a main or principal Route to it should be formed by making a Path from King George's Sound to Swan River and by establishing a Town about halfway from each place.

Concluding this private letter, he noted:

> I intend to employ the Colonial vessel which I purchased in anticipation of the *Sulphur*'s departure…in the determination of the important fact whether or not a great river exists in the Country to the Northward.[59]

There was still a strong belief in the existence of an inland sea!

Two days later, on 7 January 1832, Stirling signed the first of his official responses. His dispatch began with heartfelt thanks for his commission and the salary he had been granted, stating £800 p.a. was 'fully adequate under existing circumstances to all my reasonable desires'.[60] But given the strict instructions he had received regarding expenditure, Stirling spent the remainder of this dispatch justifying changes he had made to the previously approved civil establishment. He reported that he would suspend all payments to his civil establishment which had not been sanctioned, but added that his Government Residents were indispensable, and that he had asked them to continue their duties without salary until approval arrived. He argued that, as the colony covered such a 'great space of territory', a responsible person was necessary in each main location to keep the peace, regulate dealings with the natives and 'communicate the Orders and Instructions of Government'. He had chosen men predominantly from the services to fill these positions, knowing he could count on their loyalty to the Crown. The six Government Residents (each on an annual salary of £100) at that time were Dr Collie at King George's Sound, Captain Molloy at Augusta, Captain Byrne at York, Captain Ellis at Kelmscott, Captain Bannister at Fremantle and Captain Whitfield at Guildford.[61] When this dispatch reached England, a Colonial Office official annotated the margin, 'where are these places?'—for as yet there was no map.

As Dr Collie had originally been proposed as military surgeon for the expedition by Mr Hay of the Colonial Office, Stirling was sure his appointment as replacement Colonial Surgeon would be approved. An Acting Harbour Master, Daniel Scott, had been an essential appointment because Captain Currie,[62] the original incumbent, had been 'required in another office'. Currie had been made Auditor, Stirling explained, because his 'ability, intelligence and Integrity rendered him far more valuable to the public in that capacity than as Harbour Master'. (It also gave him a salary of £300 rather than £100.)[63] Stirling did not believe Currie's duties would conflict with the Commissary being sent out from England, as the latter would be more concerned with setting public expenditures 'on a more regular basis than hitherto'.

Another appointment Stirling had to justify was that of Registrar, an essential position when allocating grants, which he had first given to his cousin William Stirling and, after his death, to Richard Brown, the brother of the Colonial Secretary. Neither had received any salary and, as Brown had done an admirable job, Stirling would be sorry to lose him. But he had now been told that registration was the proper work of the Colonial Secretary. This, Stirling wryly answered, would be 'forthwith obeyed, as soon as the Secretary shall cease to act as Treasurer'.[64]

The major change in the Land Regulations would be implemented from the start of the year, but he noted that

> in the existing state of the Colony, I do not apprehend that any applications for purchase will be made. I anticipate however that eventually the new mode will yield a revenue for the Public Service, and will attract capital by affording a safer and more profitable investment for money than land could offer under the system of unpurchased grants.[65]

Interestingly, he believed that the new measures would be 'highly acceptable' to the settlers and that all outstanding matters connected to the grant scheme could be 'concluded by the 31st of March next'.[66] Reaction in Albany to the new land regulations was mild, for most of the small population already held grants and were thus unaffected. So when Stirling left King George's Sound at the end of January, he was totally unprepared for the howls of protest that he met on his return to Perth.

13

A Turning Point

1832

As HMS *Sulphur* was still on the mission to Van Diemen's Land, Stirling and his party travelled back to Fremantle in the *Ellen*. The newly completed Round Gaol at the top of Arthur's Head stood out like a beacon, an irony probably not lost on Stirling in this, the first convict-free colony. The family transferred into a pinnace for the long row back to Perth against the morning easterlies, arriving in the capital on 1 February.[1] Stirling found the mood in the township and its surrounds had changed. The settlement was facing real food shortages. Most people were now more settled and better pleased with the land, but they were extremely worried that their stores and savings might not last until the next harvest. As one of the wealthier settlers on the Canning reported:

> …indeed at the present time everything sells at the most extravagant price there having been no arrivals save the *Egyptian* and a small ship from the Cape for these six months…We are daily expecting two or three ships from Van Diemen's Land with supplies, but if these disappoint us and nothing else comes in, we shall be badly off for the next 12 months.[2]

Stirling was naturally worried, but he believed the *Sulphur* would soon return to relieve the situation. In the meantime he had to carry out his instructions. Accordingly, on 6 February he called a first meeting of the Legislative Council, which comprised himself as Governor, Captain Irwin as Senior Military Officer, Peter Brown as Colonial Secretary and William Mackie as Advocate-General. The Surveyor-General, John Septimus Roe, missed this inaugural meeting as he had been left at King George's Sound to complete his surveys. On his own initiative, Stirling also added Mark Currie to the list as Clerk of Council, as he 'could not find within the colony a Person better calculated than the gentleman who now fills it'.[3]

Once assembled in the Council Chambers (a room in the Governor's house[4]), Stirling had his commission as Governor and the accompanying Royal Instructions read out loud and, as directed, asked each member in turn to take the solemn 'oaths of allegiance' in which they swore that they 'did from their hearts abhor, detest and abjure the damnable doctrine that excommunicated Princes could be deposed or murdered by their subjects'.[5]

One of the first bills the Governor wished to put before his Council was an ordinance to establish a Court of Civil Judicature, to be presided over by a Commissioner. No new criminal court was established, but the Courts of Petty Sessions and Quarter Sessions, chaired by Mackie, were approved to continue as before. Stirling also wanted to establish a Commission of Peace, in order to regularise the position of the Justices of the Peace and his constables. He thus suggested that the Commissioners be those he had already made Justices, because they were either personally known to him or had come with personal recommendations testifying their suitability. Council then duly approved the appointment of Commissioners William Mackie (Chair), George Leake, Edward Barrett Lennard, Thomas Bannister, Henry Bull, the Reverend J. B. Wittenoom, Thomas Peel, William Tanner, W. L. Brockman, T. T. Ellis, Captain J. Molloy and Francis H. Byrne.[6] The first Legislative Council meeting then adjourned, but the Executive Council, comprising the same members, was to meet again the following day.

On 7 February Stirling informed his councillors that he had decided to live at Guildford and commute, as the old Government House was in such a state of disrepair it was unsuitable for residential purposes, but it would provide a suitable building for council meetings.[7] His cottage at Woodbridge had been enlarged, and as the Colonial Secretary only lived 1 or 2 miles downriver, business could be transacted as normal. Stirling then had extracts from his various dispatches read to the councillors and asked them to examine the expenses of the colony for discussion at the next meeting, set for the 11th. This would be a critical meeting, for many men who had gained government employment the previous year had been suspended and councillors were being strongly lobbied to press their claims. But Stirling had pared his civil establishment down as far as he could, and now set before his councillors a table of the actual costs of running the civil establishment—with salaries against names—to compare with the estimates prepared in England, and stressed the need for the strictest economy.[8] When the Council reconvened, members agreed that the expenditures Stirling had itemised could be reduced no further. They also agreed that certain essential positions currently earning no salary, such as the six Government Residents and the Gaol Superintendent at Fremantle, should be awarded £100 per annum in the future, as their services were 'absolutely necessary'. Stirling then asked his Council to approve the appointment of an Auditor, a position which had not been included in the estimates. He argued that the position was vital, as someone was needed to value land improvements and verify the regularity of all assignments of land and other Crown property. When Council agreed, Stirling suggested that Currie be appointed to the position on a salary of £300 per annum. Again they agreed, noting that Currie was already giving his services as Clerk to Council without pay. The next meeting was set for three days' time, when the rules to govern the courts would be considered.

Stirling had every reason to be pleased with his Executive Council, as they had so far agreed with every proposition placed before them, as well as providing the authentication and back-up he had so desperately missed in the preceding two and a half years. And he needed support, for settlers were becoming increasingly critical

as weeks passed without sight of a ship. Many blamed the drying up of immigration on the new land regulations. Now that the incentive of free land grants in return for invested capital had gone, they felt there was no incentive for British emigrants to travel half way round the world to Swan River, even if it was convict-free. Could they not, at far less cost, emigrate to Canada or the United States?[9]

Stirling was besieged by anxious people on every hand. What could be done to revive their fortunes? Could the colony continue? Would more ships arrive? In this context it was not surprising that at the next Council meeting, on 14 February, members unanimously agreed that the small colonial vessel *Ellen* should be retained when the *Sulphur* returned to England; although a major expenditure, a ship was an essential means of communication with the outposts and the outside world. One saving that was agreed to by all was the lease of the government farm at York (and most of the government livestock) to Messrs Bland and Trimmer. Rules Stirling had drafted to regulate the Civil Court were then put before councillors for discussion at the next meeting, and Stirling's choice of G. F. Moore as its Commissioner was approved.

There was much to report therefore when Stirling sent his next dispatch to London. It was signed on 14 February, the same day as his meeting, and Stirling informed the Colonial Secretary, Lord Goderich, that 'The reduction of the Civil Establishment to the scale contained in the Estimate submitted to Parliament last year is now in progress and will be effectually completed in the course of the present month'.[10] But progress had been at a cost. Even the London-appointed Commissary, Deputy Assistant Commissary John Lewis, who had arrived on the *Egyptian*, was asking to be relieved after less than two months in office. He had written to his superiors on 8 February complaining about the high price of supplies and his excessive workload,[11] and a few weeks later was suspended suffering mental derangement. All the civil officers were under pressure, most combining long hours in meetings with the many tasks associated with establishing farms and raising foodstuffs. Most of them belonged to the Agricultural Society, which had been formed on 28 May 1831 to share knowledge and give voice to common concerns. Stirling had agreed to become its patron and was receptive when representatives came to see him early in February 1832. They told him that members of the Agricultural Society had decided at a meeting in Perth that the only solution to their problems was to petition the Governor to place their concerns before the Home Government. These were stated in a memorial which was handed to Stirling, requesting:

> 1st that a Bank may be established upon the principal of the Lombard Bank at the Cape of Good Hope
> 2nd that agricultural labourers may be sent out
> 3rd that Govt. will construct roads & bridge & erect Churches and Prisons
> 4th that the Military force may be increased.[12]

Stirling enclosed this petition with his own dispatch of 14 February, stating:

> I have…the Honour to lay before your Lordship a Memorial which has been presented to me from a large body composed of the most intelligent and industrious of His Majesty's subjects in this colony…I feel persuaded that if Your Lordship could have witnessed the perseverance and patience, the courage and fortitude which have been brought into operation by the private individuals who have been concerned with the Establishment of this Settlement, which has been principally effected by the employment of private capital, your Lordship would be much disposed to grant to such persons at this moment of difficulty the assistance which I am of opinion they much need.[13]

By mid-February things were getting worse. John Okey Davis, farming on the Canning, commented in a letter home that

> Flour and biscuit…nearly all gone, no rice, and two ships that were expected from Van Diemen's Land with supplies so long over due that fears are entertained that either they are lost or gone to some other port. People talk of discharging their labourers. I am afraid we shall have some sad work, for men will steal rather than starve; this is a serious matter.[14]

Not only unemployed labourers were stealing food. The natives were feeling the shortages just as acutely, and becoming more daring in their raids on the homes and farms of settlers. The settlers' reactions were mixed, for some treated them as dangerous savages to be fought off, whilst others thought of them more as children. The same letter writer echoed the sentiments of many when describing them in the following terms:

> Now for the natives, here we have nature in its pure unadorned state…They are probably the furthest removed from civilization of any human creatures on the globe, for they have neither religion, laws or government, houses nor clothing, none worthy of the name, and yet they do not appear stupid. It seems to me that their principal mental deficiency is total absence of what we call taste, or the capability of perceiving what is beautiful…They are, in common with all savage tribes, inveterate thieves, but what is rather singular exhibit no propensity to drink strong liquors.[15]

The latter would, of course, change with time. But liquor as well as food was still in extremely short supply. As George Fletcher Moore commented in his diary on 4 March 1832, 'Prices have risen to a very serious height just now, and there is consequently a great outcry in the Colony'.[16] The *Sulphur* was still expected daily, but lack of supplies meant the young lawyer had to breakfast on bread alone (ground from home-grown grain and baked by himself) without the solace of 'butter, milk or eggs'.[17] The Governor's morning repast was probably similar, though the Government House pantry might still have had some stores of English preserves for his bread.

A few days later John Morgan, the Colonial Storekeeper, wrote to Under-Secretary Hay informing him that

> The colony is at this moment in my opinion in a state perilous in the extreme...At this moment there is not more than <u>five tons</u> of flour in the Colony...should no other vessels arrive during the next fourteen days, the people will generally be in a state of absolute starvation.

Morgan had been appointed Storekeeper prior to departure from England, but since his arrival he had been left, very much to his displeasure, guarding stores on Garden Island. He had quarrelled with Stirling over the mode of keeping accounts, complaining to Hay that:

> the system of accounts alluded to, was the Naval manner of keeping them,—of which, of course, I knew nothing—I was perfectly acquainted with the mercantile, and the Commissariat partly, but I confess I did not know, instanter, a Purser's duty...[which] gave, I have since had reason to know, very great offence.[18]

Stirling's later response, when queried by Hay, hardly bore out this last belief.

> Mr Morgan...is, I fully believe, a very honest servant to the public and has afforded me satisfaction in the discharge of his duties as Storekeeper although at first in consequence of his not keeping his accounts according to my instructions, I was under the necessity of speaking very decidedly to him...[19]

Morgan was an inveterate letter-writer and, despite his isolation, maintained close contacts with those on the mainland. He was worried about the increasing number of clashes between settlers and the original inhabitants, commenting in March 1832 that:

> The Natives are rather more troublesome than they were...blood for blood with them appears to be the order of the day. The driver of a bullock team and a boy,— going over the mountains in January last to York, were attack'd by them, apparently without any cause, the boy was killed most inhumanly but the Man, altho' severely wounded, escaped...[20]

Stirling was also very concerned about deteriorating relations, raising the matter, among other subjects, in one of the two dispatches he signed on 2 April.[21]

Annoyance to the settlers of a very serious description proceeds from the depredations of the natives on property, and the murders which they commit from time to time…It is true that greater alarm than injury is occasioned by this species of hostility, but it is a great drawback, for…even with every precaution, outrages can neither be in all cases prevented nor punished.

I have endeavoured to open up amicable communication with the tribes in this district, but hitherto with little success. I would wish to persuade them that it is safer and better to obtain those things they desire by free gift on our part, than to take them by force, but I am still unsuccessful in this endeavour. At King George's Sound where I found a good understanding established, I have caused it to be preserved and cultivated, and there the natives confide in and in fact live very much with the Europeans. In the Swan River District they sometimes meet us in amity and perhaps on the following day they commit a robbery or murder.[22]

He seemed genuinely at a loss to explain their behaviour, even though he had linked it to 'things they desired'—namely food. The small settlement at King George's Sound, where good relations had been maintained, was never in as dire need of food as at Swan River, where settlers had stopped the handouts hitherto made to natives calling at their doors, with predictable results. In February Stirling had asked his Executive Council for a ruling on the type of support that could be offered to the indigenous people, but they had shown little sympathy, agreeing that bread alone should be issued and only on the certificate of the District Magistrate.[23] Whilst Stirling tried to repress settlers' retaliatory actions, he saw his primary duty as protecting the lives and property of British subjects. Where he differed from earlier Australian Governors, and most leading colonists, was his firm belief that such protection should be a civil, and not a military matter. This belief would lead him into headlong clashes with his councillors in future years. At this stage, however, he had yet to appoint his civilian 'protectors'.

The two April 1832 dispatches are important, as Stirling outlined both the progress and the obstacles that he saw confronting the colony. The first was fairly short, informing the Colonial Office, as delicately as possible, that Commissary Lewis's appointment had been a complete failure. Charge of public monies was still in the hands of the Acting Treasurer (the Colonial Secretary, Peter Brown) and stores were still maintained by the Colonial Storekeeper (Morgan) and assistants. He suggested that expense could be cut by abolishing Morgan's department and transferring all existing government stores to the Military Commissariat. He then recommended that 'the present storekeeper be provided with another appointment', probably hoping that this well-connected complainant would be transferred to another colony.[24]

The second dispatch, also signed on 2 April, adopted a more serious tone. Hitherto, Stirling observed, the new colony 'may be considered to have been an experimental occupation of a remote and wild country…but the measures adopted…have impressed on the enterprise the character of permanency'.[25]

Since Stirling's day many writers have referred to the settlement of the Swan River Colony as an 'Experiment in Colonisation' (or the Private Enterprise experiment),[26] but few have realised that Stirling himself coined the phrase:

> The plan which was adopted in the formation of this Settlement may be viewed as an experiment in colonisation on a new principle…To the settlers generally was confided the charge of advancing and in fact of making the Settlement; the local government being established for the sole purpose of guarding and protecting them…But so small a proportion of the community being fit for the task which they had undertaken, it has been only partially successful…I have remarked thus on the plan of colonisation as it throws much light on the condition of the settlement, and may in some degree account for the contradictory reports which have been spread respecting it.[27]

The dispatch continued with a description of the territory explored to that time, which once again revealed Stirling's sound grasp of geology, and details of the number and distribution of the population—and their principal pursuits. This, he knew, would be of greatest interest to the authorities and would, in conjunction with a map Roe's department had just completed, highlight the scattered nature of his province and the consequent difficulties of administration.[28] He was not to know that it would also provide ammunition for the colonial reformer, Edward Wakefield.[29]

> The whole population of the Colony at the present time [April 1832] may be considered distributed according to the subjoined scale, the aboriginal tribes being pretty equally spread over the whole surface of the country on the conjectural average of one to each square mile.

in Perth	360
in Guildford	120
in Fremantle	400
at Garden Island	12
at Rottnest	25
at Clarence	5
at the Murray	30
at York	30
detached at stations on the Swan	300
ditto on the Canning	75
at Kelmscott	10
at King George's Sound	60
at Augusta	70
TOTAL	**1,497**

From this table it may be collected that a large proportion of persons are resident in towns. Their exertions have been applied more particularly to building, trade and mechanical arts, while the residents in the country have generally followed agricultural and pastoral pursuits.[30]

This account preceded the detailed *Return of the Population of Western Australia* dated 1 July 1832,[31] which Stirling later delivered to the Colonial Office, and indicates that rough returns reached Stirling from the various districts *before* being compiled and fair-copied by the clerks. The dispatch continued with estimates of the total value of public and private investments made since arrival:

> In Fremantle there are computed to be buildings to the amount of £15,000, in Perth about £10,000, in the smaller towns and detached stations similar investments to the amount of £15,000 more. The gross amount laid out in the improvement of the land may be stated at £20,000 and the value of the cattle, horses and sheep actually in possession £10,000. The goods in the hands of traders may be worth £30,000 and the amount of outlay incurred in passage money, in fruitless or unproductive expenses on the part of individuals, not classed in the above, may be estimated at £100,000 making a total private expenditure in the formation of the colony up to the present time of £200,000.

With this as background (as well as a detailed survey of the productive potential of the lands explored to date), Stirling entered an earnest plea for the colonists:

> …it is incumbent on me to state to your Lordship that I consider further assistance from His Majesty's Government is requisite for securing a speedy and successful issue to the experiment which has been attempted here…I fear that the plan of colonisation which has been adopted will not produce a satisfactory or brilliant result without the introduction of more people, and the use of more capital…

But he concluded optimistically, stating

> I feel fully convinced…there is no colony under the Crown, which appears to hold out to emigrants, whether stockmen or capitalists, greater attractions in agricultural, pastoral or commercial pursuits…its south western portion alone seems to be not inferior in extent, soil, climate and position, to the Spanish peninsula and consequently not incapable of containing a great and powerful colony.[32]

But even as he dictated these words, Stirling had doubts as to whether the British Government would provide the assistance the colony needed. Just a week or so earlier he had submitted to his Executive Council a proposal that he return to England to plead their cause. At this 20 March meeting his councillors 'were generally of the opinion that it would be highly desirable', though Mr Brown and Mr Mackie added 'providing Captain Irwin remained in charge of the Government'.[33] Unfortunately, Irwin had just received approval for leave to return to England, where he was hoping to marry, so he was not enthusiastic. Moreover, councillors felt that leading settlers should be consulted about the proposal, and that if there was any opposition 'it would not be advisable for the Governor to leave the Colony'.[34] A week later Stirling reported that he had had 'conversations with some of the most influential agriculturalists…[who] appeared adverse to his taking such a step', and in consequence he had decided to remain. He also reported discussions 'with various of the respectable settlers upon the subject of affording the deserving and active part of them relief or assistance'[35] which he would raise at their next meeting.

Stirling knew the food shortages and high prices that were beleaguering settlers would largely be relieved when the *Sulphur* returned with supplies. She had to be back soon; after all, she had been gone since early November. Word had arrived from Van Diemen's Land that she had been delayed by a lack of wheat on that market,[36] but that she did expect to return with a full cargo. Stirling had also taken the precaution of sending the small colonial schooner *Ellen* to Hobart to purchase even further supplies,[37] so the situation had to be relieved shortly. But once introduced, how were these supplies to be distributed so that the expense of obtaining them could be offset? The settlers had no money, and neither had the many unemployed labourers. And the British Treasury could well refuse to honour Bills for more supplies—especially as the colony was to have been established at minimal expense. So how could the expected stores be distributed in a way that would minimise the need for further aid? Stirling had pondered the problem since he had sent the *Sulphur* on her mission, and now, after discussions with the leading agriculturalists, he had had an idea.[38]

Acres under cultivation in the colony were still very limited, and settlers needed an incentive, as well as seed, to extend their efforts. If he could provide them with supplies, including seed, on a credit system based on the amount of land they had prepared for grain growing, it might work. Repayment could be made in grain after the next harvest, at a fixed price per bushel, which would give the settlers incentive to extend cultivation and at the same time replenish the Government's stores for the following year. Moreover, in view of the agriculturalists' common concern about the lack of infrastructure, roads, jetties, bridges and the like, the scheme could be extended to the unemployed. Stores could be issued as wages, and there were many hungry men with families who would gladly labour in return for food. So some of the *Sulphur*'s supplies could be used in this way for the good of the entire community.

The plan was put to the Executive Council at its meeting on 3 April, and generally approved. It was agreed to price the *Sulphur*'s supplies at the lowest that would repay the Government without a profit—which Stirling estimated would be £4 credit for every acre cleared and sown, repayment to be set at a 15 shillings per bushel.[39] A Public Notice was issued with the new terms[40] and proved very popular, so much so that at the Executive Council meeting on 22 June Stirling reported 'applications from various individuals had been received to the extent, in land proposed for wheat, of about 400 acres', and suggested that in view of this unexpectedly large response the credit offered to settlers should be reduced to £2 10s per acre.[41] His councillors agreed, but after vociferous protest from the settlers this was rescinded in favour of the original £4 credit limit.[42] Settlers simply could not take such a cut. Stirling had already raised fees and licences and placed an ad valorum tax on spirits in May[43] to raise revenue. Colonists had responded by raising a petition signed by 144 individuals begging him to rescind the tax, based on several grounds but principally because 'no Englishman by British constitution should be taxed unless by his consent through representation', and that labouring persons 'on whom duties fell most heavily' were scarcely able to find employment sufficient to subsist let alone pay taxes.[44] Stirling's reaction was to promise to raise the matter with authorities, but the taxes had remained.

With his plan for the distribution of supplies in place, Stirling waited even more impatiently than his people for the *Sulphur*'s arrival. Dr Collie, back in Albany, reported that the *Sulphur* had arrived there on 5 May and was to call at Augusta before going on to the Swan, where it finally arrived on 4 June. Stirling's displeasure at Captain Dance's dalliance would have been tempered by the necessity of seeing the stores safely housed and accounted for, and in this he was assisted by Captain Irwin and his troops. Almost immediately distribution began, but although the *Sulphur* had introduced grain and other stores, including implements and clothing, it had been unable to obtain the desired quantities of salt meat—still a staple in rations for indentured servants. Both salt and fresh meat were in short supply, which made settlers all the more annoyed with native attacks on their livestock. G. F. Moore, who lost his pigs to the natives, attended a public meeting in Guildford on 26 June, where 'strong resolutions were entered into expressive of the opinion that settlers must abandon the colony, if they be not protected in their property'. Masters, unable to supply rations they had promised by contract, were having to put off their labourers, which reduced their own production but also added to the numbers dependent on handouts from the store. Something had to be done. Ever since the Masters and Servants Act had come into force, all indentured servants had been entitled to a ration of rum, but given the masters' difficulties the Council now felt it necessary to rescind the grog allowance. But while grog could be dispensed with, meat could not. So Stirling was advised to negotiate with the Captain of the recently arrived *Cornwallis* to bring some 800 barrels of pork from Mauritius.[45]

The departure of the *Cornwallis* gave Stirling a long-awaited opportunity to send dispatches. Dispatch 13, signed on 28 June, was a very lengthy official report on the personnel and duties of each department in his civil service. It clearly indicates the difficulty he had in attracting and keeping suitable people, for time and again he had to report replacing individuals who had resigned through 'the inadequacy of the salary to maintain them'. Nevertheless, he could report that the civil establishment was now more organised, operating through eight departments, viz. those of the Secretary, the Treasurer, the Surveyor-General, the Storekeeper, the Harbour Master, the Registrar and Auditor, the Civil Engineer and the Establishment for keeping the Peace (which included Government Residents). In the case of the Department of the Civil Engineer, for example, he noted that since receiving his instructions to cut expenses to a minimum, Reveley's two assistants had been dispensed with, and the Chief Engineer's salary cut by half—and he feared his resignation.[46] Yet this small department had accomplished an impressive list of public works.

A schedule listing all the major public works that had been completed to the end of March 1832 had been prepared by this same department for transmission to England.[47] It included the temporary Government House at Perth completed by government workmen in December 1830, but now used as council chambers and in need of repair to roof and floors; four outhouses attached to the above, one used as a dispensary for the Colonial Surgeon; five public offices at Perth completed December 1830 by contract for the sum of £500; the Colonial Secretary's present office by purchase £200; a temporary Harbour Master's office at Fremantle completed November 1829 by contract; the church at Perth completed December 1829 by government workmen and in need of repairs to roof and floors; the Commissary's office completed May 1832 by government workmen; Military Hospital at Perth, July 1831, built by contract £500 and in need of a kitchen; a market house and cattle pens at Perth, November 1831, erected by government workmen; a jetty at Perth, December 1829, by government workmen; fencing of the burial ground at Perth £70; a canal at the island above Perth in 1831, by contract £330; a gaol at Fremantle completed January 1831 by contract for £1,500 (now known as the Round House); and then the bush roads, from Fremantle to Perth and through to Guildford and the head of the Swan, and from Perth to Kelmscott and through to Guildford.[48] (The lists also covered construction at the various outposts.)

In a separate dispatch signed also on 28 June, Stirling noted that, after all the cuts, his civil establishment in 1832 would cost only £440 more than the amount that had been approved for 1831.[49] It was a considerable achievement. While readying these dispatches for transmission Stirling also penned a short private note to Hay, in which he admitted 'The settlement of a new Colony is a more difficult operation for all concerned in it, than I calculated when I embarked on it'.[50]

He had had enough, and desperately wished to return to his naval career, but he was aware that the Colonial Office would only sanction him leaving his post without permission if there was evidence of exceptional circumstances. At the Council meeting on 29 June he again raised the question of representing the plight of the colony in person to the Home Government. The Council now felt that those who had previously been adverse to him leaving had 'become the most strenuous advisers of the measure'. But Captain Irwin, Stirling's second-in-command, would first have to be persuaded to forsake his longed for and already approved leave to marry in England.[51] As Stirling later informed Governor Arthur, 'at my earnest desire [he] has given up the prosecution of his private views and will become my successor in this Government'.[52]

At the meeting on 29 June, Stirling had assured his councillors that the *Sulphur* would remain in the colony during his absence.[53] But he subsequently changed his mind. At the next meeting, he told them that, on further consideration, he believed

> that great advantage would be derived by his going in the *Sulphur* to the Cape, as his arrival in England would be much accelerated thereby, and an opportunity would be afforded of her returning with supplies for the future use of the Troops and Settlement.[54]

He wanted Council's opinion. Each member spoke, as usual in designated rank order: Captain Irwin agreed, but Colonial Secretary Brown demurred, believing 'the *Sulphur*'s departure from the Colony would be very seriously felt'. Roe agreed, pointing out the benefit of additional supplies from the Cape. Mackie also agreed, believing that *Sulphur* could expedite the Governor's speedy arrival in England—so Stirling had a majority decision. A Public Notice was issued on 2 July announcing the Governor's intention to proceed to England for the purpose of promoting and forwarding the interests of the colony.[55]

Whether Stirling told his councillors that he would need evidence of very strong public support for his return is not known—it was certainly not minuted. But over the next few days public meetings were held, and petitions were drawn up and signed by large numbers of colonists, begging the Governor to return to plead their cause, as well as specifying the assistance they hoped would be forthcoming. At a public meeting in Perth on 2 July, a large proportion of the colony's landed 'gentry' unanimously passed a resolution:

> to request that the Governor would proceed to England as our representative, to state and explain to the Home Government many points which could best be represented in viva voce communication.[56]

They also presented Stirling with a petition stating that they could no longer conceal their alarm 'at the critical situation to which this Colony is now reduced'. They had 'seen with great disappointment a course of policy lately adopted which has given a death blow to their hopes'. They had 'looked for encouragement to Emigrants, but find a high price fixed upon the Land', and they were

> convinced that these harsh and impolitic measures would at once give place to more liberal and judicious ones if those who have the management of the affairs of this Colony at Home were enabled thoroughly to understand its true

situation…[which] cannot be so satisfactorily accomplished by written communication as by the personal presence of some representative on our behalf.

And they went on to beg Stirling to become that representative, concluding:

Your Petitioners humbly hope that the Extreme urgency of the case may appear to Your Excellency a sufficient justification for their making so unprecedented and so troublesome a request…[57]

On 3 July twenty-two members of the Agricultural Society lent their unanimous support,[58] while the ordinary townsfolk and tradesmen also joined the chorus, some forty-eight of them signing a memorial which applauded 'the sacrifice of domestic comfort Your Excellency is about to make for the welfare, or rather the salvation of the Colony'.[59] And there were more, from both groups and individuals. Collie, still in Albany, informed his brother some weeks later that 'the greatest excitement' prevailed in the colony at the 'grand step our Governor has taken from terra incognita to the public offices of Downing Street'.[60] Stirling now had the 'strong evidence' to justify his return to England. Clearly he wanted to go, and had engineered the decision, but it is also true that he fervently believed that only through personal intervention could 'his' colony's future be assured.

As his unauthorised return would raise many questions in the minds of Colonial Office staff, Stirling felt it was imperative to have thorough records of all his transactions, public and private, to put before them. Brown and Roe were therefore given instructions to prepare appropriate documents and Stirling, feeling his own land selections were not clear, wrote to Roe to clarify matters. On 14 July he forwarded a memorandum stating that his land claim included the 4,000-acre Woodbridge grant on the Swan, the 2,240 acres of Garden Island, 15,000 acres at Moorilup, 20,000 acres at Nornalup, 20,000 acres on the west side of Wilson's Inlet, 25,000 acres from Princess Royal Harbour west to Torbay, and 50,000 acres at a place to be determined.[61] (He had by now given back his reserved land near Toodyay.) He added that, as he was 'desirous of erecting a house near to Fremantle', he wished 5 acres of land on the north side of Arthur's Head to be reserved for him, subject to resumption if needed for fortifications.[62] Stirling hoped that the Colonial Office would approve of his change in land grant plans, as he had been forced to allocate some of his 100,000-acre reservation to the north side of Geographe Bay to other settlers, principally Colonel Peter Augustus Latour.[63] But in case the 'swap' was not approved, he sent another memorandum to Roe on the same day, reserving all the west coast land from Cape Leeuwin to the south side of Geographe Bay (excepting the township of Augusta).[64]

Stirling's land dealings in the colony have been severely criticised. He has been charged with 'grabbing the best land'[65] and making 'only one selection during his first eight years in the colony which was not subsequently cancelled'.[66] It is therefore worth noting that this initial choice of land to replace the original 100,000 acres bore a close resemblance to his final allocations, for the latter included the land he referred to at Princess Royal Harbour, Moorilup, South Geographe Bay and, of course, Woodbridge, Garden Island and part of Arthur's Head. In 1832 much land was still unsurveyed and many settlers were changing their selections, or leaving the remainder of their entitlements as unspecified 'interior'. But Stirling had already made up his mind to take land in the south which would not conflict with the needs of the majority of small investors among his colonists.

A week after writing to Roe about his own land, Stirling addressed him again. He now knew his brother-in-law, Sir James Home, was not going to join them (because of ill-health),[67] so he arranged the transfer of Home's grant at Spring Park on the Swan, telling Roe on 21 July that the 2,666-acre grant was to go to Richard Lewis.[68] Whether any money changed hands over this transfer is unclear, and subsequent events suggest it did not. With his land business now relatively tidy, Stirling turned his attention to ensuring Ellen's comfort, for she was now six months pregnant and would deliver on the voyage home. Even that prospect, however, would not have dampened her excitement at the chance to see the faces and places she had missed so dreadfully over the past three years. Andrew, now 8, could remember little of his English family while 3-year-old Frederick had been born on the *Parmelia*, and so had never met his grandparents.

On 18 July Stirling had written to Dance, Commander of HMS *Sulphur*, informing him that he would no longer be taking Captain Irwin and others back to England, as earlier instructed, but that instead a passage would be required for himself and family to the Cape of Good Hope.[69] He also told Dance that the *Sulphur* would then return to the colony with further supplies.[70] Dance was not happy. He had been preparing for a return to England, and now his instructions had changed. As he informed Stirling on 21 July, he was still unloading provisions (brought in on 4 June) and so would not be ready to depart until at least the end of the month. Stirling moved down to Fremantle with his family on 24 July for the expected embarkation, and sent a note informing Dance of his arrival. To his utter disbelief, Dance chose to ignore the note. At 9 p.m. that evening Stirling wrote again:

> Sir, I am informed, by the Gentleman who presented my letter of this Evening to you, that you have quitted Fremantle without transmitting any acknowledgment or reply. The inattention to my urgent representation on the necessity of the *Sulphur*'s immediate departure which this proceeding displays on your part, puts me under the necessity of addressing you again on this subject…

There followed a blasting, reminding Dance of the number of times he had been requested to have *Sulphur* ready for sea, and of the absolute necessity of an early importation of food supplies from the Cape. But far from agreeing to an immediate departure, Dance wrote back claiming his wife was in too debilitated a state to be moved, and that he 'must decline removing from this anchorage until the medical men are of the opinion that all risk of life...is at an end'.[71] Stirling's reply made no mention of Mrs Dance's illness, but simply reiterated the utmost urgency of his departure.[72] Called to explain this at a later date, Stirling replied that Mrs Dance had had the offer of the assistance of the Colonial Surgeon, a guard of soldiers and the attention of Mrs Brown and the other ladies of the colony. Moreover, he wryly concluded:

> if illness on the part of the Captain's lady be an admissible reason for delaying a King's Ship when required to proceed on service I apprehend considerable inconvenience would be the result.[73]

In this later correspondence Stirling also revealed that Dance had been un-cooperative from the start. The Colonial Secretary had tried to organise proper accommodation for the Stirlings early in July, but Dance had informed him that 'the Cabins for Mrs Stirling and the Governor were to be abreast of the mainmast'. The Governor had replied 'that his rank as a Naval Officer, & as a Governor of the Colony, would not allow his Family & himself being placed amongst the Ship's Company of the Ship'.[74] This was a justifiable reaction, for in naval terms it was an insult to place a superior officer abreast or behind the mast, and Stirling well outranked Dance. On 26 July Stirling had informed Dance that he would mess in the Gun Room with the other officers, and not at the Captain's table.[75] Dance protested, aware of the slight this entailed but more concerned, at least in writing, with the outlays he had made on suitable provisions for the Captain's table. This, in fact, remained a contentious point for over a year.

In answer to yet another query from the Colonial Secretary as to a departure date, Dance finally informed Stirling on 6 August that he planned to leave on the 11th. Mrs Stirling and family embarked on the 7th, but Stirling was detained in Perth that day by an Executive Council meeting which decided upon the list of supplies the *Sulphur* should bring back from the Cape. A large party then accompanied Stirling downriver to Fremantle. According to the log of the *Sulphur*, he embarked on 10 August for departure the following day, but squalls and heavy rain forced the *Sulphur* to put back, delaying actual departure until the 12th.[76] Stormy weather at the outset was a portent for the icy relations between Captain and Governor during the forty-four-day voyage to the Cape.

Not everyone had been pleased to see the Governor leave. Richard Morrell, a settler at Fremantle, wrote to friends on 8 August 1832: 'I do not know what you will think of a Governor leaving a colony when distress is likely to appear'.[77] Morrell also complained about the *Sulphur*:

> There was £24000 voted by Parliament some time ago for the use of the Colony, and we are now told that there has been £21000 deducted for the use of the

Sulphur…she has in <u>three years</u> performed <u>one voyage to Hobart Town</u> [sic] this is what £21,000 is deducted for, she was nine months away, and the rest of the time she lay at Garden Island…she is no use at all, so we have petitioned the Governor to let her go home.[78]

He was not the only one to feel aggrieved about the expenses and performance of the *Sulphur*. Stirling had been presented with a petition signed by 213 people in July requesting that the *Sulphur* be removed to save the £7,000 spent annually on her 'disbursement'.[79] But other colonists badly wanted the *Sulphur* to return from the Cape with additional supplies, which is why Stirling initially had booked a passage for his family only to that port.

Although there was no communication at all between the Governor and Commander during the voyage, Stirling could discuss matters in the Gun Room mess with two people he had learned to value highly. These were Lieutenant William Preston, who had left the *Ellen* to take his place as first officer of the *Sulphur*, and Captain Mark Currie who, with his family, was accompanying the Stirlings to England. But neither of these men could share James' real apprehension of rebuke for the step he had taken in leaving the colony without official

Richard Morrell, who drew this famous picture of Fremantle, was one of the few who were not pleased with the Governor's return to England to seek aid for the colonists

Richard Morrell. *View of Fremantle, Western Australia, from Church Hill, East of the town August 1832.*

Pen, ink and watercolour. 21 × 32.5cm.

Collection, Art Gallery of Western Australia

permission. Much of his time was spent, therefore, in crafting an explanation to the Colonial Office which he signed on 20 September, a week before arriving at the Cape. After outlining the desperate situation in the colony, Stirling stated:

> In a conversation which I had with some of the leading Settlers in the latter part of May, I was respectfully solicited to adopt certain changes in the conduct of the Government regarding the increase of Public Expenditure, the granting of lands, and the repeal of the duty on Spirits…[which] I was under the necessity of declining as a serious departure from the line of policy which had been laid down, but I stated my readiness to convey to your Lordship such representations regarding the real state of the Settlement as would enable your Lordship to judge the best course to be pursued…The difficulty of making arrangements of the kind by correspondence being suggested, I was asked whether I would undertake to represent in person to His Majesty's Government the state of the Colony and advocate its cause. I replied that it would not be proper for me to quit the Colony unless it were recommended by the concurrent wishes of the Settlers at large…Having brought the question…before my Executive Council on the 29th of June…it was the unanimous opinion of the Members that the measure proposed wou'd afford satisfaction to the Community…I determined upon its adoption and issued a declaration to that effect.

He added that a subsequent public reception by 'all classes of the people' had convinced him that his mission was necessary to restore confidence in the community and in the 'liberality of His Majesty's Government'.[80] Clearly his dispatch somewhat distorts the facts, as this account implies the settlers initiated his return, whilst Executive Council minutes show that it was initially suggested by Stirling. Nevertheless, there is little doubt that a majority of colonists felt it was the only solution to their difficulties. From later correspondence, it is also clear that Stirling had assured many that he would be able to convince the home authorities to accede to their most urgent requests.

Sulphur reached Simon's Bay, Cape Town on 27 September 1832. Leaving the heavily pregnant Ellen on board with the children, Stirling made the trip into town to report their arrival to the Governor, Sir G. L. Cole, and alert him to the colony's urgent need for supplies. He also contacted Commander Warren, the Admiralty's Chief of Staff at that Station, to ascertain the availability of ships for the continuance of his journey, and was appalled to learn that none were scheduled for return within the next month. Speed was of the essence if he was to plead the colony's cause adequately, so he believed he had no option than to plead with Dance to take them on to England (despite his earlier emphasis on the need to get supplies back to the colony). He wrote a polite note to Dance with his request on 30 September, and signed it simply James Stirling, Capt. R.N., (not Governor).[81] But Dance was not about to help, as he made clear:

I beg in answer to state that I complied with your request in bringing yourself and family to this Colony at the most serious personal inconvenience, because I conceived His Majesty's Service required my making the Sacrifice, but being now under the orders of the Commander in Chief on this Station, I do not conceive myself authorized to embark any passengers whatever from this Port without his especial order.[82]

Stirling was furious. He applied to Warren, who said *Sulphur* was not under his command, but still on service to the Colonial Department. Stirling therefore wrote to Dance again on 4 October, concluding that his refusal to comply would 'injure the settlement which you had been directed to promote'.[83] This he signed 'Governor'. Dance then caved in, agreeing to take Stirling to England but protesting about 'the extraordinary step you have taken in Messing with the Officers of the Gun Room instead of being at my table, a step as I conceive against the due and proper decorum of the Service'.[84] After finalising arrangements for the transport of supplies to Swan River, Stirling reboarded the *Sulphur*, which left Simon's Bay on 7 October.

Four days later, at 8.10 p.m., Ellen gave birth to their fourth child and first daughter, Mary, an event which was noted in the ship's log for 11 October, beneath the weather report 'fresh breezes and cloudy'.[85] On 19 October the ship reached St Helena and anchored, as was the custom, to take on water. Perhaps mindful of little William's sudden death, Ellen insisted that the baby be christened, and a small ceremony was duly held the following day just hours before departure. Mary's baptism at St Helena was later recorded in the parish of Ash in England, where her elder brother Frederick Henry, who had been baptised at the Cape in 1829, was also registered.

Leaving St Helena on 20 October, Stirling would have felt he was on the last leg of the voyage, and impatient for it to end. One can thus imagine his state of mind when, day after day, Dance chased and boarded passing ships: first a French ship, the *Echele*; then the *Princess Mary* bound for Batavia; a Spanish brigantine; *Vraca*, a Sardinian brigantine bound for the Brazils; the *Thomas Miller* out of Gibraltar; the *Royal George* bound for Mauritius; and lastly the *Countess of Chichester* returning from Botany Bay. Signals were one thing, but stopping to board these ships when urgent state business was at stake would not have pleased the Governor. At least it gave him time to complete a voluminous report on the state and condition of the colony which would be expected on his return.[86] Finally, on 11 December, the *Sulphur* anchored off the Isle of Wight and moved into Spithead the following day. Here Stirling and his family disembarked to board the coach for the two-day journey to Guildford. They had been away from home for almost four years and really had no idea how all their loved ones had fared. So joy was tempered with trepidation as they made their way to Pirbright and Woodbridge.

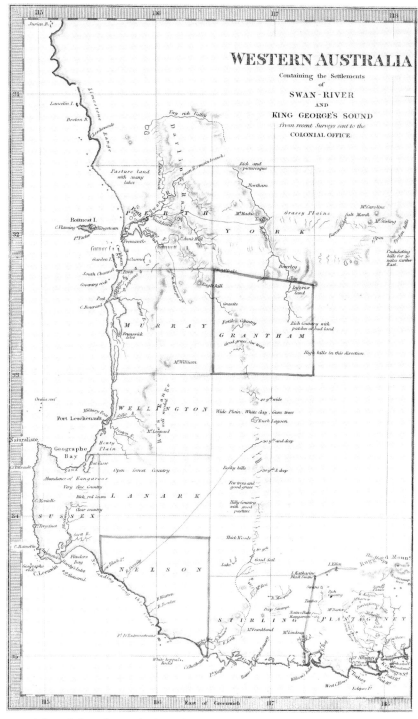

Map of the colony which Stirling took with him to England, showing
the extent of exploration and the division of the territory into counties

Courtesy Battye Library 24/1/2

14

The Interim Return

THE STIRLINGS FIRST made their way to the family home at Pirbright Lodge, where James' two unmarried sisters, Dorothea and Agnes, were still residing. In the joy of reunion James would undoubtedly have felt the loss of his mother, who had been the hub of the family for so long. Two children plus a baby, however, strained the seams at the Lodge, but James' youngest sister, Mary Halsey, who lived nearby with her children at the much larger Henley Park, quickly prevailed upon them to stay with her. As Henley Park was also only a few miles from Ellen's parents and family at Woodbridge, it was a perfect homecoming. The first few days would have passed in a haze: there were relatives to see, children to introduce, affairs to be settled, bags to unpack and news to exchange. Financially, the Stirling family were better off, for William's Manchester mills were returning handsome profits, and Stirling was able to inform brother John:

> Upon the whole I think I have found you all in a more prosperous state than I was prepared to expect…but notwithstanding all the Prosperity I find that four years absence have not elapsed without corresponding effects and that time is spreading an autumnal shade over our own generation.[1]

Above all the news exchanged in the Pirbright and Woodbridge households, Stirling was keen to know of any changes in the Colonial Office Ministry, to whom he reported. He knew that the political climate had been unstable, for news had reached the Cape that, after a stormy passage, the Reform Bill had been passed in the Commons the previous March, and finally become law in June 1832. In the course of events the Prime Minister, Earl Grey, had been forced to resign, but was recalled when Wellington could not form a ministry; in such a climate, ministerial heads were often wont to change. Lord Goderich, the Secretary of State for Colonies, to whom Stirling had been sending dispatches for some time, was by way of a 'friend at Court'. Not only was he a naval man (Admiralty 1810–17), but he had supported Ellen's father, James Mangles, who had been returned for Guildford in

1830 and elected again as part of the Whig majority in December 1832. For Stirling, explaining his unauthorised return from Swan River to Goderich would be far easier than to a stranger, so the news that he was still in office was a relief.

Leaving the family at Guildford, James went to London a few days after his return, staying at the United Services Club in Pall Mall.[2] Armed with all the petitions from settlers, the Executive Council minutes and his own reports, James lost no time in seeking an interview at the Colonial Office. His old friend Twiss had retired, but Hay was still there to facilitate an early meeting. On Saturday 15 December 1832 the Court Circular in *The Times* announced, 'Captain Stirling, from the Swan River settlement, has arrived in town, and yesterday had an interview with Viscount Goderich at the Colonial Office'. As James explained to his brother John a few days later:

> The Government is not well pleased at seeing me but I was so sure that I had taken a judicious course in coming home unasked that I did not care for the surprise which it at first occasioned and now that they are better acquainted with the reasons, they acknowledge it to have been the best course and we are such good friends that I am to make my own arrangements on all points except money.[3]

On the 18th, at the request of the Colonial Office, he met a Quaker named Edward Merrell who had written the previous September regarding the possibility of settling '200 Families with the necessary servants, labourers, merchants and others' at Swan River.[4] Other than a grant of land, his project was to be at no cost to the Government. The information Merrell received during this interview was 'highly satisfactory', and Stirling left him intending to put a formal proposition to the Government. Stirling himself had a proposal which he explained in his Christmas letter to brother John:

> Amongst other things I have asked for a Ship of War for myself and the reasons all so strange that Hay is decidedly in favour of it but it is not yet decided although between ourselves I think it will be granted, but I should not wish this to be talked of until it is decided. Such an arrangement would very much add to my own comfort & satisfaction in returning to Western Australia.[5]

What he wanted was to use a warship as a floating Government House! James had discussed the matter unofficially with Hay, who in turn informed his Minister that Stirling had a proposal 'which I am inclined to think might be advantageously acted upon, if matters could be settled with the Admiralty'.[6] But Goderich simply appended a marginal comment which read:

> I should like to see Captain Stirling…I doubt about his plan of a Governor afloat. It might do very well for a short time, but we should have to build the Governor's House at last.

And that was the last time it was mentioned. James, Ellen and the children spent Christmas and Boxing Day with the Mangles family at Woodbridge,[7] and on the 27th moved back to Henley Park. At this early stage of their return visit home, a degree of uncertainty hung over both of the Stirlings. James' sister Dorothea commented in a family letter that 'there appears every probability of his returning to Swan River for 3 or 4 years longer. Ellen is not to accompany him…'[8] Indeed, surrounded by her family, and all the accoutrements of civilisation, Ellen's initial reluctance to return to the colony is understandable, especially as her eldest child, Andrew, was now of school age and would have to be left behind. Whether James ever contemplated not returning to the colony is a matter for conjecture. There were certainly rumours to that effect, even an application to the Colonial Office to take his place as Governor,[9] and comments in letters from Swan River,[10] but there is no evidence on his side.

Aside from a short visit to Manchester for a meeting of the clan, James settled down to business in London in the short, wintry days of the New Year. Foremost in his mind was his salary for, as he informed Hay on 5 January 1833, having not been paid since leaving the colony in August, his 'private income is in some degree forestalled'.[11] Two days later he was more precise, requesting £333 6s 4d as his due for five months' salary.[12] The Colonial Office accordingly wrote to Treasury on 8 January stating:

> Lord Goderich considers that Captain Stirling is entitled to his Salary from the date of his quitting the Colony—the more especially as the greater part of his time while in this Country will be devoted to the promotion of the interests of the Colony.[13]

But Treasury queried the request on the grounds that Stirling had been paid £500 in the colony towards his passage home. Hay, in turn, replied that Lord Goderich had ordered Stirling to refund that money on his return to Swan River. Still Treasury baulked at paying, arguing that the Governor had a large grant of land as payment, and moreover, whilst in England did not have to keep open house or entertain in the manner warranted in the colony. Goderich replied that Stirling's 'Grant was not made to him (as has been erroneously supposed) in substitution for salary', but, as he could see some logic in their argument, he would recommend that Stirling be paid half salary while away. Nevertheless, he believed that Stirling had 'a fair claim to be relieved from two thirds' of the £600 he had paid for his return passage, as he had 'no alternative…than to proceed to England in compliance with the wishes of the Inhabitants'.[14] Treasury still objected,[15] but apparently paid up early in February.

Stirling was not only fighting for his own money in those first few weeks of January. He also wrote to the Colonial Office regarding promotion and/or additional remuneration for many who had assisted him at Swan River, including

William Preston,[16] James Smith,[17] Peter Belches,[18] Captain Bannister,[19] and Captain Mark Currie.[20] Most were successful, but Goderich took a dim view of the latter's appeal for additional remuneration, as Currie had had a salary of some £750 whilst in the colony, and a free passage out. Thus 'the Secretary of State did not consider himself called upon to interfere with a view to procuring for him any further reward'.[21]

Stirling was hardly going to argue; there were matters of more importance to take up with his Lordship. One of the most urgent, from a personal viewpoint, was to clarify the situation regarding his land holdings. As he explained in a letter dated 5 January, circumstances had forced him to grant to other settlers some of the 100,000 acres in the Leschenault area to which he had been originally entitled. He had therefore selected other locations for which he now sought approval, including both his land on the Swan River and land further south. Lord Goderich's reply to this request came on 23 January, generally agreeing with the change 'under the peculiar circumstances which you have represented'. But he added that the selections, 'from which he cannot authorise a future change', should be determined 'as soon after your return to the Colony as possible', and that a full report should be furnished as soon as the necessary steps had been taken.[22]

Another matter of particular concern had come up in a letter Stirling had received from the Colonial Office, dated 2 January, regarding one of the colonists' petitions. In convoluted language, Stirling was told that the colonists' appeal for additional government assistance could not be countenanced because 'the origin of the settlement must not be attributed to Govt. but was rather a concession to the representations of certain individuals'.[23] This interpretation Stirling could not allow to pass. As he informed Hay in a private letter:

> …if I had supposed at the time that I was engaging in an undertaking originated & to be supported by Individuals…& not by the Government I should have found myself under the necessity of declining such an appointment…I should have been inexcusably imprudent in undertaking it…[24]

Swan River had been proclaimed a Crown Colony from the outset, and so he believed its settlers were entitled to appeal for Crown support. This was as far as he could push the matter, and though he knew Hay was under some political pressure,[25] he was sure the reminder would find its mark. Stirling was anxious to get news of the colonists' concerns and, learning that a ship would shortly sail for Western Australia, wrote to Lord Goderich for a formal answer to their petitions. Although he agreed with the Colonial Office view that the settlers had emigrated in the knowledge that they would receive no government assistance, he argued that:

> If the prospect which was entertained at one time of a continual influx of Capital and people had been realised, no difficulty would have been experienced, nor

would the imposition of taxes, or the regulation which fixed the price of Crown Lands have been objected to…[26]

It was no fault of the existing settlers that bad Press had brought the influx of immigrants to a halt and made their current position so precarious. Though Stirling candidly admitted that he did not exactly concur with all of their requests, he felt some of the points raised were critical for the future of the colony. These he listed as: parliamentary support for the Civil Establishment; extension of the Legislative Council to include the magistrates and three nominees of the settlers; provision of a protective force, including not only troops and a ship-of-war but also a police force to stop native depredations; a more liberal interpretation of the 1829-30 land regulations to allow settlers to sell unimproved land and to average extensive improvements to part of a grant over their whole allocation; the establishment of a bank by charter to solve monetary problems; and finally, 'some official intimation of the Intentions of Government regarding the Colony in question' to resolve doubts as to its future as a Crown Colony.[27]

After several requests for clarification, particularly concerning the need for a protective force, Lord Goderich's answer came a month later, on 8 March. Its beginning was not auspicious:

> I gather from the various communications to which I have referred, that, although the absence of capital & the paucity of labourers have depressed the energies of the Settlers, & crippled their exertions…neither yourself nor any of the Colonists whose opinions are the most worthy of attention, appear to entertain any doubt as to the ultimate success of the scheme.[28]

Virtually ignoring Stirling's letter, Goderich referred only to the settlers' requests, and replied on each point. Regarding the establishment of a bank, the Government could not assist, nor would it sanction private ventures, as it might 'occasion a risk of failure'. Additional labour might be supplied, but only 'whenever sufficient security can be given for repayment'. (However, he did add that there was 'a prospect of private relief'.) Funding for additional livestock was totally out of the question; this should be left 'as it ought to be, to private enterprise'.

With reference to the new land regulations, Goderich was adamant. The Government believed the colonists' claim 'that land purchase would deter emigrants' was totally fallacious, and whilst every opportunity would be extended to settlers to sell titled portions of their estates, there was no way that improvement expenditure would be allowed to be averaged over entire grants. The improvement clauses had to be strictly enforced, for it was imperative that on one hand as much land as possible was improved, and on the other that unimproved land could be resumed for reallocation. However, he did mention that plans were being laid to allow settlers to surrender some land in return for title to the remainder, but this would take time to implement.[29] In the meantime, all deceased estates and land held by absentees of over two years were to be immediately resumed.

Before going on to items which he called 'very inconsistent demands', Goderich felt colonists needed to be reminded of the circumstances leading to the formation of the colony, to prove 'that their claims have been advanced without sufficient foundation'. Once again, and despite Stirling's earlier protestations, the government line that Swan River Colony's origin was a private enterprise affair was put forward, with some interesting changes in emphasis (underlined).

> The present Settlement at Swan River, owes its origin…to certain false rumours which had reached the Government of the intentions of a Foreign Power to establish a Colony on the Western Coast of Australia. <u>The design was for a time given up completely on the grounds of public economy</u>, <u>and would not have been resumed, but for the offer of a party of gentlemen</u> to embark in an undertaking of this nature at their own risk, upon receiving extensive grants of land, and on a certain degree of protection & assistance <u>for a limited time</u>, being secured to them by the Government. It was never, however, contemplated that the chief expense of forming a new Colony should be incurred by the Government—and accordingly, the whole of the Civil Establishment was fixed upon the most economical footing even to the extent of sending out the officer in command of the Expedition…and some of those under him, without any salary, and without any compensation whatever, except a promise of land…the first establishment of the Settlement originated in a private speculation, <u>and it would not have been undertaken on public grounds alone.</u>

He went on to add that, in publishing the regulations, the Government had 'incurred a great responsibility', and that however carefully they had been worded it was difficult to avoid 'the imputation of having given encouragement to the scheme'. Nevertheless, the clauses stipulating minimum government assistance were clear and ought to have convinced intending settlers that they could not depend with any certainty on 'the continuance of the Government Establishment there, nor look to any assistance from the public, beyond a very limited period'.[30]

Now that the colony was established, the 'limited period' of assistance from the Home Government was nearing its end, and settlers had to assume some financial responsibility. Any positions or public works not provided for by a limited parliamentary grant would have to be met by local revenue, to be raised through such means as duties on spirits and the sale of lands and public assets. Goderich continued:

> By these means…the foundation of a system will be laid, which it is to be hoped, will, in a short time, relieve the Mother Country, from all charge on account of the Civil Establishment of the Colony.

There was also a direct comment to Stirling to the effect that the 'uneasiness felt by HM Govt.' with regard to the £41,045 he had drawn in Treasury Bills to 31 March 1832, had been largely relieved by the accounts he had recently presented showing that this expense covered not only the civil service, but also the naval and military establishments.[31] Goderich went on to say that the government had given full consideration to the colony's need for protection, and had decided that the 63rd Regiment would be replaced by two companies of the 21st (a regiment recently sent to New South Wales), thus doubling the force presently at Swan River. On the other hand, there appeared no justification for a ship-of-war to be stationed in the colony, as ships from the Eastern Station would visit every six months. Stirling could, however, 'arm the colonial vessel, which will be maintained for the service of the Colony', and give its officers the necessary authority to control the crews of merchant vessels and uphold the Revenue Laws. They also approved Stirling's mounted police force, as long as it was limited to thirty men and fully supported from revenue raised in the colony.[32]

It had been noted that the Legislative Council had only met twice to sanction Executive Council decisions, and that settlers had objected to their lack of representation (particularly concerning tax matters). On this point Goderich was scathing, stating that the arrangements put in place conformed with the Act of Parliament. He was, nevertheless, 'aware of the advantages which would be derived from the presence at the Council of a few of the most leading men engaged in Commercial & Agricultural pursuits'. Accordingly he stated:

> I am induced to recommend to the King, the adoption of your suggestion, that the number of the Legislative Council should be increased—you will therefore consider yourself authorised to nominate to that body two colonists upon whose experience & discretion you can the most rely, with the addition afterwards of two more members, should you be of opinion that such an augmentation would be desirable. The total number however...should not, under any circumstances exceed eight, independent of the Governor.[33]

Taken overall, the only 'wins' that Stirling could really report back to the anxious settlers were the enlargement of the military, the institution of a mounted police force (which they would have to finance), twice-yearly visits of warships from India and four extra seats on the Legislative Council. It seemed as though the Government had totally ignored the economic predicament of the colony, which ostensibly it had, in its refusal to send out labour or livestock, establish a bank or alter the land regulations. But the decision to enlarge the military (which was put into immediate effect) was to prove the colony's salvation, though Stirling would have been hard put to see it at the time.

In the passage dealing with the request for additional labour, Goderich's reference to possible 'private relief' included both Quaker Edward Merrell's emigration proposal, and another from Robert Gouger. Gouger had earlier been involved with Wilmot Horton's schemes for pauper emigration, and had met Edward Wakefield (the author of plans for systematic colonisation) when both were serving prison sentences for debt in 1829. On release, Gouger had become Secretary of the National Colonisation Society, which in January 1831 had put forward various proposals for settling the area around the Gulf of St Vincent (South Australia), recently discovered by Charles Sturt. All had been rejected by the Colonial Office.[34] Gouger had then gone back to publicising his ideas for pauper emigration, and it was at this time that he addressed the Colonial Office regarding Swan River. His letter on 9 February 1833 was written on behalf of 'a Gentleman of great respectability and ample means' who proposed

> to defray the cost of the passage of fifty men and an equal number of women to that settlement, provided he should receive from your Lordship an assurance that he should on their arrival be entitled to a payment of twenty pounds per family to be repaid by the labourers, as in the case of artisans now encouraged to proceed to New South Wales and Van Diemen's Land.[35]

But the Colonial Office had not been interested, stating in reply that there were no funds at the disposal of the government at Swan River to effect the system adopted in the other Australian colonies.

Gouger was at this time in touch with a loose association formed by the families of some of the Swan River colonists. He was thus aware of their urgent need for labour, a desire that fitted his passionate belief in the benefits of pauper emigration. At a meeting of the 'Friends of Swan River Colony' early in May, it was decided to ask the Colonial Office to fund a position as 'Agent for Western Australia', to disseminate information and recruit emigrants, and they recommended Gouger for the position. 'His knowledge of and connection with the colonies', they maintained, 'made him an eminently suitable choice'.[36] But the reply was not encouraging. The Colonial Office had no intention of funding an appointment which it did not consider 'requisite'.[37] The proposal was abandoned and Gouger turned his attention back to South Australia. In December 1833 he founded, with Wakefield, the association that would eventually bring that colony into being.

How far Stirling was involved with the systematic colonisation movement is unknown. He certainly agreed with their belief in selling Crown lands and using the revenue to fund the emigration of labour; he had said so in earlier dispatches. It is also highly coincidental that he was in London at the same time that Wakefield was writing his book *England and America*. Published later in 1833, this panegyric for systematic colonisation juxtaposed it with the evils of the land grant system at Swan River, but in denigrating the latter Wakefield displayed a very intimate knowledge of its affairs.[38]

Although the Colonial Office had refused Gouger's proposition, it was still considering Merrell's proposal when drafting the official reply to the settlers. In fact, several individuals had written to the Colonial Office following a Press advertisement placed by Merrell inviting 'persons of moderate capital who may be disposed to emigrate to unite with several members of the Society of Friends & others in forming an extensive Settlement in Western Australia'. All were informed that

> no other arrangement has been made on the part of this Department with that Gentleman, than that he should be allowed to purchase an extensive Grant of Land in the neighbourhood of King George's Sound, at the minimum price fixed by the Regulations, and that any information...can only be obtained upon application to him.[39]

Thus the Mangles ship *Isabella*, which took the news of Stirling's progress on the settlers' behalf out to Swan River, also carried a report, subsequently published in the newly established *Perth Gazette and Western Australian Journal*, that 'A body of Quakers, of capital, had determined upon settling at King George's Sound'.[40] Actually, Merrell never reached Western Australia, possibly attracted away by the Systematic Colonisers' push for South Australia. But the interest that he and his supporters had displayed in settling King George's Sound caused the Colonial Office to look favourably on an application they received on 1 March from Sir Richard Spencer,[41] a protégé of Lord Althorp (who was Chancellor of the Exchequer and eldest son of Earl Spencer). Richard Spencer had once considered emigrating to New South Wales,[42] and after meeting Stirling in January was again keen to emigrate. Stirling would have been delighted to encourage someone with such eminent connections, and no doubt discussed the matter with Lord Goderich. But Spencer's application for the position of Resident at the Sound contained a list of demands. Having 'a numerous family of 9 children', he wanted 'the Medical attendance of the Colonial surgeon' plus free occupation of the government cottage and garden, the right to draw stores for himself and family from the Commissary for the first three years in lieu of salary, and a free passage out.[43] Although prepared to assist, Goderich was not going to sanction this sort of additional expenditure. The reply, under Hay's signature, drew attention to the fact that the Resident's position was currently filled by Dr Collie, so arrangements would first have to be made to transfer him to other duties. It also ruled out 'any facilities in respect to a free passage to the Colony' or 'the issue of rations to yourself and family in lieu of salary'.[44] Spencer was not pleased with this reply, having arranged passage on the *Buffalo*, which would land himself and family at the Sound en route to New Zealand. Writing again on 14 March, he claimed:

> I have now laid out several hundred pounds which would be useless to me in England. When I waited on you with Captain Stirling it was with the

Sir Richard Spencer

Collection: National Trust of Australia (WA); courtesy Albany Residency Museum

understanding that Mr Collie was the Colonial Surgeon, and only held the appointment pro tem. I leave Town on Saturday morning, if Lord Goderich wishes to see me before my departure.[45]

The reply, five days later, advised Spencer that his appointment had been approved by the Secretary of State, and that Collie would be so informed. Spencer acknowledged this on 25 March, but at the same time complained that the captain of the *Buffalo* wanted around £500 to take his family and freight to the Sound. To offset this heavy expense, he wanted a free grant of 'that portion of land called the Government Farm', which had been brought into cultivation by the convicts.[46] He must have heard of this farm from Stirling, but the latter would hardly have encouraged Spencer to apply for it directly to the Colonial Office, especially given the difficulties he was experiencing in justifying all the actions taken during his previous administration. Predictably, the request was refused in a reply on 3 April, a memorable date for Stirling, for it was the day he received his knighthood.

In recognition of his past service, Stirling had been made full Governor and Commander-in-Chief of the Colony of Western Australia on 15 February 1833, and

Goderich had apparently promised more. On 29 March Hay had written to Sir Herbert Taylor, William IV's private secretary, conveying Lord Goderich's request that 'you would submit to the King the name of Captain Stirling RN, Governor of the Swan River Settlement, as a fit person to receive the Honour of a Knighthood'.[47] The reply was swift, dated 31 March:

> My dear Hay, The King readily acquiesces in Lord Goderich's wish that Captain Stirling of the RN should receive the honour of a Knighthood and He may attend at the Levee on Wednesday next for that purpose.[48]

Goderich's influence was heightened by the fact that he had just been asked to sacrifice his position at the Colonial Office in favour of E. S. Stanley, one of the high flyers in Prime Minister Grey's administration. Goderich at first had refused to go, but was eventually persuaded by the offer of the position of Lord Privy Seal. He was also created first Earl of Ripon,[49] the announcement being made within days of Stirling's elevation to Knight of the Realm.

Soon after noon on 3 April 1833, dressed in his naval uniform plus regulation pantaloons and boots,[50] Stirling presented himself at St James' Palace for the Court levee. At this ceremony changes in ministerial appointments were officially approved by the King, foreign dignitaries were presented and peerages and knighthoods bestowed, each individual being presented to kiss the King's hand.[51] Possibly because of the number of presentations on that day, Stirling's name was left off the gazetted list which appeared on 4 April.[52] But he had definitely been there, for the same Gazette reported on 31 May, under the heading St James' Palace April 3, 1833, 'The King was this day pleased to confer the honour of a knighthood on James Stirling Esq. Captain in the Royal Navy, Governor and Commander-in-Chief of the Settlement in Western Australia'.[53]

One can imagine the family's pride in James at this time, even though acceptance of the honour implied a return to duty overseas. Ellen would not have been present at the levee, which was a male only affair, but would duly have been presented, as the new Lady Stirling, to Queen Adelaide at her next Drawing Room reception. Given her reluctance to return to Swan River, and the symptoms of early pregnancy, it would have been with mixed feelings that Ellen made her curtsy to the Queen, dressed in the requisite formal finery. Some of her antipathy to the return journey, however, had already been mitigated by her father. As well as a flamboyant politician, James Mangles had been one of the founding members of the Children's Friend Society, a benevolent society established in 1830 for the suppression of juvenile vagrancy.[54] Its initial aim of training and finding local employment for such children had been modified in 1832 to include seeking employment for destitute children in the colonies. First groups had been sent to the Cape of Good Hope in 1832 and reports of their reception were most encouraging. Lord Goderich had lent his support to the society,[55] and plans had been made in January 1833 to send other batches, in the care of a respectable female person, as soon as possible. Mangles knew of the Swan River colonists' need for labour, and had been able to interest his daughter in the scheme. The children, boys and girls, were all under 16 and, before being selected for emigration, were trained for a minimum of three months at the boys school at Hackney or the girls school at Chiswick. It appears that Ellen visited these schools, possibly whilst in London early in April, and eventually agreed to take on the role of Matron, supervising a group of children selected for emigration to Swan River during the voyage out.[56]

Another factor influencing Ellen's attitude towards returning was Stirling's promise that this time she would have a suitable home. Ellen had hated the small wooden building they had inhabited in Perth, and knew that living in the slightly more comfortable brick house at Guildford was totally impractical. She believed the Governor's wife, and now Lady Stirling, should not be accommodated in premises worse than servants' cottages in England, and said so. James agreed and promised to make a suitable home his first priority on their return, even encouraging his wife to order appropriate furniture.[57]

With Ellen more willing to go back, and hopes that the colonial accounts would soon be cleared by Treasury after his many detailed written explanations, it was time to begin travel arrangements. On 6 May James formally requested 'conveyance for myself and my Family on board a King's Ship', or a defraying of expenses should passage be on a merchant vessel.[58] It was a measure of the high regard in which Stirling was held at the Colonial Office (which Hay had put in writing on 9 May [59]) that they agreed to propose to Treasury that a 'half allowance may be granted to take the Governor out in a merchant ship'.[60]

Much had gone on behind the scenes at this stage, for with Stirling's strong family orientation he had seen an opportunity for his brother-in-law's shipping company. Frederick Mangles had taken over his father's business in 1829, and later been joined by his brother Charles when the latter left the East India Service to marry in 1831.[61] Having established a considerable reputation as an Indian trader in his own right, Charles initially concentrated on building up a freight business using cargo space on available vessels.[62] But by 1834 they were in a position to charter an additional ship, and with Stirling's eager participation planned to begin a yearly trading service to Swan River Colony and the East Indies.[63] Once Stirling could guarantee some government funding for the return passage of his family and freight, and was optimistic about gathering a large number of emigrants to join him, the brothers began to look for a suitable vessel.

On 22 May Stirling wrote from Guildford to ascertain progress regarding the finalisation of his accounts.[64] He had also been mulling over the official reaction to the settlers' petition, for as soon as he reached London, on the 24th, he wrote a private letter to Henry Short (who was relieving Hay at the Colonial Office). He wanted Lord Goderich to be informed of his reservations regarding certain details of two of his previous decisions. The first concerned his refusal to allow the sale of land before title had been earned through improvement. Stirling preferred allowing sale, but transferring improvement responsibility. The second issue concerned Commissariat arrangements. Goderich had stipulated that military and civil functions could be carried out by the same person, which Stirling felt would be entirely unworkable. In this same letter he listed the names of thirteen people who would be made redundant when the new pared-down civil service was implemented. He pointed out that they would include two men initially appointed by the Colonial Office, Drummond, the Government Naturalist, and Sutherland, the Assistant Surveyor, as well as Reveley, the Civil Engineer he had recruited at the Cape. All had performed to their utmost, as shown in his previous descriptions of their functions and value. Although not said, his clear implication was that the redundancies were entirely unwarranted.[65]

Expecting some discussion of the points he had raised, Stirling would have been dismayed to find himself instead called to account for his dispute with Captain Dance, who on 4 June had sent the Colonial Office a long and detailed letter of complaint.[66] Dance had, in fact, written earlier to Stirling, requesting compensation for the 'loss you yourself have occasioned me',[67] to which Stirling had peremptorily replied:

> I have to inform you that I do not admit that you have any just claim on me, individually…[for such losses, the] transaction was entirely of a public character between me as the Governor of a Colony, and you as the Commander of the *Sulphur*, and it is, as all other cases of the kind are, provided for, & governed by the Admiralty's Instructions relating to the Naval Service…It is not to me that your application should be addressed, but to the Admiralty, or to the Colonial Secretary of State…[68]

But this Dance had already done,[69] without success. Hence his reapplication in June. Stirling's formal reply to the Colonial Office, dated 18 June, refuted all Dance's claims in detail, and included copies of the fifteen letters and notes that had passed between them during 1832 'from which an idea may be formed of the general tenor of my correspondence with that officer'.[70] The Colonial Office sided with Stirling, and a counsellor was sent to placate Dance. Hay was informed on 29 June that, though Dance was 'a good deal vexed', he would take the matter no further.[71] Dance never went to sea again, although he was awarded his Post Captaincy in 1834 and eventually made Rear Admiral.

Before Stirling left London, the Colonial Office wanted his further input into the Parliamentary Estimates of expenditure at Swan River for the forthcoming year. For days on end Stirling was closeted with various officials, preparing in minute detail the estimated costs of running the colony's civil establishment. Over and over again he had had to justify the appointments, payments and allowances he had made in the past to his civil officers—and now he had to fight for their continuation.[72] And he had to be at his persuasive best, for cost-cutting was the order of the day and every proposed expenditure, even forage for civil officers' horses, was scrutinised. His advice was also sought when the first dispatch arrived from Acting Lieutenant-Governor Irwin. In contravention of current policy, Irwin had authorised increased salaries and allowances to certain civil officers, and Stirling was asked to comment. In a masterly reply on 22 June, Stirling managed to defend most of Irwin's actions by categorising some of his expenditures as 'purely military' and thus the province of the 'Army extraordinaries', and others as 'already allowed for in the estimates'.[73] But this did not prevent another interrogation from Treasury requiring a detailed reply.[74]

Therefore it would have been with some relief that Stirling accepted an invitation to dine with the 'Friends of Swan River Colony' at the Albion Tavern, Aldersgate on the evening of 23 June. When Stirling arrived he was greeted with applause and led to the dining room. 'Mr W. Whitmore was in the chair, supported by Mr Mangles MP, Captain Mangles, Dr Bland, the Hon Captain Crofton R.N., Captain Carnac and upwards of one hundred gentlemen connected with the colony.'[75] A number of them had banded together to purchase and present to Stirling 'a splendid silver Cup, weighing nearly 100 oz. and capable of holding almost a gallon of liquid'. The two-handled solid silver cup stood 18 inches (45.5cm) high, had a swan mounted on the lid and was emblazoned on one side with the Stirling coat of arms surrounded by naval emblems, while the other side carried an inscription which read:

> Presented to Capt. James Stirling RN First Governor of the Colony of Western Australia by the Relatives & Friends of the Settlers at Swan River in testimony of their admiration of the Wisdom, Decision and Kindness uniformly displayed by him and of their Gratitude for his strenuous exertions with the Colonial Department for the benefit of that settlement. London, May 1833.[76]

The cup had been made by Thomas Habgood, father of one of the settlers, and even by the fairly lavish standards of the time it was a handsome present. All forty-eight subscribers were named in the accompanying testimonial, and included Robert Gouger and, by a strange quirk of fate, William Hutt MP, the brother of Stirling's successor as Governor at Swan River. The speech that Stirling made after the presentation was fully reported in the *Observer*, and the following extracts, with inserted reactions from the assembled crowd, give a first-hand impression of the evening:

> …yes, he had in common with many of the friends of those friends he then saw round him, struggled with difficulties. They had in a great measure overcome them; and by what means? By their own exertions [cheers] by carrying to that shore, portions of that noble daring which, since the world began, had been

seldom equalled, and certainly never surpassed [loud cheers]. The colony in Western Australia had not been supported by Government outlays—by force of arms—by labour of slaves; but it had been sustained by that which was transplanted by the mother country—the intrepidity; the genius and the enduring perseverance of her sons [cheers]...

Stirling thanked them again for 'the splendid tribute offered', and before sitting down wished to give them a brief outline of 'the present intention of the Government towards Swan River Colony'. Here he embellished the truth a little,

The Swan Cup presented to Stirling by the Friends of Western Australia in June 1833

Courtesy the Western Australian Museum CH73.209; photograph by Victor France

informing them that the Government 'intended to afford it in the first place full military protection, external and internal', to provide funding for a full and just administration of the law, and to amend the constitution of the legislature so that 'instead of being as it is now, composed solely of government officers, its basis should be extended so as to include the most respectable, industrious and influential settlers in the country'. Then he stated that 'the government intended to amend the land regulations by which the early settlers would be materially benefited', an announcement that was greeted with loud cheers. Given hindsight, Stirling also sounded a gentle warning when he spoke of the Home Government looking ahead 'to the time when the colony would be able to defray its own expenses', and, in the *Observer*'s words, 'he…trusted and believed that that time was not far distant when they would be able to adopt this creditable course'.[77]

The unexpected gift would have lifted James' spirits at a very opportune time, for the Colonial Office had just received Treasury's long and detailed report on the financial aspects of Stirling's administration, of which he was speedily informed. In essence, Treasury was prepared to accept the accounts in general, but with certain exceptions—fourteen in all. These mostly related to additional payments and allowances to particular civil officers, e.g. the Colonial Surgeon and Surveyor-General, and such items as house rent for the Chaplain and a horse for Captain Bannister. They approved Stirling's purchases of wheat and rice for the colony, and even his house rent and conveyance home on the *Sulphur*, but they were singularly unimpressed with the fact that his wheat credit scheme had been extended to civil officers, who had all been given free rations from the Store. This was now to be regarded as a debt they would have to repay. Stirling was also informed that, as the estimates for the coming year had been drafted with his full participation, no deviation from them, either directly or indirectly, would be countenanced. Further-more, he was warned that he would 'be held personally responsible for any contravention of the Provisions of the Estimate that may take place under his authority'.[78]

After due consideration at the Colonial Office, Stirling was asked for an official reply, which he signed on 28 June. He sincerely believed that:

> The Deviations which were found necessary…taken with reference to the total expenditure of the Establishment, did not…exceed, according to the best of my recollection, the total amount voted by Parliament…

He then went on to explain each point with care and considerable detail, arguing, for example, that the Colonial Chaplain's house rent (item 6) accorded with the practice in the eastern colonies. As to the Chaplain's allowance for travelling expenses, this 'arose out of his performing duty at Fremantle and at Guildford, alternately on each Sunday', and since his salary was so small, relative to the cost of provisions in the colony, he could not bear 'the expenses consequent on the performance of his Duty'. For that reason, Stirling had 'made him the allowance referred to up to the early part of 1832'.[79]

During July and August, correspondence continued between Treasury and Stirling, via the Colonial Office, as the exact salaries and duties of civil appointees were hammered out and distinctions drawn between that which could be charged to the Parliamentary Grant and the Military Chest, and that which would have to be paid for from revenue raised in the colony. Instructions were also drafted regarding the types of revenue raising that would be approved, and the amounts that could be charged in various licences, fees and taxes. By the end of August all seemed settled. The Mangles brothers had successfully chartered the *James Pattison* for the return voyage, and James was finalising arrangements with his brother John to take his 15-year-old nephew Andrew back to the colony. John had given James £1,000 for his care—half for his passage and immediate living, and half to be invested in Swan River for his future benefit—for which James signed a promissory note. So much was needed to make life in the colony more comfortable that Stirling was running short of funds again. He had already asked that he be exempted from paying the normal fee for obtaining his commission as Governor of Western Australia, being ill equipped to pay the £380 10s 6d due,[80] and was still anxiously waiting a reply.

A pleasant surprise came on 1 September with the arrival of his sister Anna, her husband, Sir James Home, and their two boys. Home had been a provincial Sub-Collector in India for the past five years, and Anna had journeyed out to marry him about the time the Stirlings had first left for Swan River. There was much to discuss, for James had expected Home to follow him out to Swan River until hearing of his ill-health. What transpired between them is not known, but it is fairly certain that Stirling would have tried to involve his reasonably wealthy brother-in-law in his pre-departure planning, for he did not return to London till the end of September.

On 26 September Stirling forwarded to the Colonial Office, at their request, 'a List of those Gentlemen, who being Resident Proprietors in Western Australia, appear to be the fittest to become members of the Legislative Council of that Colony'.[81] Under-Secretary Hay was anxious to see him, as another long epistle had arrived from Treasury, enclosing instructions for the Governor of Western Australia and officers under his command.[82] Treasury was concerned about reports of paper notes circulating in the colony, and although recognising it had nothing to do with Stirling, desired him to instigate a full inquiry on his return. He was also warned 'to refrain from giving approval or concurrence to any issue of Colonial Promissory notes, or other Paper currency in future, without express permission and authority of His Majesty's Government'. Given that the Government had flatly refused to assist or countenance the formation of a bank, which Stirling thought essential for the colony's success, this was simply another shackle to be added to those already placed on his ability to govern effectively.

After the arduous process of accountability, the Treasury advice Stirling had waited months to hear finally arrived, on 13 September:

Sir James Stirling may return to his Government with the satisfaction of knowing…with regard to the accounts for the period ended 31st of March last, that all the material difficulties which have arisen on the examination of those accounts have now been removed.[83]

But the effort he had put into clearing his name and justifying every detail of expenditure, together with the dire warnings about his personal financial liability for any future deviation from the approved estimates, had dampened any enthusiasm for the task ahead. On the personal front there was also depressing news. The Admiral, his Uncle Charles, was gravely ill, and doctors had expressed little hope of his recovery. The Stirlings' own departure plans were still uncertain; their ship was in London Docks loading, but was not expected to leave there until the latter part of the following month.[84]

One pleasant outcome of the delay was that James and Ellen could play a major role in the wedding of James' protégé, Lieutenant William Preston, to his young sister-in-law, Hamilla Mary Mangles. The marriage took place in Stoke Church, the same church in Guildford in which the Stirlings had wed a decade

William Preston
Courtesy Battye Library 599P

earlier. William's father, Admiral D'Arcy Preston (of Askham Bryan, in Oxfordshire), was present with numbers of his clan, and the Mangles family turned out in force. The flamboyant James Mangles always saw to it that his daughters were married in style, and threw a lavish reception at his home at Woodbridge. Ellen, who might otherwise have been a matron of honour, was now six months pregnant, so took a lower profile, though joining all the festivities. She thoroughly approved of the match, and had done more than a little to facilitate its happy ending. But it had been arduous, preparing for a wedding and at the same time attending to the hundreds of matters that went with emigrating again for a lengthy period. Stirling's relationship with his two brothers-in-law, Charles and Frederick, was somewhat tense at the wedding reception, for he had just heard that the departure of the *James Pattison* had been postponed again.

Stirling was becoming more and more frustrated, for he had encouraged many to emigrate with him and urged them to complete preparations for departure before mid-October. Now he was forced to make excuses and placate them. It was even more embarrassing that the vessel involved in the delays was under the direction of his own relatives. Family legend tells that a large group assembled at or near Pirbright prior to departure for Swan River.[85] Many of those emigrating with the Stirlings on the *James Pattison* were either friends of the family (such as Patrick Taylor), prior service contacts of Stirling's (Peter Belches and George Elliot), returning colonists (Mr Mackie and Mr Stokes), or friends and relatives of existing colonists (such as Mrs Bussell and her daughter Mary). In addition, there were some seventy-one steerage passengers, thirty-two of them juveniles from the Children's Friend Society, while others were servants, labourers, artisans and independent emigrants of limited means. With continuing uncertainty about the date of departure, it seems more than probable that many of them congregated near the Stirling residence, for Guildford was far closer to Portsmouth than London. In fields and stables nearby, too, there were a number of valuable animals, particularly horses, which Stirling had purchased to take back with him to improve the colony's breeding stock.

During this waiting period, letters still passed sporadically between the Colonial Office and Stirling over appointments, army medicines and suchlike, addressed variously to Guildford and to London, and continued to do so through November. On 1 November Hay informed Stirling that the ten Acts passed by the colony's Executive Council prior to June 1832 had been approved by the King, though the one concerning customs needed some amendment. The time lapse was depressing. Stirling had personally delivered copies of these Acts on his arrival the previous December, and it had taken virtually a year to have them approved, even though almost all were incontestable issues. The complexities of life as Governor of a colony contrasted sharply with his experiences as Captain of a warship. So it is not surprising that when he wrote to the Secretary of the Admiralty on 5 November requesting an extension of his leave of absence, he added the following:

I take this opportunity to represent to you, for their Lordships consideration, the earnest desire which I entertain at all times to be employed in my profession, and I have respectfully to request that my name be noted by their lordships for an appointment to a ship at some early period.[86]

Two days after writing this, James heard that his beloved mentor, Uncle Charles, had died. It was not unexpected, for after a visit the previous September he had told his brother William that he thought it would be his last illness, stating, 'I much fear he will not survive many weeks. His mental and bodily feebleness are extreme.'[87] Charles left a considerable estate to his daughter Charlotte and two sons, but his affairs were confused and 'unlikely to be finalized for over a twelvemonth'.[88] James had apparently not even been mentioned in the will, despite their close connection over the years, and this added to his melancholy. Moreover, as the *James Pattison* had finally left the London Docks, the usually happy lead-up to the Christmas season was marred with all the necessary farewells. For Ellen, it was doubly difficult. She was heavily pregnant and it seemed that once more she would have to forgo her mother's help and encouragement in confinement. There was always the fear, too, that dear faces might never be seen again. The wrench in leaving her eldest son behind was probably the worst, and it was for Andrew she wavered to the last about returning.

The Stirling family had boarded the *James Pattison* at Spithead in mid-December, but sailing had been precluded by adverse winds. The vagaries of nature may have been a disaster for the ship's master, but they proved a boon for Ellen, who was safely delivered of a son at Portsmouth on 24 January 1834. This fifth child the Stirlings named Charles Edward.[89] By a sad quirk of fate, a favourite among James' sisters, Mary Noel Halsey, died on the same day, aged only 36. She had suffered a miscarriage in the past year and caught rheumatic fever, and when complications set in she had not recovered.[90] Her death would have been a severe blow, and, moreover, severed a strong link between James and Henley Park.[91]

Life on board for Ellen at the end of January cannot have been easy. Departure was still uncertain, and apart from the new baby she was also responsible for her other children—5-year-old Frederick Henry and 18-month-old Mary—as well as her nephew Andrew and at least thirty-two of the Children's Friend Society's child emigrants. Even with the help of servants it was a monumental task. The period of waiting tried everyone's nerves, but especially hers, for no real routine could be established while there was still frequent shore contact.

There was another unexpected outcome from the delay. On the day of departure, 9 February, Stirling informed the Colonial Office that

Captain Irwin, the late Lieutenant Governor in Western Australia, anchored here yesterday, and will present himself to you tomorrow…I take the liberty to remark that Captain Irwin has been employed in that country for five years, and that

I have always received from him the most zealous assistance and support. The Progress which the Colony seems to have made since the Administration of the Government has been in his hands, will recommend him I trust to your favour and Protection.[92]

Stirling had read the dispatches Irwin had sent up to the end of August, but was unaware that when the larger 21st Regiment had arrived from Hobart on 9 September 1833, its Commander, Captain Richard Daniel,[93] who was senior in rank to Irwin, had assumed charge.[94] This meant Irwin was free to leave, so he had taken passage in the *Isabella* to the Cape where he found the HMS *Buffalo* on its return voyage to England. The unexpected meeting in Portsmouth gave Stirling time to learn first hand of all that had gone on in his absence, and particularly about the escalation of tension between the settlers and the natives, which had been the subject of most recent dispatches.

Irwin reported that three soldiers, a settler and two boys (the Velvick brothers) had been murdered in the twelve months following Stirling's departure, with reprisals killing far more natives. There had also been a considerable number of raids on stock and crops. In January 1833 one of the native leaders, Yagan, had been caught and incarcerated with some of his tribesmen on Carnac Island. In March relations were not improved when soldiers at Perth Barracks opened fire on unarmed Aborigines who approached them for food. The natives had become understandably agitated when food was offered, but half taken back, and the soldiers had responded with gunfire. There is no record of reprimand. On 20 May Yagan's father, Midgegooroo, was also captured, identified as one involved in the murder of the Velvicks, imprisoned and then executed by firing squad two days later in the yard of the Barracks—with Irwin in attendance. There was no trial. This Stirling would have been aghast to hear, given his Proclamation guaranteeing equal rights. Irwin assured him (as he later put in writing to the Colonial Office) that the Executive Council had deliberated extensively before taking action, and had been

> convinced of its necessity founded on a knowledge of the character and disposition of the aborigines, after near four years intercourse. The previous lenient measures and forbearance of the Government, after they had with impunity murdered several of the settlers, having been considered to have had an injurious effect in causing the natives to believe the course pursued to be the result of fear of their superiority.[95]

The Colonial Office later disapproved of the execution, not for reasons of injustice but for fear of reprisals.[96] And more unrest had followed. Irwin had not had time to report in dispatches that Yagan had managed to escape from captivity and, after learning of his father's fate, had became even more threatening. Stirling had met Yagan and would have agreed with George Fletcher Moore's description of him as a

'Wallace of the tribe'. He managed to evade capture for two months, continuing his raids on outlying properties, but committing no murders. As Moore recorded, 'The truth is everyone wishes him taken but no-one likes to be captor…there is something in his daring which one is forced to admire'.[97] He was finally trapped on 15 August 1833 by two boys who met him in a pretence of friendship, then shot and killed him. Moore observed:

> The arrest of Yagan was *man's* work! *Boys* unfortunately undertook it, without sufficient steadiness; they were frightened at their own act, discharged their guns injudiciously, and ran away, by which the life of one of them was sacrificed.[98]

Most of the settlers were more concerned with that death, of 16-year-old William Keats, than about Yagan. Yet the power and mystique of this native had impressed all, and led to his head and body cicatrices being preserved and sent for study in England (in fact, they arrived on the very same ship as Irwin). An uneasy peace had reigned in the colony after Yagan's death, Irwin reported, which he hoped would last.

The only other matter of business Irwin was keen to discuss with Stirling concerned his soldiers. When the 21st Regiment replaced the 63rd, the married members of the latter regiment had been given the opportunity, which Stirling had sought for them,[99] to take discharge in the colony and land in lieu of half-pay. Of the twenty-seven married men, eighteen had accepted the offer. What concerned Irwin was that this opportunity had not been extended to the unmarried men, and ten to thirteen were interested in a similar discharge. He needed Stirling's support before he could put their case to the authorities. Stirling readily agreed and advised Irwin to put the case to Lord FitzRoy Somerset at Horseguards, which he did (successfully) three days later.[100]

Stirling was no doubt briefed about the main contents of the other dispatches Irwin was to submit to the Colonial Office, but he knew these would eventually be sent to him with comments and instructions from Lord Stanley, who remained in constant communication by post.[101] In fact, Stirling ended his 9 February letter to Hay with the suggestion that any further letters could be sent on to the Cape;[102] he knew that a warship would be far faster than the heavily laden *James Pattison*. Early that afternoon the winds changed, and sailing orders could finally be given. Assisted by one of the new steam vessels, the *James Pattison* wended its way into the English Channel, and the Stirlings were once again en route to Swan River.

15

A House and a Battle

1834

THE RETURN JOURNEY was uneventful and more comfortable than previous trips, though Stirling was to call it his 'longest sea voyage ever', for the *James Pattison* was cumbersome and slow.[1] At least it gave him time to mull over his myriad of instructions, and Ellen to hear the lessons and the prayers of the child emigrants.[2] Touching Cape Town on 12 May,[3] there was a chance to check on the welfare of previous Children's Friend Society emigrants, acquire additional articles and once again eat fresh food. For Stirling there were more dispatches, but also time to meet some old acquaintances, both among the settlers and the naval ships in Simon's Bay. Leaving on 22 May 1834, the *James Pattison* set a course due east, aiming not for Swan River but King George's Sound, where half the passengers were to land.

At the Cape, Stirling learned that Sir Richard Spencer had arrived at Albany on 13 September, and since then had made considerable progress.[4] Reports of the settlement at the Swan were encouraging too. The arrival of the much larger 21st Regiment in September 1833, and their coexistence with the 63rd Regiment until April 1834, had given a much needed boost to the infant economy. Army purchases of foodstuffs more than doubled, so the good harvest of 1833 had found a ready market. The billeting of soldiers had also provided a welcome addition to family incomes, as well as revitalising the social scene. Permission for the married officers to take discharge in the colony had arrived just prior to the 63rd Regiment's departure, and thirteen men had taken up the offer. Together with their wives and twenty-seven children, they added some fifty people to the colony's civilian population, which at the end of 1833 stood at 1,670. Additional immigration to the end of 1834 would increase the total European population to 2,075.[5]

The *James Pattison* finally reached the Sound on 19 June 1834. Availing himself of a ship in port about to depart for Hobart (where mail links with London were more regular), Stirling quickly wrote to Hay to put his mind at rest, in case he 'may have thought of appointing a new Governor in my place'. Explaining that his ship had to offload a large number of settlers at Albany, Stirling took the opportunity to review matters 'in this quarter'.

I do not find that the settlers have done much in this part since I was here two years ago…The arrival of some Settlers from Van Diemen's Land and the expectation of a large reinforcement from Calcutta, have latterly occasioned more bustle and spirit. I am happy to say that Sir Richard Spencer and his Family are comparatively well settled…and that as Government Resident his arrangements appear to be suited to advance the welfare of the District.

At Swan River I learn my Presence is much needed in as much as ill health on the part of the late acting Governor, Captain Daniel, has led to his Resignation of the Office, and probably to much confusion in the management of affairs. I shall not lose a moment after my arrival in putting matters upon the Footing decided upon, after which nothing short of the most urgent circumstances will induce me to depart in the smallest degree from the Instructions which you have given me.[6]

Stirling also wrote to Governor Arthur, who had been concerned about a very short communiqué Stirling had sent him from England.[7] Stirling assured him that

the objects which I had in view when I took the decisive step of going to England have been for the most part accomplished. I have succeeded at least in arriving at a clear understanding as to the Intentions of the Colonial Department in regard to the future management of the Colony, and although there is no reason to expect any considerable outlay of Public Money on the advancement of the Place, I trust its progress will be steady…[8]

This optimistic outlook Arthur was able to pass on to Richard Bourke, then Governor of New South Wales: 'Stirling…writes in excellent spirits, & tells me he has succeeded in most of the objects that led him to undertake the expedition to England'.[9] But, of course, Stirling had not achieved all he had hoped to accomplish and was mindful that many would be disappointed when they learned the full extent of the changes he was to implement. His return to Perth, however, was delayed by bad weather. For nearly seven weeks storms and high winds prevented the *James Pattison* leaving the Sound, the Master deeming it too risky to clear the heads and take the ship round Cape Leeuwin. He was well aware of the effect of bad weather on valuable livestock, and he carried on board a number of prize animals, including the stallion 'Grey Leg' whom Stirling had purchased from Lord Egremont's stud.[10]

Accommodation in Albany, initially with the large Spencer family, was cramped, and Stirling told the Government Resident on 28 June that a separate vice-regal residence would be necessary.[11] He therefore laid out £250 for a residence to be constructed on the suburban allotment that he had chosen in 1832. He also used the time to explore further the lands surrounding King George's Sound and, riding out with Spencer, was particularly pleased with the Kalgan River area, where he had reserved lands around the Moorilup Ponds (later Plantagenet Location 12). So impressed was he with this land that he later recommended several of his officers to take out grants there for their wives. Consequently, Jane Currie was assigned Location 15 and Caroline Brown Location 16.[12]

Meanwhile, news of the Governor's safe arrival at the Sound had been sent overland to Swan River, where settlers looked for him daily and with increasing agitation as the weeks passed. Finally, on 19 August, the *James Pattison* was sighted at 10 a.m. Great bustle ensued as the celebrations planned for his arrival were put in train, but in windy conditions the ship did not reach the anchorage until midnight. Undeterred, some of the principal residents of Fremantle,

> anxious to be the first to testify their gratification at His Excellency's return, although at this late hour, proceeded on board—and were received with the usual urbanity and kindness which has ever marked His Excellency's deportment, and endeared him to all classes in our community.[13]

The next day was taken up with disembarkation, the first family having to be lightered some miles from the ship to Fremantle. Further greetings no doubt took place, but on the following day, 21 August, there was a formal public function where George Leake, Fremantle's Government Resident, read a prepared welcome address. Given the dampening news that Stirling would soon have to impart, Leake's final words would have been heartening:

> In full confidence, Sir, that the same benevolence, (which has always hitherto distinguished your exertions for our welfare, though possibly restricted by powers inadequate to your wishes and over which you have no control), will continue to be exercised for the removal or alleviation of the existing evils, as well as for the promotion of our future prosperity.[14]

Stirling's short reply, though moderated by deep appreciation of their welcome and praise for their endeavours, did not hide the truth. Frankly he told the assembled traders, merchants and townspeople that:

> Debarred by considerations of policy and necessity from applying a dis-proportionate outlay of money to any particular section of Empire, all that this Colony can look for from the Government at Home is a judicious application of its share of the general Fund. The rest must be effected by individual exertion.[15]

He ended with the comment that he confidently relied on their ability to succeed, and would do all in his power to advance their welfare. The family were then rowed up to Perth, where a second formal welcome ceremony awaited Stirling on the 22nd. Speaking for the people of Perth, John Morgan waxed eloquent in an address that

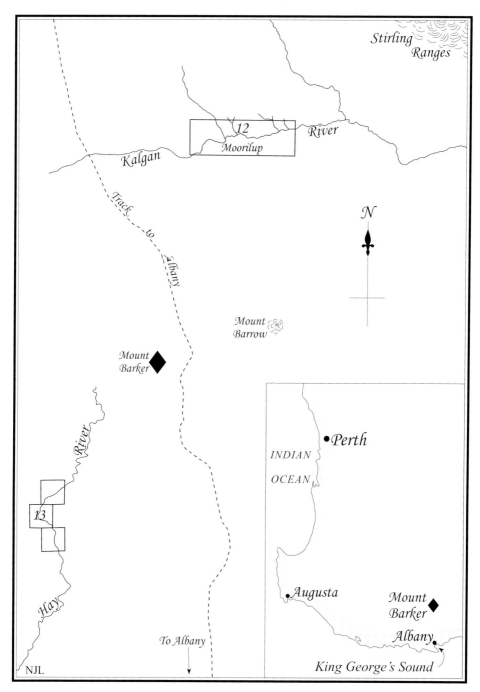

Stirling's inland land selections near Albany

must have warmed James' heart with its references to his 'parental solicitude' and 'friendly sympathy with our past suffering and present difficulties'. Identical interests, Morgan went on to say,

> which we flatter ourselves must arise from your Excellency's Fame and Fortunes being so closely connected with the prosperity of this settlement, are grounds of reliance upon which we rest our hope of the future.

Stirling's reply to the mixed crowd of civil officers, landed gentry, artisans and labourers was similar to that given in Fremantle, though not quite so direct about funding. Arrangements in future, he told them, were 'of a nature so various and complicated' that a general explanation of them was too difficult, especially on this occasion.

Great warmth had been extended towards Lady Stirling during the home-coming—and already her influence was being felt. She had seen to the immediate needs of the fourteen boys and four girls from the Children's Friend Society who had come on to Swan River (the others having been employed at the Sound), and she had also taken under her wing Mary Bussell and her mother. These two had learned at the Cape that the rest of their family, who had settled at Augusta, had lost their house and most possessions in a bad fire during the summer and then, to make matters worse, their wheat crop had failed.[16] On arrival at the Swan, Mrs Bussell had wanted to join her sons by the first possible transport, but the Stirlings 'forcibly dissuaded them', insisting the pair stay for a time in Perth. The only ships available were small colonial craft, and Stirling feared for their safety in the boisterous winter weather. Much of their cargo, however, including the family silver, was loaded onto the small vessel *Cumberland* which was lost with all hands the very evening she sailed from Swan River, wrecked off the south end of Garden Island.[17]

The Governor had other matters on his mind. On 25 August he called his first meeting of the Executive Council to inform them of the outcome of his mission. In attendance were Richard Daniel, Senior Officer of the Land Forces, Peter Brown, the Colonial Secretary, and J. S. Roe, his Surveyor-General. Stirling was brief, summarising the changes and informing them that full details of the new regulations to govern administration of the colony would be published in the *Gazette* as soon as possible. The Governor also proposed that future meetings of the Legislative Council be open to the public, who could purchase tickets (the small room limited viewers to twenty).[18] This proposal was welcomed by all Councillors and was to prove popular with the settlers. The main business of the day, however, concerned the Act placing duties on imported spirits, which had been passed prior to June 1832 but had not been sanctioned by the Home Government due to a miswording. Council readily agreed to the necessary change, and Stirling proposed that a notice to this effect be published as soon as possible for general information.[19] The Council then adjourned.

The following Wednesday Stirling travelled upriver to Guildford to receive a welcome address from the agricultural settlers of Middle and Upper Swan. It was signed by many old friends: William Tanner, William Brockman, William Burgess and Captain Meares (to whom he eventually sold his stud horse, 'Grey Leg', for £300[20]). They also hailed his return as 'the dawn of a new era', and expressed the 'universal feelings of Satisfaction and Joy pervading all ranks of the people' at his, and Lady Stirling's return.[21] In his reply, Stirling was a little more open about the changes he had been told to implement. He assured them a Parliamentary Grant would be made to cover basic administrative expenses, and that with reference to the size of the colony's population they had a 'full proportionate share of that description of outlay'. He went on to tell them that any other 'more local' expenditure

> must be met by the Colonial Revenue or those services dispensed with, but His Majesty's Treasury has been pleased to assign, as a commencement to the Colonial Fund, a very large amount; and there is reason to hope that a wise application of that sum, together with the Duty on Spirits and the Sales of Land, may be sufficient for present exigencies…[22]

He did not tell them that the 'very large amount assigned' to the Colonial Fund was no grant at all, but the debt to be collected from overpaid allowances and unauthorised rations from the Store! He mentioned the future increase in membership of the Legislative Council, and stressed the concession that had been made to allow the sale of unimproved land grants—as long as the improvements were carried out by the subsequent owner.[23] He concluded with praise for achievements in his absence, thanks for the warm welcome extended to himself and Lady Stirling, and assurance of his 'hearty participation in sincere wishes for their welfare'.

So in all of his initial speeches, Stirling had tried to prepare the colonists for change, but few suspected the extent of that change. On Saturday 30 August the *Perth Gazette* carried three pages detailing the new regulations that were to govern the management of the Civil Establishment, as well as a table stating the names, positions, salaries and place of business of all appointees. Under separate headings the duties, hours of business and records to be kept by each department were itemised in extraordinary detail. Even the daily regime of the Governor was spelt out. He would see those who had made appointments between 7 and 8 a.m. in the presence of the Confidential Clerk. Orderlies, who would attend the office from 6.30 a.m. till 4 p.m., would make appointments and keep records. The Confidential Clerk's office would be open from 6.30 to 8.30 a.m. and again from 10 a.m. to 3 p.m., and be responsible for all six sets of necessary letter books and registers. The Governor would see the Colonial Secretary at 10 a.m. 'to dispose of the business of the day', and the latter would also assume responsibility for taking the minutes of the Executive Council and its sub-committees. The Colonial Secretary would ensure the taking of all records, in duplicate, but would not keep the records, as that was to be the responsibility of a new officer, the Colonial Registrar, who would also collect and keep records from other departments. The Survey Department, which hitherto had been one of the largest and most influential departments, was to be drastically cut. Apart from the duty of overseeing the extension of the survey of the colony (which was henceforth to be carried out by private contractors), the Survey Department was to be relieved of all transactions with regard to the assignment of land. No further land was to be granted, and no purchases were to be allowed, until regular maps and surveys and descriptions of the several districts had been furnished to the Governor. Even then, the disposal of lands in each district would be the responsibility of the appropriate Government Resident, and not the Surveyor-General, whose staff was correspondingly to be cut to only a draftsman and a clerk. The duties of the Collectors of Colonial Revenue, Harbour Masters, Government Residents, Superintendent of the Mounted Police and his men, and Commander of the Colonial Vessel and his crew were all likewise detailed, even to the extent of giving examples of the format to be used in keeping the required records.

One can imagine the stunned silence and agitated whispers that ensued as this edition of the paper was distributed. The free and easy mode of transacting business in the past, and accepted as normal, was now suddenly to end. Individuals who had served faithfully, even if haphazardly, found themselves without jobs and income. Others found their incomes, and duties, substantially cut. Stirling had done his best in England to protect those who had served him well, but Treasury had been adamant about the cuts. It would therefore have been a sombre Executive Council which met that very Saturday afternoon. The minutes contain no mention of the administrative changes announced that morning, but each of the members would have been seen individually by Stirling and the situation explained. John Septimus Roe, the Surveyor-General, who had taken the largest cut in prestige and staff, was very critical of the change in his department, recognising that the lack of qualified surveyors in the colony would emasculate any private contract scheme.[24] Nevertheless, he gave the issues before the Council that day his full attention.

The first matter raised by the Governor concerned the natives. Stirling had found that a proclamation had been issued on 30 May declaring the native Weeip an outlaw, and offering a reward for his capture dead or alive. Stirling wanted the proclamation rescinded, given assurances from the tribe of future peaceable behaviour.[25] Roe agreed, believing it advisable to temporise till the establishment of the mounted police force enabled them to take a more definite position with regard to the natives in general. The others concurred, and the Governor directed that a proclamation to that effect be prepared for publication.[26]

The second major issue Stirling introduced concerned the large number of unemployed, who were at that time receiving rations from the Store to prevent starvation. It had been suggested that these men be put to work on the roads, but keeping in mind his instructions, Stirling said he felt this would be 'expensive, unprofitable & objectionable'. Instead he proposed that some of the already sanctioned public works should be 'carried forward with as little delay as possible, so as to create a demand for Labour—until the approach of Harvest should offer employment of a private character'. He laid on the table a rough plan and estimate for a wharf to join the Commissariat store now under construction, and Council members agreed this would be an excellent project to relieve unemployment in Perth. Roe, however, raised the plight of unemployed in Fremantle and Guildford, and it was agreed that in Fremantle extensions to the gaol and erections of boundary walls could be brought forward, and in Guildford road works and drainage.[27] With unanimous approval, the Governor ordered notices prepared to effect these decisions. He then raised an issue of a more personal nature.

As the previous Government House was now the Council chambers, Stirling and his family had been housed in quarters prepared for officers in the new barracks, for which the Home Government was paying lodging money. It was not what he had promised Ellen and was proving totally inadequate for his family's needs, so a more suitable and permanent dwelling was essential. At first he had thought of erecting a house on the crest of Mount Eliza overlooking the township,[28] but had been persuaded that this was impracticable from the point of view of both water supply and the daily business of government. Now he stated to Council that he wished to erect, at his own expense, a home on the town lot to which he was entitled, but had never taken. However, within the township itself 'no other position than the one previously used by him appeared to be suitable, or convenient for the despatch of business'.[29]

Stirling now took a calculated gamble. No money had been set aside in the estimates for a substantial new Government House, as his lodging fee had been approved instead. Any major public work had to have parliamentary approval, which would inevitably be parsimonious, but personally Stirling could build what he liked. So, if he purchased the prime river frontage on which the old Government House stood, and erected an imposing building, he would possess the only suitable residence for a Governor when he chose to leave the colony. He could then name his own price and the authorities would have to negotiate. It would be an almost foolproof investment of brother John's money! So he boldly proposed to Council that he buy this riverfront allotment. As such a purchase would have to take into consideration buildings already on the site, and paid for by public funds, he had called for a 'Valuation Report to be made by the Surveyor-General and the Civil Engineer'.[30] Their report initially valued the whole site at £603 6s 5d, which included old Government House at £44 16s 5d, as it was 'in a very dilapidated state from the ravages of white ants', another better preserved wooden building used as the Commissariat office at £250, three detached outhouses, a garden shed and stables at £48, and then the Government Gardens, which were 'in a high state of cultivation & partly enclosed by fence in bad repair', at £200. They added, however, that they had since heard that the Government Gardens would be leased, so that

£200 should be deducted from this valuation.³¹ Having placed the report before his councillors, Stirling asked them 'whether it would be advisable or not for the Public Interest that he should assume possession of the Ground and proceed to the Erection of a Residence', leaving it to the Secretary of State to decide whether he paid the valuation or was in turn compensated for his building expenses. Roe considered that 'no reasonable objection could exist to the proposal', and Daniel and Brown concurred.

The Government Gardens had previously been the responsibility of the Colonial Botanist, James Drummond, but his position had been one of the casualties of the new administration. Stirling had been authorised to offer Drummond a lease of the garden he had worked on since 1829, at a nominal rent. When the offer was made, Drummond was told that the house and shed he had built himself on the edges of the garden would have to be removed, to make way for Stirling's proposed new dwelling. Drummond refused, on the grounds that if he leased the gardens, he needed a place of residence and a shed for keeping seeds etc.³² Stirling apparently took his refusal as the result of pique over the loss of position and income, and made the mistake of offering the proud Scot a position as his private gardener at his former salary of £100 per annum.³³ Drummond in turn construed this as the Governor trying to gain private control of a public garden, and spurned the offer. Stirling was apparently furious, demanding in writing that Drummond vacate the house before negotiations over the lease began. Drummond was later to say that Stirling had even threatened to cut all financial support for the gardens and to throw at him 'every obstacle in his power'.³⁴ He then resigned, pleading personal infirmity no doubt due to stress. He took the £150 offered him by Council in compensation for his improvements and moved well away from Perth to his grant in the Helena Valley, sending his son-in-law to remove his property from the house and collect his most precious plants, seeds and cuttings. In this instance, Stirling's single-minded passion to realise his investment plans, and keep his promise to Ellen, meant that the people of Perth were deprived of the plants that Drummond was nurturing and an expertly planned botanical garden. Stirling did not destroy the garden, hiring another gardener to maintain the grounds that still surround Government House. But unfortunately the new man did not have Drummond's botanical skills.

With Drummond gone, Stirling then had to find a replacement for old Government House as a meeting place for Council. At the very next meeting, on 2 September, when George Fletcher Moore, recently appointed Colonial Advocate-General,³⁵ was admitted to a seat on Council, Stirling raised the issue. He claimed that the existing Council chambers were in a ruinous condition, and 'unfit for the safe custody of papers'. As any further outlay would be counterproductive, something had to be done. He had made enquiries about hiring rooms, and a person named Charles Browne had offered his building, which the Civil Engineer had deemed very suitable, and the proposed rent was extremely reasonable.³⁶ Would

The first permanent Government House—a two-storey stone building designed by Henry Reveley

Pencil drawing by Dr R.W. Clarke, RN (dated 26/3/59 on verso) by permission of the National Library of Australia R732

his councillors agree this was the best course? They did, and the way was now clear for Stirling to begin building a place that fitted his and Ellen's idea of a 'proper' Government House.[37]

Before closing the meeting, Stirling tabled a list of applications for town and suburban allotments which he had approved. Roe's 1833 map of the town and suburbs of Perth had been accepted by the Colonial Office, and it was time to regularise the position of those who already occupied allotments. This first list of names was published in the *Perth Gazette* on the 6th, well before the regulations for the assignment of town allotments were officially issued on 20 September.[38] Title in fee simple to town lots still had to be acquired by improvement, but occupancy in future was to be secured by payment of a minimum price of £2 to £5, depending on the town concerned. Of the ten town grantees put before Council that day, two were pivotal for the success of government plans. The first was Charles McFaull, who was editing and producing the *Perth Gazette and West Australian Journal*, leasing the Government's printing press to do so, and in return printing all Government Notices. In effect the newspaper doubled as the *Government Gazette*, the issue of 6 September carrying the statement under its headline that

> His Excellency the Governor has thought proper to direct that all public communications which may appear in *The Perth Gazette and Western Australian Journal*, signed with any Official signature, are to be considered as official Communications.[39]

The second grantee listed was Henry Trigg, the only master builder in the colony and responsible for most of the early construction work in Perth. Stirling would need the skills of both Reveley (his engineer) and Trigg if his imposing dwelling was to become a reality. They, in turn, needed apprentices for, as Trigg kept bemoaning in letters home, skilled labour was very scarce, and expensive.[40] But Stirling had an answer—the orphans from the Children's Friend Society. He was disappointed that the services of the fourteen boys and four girls he had brought to the Swan River had not been taken up as quickly as the eleven boys left in Albany. On 9 September he had appointed a committee to supervise their welfare, and drawn up conditions for their apprenticeship, which included food and clothing, and a payment of 1s 6d to 3 shillings a month according to age.[41] As prospective Perth employers were having difficulty in finding the £12 per annum apprenticeship fee, it was decided to drop it to £6 for suitable applicants, who would look after not only the physical but also the religious and moral welfare of the children. A notice to this effect was placed in the *Perth Gazette* of 13 September. This same issue also carried a prospectus for the 'Royal Bank of Australasia' which was being mooted in London, a development the colonists watched with serious interest as a possible solution to their constant cash flow problems. However, it would be another three long years before banking facilities would be available in Perth.

The most pressing matter at that moment was the scarcity of provisions. Whilst fish, fresh meat and vegetables were available, flour supplies were dangerously low. It had been hoped that George Shenton's newly completed flour mill at the Narrows would alleviate the problem, but on 24 April a party of Aborigines thought to be from the Murray had raided it and held Shenton prisoner while plundering 980 lbs of flour from the previous harvest.[42] Although vessels were expected daily, no reliance could be placed on the arrival of new food supplies prior to the next harvest. Sending a ship to Van Diemen's Land would be pointless, as it would return after the harvest. The Council suggested limiting rations of flour to all recipients, including the military, and that tenders be called for fresh and salted fish and vegetables to be issued in lieu of flour. The recommendations were adopted and a notice to that effect appeared in the *Perth Gazette* of 13 September.

The next edition of the *Gazette* carried the new General Land Regulations (passed by Council on 5 September). These allowed bona fide settlers to sell portions of their grants prior to improvement, on condition that improvements were carried out by the purchaser.[43] Crown resumption of unimproved lands at the end of the period was still to remain in force. Although welcomed, the amendment affected settlers in different ways. Those emigrating under the 1829 regulations had been given ten years to put in the necessary improvements, whilst those emigrating in 1830 and 1831, who were in the majority, had been given only seven years. Purchasers in 1834 would thus in many cases only have three years to effect improvements.

Land was still the major issue before Council at the end of the month. At the meeting on 30 September, Thomas Peel applied for full title to his grant under the clauses of the circular issued 5 December 1828. Council debated the extent of Peel's investment and improvements, and were of the opinion that title should be given. Stirling pointed out that, as Peel was indebted to the Government for stores, it would be advisable to take out a mortgage on his property previous to the issue of title,[44] and Council agreed.[45] Peel had come to Perth to await the outcome of the Council's deliberation, and spent some time with the Governor discussing his problems. Most of his settlers had now been absorbed into the Swan district, the township of Clarence had been abandoned, and the few who had remained with him were now settled on his land near the mouth of the Murray. Improvements had been made, but had come to a standstill after attacks by the natives on Mr Barron, a dischargee from the 63rd Regiment who was visiting from Perth, and Nisbett, a servant to Lieutenant Armstrong of the 21st Regiment. The two had been on an expedition to recover a stray horse, assisted by seemingly friendly natives, when Barron had been speared three times and Nisbett brutally murdered—'there were over 30 jagged wounds on his body and the head was mangled and crushed by heavy blows'.[46] They also cut out his tongue, then cut off his fingers and put them in his mouth.[47] Why he had been murdered was a mystery to Peel, who did not recognise the Aborigines' clear warning to stay off tribal land and leave their women alone. When the murder was reported to Perth, Captain Ellis (whom Irwin had appointed

Superintendent of Native Tribes in 1833) was sent with a party of soldiers from the 21st Regiment to the Murray, but had found no sign of the natives. Peel was at his wit's end. Nisbett's murder was the fifth fatal incident in a series of attacks on his people and theft of their scarce stores.[48] Now that his wife and children had joined him at the Murray,[49] Peel feared for their lives and begged Stirling's assistance.

Stirling had hitherto pursued a policy of conciliation towards the natives, and had even had a long interview with Weeip, whom he had ordered to be freed after his return.[50] Weeip had made it clear at that interview that his people felt cheated; they had been robbed of their tribal hunting and gathering grounds, and yet were set upon when they tried to feed themselves from the settlers' bounty. Some of his people had even been attacked and killed without provocation. Stirling knew this was true and deplored the actions of some of the soldiers and settlers. However, he had made it clear that in future colonists would be punished for such offences, just as the natives would be punished if they harmed the settlers. This interview seemed to have pacified the Swan River tribe until early October, when it was reported that a large number had congregated outside Guildford, where there had been fighting amongst themselves.[51] Captain Ellis, whom Stirling had made Superintendent of the new Mounted Police Force,[52] was sent with four of his men to investigate, and reported that the hostility had apparently been caused by the intrusion of some of the Murray tribe into the territory of the Swan River group.[53] The presence of the police, however, had led to the dispersion of the group and a relaxation of tension.[54]

On 15 October the Stirling family themselves were involved. Numbers of the Swan River tribe, driven into town after a skirmish with members of the Murray tribe, had 'held a corroboree in the Barrack yard adjoining His Excellency's temporary residence and begged the Governor to befriend them'.[55] Stirling assured them of their safety, but asked them to camp on the outskirts of town, as he was aware of many settlers' apprehensions regarding 'a more intimate aquaintance'.[56]

At this time, colonists learned through the *Perth Gazette* that the Governor intended to mount an official expedition to explore the country between the Murray and Mount William, which was reported to contain fine pasturage.[57] As a means of opening up this district, Stirling had plans to form a township at a place called Pinjarup (or Pinjarra), a fordable spot on the upper reaches of the Murray River, and this trip would provide a chance for the area to be surveyed. The expedition had been planned for some time but, increasingly perturbed at what he had heard of the Murray tribe, Stirling now decided to combine the tour with an assessment of the native situation. As he later told the Colonial Office:

> …bold by impunity and by the smallness of the force at that remote station, they threatened after the murder in July [of Nisbett] to burn the barracks and houses on the Murray and destroy all the whites in their district. There was danger that their success in this species of warfare, might tempt other tribes to pursue the same course, and eventually combine together for the extermination of the whites. It

therefore became of the most urgent necessity that a check should be put upon the career of that particular tribe. Perceiving this, I availed myself of the first occasion to proceed to that quarter.[58]

Stirling had clearly decided to apprehend members of the Murray tribe, who had been identified as the main perpetrators of Nisbett's murder, but it is telling that he gathered a civilian group for the purpose. No military officer was involved.[59]

Before the expedition set forth, a ceremony of considerable importance to the Stirlings had to be performed. Living in the cramped subaltern's quarters, it would have been with as much anticipated relief as pleasure that Lady Stirling laid the foundation stone of their new residence on Monday 20 October 1834. It was now common knowledge that the Governor was erecting the new Government House at his own expense, and his public spirit in this regard was highly commended by the colonists. The building, designed by Reveley, was to be of faced stone, 'extremely chaste, as well as appropriate to the situation…[it] will present the elevation of an edifice of considerable size'.[60] Another issue, dear to Lady Stirling's heart, was clarified before Stirling left town, and that was the management of the Perth School. Operating by subscription for the past year, it had run into difficulties in paying the master, Mr Spencer, and without funding could not see its way to accepting impecunious orphan children. As the youngest of her Children's Friend Society charges had still not been accepted for employment, Lady Stirling was determined something should be done. At a meeting of subscribers on 18 October, the Governor promised an annual contribution of £50 'to place this institution beyond a mere dependence on precarious subscriptions', on condition that the school took any orphans or destitute children recommended by government.[61] The meeting agreed.

Early on the following Saturday morning, 25 October, Stirling left Perth on horseback with Surveyor-General Roe bound for the Murray. They were joined in Fremantle by the Assistant Surveyor, George Smythe, with a soldier leading a pack-horse (who went no further), and some time later by Captain R. G. Meares (a retired cavalry officer and veteran of the Napoleonic Wars) whom Stirling had made Superintendent of Police in Guildford. As Peel settlers, Meares and his son Seymour, who accompanied him, were interested in taking up land in the new area. The Meares cut across country with Captain Ellis and five of his mounted police to meet the others just beyond Fremantle. Some of the mounted police were dischargees from the 63rd Regiment, such as Patrick Heffron, but they had been selected because they were married men who had chosen to remain in the colony rather than continue a life in the army, and they could ride. The party reached the mouth of the Murray River late on the 26th when the officials dined with Thomas Peel and his family,[62] and Ellis was able to discuss the current situation with Charles Norcott—his police supervisor at the Murray. The next day Roe busied himself surveying the township while the party waited for the ten foot soldiers of the 21st Regiment (who were to man the new outpost at Pinjarra) to arrive from a post further south at Wonup. So it was not until near noon on the 27th that the entire party, including Peel and his manservant, finally set out. Twenty-five in all, they made for the first fordable crossing, where the river widened into the inlet, and continued with Roe taking bearings all the way till they reached a place whose native name was Jim Jam—their camp site for the night.

Accounts of what followed differ considerably and, to this day, events at Pinjarra remain the most contentious issue of Stirling's governorship. To the Europeans, the ensuing clash with the Murray tribe was a skirmish which Stirling elevated to the 'Battle of Pinjarra'. To the Aborigines, whose evidence relies on oral histories, it was a massacre. There were four eyewitness accounts from Europeans: an anonymous *Perth Gazette* report of 1 November, attributed to either Meares or Norcott; Stirling's report to the Colonial Office; Roe's field book notes; and a much later account by Seymour Meares in 1868.[63] The best written exposition of the Aboriginal viewpoint (the Nyungar view[64]) can be found in a research report written for the Murray District Aboriginal Association in 1998.[65] Between the eyewitness reports and this Nyungar perspective there have been many interpretations of the battle, varying in length, detail and bias.[66] In fact, when Henry Reynolds published the first of his calls to recognise our 'hidden history' in the early 1980s (and included the Battle of Pinjarra among his examples of the 'exemplary violence' used against the indigenous people[67]), the incident already had a long historiography.[68] There had been no cover up in this instance—the story had already been told many times, mostly from the European perspective, but also by Neville Green who was the first to argue that the Murray tribe was not just punished, but ambushed.[69] In all accounts there are differences over particular details of events during the hectic confrontation. The following attempts to piece together a clearer view.

Stirling's own account of events to the Colonial Office, written on 1 November 1834 (and evidently misquoting the date of the clash), describes events after camp was broken at Jim Jam:

> In the forenoon of the 27th we reached the Upper Ford…and had just crossed the River when we heard the Natives shouting. Keeping the party out of sight, Captain Ellis, the Superintendent of the Mounted Police, was sent with Mr Norcott and three of his Corps to re-cross the Ford, and advance towards the Natives for the purpose of ascertaining whether they were the offending tribe. This he accomplished with great celerity, and on his approach towards them he recognised several of them to be of those who were present at Nisbett's murder, and amounting in all to about 60 or 70. He accordingly made a preconcerted signal to me, and advanced towards them. The Natives very resolutely stood their ground, as I am informed, and then threw a volley of spears by which Captain Ellis was wounded in the head, and one of his men in the right arm, and another was unhorsed. Stunned and dismounted by the blow, and having his horse speared, Captain Ellis's party was thus in great peril; but at this critical moment,

the men with me got into position and commenced firing, and threw the Natives into confusion. They fled to a ford about 100 yards below the other, but being headed by the Corporal's party, they were forced back into the bed of the stream. The Upper Ford being also occupied by Mr Roe, as well as the two banks, they were completely surrounded and overpowered. The number killed amounted probably to 15 men. The women were kept until after our company had been collected around the two wounded men; they were then informed that this punishment had been inflicted because of the misconduct of the tribe, that the

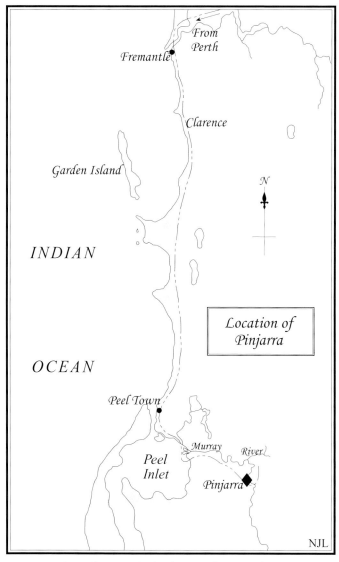

Map showing Stirling's route from Perth to
the Murray and on to Pinjarra

white men never forgot to punish murder, that on this occasion, the women and children had been spared, but if any other person should be killed by them, no one would be allowed to remain alive on this side of the mountains. Upon this they were dismissed, and after a long march, we succeeded in getting the wounded men back to the station…[70]

Stirling went on to say that he hoped the affair might impress the natives 'with the conviction of our power to defend ourselves, and to avenge violence and restrain them from the practices which have repeatedly threatened the existence of the Settlement'.

Two other eyewitness reports of the time provide more detail. Surveyor-General Roe dates the conflict as the 28th (as do other accounts), and his description generally matches Stirling's. However, his comments about the nature of the terrain crossed prior to hearing the natives at the Murray at 8.35 a.m. reveal no hint of impending conflict or premeditated action. Rather, they show that he was bent on assessing the countryside for its potential for settlement and agriculture, noting first good soil, then poorer sand and swamp and, just before the encounter, 'loamy land covered with the most luxuriant feed'. Unarmed, he remained by the upper ford and described how Ellis, Norcott and three of the mounted police rode into the camp and recognised some of the warriors.

> So soon, however, as it was ascertained that they were the obnoxious tribe, the firing commenced at full charge, in which the chief, Capt. Ellis was wounded in the temple and knocked off his horse by a spear thrown at 4 or 5 yards distance. The same native wounded one of the police (Heffron) in the right arm, so as to completely disable him. The native was however, almost instantly shot dead.[71]

He added that four or five other Aborigines were killed in this encounter. The anonymous *Gazette* report noted that it was this first shot that acted as a 'sufficient signal to the party who had halted a quarter of a mile above, who immediately followed Sir James Stirling, [back] at full speed, and arrived opposite Captain Ellis' party just as some of the natives had crossed and others were in the river'. This was Stirling's 'critical moment'. The tribe was caught in crossfire and some retreated in the direction of the lower ford, only to meet the foot soldiers who had trailed behind the mounted party on Stirling's return. According to Roe, many of the tribe who 'had immersed themselves in water having only their nose and mouth above water, nevertheless threw numerous spears with amazing precision and force'.[72] He also noted that eight women and some children, 'on being assured of personal safety…were detained as prisoners until the determination of the fray'. The *Gazette* report admitted that

> Notwithstanding the care which was taken not to injure the women during the skirmish, it cannot appear surprising that several children were killed, and one

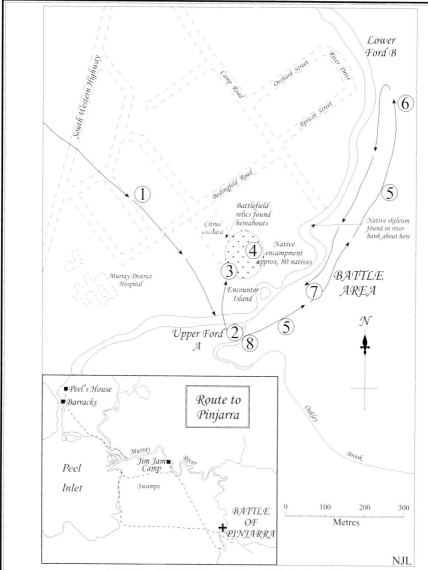

Site Plan of the 'Battle of Pinjarra' 28 October 1834
Movements Based on Eye Witness Reports

1. Stirling and Party advance, cross Murray at Upper Ford (A) and at 8:35 hear natives to the north in camp.
2. Surveyor Roe (without a gun) and four soliders left with baggage at the Upper Ford.
3. Captain Ellis, Mr Norcott and three mounted police recross the river and are seen by the natives advancing from about 200 yards.
4. Native warriors grab spears and make a stand. Ellis and party charge. Ellis mortally speared, Heffron injured and another mounted policeman unhorsed. Tribe scatters towards river.
5. Stirling and party continue north towards Lower Ford (B) estimated by Roe to be half a mile away.
6. Stirling returns with mounted men at sound of gunfire, foot soliders left back near Lower Ford.
7. Stirling's armed and mounted men line the river opposite camp site—Aboriginal warriors face armed attackers despite being able to escape through the bush on the west bank which is being held by only three men (Norcott and two policemen).
8. Some Aboriginals slip past Roe at the Upper Ford (A) where injured Ellis and Heffron are treated and eight women and children are held prisoner.

Strategic points of the Battle of Pinjarra

Based with modifications on G. Blackburn's map in Conquest and Settlement, *with kind permission to modify*

woman amongst the prisoners had received a ball through the thigh. On finding the women were spared, and understanding the orders repeatedly issued to that effect, many of the men cried out they were of the opposite sex.

After an hour of conflict Stirling ordered the bugle to sound cease fire, and the party reassembled at the upper ford, where Roe, helped by another man, had managed to extricate the spear from the stricken Heffron's arm. He made a recovery, but Ellis died of his wounds a fortnight later.[73] Roe noted that the party remounted at 10.05 a.m. and added that, 'as the idea of prosecuting the object of our expedition was now at an end', the party had to abandon earlier plans for surveying and inspecting land, and instead turn back towards the mouth of the Murray, which they reached around four o'clock.

The Nyungar view is very different from the preceding accounts. They maintain that well over fifty natives (some say hundreds) were killed, and, as the majority of the warriors were not present that morning, 'Stirling and his party attacked a group that was largely defenceless—made up of women, children and old men'. Nyungar oral accounts, handed down over generations, maintain that

> The initiated men were camped at the Peel inlet, carrying out initiation rituals with some of the older boys [and] those attacked at Pinjarra were women and children camped near a woman's ceremonial area, only protected by a small number of male guardians and older men. Stirling's men were conscious of this and therefore fled the area quickly after the massacre, anticipating that the warriors would soon discover what had occurred and pursue them.[74]

Nyungars believe the affair was a planned ambush, and it has been argued that Stirling's use in his official report of the term 'preconcerted signal' implied that 'the sighting of some of the wanted men offered the conditions necessary to legitimise a full scale attack on the camp', and that what ensued amounted to a massacre. [75]

> Nyungars had demonstrated that a large force of soldiers and police had little chance of getting close to them if they were on the run. Unless the soldiers carefully organized a trap Nyungars would scatter, regroup later and pose a continued threat to the colonizers. A place for an ambush had to be found where Nyungars would be caught in a trap with soldiers forcing them into positions of close range with enough time to reload guns and use bayonets and swords. Nyungars, particularly Nyungar women and children, for it was the men who would have been trying to counter Ellis' attack, were caught in a cross fire and 'picked off' easily by Stirling's troops on the eastern Bank.[76]

It is perhaps not surprising that in well over a century and a half so many interpretations have arisen, ranging in essence between the dictionary definitions of massacre ('the indiscriminate killing of unresisting persons') and battle ('a combat between opposing forces').[77] The correct terminology would seem to depend on whether the attack was planned in advance and intended to annihilate most of the tribe; whether significant numbers of warriors were away and hence not in a position to retaliate, leaving old men, women and children to bear the brunt of the attack; and finally, how many of the tribe were killed. These points, and related issues, need to be examined in some detail.

Planned expedition purpose

The Battle of Pinjarra has frequently been seen as a clash between tribespeople and the military, i.e. soldiers led by Governor Stirling.[78] But if a major onslaught on the tribe had been planned, Stirling would certainly have taken a detachment of the 21st Regiment with him, under their own officer. He was well aware of protocol, which demanded that armed conflict was the province of the military. It is known he did not take an officer with him, nor did he march a detachment or party of soldiers from Perth (the ten foot soldiers in the group were transferred from an outstation at Wonup). Both the military and the Executive Council were informed that the Governor was on a survey expedition, and would take members of the mounted police and their Superintendent with them for protection against the natives of the Murray region, as they had recently been very aggressive. And it has been shown that in native affairs, Stirling preferred to rely on the police, who would be under his orders. The purpose of the mission was to establish a garrison outpost at Pinjarra, in order to open up the area for settlers. His Council was told that he would use the opportunity to assess the native situation and if possible bring the perpetrators of the recent Murray murders to justice. The expedition was low-key and comprised two surveyors, Roe and Smythe, who set to work to plan a township when they reached the mouth of the Murray River. The rest of the party were entertained by Peel while they waited for the foot soldiers to join them. It was their late arrival that delayed the start on the 27th and explains the early stop at Jim Jam, as these men would have marched for most of the day. The following day the party set off towards the ford at Pinjarra, as described in the eyewitness reports.

Mostly Warriors, or Women?

Although recent Nyungar analysis has most of the warriors absent from the skirmish, being instead at the Peel inlet, the contemporary eyewitness reports all point to a good number of fighting men being present among the overall gathering of between sixty and eighty. The *Perth Gazette* noted soon after the attack that 'seven of the natives killed at Pinjarra were recognised as principals in the barbarous attack on Nisbett and Barron', and also that 'examination showed among the dead 15 very old and desperate offenders'.[79] Another report in the *Gazette* on 25 April 1835 listed the actual names of those Aborigines who had died in the incident. The names had been 'obtained from the Murray tribe' and included six Murray men, four men of a neighbouring tribe, three Murray women and a child.[80] The report is suspicious, as it is Aboriginal custom not to name the dead, but two modern anthropologists have also been able to name six men and two women killed at the time, and another man and woman who died later of injuries.[81] Archeological surveys at the site, using radar, metal detection and excavation, identified two male skeletons—one of a 19-year-old, the other between 30 and 45—with evidence of musket ball injuries.[82] Women unquestionably were present and were harmed, as the reports show, but it is highly unlikely to have been deliberate, for Stirling's naval background and honour as a gentleman made the killing of women and children abhorrent. And all eyewitness accounts testify to the repeated orders to spare the women and children.

Numbers Killed

Ellis was the only white fatality, and although reports of Aboriginal fatalities have varied, the encounter was clearly costly. The first *Gazette* account estimated 25 to 30; Roe stated that 4 or 5 were killed at first, presumably near the camp, and another 15 to 20 later; Stirling's estimate was 'probably' 15. The *Gazette* report citing the Murray informants named 14 who had died, a figure backed by the modern anthropologists who identified 10 fatalities at the time (including 3 women), though they stressed this was a significant underestimate.[83] Seymour Meares, an eyewitness who moved to the Pinjarra area later in the 1830s, believed 18 were killed at the time.[84] The real number was more likely to be 20 to 25 on the day, with 3 to 5 more Aborigines dying later from injuries. As all seem to agree that there were between 60 and 80 Nyungars present in the camp before the fighting began, the loss of this number would not have completely annihilated the tribe, which could well have happened if they had been taken by a much larger military force. It is, nevertheless, undeniable that the legacy of that day was far more traumatic than the deaths at the time, as tribal kinship bonds with those killed, and associated food taboos, would have undermined the health of the survivors.

Conclusion: Ambush or Mischance?

This issue is critical for a real assessment of the battle and has at its heart the movements of different members of Stirling's party from when they arrived near the native camp, and the question of premeditation. Why, for example, did Stirling send the initial small mounted police party into the camp, while he continued on with the bulk of the party? Had a major conflict been intended, Stirling (whose naval training had fully attuned him to tactics and strategy) would surely have remained directly opposite the camp, well positioned to follow up. As it happened, he was halted a quarter of a mile away when the first shots were fired. Stirling's report to the Colonial Office was clear in this respect: Captain Ellis' initial approach was bent on intelligence, to determine (with the help of interpreters) whether the tribe harboured, or had information about, Nisbett's killers. The *Gazette* report spoke of the desire to 'bring on an interview' (have talks) with the Aborigines. On hearing shots fired, Stirling galloped back to the scene with the mounted men, leaving the foot soldiers to return more slowly back along the east bank of the Murray (see map). Thus the Aborigines would have seen three armed groups (plus the unarmed Roe with four soldiers waiting at the southern upper ford), creating a clear impression of ambush. However, as there were only three fit Europeans on the west bank, guarding a large area of river frontage, there was ample room for skilled bushmen to escape. And their bush skills were undeniable. Stirling and others feared and grudgingly admired their guerilla-type tactics and ability to melt away unseen. Opportunities to escape would also been provided by the nature of weapons available to the European men, for the single-shot, muzzle-loading, smooth-bore, short-barrelled carbines they used[85] were cumbersome to reload, particularly in misty, damp weather, and said to be inaccurate at anything but short range. It therefore would appear, and others agree, that the Murray natives actually 'chose to take on the colonial force' rather than disperse into the bush.[86] Fleeing was not in their make up. It does the warriors an injustice, and demeans them, to use the word 'massacre', which implies the killing of 'unresisting' persons. They were not unresisting; they courageously fought an unwinnable contest—a fact which Stirling recognised when he bestowed the title of 'battle' on the events of the day. And battle honours should be accorded to those warriors today.

There is no doubt, however, that Stirling wanted to punish the Murray men, who had committed the attacks on 'his' people and were threatening the continued survival of the colony. But he never propounded a policy of extermination or eviction (as had occurred in Van Diemen's Land and elsewhere). He had ordered firing to be directed at the adult men of the tribe, called a halt to the shooting after an hour, and gave no order to round up those who had escaped. From his perspective, 'sufficient punishment' had been inflicted. He was later to comment:

> However distressing the implementation of Punishment may be to the private feelings of Individuals, there are occasions on which it is not to be avoided. Upon the one alluded to the Blow was…effectually dealt upon the Guilty Tribe, but it has cost me the Life of a valuable Officer…I await the Result of this affair with much real anxiety…[87]

Taken overall, colonists had mixed reactions to news of the 'Battle of Pinjarra'. Then, as now, there were those who believed the natives were innocent victims, murdered for trying to protect their land and livelihood. But overwhelmingly there was a sense of relief. When the news was first reported in the *Perth Gazette*, its editor referred to 'the severe but well merited chastisement…inflicted upon this troublesome people, who had rendered themselves equally the bullies of all the tribes around and the dread of the settler'.[88] The reaction of other native tribes to the encounter was carefully noted. The *Gazette* reported that the 'Natives of the Perth district' doubt the account of the numbers killed but generally evince a satisfaction that the atrocities of the Murray tribe, to which they have all been exposed, have met with this merited chastisement. Their expressions of gratification are, however, intermingled with suspicion of our good intentions toward them.[89]

G. F. Moore recorded a similar reaction from the natives on the Upper Swan who, though 'alarmed for themselves from what has occurred at the Murray, seem glad that that tribe has suffered'.[90] It was also reported that 'all the young men of the Swan and mountain tribes appear to be up in arms to obtain the women either betrothed or united to those men who were killed'.[91] No outpouring of grief was noted by any of the settlers with links to the Swan region tribes. The truth was undoubtedly that resource scarcities were pushing neighbouring tribes to take advantage of the death of the Murray men. Food taboos on remaining Murray tribespeople provided opportunities for other tribes,[92] thus destabilising inter-tribal relations and accentuating survival difficulties. Of this Stirling and his settlers were unaware.

On his return from the Murray River, Stirling visited Guildford to attend the third meeting of the Agricultural Society on 7 November. Before it began, he and others in the group, including Captain Blackwood of HMS *Hyacinth* and a Mr Taylor from King George's Sound, inspected farms in the Guildford area and stock brought in for the cattle show. At 4 p.m. the men joined society members at the Cleikum Inn for an 'excellent dinner', and to hear the annual report read out. It proved highly gratifying. Members were assured that, in only the fifth year of the colony's existence, their livestock numbers and land in cultivation compared well with any other colony at a similar stage. Moreover, the quality of stock was improving thanks to judicious importing of horses by the Governor himself, and of Saxony and Merino sheep by Mr McDermott and the late Mr Trimmer. Of particular interest to Stirling was the news that a small quantity of wool which had been exported in 1832, though dirty and badly packed, had fetched 2s 2d a pound, confirming the opinion held by many that the colony could become a major exporter of fine wool. The only impediment to this desirable object was the strange staggering disease which had affected sheep grazing on the coastal plain, and decimated flocks.[93] But this, members were told, seemed to have been overcome. No cure had yet been found for the disease, but Mr Bland, one of the largest sheep owners in the colony and keeper of the government stock, had reported that flocks he had taken over the Darling Range into the York district had been totally free of it. In fact, he had pronounced that area to be 'as healthy a sheep-run as can be found'.[94] His example had since been followed by other individuals, and there were now eight healthy flocks 'over the hills' with more expected to follow when the road was improved.

Stirling would have delighted in this news. His time in New South Wales, and his family connections in the cloth trade, had provided ample evidence of the potential wealth to be gained from the raising and sale of fine wool. An inspection trip had been planned for the York district, and he and the others were impressed with the rich valley surrounding the Avon River (so named before it was realised that it was a continuation of the Swan). Soon after his return on 13 November, Stirling announced he had been 'highly gratified with the appearance of the country'.[95] Indeed, he had decided to take out a reserve over 5,000 acres of land near the future town of Beverley, in the Dale Valley, named after its initial explorer, Ensign Robert Dale.[96] Several weeks later Stirling commented in a letter to a fellow Scot, the Hon. Alexander Macleay, who was the New South Wales Colonial Secretary,[97] that:

> Sheep-keeping answers admirably here and we have a vast range of Country well suited to it. We only need 25 or 30 thousand of your surplus Flocks to give us a good start in that line, and I wonder if some of them amongst you who are forced to go very far back with their sheep do not prefer to bring them here where Land in convenient pastures is selling at 1s an acre, and where the sheep owner is getting £2.15.0 per head for his draft Ewes & wethers from the Butcher.[98]

Stirling now urged those among the larger early grantees who, due to the restrictions on the amount of land that could be selected in the Swan district, had made up their land entitlements with unspecified acreages 'in the interior', to take them up over the hills as soon as surveys had been completed.

During her husband's absence, Lady Stirling had been attending to the cultural needs of the settlers. She had brought out a number of the latest books, including novels, to add to the small circulating library she and Matilda Roe had founded in 1830. G. F. Moore refers to reading one of these new volumes, *Arlington*, as he walked from Guildford to Perth for what would be a long Executive Council meeting on 16 November.[99] Items on the agenda included the discontinuation of the present system of issuing provisions to road parties and to agriculturalists as payment after the harvest, a plan for the future employment of destitutes, and an application for an increased allowance to Mr MacFaull, editor of the *Perth Gazette*, whose government workload had increased. Little was said about the 'affair with the natives at the Murray' on the grounds that it had already been fully and accurately made public in the Press. Discussion mostly revolved around ways in which those in debt to the Government could be made to pay restitution into the Colonial Fund. Almost all colonists had been so indebted at some stage or other, but few of Council's plans for the betterment of the colony could be realised unless more money became available.[100] Council had already updated the Act to impose duties on imported spirituous liquors,[101] but all knew that there would be insufficient revenues from this source to accomplish all that needed to be done.[102]

Settlers at the Sound had suggested the introduction of convicts as a solution to their difficulties, and sixteen of them had signed a petition addressed to the Secretary of State for Colonies to that effect.[103] But Stirling had answered that the Prayer of the Petitioners cannot with propriety be complied with, amongst others reasons because in founding the Colony of Swan River, of which King George's Sound forms part, it was an engagement that no convicts should be sent there.[104]

He was by now totally committed to the private enterprise experiment he had founded at Swan River, perhaps more particularly because news was filtering through of the calumny his colony was receiving at the hands of those behind the proposed new colony to be founded on the south coast of Australia.[105]

Despite fears of retaliation after the clash at Pinjarra, relations between the settlers and the natives remained relatively peaceable on all fronts over the following months. Stirling was keen for this to continue and had evolved a plan to give Aborigines greater independence by putting aside land for their use, and arranging employment in various useful pursuits, such as fishing and procuring wood, and even stock-keeping, under the protection and guidance of a 'proper Supervisor'. He put the plan to the Council at their final meeting for the year, on 10 December, proposing that an area under Mount Eliza (Section S on the Town Plan) be purchased for the purpose. Council welcomed the idea, Moore and Roe stating it would ease the burden on farmers and Daniel noting it would improve security. Brown was somewhat concerned that native employment might threaten the livelihood of ordinary fishermen and labourers in the town, but he generally concurred. Stirling then suggested that Mr Francis Armstrong be appointed as Superintendent of Native Tribes 'from his acquaintance with the natives and his knowledge of their language', and that he be paid £90 per annum. All agreed.

Francis Armstrong, now 21, had arrived in 1829 with his parents, four brothers and sister in the *Gilmore* as part of Peel's group. He had been interested in the Aborigines from the outset, and both at Clarence and the Murray had acquired a knowledge of their habits and language. When his parents moved to Perth in 1831, he had been employed by Moore and helped him to compile his *Descriptive Vocabulary of the Language of the Aborigines* which was eventually published in London in 1842.[106] His appointment proved an excellent one, for Armstrong was able to intervene between the settlers and the natives to their mutual benefit.

It had been a crowded half year for the Stirlings, who were looking forward to a few months' break at the Sound. The Surveyor-General would join them after surveying the country around the Hotham and Williams rivers—an expedition G. F. Moore thought would be 'interesting but very toilsome…in this very hot weather'.[107] The Stirlings did not get away until late January 1835, possibly spending Christmas at Woodbridge on the river near Guildford before heading for the cooler climate to the south.

16

A More Stable State

ON NEW YEAR'S DAY 1835 Stirling sat down to catch up on his paper work. In a long, personally written dispatch to Spring-Rice, the new Colonial Office Under-Secretary, he went through the various accounts he was sending. There had been complaints that his figures could not be filed away in London because civil and military expenditures had not been separated. Patiently, Stirling explained again that due to the paucity of resources, civil and military functions 'had perforce' been carried out in the same buildings, and stores had been shared, so deciding which expenses were military and which civil had been impossible. The problem he faced now, however, concerned the debts he had been instructed to recover from colonists. With the larger army food contracts now available, many settlers were in a position to redeem their debts, while some of the civil officers had arranged to pay through stoppages of salary. But although collection of these debts was under way, Stirling advised he could not decide their proportionate allocation to the Army Extraordinaries or the Colonial Fund.[1]

As he was desperate for funds to meet local needs, he needed an answer as soon as possible. But when this dispatch was received in London in September 1835, officials were as perplexed as Stirling, and nothing was done until 1837. Even then, there was much writing of memoranda to preserve monies due to the Crown, until it was pointed out by the eminently practical James Stephen:

> The Treasury can hardly mean that the money as it shall come in from the Public Debtors shall be disposed of after the example of…the Austrian Loan. On that occasion, it was declared that the best way of celebrating our good fortune in recovering so bad a debt wd be to build a Palace, and Buckingham House was the consequence. It wd be injurious to the Treasury to suppose that they designed a repetition of this kind of practical joke in W. Australia…I believe it will be found that the money is irreparably gone.[2]

By 1837 such funds definitely had gone: with no reply, Stirling had appropriated all recovered monies for colonial purposes. But that New Year's Day he had other matters on his mind. Addressing Hay, he raised the issue of his residence. Construction of the new Government House had proceeded apace, using timbers and glass that Stirling had imported for the purpose on the *James Pattison*. But, he explained,

> the plain truth is, that I have not at present any more money available for carrying on the building, which, although planned on a very economical scale, will require £900 more, before it will be completed; under these circumstances, I am constrained either to apply to the Public Chest, for the sum of money required to finish it for my early reception, or to desist from all further outlay, and await without a residence, the Secretary of State's further instructions on the matter, which may not reach me for a year and a half from this present time.

In the circumstances he favoured the former course of action, and begged Hay's intercession with the Secretary of State to approve such an appropriation of public money, to be repaid from his house rent allowance. At a personal level, he added that

> to me personally it is not important whether the decision in this case, be in favour of continuing the former arrangement, by which the residence was to be private property, or in favour of the construction of one at the public expense.[3]

One can see Ellen's influence behind the Governor's words. The grand investment scheme had paled in the light of the discomforts of living in the cramped officers' quarters of the military barracks. It was no place for children, and galling for the Governor's wife to be less comfortably accommodated than other ladies of the colony. Having covered his back, so to speak, Stirling could now authorise the work to continue.

Other dispatches were prepared in the next few days, as Stirling wrote notes to accompany the Executive Council minutes, letters from Spencer at the Sound, draft quarantine regulations, and arrangements for the liquidation of the debts of the Colonial Secretary, Peter Brown (who had issued unauthorised £1 notes during his absence in 1833).[4] Stirling believed that, in forwarding so much material to London, he was following his instructions to the letter. But he was to find out later that a revamped Colonial Office found his communications highly irregular, as they were not accompanied by any general report. On receipt, many of his missives were simply marked 'put aside pending report', but as Stirling did not feel it necessary to write a general report, many of the queries he raised in his covering letters were simply not answered.

On 3 January the Mounted Police Force Stirling had ordered to be stationed at the Murray, after the clash at Pinjarra, returned to Perth reporting that all was quiet. The time was propitious for the Stirlings to take their long-awaited break, but plans were suddenly thrown awry when James became quite seriously ill. Whether it was a bad summer cold, a severe reaction to an insect bite or a stomach infection—all summer hazards for Perth residents—is not known. James was rarely sick, and it caused consternation among his associates, and the colony at large, when he was indisposed for almost a fortnight. Surveyor-General Roe cancelled his plans to lead the survey expedition to the Hotham and Williams rivers, appointing Hillman instead to undertake the mission with a party of settlers. By 20 January Stirling had recovered sufficiently to attend a brief meeting of his Executive Council, and the following Saturday the *Gazette* announced that His Excellency would be leaving in a few days on the colonial schooner *Ellen* for Port Augusta and King George's Sound. He would be accompanied by Commissioner Mackie, Surveyor-General Roe, the Reverend Wittenoom and Deputy Assistant Commissary Lewis, so that a proper evaluation of these two outstations could be accomplished. Departure was set for the 27th, but unfavourable winds delayed this till the following day.[5] Lady Stirling, who greatly preferred the cooler southern climate, had intended to go but was again in the early stages of pregnancy, so remained at home to oversee work recommencing on Government House.

Stirling was away a month. At Augusta he tried to soothe the small group of somewhat embittered settlers, who felt forgotten and isolated. Some, like the Bussells and Molloys, were already looking for better land to the north, but Thomas Turner and his large family were determined to stay and were demanding greater government assistance.[6] This Stirling could not provide, so it would have been with some relief that he continued on to the Sound. Spencer, too, wanted more from the government purse, but would have been pleased that the party from Perth intended to explore further afield in search of good land. Spencer had lost many of the sheep he had imported from Hobart due to poor pasture, and was therefore elated when survey parties reported finding very good sheep country around the Hay River.[7] He and his sons quickly followed up the reports, moving flocks out to the Hay River region, where he applied to purchase 2,500 acres later that year.[8] News meantime had reached some of the agriculturalists on the Upper Swan that the Hotham River area was 'fine country', its grass green even at that time of the year, and with kangaroos and cockatoos in abundance.[9] Taken together, these discoveries of good pasture should have been welcomed by the colony's aspiring sheep farmers. But instead of returning to acclamation, Stirling arrived back on 27 February to hear that a large public meeting had been held eleven days earlier, expressing dissatisfaction with his administration.[10]

To Stirling's dismay it had been chaired by Humphrey Donaldson, a family friend who had returned with them on the *James Pattison*, in his capacity as Sheriff of Perth. Further, the principal speaker had been William Tanner, who was at that time renting Stirling's property at Woodbridge. Tanner had aired a list of grievances that the Upper Swan settlers had previously discussed at his home on the 14th, believing that Stirling had not done enough whilst in England to alert the Secretary of State to the situation they faced. Tanner, who spoke with some of the evangelical fire of the Unitarian religious group to which he belonged,[11] questioned whether the settlers' memorial had even been presented. None of the dispatches conveying the Secretary of State's responses had been seen, as these had only been circulated to councillors. He then criticised some of the Governor's early actions, especially the granting of land to officers and the 'ribbon grants' he had marked out along the Swan, which had since been found to cross one another. He admitted that Stirling had won permission for them to sell unimproved portions of their grants, but argued that they had not known previously that this was disallowed—so the 'great boon' was of little account. Stirling had been away a long time, Tanner continued, but only one of the many requests in their memorial had won approval. It was believed that through the Governor's intercession everything would be granted them except money,

> …but we have found that what was done was trifling. The Colonial Fund is increased, but how? By a present of debts; and we receive with it a twin brother, a troop of police too extravagant to be continued…but we have no representative to ask any questions…It is at least a year and a half since we asked for representatives—independent and discreet men…

William Tanner

From P. Statham, The Tanner Letters

Tanner then pointed out examples of expenditures which such representatives would never have sanctioned, citing a bridge over a stream knee deep at Guildford costing £75, while the more dangerous Helena River had been neglected. There was also the matter of the impending and unanticipated fines for unimproved land, £125 for every 5,000 unimproved acres. He ended his speech by proposing a motion that the present system of government be suspended until the Governor granted the right to return representatives by suffrage. This, and other motions, were all eagerly passed by the meeting. Finally, a committee of eighteen leading settlers was established[12] (with a quorum of five) to put the resolutions carried at the meeting into effect. It was a high-powered committee comprising at least three ex or current Government Residents, as well as large landowners, merchants and prominent tradespeople. The meeting also empowered Tanner, who was about to return to England, to act as their agent and represent their interests to the Colonial Office.

The meeting's proceedings were printed in full in the *Perth Gazette* on 21 February 1835, and must have made Stirling smart at the injustice of it all. Not only had he presented their memorial, he had sweated for months to achieve their demands. He had even nearly won the issue of additional representation, not by suffrage, of course, but at least including up to four independent men on the Legislative Council, until prevented at the last moment pending parliamentary approval. That had not yet arrived, which frustrated him as much as the colonists. His feelings were still running high on 10 March when he addressed his private letter to Hay:

> As the Governor and his measures seem to have been tolerably well abused on that Occasion, perhaps I am not an impartial Judge of their Proceeding in other respects, but I cannot help be alarmed by the Self Conceit and Absurdity of a few Individuals. The Resolutions which were adopted at the Meeting have not led as yet to any applications to the Local Government, but in my opinion the immediate Destruction of the Colony would be the consequence of granting them the Objects of their desire viz. A Representative Assembly, a Bank, & the abolition of the Police, since the establishment of which neither Robbery nor Murder have been committed by the Natives. With the exception of this Tendency…on the part of some useless People, to make themselves important by exerting discontent, the Colony is in a progressive and satisfactory state.[13]

Stirling's swipe at 'some useless people' perhaps reveals the extent to which he felt betrayed. At least none of his Executive Council had been involved, although G. F. Moore was definitely present at the meeting.[14] The Council met on 2 March, but the minutes contained no reference to the public meeting. Members discussed a new line of road along Bazaar Terrace (for which it was decided there were insufficient funds), construction of a new barracks at Albany and Augusta (which would be met by the army), and the dispatch of the colonial schooner *Ellen* to Van Diemen's Land for badly needed repairs. A second meeting on 19 March considered the need to acquire a bonded warehouse for the storing of imported spirits, and improvements to Council chambers. Plans were also made for a meeting of the Legislative Council later that month at which Stirling would lay the budget estimates before the public. It was this body, comprising the same faces as his Executive, that was to be open to the public and the Press, and Stirling demanded that all members be suitably attired in formal clothing for the occasion.[15]

The thought of retirement must have seemed increasingly attractive as the level of discontent in the colony rose. Although his house was by no means complete, Stirling knew if he did leave Swan River, his investment in it would have to be realised—hence his second letter to Hay on 13 March:

> I have now to state that viewing still more strongly than ever the advantages which are likely to result to the public service from the erection of a suitable residence for the Governor at the expense of the Crown, and the discontinuance of the house rent allowed in lieu…I have decided on transferring it to the Crown, subject of course to your approval.

This would mean, he explained, repaying him the £1,400 12s 4d he had already expended, and outlaying the £2,500 needed for completion.

> For this a substantial and suitable residence will be provided and an annual expenditure of £500 saved; the seat of Government will be fixed and no longer subject to the caprice or circumstances of the individual holding the Office.[16]

Perhaps surprisingly Lord Glenelg, then Minister, recommended that Treasury agree to Stirling's proposal,[17] but he did not hear this good news until the end of the following year.

The surmise that Stirling was thinking of leaving the colony in March 1835 is strengthened in the light of another letter he wrote to Alexander Macleay regarding his grant of land in Bathurst, New South Wales. He wished to clarify how he stood with regard to his locations, and what course he should take. Specifically he wanted to know:

> Whether I can with propriety and advantage make an arrangement…to take sheep in exchange for it, as I have a great deal of Land near this, and very few sheep… I brought out from England one of the first thoroughbred Stallions ever exported…Would it answer my purposes to send him to Sydney? Would I be likely to get £750 worth of sheep for a finer stock horse than has ever been seen in New South Wales? I brought out £1,500 worth of horses, I wish now they were converted into sheep.[18]

Stirling was by now totally convinced that investment in sheep would be the only way that money could be made in the colony, and so he intended to stock his grants to provide a future return.[19]

At 1 o'clock on 24 March Stirling took the Chair in Council chambers to preside over the opening of the budget for the financial year ahead (which then ran April to March). After a long address, he laid his estimates before the Council, and moved to have members appoint a committee to examine them. But, as G. F. Moore noted, the committee 'dissented altogether from the Governor's estimates', mainly over the expense of maintaining the mounted police, so they 'reduced that item and increased others'.[20] Stirling was not happy when the committee's report was tabled at the next meeting on 1 April. Cutting funds for the mounted police, he argued, would 'expose the colony to a renewal of the outrages which at one time desolated it—a state of things involving the necessity of resorting to extremities at which humanity shuddered…'[21]

A lengthy debate ensued in which members tried to persuade Stirling that a reduction in the police force was the only way in which funds could be made available for other services of 'paramount importance', such as exploration and the construction of roads and bridges. They believed the same police services could be obtained from the military at no cost to the settlers. The meeting was adjourned, to reconvene at 1 p.m. the following day when Stirling once again forcefully stated his reasons for objecting to any reduction in the mounted police.

> In the first place I consider an effective establishment of this kind indispensably requisite for the mutual protection of the white and the black population against each other's encroachment…In the second place the…proposed limitation… will be received by his majesty's Government as a departure from their line of policy, in regard to the natives…In the third place I received this alteration… as arising…from an idea that there are other offices and services of more importance than this…In this view I regret that I cannot concur…I consider it objectionable.[22]

But despite the Governor's objections, the councillors stood firm and the bill in its amended form was consequently adopted. Stirling would have been shocked by this defeat: he was not a man to be thwarted, but at least he could still appeal to England.

The newspaper carrying the account of the final meeting on 2 April also printed in full a 'Memorial to His Majesty's Principal Secretary of State for the Colonies', which had been prepared following the public meeting in February. Stirling cannot have missed it, and in the normal course of events it should have been submitted to the Colonial Secretary for forwarding with dispatches. Yet a month later, on 4 May, Stirling told Spring-Rice that he had 'reason to believe that some Communication to HMG is in course of preparation by the colonists upon the points on which Dissatisfaction is felt', indicating there may have been a covert delay in the memorial's transmission. He did not mention the Legislative Council stand-off, although sending the minutes of the meetings and all relevant copies of the *Perth Gazette*. When he did discuss the matter, on 15 October, his opposition to a reduction of the police force had grown even stronger, to wit:

> I assert with confidence that unless an official establishment of this description be maintained, for the purpose of controlling, managing and gradually civilising the Aboriginal Race of this Country, there will be a fearful Struggle between the Invaders and the Invaded, which will not Cease until the Extermination of the latter be accomplished, to the Discredit of the British Name...[23]

By early October he had met most of the other grievances raised at the public meeting. Relevant extracts from dispatches had been printed in the *Perth Gazette*,[24] surveys had rectified overlapping grants, and fears had been allayed about the matter of fines on unimproved land. None of the latter had been imposed, though Stirling was aware that the Home Government was anticipating revenue from such fines. He thus ended his October dispatch with the earnest plea:

> although it involves an abandonment of Right on the part of the Crown to resume unimproved lands and to lay a fine on those which are only partially improved, it will be extremely difficult if not impossible to enforce these rights.

Between the Legislative Council rebuff and writing this dispatch, the Executive Council had met twice, and Stirling had had the dubious satisfaction of placing before the men who had reduced the police force letters from Thomas Peel and Norcott, the Superintendent of Native Tribes in the Murray district, reporting further disturbances. Kalyute and Munday had apparently been making threats against the white settlers, whilst others of the tribe had congregated near the settlement. Peel was alarmed and wanted them forcibly removed, but Norcott had refused, as they were doing no harm. Both men had now written asking for direction and assistance. Stirling summed up the situation, stating it was 'requisite to decide on the best course to be pursued'. He put forward a plan to

> strengthen the party of soldiers at the Murray so as to defy attack, and to inform the Natives by some means that having punished them for former outrages, the Governor is not disposed to punish them any further, on the contrary that we will live on good terms with them if they will leave the Settlers and the Properties unmolested...In the mean time the Swan River Tribe may be employed in winning over some of the most tractable of the Murray Tribe and inducing them to exercise their influence in preventing any further mischief.[25]

The Council concurred and recommended the immediate adoption of the course suggested. At the second meeting, improvements to the ferry services then operating from Preston Point and Point Belches were discussed, as well as the question of Crown funding for Stirling's new residence. Perhaps in appeasement, all councillors not only agreed to recommend to the Secretary of State that the funds be provided,[26] but added that more should be spent to render the building suitable as a Governor's residence.[27] Work on the building had progressed considerably, aided by friendly rivalry between the artisans and labourers involved and those occupied nearby on the construction of a new Commissariat Store.[28]

Early in May Stirling had elevated his young nephew Andrew to the position of Confidential Clerk at a salary of £150 per annum.[29] The Governor was in need of a friend at court, and Andrew had developed a very neat hand. He replaced 55-year-old Humphrey Donaldson, who had taken the position earlier in the year, but been forced to resign due to ill health, and died on 24 May. A fellow pupil with Stirling at Westminster, the well-connected Donaldson had emigrated in 1833, a move influenced by Stirling. His complaints over the inadequacy of his salary,[30] and the part he had played at the February public meeting, had cost him Stirling's sympathy for a time, but during his illness both James and Ellen had rallied to the support of the Donaldson family.[31]

Whilst Donaldson's funeral was a private affair, that of Captain Richard Daniel, who died just over two months later, was very different. Daniel had been commandant of the 21st Regiment for 2½ years, thus second in rank to Stirling, and a member of the Executive and Legislative Councils. His mental instability had been a constant worry, and in a rare criticism Stirling commented to Governor Arthur that during Daniel's life 'nothing could be more unfortunate for the discipline of the Detachment, and for the public service connected with it, than the state of things on this station...'[32] Nevertheless, 'every mark of attention' was to be shown to his memory. The *Gazette* carried a notice on 8 August requesting all members of the Civil Establishment to attend the funeral, held with full military honours at 4 p.m. on Sunday 9th.[33]

Between these two deaths the colony had celebrated the sixth anniversary of its foundation. Plans had been laid weeks in advance and, during the latter half of May, grounds prepared near the flats to provide the venue for an afternoon of 'Old English Sports'. Collections were made to provide prizes for the winners of wrestling matches, foot races, gingling,[34] climbing a greased pole, catching a pig with a greased tail, etc. Several tents were erected and little boys and girls were given new clothes for the occasion. The first of June broke fine and sunny, and by noon the grounds were crowded. The *Perth Gazette* reported that the feats of skill began with a demonstration by

> a party of natives who successively, but we cannot add very successfully exhibited their prowess in the use of their formidable weapons...The Governor and Lady Stirling during this exhibition came upon the ground.[35]

In the foot races, Migo defeated his fellow natives and was afterwards pitted against the best runner among the white men—'a most interesting race, lost by the white by about a yard'. Overall it proved a highly entertaining day, unmarred by any instances of insobriety. It is interesting that this first major foundation day celebration was held on 'the Glorious First of June', the day on which Stirling had first wanted to arrive, and not the actual date that he set foot on either Garden Island or the mainland.

The same issue of the *Gazette* that reported the frolics and festivities of 1 June also announced the death of a 17-year-old native lad, Goggalee, who had been shot in the leg by John McKail, a carpenter at Perth. While pursuing natives at night in reprisal for stealing flour, McKail shot the boy, who was sleeping in his outhouse. It appeared to have been an unfortunate accident, the gun having gone off whilst McKail was confronting another native. But McKail's subsequent trial posed a dilemma for Stirling. As he told Council, it would be necessary

> to adopt a course of proceeding which would satisfy on one hand the ideas which the natives entertained of our justice, and at the same time prevent them from resorting to violent measures towards the individual if by his acquittal he should be left at liberty.[36]

The solution Stirling put to council was ingenious. Given that there was insufficient evidence to bring a successful murder or even manslaughter charge, he proposed offering the man a conditional pardon before trial, provided he would 'make such presents to the Tribe as would be likely to pacify them for their loss and then quit the Colony'.[37] Far less public concern was felt about the welfare of a young native who had been imprisoned on suspicion of the fatal spearing of George Murphy on the York road. Captured on the basis of one native's allegation (denied by others and eventually by the accuser himself), the lad was held in prison without a hearing from the first week of June until 18 August, at which point Stirling brought the matter to the attention of Council, and ordered his release.[38] The real offender was never found.

Matters before the Executive Council at this time primarily concerned the all-important ferry services across the river—determining fees for goods and livestock, and whether to relocate the Preston Point ferry to a spot closer to Fremantle. The question of building or hiring a new Court House was also under discussion, as the existing building was dilapidated. As other public buildings were also urgently needed, it was decided to request the Colonial Engineer to come up with plans for a set of public buildings, including a Court House to be built within a budget of £500.[39] Various applications for title were also considered. In June 1835 Stirling had announced completion of the surveys of a number of districts and towns, and had declared land there open to purchase. Crown land was to be sold at the minimum price of 5 shillings an acre, but private sales could now be made and registered in the Swan River district, York (in the county of the same name), Augusta, county Sussex, and King George's Sound, county Plantagenet. Town lots could also be purchased in Perth, Fremantle, Guildford, Kelmscott, York, Augusta, Albany and Kingstown (on Rottnest Island).

There was a lot of jostling over land at this time, as settlers whose grants contained large, useless tracts tried to swap or purchase the rights to better land. Exchanging land already occupied was generally not approved, but a large number of settlers had still to take out their full entitlements, having been allocated hundreds of acres at an unspecified 'interior' location.[40] Now that pressure was on to terminate the grant scheme, those still holding unspecified entitlements could sell them, but most searched diligently for the best land to claim. As a direct result of such searches, the Governor took a party of gentlemen to York on an eight-day visit on 8 September. He told Moore that they had 'passed over 300 square miles of prime grazing land'[41] and that this was the district to occupy for anyone contemplating sheep farming.

Stirling was well aware of the investment prospects his colony offered. Writing to his brother John in early August, he had named three areas where he felt greater profits could be made than in England on an investment of £1,000:

> 1st I can place it for you on Mortgage…for periods not less than 5 years at the rate of 10 per cent per annum—
> 2ndly I can buy sheep…and place them in safe hands, for which after payment of all expenses you will receive in England about 25 per cent on the average, and if the management be very good about 50 per cent…
> 3rdly Some excellent bargains in Land may be bought now when money is scarce and Land abundant. The Profit in this case will depend on the good position & skill which attend the purchase.[42]

He personally favoured the second option, as 'the Profit is so great that I do not know any investment more attractive than this'. The £1,000 he referred to was the money John had left with him for Andrew's benefit. At first he had put it into the construction of Government House, but having now been reimbursed, the money was available for reinvestment. James left it open to his brother to decide on the best course of action. He also announced in this letter that he looked forward 'to returning to England either permanently or on Leave of Absence in about 2 years from this time', and intended Andrew should return home with them.

By mid-September plans were almost complete for an expedition to open new land between the Hotham and King George's Sound. An advance party was to mark a line of road and construct temporary bridges, then be followed by Surveyor-General Roe and others, including the Governor, who would continue down to the Sound. Bad weather ended up delaying plans, and Stirling's movements were further affected by Ellen's confinement. On the morning of 1 October she was delivered of her sixth child and second daughter, Agnes—a reasonably easy birth, for within a fortnight the *Gazette* observed that she was 'sufficiently recovered…as to admit of receiving the congratulatory visits of her friends'.[43] Dr Collie, who had attended one of her previous confinements, was in Perth at the time but very ill, suffering the last stages of consumption. Stirling had arranged for him to return to England on the visiting HMS *Zebra*,[44] and he left on the 18th, but died at Albany when the ship called there en route.[45] In the meantime there had been several parties in Perth to celebrate the popular First Lady's safe delivery, though the 37-year-old Moore commented 'the weather is becoming too hot now for waltzing, which we indulge in'.[46]

Reassured on the home front, Stirling now turned his attention to the off-again, on-again southern expedition on which he planned take his two young relatives, Andrew Stirling and George Elliot. As Stirling was later to inform London, his objectives in undertaking this long overland journey were various:

> but the most important had reference to an accurate estimate of the Qualities of Soil over so large an expanse of the Country, and to the selection of the best line of Communication between the southern and the western coasts, as well as to the choice of…the most eligible point on the South Coast for facilitating the Introduction of Sheep from the other Australian colonies…[47]

The party finally set off on 19 October, and met the advance group four days later just before the present town of Williams. All were pleased with the country they saw around the Hotham River, though the advance party lost eight of their ten bullocks from 'consumption of indigestible matter'.[48] After Roe completed his survey of the region, the two parties separated, the advance group returning to Perth via York, while Stirling and Roe's party headed south. First they took a south-east direction, intending to examine land around Doubtful Island Bay, but problems in finding water caused them to swing south-west, with the aim of exploring country towards Nornalup.[49] Some thirty-four days after leaving Perth, Stirling's party finally reached Albany 'without inconvenience or accident'. The Governor no doubt dined with Spencer and his family, and Spencer would have regaled him with the settlement's problems and progress over the past year. Although a lot of land had been alienated, very little was actually being used at that time, as great difficulty had been experienced in raising crops and successfully importing livestock. More success had attended sealing ventures undertaken under the auspices of visiting ship's crews, skins to the value of some £1,500 being handled in the past year alone.[50] However, the enthusiastic killing around the Sound did not bode well for future seasons, and new locations were needed.

Stirling and Roe then set off in a small vessel to explore the territory east of Albany to Doubtful Island Bay, but found 'the appearance of the country did not realise the sanguine expectations which were entertained of it'.[51] They saw plenty of bays where sealing and whaling could be practised with profit, if the number of

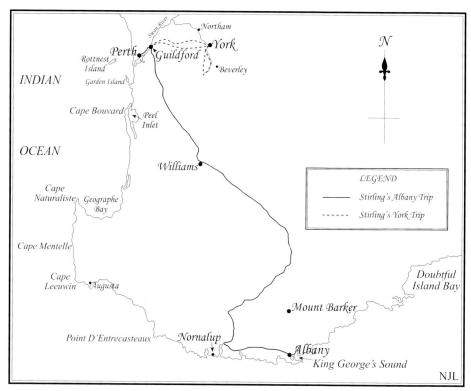

Good country was found in Stirling's October 1835 expedition between Perth and
King George's Sound, just weeks after a shorter exploration of the York area

whales sighted was any guide, but the land was patchy. On their return to Albany
on 7 December, the Governor and his entourage boarded the *Sally Anne*, hired to
replace the colonial schooner *Ellen* (which had been ruled too costly to repair), for
the return journey. Roe was to travel back overland, 'directing his course inland as
far as practicable', to continue his surveys. During the voyage home Stirling wrote
asking Roe to include in his land selections some of the good land he had seen in
the Hotham district.[52] He could not be precise at this stage about location, but
would wait to see the results of Roe's surveys. He had also asked Sir Richard Spencer
to choose for him three 640-acre blocks along the Hay River, and to send him a
precise description for registration with the Surveyor-General (Location 13).

Back in Perth on 12 December after an absence of eight weeks, Stirling could
report that his explorations had ascertained that 'sheep or cattle landed at the Sound
could be driven with the greatest of ease to the Swan River District through a
country presenting all the necessary facilities of food and water as well as clearness
from obstruction'. The news would have been most welcome, as losses from sheep
imported from Van Diemen's Land had been high, many dying from the boisterous
conditions as ships turned northwards around the Capes. There was good news for
Stirling too. Ellen would have been delighted to tell him there had been official

confirmation from her brothers that F. & C. Mangles were about to commence a regular annual shipping service to the colony to exchange goods for wool, and that a notice to that effect had been placed in the *Perth Gazette*.[53]

The settlers thus had every reason to welcome Stirling to the next meeting of the Agricultural Society in Guildford on 21 December. Their annual report was a matter of pride. The total acreage under crop had grown to 1,579 acres, 1,156 of that in wheat. Some of the wheat crops had returned 29 bushels to the acre, with the lowest averaging 8 bushels. Livestock numbers were similarly increasing, though the total number of sheep was not as great as hoped because of losses sustained in driving them over the hills, and the culling of aged and coarse-woolled sheep for meat. Thanks to a government subsidy of £100, and the efforts of the owners of several of the largest establishments, a reasonable road had been completed from Guildford to York, and the journey could now be undertaken by a loaded cart in just two days.

Stirling wrote a letter of congratulations to the Society the following day, which was published in the *Gazette*.[54] Their factual report, he said, would do more than anything else to refute the 'calumnies' abroad who had been spreading unfavourable reports about the colony. Wakefield's criticism of Swan River as 'the best example of the worst method of colonization' had run deep, and his book *England and America*, now available in the colony,[55] was being passed from hand to hand among the settlers. Though denying many of his criticisms, most colonists agreed with his basic premise that want of labour was destroying their chances of progress. The successful recruitment by a Sydney merchant of some dozen tradesmen, who had left the colony on the *Currency Lass* in November, had worried many settlers.[56]

Overall Stirling was pleased with the colony's progress, as he told Irwin in a long letter dated 22 December 1835 which was directed to him via the Mangles. In it Stirling detailed the accomplishments of the past year. He pointed to the greater stability of prices and more frequent communication, with twenty-one vessels calling at Swan River, importing cargoes to the value of £40,000. The colonial revenue had been 'put on a steady footing', £4,000 having been raised from spirit duties, and £2,000 from sales of land and fees, enabling expenditure on roads and exploration, etc. Much good land had been discovered in the interior which would pasture an 'immense quantity of sheep'. Proudly he claimed that

> Our neighbours in Sydney & Van Diemen's Land must be content with half the profit we can make…because our climate is as good, if not better, our land as suitable, & in as great abundance, and worth at present not more than one fifth of its cost there, while our meat sells steadily at 1/3 a lb, and theirs at 2d and 3d.

Crops of wheat had done well, while Sydney's had failed through drought. Stirling's Woodbridge estate, for example, had 60 tons of hay, 80 acres in wheat, and 15 in

Systematic colonisation advocate Edward Gibbon Wakefield,
whose views upset WA settlers

oats and barley. In terms of lodging and food, settlers were now far more comfortable, vegetables, poultry and eggs being abundant. A seal fishery had commenced at the Sound and whaling was likely to begin in the next season. Relations with the natives had improved:

> they have never committed any serious offence, since the famous battle of Pinjarra in Oct 1834. It is truly my wish to befriend & benefit this race, which to me if not others present some deeply interesting characteristics.

Concluding this letter, he stated:

> I have made up my mind, that there is land & grass enough to make a prosperous place, & now my task is done. The Colony grows its own subsistence, the country has been explored, & a moral certainty of its future prosperity ascertained, & a community exists enjoying comfort, abundance & security with a fair prospect before them of a continuance of these advantages to their children.[57]

Stirling really felt there was little more he could achieve. He was not by nature a man for confined spaces, constant interviews and desk work. He longed for the sea and the relative simplicity of naval life. Moreover, news from home was disturbing. Halsey, sister Mary's husband, had remarried soon after her death and, to the disgust of the Stirling family, had chosen a much younger woman who disliked country life. Halsey had virtually abandoned his children, and the Stirlings were involved in a legal battle to secure their heritage.[58] Sister Anna's husband, Sir James Home, had also died a year after his return from India, leaving another young family needing support.[59] As both James' older brothers were unmarried, as were his other sisters, he and Ellen felt their presence was necessary to see to the future of these fatherless children. It was possibly at this time that he drafted his official request for leave, which was sent in the New Year.

Christmas in their new residence, with his growing family around him, would have been a pleasant time for Stirling, but a busy one for Ellen, arranging small gifts and festivities for her household. There were fourteen indoor and outdoor servants,[60] and, as well as her own four children—Frederick (referred to as Henry) aged 6, Mary now 3, Charles 2, and 3-month-old Agnes—there were the two younger Spencer girls, Augusta aged 14 and Eliza 13, staying with her from Albany. There was also 18-year-old Andrew, almost a man but still a concern for Ellen. A friend noted he was 'a most amiable pleasing lad; but she regrets the society he is in, and the habits he has acquired, as he cannot always be under James' eye'.[61]

Ever since moving into the new Government House, Ellen had wanted to show it off and now, with James' concurrence, a grand ball was planned, ostensibly to celebrate the christening of Agnes. The ceremony was to be held on Sunday 10 January in the small rush church where the Stirlings had worshipped most Sundays. This building, which had doubled as the Court House for some years, was in disrepair and soon to be demolished to make way for a more permanent and single-purpose building, to the great satisfaction of the Colonial Chaplain, the Reverend J. B. Wittenoom. The ball was planned for the following Thursday, so the days after Christmas were busy and exciting for the whole household. The christening robes, a lacy family heirloom, were unpacked and aired, invitations to the ball were sent out by hand, the gardens and room decorations given special attention, and refreshments ordered.

On the morning of the 10th the Stirlings walked the short distance to the church, James in full dress uniform cradling his infant daughter, with Ellen and young Henry beside him. They were a first family the colonists could be proud of in looks, bearing and manners. Once the christening was over, Ellen could concentrate her attention on the forthcoming ball and welcome guests with pride, for at long last she had a home that allowed gracious entertaining. Afterwards an effusive *Perth Gazette* reported, 'we hope we shall be excused in noticing the elegant appearance of the ballroom, and the ladies who adorned it, the excellent band and the sumptuous repast, which would have done credit—without vanity for the Colony we state it—to an entertainment in any more established or refined portion of the globe'.[62]

For the Governor the rest of January was taken up, as it usually was, with report writing. He had ordered a rough census of the population to be taken on New Year's Day, and on 21 January enclosed the resultant schedule in a dispatch to England. It was disheartening. Since 1832 the European population had increased by only 230, mostly by natural increase as the number leaving the colony had balanced new arrivals. Moreover, out of the total 1,780 civilians 'a large proportion are under 14 years of age, and…there are only 780 male adults occupying…a country more extensive that Great Britain'.[63]

On this same day he signed the letter he had been mulling over for some time. Addressing Hay, he stated:

> private affairs of an urgent description will require my presence in England in the course of the next year. To enable me to accomplish this object I am very desirous of obtaining leave of absence for two or three years and trust this request will not appear unreasonable when it is considered that it is now nearly ten years since I first sailed from England on services connected with the Colonial Department.[64]

The new Government House, designed on Georgian lines by Henry Reveley, was the venue for a grand ball arranged by Ellen

Courtesy The West Australian

But by the time this letter was received (in August 1836), Hay had been replaced by James Stephen, a far tougher breed of permanent Under-Secretary. And the answer, which would be a year coming, was not propitious.

> Much as Lord Glenelg regrets the necessity of subjecting Sir JS to any incon-
> venience, yet bearing in mind that he has held the Government only 8 years and
> that during that period he has been absent for a period of nearly 2 years, his Ldshp
> cannot consonantly with the claims of the public service accede to his application
> for a renewed leave of absence.[65]

The Colonial Office had also taken a hard line on Stirling's tardy return to Perth from King George's Sound after his arrival back in the colony in 1834. James had received a letter from the Secretary to the Commissioners for Auditing the Accounts, calling on him to repay into the Public Chest the sum of £115 9s 5d because, in his words, 'I drew the salary and lodging money from the 19th of June whereas I ought not to have considered myself Governor, nor entitled to Salary or Lodging money prior to the 20th of August'. An indignant James commented to Hay:

> On the 19th of June 1834 I landed with my family at K.G.S., and being then
> within the Territory of this Government, I incurred inevitably all the responsi-
> bilities attaching to my office. On that date I gave official notice of my resumption
> of the Government and immediately commenced on the exercise of my functions,
> by remodelling the Establishment…if I was not the Governor from, and after the
> 19th of June, then the discharges, appointments and expenses which were made
> under my signature previous to 20th August were invalid, and all those Acts
> having been done without authority, I must be held personally responsible for
> them to the individuals discharged or appointed, and to the Public chest for
> having issued illegal warrants.
>   For these reasons…I trust you will consider upon a Re-examination of the
> case that I did to all intents and purposes become the Governor immediate
> upon my arrival within the Territory on the 19th of June, and became thereby
> responsible for the immediate resumption of my office.[66]

But his plea fell on deaf ears. They had paid the Acting Lieutenant-Governor's salary and house rent until Stirling's return to Perth, and were not about to pay twice. The debt would have to be paid, but this Stirling would not learn for another year. The long lags in communication were becoming frustrating on both sides of the world. In England, Stephen penned on the bottom of one of Stirling's regular notes on expenditure that

> His Lordship has had to regret for a long time past the very inconvenient
> deficiency of financial intelligence from Sir JS, and it is his Lordship's proposal to

direct that Officer's serious attention to the necessity of greater promptitude and punctuality in his communications respecting the revenue and expenditure of that Colony.[67]

Back in Perth, James was constantly making decisions that he well knew could be overturned. In the vexatious matter of land exchanges (when grantees applied to exchange their original allocations for land in newly discovered and better territory), he had decided to refer all cases to England in order to 'speedily exhaust all that are likely to come forward'.[68] The Colonial Office was not pleased, and referred Stirling to regulations, which did not in fact address the problems he faced. They forbade the exchange of land already allocated and unimproved (except in extenuating circumstances, such as inheritance after a death), and he had stuck to that line despite huge pressure from some settlers. What *he* was concerned about was exchanges of land made necessary when surveys proved initial grants had been inaccurate, and exchanges of remaining land entitlements, unallocated because the districts initially named had not been surveyed. Trying to tidy up the grant system, as demanded by superiors who had no knowledge of the practical difficulties he faced, was a daunting task. In dispatch after dispatch he outlined difficult cases and begged for advice, but the London end did not want to know about the problems of a system that had been implemented and abandoned before the current incumbents had been appointed.

They were unsympathetic on other issues too. Stirling made a special plea for reimbursement to two settlers who had undertaken at their own expense to lay a line of road from Kelmscott to the Williams River, but had lost a number of valuable bullocks to poison plants in the process. Stirling pointed out that the bullocks had perished 'while employed in point of fact on the King's Service',[69] but his argument was to no avail. Lord Glenelg refused to admit the claim.[70] As Stirling had actually approved payments from the Public Chest before this answer was received, and he was personally liable for all unapproved expenditure, the communication lags acted to compound his indebtedness. He was cheered, however, by news from Spencer containing a description of three blocks along the Hay which he had selected on Stirling's behalf. On 2 February 1836 he wrote to Roe to ask that these blocks be registered as portions of his grant.[71] They comprised Plantagenet Location 13, which remained part of Stirling's final allotment (see map page 252).

During that month several important advances were made. There had been some accusations that the *Perth Gazette* was not impartial, overly reflecting the views of government. This was vehemently denied by the editor, Charles McFaull, but a decision was taken to publish all government notices hereafter in a separate *Government Gazette*. One of the first notices in the new official publication announced that a daily postal communication was to be established between Perth and Fremantle.[72] Furthermore, the Masters of ships in port were to be required to notify their departure dates so postal deadlines could be made public.

Sultry, humid March weather was having an effect, and so the Stirlings decided to visit Fremantle for the last few weeks of the Spencer girls' stay. Ellen had expressed a desire to experience the 'benefits of Sea bathing' and Captain Scott, the Harbour Master, had 'a bathing machine in readiness'.[73] The Governor accompanied his family downriver, and Fremantle citizens were delighted, putting on a reception in their honour. It was anticipated that others would follow Lady Stirling's lead; the *Gazette* expressed the hope that more bathing machines 'will be prepared, when the number of visitors attracted to this 'fashionable resort [now called Bathers Bay] will increase'.

Although James returned to Perth for Council meetings, his family stayed in Fremantle until after the departure of the Spencer girls on 2 April.[74] But within a week Ellen would be back in Perth to support her husband. The Governor's announcements at the second meeting of the Legislative Council had provoked an agitated response from his advisers and interested colonists. Trying to balance the dictates of Colonial Office policy against the often divided but always different wishes of the colonists was a thankless task, and she prayed James would come through unscathed.

17

Dissension and Exploration

1836

The initial meeting of the Legislative Council, on 23 March, had been uneventful. The gallery had been crowded by noon, all expecting the budget to be brought forward, but they were disappointed. Stirling delivered a lengthy address summarising progress since the previous year.[1] He congratulated colonists on the satisfactory relationship with the natives, expressed pleasure that all who wanted it could find employment, and noted agricultural successes. Increased flocks on inland pastures had provided 'assurance of future pastoral wealth'. Trade had not increased, but he believed this was due 'to the substitution of domestic products for those which were formerly imported'—a good sign. Finally, he noted that despite limited funding, real progress had been made in the construction of roads and bridges, and in the extension of surveys.

The address over, Stirling put forward five bills which had been prepared by Moore, but noted that the Revenue and Expenditure Bill would be held over until next meeting. He then announced that the past year's revenue had realised expectations and, together with the previous year's balance, had met expenditures. But it would be different in the coming year, for projected income simply would not support the 'existing establishment'. In the circumstances, he believed a reduction of expenditure was more advisable than the imposition of new taxes—a course 'to which in the present state of the colony', he said, he 'did not intend to resort'.[2]

This left his councillors and the watching gallery in anxious suspense, for the outlay cuts were not to be announced until 4 April. Before that meeting, Stirling requested his councillors to re-examine the Act of Parliament that had constituted the Legislative Council, to remind them of their responsibilities. Council then adjourned.

When they met again on the 4th, the Governor put Moore's bills before them for a second reading, and followed this by introducing 'An Ordinance to provide for the Revenue and expenditures of the Colony for the year 1837'. Moore, the Advocate-General, was shocked and pointed out that 'an Ordinance…debars us from a free and full discussion'. Stirling maintained he had no right to be surprised, for under the provisions of the Act it was clear that until a bill was brought forward 'this Council can have no power to inquire into the acts of the Governor'. Moore stuck to his point, replying:

> we were called to discuss the Estimates, and the withholding of those estimates and the substitution of an Ordinance was a surprise for Council. The proper opportunity for discussing the estimates was taken away from us.

Stirling maintained that he had been in error the previous year in allowing them to discuss the estimates, and he was now only following the proper course of action. Moore promptly attacked the Ordinance Bill as 'unconstitutional' and 'injurious', stating he objected to it in principle and because it made no provision for debts. He was not alone in his opposition. Supporting him, Colonial Secretary Brown maintained that Council had a responsibility to ensure that all Ordinances transmitted for the King's approval took the form 'of an estimate passed by the majority of Council and did not in amount exceed the applicable resources of the Colony'.

Roe quickly agreed. He had calculated that, given current levels of Colonial revenue and expenditure, there was the likelihood of a £1,300 debt by the year's end if the expenditure in the Ordinance were approved. This brought Armstrong, the Military Commander, onside, so now the whole Council opposed the Governor. Stirling countered by saying, 'If I exceed the available means, I incur a personal liability—the surest safeguard against my rendering the expenditure more costly than the resources from the taxes will meet'.

Roe then intervened with a remark that enraged the Governor: 'the ground work of our opinions rests in the apparent illegality of the procedure, and upon the impossibility of providing for an accumulating debt…' The reference to procedural illegality offended the Governor, who demanded to know from his Advocate-General whether the course adopted the previous year was legal or not. Somewhat icily, Stirling remarked that if Moore could confirm that he could appropriate revenue raised for public purposes 'without the sanction of His Majesty', he would 'give his decision its full weight…'

> It may be as well to observe that I am not without authority for appropriating a larger sum than that sanctioned by the Council. The concurrence of Council is not required: they have no power to subvert His Majesty's instructions.[3]

But Council refused to budge and Stirling's Ordinance was thrown out. Recognising defeat, Stirling asked Council to form a committee to consider the estimates and report back to the next meeting.

The nub of this whole affair was again the mounted police. Stirling so believed that a civilian mounted police force was the only way to keep peace with the natives[4] that he had tried to push through (via the Ordinance) his expenditure estimate of

£830 for the pay and upkeep of a superintendent and six police and their horses.[5] Councillors were equally stubborn—they wanted roads, bridges and schools, and believed the police services should be performed by the soldiers of the 21st Regiment and paid for by the military grant. Consequently, they cut the amount Stirling had allocated to the mounted police to £479[6] and used the savings to provide for a schoolmaster at Guildford, and to add £100 for superintendence of public works.[7]

Presented with the committee's decision at the subsequent sitting, Stirling stated there was only one proper course of action—both sets of estimates should be sent to London so that 'His Majesty's Government may be enabled to decide… which shall appear to them the most eligible'. He then closed the meeting peremptorily. Curiously, nothing seems to have been said about the Legislative Council fracas at the next three meetings of the Executive Council, bearing in mind that the same men sat on both bodies. However, Moore, who had taken the firmest stand, missed the first two as he was on an expedition to explore the region further north. His diary implies that the Governor had sent him away, for he was offered police protection if he 'should be inclined to take a ten day trip anywhere'.[8] With two of his neighbours, Mr Bull and Mr Lennard, Moore had proceeded north-west from York to the coast, discovering the river which still bears his name. They returned about 11 May, pleased with the expanse of pastoral territory they had seen, and excited about the prospect of a large inland sea which they had heard of from the natives.

On 19 May 1836 the first ship built in the colony entirely from local timbers was launched into the river with due ceremony. She was called the *Lady Stirling*, but as her namesake was away with His Excellency at the head of the Swan that day, the honours were done by Matilda Roe, wife of the Surveyor-General.[9] Melville and Perth Waters were 'studded with boats richly freighted with the fair inhabitants of Perth' for the occasion, while a musical party contributed 'Rule Britannia'. Perhaps this event exhausted the enthusiasm and pockets of Perth's townspeople, for the *Perth Gazette* several times lamented the lack of any preparations for the First of June foundation celebrations. The weather was not helpful either, the last week of May being particularly stormy. Nevertheless, the seventh anniversary was celebrated, on a smaller scale but similar to the previous year, with rustic games and native demonstrations. James and Ellen attended and took refreshments in the booths that had been erected on a cleared space opposite Heirisson Island. Military officers also attended the function, and it is possible the Stirlings became better acquainted with Lieutenant Bunbury of the 21st Regiment, who had arrived from Van Diemen's Land a month or so previously.[10] Stirling was planning another expedition south to form an outpost near Williams,[11] and invited Bunbury to accompany him and others, including Mr Phillips (whom he had chosen as Government Resident for the district) and nephew Andrew Stirling, on the inspection tour.

The party returned via York, where Stirling found there had been more trouble with the natives. He reported to his Executive Council on 30 June that 'two natives

Lieutenant H. W. Bunbury,
who was often at odds with the Governor
Courtesy Battye Library 8713B

had been shot at the farm of Mr Soloman'. He had asked Captain Armstrong for a detachment to be sent to York, where he wanted one or two soldiers to be stationed on all farms in the district and a party of six to visit all the farms in rotation.[12] Bunbury, who led the detachment, described his job as follows:

> My duty is very fatiguing and disagreeable, as my men are stationed at the different farms on the Avon…a district nearly 50 miles in length…I have no fixed residence or quarters…and in the middle of winter with a pleasing alternation of rain and frost I do not find the life very pleasant. I hope, however, it will not last very long as the Natives seem inclined to be quiet since I shot a few of them one night.[13]

Stirling's concern about the consequences of military intervention was justified, for these natives were shot while retreating! Bunbury's whole attitude to the Aborigines placed him at odds with the more conciliatory Governor. And after less than three months in the colony, Bunbury voiced some scathing criticism:

> Not the slightest reliance is to be placed on the Governor's word: he changes his mind and his measures ten times a day and it is notorious in the colony that except in writing no promise of his is worth anything…personally I like him but his public character is in many respects open to censure and his weak vacillating conduct has done much harm to the colony.[14]

A warmer relationship existed between Stirling and Captain Irwin, who had deputised for him on his return to England. Since quitting Swan River, London-based Irwin had been a staunch advocate of the colony, and had applied for the position of permanent Military Commander in Western Australia.[15] The Colonial Office opposed the idea, on grounds of precedence and expense, and at first this had not worried Irwin, who was grieving for his childhood sweetheart. After years of separation he had married her on his return, but she had died just five weeks after the wedding. As an antidote to grief, and a means of refuting the disparaging attacks on Swan River, Irwin put all his energies into writing a book, *The State and Position of Western Australia commonly called The Swan River Settlement*, published in mid-1835. By early 1836 copies were available in Perth, and Stirling was generous in his praise, writing to his former second-in-command:

> Your book has made a great impression here and everyone feels assured it will do great service to the cause and be greatly instrumental in removing these unfounded and almost unaccountable prejudices which impede the introduction of fresh emigrants.[16]

At a more personal level Stirling was surprisingly open to Irwin about his own plans, writing that the absence of their eldest son, combined with looming educational needs for the other children and the state of his own health, made him 'look forward to a temporary absence of two or three years'. It was more to do with 'the mind and not of the body', he said, adding 'In point of fact the Governor and James Stirling cannot co-exist much longer in the same person without mutual injury'. As this letter was written in the middle of his fracas with Council, Stirling's feelings of stress are understandable, but it was an extraordinary comment. Long before receiving this letter, Irwin's perseverance had paid off, for in June 1836 the Colonial Office finally agreed to the appointment he sought. It was even recommended that he be promoted to Major 'in order that a successor to the Governor may always be found above the rank of Captain'.[17] Now the newly remarried Irwin could begin preparations for departure.

Back in the colony, Stirling was putting the finishing touches to a long dispatch, dated 12 July 1836, summarising the position of the settlement.[18] He commented in detail on matters listed under the headings of soils, seasons, ports, population, natives, agricultural products, spontaneous products, assignment of land, towns, Civil Establishment, Legislative Council, Clerk to the Councils, Colonial Secretaries Office, Government Residents, Civil Engineer, Mounted Police, Judicial Establishment, Military Establishment, and finally Revenue. On the sticky issue of the mounted police he wrote:

> I have stated so fully the opinions and view which I entertain upon this point that it is unnecessary for me to repeat them here. The number of persons employed in that Department at present has come…to 3 men and 5 horses…

And on the assignment of land Stirling was blunt:

> Very few applications have been made to purchase Crown Lands…[and] under present circumstances no demand for them is likely to arise. The value of land in a country where there is no money to purchase it must be purely imaginary.

This was a real problem. Local expenditures kept growing, but revenue to meet them was limited while there was no income from the sale of Crown lands. Stirling was firmly against further taxes, for 'unless considerable improvement has taken place in the circumstances of the Settlers it will not be in their power to support any additional imposts'. There were only some 300 families in the settlement, and if it was to prosper it desperately needed an injection of population and funds. He had stated this many times before, but he also felt that solutions were possible, and in closing this July dispatch he begged the Colonial Office to consider three possibilities:

1st   The augmentation of the Garrison to a Wing of a Regiment
2nd   The establishment of a convalescent station in this country for His Majesty's Forces in India
3rd   A Loan of Money from the Treasury on security of the Colonial Revenue for the purpose of introducing Labourers.[19]

The adoption of any of these measures, he believed, would 'soon attract that extent of private enterprise which would relieve the Public Purse from any further charge'. In England, Under-Secretary Stephen was sympathetic, his annotation reading:

> A Nation which has founded the United States of America & which is founding the United States of Australia, might easily be roused to the efforts necessary for nourishing this infant Settlement…To expect to settle a new country by an immediate sale of the land seems to me as rational a scheme as to undertake the building of a bridge across the Swan River by the sale of the waters.[20]

But little was done. Even William Tanner's persistent efforts in London to convince Lord Glenelg of the plight of the landed settlers seemed to fall on deaf ears.[21] Glenelg refused to accept Tanner as an agent of the colonists, and was not prepared to make Swan River an exception to the Empire-wide regulations for the disposal of Crown land. Nonetheless, Tanner's forcible presentation of the fact that much of the originally granted land was useless, and impossible to improve, must have sunk in. Tanner, together with dozens of others, wanted an equitable exchange of poor land in initial grants for new, better quality land. Glenelg was then in the process of overhauling the land regulations. Believing that administrative costs could only be contained by closer settlement, he planned to allow grantees to surrender tracts of unimproved poor land for smaller amounts of new land, but the remission scheme, as it came to be known, was not to be announced for another year.

Accompanying Stirling's July 1836 dispatch were reports from the Agricultural Society showing pleasing progress: acres under cultivation had increased to 1,579 and the harvest had come in at 19,121 bushels. Sheep numbers had increased to 5,135 with smaller increases in numbers of swine, goats, horned cattle and horses.[22] The Agricultural Society was keen to see whether there was any market in England for gums or resins from local trees,[23] and had commended Stirling for a scheme to encourage natives to collect gum in exchange for flour.[24] The Governor had just received the official response to dispatches he had written the previous year concerning the natives. The Colonial Office was adamant that they should have the same rights as the settlers and, given the recent affray in York, Stirling ordered the official instructions to be published in the *Perth Gazette*:

> It is the determination of the Govt. to visit every act of injustice or violence on the Natives with the utmost severity…Nor will it be sufficient merely to punish the guilty, but ample compensation must be made to the injured party for the wrong received. You will make it imperative on the officers of the police never to allow any injustice or insult re the Natives, to pass by unnoticed, as being of too trifling a character, and they should be charged to report to you with punctuality every instance of aggression or misconduct. Every neglect of this point of duty you will mark with the highest displeasure…Colonists in their dealings with the Natives will sometimes have to encounter conduct which in a civilized society would be looked on as highly offensive; but it will be the duty of the settler to practise forbearance & moderation &…set an example of justice and good faith.[25]

Matters of a different nature were engaging the attention of the Governor and his Executive Council. On Mackie's advice new civil court rules and regulations had been drawn up, together with a schedule of fees. Its publication caused a furore. People felt the new rules 'closed the door of justice to the poor man', and 160 individuals signed a petition against them to the Governor. Council saw no grounds for concern, but Stirling took it upon himself to reply to the petitioners through the

Perth Gazette. He assured them that the regulations had been framed deliberately to protect the poor. Higher fees were to be charged for actions 'brought forward by persons whose dealings are on a larger scale and who consequently can better afford to pay them'. However, if after a fair trial the new rules operated in any way to the prejudice of the public, he pledged their removal.[26]

The new rules had also caused offence to the colourful William Nairn Clark. A highly qualified barrister before emigrating late in 1830, Clark had practised his profession in Fremantle. He deeply resented the fact that people he regarded as less qualified had been given positions in the judicial establishment, whilst he remained in private practice. His fiery temper had involved him in a fatal duel with the naval surgeon, George French Johnston, just a month after Stirling's departure in 1832. Tried for manslaughter, and defending himself on a point of honour, Clark was acquitted. But he was involved in many more contentious suits, including Peel's defence against claims brought by his immigrants. In 1835 he had written a pamphlet entitled *Report of the late trial for libel—Clark vs McFaull*, purported to have been the first book published in the colony. It had been of wide interest as McFaull was the editor of the *Perth Gazette* and Clark one of its severest critics. Indeed, in July 1836, Clark was setting up a rival newspaper, *The Swan River Guardian*, first issues of which appeared in October. Mid-year he had drawn up a memorandum to the Secretary of State, complaining against a local ruling that allowed any educated man to represent others in court. Clark believed only members of the legal profession should be allowed to act as solicitors or Notaries Public. The Act, he claimed, meant that 'a scavenger in the streets of London may on his arrival at Swan River be found eligible to act as a practitioner in the civil court on payment of £6'.[27] Stirling forwarded the memorandum, and on receipt the Colonial Office reacted, at least in this case, in his favour. The draft reply stated that as

> there appears to be only one gentleman qualified to practise in the Superior Court of this Country, & only three more who could lay claim to the character of lawyers by profession…it appears to Lord Glenelg that as equitable a compromise has been made as was practicable.[28]

Stirling was also anxious to clarify actions he had taken to relieve the shortage of specie. He was well aware of the strictures Treasury had placed in 1833 on the issue of notes in the colony, and the use of Treasury Bills, but he was facing overwhelming practical difficulties in adhering to them. As he told Glenelg on 26 August, 'it has been found impracticable to procure a sufficiency of specie in exchange for bills for carrying on the public service'. There were 'local notes to the amount of £3,500 in circulation, which cannot be withdrawn until some means of liquidating them can be obtained'. His only possible course of action was to allow the Commissary Officer to continue issuing small Treasury Bills, 'taking care to separate in his account of disbursements those payment which are made on account of the

Parliamentary Grant from those of a Military Description'.[29] Using Treasury Bills in this way directly contravened his instructions. Treasury generally only accepted large denomination bills (i.e. over £100) and the usual course was to tender a large bill out for cash, which could then be spent from the public chest.[30] But no one in the colony had much cash. Stirling was once again in a situation where practical difficulties made it utterly impossible to conform to head-office requirements. Even the Colonial Office was at a loss as to how to reply to this situation, and referred Stirling's letter straight to Treasury for advice.[31]

Stirling's 26 August consideration of Treasury Bills was joined by another (each dispatch generally having a single subject) concerning a recent missionary development. Under the auspices of the colony's English supporters, including Charles Mangles, an Anglican Evangelist, Dr Louis Guistiniani, had arrived with his wife on the *Addingham* in June. Guistiniani has been described as 'an exotic, a sophisticated Italian convert to Anglicanism',[32] and how he came to be selected by the London group is unknown. But the settlers had been agitating for some time for more religious guidance and, as he came with high recommendations, he was immediately championed by the more prominent Anglicans on the Upper Swan. George Fletcher Moore recorded on 3 July that

> Dr Guistiniani (the missionary) and his wife have arrived. He was at death's door just on his arrival…but I trust there is yet in store for him a rich harvest in that wide field to which he has thus been munificently and beneficially sent…He is animated with zeal and full of hope regarding his success among the natives.[33]

Moore and Mackie lost no time in applying to Stirling for an assignment of land from which Guistiniani could begin his missionary work, and it was this application that Stirling now forwarded to England. He strongly supported it:

> Concurring as I do with the Promotion of this benevolent Institution in the belief that important benefit would result to that Race from the Establishment of Missionary Stations around which they might be brought in time to congregate.[34]

Stirling would later wish that the first missionary had been anyone other than Guistiniani, who became extremely unpopular for his diatribes against the colonists' treatment of the natives.[35] He also entered into local politics, siding with the radical faction in supporting the *Swan River Guardian* against the more establishment-oriented followers of the *Perth Gazette*. But all that was in the future. At this stage, Stirling and the Reverend J. B. Wittenoom were keen to encourage the new minister and, at the end of August, His Excellency laid the foundation stone of a new missionary church at Guildford. Guistiniani addressed those assembled for the occasion with the very apposite text, 'Behold this stone shall be a witness unto us'.[36] The *Perth Gazette*, reporting the event, promised to 'devote a column weekly…to communicate the progress of his mission as well as any instructive hints which may suggest themselves'.[37]

Stirling meanwhile was taken up with applications for title to grants that had been fully improved. Each week there was a list for his approval, and each case was described and forwarded in schedules to England. A junior clerk had to explain to Under-Secretary Stephen that

> Sir J. Stirling has never been required to send home these Returns though he regularly does so. They are simply put by. This is not a return of recent Grants, but of title deeds issued to old grants.[38]

Colonists were also urging the Governor to introduce elected representation, and in his 29 August dispatch he commented with some feeling that:

> A Legislative Body composed of Government Officers is usually looked upon with considerable jealousy. It is taken for granted that members of this description are under the influence of Government, and therefore opposed to the interests of the people. It would be very easy to show that this supposition is at variance with fact…yet nevertheless the notion is prevalent amongst the people, and exists in this Colony as it does in all other places

Although he was strongly in favour of extending the membership of the Council by four (and had repeated the request ever since gaining approval in principle in 1833), he did not favour elections:

> A community not exceeding 2,000 persons, and depending almost entirely on the Crown for the support of its Civil and Military Establishment could not be entrusted with the appointment of its own Governor nor with the right of interfering extensively in the administration of affairs.

It might be different, he conceded, if they were dealing exclusively with locally raised funds, as was the case in the West Indies and New England. But in the present case, he recommended that colonists be given an influence commensurate with

> the share which they take in providing for their own protection, and for the public expenditure. Upon this principle, as they advance in numbers and importance… the interests of the Crown will be conceded to the very natural wish…to exercise control over the internal administration.[39]

The Colonial Office responded by castigating Stirling for not having forwarded the names of suitable candidates to add to the Council.[40] He had left a list with them in 1833, but no one in London knew whether it was still applicable. In May 1837 Glenelg noted:

> In a dispatch which was addressed to him [Stirling] on the 7th of March last…he was again invited to recommend persons for that purpose, and there appears to be no alternative but to wait for his answer to that dispatch.

So Stirling was writing of a problem in August 1836 which could not be resolved until a letter dated March 1837 reached him (four to six months later), and his reply in turn reached London, was acted on and the directive returned to the colony. It is this which explains why he never actually saw the addition to Council that he had pleaded for in 1833, and which caused so much resentment among the colonists.[41] Instructions to expand the Council were eventually to arrive with Stirling's successor.

A much bigger issue was on Stirling's mind at the end of August 1836. He had conceived a plan that would shore up the precarious hold his tiny settlement exerted over the 3,000 miles of coast he had claimed in 1829, while at the same time reducing Great Britain's dependence on America for raw cotton. In essence, his plan was to introduce Bengalese and Chinese labour, under the auspices of British capital and management, to produce cotton and sugar in the tropical northern parts of Western Australia. He argued that Indian peasants from the upper provinces of Bengal could be obtained at monthly wages of four rupees and 60 lbs of rice, and Chinese from Canton and Fukien provinces for as little as six shillings per week. And mindful of his Whig overlords in London, he noted:

> if intertropical products could be raised in Western Australia at a lower rate than in other countries…HMG would thereby acquire the power of putting an end to the slave trade. As long as that evil is productive of profit, no extinction will be accomplished by treaty, but…in consequence of the production of sugar and cotton at lower rates…the irresistible arguments of prices will put an end to these evils without further discussion.[42]

A 'great object' indeed, and one which Stirling did not hesitate to point out 'has been acquired by the occupation of this territory'! He urged Glenelg to at least have surveys undertaken of the northern districts and experiment with crops grown by Bengalese or Chinese labour.

It is possible that Stirling had discussed elements of this plan with his father-in-law, James Mangles, and Irwin, as both had written on the subject of Indian labour.[43] But where they had suggested it as a remedy to the problems of lack of infrastructure within the colony, Stirling's plan was for a totally separate enterprise.[44] When received in England, however, there was no support for the plan. Although further exploration of the north was in accord with official thinking, and indeed had already been ordered by the time Stirling's letter arrived,[45] the remainder of his proposals were ignored.

In many ways Stirling's plan was an extension of ideas he had put up in 1828, when desperately trying to convince the Colonial Office to settle the region. Both Stirling and Irwin still held out strong hopes that the colony would benefit through a closer connection with British India. Irwin had expressed this in his recent book,[46] and Stirling never gave up. His investment in horses, brought back with him in 1834, had been based on the idea of raising remounts for the Indian Army, but it had been an idea before its time. The export of horses did eventuate, but long after he had left the colony.

In early September 1836, the colonists had another potential export in mind. For years settlers had noticed the periodic presence of whales in the Cockburn Sound-Rottnest area. In August, Murray River natives had found a whale stranded on the beach and had shown the carcass to Thomas Peel. Without any appropriate equipment, Peel had managed to extract some oil.[47] Colonists knew that both whale oil and whale bone commanded excellent prices on world markets, and had been a mainstay of the eastern Australian colonies for some time.[48] When the oil sample was shown to the captain of a visiting British whaler, the *Truelove*, he had declared that if a whaling company was set up he would take 'as many shares as would be allowed one individual'.[49] The plan was put to Stirling, who gave immediate approval, and soon the arrangements necessary to establish a shore-based whaling operation, and its possible rich rewards, were a major topic of conversation among colonists.

On 17 September 1836 the *Perth Gazette* carried in banner headlines the news that, while stealing flour from a barn, a native had been shot at York by a man stationed in the loft to prevent a repeat of a theft the previous day. An incident like this invited retribution—and a man named Knott was fatally speared some days later, resulting in even further punitive action by the soldiers. In a later dispatch to the Colonial Office, Stirling expressed 'displeasure and regret at the loss of the Native's life', but explained that he had not prosecuted his white attacker, as he was protecting his own property. Neither had he taken proceedings against Knott's killers, arguing that tolerance and prudent action in this case would suffice to prevent further outrages.[50] The Colonial Office was not impressed with either action, opining that an inquest should have been held over the barn death,[51] and stricter measures taken in the second affair.

Coinciding with the report of the York shooting came the colony's first native land claim. The *Gazette* carried a report that on Stirling's authorisation, the Native Interpreter, Francis Armstrong, had spoken with members of the Swan River tribe regarding 'making a purchase of the occupied lands of this territory'.[52] Armstrong had been told by some of the Swan River natives that they would like to dispose of the occupied lands to the Government in return for flour and clothing, 'provided they were allowed free access to such parts as were not enclosed'.[53] Exactly where the idea originated is not known. It is of interest because the suggestion followed the course taken only months earlier by Batman in Victoria, which was disallowed by the British Government.[54] The matter was discussed at an Executive Council meeting on 13 September when Stirling reminded his councillors that the natives' lands 'had to a considerable extent been taken from them in consequence of the settlements effected by the Whites', and that he was in favour of the suggested arrangement. But his councillors disagreed, believing it was

> more advisable to inform the Natives that it was not the wish of the Government to deprive them of any part of their land, beyond that which is, or maybe required by the White Inhabitants of the Territory, and upon which they are not to trespass or commit any theft on pain of forfeiting the goodwill shown, and the protection afforded by the Local Government.[55]

So nothing more came of the issue. Stirling was at this time preparing for another exploratory trip. On 16 September he left Upper Swan with a party of gentlemen who still had entitlements to choose in 'the interior', to examine the area to the north of Toodyay. He returned nine days later, so pleased with what he had seen that orders were given to form a road to the new district to provide a safer route for stock than the existing York road.[56] Within the next few weeks the Governor was off again, this time on a tour to the south, bent on tracing the Murray River inland from Pinjarra to see if its source lay near Williams. Lieutenant Bunbury, who had been given command of the station at Pinjarra, accompanied the party. On the same day this expedition left, so did another—but in the opposite direction. Surveyor-General Roe, accompanied by G. F. Moore, set out to examine the land north of Toodyay, hoping to find the inland sea which the latter confidently believed existed. Ellen Stirling, then three months' pregnant and largely confined to Government House, was left in the company of a small circle of intimates, among them her fellow 'grass widow', Matilda Roe.

The Governor was first back, reaching Perth on 25 October. His ten-day expedition had failed to find the source of the Murray, but had made some headway in establishing the line for a road from the Canning River to Pinjarra.[57] Seventeen days later, Roe and Moore returned with disappointing findings, described by the *Gazette* as 'not so promising as our sanguine expectations had induced us to anticipate'.[58]

Considerable pressure was being placed on Stirling at this time, both from the public and the new *Swan River Guardian* whose critical editor, William Nairn Clark, had made it clear that he intended his paper 'to expose abuse, curb the insolence of office and advocate the rights of the people'. In mid-October the paper had given prominence to the 'open hostility' of the natives, commenting, for good measure, 'It is not an agreeable sight to see a savage in a state of nudity approaching a person with a spear fifteen or sixteen feet long poised directly toward one'.[59]

Clark wanted action. He attacked the Deputy Assistant Commissary for selling his own sheep to the Commissariat Store, his rival McFaull for fraudulent use of postage monies, and Stirling over his land grants, and for endeavouring to promote his own private interests against those of the settlers. In one case he inferred that Stirling had given the Mangles family a monopoly on shipping to Swan River, and was thus to blame for continued high freight rates. Never one to let a linguistic opportunity pass by, Clark thundered: 'This independent settlement shall not be *mangled* by them, to suit their own selfish ends…Are second hand Wapping merchants to make a monopoly of Swan River? They never shall!'[60] Strangely, Lady Stirling, despite her Mangles connection, was never criticised by Clark. Of her, he commented:

> We cannot omit this opportunity of adding our humble meed of praise to the general acclamation which hails Lady Stirling. As a wife, a mother, or a friend of the poor, her conduct has been a shining example to all classes…wherever her Ladyship goes she will always command the respect and good wishes of the colonists of Swan River.[61]

James fared less well at Clark's hands:

> Sir James Stirling's name as a Governor is an abomination in every company. With regard to him as a private individual no one can behave better, he is a perfect gentleman, a kind husband and a kind father, but from such another Governor Good Lord deliver us.[62]

The *Perth Gazette*, which had initially welcomed its rival, was appalled after the first three or four issues, stating 'The liberty of the press was never more licentiously abused than in this production, which is truly disgraceful'.

A month after his Murray expedition, Stirling arranged a new tour of inspection that was to be linked to the maiden voyage of the new colonial schooner *Champion*. As neither the *Sally Ann* nor the *Lady Stirling* (badly damaged in a severe storm) had proved satisfactory as a means of communicating with the outstations, the Governor had successfully lobbied for the larger *Champion*, costing £1,500— some £300 more than was available.[63] Stirling justified his action to the Colonial Office by arguing that, contrary to previous assurances, no ship-of-war had visited for the past fifteen months, hence a new colonial schooner was indispensable.[64]

He had chosen Lieutenant Henry Bull, RN, a settler at the head of the Swan, to take command, and once the *Champion*'s conversion to colonial service was complete, she left on 27 November bound for Geographe Bay (Vasse), Augusta and King George's Sound. Stirling was accompanied on the voyage by D. A. C. Lewis and Commissioner W. H. Mackie.

The Governor was away a good three weeks, arriving back in Perth on 23 December much pleased with what he had seen, and more than ever determined to clarify the lands he could call his own. Accordingly, he wrote immediately to Roe describing in detail the lands he wished reserved.[65] Apart from his land in Perthshire, these were: 20,000 acres from the west of Vasse inlet to the south shore of Leschenault inlet and inland on the south shore of the Collie River (Wellington County); 20,000 acres to the south of Mt William and extending to Latour's grant (Wellington County); 35,430 acres on the Beaufort near its junction with the Arthur River (Wicklow County); 10,000 acres 15 miles north from Warnup (Hay County); 5,120 acres at Moorilup (Plantagenet); 3,200 acres on the Hay River chosen by Spencer (Plantagenet); and 5,000 acres behind Beverley (Yorkshire).

He also directed that any other claims or reserves put aside in his name were to be annulled. Most of the above claims were in the same areas he had chosen earlier, a little less at Moorilup, compensating for the land at Hay River, and less at Geographe Bay, allowing for locations in the Williams and Beverley areas.

Calling the Executive Council together on Christmas Eve, Stirling reported considerable progress at King George's Sound. There were now substantial buildings, and an increase in the revenue—mostly attributable to successful bay whaling. In contrast, Augusta had atrophied with the departure of several families to the Vasse, but American whalers had visited during the year and been supplied by remaining settlers. At the Vasse, the Bussells, Molloys and their followers were doing 'uncommonly well' on land near Stirling's initially chosen grant, and he felt assured that the country in the vicinity would be a 'valuable appendage to the colony'.[66] At this meeting Stirling was informed by councillors that some of the principal settlers intended to mount a petition to the Home Government 'to suspend the Regulation for the sale of Lands in this Colony [and] to give grants to persons disposed to emigrate on the same terms as before…'[67] The petitioners had decided, however, that it would be discourteous to agitate for signatures before the Governor's return. This time they wanted his support. As the *Gazette* reported:

> the system adopted in the older and more advanced colonies, is not suited for a young state, and that, as applied to ourselves, it has been the means of retarding emigration to our shores.[68]

Migration was a very touchy subject, as Stirling later reported to the Colonial Office:

> no fresh importation of property or population has taken place within the last three years, and the want of a market for future products together with the evils, and inconveniences resulting from the smallness of the community have occasioned considerable despondency.[69]

In fact, emigration had exceeded immigration during 1836.[70] Excluding the military, the total population was less than 2,000, scattered over a huge expanse of territory.

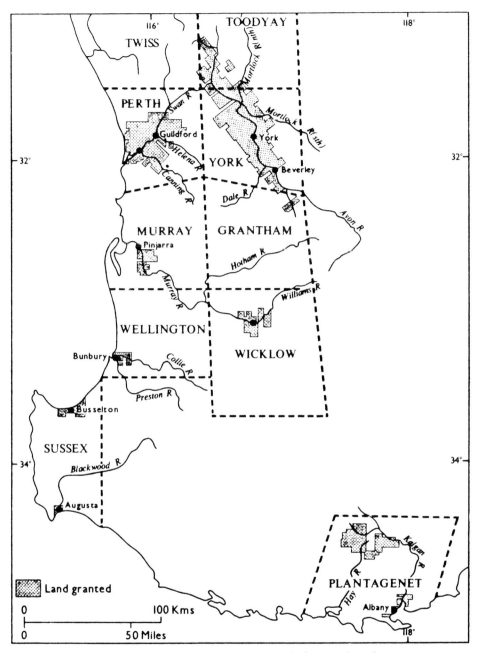

The extent of land claimed by the end of 1836, when the
total population was less than 2,000

With kind permission from James Cameron, Ambition's Fire

With such a small market, incomes were still precarious. Regular salaries were only earned by those paid from the Parliamentary Grant; moreover, many of these had to have previous debts deducted first. Those in receipt of payment from the Colonial Fund, such as the Civil Engineer, were usually on contract, so it was by no means a regular income. Landed settlers were primarily reliant on civil and military food and fodder contracts, through the Commissariat, to make enough money to buy imports and diversify into sheep. Wool exports were promising, but still confined to one or two consignments, as it had taken time for flock numbers to recover from the onslaughts made by poor pasture (and poison plants), and by the demand for meat. Families tried to be as self-sufficient as possible, and relied on relatives in England for imported needs. The few merchants who had established themselves in Perth and Fremantle were badly affected by the lack of cash in the colony. They often traded on book credit, accepting colonial produce (mostly wheat) in return for imports, and then selling the produce either to the Commissariat or to revictual ships in port. The few tradespeople and general labourers were reliant, outside harvest time, on government contracts for roadworks and suchlike, which were in turn limited by the colony's inability to raise much revenue.

The Colonial Office firmly believed that the sale of Crown land was the best way for colonies to raise the revenues required for local needs, so there was no way they would agree to the settlers' request for an extension of the grant system. However, they were sensitive to the effect that the promotion of South Australia had had on migration to Swan River.[71] The colony of South Australia had been founded on 28 December 1836, when Governor Hindmarsh had raised the flag in Holdfast Bay, on the Gulf of St Vincent. As it was established on the principle of Crown land sale, and heavily promoted, Stirling dreaded the effect that this new colony might have on his small settlement. He was painfully aware that as far as his fledgling settlement was concerned, 'although its progress continues to be gratifying, it has not as yet survived the dangers of infancy'.[72]

18

Signs of Prosperity

1837

AFTER SO MUCH time away, Stirling would have been pleased to spend the Christmas break with his family, especially as Ellen, by now eight months pregnant, was finding the summer heat very trying. Heat of a different sort was burning in the breasts of Stirling's closest advisers, who had all been attacked in one way or another by the radical editor of the *Swan River Guardian*. Was there no way to curb his outbursts? The Advocate-General, Moore had suggested that it might help if the colony adopted the English law requiring all newspapers to pay a duty which could be called on in cases of libel. A notice subsequently appeared in the *Government Gazette* stating that, at the next meeting of the Legislative Council scheduled for 10 January, three bills would be submitted for consideration: one to prevent 'Mischiefs' being published, another to outline punishments for so doing, and a third to impose stamp duties on newspapers.[1]

Guardian editor Clark naturally took this as an attempt to 'Gag the free press of Swan River', and urged the people to resist. 'The proposed Bill can never be thrust upon us unless by the point of the bayonet', he editorialised, but the bills were presented and passed the first reading. The amount required in duty further enraged Clark, who pointed out that 'in Great Britain, where the population is 25 millions, £400 security is required and here where the population is under 1,500 the security is to be £200'. The impost, he claimed, was aimed at his journal, 'for if it had not existed, this atrocious Bill would never have been thought of'.

When the bill was passed, Clark was forced to close the *Guardian*. The *Perth Gazette*, rejoicing that it had 'ceased its ephemeral existence', condemned the publication as the 'production of a man overzealous to do evil'.[2] But it celebrated too soon, for Clark managed to raise the surety and resume publication, with an even more critical pen, on 2 February 1837.

At the Executive Council meeting on 13 January, nothing was minuted regarding the Press bills, attention instead being focused on a proposition from Mr Waylen to cut a channel through the sand spit at Point Walter, if he was given exclusive rights to charge for its use. Interestingly, as this was a private enterprise colony, the Council decided to reject the proposal on the grounds that any exclusive privilege must be attended sooner or later with serious inconvenience, and might to a certain extent interfere with any future arrangement with regard to the Spit.[3]

In contrast, Council had given approval for a causeway to be built across the Swan River near Heirisson Island, if it could be paid for by public subscription. The *Perth Gazette*'s editor exhorted his readers to take up the challenge 'with energy and determination' to complete 'this most desirable work'. This same issue of the *Perth Gazette*, on 28 January, published the settlers' petition for a change in the land regulations, noting that it would shortly be handed around for signatures. Just when the petition was presented to Stirling is unclear. In any event, their plea for change was to be overtaken by new land regulations already on their way from London.

At the end of January Stirling was busy preparing the usual bundle of quarterly accounts for submission to London. On the 31st he signed the Treasurer's accounts, revenue accounts, appointments and salaries schedule, and the land returns, as well as duplicates of dispatches sent previously. With the paucity of shipping, there was no way of knowing how long it would take any dispatch to reach London, so duplicates were sent by different routes. The Colonial Secretary's office was therefore constantly under pressure as Brown, with one clerk, struggled to keep up with all the handwritten copies required. Brown was also Clerk to the Executive Council and complained that taking minutes prevented him from fully participating in Council decision-making. Stirling was sympathetic and at the next meeting, on 3 February, proposed that his own private secretary, Andrew Stirling, could do the job without increased expense. All agreed,[4] and thereafter the Council minutes became more detailed and ordered.

This Council meeting on 3 February had prevented Stirling from attending the quarterly meeting of the Agricultural Society at Guildford. Previously, he had disappointed representatives by not acceding to their request to raise the price of grain (Stirling said this would injure consumers) and to allow the *Champion* to deliver colonial produce outside the territory. When informed of these decisions, members decided, after some discussion, to petition the Governor to place a duty on the import of foreign wheat and flour, exempting only that from England and other colonies. They then went on to discuss their most pressing concern, the labour shortage, and ways it might be ameliorated.

On 10 February the Stirling family welcomed a new addition, Lady Stirling being safely delivered of a son they named Walter. Ellen now had four children under 5 years of age, as well as 8-year-old Frederick Henry to care for, and her thoughts were never far from her eldest son Andrew, at school in England. News of him was agonisingly infrequent. But ships which had just arrived from Hobart told of others en route from England, which hopefully would bring family tidings.

Information and gossip from the eastern colonies was eagerly devoured when it appeared in the local Press. On 16 February readers learned that Governor Arthur had been replaced in Van Diemen's Land by Sir John Franklin, and that Arthur would be prosecuted on his return to England for 'numerous acts of oppression and tyranny during his long 13 years'.[5] This turn of events would have perturbed Stirling, for he had liked Arthur and wondered whether he would get a fair hearing from those ignorant of the difficulties of colonial administration. He knew it had taken years for Governor Darling to be cleared by a Parliamentary Committee of Inquiry after his recall from New South Wales in 1831.[6] Stirling was now curious to know how the Governor of the new colony of South Australia was faring, but far more concerned about the effect its establishment would have on his own colony. South Australia was reported already to have over 500 settlers, and a Sydney paper had even had the temerity to suggest they expected a further influx from Swan River.

The arrival from London on the last day of February of the *Shepherd*, another Mangles ship, brought long-awaited dispatches for Stirling: nine duplicates of those sent between March and June 1836, and seven new missives written between July and September. But instead of providing guidance on matters such as the land regulations and the maintenance of the police force, they chastised Stirling for tardy correspondence and sought detailed information on a host of minor matters. His comments were desired over the substance of William Nairn Clark's claim about the conduct of the civil court,[7] on Mr Shaw's complaint of an unfair legal hearing,[8] on an unfair dismissal charge brought by one of Sir Richard Spencer's servants,[9] and on a convention regarding the removal of imposts on property transfers.[10] Among all these demands, Stirling was also asked for more detailed plans of public buildings and reliable maps of the territory. All queries were answered, at some length, in separate dispatches throughout March.

At least there was more cheer a few days later with the promised visit from the Eastern Station of the warship HMS *Pelorus*. Aside from boosting the economy through reprovisioning orders, the visit revitalised the social scene as officers and crew took shore leave. On 5 March Captain Harding entertained the Governor and Lady Stirling on board in true naval style—a refreshing reminder of the past and no doubt some solace for James, who had just learned of Glenelg's refusal of his request for furlough.[11]

In answering the request for more detailed maps of the territory, and criticism of the pace of surveying, Stirling stated forcibly that the current situation in the Survey Office was unworkable. The Surveyor-General, draughtsman and clerk were unable to keep up with the number of claims, while the system of contract surveying had proved 'highly objectionable'.[12] Politely, but bluntly, he made it clear that, without additional full-time staff and more survey instruments, the task was impossible. The draughtsman, Mr Hillman, had proved himself a competent surveyor on expeditions with Roe, so Stirling recommended he be appointed as one Assistant Surveyor, and that another, plus a replacement draughtsman, be sent out from England as soon as possible. This dispatch was received in London in October 1837, but with typical slowness a month passed before a memo was sent to Lord

Glenelg recommending Henry Ommanney's appointment.[13] But Ommanney, who had returned to England in May 1836, would not arrive back in the colony until August 1838.

Despite the shortages of staff in the survey department, the maps sent back on the *Shepherd* were detailed and informative. (They became the basis for the 1839 Arrowsmith map.) According to original instructions, the entire territory from the Moore River above Perth, south to King George's Sound and inland beyond York, had been divided into counties with rivers, topographical features and soil types all noted, together with the routes of all the exploring expeditions. Insets gave greater detail of the main townships that had been established, showing not only town lots but also surrounding country locations. Taken overall, it was a testimonial to the indefatigable energy of John Septimus Roe, the Surveyor-General, whose field books show just how difficult the task had been with inadequate staff and equipment. Records do not indicate exactly who chose the names that were bestowed on the landscape, but Stirling inevitably would have had quite an input.

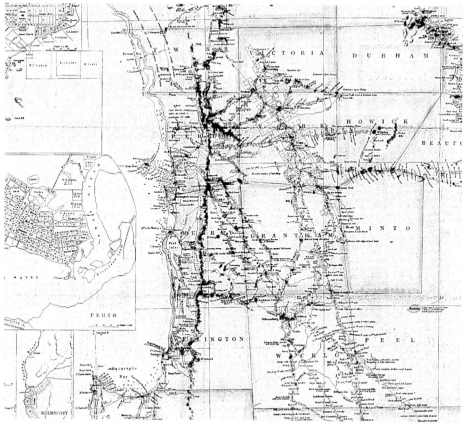

Detail of Roe's map, published by Arrowsmith in 1839, showing the growth of settlement

Courtesy Battye Library neg. 24/5/10

He seems to have used the names of British Government officials and politicians for most of the counties, such as Goderich, Murray, Wellington, Peel, Hay and Twiss, though personal preference came into the naming of Lanark, Stirling, Plantagenet and Nelson. In naming towns, Stirling often took the European interpretation of Aboriginal names, such as Mandurah, Pinjarra, Toodyay and Kojonup, but others again honoured royalty or peers such as Augusta, Clarence, Albany and York. It has already been noted that Stirling used his own family names very seldom, and Roe was similarly self-effacing. For almost a century only a rather infamous back street in Perth bore Roe's name.

Apart from running the survey office and undertaking long exploratory journeys, Roe played an active role in administrative affairs. His advice was frequently recorded at Executive Council meetings on matters as diverse as the location of jetties, or whether government funds should be deposited with the proposed local bank, to be called the Bank of Western Australia, the formation of which had been endorsed by ten leading citizens towards the end of January. They had set up a prospectus setting an initial capital of £10,000 to be raised in £10 shares (a quarter payable in April and a quarter in October 1837).[14] When the bank finally opened on 1 June, it had a paid up capital of £2,500. Its operations were to be exceedingly cautious with depositors receiving no interest on current accounts and 5 per cent on savings, at a time when 12 per cent and upwards was being offered privately. There was to be a limited issue of £1 notes and bills of exchange would be bought and sold. Loans would not be made on mortgage but only through the discount of short-term bills at a fixed rate of 12.5 per cent, and tough conditions were to be placed on renewals. The *Gazette* was supportive of the venture, commenting that it had 'reduced the transactions between all parties to a clearer understanding than the previous system of barter could possibly admit of...'[15]

Despite previous Colonial Office disapproval of the establishment of a bank, Stirling had actively encouraged its formation, even chairing the first meeting.[16] But he felt he could not allow the local bank to take custody of public funds, or use one of the public buildings for a safe meeting place as they had asked, without official approval. He was happy, however, to lend them an iron box. Most councillors agreed with Stirling; but Roe realised the problems the bank would face without sufficient liquidity, and believed that 'an early application should be made to HMG for authority to transact money affairs through the bank about to commence business...'[17] His were the views of a man fully committed to serving the colony, but without final responsibility, and they sometimes differed from those of the Governor.

On 1 April the *Perth Gazette* informed its readers that Stirling was about to undertake a three-week journey south to examine the country along the new line of road to Albany. It also carried news of further incidents between natives and settlers in the York region. Petty thieving had been the cause of most clashes, following the same pattern that had occurred around Perth as traditional food sources had been destroyed. But attempts by settlers to protect their property had led to armed clashes. In one incident two natives were shot in the leg—one, a woman, was brought to York for proper medical attention. In general, settlers were not hostile towards the natives; indeed their gratitude is recorded in many instances for help in finding people lost in the bush, or stray cattle.[18] But persistent thieving undermined closer understanding. Stirling was finding it more and more difficult to restrain the military in the district—the direct recipients of settlers' anger about theft. Taking the trip south was perhaps a welcome means of deferring action, for the Executive Council would not meet in his absence.

One of the major complaints of the people of Perth at this time was the high prices charged for grinding grain. Wheat and other grains were now available in the market for 5 to 6 shillings a bushel, but the relative ineffectiveness of the two existing water mills[19] (Reveley and Kingsford's) made grinding costs exorbitant at 2s 6d a bushel. Perth residents were therefore pleased to learn that Mr Shenton was erecting a new windmill at the point opposite Mount Eliza which, when complete, would be able to grind some 25 bushels a day. Moreover, it would have a warehouse attached, which could store grain brought by water into the adjacent small bay. But boatmen to transport produce were in very short supply. As the *Perth Gazette* commented on 17 February, 'all who could, and some who could not, pull an oar [had] repaired to Fremantle…owing to the rage for whaling'.[20]

Perth residents had set up the Northern Fishery Company at the end of March on a share basis, with each share worth £10 but only a quarter initially called. Operations were to commence on Carnac Island.[21] Almost simultaneously, Fremantle residents formed the Fremantle Whaling Company, issuing £20 shares with an initial call of £2. They began a small whaling station at Bathers Bay, at the foot of Arthur's Head. It was late April by the time both companies were set up, but despite constant watch there were few whaling sightings. Boat crews were occupied in racing each other, but observers were scathing about their efforts, stating that 'nine-tenths are not fit to pull an oar'.[22]

The Fremantle Company then decided to petition the Executive Council for permission to erect a jetty at Anglesea Point, near Bathers Bay, to facilitate landing whales. This was granted[23] and by 29 April work was underway[24] with a view to completion by the time the whales returned from their annual migration in September.

On Tuesday 2 May the Governor returned from his southern inspection, delighted that even at the end of the dry season he had found the head of the Murray River running strongly, and more permanent water at the foot of the hills further south. He had visited the outpost at Williams River and proceeded down the new line of road to Kojonup where another outpost was to be established. Stirling felt a further outpost would be necessary between Kojonup and Albany to facilitate overland transport, and favoured the vicinity of Mount Barker.[25] But before getting that far he turned back, wanting to ascertain the nature of the surrounding country.[26] On 10 May he reported to his Executive Councillors that he had found a large extent of good land which would prove 'entirely a new feature in the prospects of the Colony'.[27]

Having been forcefully reminded that the grant system had now officially been abandoned, Stirling was anxious to settle all the outstanding claims for grants. But achieving this would be an uphill task. Sufficient suitable land had first to be found and then surveyed, for Stirling did not want to run into the same problems that had ensued in Perth, when locations had been assigned before proper survey. Some of those grants had been found deficient in quantity when actually surveyed, leaving their occupants with a legitimate claim for more land. Other items on the Council agenda for that day illustrate the minutiae with which Stirling had to contend. They

In the late 1830s colonists were served by three mills:
Reveley and Kingsford's north of the river, and
Shenton's mill on the south side

Battye Library map 3/5/27 Perth mill sites

included approving a tender to supply the Court House with chairs and venetian blinds. The Court House was at the time doubling as the Anglican Church in Perth, which was a matter of concern to some councillors. There was still no official representative of other religions in the colony—they arrived after Stirling's departure.[28] There were certainly both Catholics and Methodists in the settlement,[29] but these people tended to hold services in their own homes. So it was basically an Anglican community that Stirling presided over—non-Anglicans were still officially debarred from civil and military service.

At the next meeting of Council Stirling raised the matter of his own accommodation—aware that no instructions had been received on the issue. For the past two years Government House had been left in an incomplete state, and Stirling felt it 'absolutely necessary not only for the shelter of his family, but also for the security of the building itself, that it should be completed'.[30] He had asked for this to be costed and placed the estimate on the table. Councillors unanimously ruled that the proposed alterations and additions be done immediately, 'for the preservation of the building and the bare accommodation of the family'. Tenders were called and Solomon J. Cook won the contract with a tender of £320.[31]

The forthcoming Foundation Day celebrations struck a pleasant chord in Perth society, and gave rise to other, often impromptu occasions. George Fletcher Moore gives a vivid word picture of such a scene:

> The people here...have a vile trick of sitting late at parties. I dined at a house on Thursday and was obliged to sit from six in the evening till four next morning. What occurred the next night at the Governor's, whilst they were sitting at tea, was this: some one proposed that they should get up a dance (there were two lady visitors there)…messengers were despatched to muster the neighbours, a fifer was pressed into the service, and we were dancing full fling before nine o'clock and had a very merry pleasant evening without ceremony.[32]

On the evening of Foundation Day a ball and supper were held at Leeder's Hotel, and considering that the entrance fee was a guinea for gentlemen and 7s 6d for ladies, eighty people was an admirable turnout. But few of those who considered themselves among the elite of Perth society would have missed it, for the Surveyor-General and the Colonial Secretary were among the stewards, and the Governor and his lady, arriving at 9 p.m., began the dancing. The room was decorated lavishly with commemorative symbols—a chalk drawing of the *Parmelia* sailed in stately fashion over a wheat sheaf and a lamb, representing the agricultural pursuits of the colonists. The centrepiece was a Swan, with a whale spouting on either side to represent the Perth and Fremantle companies. Even the new bank, which had opened that very day, was represented.

These frivolities, however, were overshadowed by more serious events, for two days later *Perth Gazette* readers learned of the killing of a soldier, Isaac Green, about

40 miles south of York. He had been speared three times in the back while bending to remove food from his outdoor oven. Another man who had gone to help was also attacked, but luckily the spears had only grazed his arm. While conscious, he answered questions but could give no reason for the attack. However, the *Guardian* noted that Green had been in the habit of feeding the natives more than most, and that he had refused a native on the morning of the attack. Editor William Nairn Clark observed:

> Too much blood has already been spilt in the warfare between the whites and the blacks, and we are afraid the destruction of the Aborigines has been in the ratio 10 to 1.[33]

It was one of the few times that Stirling would have agreed with Clark's sentiments.

On 5 June the Legislative Council sat, its members assembled in full dress uniform before the public gallery to hear the Governor's address on the state of the colony, and to consider the estimates for the coming year. Stirling was apologetic that no instructions had been received concerning the matters that had been referred to England the previous year. In their absence, he was forced to assume that the expenditure that had been incurred would be sanctioned. He hoped to have instructions in the near future, but in the interim proposed to adopt the same course as before, allowing councillors to consider in committee the estimates which

The relative prosperity and increased comfort of Perth people is reflected in this sketch of the capital in 1837

As reproduced in Nathaniel Ogle, The Colony of Western Australia had been prepared. They would be assisted, he was pleased to say, by various returns which had been completed for the first time. Taken together, these reports had to be considered 'proofs of a state of prosperity'.[34] They showed an extension in agriculture, an increase in livestock, the establishment of mills and whaling stations, the foundation of a bank, the opening up of new districts, the extension of communications by land and sea, the infrequency of offences against the laws and the increasing comfort of the people. The Advocate-General received the address with thanks, and particularly expressed appreciation of the returns, 'having on former occasions experienced the want of such documents'. Just before councillors went into committee, Stirling announced that he intended to introduce a bill to regulate banking in the colony and to allow directors to sue, and be sued, in the company name. This was a far-sighted move on Stirling's part, as the legislation had been accepted in England for less than a decade, and it would protect those who were behind the establishment of the bank.

The very next day, before councillors had had time to undertake their committee work, Stirling called them to an Executive Council meeting to discuss a matter of great importance, brought to his attention by the Government Resident at King George's Sound. The colony had no limits on foreign ships wishing to fish offshore, and visits by American whalers were threatening the livelihood of small local whaling ventures established down south. The Governor had therefore been asked to intervene. Stirling told his advisers he was concerned that 'any measures tending to interfere with American fishermen…would be an exercise of authority of dangerous import'.[35] Well aware of how the American War of 1812 had started, Stirling felt it would be more appropriate to address the Secretary of State on the subject as soon as possible. Council concurred. However, Roe urged Stirling to solicit the Home Government to arrange for 'periodic visits of a man of war' to protect the settlers' fishing rights, especially as whaling had just commenced near the Swan River. Stirling detailed the case in a dispatch signed on 15 June. Aware that a request would be refused if it related only to the interests of the tiny Swan River Colony, he began by reporting the potential of the area for fishing generally, and whaling in particular. In words that were later extracted and published in the British Press, he described the advantages that British whalers could reap from visiting the western coast:

> A whaling ship for instance in her outward voyage will find abundant occupation if she arrived about Christmas in the latitude 40°S and prosecutes the fishery until the end of April…between the Meridian of Greenwich and that of Cape Leeuwin. Arriving in the ports of the Settlement at the last named period she may refit and refresh her crew through the following month until the whales come into the bays in June. From thence until October, bay fishing will be found extremely profitable and the ship may then proceed through the Timor Sea and the S.E. trades towards the Seychelles…On this course sperm whales are abundant…and the ship will thus find herself at the end of this continuous season of eleven or twelve months

in the vicinity of Table Bay where she may transfer her cargo to a homeward-bound ship, and after refreshing her crew, renew again the same round of operations which, with the exception of the two short periods for relaxation, need never be interrupted until the ship is worn out.

Then he turned to Swan River:

> From this account of the matter it will be perceived that by the possession of this country, the fisheries may derive the most important advantages…not only for the purpose of promoting Colonial Interests but those of the Empire at large in as far as they are connected with maritime greatness…[36]

Having painted this profitable and nationalistic picture, Stirling went on to warn of the encroachment of the American whalers. Within the last four months at least forty American vessels were known to have been whaling in Western Australian waters, four or five even venturing into local ports. They had done so well they predicted 'an immense number of American ships' would soon follow. His Majesty's Government must therefore decide on a suitable course of action. So far he had done nothing, partly because he had no way of enforcing any prohibition, but also because it might 'embarrass a question of the greatest moment'. In the interim, Stirling continued, he would write to the Commander of the Eastern Station to ask that a ship-of-war be sent to the colony for the following year's whaling season (May to October), 'in order to prevent any quarrels between the Colonists and the Americans who may be engaged in whaling in the bays of the Settlement'.

As Stirling had correctly anticipated, receipt of this dispatch in London, on 20 March 1838, caused considerable concern. With unusual alacrity, the Colonial Office immediately forwarded one copy to the Board of Trade and another to the Admiralty. Two days later Glenelg ordered the 'substance of the information to be communicated to the principal persons…engaged in the whale fishery'.[37] By 20 April the matter had been placed before the Privy Council, and the Admiralty had sent instructions to the Commander of the Eastern Station 'to afford every protection'. Ship owners, including Charles Mangles, were also apprised of the news.[38]

But despite the high hopes Stirling had expressed for a successful whaling industry, only one whale had actually been captured in Cockburn Sound when he wrote his dispatch. On 10 June the *Perth Gazette* had reported 'the guns at Fremantle have been firing for two or three hours this morning, proclaiming the memorable event of the first whale caught near Cockburn Sound'. The report then described the pursuit which turned into high farce for the rival Northern Fishery Company and the Fremantle Whaling Company:

> Both parties assisted in its capture…the Carnac party threw the first harpoon and were obliged to cut the line from the rapidity with which their row boat—the

Spitfire—was drawn under the water. The Fremantle boat had also struck the whale & subsequently held on, bringing it in to Fremantle jetty…[with the assistance of] every boat in Fremantle.

The general rejoicing was dampened, however, by a dispute over which company should claim the catch: the Carnac Island-based group, which had attached the first line, or the Fremantle venture, which had brought it in. Books were consulted, only to find that while customs among British Greenland companies gave rights to whoever placed the first harpoon, the custom among French, American and British whalers in the South Seas was to divide it between the owners of the two boats involved.[39] Heated debate followed, but the more sensible latter course won the day.

It was, therefore, with a total catch of only half a whale that the Fremantle Whaling Company approached the Government with a proposal to cut a tunnel under Arthur's Head, to facilitate movement from their base below the cliff to the township on the other side.[40] The Governor, accompanied by the Surveyor-General and Civil Engineer, inspected the site and agreed the scheme was feasible. The company's proposal, that it would undertake all expenses of the work if the Government provided them with prison labour, was considered at the next Executive Council meeting on 22 June. Although favouring the scheme, members were wary of providing a private company with the services of prison labour for an unlimited time period, and suggested a limit of three months, with the company required to take all necessary precautions to prevent accidents during its progress.[41] The meeting concluded with the usual list of improved grants submitted for approval and conferral of fee simple title, but this time it included the 4,000 acres of Stirling's Woodbridge grant on the Swan. Approval was accompanied by a note to the effect that the Surveyor-General had readjusted the boundaries of both Sir James' and Richard Lewis's grants on the Swan, due to the discovery of certain errors in the original descriptions.[42]

Executive Council members had thus had very little time to consider the estimates, as Stirling had set the date of the next meeting of the Legislative Council for 23 June. Yet again, the key difference between the Governor and his councillors was over provision for the mounted police. As the polite *Perth Gazette* reported:

> …his Excellency felt opposed to the method suggested by the Council, of mounting a certain number of the military…as it would be the means of placing a body of men in a responsible situation who might exercise physical strength alone against the aborigines.[43]

In his actual speech to Council, Stirling had used stronger words:

> Although a military detachment may protect a post or even accompany a magistrate it was found they acquired no influence over the natives…except

Section of Horace Samson's sketch of the whaling station and tunnel
under Arthur's Head
Courtesy Mrs Godbehear

within the narrow range of their own muskets. In the meantime the evils
increased...until it became necessary...to establish and regulate upon general
principles of mutual benefit, the future intercourse between *the invaders and the
invaded* [author's emphasis].

What he wanted was a special unit including 'individuals competent to acquire
influence over savages by firmness, intelligence and zeal for their welfare', who
would be 'armed with the power to visit freely and frequently the different tribes
coercing them when requisite, and protecting them when injured, and leading
them, by degrees, to appreciate and seek the benefits of civilization'. He then said,
and clearly wanted to believe, that

> If the hope of conferring equivalent advantages of this description upon the natives
> had not entered the fixed views of His Majesty's Government, the acquisition of
> this country would never have been made.[44]

But councillors were unmoved. They were not prepared to cut expenditure on
other urgent needs in order to support a function that could be performed at no
cost by the military. If some £2,000 could be obtained from elsewhere, to maintain
a well-organised, independent mounted police corps, they admitted it would be of
'infinite benefit'.[45] But such a sum was simply unavailable. Revenue had increased
by only £606 since the previous year, to a total £5,193. Repayment of debt had fallen
from £1,035 to £800 and although duties on imports (the major source of revenue)
had increased slightly to £2,419, fees from licences had halved to £343. The revenue
increase had principally been through the sale of Crown lands, which had realised
£648, mostly from urban lots. But it was recognised that as long as immigration
remained low, and settlers could sell their own land below the Crown asking price

of 5 shillings an acre, very little could be expected from this source. On the other hand, the salary bill for those not supported by the parliamentary grant, such as the Harbour Masters, Resident Magistrates and gaolers, came to £2,165, and this did not include the mounted police. In 1836 the committee had reduced the previous year's allocation for police from £674 to £387, and this year they pared it again to £336. While expenditure on all regular contingencies—such as schools and exploration— was cut, they felt an extra £50 had to be provided for the conveyance of mails now that a regular Perth-Albany service had been introduced, and £50 more for the Colonial Hospital and Poor Relief (to a total £200). A sum of £445 was also set aside for public works.

Clearly, resources in the Colonial Fund were scanty, but settlers at large were also feeling the pinch, principally due to the paucity of shipping. George Fletcher Moore wrote on 18 June: 'We are anxiously looking for a vessel from England. There is neither salt meat nor foreign flour, nor candles nor soap in the colony.'[46] But he took comfort in the fact that there was plenty of fresh meat and colonial wheat and flour, pure clean water and even whale oil—though, as he noted, the lack of proper tackle to turn the solitary whale so far caught meant much of the carcass had spoilt, 'and smells so strongly that the inhabitants of Fremantle begin to find that there are disagreeables attending whales also'.[47] Three more whales were landed in subsequent weeks, despite boisterous weather which made their capture difficult and damaged some of the boats. Even the sturdy *Champion* had been forced to put back after six days out on her run to Albany, when all her sails were carried away in a squall.[48] Then on 8 July it was rumoured that a whaling boat with six men in it had been lost with no survivors.[49] The rumour unfortunately proved to be true, although how the accident happened remained a mystery. Surprisingly, the *Swan River Guardian*, which hitherto had taken a great interest in whaling ventures, did not report the tragedy. It was too busy castigating Stirling for his stand in the Legislative Council concerning the British Government's intent to protect native inhabitants. On 6 July Clark thundered:

> A long and bloody warfare existed between the whites and the blacks in Van Diemen's Land, which was only terminated by the extirpation of a great part of the original inhabitants of that colony…all under the express sanction of the British Government.

He immediately linked this to another grievance, the colonial administration's refusal to let the missionary, Dr Guistiniani, remove natives offshore, at the Missionary Society's own cost, to 'one or either of the neighbouring islands off the Western Coast'.[50]

This is the first known public mention of placing natives on islands off Fremantle which, at this point, were more the whale chaser's domain. Much later the native prison on Rottnest Island, set up on 22 June 1839 (six months after

Stirling's departure), became notorious for the ill-treatment of its inhabitants.[51] However, the idea was first mooted during Stirling's tenure, in a roundabout way, at the Executive Council meeting on 11 July 1837. There had been a number of thefts and attacks by Aborigines in the York and Northam districts, and settlers were once more calling for decisive punitive steps. Two offenders had been apprehended so far, and they were in gaol waiting trial, 'but…there was reason to apprehend retaliation on their part if these prisoners should be punished'. To prevent this, Stirling sent two mounted parties to York to catch the other perpetrators, one party under the direction of the Government Resident of York, and the other under Lieutenant Bunbury, 'who is not only well qualified for such a trust but who has volunteered his services'.[52] Any natives who were arrested but found not to have been involved were to be kept 'on one of the islands' until the entire operation was complete. Stirling was thus thinking of the island as a holding station, not a prison. At the next meeting of the Executive Council, on 14 July, the Governor reported they were still trying to procure horses for the York expedition. He again referred to the plan of 'sending such natives as might be taken to one of the adjacent islands', and thought Rottnest the most suitable.[53] The next day the *Perth Gazette*'s editorial proclaimed:

> It is proposed to form a prison establishment on one of the neighbouring islands to which the most notorious depredators will be removed on conviction. It will of course form part of the scheme that they should be suitably instructed and profitably employed. We shall return to this subject when the plan is more matured.[54]

Who was behind the scheme is unknown, but in the space of four days Stirling's plan for a holding station (similar perhaps to the native institution that had now run for some years at the foot of Mount Eliza) had been translated into a prison scheme. When raised again at Executive Council, it was admitted that compensation to the private occupant of Rottnest Island (Robert Thomson) posed an obstacle, and the matter was dropped.[55] The catalyst for increasing concern about isolating native prisoners was undoubtedly a rumour (later confirmed) that two settlers, Chidlow and Jones, had been found speared to death near Northam on 13 July. Worse, they had been facially disfigured and buried in shallow graves.[56] This was the first attempt Aborigines had made to disguise a murder, and it was much discussed in the small communities of Perth and Fremantle. Stirling acted quickly to stem general alarm. On the 22nd a Public Notice appeared in the *Perth Gazette* listing the various incidents that had occurred in the York district since September 1836, together with some on the Swan and Canning. It noted that there was

> no reason to believe that these several outrages were committed on any concerted plan, but, occurring about the same time, after a long period of tranquillity, it is

not unlikely that they originated in the same causes, or at least, were stimulated by similar circumstances.

Stirling's view of those circumstances was that the natives in these districts

> see but a few colonists, and those scattered over a large district…and in the few instances where conflicts have occurred they have had the appearance of being sustained only by a few individual settlers or soldiers…Emboldened by these considerations, they have never disguised their intention to take life for life, and to resent every act of the whites for the protection of their property…Their success has tended to confirm in them the belief of their strength, while the punishment received has only had the effect of irritating and uniting them.

The actions of the tribe 'beyond the Hills' was likely to have had an effect upon 'some of the natives on this side [i.e. near Perth]…It is at York therefore as the source of these evils, that the current of events must be arrested'. The Governor also had advice for settlers:

> for aiding in their own protection, by keeping their arms in order, by associating with their neighbours for mutual support, by withdrawing out of the way of the natives as far as possible any temptation to robbery, by treating them with caution, firmness, and good humour, and by not exposing themselves to attack through going about unarmed and alone. Such precautions as these…will tend to discourage offensive acts on the part of the natives. At the same time…it is especially enjoined that no act of violence be committed toward any natives by unauthorized individuals except on the strongest, clearest, and most urgent grounds of self-defence.[57]

Stirling had correctly judged the attitudes of the York natives, though not stating the cause of discontent—the loss of their lands and food supplies. Prior comments, however, about the 'invaders and invaded' show that he had some appreciation of their situation, but his duty was to protect British citizens and property. On this occasion, he felt he had no alternative other than to resort to the military. The *Perth Gazette's* editor fully supported the planned action, stating:

> a crisis is at hand, and either the white inhabitants or the aborigines must obtain the mastery. Our position is by no means a peculiar one; all newly inhabited countries have the same trying ordeal to go through. Even to this day New South Wales is in the same disturbed state, and the utmost endeavours to civilize the blacks have totally failed.[58]

Even the *Swan River Guardian's* editor believed it was time for action:

We believe that the Governor is a humane man and would not inflict unnecessary cruelty on the natives...but when the spear of the native has killed white men, and other spears are shaken in defiance by a determined band of robbers and murderers it is high time to shew our force and strike a mortal blow.[59]

He nevertheless criticised Stirling for having dispersed troops too thinly; for the scattering of their small force had induced the natives 'to arouse themselves from their natural state of timidity to commence a desultory warfare against the whites'. In truth, there were simply not enough troops to allow a significant presence in any one area if all were to be protected. The Agricultural Society's members were petitioning the Home Government for more troops, at least a full Regiment,[60] and the need for this was universally agreed. But Clark's vitriolic pen was still in action. He lampooned the choice of Lieutenants Bunbury and Mortimer to head the party bound for York, on the grounds that after Isaac Green's murder these same officers had fired on the natives indiscriminately, then 'deserted their post to attend a Ball at Perth'.[61]

Whilst the hunt began for the perpetrators of the York murders, relations with the Swan River natives returned to normal. Indeed, Stirling had rewarded three natives for their kindness in locating botanist William Morrison, who had become lost in bush north of Perth. They had found him in an exhausted state, shared their food, built a fire and shelter, and the following morning carried him into the capital.[62] Morrison, who had been brought to the colony at Stirling's expense in 1834, was collecting for the Royal Botanic Gardens in Kew, and his loss would have been a tragedy.[63]

At the next meeting of the Executive Council, Stirling reported on the activities of the military parties sent to York. Four of the perpetrators of Jones and Chidlow's murder had been shot after being named by a native who was present at the time.[64] Bunbury had also successfully repulsed an Aboriginal attack on a settler's property at Toodyay on 14 August, leaving four assailants dead.[65] A week later five natives had attacked a party of soldiers while in their tents north of Toodyay; four of the natives had been killed and the other wounded in full sight of another thirty of the tribe.[66] In York township, one of the natives involved in Green's murder was shot escaping from custody, whilst another (presumed to have been a spy) was shot in a tree. This was the military policy that Stirling had tried to avoid.

In early August, colonists' attention was diverted from affairs in York by news of a serious whaling accident. A whale fluke had struck the headsman of the Fremantle Company's boat just as he was throwing the harpoon, killing him instantly. The whale was lost, although the Northern Fishery Company successfully caught a smaller whale the same day. There had been talk of combining the two enterprises, but uneven outlays by shareholders had made agreement difficult. The loss of one of the very few skilled headsmen, however, created renewed pressure for a merger.[67] Considering the slow start, both companies had had a number of catches during the season, and the *Perth Gazette* viewed the resultant barrels of oil stored in warehouses with pride, stating:

> the Colony will this year afford a sufficient quantity of its natural productions to freight a vessel home direct. This is a matter of no slight boast and exultation… when we consider the few years it has been established and that the commodities, wool, oil and timber, are highly valuable in the parent country.

The arrival of the long-promised Mangles vessel, the *Hero*, on 22 August was thus doubly welcome. She had been delayed several times by bad weather so the twenty-three passengers, who included Captain Bannister and Major Irwin with his wife and stepchildren, had had to endure a seven-month passage. The *Hero* brought dozens of packages for the settlers, stores for the Commissariat, supplies for the merchants, English news and, most important of all, letters from home. For Stirling it also brought twenty-six new dispatches written between 29 September 1836 and 3 April 1837. He must have read till his eyes grew bleary, for four days later the *Perth Gazette* announced:

> the expectations we cherished of a favourable consideration of our many representations made to the Home government relating to the restrictions on land, we regret to learn, are not to be realized.[68]

Instead, new regulations were to come into force which, in essence, offered new land (or title to remaining unimproved land) in return for surrender of unimproved lands, but in the proportion of one acre for every three surrendered. Settlers had wanted an equal swap, and were not impressed. The editor, commenting upon the dispatch which brought the news, could have been speaking for Stirling when he said 'it contained the warmest professions of good intentions with as little practical display of them as could possibly be exercised'.[69]

19

The Glenelg Regulations

THE ARRIVAL OF dispatches containing changes to the land regulations was a forcible reminder to Stirling that the matter of his own allocation was still unresolved, and time was running out. Lord Glenelg had made it clear in previous dispatches that unfulfilled entitlements would not be recognised in future. Stirling had certainly chosen various locations in the south, and changed them from time to time, but their exact boundaries had not been officially approved. He had gained title to his Woodbridge location by virtue of improvement, and another at Leschenault was being developed by an agent, but the rest remained fairly vague descriptions in the Surveyor-General's files. The matter was the more urgent because, following refusal of his request for leave, James was contemplating resignation. It was a step not to be taken lightly and definitely not while the specification of the 100,000 acres promised him as founding Governor was still officially unrecognised. It irked James, too, that the extent of land he could claim was hardly a fit recompense for all the worry and effort he had undergone. After all, Peel and Latour had been allocated much larger grants, yet had done nothing to help the colony weather its early storms. The latter hadn't even crossed the ocean. It was thoughts of this nature that led Stirling to put the following proposal to his councillors when they met on 1 September 1837.

Alerting them that he 'had an application of some importance to bring under their notice', Stirling proceeded to put his case for an additional 132,970 acres 'on account of the expenditure of private funds on public and private objects since the commencement of the undertaking'. He concluded:

> this claim is not advanced as an appeal to indulgence. It stands simply on its merits as a question of right arising out of pre-existing engagements which imposed on me nine years of anxious responsibility and the outlay of £10,000 from my private resources.[1]

As he expected his grant would be closely scrutinised in London, he wanted his councillors' opinion on his claim. There is little doubt that Stirling believed he was entitled to additional land on the basis of all the assets he had introduced, and he certainly had introduced appropriate assets in both 1829 and 1834. But he did not give councillors a list or valuation of those assets, just the figure of £10,000 (which would have entitled him to 133,000 acres under the 1/6 per acre improvements rule). He appeared to be claiming land also on the basis of services rendered, which he himself had used as a basis for grants. Stirling asked his councillors to consider the matter for a few days, when he would raise the issue again, stressing that he wished the correct protocol to be observed. As he noted later, it was customary for such claims to be put to the colony's Executive Council, whereas he 'should have preferred a reference of the case to the Secretary of State'. He was anxious that no opinion be given on the claim 'if the grounds of those opinions be not clearly established'.[2]

After due deliberation the Council delivered its verdict on 11 September: the Governor was entitled to the original 100,000 acres of land, but it would be best

> to leave the remainder of his claim to the future decision of HMG, as some material evidence to substantiate his claim to a further assignment of land is not procurable in the Colony.[3]

Councillors were quite correct to refer the claim back to London. It was not their place to make a ruling on a grant system they knew had been firmly quashed.

While this issue was being considered, a 'welcome back' dinner for Major Irwin took place on 6 September at Leeder's Hotel, arranged by the Agricultural Society to honour the work he had done for settlers in England.[4] Most of the prominent men in the colony attended,[5] with the Governor, his private secretary, Andrew Stirling, and Captain Armstrong, the retiring head of the military, as invited guests. In toasting the Governor's health, Mr Leake, the chairman, expressed the wish that he 'might long remain with us to witness the advancement of the Colony, which owed its formation to his enterprising spirit'. Stirling's reply was surprisingly candid. After tendering his sincere thanks for the compliment paid to him, he added that 'the period might not be very far distant' when he might leave and

> that he could do so without departing from a line of duty which had been marked out, and a sincere conviction that his adopting such a measure would not interfere with the interests of any person of this community.[6]

Irwin, whom all knew had worked hard while in London to counteract false rumours about Swan River, modestly replied to his own toast by congratulating the colonists 'that a different view of our position is now taken by the public at large'.[7]

The editor of the *Swan River Guardian*, reporting the event on 14 September, was indignant that a dinner had been given for Irwin 'on his return here with a sinecure, when the Governor on arriving at Swan River in 1834, after *arduous exertions* received no such mark of respect'. He reminded his readers that when Irwin had been Acting Governor in 1832–33 'many people became disgusted with his mode of Government', and that when he left the Colony, after Daniel's arrival, 'his image was burnt in the Public Streets of Perth...to shew the rooted hatred which the people entertained against him in his official capacity'.[8]

The question of the Governor's likely retirement came up again when the dinner ended with 'one more bumper toast' by Leake. Of Stirling, 'our sincere friend and brother settler', he said:

> There is not a man in the colony who when overtaken by misfortune or depressed...has not received his warmest sympathy; and the prosperous have been congratulated by him. If fortune should so chance that he must leave us, there is not one of us but must regret his absence.[9]

Major F. C. Irwin, popular with colonists for
his staunch support while in England

Courtesy Battye Library 620P

This was greeted with long and continued cheers, and when the noise finally subsided, the *Gazette* recorded that Stirling had responded with the following heartfelt words:

> It is a source of great pleasure to me to receive this unexpected compliment, after a trial of nine years. I am gratified because I may say I am more settler than Governor of this colony. I have felt not alone in my private capacity, but in my official situation…Sometimes I have felt it incumbent on me to pursue measures in my official capacity of which it was not prudent to give explanations…I will not say that I have been wholly divested of self interest in the formation of this new colony, because I am convinced that any man who would put forth such an assertion would endeavour to impose on others a belief not entertained by himself…My study and my endeavour has been to be an honest man *(Reiterated cheers)*.

He then voiced a personal opinion he had held for some time:

> This colony has not been so fortunate as others, owing to a change in the ministry shortly after its establishment…I cannot say that the present Ministry have opposed the encouragement of this colony, but they have been beset by other interests and new schemes…indeed, I may say, the Colony fell out of fashion…It cannot be denied that we have paid a price for a ticket in the great lottery…

He concluded his long, frank address with the words:

> I have felt a curious bond of attachment to this colony, and I cannot imagine the sensations I shall experience when I am separated from it…I have felt as a father, that what I gave here would be returned to me hereafter by my children. How long I am to fill the office of Governor is at present very doubtful: my Governorship may terminate before a very long period; it is my full intention, however, to return from time to time. I cannot but admit it would be pleasing to me to shake off the trammels of office and with the characteristic feelings of a sailor, I wish for a change. One does get tired of being a Governor *(Cheers and Laughter)*. If I have played any foolish pranks as a Governor I should like once more to be set at large, to enjoy my fooleries in my own way. In whatever capacity I may again return, it will be my greatest pride to be considered as your Chairman has designated me—a settler.[10]

It was an amazing speech, clearly indicating his belief that the Home Government had almost deliberately scuppered the colony under the influence of the colonial reformers, and making no bones about his desire to quit the Governorship which he had yet to reveal to the authorities at home. The *Guardian*'s editor merely took the Governor to task for his claim to honesty, stating 'No person ever suspected you of dishonesty and the assertion that you were an honest man at a *Public House meeting* [sic] was beneath your dignity as Lieutenant of the King of England, in this part of His Majesty's dominions'.[11] There was also a shot at the *Perth Gazette* for failing to praise Mr Leeder for the excellence of the dinner and the wines!

Interestingly, nothing was mentioned in any of the speeches on this occasion of the matter that was uppermost in the minds of almost all present: the effect of the new land regulations. Glenelg's dispatch of 7 March 1837, outlining his response to the settlers' 1835 memorial and the changes to the regulations, had arrived on the *Hero* at the end of August. On orders from Stirling, it was published in full in the *Perth Gazette* on 2 September, taking up almost the entire issue. Its contents were discussed at length and caused much public disquiet. Not only did the recommendations fall far short of the colonists' requests for greater security of tenure, and the right to exchange bad land for good, but Glenelg had also demeaned their enterprise. His reply stated:

> I will not attempt to deny the difficulty which I experience in dealing with this subject, owing to the embarrassments created by the erroneous system under which the Colony was settled and particularly from the improvident manner in which land was then granted to individual settlers.[12]

Colonists were not only indignant about Glenelg's approach to their problems, they were also genuinely confused about the implications of his suggestions for reform. Councillors were thus under some pressure to examine the new regulations in depth and, at meetings on 7 and 8 September, prior to announcing their decision on Stirling's claim, the details and ramifications of the new land regulations were discussed at length.

The basic tenet of the new regulation, that every acre of grant land surrendered would entitle the landholder to a remission of 1s 6d on the 5 shilling price of an acre of new titled Crown land, was clearly understood. It meant that by surrendering three acres the landholder would be entitled to one acre of Crown land in fee simple. What was not clear, and a matter of considerable importance to colonists, was how to apply the ruling. Was one acre of totally unimproved land to be deemed of the same worth as a partially improved acre? And what if someone who already had title wished to avail themselves of the opportunity of exchange—was a titled acre to be worth the same as land totally unimproved? The matter was made more confusing by Glenelg's additional stipulation that if settlers surrendered two-thirds of their unimproved lands, they could be given fee simple title to the remaining third, improved or not. What was to happen to those settlers who held partially improved or titled grants in some places, and unimproved grants in others, due to the fact that their original locations had been fragmented? Moreover, if settlers could surrender worthless unimproved lands and select new titled land elsewhere, how was the selection process to be controlled? How long a time period should be allowed for the whole process of exchange? On all these points Stirling sought help from his councillors, for Glenelg's directive provided no guidance at all.

Speaking in the order determined in 1833, i.e. from most junior to most senior member, councillors gave their views. Moore was 'reluctantly constrained to admit' that all settlers without exception who had arrived in the colony previous to July 1831 should be permitted to effect exchanges on the terms proposed. Brown agreed, adding that settlers with partially improved lands should be able to surrender two-thirds of their unimproved acres and receive full title to the rest. Roe was more concerned about those who had already gained title through improvements, but who were faced with much useless land. They too should be allowed to surrender and claim new land. He therefore suggested that all parties be classified according to the extent of their improvements—those who had failed to improve their land in one category (who could now surrender two-thirds and gain title to the rest), and those who simply wanted to surrender some useless land in exchange for new in another. All agreed with such a classification.

The Surveyor-General then voiced his concern at the prospect of many small claims for new land and wanted a 640-acre minimum applied, with exceptions to be approved only in special cases by the Governor. Roe could see enormous problems with the scheme, as it could

> shake the security of established rights, introduce confusion of title and give rise to litigation and expense among those who have dealt with the original grants, either by sale, purchase, mortgage or other encumbrance.[13]

He also raised the issue of whether newly selected land could be chosen anywhere in the colony, or only in the parts already surveyed. Forcibly, he argued that selections should be confined to those areas which the small staff of the Survey Department could properly manage and record. Both of his suggestions were agreed to by Council. But there was dissent on the issue of the time period to be allowed for such exchanges, opinions varying from six to eighteen months. The minutes of the meeting concluded:

> The Governor informed the Council that as he concurred in the view which the majority of the Council took in the case, with the exception of a few unimportant points with regard to dates, he would direct the draft of a public notice to be prepared for carrying the arrangement into effect.[14]

He also suggested that the 'Royal Instructions in regard to the disposal of Crown Land' (i.e. the division into counties, townships and sections, etc.) should be republished with an intimation to the public that in future no departure would be permitted.[15] The appearance of the old instructions led some people to believe they would countermand the new. But they were mistaken, for the surrender and remission regulations, together with relevant council decisions, were announced in the *Perth Gazette* and *Government Gazette* on 30 September, to take effect immediately.[16]

Stirling was thus well aware of impending change when he wrote to the Surveyor-General concerning his own land on 13 September 1837.

> Having decided upon the immediate Settlement of my outstanding claim to 100,000 acres of land…I have now to report to you my final selection…and I have to direct you to cause the usual record of assignment & occupation to be made in your office on this date and to furnish me with the customary certificate thereof.
>
> 1st On the Western Side of Geographe Bay   4,000 acres
>   (bounded on the south by a west line from Castle Reach, on the east and north by the sea, on the west by a line from the Caves near Cape Naturaliste to the south boundary.)
>
> 2nd On the Eastern Side of ditto   18,550 acres
>   (on the west by Wonnerup Townsite, on the NW by a line parallel to the Sea coast about ¼ mile, on the South by another line parallel to the sea coast & at an average distance of about one mile from the NW boundary.)
>
> 3rd To the north-east of Geographe Bay   61,284 acres
>   (The eastern boundary near the base of the hills the line to be in a SW ½ west direction about 20 miles long, the location forming a parallelogram of 40 square miles, but to this block additional 20 miles on the Brunswick, 20 miles of the Corajecup and 20 miles at such points as may be most convenient on the survey of the district adjoining the location.)
>
> 4th Moorilup   4,000 acres
> 5th Dale (Beverley)   4,000 acres
> 6th Swan River, Fremantle
>   Garden Island and Hay conjointly   8,165 acres
>
> As the locations numbered 1, 2 & 3 are situated in districts not surveyed and little known, the preceding description is only general for the purpose of fixing & securing my right to the lands designated…until these districts are better known or surveyed.[17]

Surveyor-General Roe replied four days later:

> No time shall be lost in adopting the necessary measures for bringing these claims to final settlement [but] the boundaries to selections numbered 2 & 3…very materially interfere with lands already allotted to Colonel P A Latour on the Brunswick River…[18]

Poor Roe. He too wanted the matter of Stirling's lands concluded, but with such imprecise details, and claims that overlapped grants already made to others, there was little he could do but minute the changes. This claim differed a little from the selections Stirling had made in 1836. At that time he had requested 40,000 acres at or near Geographe Bay, which now was increased substantially to 83,834 acres; the 35,430 acres selected on the Beaufort near its junction with the Arthur (south of Williams) had now gone altogether, as also had the 10,000 acres he had selected at Warrenup, between Williams and the Sound. The 5,120 acres he held at Moorilup, a little further south, was now reduced to 4,000 acres, as also was the 5,000 acres near Dale (Beverley). The 3,200 acres on the Hay River in Plantagenet, selected for him by Spencer, was retained but its extent was not cited, as the Hay land was now lumped in with the 8,000-odd acres he held in various Swan River locations.

Stirling must have known that his extended Leschenault selection included part of the land initially granted to Peter Augustus Latour. Latour had sent out agents,

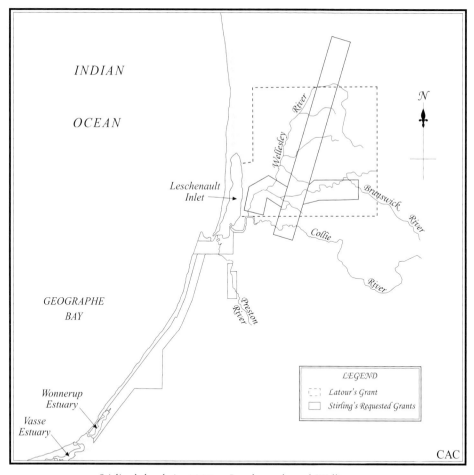

Stirling's lands in 1837 at Leschenault and Wellington,
including the overlap with Latour's selections

Based, with kind permission, on Charles Staples' map in They Made Their Destiny, *CO 18/101 f425*

labourers and assets entitling him to 113,100 acres and had been assigned 103,000 acres at Leschenault on 26 April 1830, just two months after Peel was assigned his 250,000-acre grant at the Murray. Desperate to locate the large grantees, Roe had assigned Latour part of the Leschenault land that had been chosen initially by Stirling, who obviously had approved the move. Indeed, he had later justified his choice of other locations on the grounds that he had been forced to assign his reserved land to other settlers. But he clearly liked the area and had maintained his claim over a large location to the south of Latour's grant. Now he was extending his claim into the area held by Latour, as the Surveyor-General had pointed out. From later evidence it would appear that Stirling believed Latour would be forced to surrender his still unimproved lands under the new regulations, and was thus putting in an ambit claim. He would never have approved Latour's subsequent petition, to be considered under the original 21-year improvement regulations, for Stirling believed that the 21-year clause applied only to himself and Peel. Nevertheless, the claim Stirling made at this time was to have considerable repercussions when he eventually left the colony.

With the *Hero*'s departure imminent, Stirling had to prepare up-to-date reports and answers to all the questions raised in dispatches from the Colonial Office. But first he had to write the letter he had been contemplating for some time. Addressing Glenelg on 2 October, he approached his resignation as a matter of financial necessity. With an enclosure detailing his receipts and disbursements since taking office, he began his letter with the statement that he had devoted

> nine years of my time and means to the execution of an Office the emoluments of which…have been scarcely equal to one half of my expenditure. In general no public servant can be expected to retain office under such circumstances, but in my case…as the Projector of this Settlement and as the person to whom the charge of forming it was confided, I have been bound to remain as its Leader until the service should be successfully accomplished. That event is now I trust consummated and I avail myself accordingly of the earliest opportunity to tender the resignation of my command.[19]

By this stage James and Ellen were yearning to return to England. It was three years since they had seen their eldest son Andrew, and 8-year-old Frederick Henry was now in need of more tuition than could be provided by Ellen and a governess. Stirling's determination to quit seems to have been recognised when his letter reached London, late in March 1838, for Glenelg annotated the dispatch that the Queen had given approval and added:

> I have great pleasure in expressing HM's sense of the zeal and ability with which you have discharged the important duties entrusted to you, and regret that the Colony of Western Australia which has prospered under your auspices shd be deprived of the benefit of your continued care and superintendence. 26 April 1838 GG.[20]

Glenelg lost no time in seeking a replacement. When Sir Richard Spencer applied for the position, writing just one month after Stirling, his letter was annotated 'acquaint him that Mr Hutt's appointment had been confirmed before the arrival of this letter. 23 May 1838.'[21]

Having signed his resignation letter, Stirling spent early October 1837 drafting reports for the Colonial Office on the implementation of the new land regulations. The minutes of the Executive Council were forwarded for Glenelg's attention, and it is interesting that in his covering letter Stirling made no mention of the difficulties experienced in applying the regulations to different classes of land. Perhaps it was because he had been told expressly that the Governor's opinion, and that of the Council, was only required on two matters: the period within which the surrender regulations were to apply, and the rent to be charged on Crown land leased for pasture. The latter, of course, had had important implications in New South Wales, where squatting had become widespread. But Stirling informed Glenelg it was not an issue in the West, for until stock numbers increased, it was unlikely that applications would be made to the Government 'to lease on that account'.[22]

In fact, by making new Crown land available to pastoralists in Western Australia, the surrender and exchange regulations delayed the emergence of squatting until the 1850s. As to the timing issue, Stirling stated in the same dispatch that he wished at present to leave undefined the period in which applications could be made, because there was 'not any considerable quantity of disposable land for the settlement of such claims…'

The surrender and exchange regulations actually would apply until 1841 and had an enormous effect on the status of landholding in the colony. When they were first introduced in 1837, over 1.5 million acres were held by 243 landholders in 401 different grants. Of this 1.5 million acres, 72 per cent was unimproved. By the end of 1840 only 686,877 acres, held by forty-nine landholders, remained unimproved (and subject to resumption under the 10-year improvement rule). Some 300,600 acres had been surrendered while 40,287 acres of new titled Crown land had been taken out, and the percentage of originally granted land held in fee simple had risen from 27 per cent in 1837 to over 45 per cent.[23] Stirling would not be there to see the final results of the change, but his comments to Glenelg were prophetic. He believed that although 'at present unpalatable to many individuals', and likely to pressure the Survey Department, the new regulations were 'calculated to benefit the present race of Settlers' and 'ultimately prove to be beneficial to the Colony'.[24]

On the same day that Stirling signed this dispatch, the majority of those who were to benefit from the new regulations were in Guildford for a meeting of the Agricultural Society. The main issue on their agenda was not the land regulations, but how to introduce better quality sheep. It had been accepted by this time that raising sheep to export wool to Britain was the most certain way to future prosperity, despite the problems it entailed. New finer-woolled breeds were essential to improve the quality of wool produced, but importing sheep was a hazardous business. Many died on the long sea voyage from Europe, particularly when ships ran into squally conditions rounding the Cape. Sheep introduced from Van Diemen's Land also experienced high mortality rates, and some had been infected with scab. It was thus resolved to form a company to import quality sheep from India, and a committee was appointed to effect the decision.[25]

With the first significant wool exports about to leave the colony on the *Hero*, Stirling informed the Colonial Office that statistics, hitherto collected on a 31 March year-end basis, would henceforth be made up to 31 December. At long last there were sufficient lines of communication within the colony, and enough facilities at the ports, to collect meaningful statistics. The Blue Books of colonial statistics were begun at this time and chart in detail the progress of the small settlement. Repeatedly, Stirling had been castigated by those in London for his tardiness in sending financial and statistical information. This had given him 'much pain', he stated, for it could not be attributed to any negligence on his part:

> In the first place I wish to point out that there is no direct communication from this Colony to England, nor in fact any communication with other places except at considerable and irregular intervals…For instance on the 10th of April last one vessel left this place for NSW, and on the 6th July another vessel sailed hence for South Australia but with the exception of these two, neither of which was a suitable conveyance for letters to England, no opportunity has offered for sending letters to any parts of the world for the last seven months…
>
> It is in vain to expect from a Colony thus circumstanced that regularity of communication which is practicable only under very different circumstances. With regard to the dispatches which have been addressed to the Colonial Office by me, within the last three years, upon financial subjects, I beg leave to observe that they have contained in my humble opinion the fullest information which could be given.[26]

Glenelg, however, was not convinced, as is evident from the following annotation:

> I certainly do not think that Sir J Stirling has sufficiently accounted for the absence of more regular reports…The deficiency was the more to be regretted because few persons were better able than Sir J Stirling to supply it. I think the truth is that for some time past he has been tired of his office…Sir J Stirling will soon quit his Government. It was this department rather than the Treasury which suffered the inconvenience. GG.[27]

On 20 October an event occurred in the streets of Perth which horrified the townsfolk but particularly traumatised the Stirling household. A young native boy named Yougat, who had been employed at Government House, was murdered in the street by a number of natives of the Murray tribe. The boy had been much liked and the murder was described as 'savage and barbarous', and without known cause except the hostility that existed between the Murray and Perth Aborigines.[28] The murder was all the sadder for Lady Stirling, who had worked tirelessly for disadvantaged children and no doubt had encouraged the young native lad around the household. It would have brought shock and fear too; Ellen's own young family were adventurous and could not be protected all the time. It was perhaps fortunate that a week later the Stirlings moved to Fremantle to facilitate a refurbishing of Government House.[29] The move, involving five children (including Walter, a babe in arms), plus their nurse, governess and servants, would have taken some time. Whether they rented accommodation or stayed with friends is not known, but the change of air and routine proved a happy time for Ellen, who became pregnant with her eighth child during their month-long sojourn.

James commuted to Perth weekly to attend Council meetings and deal with correspondence. As the departure of the *Hero* had been delayed, by late shearing due to inclement weather, he had had time to add to dispatches. One matter that had been of some concern was Dr Guistiniani's application for naturalisation. The latter had taken offence when Stirling had refused his application[30] but, as Stirling informed Glenelg, instructions 'expressly prohibited me from any enactment of any law, or ordinance for the naturalisation of aliens'. He nevertheless recommended that Guistiniani's application be accepted, commenting that:

> The number of foreigners likely to settle in this Colony must be so very small that I cannot anticipate any serious evil from the adoption of some general measure…and…I therefore recommend the subject to your Lordship's favourable consideration.[31]

As a direct result of this intercession, the Colonial Office devolved the power of naturalisation to the Governor-in-Council.[32]

The *Hero* finally left on 8 November, a proud day for all colonists and particularly for Ellen as her brother's ship headed out with its first cargo of colonial produce. On board were 17,920 lbs of wool, 70 tons of whale oil, 4½ tons of whale bone, 5 cwt of raspberry jam wood, 1,500 lbs of gum resin and two emus.[33] A week later Fremantle was once again alive with excitement when the HMS *Beagle*, an exploratory vessel made famous by the voyages of Charles Darwin and his subsequent evolutionary theories, came into port.[34] Darwin was not with this expedition,[35] which was intent on exploring the Torres Strait region and the north-west Australian coast, but its Commander, Captain Wickham, and his officers were warmly welcomed. The chief hydrographer on board was John Lort Stokes, whose detailed account of the voyage included the comment that

> The only conspicuous landmark visible in approaching the anchorage [at Swan River] is the Jail: rather a singular pharos for a settlement in Australia which boasts

its uncontaminated state. This building I afterwards induced the Governor to have whitewashed, and it now forms an excellent mark to point out the river, as well as the town.[36]

The extreme isolation of the new colony was made even more apparent by the belated news brought by the *Beagle* crew of the death at Windsor Castle of King William IV, and the accession of his niece, the young Queen Alexandrina Victoria. The King had died five months earlier, on 20 June, and on 18 November Stirling immediately ordered notices to be posted, couched in flowery language appropriate to the formality of the transition:

> We…do now hereby with one voice and consent of tongue and heart, publish and proclaim that the high and mighty Princess Alexandrina Victoria is now…our only lawful and rightful liege Lady, Victoria by the grace of God, Queen of the United Kingdom of Great Britain and Ireland and of this Colony of Western Australia and the Dependencies thereof, Defender of the faith…To whom we do acknowledge all Faith and constant obedience with all hearty and humble affection—beseeching God, by whom Kings and Queens do reign, to bless the Royal Princess Victoria with long and happy years to reign over us. GOD SAVE THE QUEEN.[37]

A small notice in the *Perth Gazette* had informed the public that the Queen styled herself Victoria, without the Alexandrina, while another notice announced that a ceremony to proclaim allegiance to the young Queen was to be held in front of Government House on the following Monday, 20 November, which all civil and military officers were directed to attend, and that a day of general mourning would follow on Tuesday.[38] The proclamation was read again, the military fired a *feu de joie* to a resounding three cheers by the assemblage, and Stirling then administered the new 'oaths of allegiance, supremacy and abjuration to the members of Council and officers of the Civil establishment', he and Irwin having previously administered the same oaths to each other.

Stirling returned to Fremantle until the following Monday when Council once again met to discuss the accounts. The deficit had swollen because the £750 for the Court House, charged to the Parliamentary Grant the previous year, had been disallowed and had to be repaid. This implied an increase in taxes, which would impose hardship on all.[39] The whole colony was suffering from the inevitable effects of a paucity of shipping, everything apart from local produce was scarce, and prices had skyrocketed. Even the urbane George Fletcher Moore was put to the test:

> I literally wear a hat which is half cut through by some accident or other and completely bare of beaver but there is not another to be got. The same with shoes and the same with clothes.[40]

Wages had risen in consequence and shoemakers were so besieged with business it was 'needless to give them the smallest job with any expectation of it being done in less than a fortnight'.[41] The effect on landed settlers, with no regular income, was disastrous as Council knew full well, and an increase in taxes was the last thing they needed.

The *Beagle* was still in Gage's Roads at the end of November, her planned expedition north temporarily delayed by the captain's illness. Stirling and Roe had availed themselves of her officers' expertise to conduct several surveys of the adjacent coast.[42] James would have relished the company of naval men during these all too short forays to sea—a time also to catch up on Admiralty affairs. Amongst other things he learned that a new settlement was to be established on the north coast, near the Raffles Bay outpost he had helped establish in 1827, and that Captain Bremer, who had been given command of the newly commissioned *Alligator*, was to undertake the mission.[43] On 17 December the *Beagle* was joined at anchor by the Hobart-bound *Joshua Carroll*, just in from London and the Cape. For settlers she brought much-wanted general cargo, letters, packages and newspapers, and for the Stirling family some unsettling news. Ellen's father's seat in Parliament was in some doubt, for the Whig majority had been under threat in the forthcoming elections when the ship left England. Furthermore, there had been a number of serious mercantile failures, especially among those connected with the American trade, and this would have repercussions for James' brother's textile business. It was also bad tidings for those who had sent wool away on the *Hero*, for wool prices, as well as those for whale oil, had tumbled.[44]

Hard on the heels of the *Joshua Carroll* came the *Eleanor* with thirty-three returning settlers. She dropped anchor on 23 December, just a day after the Stirlings moved back from the port to Government House.

After a dearth of shipping earlier in the year, Gage's Roads was suddenly quite busy. Next in was the *Abercrombie* from Sydney with a cargo of flour, salt meat and livestock, then the *Champion* from the Sound, and the *Eudora* from Sydney bringing the Quaker missionary, James Backhouse. He wasted no time in getting down to business, meeting Irwin and Stirling in Perth, and securing an introduction to the Colonial Chaplain, the Reverend J. B. Wittenoom, who granted permission to hold meetings in the Court House-cum-Church. In his journal Backhouse described it as a neat building with white calico in place of glass in the windows, which were fitted with venetian shutters outside.[45] The town in general he portrayed as having a slight appearance of decay, with few big houses, streets of sand mixed with soot from frequent burning, some picket fences in disarray, and many gardens overgrown and neglected. At the Quakers' first prayer meeting, on 31 December, the congregation numbered some 200—a good turnout considering the total population of Perth then was said to be only 600.

Stirling would have welcomed the arrival of the Quaker missionary, for he was sorely troubled by another outbreak of violence on the part of the natives. Just

C.D Wittenoom Esq.   J. Henshall

To Quaker James Backhouse, Perth in 1837 showed signs of decay
and neglect, with gardens overgrown

As reproduced in Nathaniel Ogle, The Colony of Western Australia

before Christmas two young shepherds had been attacked by spears near the
Canning River and had their sheep stolen. A pursuing party failed to apprehend the
offenders, but identified one as a member of the Guildford tribe. Some days later,
with the help of a member of the same tribe, the offender was subsequently
caught,[46] identified and committed to Fremantle gaol. As a recent dispatch from
London had chastised Stirling for a seeming lack of 'precision and formality in his
dealings with the natives',[47] a frustrated James on 29 December penned a lengthy
explanation of the problems he faced. Far from being trivial or accidental conflicts,
he argued,

> The true cause of quarrel is the invasion by the Whites of the country of a very
> peculiar race of people who possess, however low they may be in the scale of
> civilisation, qualities which render them extremely formidable. Hardy, active,
> quick of apprehension, fearless of death, and practised in continual warfare, they
> are fond of stratagem, and glory in its success…Women and children are
> frequently killed by men of their own tribe in satisfaction of some former grudge,
> or in pursuance of some of those dreadful rites which superstitious usage has
> established among them.

Stirling explained that but for the mutual distrust between tribes, which kept them
in arms against one another, they would 'combine for the annihilation of the
Whites'. In his view, settlers and Aborigines were sufficiently equal in numbers as to

ensure the clashes would likely be infrequent. But particularly in remote areas, a single act of violence—whether by settlers or Aborigines—tended to set off a 'train of evils', and this state of affairs could only be controlled by 'the adoption of forcible measures'. Recapitulating the earlier York outrages, he ventured the opinion that, had not the Aboriginal offenders been arrested, the local settlers would have abandoned the area.

Referring to the Canning incident, he reported that one of the natives had been apprehended and would be brought to trial within the month, but that this in turn raised problems. If a convicted offender was sentenced to transportation, rather than execution, the normal destination was Van Diemen's Land, but Stirling felt this was inappropriate for Aborigines. He wanted permission, and the funding, to establish a 'place of punishment for them on some island adjacent to the coast'.[48] Noting that he was 'without the power to remedy the defects of the system at present', Stirling said he awaited 'with much anxiety' Glenelg's decision on setting up an 'effective department for the control and protection of the aboriginal race'.

Some of the sentiments in Stirling's long dispatch he had stated before—his recognition the natives' bravery and daring, and their love of a successful strategy—aspects with which a former commander of a warship could empathise. But he does not seem to have understood the forces, such as land rights and food scarcity, that prompted such stratagems. Unlike Moore, who made an attempt to understand native beliefs and culture, Stirling was an Anglican of his times, and upholder of the faith in the colony, who decried non-Christian beliefs as superstitious rites. Both he and Ellen believed that the natives should be 'saved' from their savage state by Christianity, and Ellen particularly had appealed to her family and acquaintances in England to raise the necessary funds to build churches, and to appoint a Bishop to oversee church work in the colony. The Reverend Wittenoom simply could not attend to the needs of the whole colony, and Perth still lacked a church built only for that purpose. It was known that Lady Stirling's efforts and those of the Missionary Society had already raised over £1,000 for the erection of churches in Perth, Fremantle, Guildford, York and Albany.[49] More funds were needed, but there was enough at least to begin plans for a new church in Perth.

Meanwhile James Backhouse, getting to know his new environment, was horrified that so little had been done to 'civilise' the Aborigines who, he noted, 'not infrequently walk about Perth and Fremantle in a state of nudity', showing no 'disposition to wear European clothing'.[50] Returning to Fremantle, he became embroiled in the trial of the native who had attacked the shepherd boys. The missionary, Dr Guistiniani, had pleaded for the defendant arguing, rightly as Backhouse thought, that the taking of sheep to a native was the same as a white taking kangaroos, and that undue temptation had been put in front of the native by leaving valuable sheep in the care of such young boys. The verdict nevertheless went against the native.

On 3 January 1838 Stirling had taken passage for the Vasse on the colonial schooner *Champion*, accompanied by Surveyor-General Roe, Dr Joseph Harris, and

John Scott and family.[51] The latter, his three adult sons and stepson Daniel McGregor had been farming part of Stirling's Woodbridge estate, and were now to manage his Leschenault land. Leaving Fremantle, they took the southern passage around Garden Island, which had not been done before,[52] so Roe took soundings and bearings and then undertook a proper survey of the Safety Bay area. Such necessary survey work helped to justify the expedition, which was primarily for Stirling's private benefit. He wanted Roe to clarify the boundaries of the lands he had selected in the Vasse area, and the Scotts to be settled on his grant which was at 'a beautiful spot for a farm on the Preston river'.[53] The party closely examined the land around the Brunswick and Preston, which had not been surveyed to date, and were delighted by its suitability for agriculture.[54] To encourage more settlers, Stirling ordered that a military station be established near the entrance to the Leschenault inlet. Some of the soldiers from the Vasse were sent to man the new post, and thus became the first inhabitants of the present town of Bunbury. Stirling then visited the settlers at the Vasse, mainly to hear their accounts of recent strife with the natives.[55] Charles Bussell had taken the law into his own hands the previous year when he had mounted a shooting party to punish natives who had been stealing their property. Stirling had been appalled to hear of the loss of life, and especially that women and children had been killed in the incident,[56] and had said so to Molloy, the Government Resident. But he was sensitive also to the needs of women and children in this isolated outpost, and their need for protection. He was pleased to hear that conditions had improved over past months, as settlers had begun trading their fresh produce for supplies from visiting American whalers.[57]

Returning to his grant on the Preston, Stirling found that Scott had been able to erect the timber frame house brought from Perth to provide some comfort for Mrs Scott. Born Helen Forrest, Mrs Scott was an experienced midwife and soon became a valued member of the small Vasse community. In the future she would deliver a babe who would become Lord Forrest after being the first Premier of an independent Western Australia.[58]

Stirling enjoyed his periodic sorties out of Perth, for it was a chance to get away from paperwork and be outdoors. But there was inevitably some apprehension for Ellen, in this instance with real foundation. Stirling suffered a nasty fall from a horse during this trip which wrenched his leg muscles badly. Strapping and embrocations had relieved the pain and he could walk, but not without recurring discomfort.

On 23 January the Executive Council met to discuss the verdict of the last Quarter Sessions, in which two native prisoners had been sentenced to death, one for arson and the other for the attack on the young shepherd. Stirling felt both deserved mercy, but though his Council were prepared to grant it in the first case, on grounds of previous good conduct, they could not agree in the second. After long discussion the meeting was adjourned until the 26th when each Councillor was asked for his opinion again. Moore argued forcibly in favour of mercy, and produced an English paper dated 21 March 1837 reporting an Amendment to the Criminal Act, introduced by Lord John Russell, in which the offence of wounding with intent to do grievous bodily harm was not to be punished with death, but transportation. Roe and Brown disagreed strongly, believing an example should be made to protect the settlers, and recommended execution, but Irwin, the last to speak, sided with Moore in advising clemency. Having heard these divergent views Stirling summed up, stating:

> …according to the best of my understanding and conscience, I do verily believe that the existing law of England would not authorise the punishment of death, I am bound to mitigate the sentence which has been passed and to substitute for it transportation for life.[59]

Although pleased with this result, Stirling was faced again with the problem of where and how to transport the prisoners, who were being held in the small Fremantle gaol. It was one of the many problems on which he needed advice from England, but as so often happened the advice would arrive too late to be of use. He nevertheless spent the last week of January sending replies to all the myriad of questions raised in dispatches brought in on the *Beagle* and the *Eleanor*. The latest one was dated six months earlier, and the Colonial Office had not then received his letter of resignation. Stirling would thus have to contain his soul in patience, for no plans could be made until he heard that his resignation had been accepted.

20

Penultimate Concerns

1838

ON 1 FEBRUARY Stirling completed a supplementary report to the lengthy statistical summary he had sent the previous October, this time concentrating on the 'Revenue and Public Establishments'.[1] He proudly announced that there had been a significant increase in revenue, despite the fact that population had remained stable[2] and there had been no increase in taxation, except for the implementation of postage charges. Most of the increase in revenue had come from the sale of Crown land, as settlers used their remission certificates to obtain new lands and sometimes bid against one another at auction. These funds he hoped 'before long' could be used for 'the introduction of labouring persons', as Glenelg had intended. The colony was desperately short of labour and settlers were forwarding a separate memorial on the subject.

Government expenditure had remained within the estimates, but Stirling emphasised the need to provide soon for an expansion in the Survey and Customs departments, the appointment of a coroner, and once again an effective department 'for the Control, Protection and Management of the Aborigines'. He pointed out the extent to which colonists were providing public amenities themselves: for instance, a new church, and 'dykes and bridges' across the islands near Perth which had been built with funds raised by subscription. The whaling company also had built, at their own cost, a small jetty at Fremantle and a tunnel under Arthur's Head which was almost complete. Several American whaling vessels had called at Fremantle reporting their successes in offshore operations, but, he sadly added, the settlement had neither the capital nor the population to 'enter into extensive operations in that line however lucrative they appear to be'. In his concluding remarks, Stirling repeated this observation about the colony's needs, stating:

> although it is recovering from the distresses of its earlier years, it is not yet in the enjoyment of any considerable influx of colonists or capital, nor is there any good reason to hope for a very rapid improvement in its condition until by our increase of population & means it can bring into play those resources which are beyond the reach of its present inhabitants.[3]

Enclosed with this dispatch was the Agricultural Society report for the year 1837, which the Governor had found most pleasing. For the first time, settlers had supplied enough wheat to more than meet domestic needs. This was primarily due to a good harvest, because rural labour shortages and upwards wages pressure had increased costs and curbed any significant addition to the acreage under wheat. In his reply, read to the Society at their quarterly meeting on 2 February, Stirling promised 'to bring the matter to the attention of the Legislative Council when next they met'.[4]

Lack of labour was a constant complaint among colonists, and many blamed the American whalers who were now frequenting the port at Fremantle and recruiting local men. This put pressure on the local companies and led to calls for the closure of the unprofitable Perth-owned Northern Company.[5] It was thought that the better-managed Fremantle Whaling Company could purchase its assets and operate more efficiently when the bay-whaling season began again. Their jetty at Anglesea Point (south mole) was already proving a boon in the loading and unloading of ships, which would be further improved when the tunnel through to the High Street was completed. Past fears that American competition would erode profits had been assuaged too by the arrival of HMS *Pelorus* from the Eastern Station in early January, in response to Stirling's request.

On 4 February 1838 the *Pelorus* and the *Champion*, together with three other intercolonial ships and one American whaler, were joined in Gage's Roads by the 400-ton *Gaillardon* from Calcutta. Colonists learned that this ship had been chartered to a group calling itself the Bengal Australian Association, which intended to fit out a number of such ships

> to afford a ready communication with both countries for the convenience of passengers seeking a change of air for the benefit of their health, but who are on limited permission of absence from the India service.[6]

For Stirling this was the first sign that some of his original plans for the colony might yet come to fruition. He had foreseen the suitability of Swan River as a convalescent station for British personnel stationed in India during his first visit in 1827 and now, over ten years later, it seemed that others shared his view. The Sydney-bound *Gaillardon* had brought to Swan River Mr Thomas Little, his wife and family, Mr James Milne and a number of Indian coolie labourers. Little had been chief overseer for Charles Prinsep, a wealthy member of the East India Establishment and a promulgator of the Bengal Australian Association. Prinsep had decided to purchase land at Swan River to rear horses for the Indian remount market, and sent Little to establish the venture, for which George Leake was to be local agent. Stirling's influence was clearly at work here, and certainly in Little's selection of land, for he finally settled on Belvedere, a 380-acre location opposite some of Stirling's own land, on a peninsula between Leschenault inlet and the sea.

Movements of ships like the *Gaillardon* got good exposure in the local Press, but the stormy life of one of the two newspapers, the *Swan River Guardian*, was fast drawing to a close. On 10 February the *Gazette* announced that the *Guardian's* two guarantors, William Lamb and Dr Guistiniani, had withdrawn their surety (the latter deciding to go to Mauritius). *Guardian* editor William Nairn Clark, who had been running a series of open letters to Stirling criticising all government appointees, was finally forced to close, his last issue appearing on 22 February. With the demise of the paper, several meetings were held to establish a new free Press,[7] but they came to nothing. Clark's misfortunes continued, for in April his 2-year-old daughter died, and then his 5-year-old son in May. Broken-hearted, Clark left the colony in August 1838 for Van Diemen's Land.[8]

Early in March Stirling's troublesome leg, injured previously in the horse fall, led to him being confined to home. With time on his hands, he once again turned to the matter of his land. On 16 March Roe filed a memorandum concerning the Governor's land, noting that of his 100,000-acre entitlement only 8,165½ acres had actually been assigned, to wit:

Garden Island, Cockburn Sound	Dec 1828	2,240 acres
on the Swan River	30 Sep 1829	4,000 acres
on Arthur's Head, Fremantle	19 Jul 1832	5½ acres
Plantagenet	1 Mar 1837	1,920 acres
TOTAL		8,165½ acres[9]

Just days previously, Stirling had sent a memo to Roe stating that he had assigned 200 acres of the land he held to the west of King George's Sound to Messrs Watt, Mudie and Lees.[10] There was no mention of any monetary transaction and Roe's annotation was terse: 'directed by letter but not assigned or opened for selection', which highlighted the difficulty he had in keeping track of the various claims to unsurveyed land, not just Stirling's.

To speed the Governor's convalescence sea air was advised and, as news had filtered through of a rift between the Government Resident at Albany and his chief magistrate, it was decided to bring forward the annual visit to King George's Sound, making use of the visiting warship *Pelorus* which could at the same time investigate foreign shipping in the area. The party left on 19 March,[11] preceded by the *Champion* which was to convey Irwin and Moore on official inspections of outposts at Leschenault, the Vasse, Augusta and the Sound.

At Leschenault Moore found 'a droll sort of East India establishment', consisting of seven Indians of the 'hill coolies' class under the charge of a Scot called Miller.[12] Little and his family had not as yet come down from Fremantle. Moore took the opportunity to explore the Collie and Preston River areas, then sailed on to the Vasse in Geographe Bay, where he and Irwin were to call on the Bussell family. They stayed two days and saw 'more good land in one continued tract than we saw elsewhere'. By the time the *Champion* reached the Sound, HMS *Pelorus* had taken the Governor on several exploratory trips along the surrounding coastline. At Torbay they had found a good anchorage, and crew members sent ashore to examine the land had returned with timber samples from trees just a quarter mile inland, which 'run from 80 to 100 feet without a branch'.[13] Stirling was delighted to pronounce the timber 'of the finest description for shipbuilding', and it was, for they had discovered the tall karri trees for which this part of Western Australia is renowned.

Back in Perth by mid-April for an Executive Council meeting, Stirling faced a sensitive matter—an application from the Fremantle Whaling Company for additional land at Bathers Bay which involved the 5½ acres of his own land on Arthur's Head. As he explained, his acquisition dated back to 1831 'when Fremantle was a village and not likely to be greater'. At that point, having 'neither salary nor house' but wanting to build a residence in the port, he had made an outlay for materials, and occupied the land.

> In the Settlement of Claims in 1832 the limits of that location were defined and included in the maps and returns transmitted to England…My right to the particular portion referred to, although not requiring any particular sanction, was admitted incidentally by a letter from Mr Hay dated 23 Jan 1833.

When the whaling company had been founded, they had applied to purchase some of Stirling's grant. He had 'declined to make any sale, but offered the company a gratuitous grant of the land on which their improvements had been placed'. The problem that had arisen, Stirling said, was that the current application

> does not distinguish between the land obtained from me and that which it seeks to obtain from the Government, nor does it contain explicit statements of the works erected or prepared to be erected on the one site or the other…

He put it to Council that freehold rights should not be granted to the company in case the land was needed at a future date for port development etc. Whilst he upheld all the rights of private enterprise,

> No limitation of this right, no power to interfere with it, ought to be reserved except only…when the public welfare, derivable from the investment of private funds is less than the public inconvenience arising from the exclusive appropriation of particular spots or positions…

And the Fremantle company's proposition, he argued, constituted just such a case. He therefore offered the following solution:

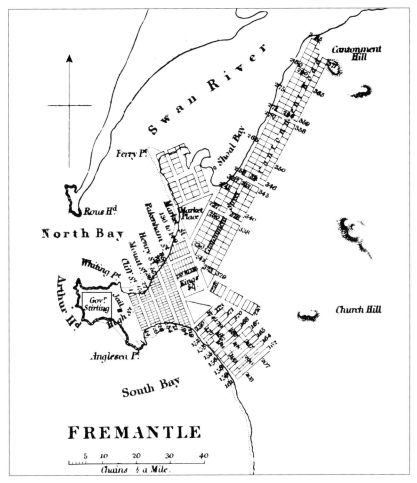

Stirling's 5½ acre grant excluded land at the point, held aside for fortifications.
From the 1839 Arrowsmith map (see also page 425)

Give the applicants a conditional Grant of the land they ask for the purposes specified. Require a statement now to be made, upon verified accounts, of the expense incurred in making the land and in the wharf, and in buildings on Crown Lands. Reserve the right of resumption on one year's notice…such resumptions being only to be made in event of its becoming necessary for public advantage.[14]

Stirling was well aware of establishing a precedent in placing long-term public good before private interests, and begged his Council to think carefully about the matter.[15] After some discussion all agreed that, despite the pre-eminence of the principles of private enterprise in the colony, there were occasions 'when private property must necessarily yield to public benefit', and that Stirling's solution was appropriate.[16]

Plans gathered apace in May for the ninth anniversary of the founding of the colony. Meetings were held to plan the balls, races and other amusements which had become a traditional part of the First of June holiday. In readiness for the horse races, a new course was selected and 'the Stud Club', a small group of Upper Swan land owners, published the pedigrees of all the thoroughbred horses in the colony.[17] It was an impressive list, tracing the blood lines of ten horses back several generations to well-known British stock. The majority were horses that Stirling had purchased from Lord Egremont's stud at Petworth and imported in 1834, or their progeny, and they were now in the hands of a select group including William Brockman, Captain Meares, George Leake, Barrett Lennard and young Andrew Stirling. Their interest in stud horses was symbolic of the Upper Swan landholders' claims to 'gentry' status, as also was their strong support for the building of a new Anglican church. Though planned for some time, this project had been delayed by disputes over its site. The spot originally agreed upon, near the Public Offices, was too near to natural springs to support construction of a suitable tower, so an alternative was sought.[18] Land on the hospital side of the barracks was deemed suitable, but Major Irwin had been loath to give up sufficient ground,[19] so negotiations continued. Nevertheless, there was such broad agreement about the need for a new church that Stirling's proposal to grant £150 from colonial funds towards the new building was accepted unquestioningly when put to the Legislative Council on Tuesday 15 May, the date set to discuss the estimates.

The public gallery was crowded when Stirling took the chair at noon; interest in the estimates was always acute, but this year another matter of widespread concern was to be raised, namely the scarcity of labour. Stirling was pleased to report that the revenue had improved over the past year and that actual disbursements, with exception of two items, 'were much within the income'.[20] The estimates were referred to Council in committee. Stirling then raised the 'Memoir on the subject of Labour', forwarded to him from the Agricultural Society, which he now had read aloud to all present.

The Society requested the Government to subsidise the passages of labourers either from England or Calcutta—men who would be carefully selected by an agent who knew the settlers' needs and be indentured to the Government. Employers would then pay between one and two-thirds of the passage money to the Government as an initial premium, and the immigrants would make a regular payment from wages. An Inspector or Guardian would be appointed to manage their employment and wages. Once the scheme had been explained, Stirling asked that a committee of the whole Council deliberate on the matter and report back as to whether the Government should be involved in the proposal, and if so, to what extent.[21]

At the 30 May Legislative Council meeting, Stirling introduced a subject he knew would meet Colonial Office displeasure. He wanted to see 'Funds created in the colony left exclusively under the management of the local Government'[22] rather than being sent to London, to be managed by the British Lands and Emigration Board, as instructed. After considerable discussion councillors resolved to hold back a sum 'of £1,000...with a view to bringing to trial the proposed experiment'. Stirling concurred.[23]

The serious procedural work of government could be put briefly to one side, for the next day, a Friday, was Foundation Day. The *Perth Gazette*'s editor reported that all the festivities went off very well, with one exception—'the pony race was a complete failure, but afforded infinite amusement from false starts, bolting and other incidental circumstances'. Both the Subscription Ball at the Public Offices and the Tradesmen's Ball at Leeder's Hotel were well attended and accounted a great success. Of the former the *Perth Gazette* paid tribute to 'a splendid repast...one of the best we have seen or enjoyed in the colony'.[24] James and Ellen attended both balls, spending some hours at Leeder's Hotel where guests reportedly 'kept up the festivities of the night until an early hour in the morning, which may be excusable as it only occurs once in the year'.

Yet more frivolities were scheduled for the Monday night—a United Services Ball in the Commissariat Store—and as G. F. Moore recorded, with perhaps a touch of world-weariness, 'I shall have to go down to it, for one has no option in these matters for fear of giving offence'.[25] It was evidently a great success, for some days later he noted that 'the company did not come away till near 6 o'clock in the morning'.[26] As officers of HMS *Beagle* were among the hosts, an undoubted talking point would have been her recent voyage in which they discovered a major river near Dampier's Archipelago, which they named the FitzRoy. The potential of good land to the north was exciting for the colonists, who would have been keenly disappointed to learn that the exploratory northern overland expedition mounted by Grey and Lushington had been terminated when Grey had been speared and become seriously ill.[27]

It was in the wake of the anniversary festivities that Stirling publicly announced his resignation. The timing was astute, for morale in the colony was high and colonists took the news with equanimity. The *Gazette*'s editorial on 9 June 1838 probably mirrored the feelings of the establishment in stating that:

> His Excellency has been so closely united and associated with every settler in our great enterprise...that we can but regret the loss of his active service amongst us; we may, however, look forward with confidence to his strenuous efforts in behalf of this territory, his adopted child, in other quarters...[28]

Having recently received a report from the Fremantle Gaoler, Henry Vincent, that a contagious illness had broken out among Aboriginal prisoners, 'probably caused by the loss of their accustomed exercise', Stirling revived debate at his 14 June Executive Council on 'the subject of the removal of the Native prisoners to one of the adjacent islands'.[29] The plan had previously foundered through fears of the compensation liable to the original Rottnest Island grant holder, Robert Thomson, but now negotiators were tackling the issue anew. On getting wind of the plan to appropriate the island as a depot 'for refractory savages', Thomson petitioned Stirling on the 18th, pleading that he had a 'young numerous female family' to bring up and, was unable to employ men to guard them, and had originally taken his Rottnest Island grant in 1832 to avoid all contact with Aborigines.[30] He nevertheless was prepared to give up his claims to the island for 'the small sum of £300' or a valuation by a jury of his countrymen. Though ill and part-blind,[31] Thomson knew the value of his island; equally he realised relocating his family would be expensive. When offered £100 or a 640-acre grant of land, he refused both. To his dismay, however, a party of five Aboriginal prisoners and a white convict, under the supervision of Constable Welsh and three soldiers, landed on Rottnest on 17 August. The prisoners had previously been detained on Garden Island where they were taught to row a boat—knowledge they quickly put to good use, for the *Perth Gazette* reported on the 25th that the five native prisoners had managed to escape in Thomson's boat, one drowning in the process.[32] The Aboriginal prisoners evidently each had leg chains attached to a tree which they proceeded to burn overnight—a feat, G. F. Moore recorded in his diary, deserving of some credit for its ingenuity.[33] Thomson was accused of carelessness in not securing his boat, which had been wrecked. He was subsequently given £10 compensation and persuaded to accept another offer, this time of both £100 cash and a remission certificate for a 640-acre grant of land. When councillors were asked to approve this offer, which they did unanimously,[34] they also sanctioned plans for Vincent to establish an institution for the reception of native prisoners on Rottnest Island. The decision was announced with approval in the *Perth Gazette* on 16 June:

> The natives transported to the island of Rottnest for any offences will be enabled to practise their old and acquired habits of hunting and fishing and their time will be profitably employed in collecting salt, curing fish, cutting firewood and in other occupations. This is one of the best, most salutary and most efficient measures the Local government could have adopted for the protection of the settlers...[35]

Stirling could now report positively to the Colonial Office on steps taken to address the native problem. He also explained that, following disturbances in the Toodyay region, he had decided to create a Government Resident in that district and had appointed Mr Whitfield, replacing him in Guildford by Lieutenant T. N. Yule 'formerly of the Bengal army'.[36] When the dispatch reached London in January 1839, the apparent increase in establishment costs met with displeasure, and even an element of peevishness, for Under-Secretary James Stephen added a note stating 'the Governor of the Colony should be desired to carry on his correspondence on paper of the ordinary size'.[37] He and others were unaware that with such irregular shipping, goods of all descriptions were in short supply in the colony, and simply finding any paper on which to submit the duplicate dispatches was difficult, let alone paper of the right size.

Luckily ignorant of this comment, Stirling was nevertheless feeling somewhat peeved himself. He felt it most unfair that whilst he and his family had lived in sub-standard accommodation for so long, his successor would walk into a Government House that had been renovated at the expense of his £300 per annum lodging money, a total of £1,100. Accordingly, he wrote to the Secretary of State on 19 June requesting some compensation. He proposed that half of the lodging money go towards the buildings costs, and the other half be returned to himself. As he was constantly short of money, this seemed a perfectly reasonable request to Stirling, but from an objective viewpoint it was a trifle over the odds when he had already received £2,828 3s 11d from the public purse in what he called 'the purchase from me of a house originally begun as a private work'. Nevertheless, his claim to have experienced

> personal inconvenience, destruction of property, wear & tear of furniture and other incidental expense arising out of the very indifferent accommodation my having enjoyed during the whole period referred to…[38]

was undoubtedly true, for after all, the engineer had reported the leaking state of the roof prior to repairs. The whole matter was not to be resolved until he returned to England.

With departure in mind, Stirling still had to clear up the matter of his land grants, particularly those in the Leschenault region. Accordingly, he arranged to visit the area with Roe, proceeding overland on 19 June via Fremantle and the Murray. Moore later reported that during the eighteen-day trip Stirling was 'greatly pleased with the country he had seen at Leschenault, especially on the upper part of the Collie river'.[39] The *Gazette* also reported on his return that:

> As grazing country, it is acknowledged to be far superior to any other portion of the colony; the establishments for rearing horses for the Indian market and our most productive dairies will consequently be found before long in this quarter.[40]

That Stirling took the opportunity to review his land holdings in the district is evidenced by a memorandum sent to the Surveyor-General's office a week after his return.[41] Essentially this outlined the boundaries of 4,000 acres that he had selected around Picton, in lieu of the same quantity originally selected on the west side of Geographe Bay which had now been set aside for the township of Bunbury.

In Executive Council meetings after his return, the problems of the natives were still high on the agenda. An Aboriginal named Helia had been sentenced to death at the last Quarter Sessions for the murder of a native woman in the streets of Perth. Stirling believed the sentence was unwarranted, arguing the murder was following tribal law, and that 'to apply strictly and impartially the British Law to this particular offender would be to pass sentence of death upon the whole race'. As sentence had already been passed, he felt the only correct course of action would be to seek a final decision from London. Councillors agreed, particularly Advocate-General Moore who noted:

> it would be cruel to take away his Life for acting amongst his own people, in a manner sanctioned and recognised as right by them, and although that conduct be in contradistinction of our Law, yet of that Law as applying to his own people he knows neither the existence, nor could he understand the force.[42]

Although a minority among Perth residents disagreed with such clemency, public opinion was slowly changing. There was a far greater understanding of Aboriginal customs now, and an appreciation also of their abilities in tracking and taking messages. Indeed, only that week a group of natives had brought mail and dispatches for the Governor overland from Albany in fourteen days.[43]

Prompted by their own growing young family's needs, both James and Ellen shared a keen interest in the development of education in the colony. There had been periodic, but shortlived, attempts to establish various schools, but in practice most settlers' children had been educated at home, if at all. The Anglican Sunday School at Perth, in which Ellen had played a major role, had been one of the few institutions that had persisted, but it had been on a voluntary basis. Stirling was therefore pleased to report at the next meeting of his Executive Council that the Reverend J. B. Wittenoom's recently established School for Boys was doing well. He had been allowed use of the Court House for lessons and was being paid by the parents of his pupils. But now Wittenoom was concerned for the boys whose parents could not afford to pay, and was asking the Government for £75 to cover such expenses and allow him an assistant.[44] At the same time Stirling had also had an application from a Miss Helms to establish a school for girls on similar principles as Mr Wittenoom's. Miss Helms[45] had been put forward by a committee of ladies as 'a person well qualified' to manage such an institution, so Stirling recommended that £30 also be granted for female children whose parents were unable 'to defray the expense of educating them'.[46] Council approved these measures and determined to devise a means of regulating the new schools.

Whilst these formative institutions were offering the chance of a sound elementary schooling, the lack of opportunity for further education concerned many prominent families. Their sons were now reaching the age that normally required enrolment in training for a specific career, like the army or navy, East India Company or Public Service. For this they needed to return to England, and in light of his impending departure, Stirling's guidance was now increasingly being sought. At the next meeting of the Agricultural Society at Guildford, which Stirling attended as patron,[47] several anxious fathers, including W. B. Andrews and Peter Brown, discussed whether he might take their sons under his wing and have them sent to appropriate schools back home.

Just days later, on 4 August, great excitement gripped the colony as news spread of the arrival of the *Shepherd* with a huge cargo and thirty-seven immigrants, including nine experienced whalers, a new minister, the Reverend William Mitchell, and Henry Ommanney, the long-awaited Assistant Surveyor. The *Shepherd*'s voyage had taken just 120 days and she brought news from England up to the end of March. Apart from private letters, dispatches for Stirling and newspapers, she also brought the welcome intelligence that the Mangles had chartered another vessel, the *Brittomart*, which was following the *Shepherd* and could be expected in October. This would have been especially pleasing to Lady Stirling, for their plans for departure could now encompass returning on one of her brother's ships.

With departure looming and Ommanney now in town, Stirling sent another memorandum to Roe asking for his new assistant to be sent to survey his Leschenault grants.[48] Possibly with Ommanney's welfare in mind, Stirling brought to the next Council meeting a request from Roe for free rations to surveyors in the field, to 'speed their activities'. Councillors were wary, fearing another rebuff from England, but were reassured when Stirling produced an extract from a London dispatch of October 1833 approving free rations for surveyors in the field.[49]

If the need to get his affairs straightened out was proving somewhat of a distraction, the situation was compounded by a disturbing incident involving Ellen, and reported by the *Perth Gazette*:

> Lady Stirling, whilst instructing the children at the Sunday school on Sunday afternoon [19 August], suddenly fell down in a fit and remained some time in a state of insensibility. We were happy to learn that she was much better in the course of the evening and on the following day was quite recovered from the effects of an attack which was supposed to have been brought on by the closeness of the building.[50]

What the paper failed to state, given the niceties of the time, was that Lady Stirling was over eight months pregnant. Although she was only 28 and had had trouble-free pregnancies hitherto, this was her eighth child and any fall at this stage could prove serious. It would have been a worrying time for James who, all agreed, was a devoted husband. He, more than anyone, was aware of the paucity of medical expertise in the colony since Collie's death in 1835. Dr James Crichton, who arrived at the end of 1836,[51] became the next Colonial Surgeon but did not have quite the same zeal as Collie, allowing the lease of rooms for the Colonial Hospital to lapse.[52] But he later gained fame as the first to introduce and dispense vaccine matter to the colony[53] and, with the support of Governor Hutt, founded a permanent hospital.[54] There were no private medical practitioners operating in the whole of Perthshire late in 1838[55] so, apart from the military surgeon, Crichton was the only qualified source of medical attention available, and he could be a day's horse ride away in any emergency. Happily, on this particular occasion all was well and Stirling was able to return to colonial affairs.

On Wednesday 22 August 1838 Council sat to consider further the question of assisted immigration, agreed to by Councillors in May but now requiring formal ratification. Stirling began by stating it was his belief that the method of introducing labour discussed so far 'would if tried, be attended with no better result here than had been found to be the case in Sydney, which by all accounts had been a complete failure'.[56] He had therefore sketched out an alternative plan for the consideration of Council. Instead of leaving the selection of labourers to an agent or to British authorities, Stirling wanted to assist only

> the relatives and friends of persons actually residing within the Settlement, or apprentices, assistants and servants whom actual Settlers may desire to procure, and for whose reception and employment they are in a condition to provide.[57]

For advances to be made by the Government, from the agreed £1,000 allocation, satisfactory security would be required and repayment strictly enforced so that immigrants would not become a public charge. Repayment would be due within two years of receiving a 'Letter of Credit' from the Government to cover passage fares. Any servants brought out under indenture were to be registered with the Colonial Secretary, who was to see to it that preference was given to applications with the shortest indenture period and offering reasonable wages and conditions.

This proposal, with which all Councillors agreed, showed that Stirling had learned from his early experiences in the colony and from those in Sydney. He did not want a repeat of unsuitable immigrants, unenforceably long indentures, and an unwaged, dissatisfied labour force. His early Master and Servant Act had been ahead of its time in attempting to provide security for indentured servants,[58] but the circumstances of some of the larger early employers (such as Peel) had left him no choice other than to cancel many indentures and support them from public funds. A recurrence of this was to be avoided at all costs. Council fully agreed, and proposed that a notice be drawn up setting out the terms of Stirling's memorandum for the information of the public.

Among a flurry of dispatches Stirling was preparing for transmission to the Colonial Office on 1 and 2 September was a long, detailed statement of accounts from 1835 to 1838 which he 'trusted would be approved', as they demonstrated

> the attention paid to the Instructions neither to exceed the aggregate amount voted, nor indeed to expend on any particular object more than specially authorised.[59]

During this period Stirling had persuaded his nephew-by-marriage, George Elliot,[60] who had been an unofficial aide-de-camp since his arrival in 1829, to take control of his grant at Leschenault and start the improvements required for freehold title. He was to work with Scott, who already had charge of Stirling's sheep and cattle in that region. Elliot dined with George Fletcher Moore before leaving and discussed the move,[61] but by setting out at this time he missed the long-anticipated 'happy event' in the Stirling household.

Ellen gave birth to her third daughter, Ellinor, on Saturday 8 September 1838. There were no complications from her recent fall, so she was probably delivered by a midwife. The colony was informed of the event in a simple one-line announcement in the *Perth Gazette*: 'On Saturday the 8th instant the Lady of Sir James Stirling RN of a daughter'.[62]

The news was overshadowed, however, by the adjacent death notices. The first entry recorded the demise of Lieutenant Armstrong, one of the senior military officers, at the Vasse on 26 August. Major Irwin reported that he had died 'after a short illness brought on by exposure in the bush in the exercise of his official duty'.[63] The second entry stated that one of the pioneer settlers, 47-year-old Joshua Gregory, had died on the 20th at his home, Rainworth, on the Swan 'after a long protracted illness stemming from service in the British Army in the tropics in his youth'.

The loss of two influential men in such a short time was felt acutely in the small colony, and just how small it was became apparent when the population return, commissioned by Stirling, was released the following week. There were only 126 landed male settlers in the whole colony. The total white population, excluding the military,[64] had grown from 1,800 in 1834 to 2,132 in September 1838, but of these only 914 were males over 14, and the workforce numbered 788.[65] Although the majority of families lived in Perth and Fremantle, the rest of the population, including the military, were scattered over a huge distance from Albany in the south, through the outposts at Augusta, the Vasse, Leschenault, the Murray and Pinjarra, and inland to Williams, York and Beverley. Claims by settlers in these regions of an acute labour shortage were well and truly vindicated by a subsequent analysis of the workforce, which showed that only half the available manpower was employed in agriculture or grazing; the rest were in trade, boating and fishing, or public duties of some kind.[66]

The same issue of the *Perth Gazette* that carried the results of the population survey led with the news that Mr John Hutt had been appointed to succeed Sir James Stirling as Governor of Western Australia. The news had been brought by the *Elizabeth*, just in from Singapore where she had collected the latest English mail. Commenting on the announcement, the editor of the *Gazette* erroneously stated, 'Hutt was said to be one of the founders of South Australia', and sought by some as successor to that state's first Governor, Captain John Hindmarsh.[67] In fact, it was John Hutt's brother William who had been involved in the South Australian colonisation proposal, though it is evident that both brothers were strong followers of Wakefield. Oddly, there was no mention of the new Governor in the minutes of the next Executive Council meeting on 20 September.

Among agenda items at this meeting was an application to build a new mill from two recent arrivals on the *Shepherd*, Messrs Schoales and Nash. They wished to buy the land under Mount Eliza, previously used by the Native Institution, for a corn and saw mill, and also proposed erecting a jetty to facilitate these activities. While welcoming the proposal, and sanctioning the purchase of the now-unused land at public auction, Stirling was concerned about their jetty proposal. He stated that 'he had always been opposed to grant the right of property to lands below high water mark', which they had requested, and suggested that they be given only a seven-year lease of the land they required, provided 'the public thoroughfare along the water's edge was not interfered with'.[68] The Council concurred, although the *Perth Gazette*'s editor took issue with Stirling's initiative, claiming it would 'impede all improvements on the waterside for at least eighteen months' (the time it would take for a reply from London) and demonstrated clearly 'the absurdity of having legislators for colonial affairs at a distance of many thousand miles'.[69] Nevertheless, Stirling's wisdom in insisting on public access to the river foreshore was upheld by subsequent legislators, and is now a much appreciated part of Perth's heritage.

Among arrivals in late September was a man with unfinished business— George Grey, the explorer and politician-to-be, who would later govern South Australia, and then New Zealand. He had been on the northern exploratory expedition with Lushington in 1837, discovering and naming the Glenelg River and

Perth citizens over generations have benefited from Stirling's decision
to grant public access to the river foreshore

Horace Samson. *Perth 1847*. Watercolour, gouache and pen and ink. 21 × 40.3cm.

Collection, Art Gallery of Western Australia. Gift of Mr D. Rannard, 1923

Mount Lyall before being speared. After recuperation in Mauritius, he had taken passage on the *Clarinda* to resume his exploration. Moore noted in his diary:

> He has greatly surprised us by giving a most favourable account of the land he saw at Lat. 16 degrees. He says…he has no doubt that some settlement will be made there…It was well watered, and the land rich beyond anything which he had ever seen before, with rivers running (sluggishly) though it was the end of summer.[70]

Stirling spent many hours with the young explorer and was impressed with his reports, although somewhat aggrieved with the way the matter had been conducted. He had been told to provide every assistance, and had expected to see Grey before his northern exploration, not after it.[71] He had already told Glenelg that when the *Champion* returned from Albany, he intended to send her north with Grey's party to the district which had been given his name. Now Grey was impatient to return north and to assist him to 'keep the peace', and to secure the territory Stirling had made him 'a magistrate…and acting Government Resident in the district of Glenelg', but without authority to assign land etc., until further instructions arrived from London.[72] Stirling was right to be cautious. His sympathies lay with Grey, for he had previously urged the settlement of the northern regions. However, the British authorities had been uninterested then, and he doubted they had any intention now of further colonisation. He was right. The draft reply from the Secretary of State said:

> I see nothing to induce me to alter the tenor of [my previous] instructions. Mr Grey will, therefore, break up the expedition and return to this country at the earliest practicable period…[73]

But Stirling still had visions of 'his colony' playing a major role in Britain's future, a vision he spelt out in a dispatch signed the very same day (30 September) as that conveying his arrangements with Grey. Ostensibly, this second dispatch conveyed the statistical report of the colony, but within it Stirling presented the following argument:

> Within a few years an immense impulse has been given to British enterprise in the Eastern Seas…the extension of the fisheries, the opening of the China Trade, & the colonisation of Australia have extended & stimulated the interest at stake in this part of the world. In this altered state of things…it is of importance that a naval post or station should be established at some commanding position.
>
> Such a position should be centrically situated with reference to India, China, the Pacific and the Cape, it ought to be in the midst of the fisheries, it ought to possess a suitable harbour capable of being effectually fortified; it ought to enjoy a climate favourable to health, vigour and discipline, and it ought to be in an

extensive territory adapted to supply the wants of shipping, and to sustain a proper colony of British origin, habits and predilections. All these essential qualifications appear to be confined within the limits of settlement of this country.

At this stage he reiterated his arguments regarding Western Australia's pivotal strategic position for both defence and trade, the suitability of its harbours, the existence of timber and other necessary supplies, all providing British forces with 'the means for effecting repairs and for recruiting men'. He concluded:

> Whether it be expedient or otherwise to form at the present time such an establishment…I cannot pretend to judge, but under the impression that the subject is one which may perhaps engage the notice of HMG at some future date, I have endeavoured to lay before your Lordship in the preceding remarks …such information on the subject as it is in my power to offer.[74]

It was remarkably similar to the plan he had presented to Governor Darling ten years earlier. Stirling had never lost his ambition to found a major naval station facing the Indian Ocean, as a bastion for the defence of British interests. And this time his vision struck a chord in the Colonial Office. When it was received in London, James Stephen, now Permanent Under-Secretary in the Colonial Office, noted 'this should be communicated to the Admiralty…and…strongly recommended to their Lordships' attention'.[75]

Colonial Office staff also praised Stirling for the comprehensive returns he had sent in the previous year. Stephen noted that Lord Normanby, who had taken over from Glenelg as Secretary of State for Colonies on 19 February 1839, was

> much impressed by the great diligence and ability exhibited in those documents, that he cannot satisfy himself without conveying to Sir J.S. his sense of the value of them, and his thanks for the labour bestowed upon them.[76]

Sir George Grey, the Parliamentary Under-Secretary (no relation to the explorer) also congratulated Stirling on the thoroughness of his statistics,[77] annotating the dispatch:

> Mr Stephen…It is singular that the little Colony of Western Australia which has so often being stigmatised as a failure should be remarkable for furnishing the best statistics of any Colony…I would beg to suggest whether it would not be worthwhile to send a copy [out] as the model of a report to be sent home annually…I despair of seeing it imitated, to do so it wd be necessary that every Governor should possess talents and knowledge equal to that of Sir James Stirling and this has never been true of more than 2 or 3 at the most of the large numbers of such officers whose dispatches I have been accustomed to read.[78]

As Stirling had so often been castigated for his tardy returns, Grey's approval would have been valuable when he returned home, but as chance would have it, Sir George Grey had left the Colonial Office by that time.[79]

The same statistical report that earned approval in London was tabled at the annual meeting of the Agricultural Society held at Woodbridge, Guildford, on 5 October 1838. G. F. Moore, as chairman, believed the report was 'so accurate in its details, so satisfactory in its arrangement, and so important in its substance' that he recommended its immediate adoption by the Society. His committee, charged with gathering information on the present state of the colony, had simply to amplify. They had found that 'notwithstanding the great scarcity of labour, the extent of agriculture on the Swan district has not diminished whilst that in the Tramuntana district, Northam, Beverley etc. has very considerably increased'.[80] The Society then released all documents to the editor of the *Perth Gazette*, who published them in full over ensuing issues.[81] Colonists were told they would find the information

> a triumphant refutation of all those statements which have been so confidently made and so industriously and perseveringly propagated to the prejudice of this colony…'[82]

This would have been of some comfort to settlers who had so recently learned that their future Governor was a supporter of Wakefield, the man who had done more than most to denigrate Swan River Colony.[83]

In the meantime the present Governor had gone to York[84] partly to check the peacefulness of the area, but also to settle the boundaries of his Beverley grant. On 10 October Surveyor-General Roe, who had accompanied Stirling, wrote a memorandum detailing the boundaries of a 4,000-acre grant on the Dale River to be assigned to Sir James.[85] It has been said with regard to another grant near Toodyay, Deepdale, which Stirling had thought of taking, that the Governor 'refused to open newly discovered areas for selection until he had looked it over for the purpose of choosing the best land for himself…'[86] But Stirling's selections in newly opened areas can also be seen as encouragement to others to take up surrounding land. For example, he had been the first to reserve land near Williams, but let it go when others followed his lead. As far as York was concerned, his cousin William Stirling had taken 4,000 acres of land there in December 1830, but this went to beneficiaries overseas after his death in 1831,[87] and not to James Stirling, who paid for its improvement.

Although race relations in York appeared to have settled down, they were fermenting in Perth, for when Stirling returned he was immediately confronted with a memorial from indignant residents wanting tighter controls over the behaviour of Aborigines in the capital. Referring to 'frequent bloody broils' and 'not infrequent murders among the natives' in Perth streets, and the effect this would have 'on the rising generation', the signatories urged the Governor to allow inhabitants 'to destroy all spears found in the hands of natives within the limits of the town and that they be not allowed to appear in a state of nudity'.[88] Stirling brought the matter before his Executive Council when they met on 17 October, first summarising the measures that had already been adopted:

> An Institution was formed some years since under the care of a Superintendent…and the Natives had every inducement held out to them to sojourn there…Many initially flocked there, but they soon found it was more to their advantage to keep in the Town, where they were constantly getting sixpences, and small portions of flour for trifling acts of service, and the result was that the Superintendent was at last left to himself…[89]

Under the circumstances, Stirling felt that the Superintendent's role should be changed to that more like a constable

> specially appointed for the management of the Natives…And to make it his duty to prevent the Natives appearing in the street in an indecent manner, quarrelling and carrying about their spears…It would also form part of his duty to interpret whenever he is required to do so by any of the Magistrates…[90]

Council members fully concurred with the Governor's plan, and recommended its adoption.

October was the month when the bay-whaling season normally ended, but for the Fremantle Whaling Company the results were disappointing. A report on the 20th revealed they had taken 50 tons of oil and 5 tons of whalebone, but because of defective gear and other causes had lost seven whales.[91] The company was limited by its lack of capital to shore-based operations, and Cockburn Sound, unlike the deeper King George's Sound, was too well protected by shoals and reefs for viable fishing. It must have irked the proprietors to see the better catches made by the deep sea whalers who called into Fremantle to revictual. Foreigners had taken 1,172 tons of black oil, 59 tons of whalebone and 177 tons of sperm oil from local waters in the preceding six months.[92] Stirling had not interfered, there being as yet no response to his 14 July 1837 dispatch detailing concerns about the American whalers. Nevertheless, the colony had earned £3,170 from its whale oil and bone in 1838, compared with £2,278 for its wool.[93] Stirling knew well the constraints on the colony's whaling industry, informing the Colonial Office 'that in a small community like this where wages are high, and provisions dear, and when the proper description of vessel cannot at present be procured', profits would never be high.[94]

Although resented by a few, the visits of foreign whalers were generally welcomed by the colonists because they relieved feelings of total isolation. Like those in similar isolated circumstances many turned to religion, but the strongly Anglican colony lacked the level of spiritual comfort which settlers had been used to in England. Attempts had been made to rectify the situation, but without success, especially on the missionary front. Stirling knew this when he chaired a meeting on 8 November to found the 'Australian Church Missionary Society'. Its new appointee, the Reverend William Mitchell, was to take Christianity out to the native tribes, although poor health had limited 'the sphere of his usefulness…to the Swan District'.[95] Ellen, in particular, supported this objective—she had been agitating for a missionary to work amongst Aborigines since 1834, firmly believing that only through education and conversion could they be 'saved'. Neither she nor James showed any great interest in Aboriginal customs or Dreamtime stories during their time in Western Australia. In fact, the only the white settlers who did show a sustained interest were Francis Armstrong, the Native Interpreter, and G. F. Moore, who also felt strongly about the Aborigines' need for conversion.

By early November the Stirlings had begun their rounds of farewell. In letters to her family Ellen had indicated she expected to leave at the end of the month on the *Joshua Carroll*.[96] But when the ship did leave, it was without the Stirlings, whose leave-takings then continued until early January.

The planned layout of Perth when Stirling left,
from inset in 1839 Arrowsmith map

21

——

A Year of Transition

1839

Farewell occasions began in earnest in November 1838. On the 2nd the Governor attended the quarterly meeting of the Agricultural Society at Guildford and, it being understood to be the patron's last visit, 'there was a numerous party much speechifying and some scenes'.[1] The chairman concluded his report by congratulating Stirling 'on the flourishing condition of the colony', whose progression from 'wilderness to a valuable appendage of the British Crown excites the astonishment of visitors'. In turn, Stirling acknowledged that the chairman's report affected him deeply,

> and will ever be remembered with pride and satisfaction. I need scarcely assure you that, whether actually resident in the colony or absent from it I shall ever retain a deep interest in its welfare, and shall study to promote it by every means in my power.[2]

In tendering his resignation as patron, Stirling asked that his name be 'enrolled in the list of its members', and the meeting concluded with a toast 'to the Governor in his private capacity, as a settler', which was 'received with considerable warmth'.[3]

Stirling had visited most of the farms in the vicinity before attending this meeting[4] and would therefore have heard of plans to build a 3 ft high dam across the islands near Perth, 'with proper sluices and tumbling bays to keep the river above Perth fresh and navigable, and raise its level to allow summer crops'.[5] He was well aware of the problems farmers along the Swan River faced in watering their crops and getting produce to market, and would have approved of the plan, subject of course to the availability of finance. One of the few people able to provide cost estimates was Reveley, the Civil Engineer, but he had 'applied for leave of absence to return to England on urgent private business'. Public works were arrested until a successor could be found, but Stirling managed to persuade Henry Trigg to take over, and at half the salary.[6]

A welcome boost to plans for a fitting testimonial to the Governor came with the return to the colony of William Brockman, a natural leader and one of Stirling's

William Brockman, leader of the farewell testimonial committee
Courtesy Battye Library 62104P

trusted early pioneers, who had been away for almost a year.[7] He chaired a meeting on 14 November at which a number of suggestions for a suitable gift to mark 'the sense the colonists entertain of his private as well as public worth' were debated. Eventually, Meares and Samson's idea of silver service plates, and McDermott and Harris' idea of a half or full-length portrait undertaken by a good artist in England, proved most popular. The meeting resolved that 'a sum not exceeding 100 guineas' be appropriated for this purpose.[8]

On 5 December another Mangles vessel, the *Brittomart*, finally arrived, bringing from London Mr and Mrs William Tanner and a large number of their friends, relatives and servants,[9] as well as parcels, mail and a large cargo. Stirling took his whole family to Fremantle when news of the arrival reached him, which led the *Gazette* to announce that 'Sir James will probably take his departure on the *Brittomart*'.[10] This is what the family wanted, but again it was not to be. There was insufficient Swan River produce to fill the holds, so the *Brittomart* had to chase cargo from the other colonies and India before returning to London. While Stirling sorted out the duplicates and originals among the incoming dispatches, Lady Stirling went ahead with packing and planning for a grand farewell ball at

Government House. The *Perth Gazette* informed readers on 15 December that the ball, to which almost everyone was invited, would take place on the evening of Thursday 20 December, and that the merchants Lionel and William Samson would hold a sale of goods by public auction at Government House on Wednesday 26th at 1 p.m. The goods would comprise 'a quantity of drawing room, parlour and bedroom furniture, plate, dinner service, glass, tea and breakfast services, culinary utensils etc'.[11] The farewell ball proved a great success, for G. F. Moore reported that

> Dancing was kept up literally till breakfast time the next day. I bathed and breakfasted and set about my daily occupation rather sleepily. Contrary to what is usual, the Governor has become more and more popular every day, and we cling to him with the more tenacity in proportion as the time approaches for his departure.[12]

At least there was the weekend to recover, but not for long. As Moore noted, on Monday (Christmas Eve) 'there was a hasty summons for Irwin and I to attend Council and we sat that night till 12 o'clock'.[13]

Stirling had called his Council together to discuss his departure, as plans had been totally upset by the early departure of the *Joshua Carroll*, and the alternative routing of the *Brittomart*. He could see only one solution—to use the colonial schooner *Champion* to take himself and family to the Cape, where he could then find passage on another London-bound vessel. But such a voyage would have to be at least partly financed from colonial funds, which he knew were low, and would therefore have to be approved by Council. Councillors were aware that the *Champion* was badly in need of repair and that it would be difficult to get to her to Sydney—the least costly destination,[14] and were persuaded that the Cape would be as good a place for repairs as Sydney. When Stirling offered at the next meeting, on 31 December, to help defray the cost of the *Champion*'s passage, they unanimously agreed that repairs at the Cape might be 'effected at considerable less expense and in a shorter period of time'.[15] With this matter and one or two other small items now settled, the Governor rose and addressed his councillors, his remarks being recorded in the minutes.

> Gentlemen of the Executive and Legislative Councils, the present meeting being in all probability the last at which I shall ever have an opportunity to address you officially, I avail myself of the occasion to express my gratitude for the zealous assistance in the administration of the Government which throughout the course of so many years I have ever received at your hands…I look back with the greatest satisfaction to the confidence, candour and consideration with which you have ever treated my communications and…the ingenuousness with which you have listened to argument…it is with pride that I assert, and I may assert it with truth, that the harmony of this Council has never been disturbed…nor the personal

esteem and regard of its Members for each other, in any degree, been shaken by anything that has occurred here.

My participation in the Government of this Colony…has nearly reached its close. Pursuant to Her Majesty's Gracious Permission I propose to embark in a few days, and the administration will become invested for the time in Major Irwin. I could not however omit this last opportunity, of recording my sentiments on your minutes, to pass without acknowledging thus deeply and earnestly my sense of the great advantage I have derived from your advice, and my sincere wishes for the health and welfare of every one of you.[16]

G. F. Moore confided in his diary that this came as a surprise to the meeting, but he rose to the occasion, saying 'what I could think of at the moment'. He began by thanking the Governor for his remarks about the Council's performance before adding:

We have ever found in Your Excellency the dignity and firmness of a Governor tempered by the urbanity and affability of a gentleman and blended with the kindness and considerateness of a friend…We cannot help feeling, now that we are about to part with one who has been endeared to us by stronger ties than those of mere political relation, that we are about…to be deprived of the warm and lively sympathy of one, who having been selected as Founder of this Colony, having shared in all our privations, having gone hand in hand in all our labours, and been foremost in our defence in the hour of danger, was so well qualified to appreciate our difficulties, and to make allowance for our deficiencies. These are the thoughts which are now uppermost in our minds.

He ended with the hope that Stirling would feel gratified by the success of the colony, and that his 'children's children have reason to feel a pride in saying they are descended from the Founder of the Colony of Western Australia'.[17] It was quite a speech for someone who had not always agreed with Stirling's views and actions. Moore probably realised, with others, that Council had been manipulated to enable the Governor to justify his return on the *Champion*,[18] but they still supported him and sincerely regretted his departure.

There is little doubt that similar feelings were held throughout the colony. The *Perth Gazette* reported on 5 January 1839 details of the public address presented to Sir James on behalf of all colonists. 'The scene was a gloomy one, and all seemed very much affected.' The large gathering outside the Government offices first witnessed the presentation of a suitably inscribed silver salver and matching entrée dishes, and listened to the long address. Stirling's administration was praised, because he had not only tackled the 'burthens common to all governments' but also the 'peculiar solicitudes and novel difficulties felt and encountered by the founder of a colony'. It had been a 'test of no ordinary severity', and

Under such circumstances, it is, we conceive no small triumph to the individual entrusted with the twofold task of founding and governing such a community to receive from them a cheerful testimony of their general and respectful approbation...the general tenor of your Excellency's administration has been highly and deservedly popular...and...in all the domestic and social relations of private life your Excellency has set an example worthy of your high station.

The address ended with sincere good wishes for the health and happiness of the Governor and his family, and a powerful tribute:

One of the two cushion-shaped entrée dishes with gadroon border and domed cover

Courtesy the Western Australian Museum

CH74.173

The presentation sterling silver salver, weighing 4.7 kg and hallmarked 'London 1786', stands on four scroll feet and has floral leaf and rococo scrolls encircling the inscription

By permission of the National Library of Australia OBJ. A4000144X Loc MS SR

Whatever may be your Excellency's future destiny you must at least retain…the proud and consolatory consciousness of…having primarily suggested, personally matured and politically founded this scion of the best and greatest nation upon earth, of having introduced into the wilderness the religious and civil institutions, the arts, comforts and refinements of the parent country, and of having opened to the savage tribes of a vast region at least an access to the incalculable blessings of Christianity.[19]

His Excellency was 'so much agitated by this address that he was compelled to sit down and request Mr Brown to read his reply'. This began with an expression of his 'deepest pride and thankfulness' for the sentiments expressed in the address, and continued with the words:

I rejoice that it hath pleased providence to permit a favourable issue to the enterprise in which we have been conjoined. If it has not been to all a prosperous adventure, it has been comparatively free from those evils and calamities so common in colonization. If it has been slow in its progress, and of limited importance, it at least affords reason to rejoice that larger numbers and greater means have not been risked in an experiment at all times so hazardous…

At some length Stirling expressed the hope that the colonists' expectation of future prosperity would be fully realised, and thanked them for their good wishes for the welfare of his family. His last words were that

if anything can add to the attachment which connects me with this country, it will be the remembrance of the generous expression of sentiment contained in the Address which you have done me the honour to present.[20]

The Stirling family left Perth for the last time on 1 January 1839. As fate would have it, they arrived in Fremantle just as the *Brothers* from London dropped anchor, its chief passenger the new Governor, John Hutt. Stirling remained in Fremantle for a few days, and so had time to talk to Hutt, but the nature of those discussions is not known. They were interrupted by tributes the Fremantle people wished to give their departing Governor and his wife, including a lunch and a ball. Almost all the local gentry came to Fremantle to take leave of Sir James and, when he finally boarded the *Champion* at 4 p.m. on Friday, 'we raised our voices to cheer him for the last time, [and] he was very much affected'.[21]

    Stirling was to sail on the Saturday, the day nominated for Hutt's proclamation as the new Governor, so most of the gentry would have departed. But Moore 'prevailed on him to wait for the newspapers of the week, as owing to the press being broken, none had been published the week before'.[22] It was worth the wait, for the *Gazette* not only published all the farewell addresses but also included the following tribute:

We forbear at present from offering any general remarks upon Sir James Stirling's administration of this colony, we cannot however, part with so old and valued a friend without adding our humble tribute of admiration and praise of his many amiable private qualities, his high talents and his manly perseverance in developing the resources of this new colony. We may safely say, there are few men in whom suitable qualifications could have been found to accomplish so great a task. May every happiness attend Sir James Stirling, his beloved partner and family is the sincere and warmest desire of every individual in the colony.[23]

Stirling's successor as Governor, John Hutt
Courtesy Battye Library 663P

The papers were brought down on Saturday evening by Moore, who would also have conveyed news of the inauguration and handed over Hutt's first dispatch.[24] The final farewell was relatively quiet, just closest friends and the parents of the boys Stirling was taking back to England for schooling. Early on Sunday morning 6 January the *Champion* finally weighed anchor for the Cape of Good Hope.

Standing on deck and looking back at the mouth of the river he had seen for the first time almost twelve years earlier, Stirling must have had mixed emotions. Behind him were friends and a landscape he had grown to love: the river in all its moods had attracted him from the beginning, and though the bush was often grey and uninviting, he had seen it burst into colour every spring. He had ridden over huge tracts of land and knew most of its secrets, the heavily timbered forests, the arid plains and the more fertile valleys. His initial perception that the landscape would prove similar to that of New South Wales had largely been vindicated. But he would be 48 years old at the end of the month. He had given the most productive years of his life to this place, and the pay-off had been small. The colony had weathered the storm of infancy but it was by no means prosperous, and any dreams he might have had of materially benefiting from the position had not been realised. He left in much the same financial position that he had been in at the outset, dependent on salary. And even that would cease when he returned to England, until he could re-establish himself with the Admiralty from whom he could at least claim half-pay. He did have his land in the colony, but much of that was still unimproved and its future value would depend completely on the colony's ability to attract new immigrants and capital. There was room for hope, as it looked at last as though a strong Indian connection might bear fruit, and he would have to cultivate this on his return to England. Hutt would have to deal with all the machinations that would arise in the colony from such a connection, and of this he was glad. The yoke of office had become very heavy over past years, and as the wind caught the *Champion*'s sails he must have felt a weight lift from his shoulders.

Ellen too would have had mixed emotions as the Western Australian coastline disappeared from view. She had risen to the challenge of First Lady and had enjoyed the role: it was very different from that of the wife of a half-pay naval officer in England. But she was young and adaptable and very keen to see her eldest son Andrew, now 14, and her parents. The family reunion would be joyful, but behind her she left the grave of baby William. Who now would take flowers in May? But she had less time for musing than James, for young Frederick Henry, just weeks away from his tenth birthday, was wild with excitement and intent on exploring every inch of the ship. His sisters, 6-year-old Mary and 3-year-old Agnes, were quieter, reacting to the strangeness of the situation, but Charles, 4, wanted to follow his older brother and was upsetting 2-year-old Walter. At least the baby, Ellinor, was no trouble for she was not yet teething and the ship's movement was soothing. The three 12-year-old boys they were taking back to England—Walter Andrews, McBride Brown and Edward Lyttleton—also needed a motherly eye. At least Sarah Hall, who was also being sent home under her protection, was old enough at 20 to be of some assistance. Nephew Andrew, who was also returning with them, spent most of his time with Stirling, to whom he remained Private Secretary.[25]

With Captain Dring in command, the passage was more relaxed than the last voyage to the Cape, as Dring was an old acquaintance, having arrived in the colony in 1831. To help subsidise his farming activities, Dring had continued merchant voyages and even had a turn in a whaling vessel before being offered command of the *Champion* the previous year.[26] He was well aware, however, of the problems the small colonial schooner faced and the need to nurse it throughout this voyage. It was a small vessel and the passage would not have been comfortable except perhaps for Stirling, who would have revelled in the return to sea. Forty-nine days later they reached the Cape.

Arriving in Simon's Bay on 24 February,[27] the Stirling party would have been happy to disembark when shore accommodation was found. There was protocol to observe, like paying respects to the Governor of Cape Town, Sir George Napier, whom Stirling had met before, and the business of finding onward passage to London. Rear Admiral George Elliot, then Commander-in-Chief at Cape Town, was also an old acquaintance but could be of little immediate help, as no naval vessels were due to return home. Nevertheless, he would have been able to smooth the way for Dring to arrange for the repair of the *Champion*, which was to prove a long, drawn-out and costly affair.

Amidst all the uncertainty of organising the homeward voyage, Stirling still found time to write a strongly supportive letter for Surveyor-General Roe, who was petitioning the Colonial Office for either a rise in salary or a transfer to Van Diemen's Land.[28] Stirling's letter persuaded Under Secretary James Stephen that Roe was worthy of promotion, as evidenced by his annotation when received in June.[29] But the Marquis of Normanby, who had taken over from Glenelg as Secretary of State for Colonies, was not of the same mind. The reply to Stirling, dated 13 August 1839, was negative. The position in Van Diemen's Land had been filled, and neither Treasury nor local colonial coffers could sustain a salary increase.[30] Fortunately for Western Australia, Roe continued in his post until 1871.

With no naval ship returning to England in the next few months, Stirling was forced to negotiate with merchant vessels in port—and here he met with greater success. By mid-March the family and their charges were again on board for the last leg of their return home.[31] It was a relatively quick and uneventful voyage, for they arrived at Portsmouth around 23 May. The Stirlings made first for Ellen's family home at Woodbridge, Guildford. The Stirling family home at nearby Pirbright was not as large, and James knew his sisters Dorothea and Agnes had taken in their widowed sister Anna Home and her two boys, now aged 7 and 10, so space there would be limited. It would have been a reunion touched with sadness, for Ellen's larger-than-life father, James Mangles, had passed away the previous September, aged 77. True to character, he had undergone one of the first operations to remove cataracts from both eyes a year before his death —and benefited from the surgery.[32] Ellen's mother Mary was still in good health at 66 years of age, and delighted to meet her grandchildren. News would have travelled fast and a gathering of the clan arranged: Mangles and Stirling brothers were called down from London and young Andrew, Ellen's eldest, brought out from school. Ellen's brothers Frederick, Charles and Albert were all now married with children to meet, but Ross Donnelly had not yet returned from India with his family. Her eldest sister Caroline was in Kent with her husband, the Reverend Arthur Onslow, while Hamilla, the youngest of the Mangles' brood, was at Woodbridge as her husband, William Preston, was serving in South America as Captain of HMS *Stag*. On the Stirling side, there was also much to relate— Charles and Charlotte, settled at Muiravonside in Scotland, were expecting their sixth child; bachelors Walter and William were doing well in Manchester and London respectively; John and Elizabeth, still at St Andrews, had a recent twelfth addition to their brood. Sadly, they had lost their 6-year-old daughter Agnes the previous January. Their son Andrew would thus have been all the more anxious to get back to Scotland. His parents would hardly recognise him after his Western Australian sojourn, for it had turned a gangling teenager into a self-assured young man. Stirling would have been sorry to lose his nephew, as there was still a mountain of paperwork to complete, and Andrew had developed a fine hand.

The business-minded Frederick Mangles, not one to overlook any promising venture, recounted to a friend an aspect of conversation with Stirling at the reunion, noting:

> He has 100,000 acres in the Colony, and we, in conjunction with him, think of starting a small company to buy sheep, and then send them out there under the care of good shepherds. Now it appears to me that men brought up in the Cheviots would be the best men that could be provided…Should you wish to venture a trifle in the speculation, I think it will probably, in a few years, pay you 20% and continue to increase. The company will consist entirely of our own family and immediate friends, and from our knowledge of the property that has been acquired, we think it must succeed.[33]

Barely a week after landing, Stirling was in London for a preliminary interview with the Marquis of Normanby,[34] the precursor of many to come. Both the Colonial Office and Treasury would question him relentlessly over aspects of his administration. On the last day of May, for example, Stirling was answering James Stephen's questions regarding WA lands which had been surrendered up to 31 December 1838.[35] On a separate issue, and much to his relief, Treasury allowed his claim for £800 for his passage fare.[36] Stirling's financial situation was tight and he desperately wanted to argue his case for more land in the Colony, but instead the Colonial Office wanted his comments on two other claims. One was from Bannister, arguing his right to more land as a result of his exploratory activities in Western Australia in the early 1830s, and the other from Colonel Peter Augustus Latour. Bannister's case was easier to deal with, as it had been heard before, and in the absence of fresh evidence, it was rejected.[37] The case was not over; it returned, but with less force than the letters from Latour which were to occupy a vast amount of Colonial Office time and temper during the rest of the year.

The first letter from Latour, dated 8 June 1839, was written soon after he was released from a charge of bankruptcy, and contained a lengthy description of the property he had sent to Western Australia. He maintained that, as he had invested between £25,000 and £26,000, he was entitled under the regulations to 400,000 acres of land. He argued:

in consequence of the misconduct and breach of contract of the persons whom I had sent out in charge of all this valuable property…my affairs in the Colony were not only neglected, but became so absolutely deranged that…an entire loss to me of the whole of my large outlay took place. But while this catastrophe as affecting myself ensued, the Settlement on the other hand derived all the benefit of my individual loss…

A 'nefarious bankruptcy charge' contested in the Court of Chancery had prevented him from taking any measures either to improve his existing grants or to obtain further grants to which he felt he was entitled on the basis of his initial shipments. He now wanted to claim that additional land, stating that

As no stipulation was contained in those Regulations as to the time at which the Grants could be claimed, the right to which had been acquired by actual shipments landed in the Colony, I am not aware that any objection <u>could</u> be raised to my taking up these Grants…but I am anxious that all possible doubt should be removed before I make the further expenditure contemplated. [38]

He ended by stating that, 'in the event of a favourable decision', he would immediately make extensive shipments of labourers, stock and implements which would be of enormous benefit to the colony. A Colonial Office annotation to Latour's letter, nearly a fortnight on, asked 'Is there any information in the Office about this subject?' and recommended that it be referred to Stirling for his report.[39] A note was added later to the file stating that

Colonel Latour was one of those persons who imported property into the Settlement of Western Australia at its formation. He received a large Grant of Land and ought *himself* to have occupied it. I believe the state of the case to be, that he…has received all the land to which he is entitled. But I think it would be impossible to act with certainty on the case without a report from Sir J S which can now be easily obtained without delay.[40]

Stirling replied, as requested, on 22 June:

On the Formation of the Settlement in 1829 the Persons and Property sent out by Col. Latour were amongst the first arrivals in that Country and his Agent in the Colony applied for and obtained in the usual course of Proceeding an assignment of Land upon the existing Regulations…The Individuals composing Col. Latour's Establishment shortly after arrival were located on certain lands granted to him on the Swan River, amounting to 10,000 acres, and the Location Duties were performed thereon and his claim to a full title thereby secured. These lands as I understand were subsequently sold by his Agent. The larger portion of his assignment was selected in the District of Wellington comprising about 105,000 acres. That portion has not been in any respect improved or occupied and is therefore liable under the original conditions to…resumption by the Crown if not improved to the extent of 1/6 an acre prior to the expiration of ten years from the date of assignment. That date will appear upon the face of the Returns and according to my recollection took place in 1830. The preceding Observations contain all that was known officially…in respect to Col. Latour's Land claim at the period of my departure from the Settlement.[41]

James clearly believed that Latour's claim was made under the 1829 regulations, which stipulated 10 years for improvement, rather than the 21-year period applying to himself and Peel under the December 1828 regulations. It was on this basis he had included some of Latour's Leschenault land in his application to Roe before leaving the colony. However, as Latour's lawyer was later to point out, Latour's first shipments to the colony had left England *before* the 1829 regulations were released, so he was in fact entitled to the 21-year improvement period. But even Latour was unsure at this stage, and Stirling certainly thought the matter closed on the 10-year rule. Normanby's official reply in July 1839 to Latour's request for more land was uncompromisingly negative.[42] On 30 June Stirling had addressed Lord Normanby regarding his own claims:

My official connection with Western Australia having ceased, I solicit your Lordship's Attention to a Memorandum drawn up by Mr Twiss on the 5th of December 1828…Pursuant to the Terms of the Agreement then made, and subsequently confirmed by Sir George Murray, I was to become entitled to Assignments of Land corresponding to my Outlay on Public or Private Objects connecting with the Undertaking. I am now prepared to satisfy your Lordship that I have expended on such Objects the sum of £17,499, by which I have entitled myself to 235,320 Acres of Land. I therefore request your Lordship will have the goodness to direct me as to the course I am to pursue in order to bring this Claim to a final Settlement.[43]

This letter caused some confusion in the Colonial Office, as shown by the annotation:

6 July. Answer that Lord Normanby would wish Sir James Stirling to transmit to this Office a copy of the Agreement to which he refers, as no document has been found here corresponding with his Statement. JS.[44]

On 5 July an official note was drawn up as an *aide-mémoire* for Normanby which detailed the dates and circumstances of Stirling's original 100,000-acre grant, the locations he had chosen (Leschenault and Garden Island), and the conditions attached, i.e. the 21-year improvement period.[45] Twiss had definitely intimated to Stirling that he would be able to claim land *in addition* to his 100,000-acre grant, on the basis of assets introduced, but Twiss had long gone from the Colonial Office. Extensive searching was to show that there was nothing in writing to confirm that understanding.

Stirling was anxious to settle his land claims, as he had made contact with members of the Western Australian Association, and through them contacted William Hutt, brother of his successor and one of the promulgators of the South Australian settlement. Hutt was keen to facilitate another Wakefieldian experiment, this time in Western Australia, and Stirling could no doubt see an opportunity to sell his land while simultaneously furthering the colonists' interests by promoting emigration. They would have had much to discuss, and their plans were outlined in Hutt's letter to the Colonial Office dated 6 July, which read:

> My Dear Sir, I enclose to you the Propositions for promoting Emigration to the Colony of Western Australia…Perhaps, after you have considered them you will allow Sir James Stirling & myself an interview with you to receive your decision respecting them.[46]

Their proposal was to allow anyone depositing £20 with the Agent General for the Colonies to become entitled to a corresponding credit in the purchase of land in the colony and, when the assisted labourer actually arrived in the colony the £20 deposit be repaid by the Colonial Treasurer. They also offered to undertake surveys of land.[47] Essentially the proposal involved a double pay-off for investors, but it would certainly have encouraged emigration. The letter was annotated, 'this should be referred to Mr Elliott for his early report. 6 Jul. J.S.', but it was some months before a reply was drafted.

Governor John Hutt had been sent out with instructions to raise the minimum price of Crown land sold at auction in Western Australia from 5 shillings to 12 shillings an acre[48] but, as the surrender and remission regulations remained in force until the end of 1840, the change had had little impact other than to increase the number of exchanges under the old scheme.[49] Moreover, the Colonial Office intention to change the system completely, by introducing a fixed price of £1 per acre for all Crown land throughout the colonies, was being mooted in the Press by late 1839, though it was not actually implemented at Swan River until June 1841.[50]

Stirling must have been aware of the change in Colonial Office thinking on land policy, either from their own staff or from William Hutt, who was a sitting MP and passionately interested in the issue. So this added some urgency to his desire to settle his own claims. As can be seen from the following correspondence, Stirling felt he had been short-changed, and when his case is compared with that of Latour and Peel he had some right to feel aggrieved. Writing from Woodbridge to Henry Labouchere (a new Colonial Office Under-Secretary) on 17 July 1839, he stated

Sir, I beg leave to inform you that the Memorandum referred to (of the 5th of December 1828) will be found amongst the Papers submitted to Parliament in 1829. That Memorandum contains the 'Terms' on which I was induced to engage in the Enterprise, and to undertake at my own Cost the Charges of Superintendent.

The Particulars of my Claims to Land on account of my Outlay on Public and Private Objects, connected with that Undertaking will be found detailed in the Statement annexed.

Statement of Claim

Amount of Disbursements incidental to the execution of the Office of Superintending the Formation of a Colony in Western Australia between 1828 and 1830 £14,499

Amount of Outlay on Unofficial or Private Objects connected with the Undertaking within the Periods specified £3,000

Charge for personal exertions and exclusive attention to the Office above-mentioned £7,500

£24,999

Deduct Amount of sums received at various times from Government on account of Salary &c £7,500

Net amount of my outlay on Public and Private Objects constituting my Contribution to the Undertaking and compounding to 233,320 acres of land at 1/6d pa as per Terms of Agreement £17,499

Note. In 1828 an offer was made to me of Permission to select 100,000 acres in advance of my Claim. It was coupled with the Condition of laying out upon it £7,500. This I have not been in a condition to effect for all my means have been engaged and appropriated as above-mentioned.

James Stirling[51]

Mulling over this claim on country rides and walks around Guildford over the next week Stirling, must have felt he had been too brusque, for on 26 July he wrote to Labouchere again. This is an important letter, as it sets out the reasons that drove Stirling to pursue his claims for the next fifteen years. He began by referring to the account included in his previous letter, stating:

although these Statements are not accompanied on the present occasion by any other Evidence of their accuracy beyond that which is furnished by their intrinsic reasonableness, I am in a condition to satisfy you of the Truth of every Fact alleged if you deem it necessary.

Stirling then laid out a detailed account of events beginning with his initial report in 1827. This part of the long letter is interesting in that it gives his recollections of the train of events. He stated that Huskisson had told him in July 1828 that the Government had no intention of colonising the area, and so he began arrangements for a 'private adventure'. Then on 12 October he had had an interview with 'Mr Barrow and Mr Twiss' and was

> informed by these Gentlemen that Government having decided on the occupation of Western Australia they had been instructed to confer with me and to offer me the command of the Expedition…In November the views of the Government were abandoned but I was informed that its Countenance would be given to the Colonisation of that Country provided it could be accomplished without expense to the Public Purse. Several Parties at the time were disposed to embark in such an Enterprise. Of these, some applied for information to the Colonial Department and others to me as the reputed Projector of the Undertaking. On the 1st of December I was visited by Messrs Peel, MacQueen, Schenley & Vincent for the purposes of discussing the subject when I learnt with much surprise that these Gentlemen, confiding in negotiations they had opened with the Colonial Office, expected to obtain an exclusive right in the Formation of a Colony.
>
> Although I perceived that they were under some misapprehension on this point I deemed it nevertheless necessary to apply to Mr Twiss upon the subject and I urged upon him the obvious necessity for some explicit declaration of the views & intentions of the Government…and I stated that the best course to put an end to all exorbitant Expectations on the part of those who had been previously negotiating would be to bring them together, and to settle their future arrangements upon one common basis. A Meeting accordingly took place in Mr Twiss's Room on the evening of 5th December and the 'Terms' bearing that date were drawn up and agreed to by the Parties present including myself.

He then detailed the agreement that had been drawn up and believed his explanation should clarify matters, but noted:

> In addition to the Evidence thus afforded of my connection with the Terms in question and of the Compensation I was to receive for my official salary there exists the incidental Testimony of Mr Hay's letter of the 6th December, and of Mr Twiss' letter of the 29th of January and Lord Goderich's of the 8th March 1833…In fact it was on those 'terms' and on no other that I went out with the earliest Party and

exposed my Family to all the Inconveniences of such a life, and continued without any other remuneration for my salary or expenses, beyond that which the Terms held out, to discharge for 3 years a costly and difficult office, rendered as it was more than usually anxious by the absence of authority, Commission, or proper Official Recognition.

As an additional justification for his claim he pointed out that

> The Position in which I stood was peculiar inasmuch as I could not retire from it as the Original Performer and Director of the Undertaking without Injury to the Service and Discredit to myself. It was in fact not until the end of 1838, that I acquired the Liberty to surrender my trust. At that Period the aggregate Amount of my disbursements calculated from the Period when I was first called from other avocations to take a part in this Adventure amounted to £17,500. This and the loss of upwards of ten of the best years of life devoted almost exclusively to public Duties constitute the sum of my contributions to the Furtherance of the Enterprise, but from this sum it is fair to deduct the amounts I have received from the Government at various times for Salary and Passage Money &c equal to about £7,500.

Regarding the originally offered 100,000 acres, he claimed that it was an 'advance on his future entitlement', and 'may in no respect be viewed as having any reference to Public outlays nor as compensation to me for my services'—a view he was to change. And permission to take the 100,000 acres had been of little benefit. He still had to perform the improvements to gain title, 'for all my Funds have been required for my support in the execution of my office'. But there was also the matter of the 133,320 acres he was due, and he wanted this settled as soon as possible. Justifying his claim, he added:

> I beg leave to refer you to [the case] of Mr Peel. He was not the Projector or Inventor of the Undertaking, he did not incur the first hardships. He did not contribute more than I did to the Undertaking. He retains the Property on which his claim to Land was based, and he possesses <u>in fee simple</u> 250,000 acres of land. I on the other hand after having entered contemporaneously with him into the same Terms, and after having expended some £10,000 out of my own pocket in the execution of a Public service, and after having performed it as I have reason to believe in a manner satisfactory alike to the Crown and the Colonists, remain with no other recompense than Permission to lay out £7,500 more upon the 100,000 acres which I have been permitted to select.[52]

It took a month for the Colonial Office to reply, a month in which they were bombarded with correspondence from Bannister, claiming more land, and from Latour and his lawyers over an extension of time for improvements on his large

Leschenault land grant. In fact, James Stephen's annotation to one of Latour's lengthy epistles would have given Stirling little cause for comfort. The memo read:

> 16 August. Answer that His Lordship is bound by the deliberate and repeated pledges of his Predecessors in office…to prevent any departure from the regulations to secure the Australian colonies against the evils which in former times resulted from the improvident alienation of unsettled lands. There is not a colony in which these evils have been more severely felt than in WA and none in which the Public Interest more urgently requires that the regulations in question shd be strictly observed…JS.[53]

The reply to Stirling was equally uncompromising. Dated 29 August, it stated:

> Lord Normanby can find no promise made to you of any further Grant than that of 100,000 acres which it was agreed that you should receive subject to certain conditions; and although it appears to have been at one time contemplated that the Colony should be formed by means of private enterprise, yet you soon assumed the character of a salaried officer, and in the year 1831 application was made to Parliament to provide such amount of remuneration as the circumstances of the case appeared to justify, including arrears from the date of your arrival in the Colony. Under these circumstances Lord Normanby can only express his regret that he is unable to comply with your application.[54]

Interestingly Stephen, the Permanent Under-Secretary who had dealt with Stirling for longer than any of the other incumbents of the Colonial Office at that time, was not altogether happy with this outcome. He noted on the draft of this reply:

> Mr Labouchere…I assume that this draft is prepared under your direction…I am not quite prepared to vouch for the soundness of the decision. JS. 7 Augt.[55]

Of this Stirling was unaware, but he was very pleased when, as a result of a reshuffle within Lord Melbourne's Government, both Normanby and Labouchere lost their places in the Colonial Office. Moreover, Normanby's successor was Lord John Russell, who became Secretary of State for Colonies on 2 September. Russell had been a year ahead of Stirling at Westminster school and had been quite close to Ellen's father, old James Mangles MP, so Stirling could anticipate a better reception. Henry Labouchere was replaced as the Parliamentary Under-Secretary by Robert Vernon Smith MP, while James Stephen continued as Permanent Under-Secretary. The change induced a flurry of correspondence, amongst which was a letter from Latour's lawyer, J. Knight, arguing strongly that Latour's grant was held under the 1828 Regulations, and hence a 21-year improvement clause. The adverse Colonial Office reaction to this claim is captured in an annotation dated 20 September 1839:

In Colonel Latour's correspondence with this Office, so recently as the 1st of August last, he stated in the most unequivocal terms that he embarked property to a very large amount to acquire land in WA on the strength of the Regulations dated on the 13th of Jany 1829 and the 3rd of Feb 1829…It is impossible that Lord John Russell should now assume and act on the assumption that not only the Official Returns and the Report of the late Governor, but even the explanation so recently given by Colonel Latour himself…are all erroneous…J.S.[56]

Stirling's first approach to the new administration, written from Woodbridge, was dated 25 September and addressed directly to Lord John Russell:

On my return from Western Australia in June last, Lord Normanby was pleased to take a favourable view of my administration of that Government, and upon my application for some mark of Favour in compensation for my success His Lordship seemed well disposed to meet my wishes, but deferred his Decision for further consideration.

I have now to request your Lordship to have the goodness to inform me, whether there is any reason for me to hope that the manner in which I fulfilled my last office, will procure for me any compensation, or further Employment under the Colonial Department…[57]

This was annotated by Stephen as follows:

27 Sept. I cannot forward this letter without stating, as there is no one else here to make the statement, that Sir James administered the Govt. of Western Australia with very remarkable ability and temper, and with more success than the inherent improvidence of that scheme of Colonisation, would have justified any one in expecting. I take him to be a man of more than average capacity. JS

Sep 29. Ans. that I view his former services favourably but cannot make him any promise. JR [Lord John Russell].[58]

But if the Colonial Office seemed united in their praise for Stirling's abilities as a colonial administrator, it was of little comfort to James who was tiring of the life of a country gentleman at Woodbridge. There were constant reminders of the need to shore up his financial situation to provide for his growing family. The boys were reaching school age, and Ellen was pregnant again. She shared her husband's sense of injustice that they had won so little from their service in Australia, especially as some of her brothers had benefited considerably from their time in India. In this frame of mind Stirling decided to press his claims once again. In London on 2 October he wrote a lengthy missive to Lord John Russell, explaining his case step by step. This was the clearest of his various 1839 explanations, and argued again that he was entitled to land on the basis of the assets he had introduced and expenses incurred, and that he would

never have taken the position of an unremunerated Governor if he had not so
believed. He ended his long letter with a plea from the heart:

> And now my Lord I beg to ask am I to be to this extent a loser? The same terms
> which were made with Mr Peel were made with me and he has received land to
> the ratio of his private outlay, and also the benefit of all that outlay; every other
> Settler has had the same advantage under their respective terms, and even every
> public officer has had land in proportion to his imported resources under express
> authority, which I alone, the Founder, Leader and Chief Supporter of the enter-
> prise remain without an equivalent…If any sufficient reason exist why my claim
> for compensation should be rejected, it is easy enough to state it, and I shall
> remain satisfied for I neither wish to uphold nor advance a claim which is not
> reasonable.[59]

When this arrived at the Colonial Office on 7 October Lord John Russell, as might
be expected, called for a briefing. A memorandum was prepared by Mr Gairdner,
the Senior Clerk, on 29 October and stated:

> His position is in effect—That he stood in a twofold character—As a
> Superintendent of the Settlement—and as one of the parties undertaking to effect
> its establishment, and as such to be repaid for the Capital which he embarked in
> that undertaking by proportionate Grants of land: that the allotment of 100,000
> acres which he did receive was merely an instalment and not taken in satisfaction
> of his claims and that the Salary which he received was merely a compensation for
> his actual services as Governor irrespective of his further claim…
>
>   This letter seems in reality to advance the case but little—and to leave his
> claim as much unproven as before. All which is on record shews, that he was to
> receive his 100,000 acres of Land—which is admitted: but as to any further Grant
> there is no agreement or trace of an agreement to that effect…

Appended to the memorandum are comments by various Colonial Office Staff,
but mostly James Stephen who, while extending 'respectful deference' to Sir
George Murray's decisions, questioned whether those affecting the settlement of
Western Australia could be justified. Murray was extremely busy at that time, he
noted, his mind was 'very slightly applied to the whole subject', and the Under-
Secretaries to whom the matter was delegated had committed serious errors.
Stephen continued:

> …seeing what were the views of this Office in 1828–9 on the subject of founding
> a new colony, I cannot but doubt whether Sir Jas Stirling may not be well founded
> in imparting to us the very absurd promise of which he now claims the
> fulfilment…there is so much confusion about the viva voce communications—

the double arrangements—and the two classes of Settlers, that it seems to me very difficult if not impossible to come to a clear decision…

Stephen's suggestion was for the entire issue to be treated 'as a question of Land', with both Treasury solicitors and Stirling to argue their case 'before the Law Officers of the Crown'. If such a judgment ruled that Stirling 'is entitled to the land he shall have it, but if otherwise, not'. Lord Russell's comments were in similar vein:

> This case seems very obscure, & almost a fit case for a Chancery suit. I would ask the Attorney General either to hear Sir James Stirling's witnesses & give me his opinion, or to name someone to whom it could be referred. Write a letter to the Atty. Gen. to this effect. JR.[60]

Russell had hardly been in his new position for a month at this stage, and letters about lands at Swan River had taken up most of his time. Lawyers for Bannister and Latour were threatening legal action, and the ex-Governor's case looked very much like another to be settled at law. From Stirling's perspective, the situation was equally galling—the Colonial Office was forever consulting him over intricacies to do with Latour or Bannister, but of his own situation there was still no word.

On 24 October 1839, from his lodgings in London, Stirling wrote to the Admiralty seeking re-employment. He pointed out that his period as Governor of Western Australia had been approved by the Admiralty and furthermore had 'originated in my Employment as a Naval Officer on that coast', and that now he held the hope 'of reconnecting myself with my own Profession'.[61]

Containing his impatience for action, Stirling returned to Woodbridge to some exciting news. Ellen's older brother, Ross Donnelly Mangles, had decided to return permanently from India and would be arriving with his family some time in the New Year. He had political aspirations, and it was felt he might follow in his father's footsteps and become the MP for Guildford. But if Ross settled at Woodbridge, there would be little room for the Stirling clan. James wanted to remain in London whilst his affairs were in such a state of flux, so he decided to take lodgings in the city that were large enough for his whole family. He found what he was looking for at No. 34 Harley Street, and early in December took Ellen to inspect the place and order new furnishings. It was planned to move the family as soon as possible after the New Year festivities at Woodbridge. Much as she loved her mother, Ellen would have looked forward to having a home of her own again and seeing once more some of the articles brought from Swan River, but left in storage during their stay with her family. The year of transition was ending and a new, though uncertain, future lay ahead.

22

The Australind Venture

1840

B͟Y S͟T͟I͟R͟L͟I͟N͟G͟'͟S͟ ͟B͟I͟R͟T͟H͟D͟A͟Y on 28 January the family were well ensconced in London, arrangements had been made for Frederick Henry to attend school, and a governess found for the smaller children. Despite his letter to the Admiralty, James was still intent on pursuing his land claims and realising some return from his Western Australian grants. Coincidentally Colonel Latour, who was also pressing his land claims, had moved into premises just a few doors away at 38 Harley Street. Three times during January Latour's trustee, Mr Knight, politely urged Under-Secretary Vernon Smith to admit that Latour's grant was held under the 1828 regulations, and was therefore still exempt from any penalties for non-improvement. On the first occasion he had stated:

> …our friends being aware of the Regulations under which Colonel Latour acted, require the best terms we can give them in respect to the land to be cultivated and managed at their expense.[1]

The words 'our friends' imply that Latour had already begun negotiations with William Hutt's Western Australian Association for the sale of his land at Leschenault. But in answer to this, and subsequent letters, the Colonial Office remained firm. As Latour had not been party to the agreement made with Stirling and Peel, he was subject as all others were to the February 1829 regulations, and his lands were now forfeit. But Knight continued to press the point that Latour's shipments for Swan River had left England before the February 1829 regulations were even issued.[2] Colonial Office staff finally gave way and on 30 January agreed to submit the case to the Crown lawyers, who took some time to deliberate as their answer was not written until 4 April.

In the meantime James had other matters on his mind. He had heard during January of the death of Sir Richard Spencer at King George's Sound on 24 July 1839. Ellen had been especially fond of the Spencer girls, and both she and James had liked and respected the family. Sir Richard had been in poor health since 1837, and

Stirling had even sent the Colonial Surgeon down to attend him.[3] His death was said to have been due to a stroke, brought on by his exertions in establishing his Hay River property. News of his death was accompanied by letters from individuals at the Sound seeking Stirling's help in obtaining the vacant position. A letter to the Colonial Office dated 3 February shows whom he chose to support:

> I beg leave respectfully to recommend to your Lordships as Sir Richard Spencer's successor Lieut. Peter Belches RN. Mr Belches accompanied me in the earliest examination of Western Australia and finally established himself as a Settler at King George's Sound in 1834 in the highly creditable Discharge of the Duties of the Magistrate and of the Office of Harbour Master. For his Integrity Discretion and Zeal I am prepared to offer the strongest assurances and I put it to be my Duty as the late Governor of that Colony to request for him Your Lordships favourable consideration…[4]

Why he chose Belches for such preferment is unclear, as he had had little to do with him since plucking him from another ship in 1827 in a contested promotion. It is more than possible there was some family connection, for Stirling was a man of his times and reacted positively when asked to favour a friend or relation. But this time his efforts were in vain for, as he learned on 13 February, Captain Grey, the explorer, had already won the post. In some ways this was fortunate, as Grey married Eliza Spencer, Sir Richard's third daughter, the following November, thus providing a measure of protection for the four younger boys and their mother.[5]

Throughout February Stirling was meeting members of the Western Australian Association, especially William Hutt MP, who wanted to form a company to promote emigration to the colony on Wakefieldian principles, i.e. where Crown land was sold at a sufficient price to fund the immigration of labour. Louisa Clifton, whose father was to play a prominent part in the venture, recorded that the object of the company was to

> attract capital investment in land at the new colony of Western Australia that the former governor, Sir James Stirling, had recommended. Once a substantial amount of land was sold, the Company would then transport the prospective settlers in ships, especially hired to charter them to the colony. It would only select 'gentlemen of capital', and they would bring their own servants, who would receive a free passage in return for their labour.[6]

Discussions with Stirling and with Latour had revealed the extent of land they held in the Leschenault area of Western Australia, and as the company's intent was to create an entirely new settlement, this land, available some 100 miles south of Perth, seemed ideal. Their ideas found favour not only among the friends and relatives of existing colonists, but also amongst some of the colonial reformers of the day.

Edward Gibbon Wakefield himself took a keen interest in the proceedings, but was apparently out of town when the first meeting of the directors of the newly formed company took place on Monday 9 March 1840. The directors were W. Hutt MP (Chairman), J. Wright, J. Stewart, Col. Latour, Capt. Sweeny RN, Capt. Brigham RN, Capt. Irving, L. Pyne and Mr Gill. Their major concern at this first meeting was to secure the land they planned to settle, and to achieve this they decided to offer shares in the company, at £500 each, of which £125 had to be deposited immediately. Most of the directors took two shares, and among the other nine names given at the meeting the Duke and Duchess of Leeds took four and the Mangles brothers two. On the basis of funds so raised, the meeting decided upon the terms to be offered to Stirling and Latour. According to the minutes:

> A letter was directed to be written to Sir Jas Stirling accepting the purchase of his land supposed to be 64,000 acres at four shillings an acre—£1,000 to be paid down & the balance in four equal payments at 2, 4, 6 and 8 years bearing 5% interest—and in the event of the first payment not being made, Sir James to keep the £1,000 & to take back his land.
>
> A letter [also] was directed to be written assenting to purchase Colonel Latour's land on the terms proposed, 25 paid up shares of £1,000 or 50 shares of £500 and £5,000 in money payable in two instalments of £1,500.[7]

Undoubtedly Stirling would have been offered the chance to take shares in the company in lieu of payment, but he was financially embarrassed at the time as his Admiralty half-pay was not covering the expenses of London living. The company's offer was most timely and their terms more than reasonable. Stirling had not been at the meeting, and whether he realised that part of the 64,000 acres he was selling to the company overlapped the acreages Latour was offering is unknown. Roe had definitely alerted him to the overlap before he left Western Australia, but at that stage Stirling had been sure that Latour's land would be resumed. Even now the Colonial Office was still refusing Latour's claim. If it was allowed, Stirling probably believed an adjustment would take place in the colony, and that his claim, as ex-Governor, would take precedence over Latour's (an absentee), and Latour be offered other land. Stirling was ever the optimist, and it is unlikely that he would have deliberately deceived a company in which his brothers-in-law had shares. But now that he was to receive some financial return from his Western Australian holdings, he was more than ever determined to press his claim for more land.

On 20 March 1840 he wrote to the Colonial Office asking Vernon Smith's help in bringing his claim, outstanding since the previous November, to a final adjustment.[8] His query was forwarded to the Treasury solicitors and Stirling informed of the fact.[9] The solicitors must have groaned, as they had just completed their review of Latour's case and been forced to reverse their earlier judgment. On 4 April they admitted that Latour's shipments had, in fact, been made before the 1829 regulations came into force, and that in consequence he was entitled to the full 21-year improvement period specified in December 1828.[10] Legally, Latour's land could no longer be resumed, and Stirling was in trouble. If this was a cause for anxiety, it was swamped by the news later in the month that his own claim had been refused. Vernon Smith conveyed the lawyers' verdict to Stirling on 30 April 1840, stating it was the lawyers' opinion

> That the 100,000 acres already appropriated would be adequate to an investment of £7,500, and that they cannot ascertain from the items set forth as investment giving…any ground to call for a further Grant of Land to you…[11]

Stirling was upset, but far from beaten (he would doggedly raise the question of his land on fourteen future occasions with successive Colonial Secretaries), and on 7 May replied, at first admitting 'this conclusion is not altogether unwarranted, because the Law Officers of the Crown had not any evidence whatsoever in place before them'. But he then added that he had been led to expect he would be 'afforded opportunity…to present evidence to the lawyers' and, that in consequence,

> my claim has been adjudicated on in the absence of the very evidence on which it rests. I therefore…request that an opportunity may now be afforded to me to produce my evidence before the Law Officers of the Crown…[12]

James Stephen was not unsympathetic, but there was a note of frustration in his terse statement that, if Stirling presented such evidence to his office, he would submit it to the Crown lawyers.[13] This was communicated to Stirling on 15 May 1840.[14]

In the interim the company formed out of the Western Australian Association had run into trouble. Uncertainty over the status of Latour's land had led some of the initial shareholders and directors to withdraw, even before the WA Company was formally constituted. Rounding up new financial support had given Hutt and his core group an anxious time. Finally, on 12 May, all was in order and the company was officially registered. Records kept by Marshall Waller Clifton, its first Commissioner, listed the new directors,[15] who included Wakefield himself, radical Members of Parliament, merchants, bankers, and shipping magnates—Buckle and Enderby replacing the Mangles in the latter category. Why the Mangles brothers pulled out is unclear, but it was possibly because the purchase of land from their brother-in-law involved a conflict of interest. Clifton's notes continued as follows:

> The Co. immediately afterwards issued Prospectus No 1…and commenced selling a portion of the Grant at Leschenault which they had purchased of Colonel Latour. This grant consisted of 103,000 acres, situated on the Eastern side of Leschenault Inlet & was described by Sir James Stirling & others as eminently

calculated for the objects of the Company. The Company also purchased of Sir James Stirling grants which he had acquired in the vicinity of this Property to the extent of 61,000 acres, & also the rights which Colonel Latour possessed to take up further grants in the same Colony. But they offered for sale only 51,000 acres of the original grant. This quantity of land was to be divided into 100 acre blocks for farming, with 500 acres put aside for 3,000 housing blocks to comprise the township which it was determined should be called Australind.[16]

The name of the town (and the settlement) had been coined to reflect the hoped for contact between Australia and India. Under Wakefield's influence the whole venture was to be carried out on 'systematic' lines: it would be concentrated (hence the 100-acre farming lots), and there was to be a due proportion maintained between available labour and capital, land and town lots were to be pre-purchased and half the monies raised 'laid out in the conveyance of passengers and emigrants to the settlement'.[17] Sales of land were to start as soon as possible, and it was hoped that the first ship carrying the Commissioner, the all-important surveyors and first settlers would leave before Christmas—so there was much to organise. The property was drawn on a map and subdivided on a grid basis into rural sections to

Louisa Clifton, daughter of the Australind Commissioner and avid diarist

Courtesy Battye Library BA1073

Marshall Waller Clifton, the first Commissioner of the Australind Company

Courtesy Battye Library 225184P

sell at £1 per acre, and town lots at £10 per acre. Sales began in July, and within two months 400 rural sections (which included a town lot) had been bought, together with 1,500 separate town lots, raising a total £18,375.[18]

Meanwhile, Stirling had raised his own land claim again, submitting to Russell on 3 June 1840 a detailed statement of claim, plus 'sundry documents', with the advice that in fact the 'accounts & vouchers remain in the control of the Accountant'. He expressed the hope that Russell would see the justice of his claim, and not 'delay its final adjustment, by any further reference to legal advice'.[19] Russell, however, simply forwarded the letter to the Solicitor-General for an opinion, so once again Stirling had to wait.

A letter from brother Walter to his niece on 16 June gives an insight into family doings at this stage.[20] He had heard that Andrew had decided to return to Swan River, as James had offered him the chance to manage some of his grants. Stirling knew he had to fulfil the improvement clauses in the next ten years, or lose

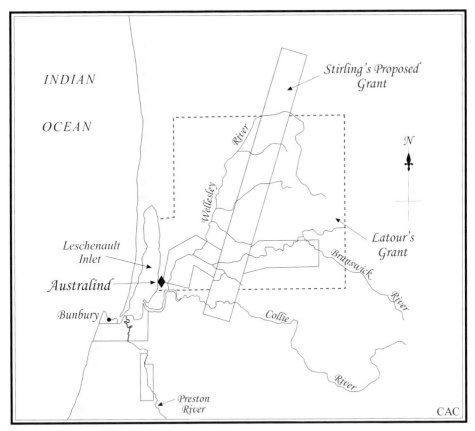

Map of overlapping Leschenault grants, the source of problems for the
Australind Company, and the location of Australind and Bunbury

Based, with kind permission, on Charles Staples' map in They Made Their Destiny, *CO 18/101 f425*

his lands. Although Andrew had been told of the Australind venture, he had decided, probably on the advice of Frederick Mangles, to go out with a group of private settlers who were independently preparing to migrate to Swan River. James, who had been *in loco parentis* for many years and regarded his nephew with much fondness, expressed considerable concern over Andrew's departure. He told his brother John that he had inspected the *Shepherd*, which Andrew was considering joining, but found that 'he would not make a comfortable passage' in it. Instead, he advised the *Napoleon*, 'a much better and faster vessel'. With some meticulousness, James then outlined a statement of account in respect of the £500 his brother had, in 1833, entrusted him to invest in Swan River for Andrew's benefit. As of 1 July 1839, his brother was due £853; interest at 5 per cent had increased this to £901 13s, while various debits, including amounts paid to Andrew during his stay in the colony, and money expended in Mangles' shipping activities on Andrew's behalf, had reduced the overall sum still in Stirling's hands to £150. Stirling went on to say of his nephew:

> He is now poor fellow started on his journey and like some others I could name has his way to make in the World. I do not doubt in the slightest degree his good sense and principles, and I have great hope that necessity the Mother of Invention will enable and induce him to find or make some way of pushing himself forward.[21]

Before Andrew left in late August, Stirling had taken him to dine with the Clifton family. Louisa Clifton noted in her diary that she had been seated between the two, and Andrew had promised to present her with 'a water melon on landing'.[22] Andrew would also have met the newest addition to the Stirling family before he left—Anna Hamilton Stirling, James' and Ellen's ninth child and fourth daughter, born in London early in July.[23]

But while new horizons were opening for his nephew, more intransigence awaited Stirling who had received word from the Colonial Office that Treasury officials had once again refused his land claim.[24] His resolve to continue fighting appears to have been strengthened at this time, although his reply had a more conciliatory tone. He expressed satisfaction that the case had been treated 'with candour and impartiality' but added, 'I must aver that my opinion of the Justice of my claim remains as strong as ever'.[25] He asked for a copy of the grounds upon which the refusal was based, and in annotations Stephen recorded that he saw 'no objection to this, although it threatens a protracted correspondence'. It befell Vernon Smith to undertake this chore, which he did in a lengthy letter dated 29 August. This made it clear that Stirling's claim was vetoed, first because the initial grant of 100,000 acres had been 'only by way of advance and not in compensation of a prior claim'. In other words, that it was not a grant in reward for his previous services, but an advance on land he would be entitled to on the basis of assets introduced and services performed (which in fact Stirling had originally claimed). Second, although the language of the 5 December 1828 document was 'very loose & indefinite', and what was meant by 'investment upon public or private objects' was nowhere defined, the Treasury lawyers believed

> that the items of expenditure set forth in your Account…can in no reasonable sense be considered as an investment entitling you to any further Grant of Land. That they consist merely of expenses of living during your residence in the Colony…[26]

As a result they could find no reason to alter their previous decision.

This whole matter was somewhat of an embarrassment to the Colonial Office, as they were simultaneously sounding Stirling out on his willingness to take on the Governorship of New Zealand, the incumbent having become seriously ill. In fact, Stephen sent a memorandum to Lord John Russell to this effect early in September:

> I have seen Sir James Stirling, and have asked him whether in the event of Captain Hobson's incapacity being reported as final and incurable, he would be willing to accept the Office of Lt. Governor of New Zealand. He answered that he was much gratified by the communication; and that if the contingency should arise, he would gladly accept the Office.[27]

In the event, Hobson recovered and was able to continue, but as Stirling later informed brother John, the Colonial Office, 'having a much better opinion of me as a Colony Builder or Tinker than I have myself', had also offered him the South Australian post.[28]

Early in September, the first of the Australind-bound ships, the *Island Queen*, was scheduled to set sail, and to celebrate the event the directors had invited all involved with the company to a grand fete.[29] James and Ellen, who were about to begin a month's stay at Woodbridge, mingled in august company on the day, for it was recorded that Lord John Russell, Lord and Lady Petre, the banker Samuel Guerney and his sister Elizabeth Fry and many others attended a 'dejeuner at Lovegrove's West India Dock Tavern where chairman William Hutt gave a rousing speech'.[30] Land sales were booming and everything looked bright for the company and the colony.

With the quieter pace of country life at Woodbridge, Stirling had time to review the grounds the lawyers had used to dismiss his case. He still felt it was unfair, particularly the finding that his grant was in return for investments, rather than remuneration for his services. He probably realised that his initial tack—that the grant was an advance—which he had made to stress the point that he was *also* entitled to land in return for imported assets, had been unwise. He had had no other remuneration for his efforts in founding the colony. On 21 September he expressed this in a letter to the Colonial Office, enclosing also a lengthy 'further statement' of his case. His letter argued that his grant had been a reward for his 'services prior to the receipt of salary' and was 'expressly exempted from any obligation and condition whatsoever' except for the 21-year improvement clauses.[31] He therefore requested that his letter and the appended 'Further Statement' be put again before the Law Officers. In the additional statement, Stirling tackled the various grounds raised by the lawyers one at a time, detailing again the dates and circumstances in which he had been granted the 100,000 acres. He noted that in April 1831 Viscount Goderich had stated that he was to have a salary of £800 per annum, a rate far below the expenses of his command but offset by the fact that he had his large grant 'in consideration of having volunteered his services without salary'. Moreover, he added, he had had to spend most of his private resources 'in the unproductive and very unprofitable location of…Perth, instead of investing the whole of his capital in cultivation, buildings and livestock as private colonists were at liberty to do'. He then tackled the other criticism made by the Law Officers, that his expenditures could not be 'considered as investment' entitling him to additional land. He argued again that there had been no constraints on the importations of other private investors, especially Peel, and that:

> I am equally entitled to an apportionment of land on the ground of having imported property whatever I may have made of my property after importation.[32]

After submitting this document personally to Vernon Smith,[33] Stirling returned to Guildford for his baby daughter's christening on 29 September. Before a gathering of the clan, Anna Hamilton was baptised in the same church her parents had been married in sixteen years previously.[34] As he stood at the font with Ellen beside him, James had every reason to feel quietly confident. He had several irons in the fire. Not only was the Colonial Office interested in his services, the Admiralty had also been in touch about a possible command. He was therefore totally unprepared for the furore that descended soon after the family returned to London in early October.

News apparently reached London on 12 October that Latour's lands had been resumed by Governor Hutt in May 1840.[35] This was devastating for the WA Company, whose first ship was already on its way to Leschenault. Even more disquieting was a report from the explorer, Captain George Grey, condemning the Leschenault lands as totally unsuited for the venture, and recommending instead land around Champion Bay that he had seen in 1839.

Even though Lord John Russell had attended the Australind celebrations to mark the *Island Queen*'s departure on 2 September, the Colonial Office had, as late as the 26th, seemingly distanced itself from the venture. In reply to one query about the company's activities, it advised that the Government had not authorised sales, nor had they 'any official knowledge of the constitution, the objects or the proceedings of the Company'.[36]

Mindful that Russell could well be questioned in Parliament about the downturn in events, James Stephen prepared a long memorandum on 14 October reviewing the situation. Stephen recounted William Hutt's role as the 'principal projector' of the Australind venture, due to take effect on land purchased from Colonel Latour at 5s 3d per acre, and how 'a great body of emigrants' was ready to sail. The negative reports just received, Stephen wrote, had branded Australind 'a tract of land utterly worthless and barren…the Sahara under the influence of a milder climate'; Grey had lived 'for two years in the vicinity' and his examination of the land was made 'with perfect impartiality and as a man of science'. As the new company had resold the land

> at a higher rate (so I understand) to the more wealthy emigrants…Ruin to these ignorant and inoffensive people, disgrace and grievous loss to the Company, are therefore impending. Mr Hutt himself will be the chief loser. I found him quite overwhelmed with anxiety and distress. If the facts I have mentioned should become known before any remedy has been provided, the mischief would be irremediable…To avert this ruin, your Lordship's aid is now invoked.

Stephen's suggestion was that the Land Commissioner should investigate and report on the actual labour emigration expenses incurred by the company, and that for every 12 shillings thus spent, the Land Commission

> might, I think, be told to give them an order for one acre of land…on the condition of their placing the emigrants on the lands so to be granted by the Government. To the Governor the whole story might be confidentially communicated, with instructions to give effect to the Order only if the settlement of Australind should really prove good for nothing…If they stand by the place which they have bought of Colonel Latour, then it is a mere private transaction from which I think the Government cannot too studiously stand aloof.

Stephen cautioned that the Government probably would be held to blame for the misfortune, although he believed that 'your Lordship is as ignorant, as all those serving under you are, of all that has been going on about Australind'. He went on to refer to the resumption order which Governor Hutt had imposed on Latour's land, warning Russell that:

> It will be argued that the Governor has proceeded illegally, and that to his intervention in resuming the land the disappointment of the emigrants is owing…[but] the Governor has long since been instructed to place Colonel Latour's Trustees in possession of the land. The forfeiture and resumption must therefore of course be regarded as mere nullities, and the new grantees, if any such there be, must make way for the old proprietors.[37]

It was just as well Stephen prepared this detailed memorandum for Russell, for the very next day, 15 October, William Hutt himself delivered a long and impassioned plea for help. Grey's poor evaluation of the Leschenault land, he said, had led him

> almost to rejoice at the previous news of the resumption of Latour's Grant because I trust it will justify the Government at home in helping us out of the disaster into which we have fallen…This might happen if the Company were allowed promptly to exercise Col. Latour's right to land in another part of the Colony as fit as Leschenault was supposed to be for the purpose of a settlement. If he should approve of that suggestion everything will remain in status quo… excepting only that the surveyors must be removed from Leschenault to the new location…[38]

Russell was disposed to lend assistance and, after re-reading Stephen's earlier memorandum, placed the following annotation on file:

> …it appears to me that we may consider this company as purchasers of land to the extent proposed by Mr Stephen…The Government will in a pecuniary sense not be losers to any considerable amount—they will be gainers by the acquisition of a good body of emigrants…but it must be an indispensable condition that the Emigrants are informed of the terms & agree to them…J.R.[39]

Advising Hutt of this decision, Stephen minuted their conversation for Russell, saying he had concluded that the best all-round outcome would be to

> either direct that the act of resumption be cancelled and the land restored, or direct that some other tract of country of equal extent, should be assigned to them in exchange for it…I understand that Mr Hutt would be perfectly satisfied with this, and very grateful for it.[40]

This solution would definitely suit the company—as yet unaware of the unsuitability of the proposed alternative northern land—but it was detrimental for Stirling, as part of his own land sale to the company would now be null and void.

There was further bad news for Stirling. Stephen had heard a disparaging rumour about his choice of land from William Hutt and a Charles Buller, and mentioned it in a memo to Russell on 16 October:

> I am sorry to do so, as it may seem to throw some shade over the conduct of Sir James Stirling. But it is particularly incumbent on me to keep back nothing of that kind, as I have more than once borne my testimony to his great merits as Governor of Western Australia.

The charge was that Stirling had selected his land 'in a manner most unfair to the Colony at large' by taking all available river frontage and thus 'the best alluvial land of a whole district'. Stephen did not believe the claim, stating:

> I think it far more probable that Messrs Hutt & Buller have been misinformed, and that Sir James Stirling has been slandered…But I have every reason to think that the story is very generally told to his prejudice…Nevertheless I would suggest the propriety of a letter being written to Sir James Stirling…requesting him to supply your Lordship with the…landmarks of his grants, as may enable you to remove from the minds of others the unfavourable impression which appears to prevail in some quarters…16 Oct 1840. JS.[41]

Although it is true that Stirling's choice of Latour's land contained parts of the Brunswick River, this was not the large river the rumour implied, and the grant boundaries by no means took in 'all available river frontage in the district', as the Wellesley River and others lay outside the boundaries.[42] It would appear that William Hutt and Charles Buller, neither of whom had been to Swan River, were deliberately undermining Stirling, whose grants, after all, had been correctly submitted to the Colonial Office in writing and clearly marked on the maps. But it is also likely that when news of the resumption came through, William Hutt had also received private correspondence from his brother, Governor John Hutt, complaining of the mess the survey department was in and the number of disputed land claims with which he had to deal. It is not hard to envisage the new Governor privately blaming the state of affairs on his predecessor rather than on the real cause, the lack of resources available initially to explore and carefully mark out boundaries. To blame Stirling was to create a convenient scapegoat —a welcome ploy for a brother in England facing a ruined reputation over resumed grants. Moreover, with his honour smeared, Stirling would be in no position to argue that the proposed alternative to the Leschenault land was impractical. He knew that the area Grey had examined was a long way north of Perth—dry, hot and on a dangerous coastline—and that transport would be an overwhelming obstacle to progress.

Following the explorer's condemnation of the Leschenault area as 'unsuitable for rural pursuits', and praise for the northern land he had discovered, the company decided to ask Lord John Russell to change their allocation to that lying between 'the river Arrowsmith and Gantheaume Bay' [above Kalbarri],[43] equal in extent to that resumed from them by the Crown.[44] Under-Secretary Vernon Smith replied immediately, conveying Russell's agreement to the proposal, but adding

> that the substituted land shall be granted only to the extent to which Colonel Latour may substantiate his claim to the lands, originally assigned to him…[45]

There was no reference to any substitution for Stirling's land, though the £1,000 the company had paid him initially had been on non-refundable terms.[46] Under the circumstances, they were hardly likely to accept Stirling's advice on their new choice of land. Nevertheless, questions must have been asked, for on 23 October the company secretary wrote to Russell asking to see Grey's actual journal.[47] Permission was granted and the journal contents soothed frayed nerves. The directors felt all would be well and sought a public meeting of shareholders and intending emigrants to clarify the whole situation, and allay the rising tide of panic. (As disparaging news about Australind had spread, several land purchasers had demanded their money back, and new sales had halted completely.) To provide cast-iron evidence that all would be well, the company secretary hastily wrote again to Russell asking for a copy of the instructions he had sent to Governor Hutt over the substitution.[48]

Speed was important in view of the company's looming general meeting, scheduled for 12 November 1840 at the City of London Tavern in Bishopsgate Street. William Hutt took the chair, explaining events and the plans for redress.[49] To reassure investors, he called on various supporters to speak to the assembled group—among them Edward Wakefield and Charles Mangles.[50] The latter noted that it was his opinion

> as a nautical man that if the land at Port Grey was inferior, the superiority of the harbour there over Port Leschenault would turn the scale in his opinion for there ships might remain in perfect safety in every season.[51]

It was a strange comment from one who had never been to the colony, though his ships had visited and perhaps sent in reports. There could well have been a rift between Stirling and his brother-in-law at this stage, for Mangles had been heavily involved with the company and might have been unwilling to listen to advice that the proposed land near Gantheaume Bay was untenable.

Though he knew of, and had privately commented on the substitute arrangement, Stirling was not party to any of the company's dealings after mid-October. He had been approached by the Admiralty regarding a posting to the Mediterranean, and had gladly accepted the commission. During the following weeks he ended the lease on the Harley Street premises and moved his family back to Woodbridge. Finally, on 2 November 1840, he took command of the HMS *Indus*. She was docked at Portsmouth and Stirling joined her in stormy weather which lasted nearly a week. His two Lieutenants, Brown and McKenzie, boarded the following day and the three would have spent some time checking the 3,653-ton and 51 ft long ship from stem to stern before the Master (Quinlan) and crew arrived, and victualling and other procedures began.[52] A totally new life now beckoned Stirling.

The WA Company went ahead with its plans, and Clifton, the Commissioner, with his large family[53] and the first shipment of emigrants left on the 600-ton *Parkfield* on 5 December. Although two more ships were to follow (the *Diadem* and the *Trusty*), the huge initial interest in the new settlement had been severely dampened by news of the company's land difficulties. Eventually, some £30,808 had

to be repaid to investors, which drove the company's bankers to near insolvency.[54]
The advance party of surveyors on the *Island Queen* arrived in the colony in
December 1840, unaware of the crisis that had occurred in London. They had begun
surveying the shores of the inlet for the town of Australind, but had not completed
their surveys, or erected any permanent shelter, when the *Parkfield* arrived on
17 March 1841 with Commissioner Clifton and the first immigrants. Clifton was
despondent, anticipating a northward move soon after arrival and lamenting the
lack of supplies to keep the isolated group going until the arrival of further ships.
In contrast, his artistic daughter Louisa was enchanted with the colours of the land
in front of her, and pleased to see in the distance 'Mr Elliot's and Mr Stirling's little
dwelling'[55] just as Andrew had described it in London.

Leaving the women and children on board the *Parkfield*, Clifton inspected the
survey work and surrounding land. He soon learned from George Elliot and
Andrew Stirling that, although Latour's land had been resumed the previous year, it
had not been regranted. Moreover they told him, and showed him, that the area

Stirling's nephew George Elliot
Courtesy Battye Library 4069B

contained much good land. Louisa, who was party to some of these early
conversations, recorded in her diary that Grey's assessment of the land had proven
'abominable misrepresentations'. The whole debacle in London had been
unnecessary. With the Governor's permission the whole settlement could go ahead
as originally planned, so Clifton set out overland with some of his party to see
Governor Hutt in Perth. Given the new directive from the Colonial Office,
Governor Hutt agreed that the settlement should go ahead on Latour's Leschenault
land, which would now be transferred to the company. In fact, Hutt was personally
opposed to any movement to the north as it would further disperse the already
scattered colony. So Clifton was given permission to establish the settlement of
Australind some little distance north of the outpost Stirling had created at Bunbury.

Returning to Koombana Bay, Clifton set all the adult males to work, and the
women and children on the *Parkfield* finally disembarked a month later. That
evening, seated in a tent and writing on a packing case, Louisa recorded in a letter
to her brother in England, 'I cannot tell you how truly kind Mr Elliot and Mr
Stirling have been. The former is a very agreeable gentlemanly man, and the latter
is most pleasing, and though a colonist no less a gentleman.'[56] Stirling's relatives had
helped the newcomers through the first shock of arrival in a strange land and would
go on helping the family, even though conditions became more and more difficult.
The near bankruptcy of the company meant that the other two emigrant ships
arrived without the capital assets and finance that Clifton so desperately needed to
establish the settlement. The 100-acre farming lots proved too small and poor for
crop farming and many of the settlers and their labourers and servants drifted away,
either to the Perth region or south to Bunbury and the Vasse. By 1843 the dream of
a Wakefieldian settlement in Western Australia was finished. For Daniel Scott, who
was managing Stirling's land with Elliot's help and cultivating the acres he believed
Stirling had given him at Eelup,[57] it was a tragedy. He watched the entire drama
unfold and the hopes of many ruined. As an experienced midwife, Mrs Scott helped
many of the women through uncomfortable pregnancies, in unaccustomed heat and
poor accommodation. For George Elliot, Stirling's nephew, it brought a new life as
he courted and married Louisa Clifton and remained to become Resident
Magistrate of the now slightly more populous region.

Surveyor-General Roe had had the difficult task of reassigning land to allow
not only for Latour's now approved grant (Wellington Location 1), but also for
Stirling's entitlement. This he did by placing Stirling's land in separate grants above
and below Latour's (Wellington Location 50A above and his earlier choices,
Leschenault Locations 41, 26 and 12 below—see map opposite page), though all was
not finalised until 1853.[58] Part of Stirling's claim running along the inlet became the
land he sold to the company, but it was much smaller than the amount initially
agreed upon, so additional lands were allocated to the company in lieu (Locations
48, 50, 51 and 56). Stirling could have had no idea that the claims would take so long
to sort out when he again took command of a ship after an absence of twelve years.

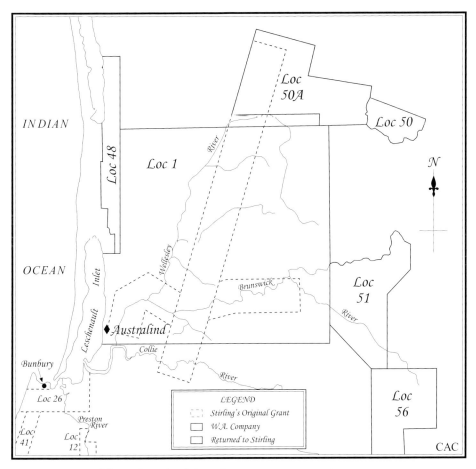

The end result of the mix-up over compensating grants

Based, with kind permission, on Charles Staples' map in They Made Their Destiny,
CO 18/101 f425 and WAA 45/15–16, 298C/S16 Map L157

23

Third Command: HMS *Indus*

1841–1843

STIRLING'S RETURN TO the sea took place at a time when Britain was 'dangerously over-extended' on the international stage.[1] She was at war with Afghanistan and with China, in dispute with the United States over the slave trade, the Canadian boundary and maritime rights, and, even more seriously, had come nearer to a break with France than at any time since the end of the Napoleonic Wars. Differences over power-sharing in the arrangements of royal marriages in Europe played a small part in this, but the major issue of contention became known as the 'Eastern Question'. There were in fact two theatres where Britain and France were at loggerheads: one involved Turkey, the other Sicily, and both came to a head in 1840.

At the heart of matters were shifting alliances and the delicate balance of power. Relations with the Turks, whose Ottoman Empire kept Russia out of the Mediterranean, had deteriorated in 1839. The Turkish Sultan had been challenged by the Egyptian Pasha, Mehemet Ali, who had invaded Syria and then part of Turkey. When the Sultan asked Britain for help, she had been slow to respond. Mehemet Ali was supported by the French, so any action threatened the balance of power. The matter dragged on until June 1840 when Lord Palmerston (Foreign Secretary 1835–41) engineered a treaty between the other great powers—Russia, Austria and Prussia—to force Mehemet Ali to withdraw from Turkey. This left France out on a limb, as she had to accept the treaty or declare war on the allied powers. When Mehemet Ali refused to leave, still believing in French help, the British intervened and attacked Beirut in September 1840 to try to force his submission. Within a matter of weeks Palmerston gave orders to bombard Acre (just north of modern Haifa). As he had anticipated, France did not intervene.[2] War ceased in November with surrender to the British.

France was also distressed by Palmerston's successful manoeuvring to retrieve the Sicilian sulphur contract. Sicily's sulphur mines furnished some four-fifths of the world's supply of this essential ingredient of gunpowder. English companies had run the mines for years until the new King of the Two Sicilies, Ferdinand II—

HMS *Indus*, Stirling's third command, pictured here leaving the Bay of Naples in 1843, was just eight months old and had the latest firing technology

Courtesy National Maritime Museum, Greenwich PAH 0894

otherwise known as the King of Naples—had awarded the monopoly to a French company in July 1838. British diplomatic efforts to terminate the contract proved unavailing. In April 1840 the British Navy had been called on to blockade Ferdinand's capital, Naples. The blockade lasted just over a month and, as Ferdinand was related to the wife of the French King, and indeed had just returned from a visit to France, this again put pressure on France to act against England. They didn't, and the French sulphur contract was finally terminated on 11 July 1840 and restored to the British.

So when Stirling received his commission to the *Indus*, on 2 November 1840, Anglo-French relations were at breaking point. Anything could happen, so he must have expected a rapid deployment. Fortunately, Lord Palmerston believed that the best guarantor of peace was a large and superior naval presence,[3] and at the end of the 1830s had ordered increased numbers of line-of-battle ships,[4] Stirling had been given command of one of these new ships, as the *Indus* had only been completed at Portsmouth dock the previous March. She was a second-rated ship with 80 guns (first-rated ships carried more than 100 guns), but her guns were more modern than many other ships of the line, incorporating some of the new firing technology. At 189 ft long and 51 ft wide (3,653 tons) she was a fine example of her class. The Admiralty seemed anxious to give her a good start, for her initial crew of 122 seamen, and some officers, were transferred from the famous HMS *Victory*, while others were seconded from HMS *Queen*.

The *Indus* was also marked out to take more than the usual number of trainees, and thirty first-class and fourteen second-class boys were sent aboard early in November, among them Stirling's eldest son. Young Andrew had enlisted the previous July aged 15 years and 1 month. He was described as of dark complexion, with dark eyes and hair, normally resident in London, and vaccinated.[5] He joined the *Indus* as a first-class volunteer on Monday 9 November.[6] For the Captain's son, it was probably just as well that Stirling did not remain for any length of time on board during the first weeks of his commission. Most of November was spent fitting out the ship in Portsmouth, a task exacerbated by storm damage on the 17th. Stirling certainly visited the ship periodically, as he addressed another letter to the Colonial Office from the *Indus* on 8 January 1841.

This letter makes clear that he had spent the previous weeks in seeking legal advice on his claim for land compensation. He had gone to the top, approaching Sir Frederick Pollock, the chief legal adviser to the Queen, for advice. His letter now emphasised the services he had performed prior to receipt of salary, and concluded:

> As a British Subject deprived of my Right by some strange misapprehension of the Facts of the case on which my claim depends, and a Public Servant of many years standing and now labouring under the Imputation of having made unfounded Allegations with a view of obtaining Property, I am compelled to claim from Your Lordship a fair opportunity to place the Truth of my Allegation…[7]

This monochrome copy of the original 'Swan Cup' portrait, painted c. 1840,
shows Stirling in naval uniform. He turned 50 on 28 January 1841.

Courtesy Margaret Lenfestey

And again he set out, quite forcibly, his belief that the initial grant was a reward for his efforts in establishing the colony, and that he was still entitled to additional land on the basis of the property he had introduced and services rendered. But the Colonial Office was unmoved, Stephen annotating the letter:

> on comparing Sir J. Stirling's present tone with that which he adopted when he was still a candidate for employment here, and had not obtained the command of a ship, there is, I think, a very perceptible difference which should, I think, rather dissuade than recommend concession even in a less doubtful case. 20 Jany JS.[8]

As he turned 50 on 28 January, Stirling probably combined a low-key celebratory visit to his family at Guildford with some unfinished business. His sister Dorothea was unwell, and he was also concerned about supervision for his young brood while he was at sea. It was not until the end of February 1841 that he was called to the Admiralty to receive orders, confirmed later in writing, to proceed to the Mediterranean and place himself under the command of Rear Admiral Sir John Ommanney at Malta. (Britain had acquired Malta during the Napoleonic Wars and it had since become a major British stronghold in the Mediterranean.) It was welcome news, for Ommanney was related to both his own naval agent and the young man who had been his surveyor in Western Australia.

On 6 March the *Indus* slipped from her moorings and, with the help of two steamers, was moved to an anchorage at Spithead. In accordance with navy protocol, the new vessel then fired a salute of 15 guns—the first of many gun salutes to come. Gun salutes were fired to mark movements in, out and within the harbour—the number of shots per salute varying according to a strict code which acknowledged nationality, seniority of commanding officers and their guests, etc., as well as occasions like royal birthdays, national days and other diplomatic niceties. Flags were flown to carry such information, and all Admirals insisted that correct procedures be observed—Stirling on one occasion was reprimanded for firing too many shots! Salutes served a double purpose, as they provided invaluable training for a ship's company in the firing of the 18 lb and 32 lb cannons, but it was an expensive exercise, and thus had to be strictly monitored.

Initially *Indus* was understrength, and an officer had to be despatched twice to raise more men.[9] By 10 April, with the target nearly reached, a muster was called for the men to be paid. There would have been some stirring speeches on this occasion, for Lord Minto, First Lord of the Admiralty, visited the ship. He took a keen interest in the trainees on board, and sent a naval instructor to join the ship a week later. The log entries record drills for the 'young gentleman at the guns' during this period, which were put into practice on 21 May with a 21-gun salute for Queen Victoria's birthday.[10]

Between May and the *Indus*'s eventual departure in early August, Stirling made several more approaches to the Colonial Office. It was clear he still felt slighted, and on 7 May, while on a visit to London, he wrote to Lord Russell, at first stating that if his grant continued to be judged as an advance on investment, and not a payment for services, then it left him 'a claimant of Her Majesty's government at present uncompensated'. He pointed out:

> there is scarcely an instance amongst officers, similarly circumstanced, who have not received by your Lordship's intercession, honorary distinctions, pensions, or more profitable offices…I appeal to your Lordship's justice whether I ought to be permitted to retire from the Colonial Department after so long a connection without notice or reward.[11]

Stirling was clearly thinking in terms of public service in India rather than Australia, for most of the early Australian Governors had had to fight criticism and disgrace before gaining meagre recognition.[12] But he had not been recalled, and his administration had been praised. Was he to gain less than his problem settlers Peel and Latour for all his effort? As his land claim seemed to be of no avail, Stirling privately told Stephen that he would like to be remunerated in money or made a Baronet. When this was intimated to Russell on 11 May, he annotated Stirling's dispatch:

> Sir James Stirling is a very good & honourable man, but I do not know he is entitled to be made a Baronet. As to money, I thought he had large grants of land. JR[13]

The official reply of 20 May stated that his Lordship 'would have felt pleasure, if it had been in his power' to recommend a mark of approbation, but regretted that he had no means at present to comply.[14] Personal matters would have done little to assuage Stirling's disappointment, for his favourite sister Dorothea died on 10 June at the age of 48—a severe emotional blow. It may have also affected his son, for Andrew's service record indicates he was discharged to Haslar Hospital on 11 June 1841,[15] though this could have been coincidental. The loss of his sister, combined with the inactivity on board in the absence of sailing orders, compounded Stirling's sense of injustice, and he once again wrote to the Colonial Office, asking them on 5 July for a copy of the letter Hay had written to him on 2 January 1833. This letter, he felt, would authenticate his claim, but he had no copy.[16] When no reply came, he wrote again, on 22 July, asking that his case be resubmitted to the Law Officers with all relevant correspondence.[17] Somewhat perfunctorily, Under-Secretary James Stephen noted 'this was one of a succession of claims which had each been rejected by the law officers', observing that the matter needed to be brought to a close. But the official reply, on 9 August, still left a door open:

> Lord John Russell regards it as absolutely necessary that some limit should be put to the discussion of this question. His Lordship can therefore advance no further unless upon a distinct assurance that you have at last advanced all the testimony

in your possession…[and] explain why the testimony, to which reference is now made, was not referred to before.[18]

This letter was addressed to Portsmouth, but by the time it arrived, Stirling and the *Indus* had departed.

Sailing orders for the *Indus* had been finalised at the end of July, and on 4 August 1841 she headed, without escort, into the English Channel, reaching Gibraltar eighteen days later. From there, Stirling had instructions to make their presence felt along the coast of Algeria. He also used the time to inspect the defences at Orum (modern Oran) and environs, writing a long report for submission to the Admiralty. On 2 September there was a brief engagement with the French, welcomed after so much inactivity, and five days later the *Indus* entered Valletta harbour. Stirling lost no time presenting letters to Admiral Ommanney from the Lords of the Admiralty, together with reports from Gibraltar and his own report on Orum's defences, which instantly won approval from the Admiral.[19]

So began a period in Stirling's naval career of almost non-stop activity in which he criss-crossed the Mediterranean, 'showing the flag', undertaking manoeuvres and engaging in subtle diplomacy of the sort that he had found challenging in his earlier commands in the West Indies and South America. His ability to communicate and negotiate, which had served him well during his Governorship of Western Australia, was to be be put to even greater use during his Mediterranean commands.

For Admiral Ommanney, maintaining peace among rival states who thought little of plundering each others' shipping, was a difficult task—and one that

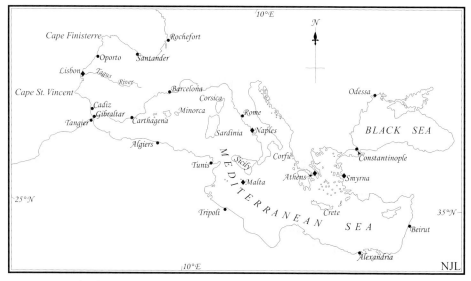

Stirling's voyages in the *Indus*, and later in the *Howe*, covered most of the Mediterranean from Gibraltar to the Levant

required constant patrolling by his squadron. In July, just before Stirling had left England, France had signed the Convention of the Straits,[20] joining the Quadruple Alliance with regard to Turkey and agreeing that the Straits of the Dardanelles and the Bosphorus would be closed to foreign warships in peacetime for all except Russian ships.[21] But there was still trouble with insurgents in Syria, and the French had to be watched as they had only agreed to co-operate with respect to Turkey. Ommanney's patrol options were limited—the fourth-rated *Vernon 50*, third-rated *Vanguard 78*, second-rated *Monarch 84* and *Powerful 84*, and the first-rated 120-gun *Howe*, his flagship.[22] Hence the *Indus 80* was very welcome. Her initial instructions were to join the *Vanguard* in patrolling between Malta and the boot of Italy, and in the course of this to visit Syracuse, where Stirling was to meet the King of the Two Sicilies, Ferdinand II. Stirling would have been most interested to meet the man who had been at the centre of the sulphur contract crisis the previous year, particularly as opinions of him differed widely. Ferdinand II was then 31 years old, 'stout with light reddish brown hair, florid complexion, whiskered and rather young-looking'. He had charming manners, was intelligent and perspicacious but also had 'an over lofty idea of his own importance',[23] and his sacred right to rule the Two Sicilies (which had been united since the Congress of Vienna). Ferdinand trusted no one, had no ministers or allies, and enjoyed playing diplomats off against one another—a ploy which made some think he was weak and vacillating. On the other hand, he was a devoted family man and had personally supervised improvements in infrastructure throughout his realm. He was known to love pomp and pageantry, which was not spared in this visit to the other half of his Kingdom. So Stirling would have donned his full dress uniform for the entertainments that followed the official hand-overs of dispatches and briefings at their meeting on 7 October. Diplomatic tension had eased by this time,[24] so the social pleasantries that cemented international relations could be played out in full.

The following Sunday *Indus* set sail for Malta, arriving just before Ommanney's replacement, Rear Admiral Sir Francis Mason. Among letters awaiting Stirling was the reply he had missed earlier from the Colonial Office. The curt tone of the letter would have hurt his pride and exacerbated his sense of injustice when ordered by the new Admiral to place himself under another Captain of the same rank as himself (Sir Samuel Robarts), rather than receive orders directly from the top. He was already missing Ellen's support, and eagerly looking forward to their planned meeting in Lisbon in December. To clarify their position regarding his WA lands, he wrote to Russell on 20 October, thanking him for being 'willing to admit my case to further consideration', and adding the important new information that his own opinion had now been confirmed by the Queen's Attorney-General, Sir Francis Pollock, who was 'clearly and decidedly of opinion that I could not be negatived without Injustice'.[25] Pollock's involvement caused some concern at the Colonial Office, and the reply of 23 November was carefully phrased. Stirling's case would be reopened only when you are able to give the distinct assurances required by Lord John Russell…To neither of these points have you adverted in the letter under acknowledgment. It may also be proper to observe that, should such further reference be made, as HM's present Attorney General has acted as your private Counsel and Adviser in the case, he may perhaps decline to accept the reference.[26]

The reply was addressed to Malta, but Stirling had gone before it arrived.

Before leaving Valletta for Lisbon, on 10 November, Stirling met a man whose mission interested him greatly. This was Charles Fellows, the cartographer and archaeologist who had discovered the Xanthean marbles during a visit to south-western Turkey in 1838, and who was now on an expedition to retrieve these sculptures for the British Museum. Fellows had arrived in Malta on 30 October 1841 and, while waiting for transport to Rhodes and the Xanthus River, had found ready company among the captains of the various British ships in port, including Stirling who had long had an interest in antiquities. Fellows' discovery of the ruined ancient Roman province of Lycia and its great treasures dating back to the

Eminent archeologist Charles Fellows, whom Stirling met in Malta
From Enid Slatter, Xanthus: Travels of Discovery in Turkey

fifth century BC[27] had caused a tremendous stir in Britain, and the Government was anxious that the marbles should not fall foul of rampaging tribes in the area. Their removal was now a matter of priority for the British Navy[28] and it was only by chance that Stirling was not given the commission to undertake their return the following year.[29]

Stirling's new orders were to proceed to Lisbon, which he reached on 18 December in the company of the steamship *Revenge*. He was to remain there as replacement Senior Naval Officer for some time. Although the British naval base at Lisbon had been withdrawn in 1828, a presence was still maintained and a wary eye kept on relations between Portugal and Spain, which had been shaky since the latter's support of reactionaries behind a Portuguese constitutional and succession embroilment. That dispute had reached its peak in 1829 when the reactionaries, with Spanish help, seized power and ousted the child Queen, Maria di Gloria,[30] only to see the country caught up in civil war. In adult life Maria entered into a second marriage, to Ferdinand of Saxe-Coberg-Kohary, cousin of Prince Albert, Queen Victoria's consort, and during the 'Septembrists' revolt in 1838 they had had to seek sanctuary on a British gunboat. Under a new government, which introduced yet another constitution, the situation calmed down until new elections in June 1841 again brought in reformists whose financial and administrative changes stirred up rebellion. By the end of June 1841 the British Admiralty had received information that the Portuguese Government was actively preparing for conflict, strengthening the frontiers and arming ships for war.[31] This was the situation Stirling had been sent to monitor.

Stirling had been prone in the past to what his mother used to call 'wife-sickness', so now, when arrival formalities were complete, he could look forward to a joyful reunion with the very pregnant Ellen, who had arrived some time earlier. The Stirling family had connections among the English community in Lisbon, so she had been in good hands. The beautiful city was in a tranquil mood and the leafy gardens and sunny squares made a wonderful winter haven. However, their time for relaxation was brief, for not even a week had passed when Stirling had to report the presence in port of three French warships whose visit, he thought, could be linked to the dire financial straits Portugal was rumoured to be in, and trying to overcome with outside loans. This first report from Stirling, sent both to Malta and London, was dated 3 January 1842. His second, on 31 January, was more alarming, as he had heard that signs of insurrection were evident at Oporto, where opponents of the Government had reinstated an earlier charter, and large-scale troop movements had been observed.[32]

The prospect of armed troops threatening the capital was a matter of concern to Stirling, particularly after Ellen had given birth to Dorothea, their second last child, in the British Hospital in Campode Ourique, Lisbon. No exact date of birth is known, but her baptism was recorded on 12 February 1842, at St George's, the small Anglican church near the Jardin Da Estrela.[33] It was the first child Ellen had borne in a hospital, and this one was well known for its care of expatriates, so both mother and child prospered. The period of family togetherness, and the strength that Ellen brought to their marriage, was no doubt a boost to Stirling in Lisbon. She had supported him in the past in his impasse with the Colonial Office over his lands—and now, once again, Stirling returned revitalised to that unresolved issue. On 17 January he wrote asking whether or not the most recent decision of the Law Officers had been influenced by communications from the Colonial Office. He ended with the comment, 'I hope your Lordship will not deem me impertinent in seeking to remove all doubt on the point in question…' [34] But the Colonial Office was not impressed, the letter being somewhat drily annotated, 'Sir James Stirling is in my mind, pertinacious to such an extent as only to preclude any hope of satisfying him…'

James was indeed 'pertinacious' at this stage—he had even written to Sir George Murray in the hope that the former Colonial Office head might have further evidence to support his cause. But the reply dashed any such hopes. Writing from his Berkshire home on 19 February 1842, Murray's letter expressed regret that Stirling felt 'aggrieved' over the non-fulfilment of some of the arrangements made when the Swan River Colony was founded. He had considered Stirling 'particularly well qualified for the undertaking at the time of his appointment' and had been 'confirmed in the judgement by the result'. But he was

> not in possession of any of the public documents relating to that transaction; nor is it probable, indeed, that any statement which I might be enabled to make… would be held to counterbalance the opinions of the law officers of the Crown… [35]

The formal Colonial Office reply, when it came, was even more discouraging, advising Stirling:

> if…you are not prepared to acquiesce in the decision of the Law Officers of the Crown on four successive references of your case to them, his Lordship must refer you to legal remedies, and must decline to communicate with you further… [36]

Meantime, in Portugal events were changing quickly as the political crisis worsened, and Stirling was kept busy updating the Foreign Office and Admiralty. At one point, as he noted in a 7 February report,[37] a 5,000-strong 'Army of the Charter' was rapidly moving south and violence was feared in Lisbon, hitherto without disturbances. Stirling's warning that British citizens and trade interests could be at risk both in the capital and Oporto was received in London with alarm, for just five days later the Foreign Office urged the Admiralty to direct the Senior Naval Officer 'to take no part in any contest which may arise between the different Political Parties in Portugal'.[38] Rather, Stirling should look to protecting 'the prosperity and persons of British Subjects', and to safeguard members of the Portuguese royal family should they seek refuge. As it happened, after much see-sawing and intense political struggle between opponents and supporters of the 1826 Charter, the latter group prevailed. Stirling was able to report on 14 February that Lisbon 'has been entirely free from any disturbance'.[39] Events, and Stirling's duties, returned to normal and several times he was received at Court, where King Fernando II was more than gracious. His wife, Maria II, had been on the verge of confinement, and on Wednesday 16 March it gave Stirling real pleasure to lead the British squadron in a 21-gun salute 'in honour of Her Most Faithful Majesty the Queen of Portugal giving birth to a prince'.[40]

Stirling would have had time during these early months of the year to take drives with Ellen, exploring the older parts of the city and its surrounds, including the village of Sintra where the Royal Family had a summer residence. On such trips they could have discussed their future, including the problem of their Western Australian lands. Mail exchanges were far quicker now, and the Colonial Office's answer to James' January letter probably arrived early in April, as also would two letters from the Western Australian Company. In the first of these, dated 26 January 1842, secretary C. H. Smith informed Stirling that out of the 62,284 acres of land the company had purchased from him, only 13,364 fell outside Colonel Latour's grant, and of that only 424½ acres were contained within the deed of sale as lying between the Collie and Preston rivers:

> As therefore a large quantity of 48,444 will remain for selection in situations not defined, the Directors instruct me to communicate this intelligence to you because it will very materially affect the amount of the instalment that will become payable to you on the 19th of June, next, as...provided for in the deed.[41]

This was unwelcome, but possibly not unexpected news. The second letter, dated 25 February, answered some questions Stirling had raised earlier. He was informed that 'the Governor of Western Australia...has acknowledged the Company's right to select the quantity of land which interferes with Colonel Latour's Grant, in some other situation'; and further that they could then hold these compensating grants (see map page 401) 'on the same terms as the remainder of the grant'. The letter then continued:

> you request to know the amount which under the contract of sale will be payable to you & the time when payable including interest. The following is a statement thereof based upon the terms of the Deed of Conveyance:

Total quantity of lands purchased and conveyed	62,284 acres
do authorised by the local Government	
to be taken possession of by the Co, 1st	424 acres
2nd	12,840 acres
	13,264

Remainder of selection	49,020 acres
Brought down land authorised to be taken possession of	
by the Co. (13,264½ at 4/-)	£2,652.18.0
Deduct paid on execution of deed	£1,000
	£1,625.18.0
1st biennial payment of £1652.18.0	
due on 19th June 1842—one quarter	£413.4.6
Interest on £1652.18.0 for 2 years at 5% pa	£165.5.9
Total sum due from the Company on 19th June 1842	£578.10.3
C H Smith.[42]	

Seeing this in writing would have been a relief, as early intimations had led the Stirlings to expect little, or nothing. It would also, however, have provided an incentive to continue pressing for the additional land to which they felt entitled. Accordingly, Stirling wrote again to the Colonial Office on 9 May, acknowledging the previous letter advising him to take 'legal remedies', but pleading:

> as there is no legal remedy against the Crown of England I venture to appeal to your Lordship's sense of Justice against the Course taken by the Colonial Department in respect of my Right to Compensation for my Services.

Yet again he went through the course of events, citing letters and dispatches as proof, but his frustration was showing as he noted:

> In the hope of adding another Territory to the British Empire, and upon the Inducement held out, I went to Australia—I undertook for the success of a half starved and disjointed Enterprise—I dedicated to it my exertions and my means, and I struggled for three years with all the natural Difficulties of the Undertaking enhanced by the absence of Salary, Commission or proper Recognition on the part of the Government.
>
> At length on the successful Establishment of the Colony I returned to England in full legal Possession of the lands granted before I went out, and then I learnt for the first time that my Right to hold those lands upon the Terms of the original Agreement was denied by the Colonial Department on the opinion of the Law Advisers of the Crown.

As he had now been given the grounds for dismissal of his case, he felt some 'observations would not be improper', and here he pushed his points home.

> ...the Law Officers reported that...I had no Right to Land in compensation for my Public Service [but]...a long series of official documents show not only that

my Services were first engaged upon the Promise of a Recompense in Land but that this Promise was fulfilled and the Land given before I left England….by an assignment from the Crown…The Interest so constituted and acquired cannot be modified, diminished, nor taken away, except by course of Law in the Ordinary Courts of Justice…With respect to the further appropriation of Land to me on the ground of my investment of Capital in Western Australia, I beg again to refer to the Admission of that Right by your Lordship's Predecessor, and to request that the proper Assignment be made to me in liquidation of that Claim. If your Lordship has any further doubt…I beg to refer you to the clear and decided opinion of Sir Frederick Pollock, which I had the Honour to submit to Lord John Russell in the year 1840.[43]

The arguments were much the same, but the tone was now more authoritative; Stirling clearly felt he was in the right and would eventually succeed. But he did not know that the Colonial Office was also under constant barrage from Latour and his lawyers,[44] and others who were simultaneously pushing their claims. They were completely fed up with the Swan River mess. If Stirling had been the only appellant his treatment would no doubt have differed, especially with Pollock's support, but in the circumstances their intransigence was understandable.

Early in June 1842 Stirling received orders to return to Malta, where Vice Admiral Sir Edward Owen had taken over as Commander-in-Chief. Arrangements were made for Ellen and the baby to return to London, and on 10 June *Indus* weighed anchor and sailed out of the Tagus, stopping briefly at Gibraltar before reaching Valletta harbour on 2 July. This was the start of a two-month period of relative inactivity, broken only by repetitive exercises and offshore manoeuvres. The naval station at Malta was a small, isolated community, and as tensions rose with boredom and the summer heat so did the number of courts martial which James and other captains had to attend. Stirling appears to have raged at the purposelessness of it all, and requested six weeks leave of absence. This Owen refused, so Stirling asked that his application be referred to England,[45] but there it met a similar fate.[46]

After another round of exercises extending for two weeks to 6 October (this time more intensive in-line tacking), the squadron returned to harbour. Awaiting Stirling was a disappointing reply to his May letter to the Colonial Office. He was told that nothing more could be done, and he was to consider the correspondence closed.[47] Disappointment was assuaged by distraction, for his son Andrew, who had finished his training, was ready for his Midshipman examination. As it was accepted that this should not be done on his father's ship, Stirling wrote to Owen on 20 October 1842 requesting a transfer for the lad to the *Belvedere*, which had recently arrived from Syria and obviously met with his approval. Owen complied, and the *Belvedere* left for Naples with Andrew four days later. It would be another week before the *Indus* too received sailing orders, which were to proceed to Smyrna (Izmir) in Turkey to strengthen the British forces there.

Britain maintained a consulate at Smyrna, as it was a useful station both for mail transfer and reprovisioning ships bound for nearby Constantinople (Istanbul), itself a valuable trading port and a base for intelligence concerning Russia. As there had been another insurrection in Syria during the year, and rumoured strife between the local Pasha and the Sultan, the consulate and its important diplomatic role were considered at risk, as were British subjects and property in the region.[48] Consequently, it was considered necessary to strengthen the force at Smyrna with another warship. The *Indus* anchored there on 8 November at the start of an eleven-week tour of duty. The city had a distinctly oriental feeling, with consulates and foreign merchants ranged along the foreshore in overhanging houses reminiscent of Tudor England,[49] while minarets soared above buildings further back from the water. Soon after arrival, Stirling presented himself at the British Consulate and handed over dispatches, but finding no instructions from the Ambassador in Constantinople, Sir Stratford Canning, he decided to write directly to him to offer his services.

Shore leave for the crew would have been exciting, as the port, bazaars and cafés buzzed with the city's cosmopolitan population of Turks, Greeks and Armenians, plus the small European enclave of Russians, Italians and English. Streets were described as 'pulsating with the movement of white veiled women and their children, often accompanied by black slaves, the urgent scurry of donkeys and the stately plodding of camel trains bearing bales of merchandise—corn and cotton, wood and iron—on their way to and from the Caravan Bridge'.[50] The Governor of Smyrna was particular in paying homage to his various foreign visitors, and Stirling would have attended one of his regular levees at the Casino Club, where members of the Turkish Court, consuls, naval and military officers and the elite of the European community gathered together in a 'great profusion of diamonds, gold embroidered fezzes and velvet bodices'.[51]

By 28 November definite orders had still not materialised; indeed, it took a further eleven days before Canning finally requested that dispatches be sent to Beirut, a task carried out by HMS *Devastation*. During this time the *Indus* went south to Vourlu (modern Urla) to take on water, which was becoming scarce, and costly, in Smyrna. It was not the only commodity—or service—to be problematic. Back in Smyrna on 21 December, Stirling found five vessels at anchor, yet despite this seeming wealth of available shipping, correspondence was simply not getting through. He complained to Canning that 'the French Post Office here seems to be unable at present to afford any explanation upon the subject'.[52] Furthermore, there was trouble with provisions, not only for the *Indus* but for the other British vessels at Smyrna and Beirut, for which Stirling was also responsible. He only had sufficient provisions for about six weeks from the end of December, so, anxious to settle arrangements, he wrote to Canning asking 'how long the *Indus*'s presence in this quarter is likely to be required'.[53]

Canning's reply evidently released the *Indus* from its immediate duties, for Stirling later advised Admiral Owen that, as the Ambassador saw no reason to detain the *Indus* any longer, she was free as per the original orders 'to fall back on

Athens'.[54] With permission given, Stirling lost no time. After sparing water and provisions for the other British vessels at anchor nearby, the *Indus* left Smyrna harbour on 26 January 1843 bound for Greece, anchoring in Piraeus harbour two days later.[55] The latest mail was waiting—disappointment from Ellen over the refusal of James' request for leave and, either through her or the Mangles brothers, disturbing news from Western Australia which galvanised him to write again to the Colonial Office. Addressing Lord Stanley on 1 February he stated:

> I have received within a few days Official Notice from Western Australia that the Governor had directed the Surveyor General to expunge from his returns the recorded assignment to me of a portion of the Grant [at Leschenault], the same having 'under Orders from the Secretary of State reverted to the Crown'.
>
> These proceedings are a breech [sic] of the Engagement under which I went out to Australia, and I now look back with Indignation and Contempt to the Broken Promises and the delusive assignment on the faith of which I gave my time and money to the enterprise. But these proceedings are moreover an invasion of the Sacred right of Private Property, for which it behoves any Member of a free Country to seek a Remedy. I accordingly request your Lordship to inform me whether the Proceedings represented to me by the Governor of Western Australia aforesaid, have in reality received your Lordship's Sanction and Approval.[56]

The tone of this letter, quite apart from its content, did not meet with approval in London. James Stephen, still Under-Secretary, annotated the letter that Sir James 'should be reminded of the impropriety of so expressing himself' to the Secretary of State, but continued:

> I must add, however, that Sir James Stirling was an excellent Govr and that if this kind of notice of his style be not necessary, I for one should be very glad if it were avoided. JS. Ld S. Mar 24. My opinion is that it will be better not to answer this letter at all.[57]

So no reply was sent and, kept in the dark, Stirling bent his energies to his new post as Senior Naval Officer at Piraeus. For two months or so he was responsible for ordering the various salutes to incoming shipping and the deployment of men on all British naval ships in harbour. One of his more testing tasks was to call on the British Consul in Athens, Sir Edmund Lyons, and report the outcome to Admiral Owen.[58] Lyons was described as a 'bluff, not to say domineering sailor, quite unfitted for a diplomatic situation'[59] who had caused dissension among the other consuls in Athens, and earned a reprimand from the Foreign Secretary. London was keen to learn how effectively Lyons was fulfilling his role. Given his experience with dissenting councillors in Western Australia, Stirling was well equipped to undertake this delicate mission, and the associated court intrigue.

At a personal level, James could rejoice in some welcome news, and share it with his brother John in Scotland. The Western Australian Company had paid the second instalment on their purchase of his lands. He wrote:

> I am therefore now more flush of cash, and I have accordingly directed Ommanney to pay…you the sum…you were so kind as to lend me in August 1841. It has been of the utmost accommodation to me for I really do not know what I would have done without it. This payment of theirs puts an end to a long and painful state of anxiety upon the subject of money matters, in which I have been involved ever since I last saw you, for what with disappointments as to remittances from Australia and with the unexpected Bills instead I have been scarcely able to get on.[60]

Stirling confided to his brother that his time on the *Indus* was fast drawing to a close, and there was no chance of 'turning the command to any account'. He regretted being apart from Ellen, who was now living with her mother at Brighton, and who 'grumbles much poor thing at the loneliness of living in the house with no one to speak to but young children'. Stirling was clearly concerned at what lay in store for his two eldest sons, both of whom he told John were with him in Piraeus. Andrew evidently had now rejoined the *Indus*, and 13-year-old Frederick Henry had joined as a 'young gentleman'. But, as he remarked to his brother, 'they have no sinecure of it for we are all, like our neighbours, very short of young officers, and we are obliged to bring the youngest into War'. He continued:

> I do not know that I have chosen wisely for them in allowing 2 to come into the Navy but in fact I have no choice for they must either take to that or go to Australia and they can go there when they grow up if they do not wish to stay where they are.

Being more 'flush of cash' was a relief, but having his land appeals rejected and some lands resumed was not. A fulminating Stirling now took the extraordinary step of writing a petition to the Queen. Signed on 3 March and enclosed in a letter to Lord Stanley of the same date,[61] it began by stating the circumstances of his initial grant and subsequent events, and continued:

> …the Governor of Your Majesty's Colony of Western Australia, has lately caused a Portion of the Grant aforesaid to revert to the Crown by which Your Majesty's Petitioner and others who had expended considerable sums on that property have been materially injured.
>   Your Majesty's Petitioner is advised that these proceedings are opposed to the fundamental Institutions of the Land, and to the invariable practice of Your Majesty's Government whose Proud and Glorious Distinction it hath ever been

to…respect the sound right of Private Property, and to secure for the Public Service, a just and generous recompense.

Your Petitioner is persuaded that such Severe Measures against an Old and Faithful Servant of the Crown, would not have been adopted, if the circumstances of this Case had been accurately understood.

Your Majesty's Petitioner therefore humbly prays that Your Majesty in your Goodness and Justice will be pleased to cause due inquiry to be made …in order that such Remedy may be applied as the Case may be found to deserve. And Your Majesty's Petitioner as in Duty Bound will ever Pray for the Safety, Honour and Welfare, of Your Majesty. James Stirling. Athens. March 3rd 1843.[62]

In sending his petition via Lord Stanley, Stirling must have been aware from his years of government administration that Stanley's advice would be sought and reference made to previous files. That he still hoped for a positive outcome shows a degree of naivety, a belief that constant repetition would eventually win. He was clearly wrong, for the reply on 30 March read: 'HM has not been advised to issue any directions on the subject to which the Petition refers'.[63]

Stirling's term as Senior Naval Officer at Piraeus having ended, the *Indus* finally weighed anchor and left the harbour on 21 April. Five days out she encountered a severe storm which split the main topsail and stripped away another, delaying her arrival in Valletta harbour until Tuesday 2 May. As one of the sailors had died of fever during the voyage, the whole ship was then quarantined for a week.[64] She was out and being refitted when the *Oriental* arrived with the latest English mail, including the news that Queen Victoria had been delivered of a princess, and that HRH the Duke of Sussex had died. In consequence, orders were given to the whole squadron to hoist the Royal Standard at noon on 13 May in honour of the birth, then to lower all flags to half mast and 'dishevell the rigging' in mourning for the Duke on the following day.

Stirling's new instructions were in lighter vein—to proceed with dispatches to Naples, and then to take part in the formalities associated with the departure of Princess Teresa (sister of King Ferdinand of Naples) for Brazil, where she was to marry the Emperor. The *Indus* joined a crowded Naples harbour on 3 June. There was an entire line of Neapolitan battleships, plus brigantines and frigates, as well as Brazilian frigates and a corvette, a visiting American warship and British ships. It was an occasion replete with protocol: the British Ambassador and Consul both visited the *Indus*, and Stirling was required to attend interviews and meetings onshore, including one with the King. Court dealings of this nature required subtlety and detailed knowledge of the complex Bourbon alliances, and family relatives. King Ferdinand was at that very time trying to negotiate the marriages of his younger brother to Isabella of Spain, and his sister Caroline to the Duc de Bordeaux,[65] and would have been pressing for information, so newcomers were interrogated closely. The Admiralty was also keen for news, especially about other countries' vessels, so Stirling compiled a detailed report on all foreign men-of-war he had encountered in Naples harbour before returning to Malta on 18 June.

The stay was short, for Owen had decided to send the *Indus* to relieve HMS *Formidable* at Gibraltar, to allow that ship to proceed to Lisbon. It was a posting beset with confusion. Stirling left Valletta harbour on 1 July, but between then and the *Indus*'s arrival in Gibraltar on the 21st, Owen had changed his mind, directing another ship to relieve the *Formidable*, and recalling the *Indus* to Malta. Unaware of these new instructions, Stirling began his duties as Senior Naval Officer. Hearing that anti-royalist rebel Spanish troops were being massed at Algeciras for a planned blockade of Cadiz harbour,[66] Stirling decided to take the *Indus* directly to Cadiz to show the flag. He sent a brief note to Owen, apprising him of this before leaving. *Indus* anchored in Cadiz harbour on 2 August, and together with some French men-of-war made a persuasive presence, certainly enough to diffuse the situation when, a week later, a steamer arrived bearing the rebel troops. Nevertheless, it seemed dangerous to leave Cadiz, and Stirling's command of Spanish was valuable in gaining information, so he remained until 14 August, then sailed back to Gibraltar where, a few days later, Owen's change of instructions turned up.

When the *Indus* arrived back in Malta on 3 September, Stirling faced a reprimand from Owen for having spent extra time at Cadiz and 'having left Gibraltar without leaving orders for ships arriving after'.[67] Stirling vehemently upheld his actions and expressed disappointment with Owen's stance, especially as he presented a detailed report of improvements that might be made to the anchorage at Gibraltar.[68] Amicable relations were restored by 13 September when Stirling attended a levee on the *Queen*, Owen's flagship, to mark the visit of the American Ambassador for China and the US Consul. Three days later the squadron was sent cruising for target practice, where to Stirling's surprise he met, while at sea, Captain Ommanney of the *Vesuvius* (son of the Admiral and nephew of his naval agent). Ommanney had actually been sent from Lyons in Athens with urgent dispatches for Owen, informing him that a revolution had taken place against the Government of Greece and requesting immediate assistance.[69]

From the flagship, a concerned Owen sent for Stirling and gave him instructions to proceed, in company with the *Vesuvius*, direct to Athens where he was to place himself at the disposal of Sir Edmund Lyons, and arrange for the protection of British subjects. Stirling returned to his ship and mid-morning on 24 September the *Indus* broke from the squadron to begin what was to be a memorable posting.

The popular uprising which King Otho II faced on 15 September 1843 stemmed chiefly from resentment over his personal extravagance and rising government debt. Otho had been only 17 when appointed to the throne in 1833, and his Bavarian ministers had indulged him, allowing him to pour money into a palace and a garden which took much of Athens' water supply.[70] The British had tried to nudge him into accepting constitutional government, but he opposed this, believing he had French, Austrian and Russian support. Far from providing financial aid, this triumvirate had, as recently as 5 July, joined England in demanding repayment of existing debt from Greece.[71] Events reached flashpoint when unpaid troops joined the resistance movement, sparking the revolution in Athens.

By the time Stirling reached Piraeus on 29 September, the situation had calmed down. A new Greek ministry had been formed and was working on a new constitution, which King Otho had promised to accept. There was still latent hostility to King Otho, however, as he had refused to see all diplomats at the height of the revolution and had behaved reprehensibly to some of his ministers. He was also threatening to reject the new constitution. Lyons was extremely worried and explained to Stirling and Sir Charles Sullivan of the *Formidable* (the two senior officers at the station) the delicate situation he faced in trying to persuade the King to accept change for his own good. Stirling lent the considerable charm he could call upon in such situations to assist the somewhat unpopular Lyons[72] in speaking to the King, and it was a relief to all when, on 19 October, King Otho addressed his ministers and embraced the formation of a new constitution. But there were still problems for the monarchy, as Stirling outlined in a report to Admiral Owen, for while one group wanted to carry the revolution further, another was attempting a counter-revolution. But the presence of three British warships (the *Formidable*, *Indus* and *Vesuvius*), known to stand for the King, provided a calming effect.

The new constitution was presented for the King's approval on 7 March 1844, but, when he sought to make changes, there was such opposition in the Assembly that it threatened to disband. Again, British persuasion, particularly from Stirling and Sullivan, not only won the King's acceptance of the document on 19 March, but also assisted in pacifying rival factions and their consular advisers. Not long after, the Admiralty was informed[73] that King Otho intended to bestow Greece's most distinguished honour, the Order of the Redeemer, on Stirling and Charles Sullivan, for their diplomacy in the crisis. (It was the second time Stirling had been thus acknowledged—towards the end of 1843 he learned that the King of Naples had presented him with a gold medal related to his mid-year diplomatic efforts.)[74] The Order of the Redeemer went to those who had rendered outstanding service to Greece, and came in five classes. That of Commander, which was formally awarded to Stirling and Sullivan, appears to have been exceeded only by the Grand Cross (generally reserved for Heads of State).[75] But the men were never allowed to display the award in public outside Greece. Existing regulations precluded British subjects from accepting foreign honours unless they resulted from 'active and distinguished Services before the Enemy at Sea, or in the Field'.[76]

The captains continued to assist with thorny negotiations between the King and his ministers over the issue of the succession to the throne (Otho had no children), and in helping to secure a loan to restore Greece's financial stability. Admiral Owen was keenly aware of the diplomatic success that Stirling had achieved, reporting that his influence had been invaluable in restoring 'cordial co-operation', and even telling Lyons that 'parting with the *Indus* may be prejudicial to the objects of our Government, or the Confidence of His Hellenic Majesty'.[77] However, a month later, at Owen's instruction, the *Indus* was recalled to Malta.[78]

Arriving back in harbour on 8 April, Stirling was given the welcome news that he was to prepare his ship for the homeward voyage. Six days later she left, carrying a number of invalids from Malta Hospital—wounded or ill sailors being repatriated, and many in poor shape for the voyage. In fact, two died in a matter of days— distressing for Stirling, as he had lost only four men throughout his entire *Indus* command. After a brief stop in Gibraltar to deliver dispatches, and another at Lisbon to take on water and provisions, the *Indus* set sail for England, reaching Plymouth Sound on 31 May. A little later a steam tug took *Indus* in tow up the Hamoaze where she was stripped, cleaned and finally paid off on 13 June 1844.[79] At last Stirling and his two boys were free to rejoin the family.

24

A Gentleman's Estate

WHEN STIRLING LEFT the *Indus*, Ellen and the rest of the family were still living at Brighton, where Ellen's mother had taken a house when her son's growing family had made Woodbridge too crowded. James' sisters had left Pirbright after Dorothea's death and were living with their brothers, Walter in Manchester and William in London. So when the excitement of reunion had subsided, Stirling moved his family to London, staying initially with William and Agnes at Upper Baker Street. By the end of June he was again pursuing his Western Australian affairs, but this time with more tact as a half-pay officer did not have the clout of the captain of one of Her Majesty's warships on diplomatic duties in the Mediterranean. He had contacted new lawyers, recommended either by Pollock or family connections, and on 27 June Messrs Baxendale, Tatham & Co. of Great Winchester Street addressed Lord Stanley on his behalf:

> …It is obvious that on constitutional grounds, a subject cannot maintain an Action against the Crown…But there can be no doubt that…under the direction of his Lordship the question might be raised as to admit of the decision through a Special Case submitted to one of HM's Courts of Law.[1]

And they asked for such a direction. But Lord Stanley and his advisers were not prepared to move, and said so in a brief reply on 8 July.[2] What Stirling's lawyers thought of this is unknown, but the Colonial Office was to be reminded of Stirling's claims just days later.

Daniel Scott, previously Harbour Master in the colony and a major shareholder in the Fremantle Whaling Company, had returned to England to clarify with the Colonial Office the company's claim to Stirling's Arthur's Head land. When Governor Hutt had been pressed by the Fremantle Whaling Company for title to their land in 1840, he had refused to recognise their right to it even when Scott pointed out that the company had outlayed a considerable sum (over £3,000) on the strength of the original assignment from Stirling.

Scott now detailed the grounds upon which Stirling had been given the grant, and how it related to his part in the formation of the colony, then continued:

> In 1840 Captain Stirling's agent applied to the Local Government for the deed…But it appears that the Deed was…refused, and it further appears…that the Governor [Hutt] had caused the record of assignment of the aforesaid portion of Sir James Stirling's Grant to be expunged from the Colonial Returns alleging that it was reverted to the Crown by order of the Secretary of State.
>
> By this act of confiscation Sir James Stirling and those who hold derivative interest in that portion of his land, have been deprived of their property…In this proceeding there is surely some mistake…the Secretary of State cannot have intended to authorize the resumption of that Grant with all the improvements upon it, for proceedings of this nature would tend to destroy all confidence in Colonial property, and to put an end to Colonial Enterprise.[3]

There is little doubt that Stirling had briefed Scott before this letter was written, as some phrases are similar to those he used in his own case. And by July Stirling was back in contact with the Friends of Western Australia, the association that the Mangles brothers had championed since the early 1830s, and which Scott had now joined. Enclosed with Scott's letter, as proof, was a copy of the Governor's resumption order.

Hutt had indeed had approval for his action. On 29 November 1839 Lord John Russell had approved withholding title to the Arthur's Head land on the grounds that

> Neither in this nor in any other case ought an alienation to be made of any land which there is sufficient cause to anticipate may be hereafter required for the security, health or general convenience of the Public at large.[4]

What was forgotten in this exchange is that Stirling himself had objected to selling this land to the company for the same reason, and that the land he had allowed the company to occupy was not on the actual point, but on the southern side, abutting the Round Gaol. This was patently clear in all the maps sent to the Colonial Office before Stirling's return.[5]

Scott's letter caused some consternation at the Colonial Office, and they appear to have sought legal advice before replying. A memorandum was written on 17 October which acknowledged that

> If…the Company or their representative wish to continue the occupation of the land, a small rent should of course be paid to the Crown as an acknowledgment of the title under which the property is held.[6]

The formal reply, offering the lease, was finally written on 2 November and included the following total misrepresentation:

When therefore Sir James Stirling sold 5½ acres of land to the Fremantle Whaling Company the Deed of Grant was very properly, as Lord Stanley conceives, refused by the Governor as it was considered that the land which commands the entrance to the River Swan and the Town and Roadstead of Fremantle would be required for works of defence.[7]

At no stage had Stirling 'sold' his Arthur's Head land. He had ceded one acre to the company at the beginning, and when the tunnel was constructed, had agreed to lease more of his and adjoining Crown land. Despite the error of fact, it had taken Colonial Office officials nearly four months to reach this decision. But the matter was far from closed.

While the Colonial Office were considering their answer, the Stirlings had returned to Brighton to escape the heat of London. But staying with his mother-in-law was not a long-term option, so Stirling began to look for a suitable residence. Either he had decided to take furlough, or had been told that another

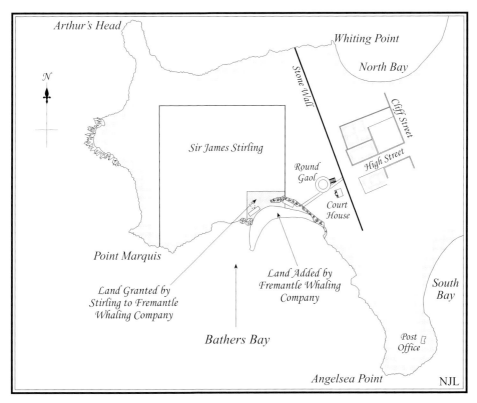

Land on Arthur's Head, granted to Stirling and sought by the
Fremantle Whaling Company, became a contentious issue when Colonial Office
bureaucrats endorsed its resumption

Redrawn from surveyor A. Hillman's 1838 map of Fremantle 19c

command would be some time coming, for he decided to look for an estate where he could supervise farming activities and live the life of a country gentleman. But he still wished to be near enough to the sea and his naval acquaintances to stay abreast of world affairs and the diplomatic intrigue he had grown to love. A naval colleague and fellow Scot, Sir Charles Napier, had recommended the Havant area where he had taken up residence in 1836,[8] and possibly alerted Stirling when the Belmont Estate, at Bedhampton, just outside Havant, became available for lease. The property had belonged to the trustees of Sir George Prevost (who had been Baronet of Belmont in 1805, a Governor of Lower Canada and Governor-General of British North America).[9] Sir George had died in 1816, leaving a widow and three children, the eldest only 11 years old. The estate had been managed by trustees and the family had continued to live there until early in 1844, when they decided to lease the property and live elsewhere.

When James and Ellen first saw the Belmont Estate, they were entranced. The large Georgian house was approached by a double carriage drive lined by elms. The surrounding finely timbered 30-acre park was similar to Henley Park, and the total estate included two working farms with all associated outbuildings and cottages. At the peak of the gently rising land, on the eastern edge of Portsdown, a 'Belvedere' or tower summerhouse had been built around 1789 to take advantage of the view of

The late Georgian Belmont House, not far from Portsmouth,
where the Stirlings lived for sixteen years

From P. Rogers, The Borough of Havant in Old Picture Postcards the land and sea. It was so visible that it had been used as a trigonometrical station by the Ordnance Survey of 1794, and as a landmark for navigation,[10] and as such might have already been known to Stirling. Negotiations to accept the lease must have occurred some time in August 1844, for James mentions taking it in a letter written to his brother John early in September. It was just a short note, and implies either that John knew the property, or that Stirling had previously spoken about it at length. The letter read:

> My dear John…Our late losses in London…make me rather low spirited…We have taken Belmont for 3 years…Ever most affectly yrs Js Stirling.[11]

The 'late losses in London' probably refer to the textile trading business that William was still running from Bow Church Yard, which had been hit hard by a trade downturn. This same slump was blamed for the depression experienced by all the Australian colonies during the 1840s. Western Australia had been somewhat protected by a surge of immigration and funds associated partly with the Australind venture, but also with schemes sponsored by the local government and the Agricultural Society. But when those inflows ceased mid-1843, the colony too felt the impact of falling export markets.

News of the colony's predicament reached London at the end of September 1844 and, after several anxious discussions, the Friends of Western Australia decided to act. A meeting was convened which Stirling attended with his Mangles brothers-in-law. With William Hutt in the chair, it was decided to petition the Colonial Office for help. Signed on 12 December 1844 by seven individuals, including Stirling and the Mangles, the petition summarised the plight of the colony, stating that in the space of a few months it had 'passed from a state of prosperity, to one of extensive and severe distress'. Its position, they argued, was readily explainable:

> the Colony has now arrived at a point when the supply nearly equals the demand, but from the scarcity and consequently high rate of labour in Western Australia, as compared with the neighbouring colonies, we are unable to compete with them in agricultural operations…Henceforward, we must look for prosperity in the growth of wool and tallow, and other exportable articles such as timber, bark &c, and of these we do not doubt the territory is calculated to afford a large supply, but in the present crisis, the great and urgent want of the Colony is an annual addition to its labouring classes.

And this the petitioners wished to address. They knew that in other colonies proceeds from the sale of Crown land were being used by the Emigration Commission to supply them with labour, but Western Australia had no such funds to apply. They therefore asked whether the Emigration Commission would use funds raised by subscription among themselves for the conveyance of labour to the colony, ending:

> But as we cannot afford to make the advance without a prospect and assurance of remuneration, we propose that the Colonial Revenue of the Crown be made chargeable with an annual payment in liquidation of this loan…[12]

They believed that their scheme 'would be the means of increasing the general public income of the Settlement beyond the amount required for the liquidation of the loan'. And in the circumstances the colony then faced, they were probably right, but the Colonial Office was totally unsympathetic. None of the Under-Secretaries through whose hands it passed was prepared to recommend it. The official reply on 30 December stated categorically that

> the scheme of raising money for emigration on the security of a Revenue which is deficient, is open to such conclusive objections that his Lordship must decline on the part of HMG sanctioning such an arrangement.[13]

Before this answer was received Stirling had returned to Belmont where Ellen, five months pregnant with their last child, had settled into quiet village life. Bedhampton, near the northern shore of Langston Harbour, had a population of not much more than 500, and 'several neat and pleasant mansions and scattered farm houses commanding picturesque views of land and water'.[14] The woodlands area, called Bedhampton Park, was once part of Beve Forest. The manor house was 'an old brick mansion near the church where there is said to have been a nunnery', evident from some monastic remains in one of the boundary walls where a passage supposedly led into the church. A number of retired naval captains lived around Havant, and one was residing in Bidbury House, a small mansion opposite Bedhampton's church, St Thomas, which stood on medieval remains. Social life probably revolved around the church, and Ellen would have got to know the Snooks, owners of the mill at the bottom of the village who had rented a small turreted building on the edge of Belmont estate, just before the Stirlings arrived.

As the year 1844 drew to a close and pregnancy circumscribed outings, Ellen would have rejoiced in the spaciousness of her new home. Belmont effectively comprised three stories with a large entry hall, drawing room, dining room, library and conservatory at ground level, a wide staircase to the first floor which contained six bedrooms, while above this again was a nursery and three servants bedrooms.[15] It is likely that various family members and friends visited over the New Year period, some staying for Stirling's 54th birthday on 28 January 1845. Mary Mangles was certainly a visitor, for she was present at the birth of Ellen's fifth daughter on 7 April. The child was christened Georgina Janet Stirling at St Thomas' Church on 27 May. This completed the family.

James and Ellen Stirling

m 1824

Andrew	Frederick Henry	William	Mary	Charles	Agnes
b 1824	b 1829	b 1831	b 1832	b 1834	b 1835
		d 1831			

Walter	Ellinor	Anna Hamilton	Dorothea	Georgina
b 1837	b 1838	b 1840	b 1842	b 1845

Georgina's christening should have been a joyful affair, but the spirits of the whole family were crushed by the news that Andrew, their nephew and cousin, had died at Swan River. James was the first to hear, and on 1 May he wrote to his older brother Walter in Manchester:

> My Dear Walter, It is with the deepest sorrow that I now forward to you the enclosed letter from Swan River. It tells its own very distressed Tale in better words than I can put it in, and so I send it with one for John which I presume is from Mr Samson, and as these are probably the only accounts from the Colony, it will be for you to relate their contents to John and Elizabeth for both of whom I feel most deeply. Perhaps it may be necessary to explain that Mr Samuel Moore the writer of the letter to me is my Agent…It seems but a very short time since poor Andrew was a child in petticoats on his Grandmother's knee at Henley. His Race has been soon accomplished and may the Blessing of God be with him…'[16]

In the colony, Andrew's death had been reported in the *Perth Gazette* as follows:

> DIED. On Wednesday the 6th instant, at the residence of Mrs Boyd,[17] Guildford, Andrew Stirling Esq. Eldest son of John Stirling Esq. of St Andrew's Fifeshire, in the 26th year of his age, deeply lamented by a numerous circle of friends and acquaintances.[18]

The editorial recounted Andrew's role as James' Private Secretary between 1834 and 1839, 'which office he held with much credit', and his return in 1840 to look after Stirling's flocks at Leschenault. It described how

> He there met with a serious accident, to which may be attributed the serious illness which prematurely closed his mortal career. His remains were interred yesterday at Guildford, followed by the most respectable inhabitants of the Colony, and many of his most immediate friends. The coffin was carried to the grave by the sons of the oldest tenant of Sir James Stirling.[19]

The official cause of Andrew's death was 'icterus or jaundice',[20] but how he acquired the illness after the accident (a fall from a horse) is a matter for conjecture.[21] Andrew's closest friend in the colony had been George Elliot (a family connection), and Stirling urged his brother to deal with him when winding up Andrew's affairs, 'as he is strictly honest and knows more of the state of things than anyone else'. He concluded:

> Having thus disposed of business, permit me my Dear John, to say to yourself and Elizabeth how deeply I participate with you in this great affliction, nor am I alone in this for Andrew was for years to Ellen and myself as one of our own children, and no one ever possessed a more amicable or more honest heart. God Bless and comfort you…Your ever affectionate Brother Js Stirling.[22]

By the end of May Stirling was back in London to see his solicitors, who had been pursuing his claims with the Colonial Office. On 14 January the lawyers had sent a letter arguing against the grounds given for refusing to reopen the case.[23] The Colonial Office reply on 31 January was of course negative, but phrased with care. Essentially they could 'not assent to the correctness of your summary', i.e. the case put by the solicitors, and argued:

> His Lordship has not refused 'to permit the Case of Sir James Stirling to go before a Court of Law'…If Sir James Stirling has no such right of action, there is nothing in his case, which in Lord Stanley's judgement, imposes on the Executive Government the duty of affording him facilities for litigation which the law has not given.[24]

It was bureaucracy at its obfuscating best. On the very same day, no doubt having heard about the Colonial Office's reaction, James wrote unofficially, from the United Services Club, to his old sparring partner, Under-Secretary James Stephen:

> Acquainted as you are with all the circumstances of my case you will readily believe me when I say that matters over which I scarcely have control, will shortly lead me before a Court of Law and possibly before the Legislature upon the subject of my lands in Western Australia.
>
> I confess Sir that I entertain the greatest repugnance to any exhibition of the kind, for although I feel the fullest confidence in the eventual assertion of my right, I know that I should have to take it by measures painful to myself as well as to others.
>
> Prompted therefore by these sentiments, I venture to ask if there be no way short of an appearance before the Public by which my Case may be adjusted? If you think that such a way exists perhaps you will allow me to see you, when I bring this note. If not I feel at all events that I shall have done my duty in asking you this question.[25]

Stephen made a note on the file on 1 February:

> I answ'd this letter by a message to the effect that it wd rest with you [Lord
> Stanley] and not with me to receive him if you shd think it right to do so. On
> receiving that message I understand he went away. I presume that this should be
> put by? JS.[26]

A few days later the Colonial Office received a letter from another
representative of the Fremantle Whaling Company, again demanding clarification
of Stirling's right to the Arthur's Head land so that they could obtain title to their
own holding.[27] The writer, Alfred Waylen, was a major shareholder and said so, but
Lord Stanley refused to 'enter into a correspondence & explanations with separate
& individual members of that body on the subject'.[28] This infuriated Waylen, who
took the matter to Stirling. On 21 February Waylen wrote again to the Colonial
Office enclosing a letter from the ex-Governor himself. The enclosure contained a
repetition of the original grant conditions, the land selected and exchanges made.
Stirling's letter continued:

> …the Government of Western Australia in 1842 addressed a letter to the Surveyor
> General, commanding him to falsify the Colonial Returns by leaving out of them
> the Record of the original assignment to Sir James Stirling of the 5½ acres of land
> on Arthur's Head, the same (as the Governor alleged, having reverted to the
> Crown, by order of the Secretary of State)…It appears that on the 19th of July last
> a member of the Fremantle Company addressed…Lord Stanley complaining of
> this invasion of their property, and in November Mr Stephen acknowledged
> receipt of that complaint. But Mr Stephen's letter is not an answer to—but an
> evasion of—the question that was submitted. It is sufficient to observe that his
> account and mine are opposed to each other in several important matters of
> fact…and wherever they differ Mr Stephen's statements are contrary to fact and
> evidence, and this assertion, I hold myself in readiness to prove.[29]

On 28 February the Colonial Office again replied that they could not address the
matter with Waylen unless he was an authorised representative of the Company.[30]
When they received this assurance on 5 March, they simply referred the whole
matter to the Land and Emigration Commissioners, advising Waylen of this move.[31]
In the meantime, Stirling had taken the issue to his own solicitors. It provided just
the ammunition they needed. On 10 March Baxendale, Tatham & Co. addressed
the Colonial Office, stating that Sir James had received a 'grievous injury'.[32] They
restated the contradiction between the Colonial Office's current view and those of
Viscount Goderich, Hay and Twiss, then added that Stirling had instructed them to
raise an 'additional case of wrong inflicted on him', namely the resumption of land
at Arthur's Head:

The result is that although Sir James Stirling was in possession of the 5½ acres of land on Arthur's Head under the Crown's assignment, yet that the Colonial Department have deprived him of it.[33]

But to the Colonial Office this was just a new twist to an old tale. The letter was annotated on 12 March, 'I rely confidentially on the various facts stated in the precis of the 25th Jany last to prove that no injustice has been done…JS'.[34]

By 17 March Waylen had received the peremptory reply from the Colonial Office and was fuming, as probably was Stirling. Waylen's response, written that same day, reveals his state of mind, though it is ambiguous as his use of the plural could be taken either as himself and the company, or himself and Stirling.

Your Lordship has thought fit to quench our title to a certain property by which we have sustained a great amount of injury and loss. We have neither claims to be considered of, nor business to be settled by the Land and Emigration Commissioners, nor have we any intention to submit our case to their Determination.

   We look to your Lordship as the party by whom we have been deprived of our said property in an arbitrary and illegal manner, and if your Lordship will not grant us compensation for that wrong, our only appeal is to the Legislature by Petition.[35]

It elicited a stiff reply on 27 March.

His Lordship will direct the Colonial Land & Emigration Commissioners to investigate and report on the claims of the parties on whose behalf you write, without awaiting further communication from you…and, when in possession of their Report, his Lordship will convey to you his final decision on the question.[36]

Over the following months there must have been many meetings between Stirling, Waylen and the lawyers at Great Winchester Street. It would have been an expensive exercise, for additional legal advice was sought, as Baxendale & Tatham's next letter to the Colonial Office, dated 21 May, made clear. They stated they had submitted the case and all pertinent documents to the eminent lawyer, Mr John Leyster Adolphus, who had agreed that Sir James had been done an injustice. His view was enclosed with their letter, and they hoped its perusal would persuade Lord Stanley to 'submit the case to the Law Officers of the Crown for further consideration'.[37] But Lord Stanley found nothing in it 'to call for an alteration of the decision already intimated to Sir James Stirling', and so informed Baxendale & Tatham on 31 May.[38]

In the meantime, the contentious matter of the Arthur's Head land resumption had been directed to the Land and Emigration commissioners for review.

Their report of 4 June to the Colonial Office was lengthy, but contained a concluding summary that did not further Stirling's cause:

> We think it more becoming our position to leave it for the Secretary of State to decide, whether in appropriating to himself apparently the most important spot in the whole colony for its military defence, Sir James Stirling has so far infringed his duty as Governor that he has no right to the confirmation of that choice by a deed of grant from the Crown…Nevertheless…we think that as the ground is not at present required by the Government, and as the Company have invested money in buildings upon it, it may still be fitting to allow them as an indulgence…a continued occupation of this site, upon lease, subject to resumption if wanted… for works of defence.[39]

Colonial Office staff were more than pleased with this report, Stephen's annotation reading:

> He selected a large tract, and in that tract, the most important military situation in the whole colony. He reported his selection but totally concealed this circumstance. If he had been nothing more than a private Settler, I think that this condition and this concealment wd have been fatal to his claim. But he was also the Governor and had positive Instructions to alienate no land required for the purpose of public utility. Therefore he had no right to make this grant to any other person. Still less had he the right to take it for himself and to conceal from the Govt. the peculiar character & importance of what he so took. 5 June JS.[40]

The fact that Stirling's Arthur's Head grant had been clearly marked on every map sent back to the Colonial Office during his regime, and had never before caused comment, was completely ignored.

The Commissioners' views were conveyed to Waylen on 12 June and no doubt transmitted to Stirling soon afterwards. Rail had made an enormous difference to the ease with which people, and mail, could travel between London and Portsmouth, and the link to Havant had been completed in 1842. Belmont Estate was only a mile or so from Havant Station, so Stirling was able to go fairly regularly to London, where he had a convenient base in the United Services Club. Another frequent guest at that club was Peter Augustus Latour, who was still warring with the Colonial Office over his Swan River land claims. From the club on 12 August Latour had written an impassioned letter to the Colonial Office defending his position and requesting another hearing from the Law Officers of the Crown, as he was totally confident 'of the justice of my claim in law and equity'.[41] But he too was told on 21 August that Lord Stanley saw 'no reason for altering the decision already communicated to you on your claim'.[42] One can see the rising irritation of Lord Stanley and his Under-Secretaries as so much correspondence and time was taken up by the insignificant colony of Western Australia—and summer heat would not have improved matters.

Recognising temporary defeat, Stirling returned to Belmont where his eldest sons were learning the ropes of practical farming. Young Frederick Henry was still a long way from qualifying for a naval position, whilst Midshipman Andrew, whose health was not strong, had declared his unwillingness to return to sea. The family was growing up; the eldest daughter Mary was now 13, and Stirling was not unmindful that his own mother Anne had married at 14. Mary's sisters, Agnes aged 10, Ellinor 7, Anna 5, Dorothea 3 and the baby Georgina could be looked after at home by a nurse and governess, but the other two boys, Charles, now 11, and Walter, 8, were almost beyond the nursery schoolroom. Belmont suited them all, and riding around the property, Stirling could see its potential. Just when he decided to try to buy it is unknown—but it was probably some time in the second half of 1845. Such a purchase would be costly, however, so it meant a hard look at finances, which once again brought him back to the question of his assets in Western Australia. But the cloud over his name raised by the Land and Emigration Commissioners' verdict over Arthur's Head had to be removed first. Accordingly, on 13 December 1845 Stirling wrote directly to Lord Stanley, outlining the case and stating:

> The effect of this decision and of the imputations thus made public…is to destroy the reputation of a public servant, and to deprive him of a piece of land which has been for years in his possession…neither in the instance of the land in question, nor in any other instance, have I merited your Lordship's imputations on my conduct as having been 'inconsistent with the Royal Instructions under which I was acting, and with the obligations and duties incumbent on me as Governor of Western Australia'.[43]

It was not a humble letter, and when asked whether it required a reply, Lord Stanley responded, 'I think not'.[44]

The end-of-year family gatherings were important for Stirling, as they gave him the opportunity to discuss his plans to purchase the Belmont Estate with his brothers and brothers-in-law. It was up for sale for just on £10,000, but this was more than he had hoped to spend. In all likelihood, Stirling had received another return from the WA Company—a sound basis for such a purchase—but no actual records of a payment at this time have been found. Nevertheless, official letters indicate that, before leaving office in 1845, Governor Hutt had cleared the reselection of lands that overlapped Latour's grant.[45] Stirling had thought that the company would be able to select the 61,284 acres elsewhere in the colony on good land, but the Surveyor-General, on advice from London, had only allowed it to choose land adjoining Location 1, which had been transferred from Latour. Location 1 had contained all but 12,800 acres of Stirling's overlapping Locations, and in the reassignment this 12,800 acres was returned to Stirling as Location 50A. The company selected as replacements 7,700 acres in Location 48, 13,000 acres in Location 51, and 15,000 acres in Location 56 (see map 'Compensating Grants' on page 401). So by 1845 they had claimed 35,700 acres of Stirling's land.[46] At the originally negotiated price, they thus owed him a total £6,604—of which £1,578 had already been paid.[47] Under the initial agreement £8,592 had been due in June 1844, but this would have been delayed while the reassignment took place in the colony. As the company had been unable to obtain the full amount of land they had negotiated from Stirling, and were already in financial trouble, they would not have paid the full sum, but might have paid a couple of thousand pounds. In the event, Stirling never received the full amount he was owed, for the company went bankrupt in June 1846.[48] If part of the money Stirling paid for Belmont came from the WA Company and his savings, the remainder was borrowed from the Mangles brothers on the security of some of his Western Australian lands.

On 23 April 1846 James Stirling completed the purchase of Belmont House and Estate from the trustees of Sir George Prevost for the sum of £9,750.[49] Three months later, on 25 July, he took out a £4,000 mortgage on Belmont from Messrs William King and Joseph Blunt, whom the Mangles brothers used in business affairs.[50] Part of this money was needed to finance the improvements on his Western Australian lands, which to date had been handled by both his own and the Mangles' agents. The rest went into the estate, as tithe maps show considerable improvements. The purchase of Belmont meant a lot to Stirling, who appears to have remained there for most of the year, paying occasional visits to his brothers in St Andrews and Manchester, and certainly visiting London.

In February 1846 there was a little excitement, for the prestigious *Illustrated London News* published a picture of St Mary's Church in Busselton with an article stating that part of the £300 it had cost to build had been raised by Lady Stirling and her friends in London.[51] Publicity of this nature was a godsend for the growing colony, and numerous copies of the journal were purchased to ship out to friends. From their connections Stirling would also have heard that Latour had made no headway with W. E. Gladstone when Secretary of State for Colonies, or with his successor, Earl Grey, who took over in July 1846.[52] There had been much talk of the change in Government, for Sir Robert Peel had resigned as Prime Minister in June 1846 and been replaced by Lord John Russell, who then had to face elections the following year. Ellen's brother, Ross Donnelly Mangles, was keenly looking forward to this 1847 election, as he intended contesting his father's old seat as Liberal member for Guildford.

One subject Stirling appears to have discussed with his brothers-in-law and various members of his family and political acquaintances during 1846 was the Navigation Laws and their impact on trade and shipping. These laws were regarded by some as a last bastion against free trade, but many British ship owners feared that complete removal would result in fierce competition that would undermine their

Funds raised by Lady Stirling and her London circle helped construction of St Mary's
Church, Busselton, pictured in the *Illustrated London News* on 21 February 1846

prosperity.[53] The large Mangles family held divergent views. Charles and Frederick,
as ship owners, were wary of a change in the laws, but Ross Donnelly was right
behind his party's drive for reform. Another Select Committee had been called by
Parliament to investigate the operation and effectiveness of the laws, and at some
time during the second half of 1846, James Stirling's name was put forward as a
useful witness. The increasing use of steam power, and its transformation of the
speed of communication, had raised new challenges for the working of the
Navigation Laws and also had huge implications for naval administration—both in
terms of defence planning and manpower requirements. As he was so near
Portsmouth, James was able to discuss such matters with his fellow naval officers
and so keep abreast of developments.

Hitherto steamers had been used by the navy mainly for towing the sailing
ships-of-the-line in and out of harbour and for coastal work, such as the rapid
delivery of dispatches. Having worked with them in the Mediterranean, Stirling
conceded they were of enormous assistance in this regard, but he firmly believed
they could never replace large sailing ships in actual warfare. In this respect, his
views matched those of his mentor, Admiral Sir George Cockburn, who was just
coming to end of his five-year term as First Lord of the Admiralty. Cockburn had
overseen a 48 per cent increase in the number of paddle steamers employed by the
navy,[54] but he was concerned that, as there had been no real armed conflict since
they had been adopted, their role under fire was untested.

By now, Stirling was one of the few active senior naval officers who had experienced close combat. Many of his peers in roughly the same age group had not served afloat for fifteen years or more, and were unfamiliar with technological developments. Some had been taken off the active list under a new retirement scheme introduced in 1845 following a campaign by Stirling's friend, Sir Charles Napier MP;[55] others were still on half-pay, waiting until seniority brought them Rear Admiral status before retiring. Even line-of-battle plans and other strategies which had triumphed in the Napoleonic Wars a quarter of a century earlier had not been revised.

This changed with Lord Palmerston's return to government under Russell in July 1846, for, as Foreign Secretary, he brought back an emphasis on 'gunboat diplomacy'. He was wary of a French invasion, frequently stating that 'steam power permitted a steam bridge to be constructed across the Channel capable of landing 30,000 troops overnight'.[56] Believing that Britain was currently incapable of repelling such a force, he advocated a major increase in defence spending.[57] Not only did he want more ships with the latest technology, he was also very concerned about manning. Raising crews at short notice was difficult because there was no system of reserves. As a result, impressment or some form of compulsion was the only way that warships could be manned in less than two or three months.[58]

With this same problem in mind, the Admiralty had decided in 1845 to form a 'Squadron of Evolution', intended to train officers and men, test the merits of new ships and provide a genuine reserve force for home waters. Command of the Evolutionary Squadron was first given to the veteran Sir William Parker, then Mediterranean Commander-in-Chief, who began exercising the sailing fleet in line-of-battle routines, signalling and gunnery around mid-1846.[59] In Parliament Sir Charles Napier argued forcefully that the squadron was being misdirected, for it should be concentrating on the interplay between steam and sail under battle conditions. By November 1846, when he was promoted to Rear Admiral, Napier had left Parliament, but his advice continued to be sought by the Admiralty, which was in limbo after the resignation of Cockburn in July.[60]

As yet Stirling had no compelling desire to return to active command, for he was busy building up his stable of stud horses and attending to the beautification of Belmont. But his naval career was still important, and he would have watched for opportunities of advancement. Like Napier and Cockburn, he was also concerned about the poor state of readiness of the navy if anything should threaten the peace, and he appears to have discussed this with Napier towards the end of 1846. At that time the balance of power had been disturbed by an alliance between France and Spain through a royal marriage[61] which contravened an earlier undertaking to Great Britain.[62] Anglo-French relations had reached a new low and strengthening the navy appeared imperative. Called to the Admiralty in the New Year, Napier pushed home the point that other nations, particularly France, were using steamers in an active role in naval defence, and he strongly advised revamping the Evolutionary Squadron to include more steam ships and experiment in their effective defence use. His arguments were persuasive, and the Admiralty not only agreed but also offered him command of the combined squadron.[63] It would seem that Napier immediately suggested Stirling as his second-in-command, for on 28 April 1847 James was formally offered command of the 120-gun HMS *Howe*[64] in the Evolutionary Squadron. The first-rated *Howe* was larger than any ship Stirling had yet commanded, and one he knew well, as it had been Vice Admiral Owen's flagship in the Mediterranean. It was an exciting commission, and he accepted with pleasure.

On 4 May 1847 Stirling was at Sheerness to officially take command of the *Howe* and bring her into commission,[65] for she had been lying stripped of all rigging since her last voyage. At 205 ft long and 56 ft wide, she would team well with Napier's flagship, the *St Vincent 120* (205 ft × 54 ft), which was commissioned about the same time. The following weeks were hectic as the *Howe* was fitted and rigged, officers and crew joined, marines from Chatham and Woolwich were mustered, and provisions and water stowed, the whole process made more difficult by squally weather and strong tides. Stirling left supervision of these activities to others, as he was called at last to give evidence at the Parliamentary Select Committee of Enquiry into the Navigation Laws.

The Navigation Acts had protected British merchant shipping rights since 1651, but amendments and alterations over the years had made them increasingly unworkable. A Royal Commission in 1844 had upheld their continued use, but a groundswell of *laissez-faire* thinking had increased opposition and led to this second inquiry in 1847. There would be yet another Royal Commission before their eventual repeal in 1850, but the 1847 report was to be important in paving the way.

Stirling was the second witness of eight called before a twelve-member committee chaired by the Hon. Thomas Milner Gibson, MP for Manchester and an active reformist.[66] It was an impressive and powerful group, including seven former or standing MPs, former Admiralty Lords, Major Generals and other senior public servants.[67] Stirling was introduced as a Post Captain in the Royal Navy who had been in command of several ships of war, and as a past Colonial Governor. His evidence was lengthy,[68] and took up the whole of 13 May. He had thoroughly researched likely questions and had facts at his fingertips to support very definite views. Clearly a firm believer in Adam Smith's doctrines, and the virtues of free trade, he was strongly in favour of reforming the laws, stating that in his opinion they were of no benefit to shipowners, to the navy and to seamen generally.

One argument he forwarded, on the basis of his experience in Australia, was that the Navigation Laws and the Shipping Registration Act together had brought about the demise of the British whaling industry. He pointed out that as three American ships could be fitted out for the same price as two English ones, the former could undercut the latter and so 'drive us out of that fishery entirely'. The Navigation Acts had contributed to this cost differential, and

The political consequences I conceive are serious; the Americans have a standing naval army of 10,000 men employed in their whaling ships, ready for war, while the number of Englishmen is not more than a fourth part of that…

This struck a chord with Admiralty representatives, who believed that the merchant (and fishing) fleets constituted 'a nursery for seamen for the Royal Navy'. Stirling was closely quizzed on the movement of seamen between naval and merchant service, as it was thought that naval men who had been laid off at the end of their ship's commissions could seek work on merchant or fishing vessels until needed again in the navy.[69] Stirling argued that this was not common practice, and that for merchant seamen 'our wages are too low; and other circumstances [such as discipline] are opposed to them entering the navy'. Furthermore, of those entering the merchant service for the first time, 'one half desert from their first ship; consequently we are not very anxious to obtain men of that description'.

When told that the inability to rely on men from the merchant service meant that the navy could only add to its force by impressment, the committee was most concerned, especially when Stirling said that warships sometimes took five or six months to complete their complement. But he offered a solution: instead of the present system of an annual vote for naval funds (resulting in a constantly fluctuating number of seamen), a permanent peacetime establishment of about 4,000 trained and able seamen could quickly train others in the event of war, leaving the two services independent of one another to Britain's advantage. This suggestion (which was eventually adopted with the establishment of the Naval College at Greenwich in 1873) Stirling believed could be achieved without undue expense by reducing the disproportionately high number of officers currently on the navy lists. Of the total naval establishment in 1846 amounting to 44,476 men, he pointed out that 15,548 were officers and 4,476 of them on half-pay reserve (despite the new retirement scheme).

Asked whether the American naval service was more popular than the British, Stirling replied:

In American ships the seamen obtain much higher wages; but I believe except on that one point, Englishmen do not like the American service so well as their own; they are not treated with the same consideration and justice, as I am given to understand, and though many go there I believe a large proportion return…I do not think that seamen are more mercenary than their fellow subjects; but I believe that with very few exceptions the world at large is influenced by motives of self interest…

This led a committee member to ask Stirling whether he thought that raising the wages of sailors in the British Navy would increase supply. Stirling demurred—any increase in naval pay rates would simply result in 'a leap-frogging'[70] between the navy and the merchant service.

Asked whether the introduction of steam navigation had made the navy less reliant on merchant seamen, Stirling pointed out that 'a very great change had taken place', one that minimised the advantages of going into action 'with mere seamen'. Now it had to be with men who comprehended the use of guns; '…we do not, therefore, require the same proportion of seamen to man our ships as we did formerly…provided we have landsmen and sufficient time to train them to the use of the guns'. Stirling was well aware of the new shell-firing guns that had been mounted on naval warships since 1841, as the *Indus* had been so equipped. They had less range than the old cannon-fired shot, yet were far more powerful and current work to extend their range held promise.[71]

He knew that the new shell technology made wooden sailing ships more vulnerable than before, and that attempts to provide protection with iron cladding had so far been relatively unsuccessful. Since 1845, however, there had been a programme of purpose-built iron frigates and paddle steamers, as well as some of the new screw propeller steamers, and there were now 1,642 stokers in the navy to reflect the rapidly increasing importance of steam. Stirling agreed with the suggestion that steam navigation would 'still more extend itself and become used for naval warfare'. But he could not see them totally replacing the sailing men-of-war, though he stressed that practices on those ships would have to change—just as would the law.

It had been a long, gruelling day, but overall Stirling could feel that he had played a part in the eventual abolition of the Navigation Laws.[72] Now a new challenge awaited him.

25

Fourth Command: HMS *Howe*

1847–1850

AFTER A FEW days home with his family, James received news that the *Howe* was ready, and on 25 May 1847 he moved on board. She was a magnificent ship, a three-decker with a builder's measure (BM) of 2,629.[1] The full ship's company of the 120-gun *Howe*, of over 800 men, was larger than the entire population of Perth when Stirling had left. But on the *Howe* his word was law. The day after he joined the ship, it was inspected by the Vice Admiral of Sheerness, Sir Edward King, and declared ready to join the rest of the Evolutionary Squadron at Portsmouth. Towed by the HMSV *Terrible*, the *Howe* left Sheerness the following day and arrived at Spithead at 5 a.m. on 28 May, in time to salute the Commander of the Port and anchor near the *St Vincent*.[2]

Napier had taken command of the *St Vincent 120* and hoisted his flag on 20 May. His squadron consisted of the *Howe 120*, *Caledonia 120*, *Queen 110* and *Vengeance 84* and three wooden paddle steamers, the *Vixen*, *Stromboli* and *Avenger*. All told it commanded 590 guns and a total complement of just over 5,000 men.[3] Over the next few days there was much saluting as the squadron assembled and commanders boarded their ships, and even more when HRH Queen Victoria and Prince Albert passed to and fro on the Royal Steam Yacht *Fairy* between Osborne House and the mainland. The royal couple even paid a visit to the *St Vincent* on 27 July, passing through a flag-emblazoned squadron on the way, the ships fully manned on yards and decks by a scrubbed and polished crew. Less than an hour after their departure the squadron proceeded to take up battle lines, the *St Vincent* and *Vengeance* on the starboard line, the *Howe* and the *Queen* on the port side, followed by the trio of paddle steamers. Orders had been given to sail in company to Plymouth from where, Napier told his squadron commanders, they would head for Lisbon, keeping strictly to the line-of-battle sequence.

On 1 August 1847 the squadron left the Sound, the steamers towing the rated ships, which then fell into pre-arranged lines following Napier's lead. This became difficult for Stirling, as the faster *Howe* had to shorten sail and tack to keep station, so at 2.45 p.m. he called for a boat to take him to the *St Vincent*. The subsequent

The triple-decked HMS *Howe*, the biggest ship of Stirling's commands, pictured off Sheerness

Courtesy National Maritime Museum, Greenwich PAF 8023

interview with Napier must have been successful, for although the squadron kept 'generally together', the *Howe* was at times some 30 miles ahead.[4] En route, Napier received instructions by steamer that he was to take command at Lisbon. Stirling was called aboard the *St Vincent* and told of this the following day. When the squadron entered the broad waters of the Tagus River on 21 August, they presented an impressive sight as the large sailing ships were towed upriver in two columns, one headed by *St Vincent* and the other by the *Howe*, to anchor off Lisbon in order of sailing.[5]

Already there were six other British naval ships, plus three French and three Spanish ships of war and a Portuguese flagship. The customary salutes were given and the next five days given over to official visits. As Stirling had met King Fernando and the British Consul on his previous visit to Lisbon, he would have been included in the formalities and no doubt played his part in the diplomatic niceties. Before long the squadron was enlarged by the addition of one extra ship-of-the-line, the *Canopus* and three more paddle-steamers, the *Dragon*, *Sidon* and *Odin*. As Napier was anxious to begin exercises, the ships all weighed anchor on 10 September and left the Tagus, the sailing ships under tow by the steamers. But the Admiral must have received a last-minute dispatch before leaving, for he signalled the *Howe* for Stirling to come aboard and told him that he was to return immediately to Spithead on special duty.[6] Back on the *Howe*, Stirling arranged for the marines on board to be transferred to other ships in the squadron, informed his officers of the change in plan, and parted from the group at 3 p.m. on 11 September.

Without the need to keep in line, the *Howe* fairly flew on the homeward journey, reaching Spithead in just eight days (compared to the twenty-day outward journey). Stirling's new instructions were to conduct Her Majesty the Queen Dowager (Queen Adelaide, Victoria's aunt) on a visit to Portugal. She had not been well, and on medical advice was to holiday in a warmer climate, and the Portuguese island of Madeira, off the coast of North Africa, was deemed a safe destination. Some refitting of the *Howe* was required to meet royal needs, and on 1 October the Queen Dowager paid a short visit and pronounced herself satisfied. In the following week the royal baggage, and that of attendants, was taken on board and arrangements made for the official reception.

Shortly after lunch on 9 October, a 21-gun salute welcomed the Queen Dowager as the *Fairy* brought her out of the harbour to board the *Howe*, while the crew manned the yards and officers stood stiffly to attention. The Royal Standard was displayed at the main and the royal guest made comfortable. But the southerlies were so strong that the smaller steamers entrusted with towing the *Howe* out were likely to have been battered to pieces, so she was held back at Spithead for two nights before getting under way.[7]

Throughout the voyage Stirling was strict with his men, insisting on privacy for their royal passenger, whose health improved with daily walks on deck. They entered the River Tagus on 22 October, passing through Napier's squadron and firing the royal salute before casting anchor just off Belem Castle. In accordance with protocol, Napier boarded promptly to pay his respects, followed two hours later by the King of Portugal with his suite, including the two princes.

The five-day visit passed with a mixture of formal and informal occasions. The day after arrival all squadron captains were obliged to don full dress and white trousers for presentation to the Queen Dowager, who was then escorted by Napier and Stirling to the royal palace, Necessidades, a few miles out of the city, where she was received by the Queen of Portugal. She excused herself from a grand dinner on the fourth evening, but took part in a day trip to the nearby picturesque town of Sintra, much favoured as a summer retreat for the royal family who loved its fourteenth century royal palace built in a distinctive Moorish style, with open courtyards and running water. Above Sintra another and very different royal palace was rising from the ruins of a convent bought by Queen Maria's husband Ferdinand in 1839. The amazing Palácio da Pena (Pena Castle) was said to mix 'Manueline style with Muslim and Indian Orientalism, Renaissance and Mudejar styles',[8] and hence was a worthy showcase for royal guests. It was evidently a jolly day in which Queen Adelaide and her party mounted donkeys and ponies to get to the castle. As the Queen later recounted, on their return the King of Portugal 'sang the whole way with a very fine voice all our favourite songs from operas...'[9]

On the day of departure for Madeira, the British Consul in Lisbon, Sir H. Seymour, wrote that 'the *Howe* weighed anchor at three o'clock [and] Her Majesty sails with a fair, though light wind...'[10] However, Seymour's confidence in

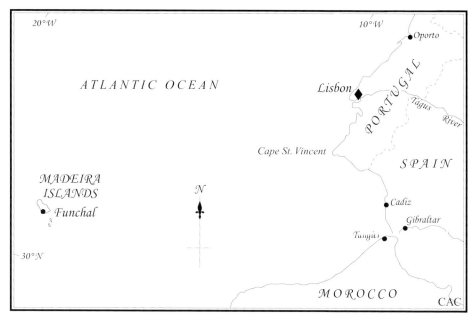

Sojourns in Lisbon and Madeira proved beneficial in the convalescence of
the Queen Dowager

a smooth journey was to prove misplaced, for just as the *Howe* left the Tagus, under
tow to HMSV *Terrible*, she encountered a heavy swell and very strong tide which
carried away the tow ropes.[11] The *Howe* lurched to one side and the Queen Dowager,
on deck for departure, nearly fell overboard but was rescued by Stirling's quick
thinking. In doing so, Stirling lost his ceremonial sword overboard, and later in the
day a grateful Queen Adelaide presented him with a new one—a fine gold-plated
dress sword and scabbard which was one of several made especially for the Queen
Dowager early in 1847.[12] In addition to the sword, Stirling afterwards was presented
with a silver snuff box decorated with blue glass beads, with the royal initials on the
lid and an inscription inside which read:

> Presented by Queen Adelaide to Captain Stirling in 1847 in recognition of his
> presence of mind when she slipped and nearly fell overboard on a visit to Sir
> James' ship. The sword presented at the same time replaced the one which fell into
> the sea at the time.[13]

Once safely anchored in Madeira's Funchal harbour, reached on 1 November,
Queen Adelaide wrote to Queen Victoria, mentioning the incident at the mouth of
the Tagus but minimising her personal danger.

> The tide was so strong that the waves were from both sides like high walls & the
> hawsers, ropes, which attached us to the steamer which was to tow us out of the

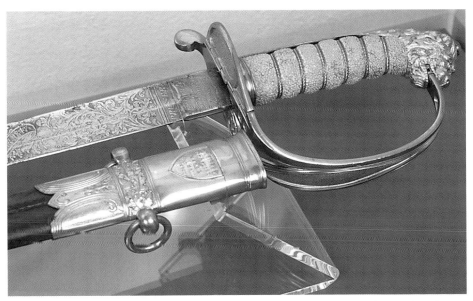

Detail of the Wilkinson's/Prosser steel sword and scabbard, presented to Stirling by
Queen Adelaide to replace the one lost overboard

Courtesy the Western Australian Museum CH73.207/Victor France

River & over the Bar broke off at once, which gave us a great shock & might have
been fatal had not the Captain been skilful. The ankers [sic] were thrown out and
we were obliged to remain for the night, which was not a safe anchorage, but
nothing else could be done as there was not sufficient wind to carry us beyond the
Bar…I am well & feel already much better from the change of air. I have good
appetite & have never been sea sick…[14]

When the Queen Dowager and her attendants left the *Howe* the following morning,
the crew spent a busy day offloading baggage and restoring order to the ship. Late
in the day on 2 November they were ready to depart, and after a smooth passage the
Howe reached the Tagus on the 9th to rejoin the squadron. Stirling had had time to
think about the towing accident, and had prepared a report for Napier which
contained suggestions for improving steamer-towing, and establishing some kind of
uniform system.[15] His suggestions were warmly received and offset the reprimands
from an anxious Seymour!

The period between dropping off and retrieving the royal party was brief, and
uneventful. Throughout December and January Napier ordered the squadron to
exercise the guns and undertake various manoeuvres with the steamers. By late
March the *Howe* was prepared to collect the Queen Dowager for her return voyage,
but Stirling had to beg Napier to reduce the four months' provisions he had been
assigned on account of the crowded state of the decks when the Queen Dowager's
luggage was embarked.[16] On 1 April Stirling took the *Howe* out of the Tagus,

escorted by the steamers *Scourge, Jackal* and *Comet*, arriving in Funchal harbour a week later. After collecting baggage and stores, *Howe* set course for Spithead escorted by the *Scourge*. The homeward journey took only thirteen days, and on 27 April Stirling signalled for the royal steam yacht *Fairy* to collect the royal party. The Queen Dowager was conveyed to Osborne House, but returned later that evening to depart officially with her attendants the following day, after thanking Stirling and his officers and being cheered by the crew. Stirling clearly had made an impression on the Queen Dowager, for twelve months later he learned from the Admiralty that he had been appointed her naval aide-de-camp.[17]

With the royal tour over, the *Howe* had to return to the dockyard for refitting. Crew were given leave and Stirling took the opportunity of returning to see his family at Belmont. But on 28 April 1848 he learned from the Admiralty that they wanted him back in the Mediterranean as soon as possible. Europe was in the grip of the 'year of Revolutions' and Vice Admiral Sir William Parker, who had replaced Owen in 1845, needed help. Some of the Evolutionary Squadron at Lisbon had been sent down already,[18] though Napier had been recalled to Ireland where affairs looked threatening. Ellen was not happy about James returning to sea. She wanted to see her husband rewarded for all his past efforts, not only in a financial sense but also with social recognition in the form of something more than a knighthood. In response to family urging Stirling wrote on 13 May to Lord Grey, now Secretary of State for the Colonies, addressing the letter from the *Howe* at Portsmouth rather than from Belmont. His letter stated that on his return to England in 1839 the Minister for Colonies had 'announced an intention to confer on me some mark of approbation' for administering a colonial government 'under circumstances of no ordinary difficulty, for the long period of ten years without a single instance of complaint or reprehension'. Furthermore, the Governorships of New Zealand and South Australia had been offered to him 'in flattering terms' in 1840. With regard to the latter, he had advised Lord John Russell that he would, if the Government wished, go out to the colonies again, even to the detriment of his professional prospects and the interests of his family. He continued:

> To this his Lordship replied that he was aware of my previous services, and that it was in consequence of the view taken of them that the Government desired to avail itself of my assistance in the present case. That the terms should be entirely satisfactory…and with reference to my previous services, His Lordship undertook to submit my name to Lord Melbourne for a Baronetcy…

Stirling then asked that, at a time when 'the honours of the Bath are so liberally conferred upon all who are supposed to have rendered colonial services of any value', could the 'expectations which were held out to me by the Colonial Minister' now be realised?[19]

Stirling's reference to the liberal conferral of the honours of the Bath could well have been prompted by the reward bestowed on Governor Darling who, once cleared of charges in 1837, had been awarded Knight of the Grand Cross of the Guelphic Order, a new order just below that of the Bath.[20] Unfortunately for Stirling, most of the 1840 communications he had referred to had been verbal, and by now even the long-serving James Stephen had been replaced as Under-Secretary. The official reply of 20 May 1848 read:

> I am directed to acquaint you, that, as there is no record in this Department of a baronetcy having been promised to you by Lord John Russell in the period to which you allude, Lord Grey must refer you to Lord J Russell himself who will no doubt be prepared to decide whether he can properly advise the Queen to confer that honour upon you.[21]

This letter may have reached Stirling before he left Belmont, but he would have had no time to take the recommended action, for the *Howe* was ready by 22 May, and the ship's company mustered. Later that same day she was moved out to a mooring off Spithead and began the regular salutes as Her Majesty plied to and from Osborne House in the *Fairy*. On the 'Glorious First of June', orders came for Stirling to take the *Howe* to Malta, where he was to meet Vice Admiral Parker.[22]

The international situation at this time was turbulent and worrying. Following riots in Paris, King Louis Phillipe of France had abdicated in favour of his grandson the previous February, but as the public were still not happy with the pace of democratic reform, tensions remained high. In March republican revolutions had broken out in Vienna, Venice and Milan against Austrian rule, culminating in April in a battle where Austria was defeated by the Piedmontese. Things Italian continued to simmer through April and May: Ferdinand I, the King of Austria, had to flee for safety to Innsbruck, following public dissatisfaction with a new constitution, while the King of Naples came under attack when the Sicilians announced their independence in April, after a revolt in Palermo. British policy at this stage was to maintain peace, and the balance of power, by supporting monarchies where possible, and gunboat diplomacy was their major tactical weapon.[23] So Vice Admiral Parker was under enormous pressure and needed help. Stirling's inducement was, that if all went well, he would be in line for promotion at the end of his term. Thus, on 11 June 1848, after reprovisioning and seeing that the crew were at full muster, Stirling took the *Howe* out of Portsmouth harbour.

Again the *Howe* proved her sailing prowess, for she ran through the Straits of Gibraltar to enter the Mediterranean on the 26th. En route, as was customary, the ship's company was put through its paces in various drills, but not always, as it transpired, to desired effect. On 27 June the 'young gentlemen' were set to exercising with blank cartridges, and the log records that they

broke by accident in firing in the Captain's pantry 8 wine glasses, 1 liquor glass,
one half pint tumbler…also broken in Captain's fore cabin 1 pint decanter stopper,
6 claret glasses, 3 wine glasses, 2 tumblers, 2 liquor glasses, 1 vegetable dish cover,
1 quart decanter, 1 pint decanter.[24]

It was some accident, but as there was no recorded punishment it probably
reminded Stirling of his own son's escapades. Andrew had never gone back to sea
after his initial voyage, choosing training for the East India Company instead. But
Frederick Henry had gone with Napier in the expeditionary force on the *St Vincent*
as Mate and gained his Lieutenancy on that ship in May 1848.[25] Destined for a
distinguished naval career,[26] Frederick had gone far beyond firing blanks! The *Howe*
finally entered Valletta harbour, Malta, on 12 July when crews took on water and
provisions, and instructions were received to proceed to Sicily.

A degree of instability still prevailed in the region since Stirling's previous tour
of duty, and once more the focus was on rivalry between Neapolitans and Sicilians.
The Sicilian independence movement had chosen the Duke of Genoa to be their
new King and Admiral Parker had gone to Palermo for the announcement, leaving
orders for Stirling to join him. When Stirling met his Admiral on 23 July he found
him most concerned about two issues. First, a Sicilian deputation was preparing to
go to Genoa to see their chosen King, but had asked the French to help with this
delicate mission instead of the British. Second, the Neapolitan Navy, refusing to
recognise the independence movement, was capturing Sicilian prisoners by using
false colours, and had ventured 'so near to Corfu as to involve a violation of HM
Territory'.[27] (Corfu had been a British protectorate since the defeat of Napoleon.) In
Parker's view, the Neapolitan Government was not showing proper respect to the
British flag, so he ordered the squadron into the Bay of Naples. The move had the
desired effect, for a note of apology from Prince Cariate and the Neapolitan
Government soon followed, enabling the squadron to move down to Castellammare
(just west of Palermo) on 30 July.

The *Howe* remained at Castellammare, with most of the squadron, until 6
September. As the weather continued warm, the crew were allowed to bathe in sails
lowered over the side for the purpose. On 30 August the Neapolitan squadron of six
steamers, fifteen gunboats and several launches was spotted leaving the Bay of
Naples, causing the Admiral to hurry to the capital. On 4 September he learned that
the Neapolitan fleet was preparing to attack Messina, at the tip of Sicily, where the
British paddle steamer *Gladiator* was on guard. By the 9th Messina had fallen and
the French squadron asked the British for immediate on-site action. Instead, Parker
took his squadron into the Bay of Naples where, in company with his senior
officers, he urged the Neapolitan Government to cease hostilities immediately or
face an enforced armistice. In this, he had total support from the French Admiral
Baudin. A dispatch was sent to Palermo to give similar instructions to the Sicilians,
and a tense few days ensued until a truce was declared on 11 September 1848.

Belmont House, home to the Stirlings between 1844 and 1860.
This rendition, by Rose Paynter, appeared in 1882

Courtesy the Havant Museum

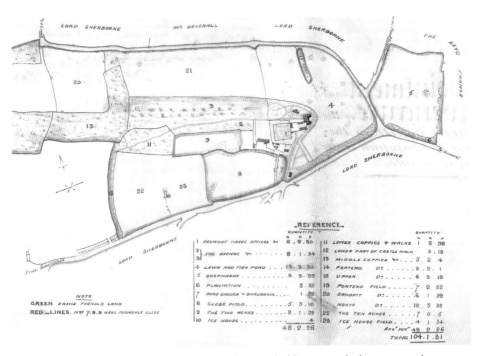

The 30-acre Belmont Estate, showing the main buldings towards the eastern end.
On this working farm Stirling indulged his love of horses

Portsmouth Museum and Record Service, Major Browne Collection PCRO 1115/A/1/39

Portrait of Ellen Stirling c. 1840.
Courtesy Edward Buckley/photograph Murray Glover

Ellen's mother, Mary Mangles
Courtesy Robin Mangles

Andrew Stirling and Anne c. 1820s
with their five eldest sons:
William, Walter and John (above)
and Charles and James (below)

*Courtesy Marion Leeper (Charles);
Lenfestey/Government House, Perth (James);
rest Mrs Stirling Aird*

The ceremonial sword and scabbard (detail top) presented to Stirling by the Queen Dowager. The sword measured 91 cm and had a gold-plated hilt

Courtesy the Western Australian Museum CH73.207; photograph by Victor France

The silver snuff box engraved on the inside lid, commemorating the Queen's gratitude

Courtesy the Western Australian Museum CH73.210; photograph by Victor France

Stirling does not appear to have been officially engaged in any of the negotiations over the 'Sicilian Question', but it is unlikely that a man with his language skills and experience was not involved. He remained the Senior Naval Officer in Naples harbour for more than three relatively uneventful months, though Admiral Parker came and went, and there were interchanges among ships in the squadron. The only incident worthy of remark in the ship's log was a 'serious insubordination on the *Rodney* on Christmas night',[28] likely a party that got out of hand and which drew Admiralty disapproval of 'the issue of extra grog' on that occasion.[29]

Late in February 1849 came the news that there was a new Government in Palermo, committed to regaining Messina. The King of Naples had been held to his Sicilian truce with difficulty over past months, so when he asked the British and the French to help by delivering his terms to the new Government, they agreed. Admiral Parker took most of the British squadron, in company with Baudin's ships, to Sicily for what proved to be fruitless and long, drawn-out diplomatic efforts. Stirling, meanwhile, remained in charge in Naples with only a couple of steamships until orders finally arrived to return to Malta early in May.

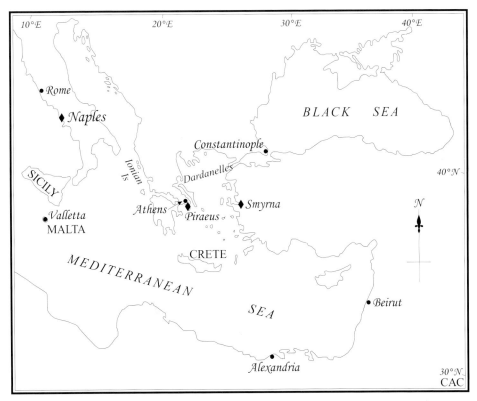

Eastern Mediterranean, where Stirling served as Senior Naval Officer in Naples, and was involved in a blockade of Salamis harbour into Piraeus

The *Howe* finally left Naples on 6 May 1849, one month short of a year since she had first arrived. With no steamer escort and with little wind, she found the going difficult and did not reach Valletta harbour until the 11th. The following day, with assistance from steamers, she was towed to a closer mooring for a full survey of stores, guns and gear. By this time Parker's flagship had changed to the *Hibernia*. Around her the *Howe* found the *Thetis 56*, the *Spartan 26*, the iron paddle sloop *Antelope*, the large wooden paddle steamer *Terrible*, and the small wooden paddle packets *Merlin*, *Medusa* and *Medina*. Over the following three months the squadron undertook various training manoeuvres, brought to a halt in late August by orders for Parker to move to the Ionian Islands, where trouble had been reported. On 1 September 1849 the steamers towed their charges, one at a time, out to sea for the start of a week-long voyage to Corfu.

During 1848 and 1849 there had been rising feeling in the Ionian Islands against British rule, imposed in the Treaty of Paris in 1815. The islanders' increasing desire for union with Greece had led to escalating conflict until an amnesty, promising greater concessions, was declared on 1 August 1849 by the High Commissioner. By late August, however, a more serious rebellion had broken out on the island of Cephalonia, although when the *Howe* arrived there on 10 September as part of the squadron's reinforcement, it had been quelled. Further attacks on the British garrison were not ruled out and the Commissioner was relieved to have a back-up at hand.

An opportunity to show force and thus deter potential disturbance arose the next day, albeit in sad circumstances. One of the *Howe*'s 'young gentlemen' had died after a short illness and arrangements were made to bury him ashore. With the burial party went 100 marines who would undertake two days of exercises with field pieces and howitzers in full public view. They remained at Cephalonia until orders were received for a change-over in the squadron's ships, causing Admiral Parker to send out instructions for a meeting at Corfu. Just after the squadron left Cephalonia on 18 September they ran into a heavy squall. It was so sudden and so fierce that considerable damage was done to the ships, and lives were lost: three boys and one seasoned sailor on the *Howe* died of injuries received falling from the rigging.

While still at sea Stirling was called on board the *Caledonia* to be briefed on the squadron's new mission, to the Dardanelles, as diplomatic relations in Constantinople between Austria and Russia had been suspended, potentially harming British interests. The stand-off, Admiral Parker learned, had arisen because the Turkish Government had not complied with those two countries' demands for the extradition of Hungarian and Polish refugees. Showing the flag, therefore, was an important priority.

On 26 September, three days after arriving at Corfu, Admiral Parker shifted his flag from the *Caledonia* to the *Queen*,[30] a move that must have bemused Stirling, for the 110-gun *Queen* was lower rated than his 120-gun *Howe*. By 10 October all the change-overs were complete and the squadron made its way towards the southern tip of the Peloponnesian Peninsula (Cape Matapan), rounding the island of Kithira on 18 October and anchoring at Besika (also Bashika) Bay, near the entry to the Dardanelles, ten days later. From here Parker sent a dispatch to the British Ambassador in Constantinople, Sir Stratford Canning (with whom Stirling had corresponded in 1843), alerting him of his intention to bring the squadron inside the Dardanelles. Canning favoured the idea, although aware that Palmerston had urged caution because of the 1841 Straits Treaty (which prevented any other than Russian warships through in peacetime). He advised Parker at first to find a less exposed anchorage than Besika Bay, preferably under the outward castles of the Dardanelles.[31] But Parker, believing that easy access to Constantinople was all-important in case of emergency, ordered the squadron to move into the channel. During this manoeuvre the *Prince Regent* and the *Howe* collided, with the result that 'four channel rails, stanchions of sheet anchor and martingale &c. had to be cut away' from the *Howe*. Both ships came to and repaired damage,[32] and by 2 p.m. the squadron proceeded slowly into the Dardanelles, anchoring in Charnak (or Havouzlah) Bay that evening.

It did not take long for the squadron to attract criticism, albeit over trivial matters. For example, complaints were received that bumboats were taking advantage of privileges granted only to Her Majesty's boats, by claiming they were transporting officers.[33] So Parker issued strict orders to use only the ships' boats in shore forays. When further complaints arose that trees had been destroyed by crews fetching water, Parker replied defensively that 'no whole tree had been destroyed but boughs had been cut for firewood'.[34]

To clear the air, the Admiral decided the squadron should retreat to a position outside the Dardanelles, leaving the *Ardent* and the steamer *Tartarus* behind as communication links. The withdrawal was not without incident, for at 11 a.m. on 13 November, soon after weighing anchor, there was a blast from a cliff-top Turkish fort, which fired a single large cannon-shot down into the passage. Fortunately it missed all eleven ships. In response, orders were given the following day to 'exercise the great guns', and on the 15th the marines with their field pieces were landed for further exercises. That evening the *Ardent* arrived from Constantinople with Canning, who spent six hours on the *Queen* discussing strategy with Admiral Parker. As the pair decided the squadron's continued presence just outside the Dardanelles would smooth the way for continuing negotiations between Turkey and Russia, it remained in the bay for over a month, with the battleships undertaking exercises.

Late November saw bad weather set in, with days of strong gales and rain. As it eased, a Turkish steamer was seen coming through the Dardanelles, and on 2 December the Turkish Pasha boarded the flagship to speak to the Admiral. The latter was forcibly reminded that Besika Bay was in Turkish territory, so Parker sent his steamers out to look for possible alternative anchorages. He had received orders from the Admiralty to return to Malta, but news to hand that the Turkish squadron had moved into the Golden Horn made it imperative to stay in the region a while longer. Informed by his scouts that Moskonisi harbour, though still Turkish, would be a suitable alternative anchorage,[35] Parker gave the order to leave. On Saturday afternoon 15 December the squadron moved out in two columns, running south-ward toward Morlivi. On the 18th they entered the south roads of Moskonisi harbour (Mosko South Roads).[36] In company with the *Queen* and the *Howe* at this stage were the *Caledonia*, *Powerful*, *Vengeance*, *Ganges* and *Bellerophon*, plus the steam vessels *Odin*, *Firebrand*, *Dragon*, *Spiteful* and *Bulldog*.[37] The following day the Admiral, together with his senior captains, waited on the Turkish authorities. Diplomacy was essential and gifts were probably exchanged, with the need for provisioning given as an excuse for their presence. On the 22nd the *Tartarus* arrived from Constantinople with the latest dispatches. One from the Admiralty insisted that Parker proceed immediately to Athens to enforce certain demands on the Greeks, while another from the Home Office informed them of the death of her late Majesty the Queen Dowager. Parker summoned his captains to pass on the news, ordering the Royal Standard to be struck at half mast and all ensigns, jacks and pendants likewise for the next five days, to be followed by full honours on 28 December.

The news would have especially devastated the ship's company of the *Howe*, who felt as though they knew Queen Adelaide, but no one more keenly than Stirling. He had liked and treasured his royal connection and, in those days of patronage, had hoped for her assistance in preferment. Bitterly disappointed, and grieving for the woman who had been his Queen for many years before Victoria, he watched the flags hoisted and lowered every day until the 28th. On that day the battleships of the squadron commenced the royal salutes at 1 p.m., firing their guns at 30-minute intervals, the guards on each ship 'drawn up on the poop with arms reversed until the last ship's firing'.[38] It was a sad ending to the year. Stirling could only hope that the new year and the new decade would bring better prospects.

Early in January Stirling learned that negotiations with the Turkish Pasha had reached the point where the squadron's presence was no longer deemed necessary, and instructions were given for all ships to prepare to leave for their next assignment, in Greece. The inactivity of recent months had made time drag, but now there was much to do—rigging to be checked, food and water replenished, assistance provided in recoaling the steamers, and crews inspected.[39] On 8 January the steamers towed the squadron's line-of-battle ships out of the channel, ready for the three-day voyage to Salamis Bay.

The call for Admiral Parker's assistance arose from efforts to get the Greek Government to repay the 1831 loan, and provide restitution for property lost by several British citizens in the 1847 riots.[40] Palmerston, the British Foreign Secretary, had taken a hard line which was being pushed by the new Consul, Thomas Wyse, who had recently replaced Lyons as British Envoy in Greece. The appearance of the squadron, seven ships-of-the-line and four steamers, would send a powerful message. But it was a delicate situation, for France and Russia (also signatories to the 1831 loan) could resent Britain's action. Indeed, King Otho sought their help[41] after officially refusing to accede to Britain's demands just a week after the squadron's arrival. Parker then set up a blockade on all Greek Government vessels putting to sea,[42] quickly extending it to Greek merchant vessels.[43] By 8 February he advised the Admiralty:

> We have now under detention in Salamis Bay the Government steamer *Otho*, one schooner of 3 guns, two small gun boats, ten loaded and twenty light merchant vessels. Two Government schooners and five merchant vessels have been seized by the *Rosamund* on patrol...[44]

Soon Russia and Austria were protesting, but despite claims that their cargoes were being held up on detained Greek vessels, the blockade continued.

The situation remained unsettled for almost three more months. Critics in London thought Palmerston and his gunboat diplomacy had gone too far, and on the 12th the British Government agreed to mediation attempts by the French. Orders were given to suspend the blockade, and on 5 March the French Envoy, Baros de Gros, arrived to undertake month-long settlement talks in Athens.[45] The first figure which de Gros proposed as settlement of the outstanding Greek loan proved unacceptable to the British, so on 25 April the blockade was temporarily resumed.[46] This meant that Stirling's 16-year-old son Charles, who had just been transferred as a midshipman to Parker's flagship *Queen*,[47] could witness some action. So vigorous was the blockade that King Otho gave way, agreeing to settle the claims for the required 180,000 drachmas plus an apology. At 3 p.m. on the 27th Admiral Parker removed the embargo on the port of Piraeus and ordered the release of detained Greek vessels.[48] The squadron was now free to return to headquarters.

Leaving two warships behind, the rest of the squadron weighed anchor early on 4 May to return direct to Malta. As the *Howe* and the *Vengeance* had been officially recalled,[49] arrangements were immediately put in train for their departure. On the morning of the 18th both ships (with young Charles permitted to return with his father on the *Howe*) sailed out of Valletta harbour bound for Spithead. After some delay in Gibraltar they reached England on 2 July.

Three days later the Admiral of the Nore boarded the fully-dressed *Howe* and expressed himself satisfied. Orders were then given for the ship to be taken in tow to Sheerness for official inspection, and on 12 July 1850 the ship's company was paid off. The marines left for Chatham and Stirling quitted the ship which had been his home for three years, two months, two weeks and two days.[50] Any sadness at leaving the *Howe* and his officers, however, would have been far outweighed by the prospect of being reunited with Ellen and his family.

26

Belmont and Family Tribulations

News of her husband's arrival would have reached Ellen at Belmont soon after the *Howe* reached Spithead, and prompted her to take the London train for a joyful reunion. In their years apart, James' hair and sideburns had turned from pepper and salt to a distinguished pure white,[1] and his neat-waisted wife was now dressed in the new fuller-skirted fashion. Family news inevitably took pride of place, and Ellen could tell James that while most of the girls were at home eagerly awaiting his return, 15-year-old Agnes had a heart condition for which sea air had been prescribed. She had been sent to Brighton, near her 14-year-old brother Walter's school. Andrew, now 25, would see his father at Belmont, while latest letters from Frederick Henry indicated that his ship, the HMS *Castor*, was currently stationed at the Cape of Good Hope. Young Charles would have been just as delighted to see his mother, so a happy trio headed for brother Walter's home at 18 Upper Baker Street, Marylebone. James' younger sister Agnes (now 58) had been housekeeping for 70-year-old Walter for some years[2] and James would have been anxious to see them, for Walter had always been his favourite brother and an anchor to the family.

James soon caught up on all the latest family news. Brother William was still living in Manchester near the cotton textile business he had founded, but its day-to-day working had been passed to Thomas Mayne Stirling, John's 26-year-old bachelor son. William had not been well and James was urged to visit him as soon as he could. Sister Anna, the widowed Lady Home, was living in Scotland but had suffered a tragedy the previous year when her eldest son John had died at sea, aged just 19. Her second son George, now the 10th Baronet of Blackadder, was studying to join the Bar. Brothers John and Charles and their families were still in Scotland, at St Andrews and Muiravonside respectively, and looking forward to seeing him, whilst their youngest brother Edward, now 53, had retired from the East India Company and was living in Jersey.[3]

Whilst in London James tried to reach his brothers-in-law at the Wapping premises of their shipping concern, F. & C. Mangles and Co., but London's summer heat had driven both to their respective country estates—52-year-old Charles to

Poyle Park near Guildford, and Frederick, four years his senior, to Downs Farm at Compton, Surrey. James would see both when he paid a visit to Woodbridge, where Ellen's brother, Ross Donnelly Mangles, now 49, had taken residence on becoming Member for Guildford in 1841. The rest of the Mangles clan, including his redoubtable mother-in-law, he would catch up with once he had settled into Belmont.

Sending a telegraph to announce their arrival, the Stirlings took the train to Portsmouth, changing there for the short trip to Havant.[1] One can imagine the scene when the pony trap entered the driveway to Belmont Park and drew up at the main entrance. Five-year-old Georgina and 8-year-old Dorothea would have been on the lookout and excitedly called to their older sisters Anna, 10, and Ellinor, 13. Mary, now 18, would have hung back a little, very conscious of the fact that she was now meeting her father as a young lady and not a child. There undoubtedly would have been presents for all and much for father to see and hear in the first few days. Ellen had engaged a governess for the girls, German-born Miss Elizabeth Blackwell, who was proficient not only in languages but in all facets of a young lady's curriculum. James was well pleased with their progress and took particular interest in their music and drawing skills. Interviews with the tenants and his bailiff were also satisfactory, though there was still a lot to be done to complete the plans made when he had first purchased the estate. There had been additions to the stables in his absence, and quieter horses for Ellen and the children, but his own favourite had grown older and out of condition. Discussions with his groom, therefore, would get top priority, for James had always taken pride in his horses and now had the money to buy well.

Another priority was a visit to his mother-in-law. Mary was now 77 and living with her youngest daughter Hamilla and husband William Preston at Borde Hill, a 350-acre farm in Cuckfield, Sussex. William Preston had given away the sea and was now a magistrate with a large house providing ample accommodation, and it was obvious that he and Hamilla were very happy. Their eldest daughter, aged 15, had been named Ellen after Lady Stirling but, like her sister, Hamilla had also had a long gap between her first and subsequent children. Her next child Henry was only 5 and the youngest son just 2.[5]

Preston was able to update Stirling on the political ramifications of Palmerston's gunboat diplomacy in Greece. This had led to a censure motion in the House of Lords on 18 June, carried by 37 votes.[6] But when the matter reached the Commons on 29 June, Palmerston had confounded his critics and won universal acclamation with one of his most memorable speeches on the rights of British citizens abroad.[7] Stirling would have been pleased, for his entire career had been governed by the need to protect British personnel and property in other lands. Moreover he believed, like Palmerston, that the navy was Britain's strongest weapon and that its mere presence was a powerful deterrent to international conflict.

The Stirlings' eventual arrival at Woodbridge saw heightened activity as the large Mangles clan gathered for the occasion. Given their mutual interests, it was not long before the talk turned to Western Australia. The last Mangles vessel to visit Swan River had been the *Trusty*, in late 1848, which had brought home news that sandalwood exports had rescued the colony from the slump of 1843–44. Pastoralists were now agitating for convicts to alleviate the shortages of labour brought on by the sandalwood boom.[8] The idea was at first unpopular amongst the gentry, and opposed by Major Irwin who had stepped in as Acting Governor when Hutt's replacement, Andrew Clarke, died of consumption. However, a new Governor, Charles Fitzgerald, had since been appointed by the Colonial Office, and he had been convinced before departure that the colony's salvation lay in the acceptance of 'exiles'—prisoners who had already served the bulk of their sentences and who would be free on arrival. Ross could add that pressure from Jebb, the Comptroller of Her Majesty's Prisons, and a petition from Friends of the Colonists in England (including all three Mangles brothers)[9] had led to an overthrow of the plan to send exiles only. It was realised that labour alone, without supporting finance, would be of little use. An Order-in-Council constituting Western Australia a fully financed penal settlement had eventually been signed by the Queen in May 1849.[10]

Stirling welcomed the news[11] and it must have seemed oddly coincidental when he learned later that the *Scindian*, carrying the first batch of convicts, anchored off Fremantle on 2 June 1850, exactly twenty-one years after his own arrival in the *Parmelia*. He was well aware of the colony's desperate need for the sort of public works that he had seen completed by convicts in New South Wales, and had not been averse to the idea of a convict settlement in the very beginning. He could understand the disappointment of many pioneer settlers who had taken pride in their 'First Free Australian Colony' status, but he was pragmatic. The future of the tiny, isolated colony, which had a total of just 4,622 European inhabitants in the census of 1848,[12] needed to be assured, and becoming a convict settlement was about the only way this could be achieved. It was especially important if his lands in the colony were to increase in value and provide for his family's needs.

James also heard from his brothers-in-law that Samuel Moore, his agent in Western Australia, had died of a heart attack the previous July,[13] and that George Fletcher Moore, Sam's brother and the former Advocate-General, had married Governor Clarke's daughter and was intending to return to England. George Elliot, his relation by marriage, had been appointed Resident Magistrate of the Bunbury region, which now included settlers from the failed Australind venture. Though George was still overseeing the management of Stirling's Leschenault estates, he did not have time to attend to all of his affairs, so another agent would have to be found to replace Moore. As the time delays in receiving and sending instructions made everything so very difficult, James would have been delighted to hear that his brothers-in-law, in conjunction with agents for the Western Australian Bank in London, had petitioned the Colonial Office just the previous April to ensure 'that the proposed steam communication with Australia for conveyance of mail be allowed to touch at Swan River'.[14]

Moreover, it was now known that the Government had agreed to send free emigrant women as well as male convicts to Swan River, to balance the sexes and lessen the moral taint on the colony, so shipping was bound to be more frequent. Although Mangles ships had been involved in transporting convicts to New South Wales in the 1820s,[15] Charles and Frederick were not interested in further contracts and were scaling down their shipping business. In fact, the *Trusty* had been the last of their ships to visit Australia. Charles Mangles was now more interested in following his brother into politics.[16]

Stirling would thus have had much to cogitate when he returned with Ellen to Belmont. The ensuing months were busy with visitors: friends and family, naval officers and Western Australian connections such as Caroline Brown, widow of Peter Brown,[17] Stirling's former Colonial Secretary. She wanted support for her claim to a pension, hitherto denied by the Colonial Office.[18]

For James the end of the year was clouded by the passing of his eldest brother. William died of spinal paralysis at his home, Cornbrook Bank, in Stretford near Manchester on 19 December 1850, aged 71. Described as 'of Drumpellier' in the Family Bible, William had been the 22nd Baron of Cadder, inheriting the title on his father's death, and the family wanted a fitting farewell. He was interred in a private vault of pink granite in the recently opened Kensal Green Cemetery near London.[19] As William had had no issue, the Cadder title now passed to Walter who, as William's sole beneficiary, also inherited the textile business.

At Belmont, 1851 entered quietly. Soon thousands of homes were caught up in the sharp gaze of officialdom—census night of 10 March. The Stirling family, and their activities, became a set of statistics: four younger girls at home, two older ones (Agnes and Mary) absent, and none of the boys in residence. That night Stirling had a visitor, 23-year-old George Parker RN who, like himself, was on half-pay. The governess, Elizabeth Blackwell, was shown to have been born in Holstein. Ellen's personal maid, Justine Muchard, was identified as French. In addition, the household had a cook, two housemaids (one aged just 11) and a groom. Stirling himself was described as 60 years of age, retired Captain RN and farmer of 50 acres employing four labourers.[20]

Barely a month later, James' quiet country life had a rude interruption—a rumour that the Government might rescind its decision to make Western Australia a penal settlement. It was said that only Gibraltar and Malta, and no other British colony, would get this facility. Stirling headed straight for London and threw all his energies into raising a petition against such a move. The petition, lodged on 6 April, stated that a penal settlement on a large scale was the only way of saving colonists in Western Australia 'from utter ruin'. The petitioners argued that:

> Unless Western Australia can offer some inducement to the higher classes of emigrants, she can never become of any importance or advantage to Great Britain; inasmuch as it is absolutely impossible to maintain a large body of ticket-of-leave convicts in a country where there are no employers.[21]

Stirling's name headed a list of thirty-seven signatories, including all four Mangles' brothers. A requested interview was granted on 10 April, at which Stirling and Ross Donnelly Mangles were relieved to hear that the rumour had been a mistake.[22] Lord Grey had referred to convicts in the *earlier* stages of punishment being sent to Malta and Gibraltar, not that other destinations would be abandoned, and this was confirmed in the formal reply of 14 April.[23]

Stirling's visit to London was well timed, for Queen Victoria was about to open the Great Exhibition at the recently completed Crystal Palace, a radical design of glass and iron inspired by Prince Albert. During its nine-month span, the exhibition would attract some six million visitors, and as the Glasgow Stirlings were displaying their famed Turkey-red dyed cloth in the manufacturing section,[24] James and Ellen would almost certainly have been among the 25,000 ticket-holders at the 1 May opening. Few could fail to be impressed, for the audacity of the immense glass building, the sumptuous internal decorations, and the range and size of exhibits from all over the country and the Empire, were quite awe-inspiring. Three-guinea season tickets were available, and the Stirlings probably visited on several occasions to view the Australian exhibits, though perhaps disappointed that there was nothing from Western Australia.[25]

While in London Stirling caught up with colleagues and no doubt learned that his name had advanced significantly in the naval lists. Naval promotion came with seniority among both serving and half-pay officers, and on 8 July 1851 James was finally named Rear Admiral.[26] The news delighted Ellen, who had always pushed his advancement, but it made James long for a more active role. On the 30th he wrote to the Admiralty asking for an appointment,[27] but at that time there were simply no vacancies. For Ellen this was a blessing, as James was with her when they learned that her mother had suffered a bad fall early in August. Her pony carriage had toppled over and Ellen was informed 'She was much shaken and bruised, alarming for one of her age, and in a weak state, more especially as the Dr. had to apply 12 leeches'.[28]

Mary Mangles never fully recovered from this fall, her normally strong constitution being undermined further by the deaths of two sons-in-law. First, her eldest daughter Caroline's husband, the Reverend Arthur Onslow, died in November at 77, the same age as herself. Then, less than a month later, William Preston, Mary's host at Borde Hill and husband of her youngest daughter, died suddenly on 12 December 1851, aged only 50. At the funeral James would have drawn some comfort from the fact that two places in Western Australia, Preston Point on the Swan and Preston River in the south, would perpetually commemorate his name. Despite overtures to the bereaving Hamilla to shift to Woodbridge, she opted to remain at Borde Hill where it would be far less traumatic for her three children and her mother.

Early in the New Year James learned that Vice Admiral J. W. Dundas, then Second Lord of the Admiralty, had been appointed Commander-in-Chief of the

Mediterranean Station.[29] Aside from his own interest in naval matters of this region, James knew it would necessitate a reshuffle of the Admiralty Board. As Lord John Russell was still Prime Minister and the appointments were his to command, Stirling had good reason to hope for preferment. He probably heard the news even before the London *Times* stated in its Naval and Military Intelligence column on Monday 9 February 1852 that:

> Rear Admiral Stirling is reported to be the new Lord of the Admiralty…Sir James is a very upright man and experienced Officer.

On Saturday 14 February *The Times* printed an excerpt from the *London Gazette* containing the official announcement, dated Whitehall on the 12th. It read:

> The Queen has been pleased to direct letters patent to be passed under the Great Seal of the United Kingdom of Great Britain and Ireland, constituting and appointing the Rt. Hon. Francis Thornhill Baring Bart, MP; Rear Admiral Maurice Frederick Fitzharding Berkeley CG; Rear Admiral Houston Stewart CB; Rear Admiral Sir James Stirling Knight; Captain Alexander Milne; and the Hon. Francis William Cowper, to be Her Majesty's Commissioners for executing the office of Admiral of the United Kingdom, Great Britain and Ireland, and the Dominions, Islands and Territories thereto belonging.[30]

Stirling was officially the Fourth Lord of the Admiralty.

It was to be a remarkably short term of office. Just a week later, on 21 February, the Government fell. Nevertheless, it was a week that provided Stirling with a real insight into Admiralty procedures and the myriad of matters that required attention. There were shortages of sailors, delays in departure, smallpox among some crews, accidents in various harbours,[31] and even Australian news. The *Emigrant* had arrived at Portsmouth from Tasmania with the largest piece of timber ever seen: 148 feet long, 22 inches wide and 6 inches thick. It had been intended for the Great Exhibition but no available vessel was capable of carrying it in time for the opening.[32] Though he did not know it, Friday 20 February 1852 was Stirling's last day on the Board, which had before it dispatches reporting the destruction of Lagos by Her Majesty's forces.[33]

On the evening of that same day Lord John Russell lost a vote of confidence in the House over the Local Militia Bill, and after a short Cabinet meeting the Prime Minister tendered his resignation to the Queen. Lord Derby, Leader of the Conservatives, was recalled to London by telegraph and given the task of forming a new Government. *The Times* carried a list of new appointments on 24 February, including that of the Admiralty Board. The Duke of Northumberland was announced as First Lord of the Admiralty while remaining Board members were gazetted on 2 March. Only Captain Alexander Milne, the most junior member, retained his place.

At least the release from full-time duties enabled James to be with Ellen at Belmont for the sad news of Mary Mangles' death. She had never fully recovered from her fall and passed away at Borde Hill on 13 March 1852.[34] Mary was interred in the new church at St Mark's, Wyke, Normandy, in the Parish of Ash.[35] She could well have been a benefactor of St Mark's, for there are large plaques inside commemorating both husband and wife.[36] As they had always been close, her mother's death hit Ellen hard and there were many letters of condolence to answer. It was Mary who had emphasised a family tradition, that as a service wife she should destroy correspondence once answered.[37] Unfortunately, this has denied us insight into the lives of these charming and strong-willed women.

By coincidence, it was on the day that Mary died that the War Office contacted the Colonial Office over a matter that would once again involve Stirling. The Pensioner Guards who had accompanied the convicts to Western Australia had been promised cottage accommodation, and whilst Edmund Y. W. Henderson of the Royal Engineers had attended to this in Fremantle,[38] Pensioners stationed near Bunbury had not yet been housed. The problem was that the most suitable land for such accommodation belonged to Sir James Stirling. The Colonial Office were asked to ascertain whether he would agree to granting some 30 to 40 acres 'on very favourable terms', and instruct his agent in Western Australia to make the necessary arrangements.[39]

No doubt in view of past dealings between Stirling and the Colonial Office on his land holdings, the request caused some consternation, with one official urging 'great caution' on the matter. Stirling consented to travel to London, where he agreed to 'place any land required for this purpose entirely at the disposal of the Government'.[40]

A note dated 26 May mentions that Stirling had told the Colonial Office that his Bunbury (or Leschenault) lands were now the 'joint property of himself and others', but that they would be in favour of placing 'any modest quantity of land' at the disposal of the Government.[41] Later legal documents reveal that Stirling had signed a memorandum on 19 May 1852 to convey 'four undivided eighth parts of his Estates in Western Australia' to his brothers-in-law Frederick Mangles, Charles Edward Mangles and Ross Donnelly Mangles, and to William Stanhope Stockley (who had been the Mangles' agent in WA).[42] This agreement was partly related to mortgages James held with the Mangles brothers over Belmont, and to improvement of some his Western Australian land, but it was also to provide for Ellen's future if anything happened to him. The recent spate of family deaths had been unnerving and had also delayed his appointment of a new agent to handle his affairs in the Colony. This Stirling rectified some time in mid-1852, choosing (or persuading) Robert King, who had acted as English agent and man-of-affairs for himself and the Mangles brothers for many years. King arrived in Western Australia on the *Travancore* on 13 January 1853, and among other things dealt with the transfer of the Bunbury lands.

As James' brothers John and Charles had each lost a child the previous year, he and Ellen took the opportunity to visit Scotland to strengthen family bonds. Love of Scotland ran deep in James, and here was a chance to show his children the landscape he had known so well as a boy. And there were many cousins to meet. At St Andrews, John and Elizabeth's family had mostly left home, but Charles at nearby Muiravonside still had children of a similar age to James and Ellen's.[43] This happy interlude was overtaken by another family milestone requiring the Stirlings' presence at home—the wedding of Ellen's widowed sister Caroline to a man twenty years her junior on 17 February 1853.[44]

Back at Belmont, the quiet life of a country gentleman was shattered for James just three months later, with news that his frail second daughter Agnes had succumbed to her heart condition and died at Brighton, aged only 17, on 9 May 1853.[45] For a parent, losing a child is always traumatic, and James and Ellen were no exceptions. Both would have drawn on their religious convictions to get them, and the family, through this distressing time.

Just a month after the funeral, Western Australian matters of particular interest to James were being discussed at the Colonial Office. Apparently King had issued a 'no trespassing' notice on Garden Island, which had alarmed the local government—partly for defence reasons but also because the Peninsular and Oriental Steam Navigation Company had approached them to use the island as a coaling station.[46] They knew it was part of Stirling's original land grant, conveyed to him by deed dated 31 July 1832, but could find no copy of the deed, and hence sought help from the Land and Emigration Commissioners, who now asked the Colonial Office if they had a record. The Colonial Office did not, but they had it in writing that:

> the Title Deed granted to Sir James Stirling gives the Government an express right to 1/20th of the island whenever it might be thought desirable to claim it.

The then Secretary of State therefore felt that using Careening Bay on Garden Island for the purpose outlined would be quite legitimate.[47] Although retention of his right to Garden Island was important to Stirling, who had originally seen it as a future Isle of Wight in southern seas, he had always understood that a part might be needed for public and defence purposes. He was therefore quite happy to instruct King to release the agreed portion around Careening Bay to the Government.[48]

Unhappy news soon followed. Stirling was shocked to hear that his brother John had died suddenly in Manchester on 18 December 1853 of a stomach haemorrhage. John had been visiting his son, Thomas Mayne Stirling, who was managing the family textile business. Thomas now had the sad task of accompanying his father's body back home to St Andrews to his shocked mother and sisters. Once again the family would have assembled from all directions for the funeral, as John had been loved by all for his unconventional outlook and rakish humour. John had been the hoarder in the family and kept every letter he had received, a legacy he left to his eldest son, who fortunately kept them for posterity.[49] John was buried in the family vault at the cathedral at St Andrews—in reality, the remains of an immense medieval building lying derelict since the Reformation.[50] John had lived opposite the cathedral ruins for most of his adult life and, with his quirky sense of humour, doubtless relished the idea of establishing a family vault in a cemetery without a church.

After attending to things spiritual and temporal in Scotland, James returned to Belmont where he heard early in the New Year that he was to be recalled to active duty. It was a surprise, however, when he learned that his next command would not be the Mediterranean, where tensions were escalating prior to the Crimean War, but in the Far East. His appointment was gazetted on 19 January 1854 and read:

> Rear Admiral Sir James Stirling is appointed Commander-in-Chief, China and the East Indies Station (vice Sir Fleetwood Pellew, summarily retired)—Flagship *Winchester*.

Stirling's knowledge of China was scanty when first appointed, but he was quickly briefed. Throughout 1852 and early 1853 activities by the Taiping rebels in China had seriously concerned the Foreign Office. The then Governor of Hong Kong, Sir Samuel George Bonham, had urged non-interference in what he saw as a civil war, but was extremely worried about the safety of the ports secured by the Nanking Treaty of 1842, and that of British residents and their property.[51] In response, the Foreign Secretary had given orders in May 1853 for all war vessels that could be spared from Indian waters to join the flag of Vice Admiral Sir Fleetwood Pellew 'to provide adequately for the protection of British subjects and property in Canton, Amoy and Shanghai'.[52] But an over-zealous and imperious Pellew had relentlessly patrolled the coast in hot, humid conditions, enforcing strict discipline and denying all shore leave, which incited near mutiny by his crew. Officers and men had complained bitterly in letters home, and when their views were picked up and published in *The Times*,[53] the Admiralty was forced to act. They were aware that this was the third time that crews had become mutinous under Pellew's command, and so he was relieved of his post.[54] He was ordered to sail for Trincomalee where his successor, Rear Admiral Sir James Stirling, would take command.[55]

Just before Pellew's command, the responsibilities of the former Eastern Station (based at Trincomalee) had been divided. The need to protect the rapidly increasing trade in the five Treaty ports—Canton, Amoy, Foochow, Shanghai and Tientsin (near Peking)—had led to a split in responsibilities. China and the Malayan seas became a separate China Station, headquartered in Hong Kong, while the Eastern Station, still based at Trincomalee, commanded the rest of the Indian and Pacific Ocean regions, including New South Wales, New Zealand and adjacent islands (which were also given a semi-independent command).

The force that Stirling would have at his disposal on the China Station consisted initially of one third-rated ship-of-war (his flagship), two frigates, five sloops and one steam vessel,[56] and their primary duty was to check piracy both in the Malayan seas and along the coast of China. The Admiralty Board had made it clear in its standing orders, however, that the purpose of the warships' presence was far from belligerent. Naval officers were to work with the Chinese authorities, and study Chinese wishes and feelings, in order to preserve amicable relations, and hence protect the valuable trade links between Britain and China.[57]

The new appointment was thus very different from Stirling's previous experience, and it would be complicated too by increasing tensions with Russia, and rebelliousness among the crew of Pellew's flagship. But one thing was cheering. Family advice in Manchester held China to be the key to future fortunes in the cotton trade. Soon after the Treaty of Nanking the former Governor of Hong Kong, Sir Henry Pottinger, had lectured in Manchester and pointed to a vast potential market in China, as the inhabitants presently wore cotton homespuns made from Indian cotton.[58] British cotton exports to China had since increased, but not to the extent anticipated, and this new command would give Stirling a chance to unearth some useful information.

On the day that his commission was officially gazetted, Stirling began his 'Journal of Proceedings', noting on 19 January that he had hoisted his White flag on the mizzen mast of HMS *Fishguard*[59] as the *Winchester*, his designated ship, was still in the China seas.[60] James had initially been a Rear Admiral of the Blue, but had gone up a step to Rear Admiral of the White on receiving his command. (Each naval rank had three colour classes at this time, of which red was highest.) Stirling also wrote on that day to the Admiralty applying for Captain M. J. Currie to be his secretary—the same Mark Currie who had been his Harbour Master during the founding years of Swan River Colony. On 21 January Stirling learned that he was to go out on a steam-packet rather than a navy vessel to save time, so he immediately hauled his flag down, took leave of the *Fishguard*, and returned to London.

There was much to do in the ensuing days: reports from the Foreign Office and the Admiralty pertaining to the recent Chinese insurrection, similar dispatches covering the conduct of British ships in the event of war with Russia, and a special request to the Admiralty (granted on 31 January) that his son Frederick Henry be appointed his Flag Lieutenant. It would have pleased Ellen immensely that the two would be together for James' term of duty in the remote China seas.

Information received early in February 1854 had caused the Admiralty to rescind its earlier order for a meeting with Pellew in Trincomalee, and instead urge James to proceed directly to Hong Kong.[61] Under a previous Act of Parliament,[62] £20 in prize money had been awarded for each 'piratical person captured or killed',[63] but the suppression of piracy on the China coast had cost the British taxpayer a total of £149,243 in bounties until the law was amended in 1850, and was to be reduced further in the *Naval Prize Act* of 1854. Not surprisingly, by early 1854 piracies in

Hong Kong waters were once again occurring at the rate of fourteen a month.[64] The two largest merchant houses (Jardine Matheson & Co. and Dent & Co.) were demanding action. It was a delicate situation, as both were known to be involved in the opium trade, of which Britain officially disapproved but unofficially sanctioned as a necessary link in the trading chain. Britain could not afford to ignore their pleas. It thus became imperative for Stirling to assume his command quickly and set in train actions to control the pirates.

Arrangements were made for Stirling to travel privately by the fastest route. Passage was booked for him aboard the P&O vessel *Sultan*, bound for Alexandria in the Mediterranean, where he would be transferred across country, along the route of the future Suez Canal, to meet other P&O packets which would transport him and his retinue to Hong Kong. In the rush to prepare for departure, which had to include fittings for new tropical uniforms, there was no time for long farewells as James left England on 24 February 1854.[65] Another chapter in his long career lay ahead.

27

Fifth Command: HMS *Winchester*

1854–1856

STIRLING'S JOURNEY TO Hong Kong was broken by two transfer stops: first in Galle, Ceylon, which his P&O steam packet *Hindustan* reached on 28 March 1854 (the day before the Crimean War was declared), and then Singapore, where a second packet, the *Cadiz*, docked on 5 April. There he hoisted his flag on HM brig *Rapid* and was received with full ceremony.

Alongside the *Rapid* at Singapore were the *Sibella*[1] and the *Lily*, whose commanders apprised him of the distribution of the remainder of the squadron. The *Encounter*, *Grecian* and *Styx* were at Shanghai, the *Bittern* at Amoy, the *Comus* at Canton, while the *Spartan*, *Barracouta* and *Rattler* were in transit between Singapore and Hong Kong, as also was the *Winchester*, his future flagship.[2] Of these, the *Spartan 26*, *Sibella 20* and *Winchester 52* were line-of-battle sailing ships, the *Comus 14*, *Grecian 12*, *Lily 12*, *Bittern 12* and *Rapid 8* were sloops, and the rest were steamers. It was a much smaller squadron than those Stirling had been used to in the Mediterranean, and most were short-handed as he soon informed the Admiralty.[3] But they were his to command, and he must have taken pleasure in transmitting on 5 April a memorandum to all his captains informing them that he had assumed command of the Station.[4]

During his month-long stay in Singapore Stirling was alerted by the Governor of the threat of Chinese pirates, a threat as real there as he would encounter in Hong Kong. P&O ships had virtually stopped carrying passengers after two of their vessels had been attacked, and all on board put to death. He also had his first taste of the type of incident which would engage his attention as head of the China Station. Urgent intelligence had been received that the protectorate at Shanghai was practically under siege from insurgent forces and the British Consul there, Sir Rutherford Alcock, had authorised a sortie by British naval forces, under the command of Captain O'Callaghan, which had crossed international boundaries. Assisted by Americans from the sloop *Plymouth* and by civilian volunteers, O'Callaghan and his men had rushed the insurgent Chinese soldiers' encampments around Shanghai. This was unwelcome news for Stirling, as he had been given strict instructions to avoid acts of hostility towards the subjects of a foreign country, even when provoked. This ruling he immediately conveyed to O'Callaghan:

> …it is my duty to point out that it belongs to the Crown alone to declare war…No such acts can be…recommended or called for by any consular officer…I have considered…the circumstances you relate, and I am bound to acknowledge that they appear to have been such as to have left you no alternative…I have therefore to inform you that your personal conduct, and that of the gallant captain, officers and men who co-operated with you from the United States ship *Plymouth*…has elicited my warmest admiration…[5]

However, the incident had a constructive outcome. With the help of the Americans, a non-interference policy was subsequently worked out to the satisfaction of the Imperial authorities in Shanghai.[6] Henceforth, Stirling reported, 'British French and American subjects could live in peace and their ships move safely to and from the port to the open sea'.[7]

On 3 May Stirling transferred his flag to the *Barracouta*, which would take him to Hong Kong. On his way to the same destination, aboard HMS *Winchester*, was the newly appointed Governor of Hong Kong, Sir John Bowring, with whom he would have close dealings. At 62, just a year younger than Stirling, Bowring was an unusual man, by one account literary-minded, a linguist and 'would-be man of action' with a penetrating mind, whose 'judgement could be capricious',[8] and by another, as a man whose 'great failing in matters great and small was that he could not judge the time to act and the time to pause'.[9] This Stirling was to experience in no small measure. Between 1841 and 1849 Bowring had served on a Parliamentary Commission inquiring into commercial relations with China. In 1849 he had been appointed British Consul at Canton—responsible to Sir Samuel George Bonham, Governor of Hong Kong—and when the latter retired in early 1854, Bowring was given his position.

When Stirling arrived in Hong Kong on 11 May, officers on board HMS *Winchester* fired a gun salute to their new Admiral as the wooden paddle sloop *Barracouta* came to anchor alongside. Stirling's flag was then shifted to the *Winchester*[10] and he could finally inspect his new ship. She was much smaller than the *Howe*, being only fourth-rated with 52 guns compared to the *Howe*'s 120. She was also one of the oldest ships still in use, with lengthy battle honours to her credit.[11] She had last been coppered in 1850 and had a total complement of 450 men.[12] Her Captain at this time was John Fitzgerald, with Lieutenants Francis Marten, James Bushnell and Horatio Nelson.[13] Many of her officers and seamen were due for furlough, so the ship's company would change when new appointees arrived, including his son Frederick Henry. In his first dispatch from Hong Kong Stirling informed the Admiralty that

Sir John Bowring, Governor of Hong Kong during Stirling's term as
Naval Commander-in-Chief

the sick list on the *Winchester* is 55. Ever since service in Burma the sick list has been enormous, and the surgeon is of the opinion that it will continue until we have a complete change of climate.[14]

They were now at the beginning of May and the stifling summer weather to come would provide little relief. Whether or not heat was a factor, Stirling once again found himself at odds with the protocol of sending dispatches to London. He had failed to state his exact location and included more than one subject in those previously sent, earning an Admiralty rebuke similar to those he had received so many years earlier, as Lieutenant-Governor of Swan River Colony. Ever particular, the Admiralty spelt out the procedure for all future correspondence—one subject per dispatch, each dispatch numbered sequentially (and each paragraph within them), and all to be returned in duplicate.[15]

His immediate concerns were two-fold: piracy, which required some semblance of control, and the problem of Russia's expansionist plans around the Eastern Russian-Japanese border. Governor Bowring, who returned on 17 May from a short visit to Whampoa (the entry to Canton), reported further alarming acts of piracy—one involving a Dutch ship set upon by nineteen pirate junks with many killed.[16]

The second problem was potentially far more serious. The arrival on 24 May of the latest English mail brought the news that war had officially been declared on Russia. James learned that his son Charles, recently promoted to First Lieutenant in

Stirling's flagship HMS *Winchester*, shown above in an 1835 watercolour

Courtesy National Maritime Museum, Greenwich PAD 6130

the Royal Artillery, had orders to embark for the Crimean Peninsula, as had his two nephews, John's sons William and John (the latter, sadly, to die aged 18 in one of the early, bloody battles of the war).[17] Even as recently as the end of March, Stirling had received reports of Russian ships spotted off Shanghai, and had immediately sent one of his patrol ships, the *Rattler*, to investigate. Soon afterwards, other reports confirmed the presence of a Russian steamer near Shanghai and the expected arrival of three more ships from the Russian Far Eastern Fleet.[18] This intelligence produced near panic in Hong Kong, resulting in a flurry of activity to strengthen defences against a possible Russian attack. Stirling did not share the panic. He was too politically astute to believe that Hong Kong was a target. He could see that Russia was attempting to consolidate her claims southward through Manchuria, so that she could put pressure directly on China and Japan from home territory.[19] The threat was therefore well to the north. In consultation with Bowring, Stirling decided on a show of strength and ordered the squadron to make ready for sea.

With Bowring also on board the *Winchester*, Stirling and four other vessels headed out of Victoria harbour on 25 May, anchoring off the mouth of the Yangtse River twelve days later. Early on 7 June Bowring and his suite transferred to the paddle sloop *Styx* for the journey up the Huangpu River to Shanghai to confer with Consul Alcock. Stirling, who had issued orders for 'the capture of all vessels under whatever flag carrying Russian sailors intended to reinforce Russian Cruisers',[20] was himself then asked to visit Shanghai where he shifted his flag to HMS *Grecian*, a small brig moored at the docks of the British enclave.

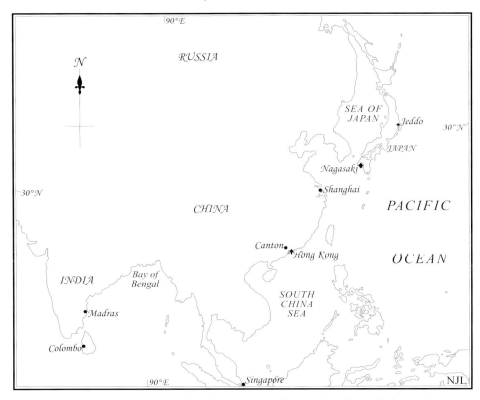

Map of the area under Stirling's China command, extending from Ceylon to Japan

His talks with Alcock mainly concerned establishing accurate information about Russian movements for the Admiralty, but others impinged more directly on his command. In the previous September the work of British consular and customs officials had been disrupted when pirates and insurgents overtook the city. Some foreigners had supported the insurgents, and supplied them with arms.[21] As a result, with confidence in the British reduced, the foreign settlement began to suffer 'the aggressions of the Imperial Soldiery'. In response to complaints about Chinese soldiers transgressing the boundary of the British settlement, Stirling had had to interview the Commander-in-Chief of the Chinese Imperial Army. It was a delicate line to tread, trying to protect British interests and the obvious trade benefits, while at the same time refraining from 'any act which may be fairly deemed offensive or injurious to the inhabitants of a country with which Her Majesty is in a state of Amity'.[22]

Stirling's intercession had a positive outcome, for in conjunction with the relevant Chinese authorities, he organised the formation of a municipal council and a civilian police force for the foreign settlement. His views in this respect had not changed from his days as Governor of Western Australia—Her Majesty's forces were not the proper authority to undertake civilian peace-keeping responsibilities. That was a task better suited to civilians with an intimate knowledge of local affairs and hence the ability to negotiate to avoid conflict.

In Shanghai at this time was the American sloop *Plymouth*[23] from whose officers Stirling learned details of Commodore Matthew Perry's 1853 expedition to Japan. In fact, some of the American ships at Shanghai had just returned from ratifying the Treaty, the first to be negotiated with previously isolated Japan. As a result of their negotiations, two Japanese harbours had been opened to American ships, and Stirling heard first-hand accounts of the reception and difficulties they had encountered. Perry's actions, which would vastly increase the United States' naval authority in the area, had yet to be fully comprehended. However, in late July Stirling prepared a report for the Admiralty, headed 'On the late Treaty between the United States and Japan'. He clearly saw the future potential of the treaty, but reported:

> At the present it is hardly more than an engagement that shipwrecked Americans shall be well treated; that American ships in need of supplies may resort to two ports indicated…that a thousand tons of coal shall always be ready for the use of American steamers; and that in future a tariff of prices for supplies shall be established. The Japanese denied that they had any articles of commerce to export, or any need of imports from other countries, and the American Officers appear to think that this is substantially true…[24]

As a mark of respect to the Americans in port, Stirling ordered all British ships to be dressed and to fire a 21-gun salute on 4 July—Independence Day.

The next day was time for a family celebration, for among the replacement ship's company sent out from England and welcomed aboard the *Winchester* was Commander F. H. Stirling.[25] James would have been delighted to see his son and quickly briefed him on the situation they faced. Not only was there the Russian threat to worry about, but British trade in the area was being seriously undermined by persistent pirate raids, which somehow had to be brought under control. This was an exciting challenge for 25-year-old Frederick Henry who, thanks to his father's intervention, would have some say for the first time in the actions of his ship.

Throughout the latter part of his time in Shanghai, Stirling had been giving considerable thought to Perry's successful negotiations with Japan. He had had no official orders to follow suit, but he *had* received orders to transmit details of the declaration of war against Russia to all Far Eastern ports. Using this as his objective, Stirling called the captains of his ships to the *Winchester* late in August and announced his intention of visiting Nagasaki in Japan. Both Bowring and Alcock had shared his belief that, as things stood, Russians could shelter in Japanese harbours and menace allied shipping. If he could win similar concessions to the Americans and strip Russia of any preferred position in Japanese ports, Stirling could make a significant contribution to British defences in the area and hence to the war.

On 2 September 1854 Stirling took the *Winchester* and steamers *Encounter*, *Barracouta* and *Styx* out of the mouth of the Yangtse, and bore east for Japan. On the afternoon of the 7th they sighted the island of Kyushu, and the Admiral signalled the squadron to form the 'line-of-battle', and for all ship captains to board the flagship. A memo was given to each captain setting out rules to govern the behaviour of officers and men during their stay in Japan, as 'the utmost prudence will be necessary to avoid injurious mis-understandings with that peculiar people'.[26] His instructions on this occasion were forwarded to the Admiralty Lords, and included the final directive that he would

> reject as foreign to my business all reference to commerce, [and] limit my own attention and that of the Authorities, to the Military question intimated in my first communication, and simply to seek its solution by a firm and consistent course.[27]

The squadron then proceeded slowly towards Nagasaki, nearing the port on the evening of 7 September. Lieutenant J. M. Tronson, from the *Barracouta*, recorded subsequent events:

> As we entered the…[outer anchorage of Nagasaki] many official boats approached, and by waving flags and bunches of paper warned us not to enter the inner or middle anchorage. One personage who appeared to be a custom house officer, held up a white wand with some document attached, written in the Dutch language; this was passed on to the flagship. It contained a list of questions as to where we were from, our business, our intended stay; and ordered the ships to anchor…A line of guard boats was placed around the squadron, for the purpose, the authorities informed us, of keeping away intruders, such as smugglers; the real object being to prevent any person landing from the ships…The Admiral received some of the principal Japanese officials on board the *Winchester*…[28]

Stirling had brought with him a Japanese-born interpreter, John Ottoson, who was employed by the Hong Kong merchant house, Dent & Co., which had released him for the expedition.[29] He was mainly used in verbal exchanges, as all the documents Stirling handed over to the Japanese officials were in English. In this first meeting, after a ceremony of introduction, Stirling gave the Japanese officials a letter, written on parchment and tied with silk ribbon, which he had previously prepared for the Governor of Nagasaki. He began by explaining that:

> HM the Queen of Great Britain (in conjunction with all her allies) has been compelled, by the ambition and rapacity of Russia, to declare war against her, in defence of the liberties of Europe…large military forces have been called into action [and] the fleets of Russia have been forced to retire within their own Harbours…In a similar spirit measures will be taken for the capture and destruction of the Russian ships and settlements in this vicinity, where the gradual encroachments of Russia…point very clearly to their ulterior designs upon Japan.

As the 'Commander-in-Chief of the naval forces of Her Majesty the Queen of Great Britain, appointed to carry on the war in the Eastern Seas', Stirling stated that he would have

> frequent occasion to visit the coasts and ports of Japan, in order to prevent the Russian ships of war and their prizes from making use of those ports, to the detriment of the interests of Great Britain and her allies.

It was his anxious desire to avoid, as far as possible, the commission of any act which might give offence to His Imperial Majesty the Emperor of Japan, or his subjects, but to accomplish this he needed to know the intentions of the Japanese Government with respect to the admission into its ports of the ships of war of the belligerent parties. He therefore requested the Governor of Nagasaki

> to take all necessary measures for ascertaining and communicating to him the views and intentions of your Government upon this subject, not only in reference to the port of Nagasaki, but also in regard to all other ports and places within Japanese territory.[30]

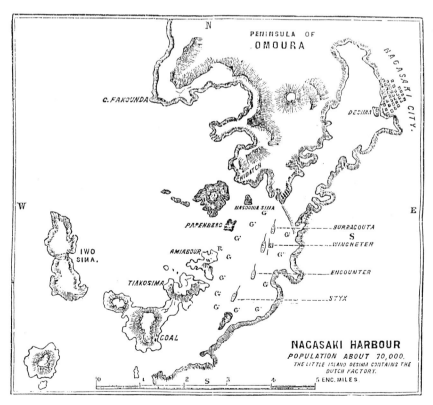

The position of Stirling's squadron in Nagasaki harbour, published
(with ships' names misspelt) in the *Illustrated London News* on 28 April 1855

Requesting entry to *all* ports[31] was a bold move on Stirling's part. The American, Perry, had had to resort to a certain amount of bullying to push through the treaty he had signed on 31 March 1854, and that treaty had only opened two (later ratified as three) of Japan's harbours to American shipping. Stirling was now pushing them further.

In this first contact with Japanese officials, Stirling had sought, and won, permission to move his squadron to a safer anchorage, and at 9.30 a.m. on 8 September the squadron tacked into the picturesque middle harbour at Nagasaki where there were numerous islets covered by 'pine, camphor tree, and luxuriant camellia'. A row of chained junks barred passage to the inner harbour, and the surrounding hills 'were decorated with batteries in terraces, each having from six to ten guns'.[32] Once the *Winchester* had anchored, a Japanese officer came aboard with a present of fresh provisions and a message from the Governor of Nagasaki to the effect that Stirling's letter had been translated, and been sent on to Jeddo (modern Tokyo), but no answer could be expected for a month as it was an overland, mountainous journey of nearly 400 miles.[33] (A few days later Stirling learned that his letter had been translated first into Dutch, then Japanese, and that in fact a normal round trip to Jeddo in fine weather was more like ten days.)

That afternoon the Governor sent fresh provisions for the crews, including three pigs, fifty fowls, 500 eggs, six boxes of cake and a generous quantity of fruit and vegetables which Stirling acknowledged as a 'very acceptable present'.[34] But the Governor did not accede to Stirling's request to allow small parties of his men on to one of the nearby islands for recreation and exercise. Existing port regulations forbade the landing of foreigners, and no rule could be relaxed without the Emperor's permission. Another request, for a boatload of sand to clean the decks, was allowed, but not with the desired result. Delivered on 14 September, it was found to be gravel, much to the amusement of the Japanese authorities, who wished to rectify the mistake. As the waiting game dragged on Stirling had to keep tight rein on his men, who were still forbidden to go ashore. Permission for them to fish was also refused, and Stirling had to decline the Governor's offer to provide fresh fish if ordered, on the grounds that he could not trade until the standing of the two nations had been established.

On 22 September word came that the Governor would, at the Admiral's particular request, allow some boats to pull about the harbour within specified limits, providing no one landed or went too close to shore. Unasked for baskets of fish were delivered over the next two days, but Stirling's offer of some English newspapers was rejected—this would have to be cleared from Jeddo. By the 27th Stirling had had enough. He sent a brief note ashore thanking the Governor for his 'civility and courtesy', and advised him that, as twenty days had passed without answer to his dispatch, he planned to proceed to Jeddo 'with a view to demand an answer from the Imperial Government'.[35] That afternoon he ordered the squadron to ready for departure next day, instructing captains to rendezvous in Shimoda Bay (near Jeddo) in the event of being separated. This initiative, and signs of activity, drew a quick response, for early next morning an emissary of the Governor arrived with an urgent message, which was minuted by Stirling's secretary, Mark Currie. In essence, the message sympathised that 'the Admiral's patience had been tried', reiterated that Jeddo's 'great distance' from Nagasaki took time for replies to get back, and pointed out that public dispatches went slower than merchant letters because of 'the greater ceremony observed in passing the dispatch from hand to hand'. Stirling should stay another ten days, but if he persisted in leaving straight away, the Governor could face 'great trouble'.

Stirling replied that he would stay at least another day. The emissary returned with an urgent response which included a sweetener. The Governor would 'on his own responsibility' try to find a small spot for the sailors' recreation on condition that Stirling consented to remain ten days longer. As to supplies, whatever the squadron required could 'be purchased through the Dutch Superintendent for Trade until the Emperor's answer arrives, as the Admiral declines accepting them from the Japanese Government'.[36]

The Dutch, who since the seventeenth century had maintained a small trading post at Hirado, had been exempted from Japan's total ban on foreign intercourse but forced to contain all operations to the tiny island of Deshima in Nagasaki Bay. Although traders and their families were kept in virtual confinement, they were allowed limited trade with Europe through Java and, as such, had been Japan's one window to the West during some two centuries of seclusion.[37] Stirling accepted the olive branch in a letter he desired to be put into the Governor's hands. It read:

> The Admiral is deeply sensible of the kind feeling evinced by the Governor's message now delivered. If he understands it rightly, it is, first, that his people shall have a place assigned to them where they may land for exercise and recreation; and secondly, that he shall be allowed to purchase from the Dutch superintendent what he may want. And to show his sense of the Governor's goodness in these concessions, he consents to remain ten days, in compliance with his request.[38]

There is a gap in Stirling's journal between 27 September and 2 October, but Currie's diary records a significant letter from Admiral to Governor dated the 30th which Stirling insisted be explained to the Japanese officer-emissaries before transmission. It read:

> The Admiral hopes the Governor sees clearly the great difference between the business which brings this Squadron here, and that which all former foreign ships have come. All former visitors—English, French, Russian and American—come as mendicants, soliciting some relaxation of the laws, or other accommodation. We come, as it becomes the Public Officers of a great country, asking for nothing, and unwilling to accept anything but an answer to a question arising out of the war, which concerns Japan as much as England; not to beg favours but simply to

have the important question contained in the Admiral's first letter to the Governor candidly answered; and if he sees this difference between us and our predecessors in a proper light, he will know how we ought to be treated.[39]

By 2 October agreement had been reached on a place for the men to exercise. Tronson noted that they dubbed the small island they landed on that afternoon 'Little Britain', and that the food purchased from the Dutch was 'scanty and of indifferent quality'.[40]

Finally, on 3 October, the Governor of Nagasaki sent a message that he would be glad to receive the Admiral the following day at about 9 a.m. if convenient. He wished to be informed on the numbers of officers and men accompanying Stirling and would provide chairs for the visitors, unless he preferred to bring his own. Stirling replied immediately, presenting his compliments and accepting the invitation. He added that he proposed to proceed on foot from the landing place to the palace. His party would consist of thirteen officers and four orderlies, there would be no military guard, but all officers would wear their swords. He 'accepted with pleasure the Governor's offer to have chairs provided'.[41]

Early next morning the party was assembled and inspected minutely before entering the flag-bedecked boats. The band went first, playing a medley of British airs, followed by five boats in line carrying the shore party. Stirling, with his son as Flag Officer, and secretary Currie were in the last. Almost as soon as they took to the water they were surrounded by a flotilla of small boats which accompanied them to the shore. Tronson from the *Barracouta* was among the officers in the party and noted that on landing the band played 'God Save the Queen', and the Admiral was received by a guard of honour and a body of Japanese officers in court costume, after which

> The procession passed through a suite of rooms to an antechamber where each individual was presented with a chair…the Admiral and the Captain were ushered into the presence chamber, a large apartment, with the usual festoons; a row of soldiers lined the sides, and near the audience seat were many of the grandees and courtiers, squatted down before the Governor and Chief Inspector, who stood waiting to receive the Admiral. His Excellency advanced and saluted the Governor, who returned the salutation by a slight inclination of the head. Conversation was carried on through the medium of interpreters…[42]

After an exchange of compliments the audience concluded and the company was offered 'Tea and pipes…followed by fish and sweetmeats; forks, chopsticks and napkins being supplied'. Currie noted that the Japanese party were all without shoes, but no sign was given that the visitors' naval boots should be removed. In the more intimate discussion that followed refreshments, Stirling was attended only by his son, Captain Wilson and secretary Currie. The Governor apologised for the time

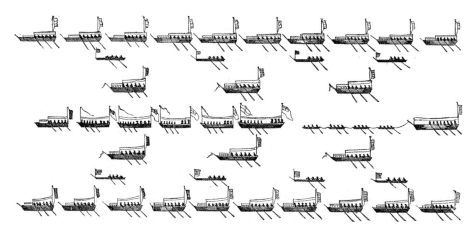

The procession of boats into Nagasaki during Stirling's second visit there,
for the signing of the treaty. The Japanese sketch was reproduced in
the *Illustrated London News* on 28 April 1855

it was taking to receive an answer from Jeddo. Stirling replied that the delay was
understandable as it was a very important question. The Governor agreed, remarking that the 'important information so kindly communicated by the Queen of
England…had created great astonishment'. The conference, which lasted nearly two
and a half hours, then got under way.

Stirling began by stating his desire to explain anything that was not perfectly
clear, and went on to say:

> he was quite sure the Government of England had no wish to intrude their ships
> into the ports of Japan; but that a new order of things had arisen out of a state of
> war, which had brought the English ships into these seas…his Government were
> anxious to act against Russia…[but] in a manner to avoid giving offence to the
> Japanese Government or to the subjects of the Emperor…

The Governor said he saw 'some little difference between the letter as translated to
him and the observations which had just dropped from the Admiral', and would
like further explanation. He understood the exigencies of war had caused the visit,
but wanted to know whether the Admiral's object was to gain access to Japanese
ports to look for Russians, or to anchor in them to obtain supplies. Stirling
answered at length:

> If the Russians be not permitted to enter, he will not seek to do so for the purposes
> of refitting, harbouring prizes etc; but must be permitted to enter Japanese Ports,
> as belonging to a neutral, to see that no Russian be present, and that they do not
> bring their prizes in; and this is what the Admiral has come to arrange with the
> Government of Japan.

The Governor said he now understood, but thought he could only have one or two ports for the purposes mentioned. The Admiral replied that it might be best if he embodied what he had said in a letter, but then asked whether the Governor had authorisation from Jeddo to settle the matter. The Governor replied that he had received instructions and was empowered to discuss and settle matters with the Admiral. After many pleasantries on both sides, the party repaired to the outer room where Stirling's men were served pudding with a silver fork and spoon in addition to chopsticks. At 2.45 p.m. they made their way to the boats and were escorted out of the inner harbour in the same way they had been ushered in, though with fewer attendant boats.[43]

Real negotiations appear to have begun on 5 October when Stirling sent a draft of his proposed convention for the admission of British ships into the ports of Japan, formally addressed to Mezi-ro Chekfu-no Kami, the Governor of Nagasaki.[44] The draft convention had six clauses dealing with the ports to be opened to ships of war, the expectations of the British regarding supplies, their responsibility to obey any port regulations set down, and to conform to the laws of Japan. It was prefaced by a note stressing that an agreement was necessary because of the exigencies of war.[45]

On the 8th the Governor sent word to invite Stirling to an interview at noon the following day. After preliminaries the Governor produced a response to the Admiral's draft and suggested that Stirling should have it read to him prior to discussion. The interpreter then translated, and Currie minuted the Governor's detailed comments on each of the points Stirling had raised. His main concern was Stirling's emphasis on war needs:

> Japan not having an enemy in the world, would, by opening her ports for the purposes of War, be creating them; and not only Russia, but other nations might become her enemies, to the great distress and trouble of her people. And as the Queen of Great Britain is desirous that the whole world should enjoy peace and quiet, she would regret much should a war rage in Japan; therefore any harbours to be opened cannot be used for the purposes of war…

The Governor then asked whether the Admiral understood that, while he could not open any ports for the purposes of war, he could do so for the purposes of supplies like provisions and water. Further, he could not distinguish between ordinary supplies and those arising from distress occasioned by acts of war. Stirling said he understood. The Governor was also concerned about the suggestion that 'ships of war of Great Britain are to be treated equally with other nations'. He stated, with clear reference to the Dutch, that

> What the Admiral suggests is reasonable…but just as there is a difference between one's own family and strangers, so there is between nations with whom there may

have been intercourse of long standing and others where it has not previously existed, which renders it difficult to treat all parties alike.[46]

Stirling agreed with his point. The Governor then added that, though both Nagasaki and Hakodadi would be opened, the latter port was a long way off and he could only make arrangements regarding Nagasaki.

At the end of their discussions the Governor intimated that he would have a new agreement drawn up, and sent to the *Winchester* for the Admiral's signature. Refreshments were then offered and the party escorted, under umbrellas due to heavy rain, to a covered boat provided for their return. Currie noted that during the conference the Japanese had taken the boats' crews and the band (amounting to almost 100 men) to shelter in the palace, and had provided them with refreshments.

Over the next two days there were several queries from the Governor, and replies by Stirling, on various matters. The Japanese were particularly wary about granting to Britain the same privileges extended to other nations, but Stirling insisted on retaining this clause, stating:

> an English Officer must not sign, and his Government would not ratify, any engagement whatever which would place British subjects in Japan in a worse position than Americans or those of any other nations.

Various minor issues were also raised: from Stirling, a request that a 'fenced…and properly protected'[47] burial ground for the British be reserved on Medsume Sima (the island where they had been allowed to land); and from the Governor, a request that an identity stamp or licence be issued to authenticate British vessels entering Japanese ports. The latter also wanted it to be understood that the treaty would be ratified by a high officer under the Emperor's instructions, and not by the Emperor himself, as was the custom in Japan. The visiting officials then intimated that the Governor was greatly interested in steamships, and that he would like some of his Japanese mechanics to be allowed to inspect the machinery. Stirling readily agreed and said he would also recommend that the Queen of England send out to Japan, for the Emperor, a small engine with a screw-propeller adapted for a boat.

Formal signing of the documents was set for 11.30 a.m. the next day, 14 October, and once more Stirling and his officers, in full dress uniforms, left the *Winchester* to be taken in barges to Nagasaki for the signing. In this procession, as one of the party later described, five boats bore the British flag. 'The Japanese boats took up their stations in the most perfect order, every one of which was distinguished by some flag…brilliant in red, blue, black and white', denoting different guards and departments.[48] On arrival at the landing place, the British party were ushered to the reception rooms where the Governor (or Obunyo), Inspector (or Omedski), and other Commissioners of the Emperor and their retinues greeted them. The Conventions, both English and the Japanese versions, lay waiting for signing.

Convention for Regulating the Admission of British Ships into the Ports of Japan

It is agreed between Sir James Stirling, Knight, Rear Admiral and Commander-in-Chief of the ships and vessels of Her Britannic Majesty in the East Indies and seas adjacent, and Mezi-ro Chekfu-no Kami, Obunyo of Nagasaki and Nagai Evan Ocho, Omedski of Nagasaki, ordered by His Imperial Highness the Emperor of Japan to act herein; that—

1st

The ports of Nagasaki (Fisen) and Hakodadi (Matsmai) shall be open to British ships for the purposes of effecting repairs and obtaining fresh water, provisions and other supplies of any sort they may absolutely want for the use of their ships.

2nd

Nagasaki shall be open for the purposes aforesaid from and after the present date; and Hakodadi from and after the end of 50 days from the Admiral's departure from this port. The rules and regulations of each of these ports are to be complied with.

3rd

Only ships in distress from weather, or unmanageable, will be permitted to enter other ports than those specified in the forgoing Articles, without permission from the Imperial Government.

4th

British ships in Japanese Ports shall conform to the laws of Japan. If high officers or Commanders of ships shall break any such laws, it will lead to the ports being closed. Should inferior persons break them they are to be delivered over to their commanders for punishment.

5th

In the ports of Japan now open, or which may hereafter be opened, to the ships and subjects of any foreign nation, British ships and subjects shall be entitled to admission, and to the enjoyment of an equality of advantages with those of the most favoured nation, always excepting the advantages accruing to the Dutch and Chinese from their existing relations with Japan.

6th

This convention shall be ratified, and the ratifications shall be exchanged at Nagasaki on behalf of Her Majesty the Queen of Great Britain, and on behalf of His Highness the Emperor of Japan, within 12 months from the present date.

7th

When this convention is ratified, no high officer coming to Japan shall alter it.

In witness whereof we have signed the same and have affixed our seals thereunto, at Nagasaki, this fourteenth day of October, 1854.[49]

Even at this stage the Governor of Nagasaki had reservations. In Article 1 he wanted it understood that by supplies was meant absolute necessities, not spars or naval stores. The Governor was perfectly happy with Article 2 but the Admiral asked that the port regulations be furnished as soon as possible, to which the Governor agreed. Both agreed on Articles 3 to 6 but the Governor hesitated over 7 which had originally said 'This Agreement, being settled, cannot be altered'. The Governor argued that the next Admiral or some high officer coming to Japan might wish for other arrangements, so Stirling agreed to change the wording slightly. While the alterations were effected, the Governor said that he much regretted that he and the Admiral had not been able to converse in a language known to them both. Stirling had replied that he was too old to start studying Japanese now, but he would recommend that his son (whom he presented to the Governor) do so at once. The Governor of Nagasaki also agreed to await Her Majesty's directions regarding the stamp or proof of identity to be furnished by British ships.[50] Arrangements were also made for a party of Japanese to be taken out on the *Encounter* on 16 October to witness the workings of the screw-propeller.

The documents were then examined by all to ensure they were true copies, the Governor and the Inspector signed and sealed every page of the Japanese version, and the accompanying letters, and Admiral Stirling did the same on the agreement bound for the British Government. The Governor asked that when the document was returned for ratification a Dutch translation should accompany it, to which Stirling agreed. Stirling formally thanked his co-signatories, and expressed the hope that the Convention would prove evidence of a lasting friendship between the two nations. When the signings were complete, dinner was served, European style. Tronson recorded with some surprise that the meal consisted of 'soup, fish, meats and pastry with wines: the latter I presume, procured from the Dutch'. The pleasantries ended well after dark and a guard of honour, holding elegant paper lanterns, escorted the Admiral and his suite back to the waiting boats. Later some gifts were sent to the ships; including pieces of fine silk, delicate Japanese china, and, for the junior officers, less valuable 'cups, saucers or plates of porcelain'.[51]

There were still a few loose ends to tie up, but the squadron could now prepare to leave. On the 16th, as promised, Stirling accompanied a party of Japanese officials and mechanics on a visit to the steamer *Encounter* which, to their delight, was run through her paces for well over an hour.

One of the most important issues to clarify before leaving were the port regulations to be observed in future by incoming ships. On the 17th Stirling sent a memorandum requesting the Governor to have them readied immediately, or he would return for them in two months' time.[52] The Governor replied that the Regulations for the Port of Nagasaki would be ready the following day.

True to his word, the Governor sent the Standing Port Regulations for the Port of Nagasaki on 18 October. They contained five clauses:

1st That ships wait in the outer harbour for directions from the Governor,

2nd That no firearms be discharged,

3rd No person to land on any of the islands without permission,

4th No soundings to be taken or boats to be pulling about,

5th No communication be held with merchant boats and no exchanges or trading of any sort.[53]

The Port Regulations for Hakodadi were to be communicated at a future date. Stirling acknowledged this the following day, but added that he would like to know whether French ships would be admitted to the two ports to be open to the British.[54] The Governor's reply, just as the squadron was ready to weigh anchor, said this matter would have to be referred to Jeddo.[55] The fact that the Japanese Government had decided to treat each nation separately made Stirling's achievement all the more remarkable.

The Admiral had proposed firing a 21-gun salute as a mark of esteem as the squadron left the harbour, but a polite message from the Governor said it was contrary to Japanese custom for any firing to take place. As officials delivered this advice, two little spaniels—a gift from the Governor—entered the cabin, prompting Stirling to say he was thinking of sending them to the Queen of Great Britain. One of the officials replied that 'it would be a good chance for the dogs'! The Admiral then presented the officials with two revolvers for the Governor and the Inspector, as examples of British manufacture, regretting he had no other gifts. In acknowledging this gesture later, the Governor said it was not customary in Japan to accept presents, but as a token of remembrance he would accept what the Admiral had so kindly sent.[56]

With all negotiations completed, the small squadron weighed anchor at 8 a.m. on 20 October 1854 and was escorted out of Nagasaki harbour to the open sea.[57] The following day strong gales from the north-east split up the ships and forced the *Winchester* to hove to for three nights, so delaying their return to Hong Kong. When the wind died sufficiently to give his desk stability, Stirling prepared a report for the Admiralty on the subject of his Convention. Dated 26 October 'at sea' aboard the *Winchester*, it first summarised the reasons behind his visit to Japan as being:

> the chance it offered of finding the Russians in a quarter in which they had passed considerable portions of the previous 12 months; and in the second place the opportunity it gave me of making such arrangements as should prevent the enemy from making use of the ports and resources of Japan…

He went on to describe the Convention, as executed in both English and Japanese, and summed up the effect of the seven articles as follows:

> It opens absolutely and at once to British ships of every description two of the most convenient harbours in Japan. It opens inferentially to British ships in distress any

other Port in Japan it may be expedient for them to seek shelter in…It secures eventually to British ships and subjects, in every port of Japan which may hereafter be open to foreigners, equal advantages with the ships and subjects of the most favoured nation, excepting only the advantages at present accorded to the Dutch and Chinese; and it imposes in return for these concessions no obligation on British ships and subjects than of respecting the laws and ordinances of the ports they visit. This agreement will cease at the end of 12 months from the date of execution unless it shall be honoured with Her Majesty's ratification; but in this latter event it will acquire thereby a permanent character.

He also noted that

although it makes no sort of provision for commercial intercourse, it affords the means of cultivating a friendly understanding with the Government and people of an extensive Empire, whose neutrality in War and friendship at all times are matters of vital importance to British interests in the adjacent seas.

In conclusion he stated that while he hoped the Convention would be adopted, he wished to point out that

in no part of the negotiation did I pretend to have been sent by Her Majesty's Government in any other capacity than that of Commander-in-Chief of Her Majesty's ships and vessels on this Station…and although at the suggestion of the Japanese Government the negotiation ultimately took a more extensive and important character than that which I originally contemplated I trust the Convention finally agreed upon may appear to their Lordships as nothing more than a proper provision for the security of interests confided to my care.[58]

When this dispatch with all its enclosures reached London at the end of December 1854, the news was initially welcomed. The Foreign Office informed the Admiralty:

Lord Clarendon is of the opinion that the tact and judgement shown by Sir James Stirling in this matter are deserving of entire approbation, and the success of this important negotiation appears to be due to the manner in which it was conducted.[59]

The Foreign Office was to immediately put steps in train to see the Convention ratified, and when the documents were ready they would be sent to the Admiralty for forwarding to Stirling to take to Japan for ratification.

Unfortunately, problems emerged in England over the New Year. Questions were raised regarding the Convention and hackles rose, as Stirling had anticipated, over the fact that Foreign Office staff had not been involved in such an important negotiation, and that it held out no opportunities for trade. Stirling explained his views on the latter issue in a private letter to Sir James Graham of the Admiralty:

> To those who attach no other value to Japan than that which rests upon the opening it may appear to offer for commercial enterprise it may seem strange that I pertinaciously neglected every opportunity to open trade. But I respectfully submit that Japan is far more important in a Political, than in a Commercial sense…it may with truth be said, whatever Maritime Power may gain predominant Influence in Japan…will be the mistress of the China Seas, and of the commerce carried on upon them…but I am clearly of the opinion that if we or the Americans attempt to force a trade upon them in opposition to the long established Institutions of the country, either we or they by so acting will lose their confidence, and may be made to feel the evils of their enmity.[60]

The day this letter was signed, 27 October, the *Winchester* was towed by the *Styx* into Hong Kong harbour to confront, after forty-four days on the Japanese mission, voluminous mail and reports requiring Stirling's attention. There were dispatches from the Admiralty, some specific and others routine, and reports from all his senior naval officers. Keane on the *Grecian* at Shanghai reported testing new supplies of coal for the steamers, while Vansittart on the *Bittern* at Amoy reported surveys of a dangerous rock near Koolansoo. Fellowes on the *Comus* at Canton reported further searches to find boats which had been seized by pirates. Hoste, who had been left in charge at Hong Kong, reported various attacks by pirates, and that a French lady missing from the ship *Caldera* (captured by pirates and burnt) had been successfully rescued by Lieutenant Palliser on the *Spartan*, which had also destroyed one of the piratical forts.

All these reports Stirling was pleased to hear and quick to praise.[61] But the Press had complained bitterly about levels of piracy in his absence[62] and it was this overriding issue—the problem of pirate attacks—that would occupy him fully over coming months.

28

Pirates, Rebels and Russians

THE PROBLEM OF pirates in Hong Kong and neighbouring waters was very much one of detection. As the editor of the Hong Kong *Times* pointed out, Victoria harbour was home to more than 200 coastal trading junks, and every one of them was armed with at least two heavy guns for attack or defence, according to the circumstance. Of these, up to a quarter were thought to be involved in piracy[1]. Stirling estimated that at least 5,000 people in Victoria lived by that means,[2] so it was an immense problem. Pirate depredations were costing legitimate traders thousands of dollars a month, but unless caught in action these vessels were difficult to track down, as they looked similar to the hundreds of regular junks plying between Canton and Hong Kong on ordinary business. It seemed the temptation to hijack rich cargoes of outward bound opium, tea and silk, and inbound spirits, oils and spices (as well as the silver that the Chinese accepted in exchange), was powerful and pervasive.

Aside from detection, other issues hampered Stirling's fight against piracy. In the first instance, with the looming certainty of hostilities against Russia, the ships and manpower required for the job were limited because Britain wished to preserve her resources for that contingency. Secondly, there were complex regional politics to consider, for the distinction between pirates and rebels (or Chinese anti-Imperialists) was considered 'very finely drawn' and in the coming months would involve the safety of European citizens in mainland China.

Stirling first approached Yeo, the Viceroy of Canton, asking him to take the onus of controlling the illicit activities 'within the Imperial jurisdiction', but the latter pleaded 'want of force'.[3] Next he suggested a co-operative effort, agreed to by the Chinese: a 'Mandarin of Rank' was appointed to accompany his ships to check 'every port and place upon the coast known or suspected to be haunts of pirates'. With the 'legal sanction afforded by an Imperial officer's presence, and his acquaintance with localities and persons', plus the support of British warships, Stirling believed 'a stop might be put to an evil which threatened to increase to a most destructive extent'.[4] An eye witness later humorously described the assisting

Mandarin sent with one expedition, 'picking his way fan in hand over the muddy flat' in satin shoes.[5] But the initiative was considered a success, and numbers of pirate junks were identified and apprehended.

Offers of help to combat pirates came in from various sources: from Hong Kong's Lieutenant-Governor, the Portuguese Governor of Macao, the American naval commander, Commodore Abbot, who placed a steam vessel, the *Queen*, at Stirling's disposal, and from leading Cantonese merchants who sent $5,000 for use as he saw fit. One wealthy Chinese trader even chartered two P&O steamers to accompany any expeditionary force.[6]

The first successful sorties against the pirates occurred early in November 1854 after Stirling had learned of a pirate stronghold just outside Portuguese-held Macao. The subsequent engagement, in the Bay of Tyho on Lantau Island, involved Captain O'Callaghan of the *Encounter*, whom Stirling had sent to investigate, and an American naval officer, George Henry Preble, Captain of the seconded *Queen*. According to Preble, who kept a detailed diary during his time in the Far East, Stirling's orders to his own captains were 'not to attack a Chinese pirate unless they had first attacked a British vessel or British Officer'.[7] He recounted how a fleet of ten pirate junks opened up with heavy guns while the *Queen* was 'standing into the Bay of Tyho'. After seeking *Encounter*'s assistance, he returned to the area a second

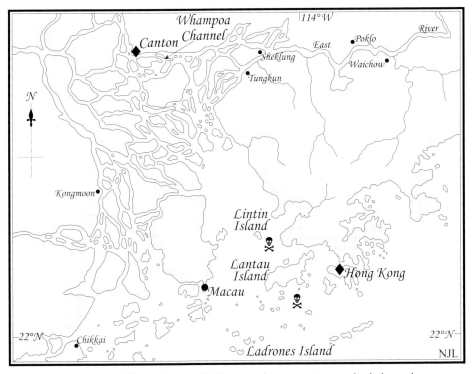

Area between Hong Kong and Canton subject to pirate and rebel attacks

time at dawn next day, only to find the pirate fleet reinforced by seven more junks. During a second exchange, the Chinese howitzer found range and he backed off, returning later that afternoon to find that the *Encounter* had shelled the area. Between them, the two boats then 'effected a landing and set fire to the junks lying in the creek and to the pirate storehouses on shore'. O'Callaghan's summary of the physical damage inflicted, as reported to Stirling, gives some idea of the ferocity of the attack:

> At Tyho the whole of the junks, 17 in number were destroyed; 6 guns taken by *Winchester's* boat delivered to Marshal of Admiralty Court at Hong Kong; 7 guns taken by *Spartan's* boat disposed of in like manner; 2 guns taken and retained by the US steam vessel *Queen*; and 10 guns destroyed with the junks and sunk. Number of pirates killed unknown, from 50 to 60 prisoners taken by the Chinese Authorities.[8]

Another major victory occurred almost simultaneously in Tymoon Bay when a joint action involving the *Winchester* and the *Spartan* razed a pirate stronghold. In this clash fifty junks were destroyed, many guns seized or sunk, fifty to sixty pirates killed and thirteen taken prisoner. Stirling was able to report to the Admiralty that, in the space of not much more than a week, sixty-seven pirate junks had been burned. As each was capable of carrying crews of thirty or more men, there were some 2,000 pirates involved in the two incidents 'of whom 115 may be said to have been either taken or killed'.[9]

In the same month as these successful outcomes, the Hong Kong Governor, Sir John Bowring, had gone to Peiho (near Peking) for a conference with Chinese officials and the American Commissioner McLean aimed at negotiating a revision of the Nanking Treaty. Bowring had largely ignored instructions not to push for changes to the Treaty, and took the Chinese refusal to open the doors of some of their key walled cities to Europeans as a personal insult. At Peiho, Bowring presented his revised Treaty conditions, all eighteen of them, and urged the Chinese High Commissioner to accept them, especially as the Imperial Government might need foreign help, given the rebellions occurring in many Chinese provinces. The High Commissioner was unmoved. Reporting their lack of success, both Bowring and McLean asked their respective governments for a more aggressive policy to force the Chinese into negotiating. However, Britain's Lord Clarendon told Bowring that warlike demonstrations would be 'doubtful policy as a matter of right and very questionable as a matter of policy', and the Americans agreed. In Clarendon's view, because of the Russian problem any demonstration in neighbouring China would be 'singularly inopportune'.[10]

The focus shifted from pirates to insurgents on 19 November 1854 when Stirling received a worrying report from Robertson, the Consul at Canton, concerning the advance of the Taiping rebel forces. The Consul wanted a naval force to be stationed at Whampoa, the deepwater port at the entrance to the Pearl River leading to Canton.[11] Stirling took immediate action, sending the *Barracouta* as well as the seconded *Queen*. When Captain Preble reached Canton he found trade 'now entirely cut off, no tea or silk being allowed to come from the interior without a payment of so heavy a blackmail as to amount to a prohibition'.[12]

In fact, the Imperial Manchu forces at Canton were under attack from two sides—the Taiping rebels and the Triads. The Taiping rebels were a fanatical quasi-Christian group inspired by their leader Hung to believe in fighting for the great peace (or Tai-p'ing).[13] They had taken Nanking in 1853, thereafter to become Hung's headquarters, and were ousting the Manchu Imperialists in combats across the countryside. They were now taking control of the river approaches to Canton, while inside the city another group, the Triads, were raising mayhem. The Triads, who wanted the restoration of the Ming dynasty, had held Amoy for five or six months in 1853, and were now challenging for Canton.[14] Stirling decided to see the situation for himself, and accordingly, on 11 December the *Styx* towed HMS *Winchester* out of Hong Kong harbour, accompanied by the *Comus*, arriving off Whampoa three days later.

Transferring his flag to the *Styx*, Stirling proceeded up the Pearl River to Canton[15] where he met Governor Bowring and Commodore Abbot to discuss the situation, and to plan 'certain measures for the defence and protection of Foreign Interests at Canton'.[16] In a preamble to what was agreed, Stirling was careful to note that 'the forces of our respective Countries here present' were there to help the Chinese quell disorders and maintain security and peace 'within the limits of the Foreign Settlement'. They were *not* there 'to interfere between contending Parties in this Country', nor to relieve the Chinese authorities 'from the responsibility they are under…for the security of our countrymen'.[17] This clearly set out the limits of what Stirling believed to be his duty. The defence measures he put in place were made more difficult because the 'factories' in the foreign enclave, which supported and contributed to trade, were situated outside the walls of the city in a very extensive and populous suburb. Chinese houses of very combustible materials 'surround, and even intrude into and amongst the houses of the Foreign Residents, and deprive the site of the factories of any continuous or definite boundary'.

As Stirling had given orders for the captains of the *Comus* and *Styx* to see what could be done to remove the artificial obstructions rebels had placed in the Blenheim passage leading to Canton, he had to call again on the services of Preble and the *Queen* to take him back to rejoin the *Winchester* which was anchored in deeper water downriver. Stirling was thus back at Whampoa when the Taiping rebels managed to block the Pearl River completely on 29 December and rout the Imperialist fleet.[18] Later Stirling advised the Admiralty that a squadron of forty insurgent gunboats defeated eighteen Imperialist junks so speedily 'there was not time to interfere'.[19] The following day fighting extended to Whampoa Reach, but the presence of the large foreign vessels quickly dampened hostilities.[20]

Although Stirling regarded the fighting as a civil matter between two Chinese groups, when it threatened the lives and property of British subjects he had to act. On 1 January he instructed Lieutenant Fellowes to advise Chumninlung, chief of the insurgent force, that foreigners were to be immune from the existing hostilities.[21] They deserved 'entire exemption from the hazards and evils of war, and to unimpeded navigation in the river', and 'any violation of these rights or any pretence whatever will be deemed an act of war and lead to immediate reprisals'.[22] Chumninlung agreed to comply, saying his forces would 'not interfere with any boats or vessels…flying any European flag' and that they would give advance notice of any hostilities.[23]

But now the focus had shifted from Canton to Shanghai, where Stirling was advised of an outbreak of hostilities. On 6 January some 400 French marines had supported Imperialist troops in breaching the city walls and engaging in combat with the rebels who held it. Worse, the French were blaming the British and Americans for not providing assistance. A precarious peace had held in the walled city of Shanghai since 7 September 1853 when 1,200 members of the Small Sword Society, an offshoot of the Triads,[24] had taken it over in the face of little opposition and even less bloodshed. The overtaxed people regarded them more as saviours than oppressors.

Ever since the rebels (called by Stirling either the 'City Party' or 'Insurgents') had taken Shanghai, the Imperialists had been trying to regain control. Believing that the Insurgents were being supported in a 'moral and material sense' by the foreign settlement, the Imperialist General Keih had approached the consuls of England, France and the United States in October 1854. He had suggested that, in exchange for some concessions, and for their own protection, a wall should surround the foreign settlement, thus severing the insurgents from their chief market. Consuls agreed that the erection and maintenance of the wall 'was to be protected and secured' by the naval forces of England, France and the US.[25] Despite requests by Governor Bowring and Consul Alcock to Captain Keane, Stirling's Senior Naval Officer, to provide a guard to protect workers building the wall, the latter refused— as did the Americans. The French went ahead, however, and the wall on their side progressed to the point of threatening communication between the city and the settlement. In response, the insurgents began to construct another line into the city, but the French pressed them to dismantle it.[26] When this failed to happen immediately, the demolition was effected under protection of a French force, prompting a clash with considerable loss of life. According to Stirling, 'the French Admiral declared the city in a state of siege and proceeded to Bombard it…in consequence these 2 parties are in a state of open and uncompromising hostility'.[27]

Bowring and Alcock cast blame for the entire conflict on Stirling, and his officer, Captain Keane, for causing a split with the French and 'impressing the Chinese High Authorities with a conviction of our bad faith'. Stirling defended his officer as having correctly obeyed orders to refrain from interfering in local political affairs. He reminded the Admiralty that only a portion of Shanghai's inhabitants were British subjects, and 'any interference in the affairs of the Settlement was to be avoided on his part, except when absolutely necessary for the safety of the lives and property of British subjects…'[28]

In the event, the Admiralty fully supported Stirling, on 28 March approving of his 'directions to the Senior Officer at Shanghai to take no part in the contest between the Imperialists and the Rebels…'[29] The Imperialists ultimately recaptured Shanghai with the help of the French marines.

Meanwhile, in Canton the European community was alarmed to learn that by 20 January the Taiping rebels had closed all approaches to the city. Some 200 rebel junks, many of them ex-pirates, had pushed an opposing force of fifty of Viceroy Yeo's war junks to within 3 miles of the city gates.[30] According to Stirling's estimate, the insurgent force amounted to '10,000 or 12,000 men in 400 vessels of various sizes well armed and suited to river service'.[31] Fierce fighting occurred over the Barrier Forts from 23 to 28 January, with the Imperial Mandarin forces just managing to repulse the attacking rebels. This rebellion forced the proud Viceroy Yeo to seek assistance from Governor Bowring in protecting Canton against the impending assault.[32] Bowring sent word to Stirling, who on 24 January left Hong Kong with orders for as many of his squadron as possible to gather at Whampoa. By the 28th the *Winchester*, *Barracouta*, *Comus*, *Styx* and *Rattler* had grouped ready to proceed upriver, obliging the rebel junks to withdraw with Canton 'almost in their grasp'.[33] Stirling knew from previous contact with the rebel chief that his forces did not wish to molest Europeans or Americans, and believed he would keep his word.[34]

On 9 February intelligence reached him that an Anglo-French flotilla, under Rear Admiral David Price, had attacked the Russian Pacific Squadron, led by Rear Admiral Poutiatin, in August 1854 at Petropavlovsk.[35] The operation had had to be broken off, however, when Price committed suicide, and so the action had only been partially successful.[36] The Admiralty had already appointed Rear Admiral Bruce to succeed Price and given instructions that in the spring of 1855 there should be an allied offensive against 'the Russian settlements on both sides of the Kamchatka Straits'.[37]

On 1 March Stirling received instructions to send two of his steamers to join Bruce in this manoeuvre,[38] and also to investigate reports of two Russian warships in the River Amur which, in conjunction with the French Squadron, he should find and attack. To assist him, Captain Charles Elliot of HMS *Sybelle 36* had been sent to join his flag. For Stirling, news that another warship would join his command was very welcome. The *Sybelle* arrived from Singapore on 4 March (confusingly, the similarly named French naval frigate *La Sybille* also showed up the next day) and orders also went ahead to free the best ships for a journey northwards. The *Encounter* at Shanghai was directed to move down to Woosung and await the arrival of the *Barracouta*, under the command of Captain F. H. Stirling, and both were then to provide reinforcement for Bruce's squadron off the north Japanese coast.[39] Closer at hand, the *Spartan* at Canton and the *Bittern* at Amoy were ordered to return to Hong Kong. The British squadron would also comprise the *Winchester*, *Sybelle*, *Hornet*, *Styx*, *Saracen* and *Rattler*. On 6 March Stirling wrote to the French Commander, Rear Admiral La Guerre, conveying his instructions and arranging to meet him in Nagasaki where, he explained, 'Her Majesty's Government have entirely approved the convention I made with the Emperor of Japan in October last'.[40] To cement relations, Stirling included a copy of a letter he had sent to each of the Senior Naval Officers at the Treaty ports to 'afford to the ships and subjects of France aid and protection as far as orders permit'.[41] Stirling's intention was from there to 'move up to Hakodadi by the middle or end of May in time to have the whole of the approaching season available for future operations'.[42]

On 2 April the incoming mail brought news that sparked Stirling's interest, that of insurrection amongst the gold diggers at distant Ballarat, in Australia. When Stirling had first heard of the discovery of gold in eastern Australia, he had been concerned about the possibility of violent theft, and had written to the Admiralty suggesting that all remitted gold be carried by British warships. But the Admiralty had not been impressed, noting that his suggestion would be 'reserved for future consideration'.[43]

On 7 April Stirling dispatched Commander Elliot in the *Sybelle*, attended by the steamers *Hornet* and *Bittern*, to Shanghai as a base for their intelligence mission. He believed that the Russian Admiral, Poutiatin, and the crew of his warship *Diana* would try to reach Petropavlovsk, where Bruce's squadron was headed, or the Russian settlement opposite the island of Sakhalin near the River Amur. Elliot was thus to check for any Russian bases in Sakhalin, and obstruct landing of munitions by Russian or neutral ships. He was then to leave reports of his findings in cypher at Hakodadi, on the northern Japanese island of Hokkaido, where Stirling hoped they would be afforded a comfortable reception, given the treaty signed the previous year. Elliot was authorised to engage a Japanese interpreter 'for a sum not exceeding $50 a month without rations'.[44]

Five days later, on 12 April 1855, Stirling instructed Sir William Hoste on the *Spartan* to stock up with ammunition and then to proceed to sea in execution of sealed orders.[45] He was to head north to the Kuriles Islands, camouflaged in black paint, where he was to scan the coast for Russians, gather intelligence and then rejoin the squadron in Hokkaido by 31 May.[46] The steamer *Saracen* was to leave Hong Kong as soon as possible and proceed to Hokkaido, to survey the headlands while awaiting the arrival of the remainder of the squadron. These various orders accompanied a dispatch Stirling addressed to the Admiralty on 15 April. He had moved earlier than proposed, he stated, because of new intelligence concerning the Russians, confirmed by Captain Adams of the US Navy, and Admiral Lobscheid, a Prussian missionary who had recently returned to Hong Kong from Japan. The Russian warship *Diana 52*, 'the largest and most efficient ship in these seas', had been wrecked near the Bay of Shimoda, and Admiral Poutiatin and his large crew had escaped. As information trickled in, the wrecking turned out to be no minor mishap, but the aftermath of a terrifying earthquake and tsunami which, for the Russians, could not have occurred at a worse possible time.

As early as 1853 Poutiatin had been seeking trade openings with the Japanese, but had met with resistance.[47] And in any event, the Americans, under Perry, and the British, through Stirling, had pre-empted him. In renewed pursuit of negotiations, he had arrived in Osaka on the *Diana*, where the Japanese told him that further talks would now only take place in Shimoda, one of the ports opened by the American Treaty. Arriving early, and unhappy with the unprotected anchorage, he had to wait until 22 December 1854 for discussions to finally get under way. They did not last long. The next day an earthquake struck, and the resultant great tidal wave, rising 21 feet above sea level, inundated the coast and all but wiped out Shimoda, leaving by one account only sixteen houses standing.[48] The *Diana* had been caught in a furious whirlpool offshore, spinning some forty-two rotations in half an hour and losing her sternpost and rudder. With the help of a hundred Japanese boats she had been taken around the peninsula towards the Bay of Heda, some 45 miles away, for repair, but just as she reached the safety of the harbour a sudden storm blew up on 19 January and the badly listing frigate sank.[49]

The treaty negotiations resumed at Heda, where the Japanese, appreciative that the Russians had rescued several of their citizens from drowning during the tidal wave, extended great hospitality. But Poutiatin was unable to gain entry to any more ports than those finally agreed to with the Americans (Nagasaki, Shimoda and Hakodadi), though he did win the right to barter and purchase goods, and appoint a consul, at the last two ports. Most important to Poutiatin, however, were the negotiations over common boundaries which entailed considerable debate, as the Japanese initially claimed all the Kuriles Islands. Eventually it had been decided to divide the Kuriles Archipelago between them, the southern islands staying with Japan and the northern islands with Russia, and to leave the large island of Sakhalin, which both parties adamantly claimed as theirs, in joint possession.

The Russian-Japanese Treaty, embodying all these clauses, had been signed on 7 February 1855.[50] However, it still needed ratification from the Russian Government. Eventually it was shipped out by the Americans, who visited Shimoda at the end of January 1855 with the ratified Japanese-American Treaty, but the Russian Admiral had refused to accept their offer of transport to Shanghai, fearing capture by the allies. While in Heda his crew had managed to build a small schooner, enabling a select party, including Poutiatin, to reach Petropavlovsk on 22 May, only to learn that English and French ships were gathering nearby. Under cover of darkness they slipped past the English squadron, and arrived at the mouth of the Amur River in the Sea of Okhotsk on 20 June 1855.[51] Later it became known that the remaining majority of the crew of the *Diana* had also escaped, some on the American ship, the *Caroline Foote*, and a second, larger group on a German trader, the *Greta*.

Stirling's journey north to Nagasaki in fact was delayed until 1 May 1855,[52] partly on advice of the Americans who felt that the Russian fleet was no longer a threat with the *Diana* gone, and partly because he was still waiting for the documents from England that would ratify his treaty with Japan. There was another matter of concern as well. Aware that his squadron had 'too much draft and too little speed' to serve for reconnoitring work,[53] Stirling had already approached the P&O office in Hong Kong to charter a steamer, preferably the relatively new *Tartar* which, he had argued to the Admiralty,[54] was said to have a speed of 13 knots an hour. She also had just an 8 ft draft, and hence was ideal for reconnoitring duties. By comparison, the steamers currently with the squadron drew too much water, were slow and coal-hungry, requiring 24 tons a day to go 150 miles—a distance the *Tartar* could achieve with 7.5 tons. Furthermore, he argued, for the navy to purchase her would be extremely useful in the fight against piracy. But P&O held out, claiming that the *Tartar* was engaged in a very remunerative trade, and her loss would disadvantage the company.[55] When Stirling wrote to the Admiralty on 15 April negotiations were still continuing, but two days later he got his way with an agreement to settle for some £26,000,[56] which included loss of commercial revenue. Stirling immediately ordered the master boatswain, carpenter and sailmaker from the *Winchester* to survey and refit her so she could accompany the squadron to Nagasaki. *Tartar* was to be the steam tender to the *Winchester*, and after due consideration Stirling appointed the Master of the steamer *Comus*, T. R. Collingwood, to take command.

Early on 26 April the French frigate *Jeanne d'Arc* arrived, bearing the flag of Admiral La Guerre who then met with Stirling on board the *Winchester* to exchange the latest news on Russian movements. Stirling had just received dispatches from the Admiralty, dated 20 February, transmitting information on Russian movements in the River Amur and the existence of a Russian naval establishment in the Gulf of Sakhalin.[57] La Guerre, whose planned rendezvous with the British squadron in Nagasaki was now overtaken by his recall to France, doubted its accuracy.

The impending departure of the British naval vessels alarmed Hong Kong merchants, who feared it would expose them to pirate attacks and seriously injure trade. When Messrs Jardine & Co. and thirteen other merchants petitioned Stirling to leave a steamer and senior naval officer behind in Hong Kong for protection, he replied that this had been his intention all along, and the duties would be shared in turn by the *Rapide* and the *Comus*.

With the *Sybelle*, *Hornet* and *Barracouta* also already deployed, the ships to comprise the northern expedition—the *Winchester*, *Styx* and *Tartar*—were instructed on 30 April to prepare for departure. A gap in Stirling's journal obscures the actual date they left, but by 3 May the small squadron was at sea in the Taiwan Strait (Formosa) bearing north for Nagasaki. The *Winchester* and *Tartar* reached the outer anchorage at 6 p.m. on 10 May and found the *Styx* already there together with two French vessels, the corvette *Constantine* and steamer *Colbert*. Once again the ships were met by Japanese officials, to whom Stirling gave a letter addressed to His Excellency, the Obunyo of Nagasaki, announcing their arrival and requesting an interview to discuss procedures for ratifying the treaty.[58]

As before, there was no immediate response to this communication, although permission was granted over the next two days for the *Winchester* and her escorts to move to the middle anchorage. Stirling was disappointed, as he had expected a warmer reception. On the 13th he sent a message to the Governor stating that he would remain until the 17th, and 'should it not be convenient to the Governor to grant an interview by that time', he would communicate with the Imperial Government at Jeddo. This had the desired result, for on 15 May Stirling recorded receiving a missive from 'HE the Obunyo of Nagasaki suggesting the revision of the Port Regulations' prior to ratification of the Treaty. This probably referred to the regulations for the other ports which had been left pending. But it left room for negotiation and Stirling's reply on the 17th was more conciliatory, proposing 1 October as the date he would return to exchange ratification documents and finalise port regulations.[59] There was no official meeting on this occasion.

Early on 19 May the *Winchester* and her escorts left Nagasaki harbour. The *Styx* had orders to return to Shanghai with dispatches and wait for the English mail, then rejoin the squadron at Hakodadi. After more than a week at sea, working their way up the western coast of Japan, the *Winchester* and her escorts anchored in Hakodadi Bay on the southern point of Hokkaido Island. In the summer evening light they were able to take stock of the bay, which was a haven for whalers in the North Pacific.[60] Almost before the ships had been made secure, they were joined in quick succession by the *Bittern* and the *Rattler*. Late that evening, 29 May, Vansittart of the *Bittern* boarded the *Winchester* with dispatches for the Admiral. He brought exciting news.

Vansittart had met the *Sybelle* en route and heard from Elliot the results of his reconnoitring mission around the Sea of Japan and the Gulf of Tartary. In De Castries Bay (sometimes spelt by Stirling as De Kastries Bay) on the mainland opposite Sakhalin Island, Elliot had discovered a Russian squadron of six vessels at anchor, mounting together 102 guns.[61] Later accounts cast doubt on the finding, referring to the 'Phantom enemy',[62] but there is no doubt of the Russian presence. A description of Elliot's expedition appeared in the *Illustrated London News* a few months later, and was quite specific in its detail, the writer counting 'one 44 or 50 gun frigate, two or three 22 gun corvettes, one barque of 15 guns a store-ship a steamer and a schooner'. Although the *Hornet* managed to get in quite close, firing three shots at the Russians and challenging them to come out, the passage was too narrow for the *Sybelle* to approach further. The Russians fired two guns in reply, and Elliot decided on the tactic of withdrawing 'a sufficient distance to allow the Russians an opportunity of coming out into deeper water'. But despite an all-night wait with 'shell, grape and canister' ready, the enemy would not take the bait.[63] Elliot had then retired out of sight and sent for immediate reinforcements, reporting to Stirling that he had 'deemed it to be imprudent to attack this superior force'. Elliot's assessment of the situation was that the squadron, not being able to get into the Amur by the north at this season, has taken refuge in Castries Bay…either with the view of getting their ships into the river by lightening them and taking them through a channel from the south (if such a channel exists) or of concealing themselves till circumstances afford them an opportunity to get through the straits of Perouse to the Amur, or some other safe position…My opinion is that if they move they will do so at once and try to make their escape through the Straits of Perouse.[64]

This news changed Stirling's plans completely. A chance to have a crack at the Russians, who were doing such damage to British soldiers in the Crimean Peninsula, was not to be missed. He ordered his ships to be ready to leave the following day and penned a polite note to the Governor of Hakodadi stating 'the necessity for my proceeding to sea immediately', but assuring him that 'on my return I trust to have

The area in the Sea of Japan and Sea of Okhotsk
where Stirling's squadron sought Russians, and the
disputed channel between Sakhalin and the mainland

the pleasure of visiting'.[65] Then, with orders to the *Spartan*, *Bittern* and *Tartar* to follow the *Winchester*, and not to part company if possible, he set course for Sakhalin. The *Spartan* had just completed its mission to examine the Kurile Islands and the Sea of Okhotsk, and its commander, Sir William Hoste, had been asked to record 'the tracks and soundings he had made' on maps for the benefit of the squadron.

On 5 June, in latitude 44.4°, longitude 139.5°, a thick fog separated the ships, but they managed to regroup the following day. At daylight on the 7th the lookout on the *Winchester* observed a strange sail on the windward bow, which proved to be the *Sybelle*. Shortly Elliot boarded the *Winchester*, conveying the news—and his extreme disappointment—that the Russian squadron he had seen anchored in De Castries Bay had managed to escape. He reported to Stirling:

> I may confidently affirm, that in the heavy weather, with thick fogs we experienced, the Russian squadron must either have come to an anchor in some bay or have separated from each other. I therefore still consider it improbable that they should have passed south and my suspicions are that they have made for a northern passage, though it seems evident that if such a passage exists, it is intricate and shoal.[66]

A correspondent to the *Illustrated London News*, reporting well after the event, took a different view, that the Russians were believed to have 'got through the passage at the head of the Gulf of Tartary and so into the River Amur where they are known to have large settlements'.[67] It was later proven that this indeed was the case, but Elliot's own account is not as positive. He was able to tell Stirling, however, that on returning to the area with HMS *Hornet* 'he had visited and destroyed all of the enemy property…left behind at a kind of settlement found' at De Castries Bay.[68]

With three sailing ships, the *Winchester*, *Spartan* and *Sybelle*, and three steamers, the *Bittern*, *Hornet* and *Tartar*, the squadron made an impressive sight as they passed Cape Krillon, (the south-west point of Sakhalin Island) on 16 June. At this stage Stirling was concerned about the French ships and ordered Vansittart of the *Bittern* to proceed to a prearranged rendezvous off Cape Krillon and wait for them for seven days. After a week Vansittart, with or without the French, was to rejoin the squadron at Jonquiere Bay, on Sakhalin Island.[69] The 17th had dawned stormy and thick fog the next morning cut vision; as *Tartar* was struggling to hold position, Stirling signalled *Spartan* to take her in care. Reports from his captains revealed the problem to be in her paddle wheels, and being a heavy ship she had to carry full sail to keep up. It was now obvious that the vessel Stirling had personally commissioned from P&O would have to be towed back to Hakodadi, a task given to Commander Bruce of the *Styx*.

The remaining four ships, *Winchester*, *Sybelle*, *Spartan* and *Hornet*, the latter dependent on sail now that coal supplies were low, continued on towards the head of the gulf. Towards nightfall on 25 June they reached Jonquiere Bay, some 50 miles short of De Castries Bay, where the squadron was able to anchor in safety. As this bay was well timbered, Stirling sent parties ashore next day to cut wood for fuel.[70] They were lucky enough to find a cache of coal, probably left by the Russians, so the following day the boats of the squadron were fully employed shifting two tons of it to the *Hornet* to replenish exhausted stocks.

Early on the 27th *Bittern* arrived back from its mission to contact the French. The news was not promising. The French frigate *La Sybille* had lost the services of the steamer *Colbert*, which was on the way back to Shanghai for repair, while *La Sybille* itself had 120 men sick on board and needed to go back to port.[71] Stirling had to act on his own. As the *Hornet* was the only ship with a small enough draft to reconnoitre the shallow coastline, and sufficient power to cope with the weather, he decided to send it up the gulf alone. Its mission, to search for Russians and any escape routes through to the Pacific, required a senior officer with some inside knowledge, and at his own request Commander Elliot was given charge of the *Hornet*, and Captain Forsythe of that ship ordered to follow his instructions.[72] Elliot lost no time and took the *Hornet* out that afternoon under sail, bound for De Castries Bay.

It must have been a cursory examination, for Elliot returned two days later, on 29 June. Stirling's journal simply notes that Elliot had examined De Castries Bay and the northern part of the Gulf of Tartary without finding the Russian squadron or discovering a passage into the River Amur, 'the water being excessively shoal on entering the narrows at the head of the Gulf'. In subsequent discussions Elliot expressed his opinion that 'if a passage for large ships existed, it could not be entered', which was also recorded in the journal.

Stirling totally accepted Elliot's advice. He therefore had no idea that a channel *did* exist at the northern end of Sakhalin and that the Russian ships had been able to escape through it into the Sea of Okhotsk. The Admiralty later took him severely to task over this matter, but there was little else he could have done, for his three line-of-battle ships simply could not have traversed the narrow and shallow passage.[73] Stirling never blamed Elliot. In a later lengthy report to the Admiralty, he stated that he had 'never intended to assign to the *Hornet*'s search for a Channel, a character of completeness it did not deserve'. The task

> of re-examining and reconnoitring De Castries Bay and the anchorages to the northward of it for the purposes of ascertaining whether the Russian Ships were there or not, had been effected in the most complete manner; but I did not extend this description to the search for a channel...

He explained that he had intended taking the *Hornet* up the gulf himself. However Elliot, who 'had some acquaintance with the place', had expressed a wish to go also, and it would have been 'objectionable' for both to be absent from the main party at the same time. The dispatch, based on written and verbal reports from both Elliot and Forsythe, detailed how those officers had checked De Castries Bay and found nothing more than had been seen in May, and then proceeded further north in search of the channel:

> After having steamed about 30 miles from De Castries Bay they were stopped by shoal water and backed out, stirring up the mud. Attempts were made further to the eastward without success…To me it appeared most probable that there was no channel to the northward, and consequently most probable that the Russian ships had gone down the Gulf, in which direction besides the chance of overtaking them, we had services to be performed, arrangements to be carried out, and interests to be guarded. On the other hand there did not seem to be any reason in favour of a northern course, for even if, by any way unknown to us, the Russians had escaped to the northward a month before, they had acquired thereby the power of placing themselves in a position unassailable by any force I could direct against them with a prospect of success…[74]

But there was still no sympathy when this explanation reached the Admiralty in London.[75] Meanwhile Stirling, as he explained, had ordered his squadron back down the gulf. However on 29 June, the very day the *Hornet* returned, he had given in to Elliot's urging and allowed him to take his *Sybelle*, with the *Spartan* and *Hornet*, ahead to meet the French Commander and proceed to the Sea of Okhotsk searching for Russians.[76]

When Ellen read about the whole episode in the *Illustrated London News* on 6 October 1855, she would have been aghast at the unfavourable account it gave of her husband's activities. The following passage, again received from one of Elliot's ship's company, would particularly have raised her ire:

> The Admiral made all sail for the southward down the gulf of Tartary, but as we believed far from the scene of the expected fray…the report was spread that the Admiral was going to leave the squadron; so it proved, for presently Commodore Elliot, who had already been ordered to take *Spartan* and *Hornet* under his orders, received permission to part company and beat through the Strait of La Perouse, going thence to the Sea of Okhotsk to destroy Russian settlements. The French frigates accompanied him and his five ships worked gallantly away, while the *Winchester* and *Bittern* were unwillingly running to the southward 'to rest on their laurels' that is we suppose, to ground on their beef bones in some port in China or Japan.[77]

To Ellen this was a travesty. Her husband had never run away from conflict in his life. She knew that his sense of responsibility for the safety of his ships and men would have weighed heavily, and knew too that he would stand by his officers, no matter what criticism was levelled from outside. What made this different from past wars and naval operations, however, was the coverage provided by the Press, and the way unofficial and incomplete information was made available to a mass audience. Moreover, as one historian put it, 'To a British public reared upon memories of the Nile and Trafalgar the Navy's role during the Crimean war appeared most disappointing and inglorious'. Few realised 'it couldn't tackle Russia by sea', yet exaggerated expectations remained.[78]

And it was unfair criticism. When Elliot had completed his mission, he reported to Stirling that he had gleaned further (and admittedly imprecise) information about the channel from a party of whalers. They said the tidal movement in De Castries Bay was about 5 feet, and to Elliot this factor, allied with the strong south winds blowing at the end of May (on the occasion of his earlier inconclusive reconnaissance) 'no doubt caused the waters to rise, [and] the Russian Squadron by lightening may have got through'. Elliot added that this information 'confirmed the opinion I have always held that the Russian squadron had never escaped south out of the Bay of Tartary'.[79]

Unaware of all the controversy that would transpire about the navigability of the northern passage, Stirling had taken his remaining battered and short-rationed squadron back to Hakodadi. On 1 July they had sighted Elliot with two French ships, the corvette *Constantine* and frigate *La Sybille*, and that evening Stirling conferred with Elliot and the French Commodore over dinner on the *Winchester*. When they parted company the next day, Elliot and the French sailed for the Sea of Okhotsk (stopping at Arnowa in northern Hokkaido for supplies), while the *Winchester* and *Bittern* proceeded to Hakodadi.

As they were nearing their destination, Stirling instructed Captain Vansittart and the *Bittern* to return to Shanghai to take over the duties of Senior Naval Officer at that port. Before they parted, however, Stirling told Vansittart that he had received a serious complaint from an officer on the *Bittern*, and he could expect a court martial to investigate the matter at the earliest convenient opportunity. Although sure he would be cleared, Vansittart knew this could take many months to arrange and would be unpleasant for all concerned. So it would have been with a heavy heart that he returned to the *Bittern* to part company with the *Winchester* on 7 July. That evening the flagship entered Hakodadi harbour and found there at anchor the *Encounter*, *Styx* and store-ship *Singapore*. An hour or so later the repaired *Tartar* also came in to anchor.[80]

Stirling was anxious to hear of the *Encounter*'s exploits and interviewed her captain that same evening. O'Callaghan reported that having joined Rear Admiral Bruce, as directed, they had found Petropaulski abandoned and had proceeded into the Sea of Okhotsk until 13 June, when he had been ordered to return to Stirling's command with a letter for the Admiral.[81] This contained Bruce's official release of the *Encounter* and *Barracouta*, but said nothing of their location. Stirling thus still had no news of his son, the *Barracouta*'s commander.

On 8 and 9 July the British ships were restocked from the steamer *Singapore* and approaches were made to Japanese harbour officials to obtain water and fresh food. With green vegetables and fruit available, Stirling could order a stoppage to the issue of lime juice and lime sugar which all the men had been taking since the beginning of June.[82] The officials were also asked to arrange a meeting between the Admiral and the Governor of the province, which was set for 1 p.m. on 10 July. At the appointed time Stirling and his suite, all in full dress uniform, paid their first visit to the Governor of Hakodadi. Stirling found him reasonably informed, as Elliot had paid his respects when he had put into Hakodadi for supplies between 29 April and 2 May. That had been the first time the Governor had met an English officer, and he had needed reassurance that the war with Russia would not be conducted anywhere near his people.[83]

Stirling found the Court at Hakodadi a little less formal than Nagasaki, and when the Governor expressed curiosity about the Admiral's shipboard life, Stirling extended an invitation for him to tour the *Winchester* and inspect the machinery in detail. Over the next few days officers and crew from the British ships were granted shore leave, reporting that everywhere they went they were avidly followed by Japanese officials and the simply curious. One noted that 'indeed we kept them continually under a species of physical training during our stay'.[84]

On 14 July Stirling and his suite were once more entertained by the Governor of Hakodadi with a meal that they thought surpassed that provided at the official reception at Nagasaki. In his letter of thanks to the Governor for 'his recent agreeable entertaining', Stirling advised that British ships in port would leave 'at an early opportunity', but first he needed to be 'furnished with a copy of the Treaty lately entered into by the Japanese Government and the Russian Admiral'. Without this, he explained:

> I am at a loss to know whether I am to consider the island of Urup [in the Kuriles] as Japanese or Russian. That if Russian it will be my duty to take it from them. If Japanese I do not wish to interfere with it—and that in the absence of the Russian Treaty, I am also at a loss to know what part of Sakhalin belongs to Japan and what part belongs to or is claimed by Russia, it being my intention at a convenient time to take the Russian part. I shall therefore be much obliged if the Governor will either give me a copy of the Treaty if it settles this point or at least a distinct explanation as to that part of Sakhalin which the Japanese consider to be their territory.[85]

The reply, evidently satisfactory, was most likely a verbal one, and having requested a written copy when the Governor had confirmation from Jeddo,[86] Stirling decided to wait at Hakodadi for the information to come in. He was also aware that the French Commander, Commodore de Montravel, needed urgent assistance. The scurvy afflicting his crews had grown serious, and *La Sybille*, with more than 100 men in hospital, was being sent back to Hakodadi. As de Montravel desperately needed 'bullocks and fresh provisions', Stirling gave immediate orders for Captain O'Callaghan and the well-stocked *Encounter* to undertake the rescue mission.[87]

On 27 July two ships entered the harbour. The first was HMS *Nankin* direct from London with dispatches, including the all-important treaty ratification documents, and additional men and supplies. It had called at Hong Kong and then followed Stirling north. The second arrival was a French frigate, *La Virginie*, bearing the flag of Rear Admiral Guerin. Stirling was delighted to meet the new French Commander-in-Chief, and that very afternoon sent an invitation to Guerin to join him on the *Winchester* for a full update. Stirling did not have precise knowledge of the whereabouts of the ships he had sent to the Sea of Okhotsk, and was certainly unaware that at that very time his son was embroiled in some exciting action.

On 1 August, F. H. Stirling, Commander of the *Barracouta*, had captured the German brig *Greta* carrying more than 280 Russians from the shipwrecked *Diana*. The incident had occurred just off the northern tip of Sakhalin. A dense fog had obscured vision and the two ships found themselves within firing range when it lifted. The German captain had then raised an American flag, but young Stirling had not been fooled. He had boarded the *Greta* and found the Russians in the hold, 'given away by some of the Chinese members of the brig's crew'.[88] The *Greta* was declared a prize and the Russian seamen and officers declared prisoners of war.

Between the departure of the French Admiral and 14 August (when the squadron finally quit Hakodadi), Stirling had time to examine in detail the treaty documents delivered by the *Nankin*. They contained a disturbing directive: contrary to the previously agreed procedure, the Admiralty Lords had delegated the task of delivering and signing the ratified treaty to Elliot, without a word of explanation. Although Stirling had much to cogitate, he also had the loading of supplies and coal to oversee, and the two new arrivals, the *Nankin* and the *Pique*, to check over. When the squadron was finally out to sea, he ordered the latter's captain, Sir Frederick Nicholson, to divert to the island of Urup in the Kuriles and, in conjunction with the French, take formal possession of it before proceeding on to Nagasaki.[89]

Stirling's own plan over the ensuing month was to take the rest of the squadron slowly down the Japanese coast searching for Russian ships, and calling in at several ports. It was during this period that his ideas concerning British maritime policy in the Far East crystallised.

Stirling saw expansionist Russia as a major threat to British interests in the East. At that time Russian influence over the valuable eastern trade was constrained by lack of a secure outlet to the eastern seas—all her ports in that area faced the often ice-bound Sea of Okhotsk. But the coast of Chinese Manchuria offered a solution. In his 'Memoir on the Maritime Policy of England in the Eastern Seas',[90] Stirling argued that Russia had the power to call together 'enormous armies and to render them efficient by European skill and Training'. Her forces could easily overcome those of the Chinese Imperial Army, whose weaknesses had been shown by past British experience. And this was despite the fact that Manchuria was 'the Birth Place of the Race which governs China' and equated with 'Dynasty and Empire'. Stirling believed Manchuria was the 'Turkey of the Eastern Seas'. He had seen for himself the value of the Manchurian coast near Sakhalin, and argued that it offered

> admirable sites for Naval and Military strongholds: the adjacent country is capable of supplying the wants of an immense population: it is known to produce Gold and probably contains minerals of other sorts…it would become the outlet for the commerce of all Eastern Asia.

China's possession of Manchuria had to be protected, but he warned:

> if China be not electrified and organised by British Energy and Management, and brought under the Influence which a more extended commerce will give us, she will soon fall within the Dominion of Russia.

Moreover, once Russia overcame Manchuria, she would

> lose no time in…over-awing and controlling the surrounding Nations…Our Trade with China would be destroyed and even India would be menaced with Armies as numerous as those of Attila or Ghenghis Khan but far more powerful.

His memoir then suggested various means to counteract this threat. The first and most urgent need was to establish a better understanding with the Chinese Government, though he was 'not unaware of the difficulties which oppose this' and 'prepared to admit that something must be left to time'. He believed Britain should move quickly to establish first

> a new Treaty and a more intimate alliance with the Imperial Government in China: Commerce for the sake of the influence it gives and the revenue it yields must be greatly extended: All the Ports of China, Corea [sic], Manchuria and Saghalien [Sakhalin] must be opened to use: We must repress Piracy and employ the Pirates in the Fisheries or other occupations: We must assume the Protection of the Coasting Trade by regular convoys of Ships of War…

Secondly, the naval base at Hong Kong should be enlarged so as to

> maintain an undeniable superiority over all other nations: In other words we must establish a Maritime Empire with all its concomitant adjuncts of Naval Positions, Postal Communications, Hydrographical Surveys, and Steam Factories and Dock Yards…

This, he admitted, could cost up to half a million pounds a year, but if England was 'not prepared to encounter such expenses'

> we must not wonder if we see a few years hence, Russia the dominant power in the Eastern Asia, our trade with China abandoned, our Indian Empire seriously menaced, and our maritime supremacy annihilated in this distant quarter of the world.[91]

All told it was a strong and far-sighted document which Stirling forwarded by the first mail out of Hong Kong on his return, 15 November 1855. At an earlier date it would have received deserved attention when it arrived in England, but the memoir reached the Admiralty in March 1856, when the messy Crimean War was over and Russian affairs no longer took priority. Once again Stirling's efforts would be overlooked.

While Stirling was composing this memoir, the squadron had proceeded slowly down the Japanese coast, checking each bay for Russians. None were seen, though excitement levels among the crews rose each time they entered a new Japanese port. Finally, on 28 September the *Winchester* and her escorts reached Nagasaki for the treaty ratifications, almost a year after its first negotiation.

Reproduced in the *Illustrated London News*, 20 October 1855: Stirling's ships
Hornet and *Bittern* near Jonquiere Bay

From Treaty Ratification
to Resignation

WHEN STIRLING ENTERED Nagasaki harbour, he found the *Sybelle* and the *Barracouta* already at anchor. At last he could hear first-hand of his son Frederick Henry's exploits in capturing the German brig *Greta* and taking its 280 Russian passengers as prisoners of war. He also formalised Captain Fortescue's command of the *Barracouta*—an order he had previously received but been unable to implement, as he had already sent the *Barracouta* north under his son's command. Captain Stirling would now 'fall back into his old position as Commander of the *Winchester*'.[1] Fortescue was then to take the *Barracouta* on to Shanghai, where the *Greta* and the majority of prisoners had been left. Captain Nicholson of the *Pique* also rejoined the squadron and reported that, in company with the French ship *La Sybille*, he had successfully taken the island of Urup in the Kuriles for the Allies.

The main objective of this visit to Nagasaki was to exchange the treaty ratification documents that had been sent from Britain on the *Nankin*. But Stirling had expected updated instructions, which had not yet arrived, so he detailed the *Styx* to proceed to Shanghai, recoal and return with the most recent mail.[2] The Admiral was well aware that his 'Convention' of 1854 would not have been greeted at home with the same fanfare as Perry's initial American-Japanese Treaty, for he knew the English would not take the same view as Americans of foreign affairs being conducted by a naval commander. And he was quite correct, for despite Lord Clarendon's initial 'entire approbation' on 24 December 1854,[3] various quibbles had emerged in the Foreign Office during January 1855. The first—whether Sir James had full power to make the treaty—was put to the Advocate General,[4] whose reply found no objection to its legitimacy.[5] Then, after Foreign Office staff questioned Stirling's condition that British ships entering Japanese ports should carry a stamp or licence, this matter was referred to both the Board of Trade and the Admiralty. A third concern was that Stirling's treaty documents stated that the Japanese ratification would be 'executed by a High Officer under the Emperor's instructions', and not by the Emperor himself—so it would be inappropriate for the British document to be signed by the Queen. It was settled that it should instead be executed by Lord

Clarendon. Then the matter of a Dutch translation of the English ratification, agreed to at the time by Stirling, was raised. In a cryptic file minute dated 23 January Clarendon noted that he had informed the Admiralty that Elliot should be told to procure one.[6]

The actual signing of the British ratification document occurred that same day, and the original, and a copy of the signed convention, were transmitted to the Admiralty two days later.[7] An earlier draft of the letter accompanying the documents made it clear that Sir James Stirling, 'The officer sent with the ratification should further be instructed to state that the form of the stamp or licence…has not yet been arranged, but it will be communicated hereafter to the Japanese authorities'.[8] On 25 January the Foreign Office again contacted the Admiralty stating that, although the matter of the 'stamp or licence' had been sent to the Board of Trade to arrange, it was up to the Admiralty Lords to consider 'whether it be necessary that ships of war should be furnished with the document in question'.[9] Before they responded to this issue, the Secretary to the Admiralty sent the Foreign Office a copy of the orders given to Stirling in a dispatch signed 27 January,[10] the one which had so shocked him when it arrived via the *Nankin*. The dispatch read (author's emphasis):

> I am commanded by my Lords Commissioners of the Admiralty to transmit to you a copy of a letter from Mr Hammond, inclosing a ratification of the said convention on the Part of Her majesty; and I am to signify their Lordships direction to you, if the service will permit, <u>to order Captain the Honourable C Elliot, of the *Sybille*, to proceed, as the Queen's representative, to Nagasaki, and there to deliver to the Japanese functionaries the ratification in question,</u> in exchange for a ratification on the part of the Emperor of Japan. Captain Elliot is to conform himself to the instructions of Lord Clarendon, contained in Mr Hammond's letter and be very careful in complying with Japanese observances.[11]

Although the Lords of the Admiralty were correct in assigning this duty to Elliot, who was Stirling's second-in-command if he had been absent, they had clearly misread the conditions Stirling had explained in his earlier letter. He had promised to return himself, and this had clearly been Clarendon's original intent, as stated in his note to the Admiralty on 26 December 1854, viz:

> the necessary instrument of ratification will be sent to the Admiralty, to be forwarded to Sir James Stirling, by whom the ratification should be carried to Japan.[12]

So what went wrong? Why was the original order by Clarendon changed? The episode in the Gulf of Tartary did not occur until well after this time, so it had no influence. Was someone on the Board anti-Stirling and pro-Elliot? Or was it that the Lords were simply annoyed with Stirling for agreeing to the condition that

British ships entering Japanese ports should bear a stamp or licence? The Admiralty, writing to the Foreign Office, clearly was unhappy that ships of war, like merchantmen, should 'be made dependent upon a pass or a stamp'. It suggested explaining to the Japanese authorities 'that ships of war, in addition to ordinary armament as such, are distinguished by the national colours and pendant, or by the flag of a flag officer'.[13] This Clarendon accepted, stating 'their Lordships will instruct Sir James Stirling to convey a suitable explanation to the Japanese authorities on that point' when he forwarded a Certificate of Registration for merchant vessels, designed by the Board of Trade, for forwarding to Japan.[14]

Stirling's first communication to the Governor of Nagasaki regarding the exchange of ratifications was on 29 September 1855.[15] He had received the order for Elliot to conduct the process, but as they were both in Nagasaki harbour at the same time, and Stirling was the Senior Naval Officer, the order could quite properly be put aside. Moreover, recent mail had brought the Admiralty's censure of operations in the Gulf of Tartary the previous summer, so Stirling determined to kill two birds with one stone. He decided to send Elliot to double-check the existence of a passage at the northern end of Sakhalin, and thereby eliminate his presence at the ratification ceremony. He gave the order on 1 October, noting it in his journal together with a memorandum which indicated that there had been some unofficial communication from the Japanese, and that he had been told of a change in government.[16] The memorandum was addressed to their Excellencies Alas-Jirani-no-kami and Nazai-Evan-Ocho, and acknowledged receipt of a Dutch translation of 'the intended Act of Ratification on behalf of the Emperor of Japan'. However, Stirling noted that he had found it 'not according with the intent of the English Version of the treaty', and so he could not 'proceed to an Exchange of Ratifications'.[17]

Stirling was singularly fortunate in having aboard a Dutch-speaking surgeon, Mr R. W. Clarke, whose services were later praised by the succeeding head of the China Station, Admiral Seymour.[18] Clarke had immediately spotted divergences between Stirling's previously agreed Treaty and the Dutch version now presented by the Japanese. Whether Elliot had produced a Dutch translation, as Clarendon had asked, is not known. But as there was now no further need for Elliot's presence, the *Sybelle*, with escorts *Hornet* and *Encounter*, left Nagasaki Harbour at 6.30 a.m. on 2 October.

Some of the Japanese hesitation in agreeing to the ratified Treaty was due to the fact that the Emperor who had authorised the signing of the original document had died and been replaced by a new Emperor, and due ceremonies were not yet completely finalised. But it was due also to the fact that Stirling had insisted on certain 'understandings' in relation to each of the clauses. These, in italics below, had been made available to Lord Clarendon before he signed the Convention agreement and, read in conjunction with the actual article, extended their meaning considerably, viz.

Convention for Regulating the Admission of British Ships into the Ports of Japan

1st

The ports of Nagasaki (Fisen) and Hakodadi (Matsmai) shall be open to British ships... *This opens the whole and every part of those ports; but ships must be guided in anchoring by the directions of the local Government. Safe and convenient places will be assigned where ships may be repaired. Workmen, materials and supplies will be provided by the local Government according to a tariff to be agreed upon, by which also the modes of payment will be regulated. All official communications hereafter, when Japanese shall have time to learn English, be made in that language. A British burial ground shall be set apart on Medsume Sima fenced in with a stone wall and properly protected.*

2nd

...The rules and regulations of each of these ports are to be complied with... *The Japanese Government would take care that the port regulations would not create embarrassment nor contradict the general tenor and intent of the treaty, the main object of which is to promote a friendly intercourse between Great Britain and Japan.*

3rd

Only ships in distress...will be permitted to enter other ports than those specified... *Ships of War have a general right to enter the ports of friendly Powers in the unavoidable performance of public duties, which right can neither be waived or restricted, but Her Majesty's ships will not enter any other than open ports without necessity, or without offering proper explanations to the Imperial Authorities.*

4th

British ships in Japanese Ports shall conform to the laws of Japan... *All this is as it should be; but it is not intended by this article that any acts of individuals whether high or low, previously unauthorized or subsequently disapproved of by Her Majesty the Queen of Great Britain, can set aside the Convention entered into with Her Majesty alone by His Imperial Highness the Emperor of Japan.*

5th

...British ships and subjects shall be entitled to...an equality of advantages with those of the most favoured nation, always excepting the advantages accruing to the Dutch and Chinese... *If therefore any other nation or people be now or hereafter permitted to enter other ports than Nagasaki and Hakodadi, or to appoint Consuls, or to open trade or enjoy any advantage or privilege whatever, British ships and subjects shall, as of right, enter upon the enjoyment of the same.*

There was no comment attached to the two last clauses. On 6 October a new Dutch version of the Japanese treaty document was sent to the *Winchester*, and this finally gained the Admiral's approval.

Arrangements could now be made for the ceremony, which was set for 9 October. Stirling had been given authority to offer the Emperor of Japan, as a gift from Her Majesty, a 'Screw Steam Yacht', which he did, as soon as he had cleared up a situation where the Japanese were trying to exclude steamers from the ships allowed in the harbour. His objection to the ruling, and the offer of the steamer which would come with 'an officer acquainted with the machinery', were made in separate letters on the same day, 8 October.[19] Negotiations were complicated by the fact that the Governor and Omedski, whom Stirling had met the previous year, had been replaced, but agreement was finally reached. One of the officers on the *Winchester*, in reporting the ensuing events, described how the twenty-one-man British party proceeded by boat to the city where, after anchoring, 'Friendly greetings were exchanged and inquiries duly made for the health of the Queen, the Admiral and others'. Armchairs and smoking materials were made available to the visitors.

> The conference began and after some conversation our ratified treaty was produced in the simplest style from an envelope, and the seal and subscribed names of Clarendon shown to us. Meanwhile the Japanese Treaty was brought in by their officials. A large box was opened, and the silk covered book or treaty carefully unwrapped from its crape cover inside a lacquered case, its silken cords loosened; and all being ready, our Admiral stood forth, surrounded by his officers, and tendered to the Governor, Araoo Iwamino Rami, the Treaty of Friendship in the name of her Majesty; and the Governor of Nagasaki, on the part of the Emperor, presented the Japanese version. Several well turned speeches were then made by the new Governor, and we had the satisfaction of seeing the affair successfully closed.[20]

A formal minute of the ratification process requested by the Foreign Office (and taken by Captain Wilson of the *Winchester*) had twenty-one signatures attached, beginning with Stirling's and followed by those of the captains and officers from all ships in the squadron, including his son Frederick Henry.[21] A banquet hosted by the Governor followed the formal signing, and was described in detail in the *Illustrated London News*:

> The food consisted of rice, fish soup with mushrooms, stewed fish, a whole fish baked, pickles, omelets, raw fish with vinegar and pomegranates; cake, hot and sweet, was served…We had a further cup of tea, and…a display of presents for the Admiral and officers…the Admiral was to touch them as a mark of acceptance. [22]

In his official report of the proceedings, Stirling intimated that things had not gone smoothly after the signing, for the Japanese had been unwilling to accept two of the 'understandings' he had put to them. He had therefore agreed 'to leave those passages unpublished for the present without any relinquishment of claim', leaving it to 'Their Lordships to decide on the propriety or impropriety of the course I have taken in the Transactions herein reported'.[23]

The two sticking points were the Japanese reluctance to allow the same freedom to land at Nagasaki as had been granted at Hakodadi and Shimodo, and their unwillingness to extend to the British concessions that had been granted to the Dutch and Chinese *after* his agreement on 14 October 1854 (for there had been a distinct loosening of restrictions previously imposed on these two long-term commercial partners). Stirling felt that the Japanese were now violating the first and fifth articles of his Convention, and he urged that the British Government should insist that the two issues be resolved. He believed some 'unfavourable influence' had been involved in preventing agreement,[24] but what the unfavourable influence was is unknown, for Captain Currie's separate diary of proceedings was not published with the rest of the Treaty documents that were put before Parliament in 1856. Captain Wilson's official memorandum of events stopped with the ceremony on the 9th, whereas Currie's diary had continued, as Stirling reported in his dispatch, to at least 18 October.

On the day following the signing ceremony, Stirling sent the *Spartan* back to Amoy, where there had been more trouble with pirates, with orders to proceed on to Hong Kong.[25] Stirling, meanwhile, waited for further clarification from the Governor over the above two issues. Perhaps hoping to break the stand-off regarding landing at Nagasaki, he sent a memo to the Governor on 14 October seeking permission (which was granted) to buy artworks for the British Government.[26]

Stirling was also concerned that he had not yet been given a written copy of the Russian-Japanese treaty he had requested in Hakodadi. On the 16th he sent an ultimatum that 'if at the end of 60 days a Full and Distinct acceptance of the Exposition together with the Russian Treaty is not forwarded I shall go to Jeddo for it myself'.[27] This prompted an invitation to a conference on the following day—a stalemate, as it turned out, for the Japanese refused to make a decision without instructions from Jeddo.

As nothing more could be done, Stirling gave orders for the squadron to prepare for departure, and at daylight on 20 October the *Winchester*, in tow to the *Tartar*, together with the *Barracouta* and the *Styx*, made their way out of Nagasaki harbour. Once at sea Stirling drew up a general memorandum 'conveying a copy of the Ratified Convention and an Exposition of the effect of the Several Articles as agreed to by their Excellencies the Four Japanese Commissioners and the Rear Admiral Commander-in-Chief'.[28] One copy, with a covering letter dated 20 October, he sent to Hong Kong's Governor, Sir John Bowring.[29] But he delayed signing his account to the Admiralty until 8 November—a possible indication of the degree of frustration he felt with his superiors.

At 8 a.m. on 25 October the *Winchester* anchored in Hong Kong's Victoria harbour, where a host of reports awaited him. Commanders Fellowes, Barnard and Vansittart had all had successful clashes with pirates and made significant inroads on their traffic, though in some cases losing marines and seamen in the fray. Lieutenant Brock was also up for honourable mention, having succeeded in capturing three pirate junks, each with a cargo worth over $12,000.[30] The commanders of the *Spartan* and the *Pique* were anxious to see their Admiral, as both had had disciplinary problems with officers and wanted courts martial arranged.

Answering the flood of mail and attending two day-long courts martial kept Stirling busy during his first week. According to naval discipline, any officer accused of misconduct had to have a full hearing in front of all senior officers available. Tensions had been high on the ships that had accompanied Stirling on the northern expedition, for there had been little or no shore leave and provisions had been scanty. Even his own son Frederick had been in trouble, for on 28 October Stirling recorded in his journal a memo sent to Captain Wilson of the *Winchester* 'to remove the check from Commander Stirling's name and order him to return to his duty'.

On 11 November he signed a report on the disposal of Russian prisoners captured on the *Greta* and brought to Hong Kong, a matter he obviously had given considerable thought. Acknowledging that the men were 'for the most part amongst the best description of seamen in the Russian Service', Stirling argued that freeing them to return to Russian settlements would not be in the best interests of trade. Equally, it would be dangerous to keep them in Hong Kong 'where there are neither prisons nor guards', for merchant vessels in port could be carried off. There was, therefore, 'no course open but to send them to England…with the least possible delay…in a ship or ships of war of sufficient size and power to carry them and keep them in subjection'.

He proposed assigning this duty to the *Winchester*, not just because she was the right size but, being nearly four years in commission, she urgently needed repairs and recoppering. In her absence he proposed that the *Nankin* should become his flagship, and that its captain (the Hon. Keith Stewart) should be transferred to the *Winchester*.[31] It was a clever suggestion, as it would allow Stirling to move from the slow and crowded *Winchester* to the fast new steamer *Nankin*. It was written in the clear knowledge that the Admiralty had already ordered the *Rattler*, *Styx* and *Grecian* home,[32] but phrased in such a way that it could not be (and was not) refused.[33] It was typical of Stirling, however, that he requested favourable treatment for Commander Stewart and shows that he understood the effect on a young officer of losing command of a brand new ship.

On 12 November Stirling dined with Captain Preble, the young American officer whom he liked and respected, and who had just returned from duty in Shanghai. The liking was mutual, as Preble had noted in his diary, accompanying the comment with an apt description: 'Sir James is a good old man and a true specimen, with his rosy cheeks and long silver hair, of the fine old English

Despite their age gap, the silver-haired Stirling (left) enjoyed the company during
his China command of US Captain George Henry Preble, to whom he was
a 'fine old English gentleman'

Courtesy Battye Library 668P and Massachusetts Historical Society

gentleman of the olden time'.[34] Talk centred on the declining health of the Commander of American naval forces in the Far East, Commodore Abbot, Stirling's counterpart in the region, who was a man of long experience both held in great esteem. Stirling had visited the sick Commodore and undoubtedly discussed both with him and Preble his ideas regarding British maritime policy in the area, for he was preparing at that time to sign his memoir on the subject.

On the very day that he signed the dispatch covering his Maritime Policy memoir, Stirling also informed the Admiralty that Commander F. H. Stirling had 'proceeded to England in charge of the Act of Ratification of His Imperial Highness the Emperor of Japan'.[35] The significance of this document fully justified Frederick acting as courier to the Admiralty, but he also took to them another important missive: his father's request to be relieved of his command. Like many men serving in the Far East, Stirling had suffered recurrent fevers which had undermined his stamina. He had also been under constant pressure, and the stress was telling. He had therefore written to the Admiralty expressing his wish to be replaced as soon as possible, and sent the letter with his son.[36] Young Stirling left Hong Kong on the returning mail steamer to Singapore, where he would catch P&O steamers to the Middle East and return to England overland and through the Mediterranean. He would therefore reach England much earlier than the three steamers (*Rattler*, *Styx* and *Grecian*) which had been ordered home via the Cape of Good Hope.

Just after Frederick left Hong Kong, Preble had called on Governor Bowring, only to find that Sir John and his daughters had 'gone with the Admiral on an excursion around the island in the *Coromandel*'.[37] This was the *Tartar* in her new guise, and it is possible Stirling was inspecting the repairs and conversion that had taken place. He would have enjoyed the company of Sir John's daughters, as he had recently been reminded of how fast his own children were growing up. A parcel had been waiting at Hong Kong containing pictures of his sons and daughters, which sharply reminded him of home and which he had displayed with pride. Captain Preble noted in his diary on 25 November that he had been one so honoured, stating:

> Admiral Stirling showed me on board the *Winchester* some stereoscopic pictures of his family. He certainly can boast of the handsome faces and intellectual expressions of his children.[38]

On 26 November Stirling ordered a muster of all the ships in harbour to take place the following day. Standing on the decks of the *Winchester*, it would have been a time for quiet pride, as his squadron was now far larger than the one he had initially commanded. The following day he reminded his captains and commanders to send in their returns of the number of discharges and entries in their respective ships, and two days later ordered an inventory of stores controlled by the naval storekeeper.[39] He was clearly trying to tidy up accounts before the year's end.

With the first day of December 1855 came the mail steamer, all the more welcome because her flags signalled 'Sebastapol Fallen',[40] which heralded an end to the Crimean War. Papers and letters were distributed the following day and perused with great attention. However, Britons in this small outpost of Empire were dismayed to learn that the victorious action on 8 September had been due almost entirely to the French, as the British army 'had been in no condition to repeat the heroism and disciplined fury of earlier battles'. But they had followed up the French attack and seen the Russians abandoning Sebastapol, blowing up their arsenals in retreat and wrecking those defences still intact.[41] In acknowledgment of the decisive victory, Stirling ordered all his captains to dress ship and fire a celebratory salute of 21 guns on 3 December. It was not the only gun salute fired that day. The mail had also brought news of Stirling's promotion to Rear Admiral of the Red (the highest in this grade),[42] and in a memorandum he directed that 'HM ships and vessels under my command will hoist a red ensign at 8am and *Sybelle* will salute with 15 guns' (previously it had been 13). It was a subtle, perhaps ironic, touch as the *Sybelle* was commanded by Elliot, who had just returned from his second surveillance of the Gulf of Tartary.

Less than a fortnight later, Stirling was called on to take charge at a more sombre occasion. The ailing Commodore Abbot finally died on 14 December from an ulcerated stomach and, as Preble noted, Stirling took charge of arranging the funeral procession set for the next day. It was an elaborate affair, headed by the

Winchester's band playing the Dead March, and followed by the late Commodore's coxswain bearing his broad pennant, Sir John Bowring, Stirling, the US Consul and various other diplomats and officers—even Russian officers being held as prisoners.[43] Organising this event may have reminded Stirling of the sudden death of Sir James Brisbane in Sydney all those years ago, in December 1827. At that time he had just been thrust into a senior position and had had to make similar funeral arrangements, but with four days to do it, not just one. That he managed to achieve the efficacy and scale of Abbot's funeral in such a short time is indicative of the close relationships he had built up with high-ranking service personnel in the region—not only British, but from various nations. Even Abbot had left instructions for Stirling to be included in the distribution of his best 'wine and seegars', which Preble ensured were delivered.[44]

Just before Abbot's death Stirling had been preparing dispatches to the Admiralty on the results of Elliot's second mission to the Gulf of Tartary. Elliot's report, and another from Captain O'Callaghan, had confirmed the discovery of a channel

> from the so called Gulf of Tartary into the hitherto designated Gulf of Amur…as shewn by the accompanying charts. It is worthy of notice how adroitly the Russians have managed to keep this fact so well concealed from the world, for it has never appeared on any of their charts, or even in the most recent Directory, that of Findlay published in 1851, Sakhalien [sic] is expressly designated a peninsula and said to be connected to the main by a sandy isthmus.[45]

When received by the Admiralty on 4 February 1856, this still did not improve their Lordships' opinion of Stirling's earlier activities, the annotation reading in part:

> this discovery adds to the feelings of disappointment and regret that they have already expressed at the manner in which part of the Gulf was examined in June. It is obvious now that the survey which he described as complete was most imperfect…[46]

Stirling had received several requests for copies of Elliot's report and charts of the northern seas. One was sent to the French Commander Guerin on 10 December and, a day or so later, to Sir John Bowring. But even though the channel had now been proven, Stirling was convinced that the Russians posed no immediate threat to British shipping in the Far East. It was their land aspirations that concerned him. Their ships were trapped by the weather during winter, whilst at other times of the year they could be held at bay by Japan's neutrality combined with British naval superiority. He knew that others did not share his views and was growing tired of the constant need to justify and defend his opinions.

Abbot's death cemented Stirling's decision to retire. He would be 65 in the coming January and had been away from his family for nearly two years. The heat and humidity of summers in Hong Kong and China had taken a toll on his normally strong constitution, and he longed for home. He hoped Frederick would inform the Admiralty, when he handed in the treaty documents and his request to be relieved, of his father's fatigue and increasingly frequent indisposition. No record has been found of either Stirling's resignation or his son's report, but it proved enough to move the Admiralty, early in February 1856, to release James from what was usually a minimum three-year period of service.

In the meantime Stirling's spirits had been lifted by a three-day regatta which started in Victoria harbour on 19 December, and had involved ships of all nations. The *Winchester*'s company took a leading role in organising the proceedings, and her crews performed creditably in various events. Stirling attended the regatta ball on the Saturday night and, at Lady Bowring's invitation, spent Christmas dinner at Government House. Preble was also invited, noting in his diary how

> Lady B's plum pudding was praised as a matter of course by all the guests, and discussion as to the orthodox method of cutting it was had. The Admiral siding for slices instead of wedges as that left the remainder right for the fry next day.[47]

It was mercifully cool over the Christmas period, making walking a pleasure. Preble recorded meeting Sir James and Captain Currie on the 28th when they were out taking a 'constitutional' over the hills. On Stirling's mind was a plan he had discussed with Bowring to foil the constant inroads of local pirates. His idea was for the navy to provide protection for convoys of merchant ships 'at periods to be arranged and from place to place as fixed upon'.[48] But he would need to have his three steamers replaced to provide anything like an effective escort. Nevertheless, the last of his outward correspondence for the year 1855 was a draft Public Notice, submitted to Sir John Bowring, on the subject of 'affording the protection of convoys to the coasting trade'.

Stirling had wanted to introduce this service much earlier in his command, but during the Russian crisis too many ships had been involved in surveillance work to implement it. Now the control of pirates had top priority[49] and the convoy protection system came into effect in the first week of January 1856. Under the arrangement 'all vessels of every nation' wanting safe passage could join a convoy protected by a British Navy warship. During both monsoon seasons (north-east and south-west) the convoy would depart from Woosung and Whampoa on the first day of the month, calling in also at the ports of Ningpo, Foochow, Amoy and Hong Kong. Stirling's notice also stated that

> Orders will be given that the Ships-of-war shall not permit any sort of piratical interference whatsoever with the vessels under their protection. And Notice is hereby given, that Ships-of-war…will seize every armed vessel suspected of being so engaged, and will deliver them over, together with their crews, to the proper Tribunals.[50]

One contentious issue related to piracy concerned the disposal of spoils gained in the capture of pirate vessels. Stirling had been wary of allowing his men to keep any of the property seized, and had referred the matter to London. The Admiralty, having sought advice from the Queen's Advocate, now ruled that all property seized from pirates had to be treated in exactly the same way as prizes, and be processed by the Vice-Admiralty Court. It was a reasonable solution, but extremely difficult to police as many of the goods involved were small valuables or spirits.

One of Stirling's most active commanders in the fight against pirates, Captain Vansittart, was due to appear before a court martial on 18 January, and the man bringing complaints against him, Lieutenant Brock, now in charge of the *Hornet*, was ordered to return to Hong Kong for the hearing. Brock risked unpopularity, for Vansittart had earned the respect not only of his men but of the entire community. Among gratuities he had earned for himself and his crew was $22,000 from Dent & Co. in appreciation of the *Bittern's* part in action against a piratical fleet at Sheippoo the previous September. Vansittart had recommended that the equivalent of £1,000 go to the mother of ship's master, Charles Turner, who had lost his life, and £200 each for the men who lost limbs.[51] Stirling had forwarded Vansittart's reports of his clashes with pirates the previous November, with covering letters of strong approbation,[52] and the details of action leading to Turner's death had particularly caught the public imagination. The *London Gazette's* report of 11 January, quoting Vansittart, gives an insight into the dangers Stirling's men faced when engaging an elusive and dangerous enemy. Spotting the pirates, the *Bittern* found them

> moored in an excellent defensive position…with crowded decks, men, at their guns, pointed for the passage. I ordered Mr Turner the master, who…was towing ahead and piloting us in, to keep her at fullest speed, and with sail on the *Bittern* to the last moment, we were still exposed for more than 10 minutes to a heavy raking fire before…the ship could be brought up and sprung into position; then we found our port broadsides engaged at about 500 yards…this they kept up with astonishing spirit for some time, and it took more than an hour to silence them altogether…On taking possession only one of the whole 22 vessels was found uninjured enough to move; she had 11 guns, which had evidently been well served…[53]

Unfortunately, Turner had received a 'shot, which tore away part of his right side'.

Vansittart prepared a separate report assessing the pirates' defence capabilities, which explains the concerns of the merchants and the necessity for the protection Stirling had implemented. The pirates could, he said, easily maintain three to four knots, sufficient even to outspeed the *Bittern*, and their guns varied from the occasional 32-pounder down to 18 lb. Prisoners taken spoke of booty worth between $200,000 and $300,000—sunk during the action—while other pirated goods, like rich furs, were burned.[54]

Commander Fellowes of HMS *Rattler* had also earned Stirling's warm commendation for attacks on pirates. In a joint action with the American frigate *Powhattan* at Tyloo the previous August, he had reported capturing 'Nine war junks, mounting 130 guns of all sizes, and nine small junks (traders) the pirates had detained'. Their own losses—five men killed and eighteen wounded—paled in comparison to those of the pirates, for Fellowes estimated that at least half of the 1,000-strong enemy force were killed, wounded or drowned.[55]

The Times editorial on 13 January 1856, commenting on these reports in the *London Gazette*, could not resist rubbing salt into old wounds. Stirling's dispatches, it said, showed that his officers and crew 'were not deficient in dash and enterprise' when distinction was offing. On the other hand,

> We remember, not without a certain degree of humiliation, the futile cruize of this very squadron in the Japanese waters, and *journée des dupes* in Castries Bay. Never was there a fairer occasion for crushing the power of Russia on those distant seas, but it was allowed to escape unimproved...All this however is a matter of history, and...If we recur to the subject at all it is because the despatches from Admiral Stirling give ample proof that the officers under his command are capable of contending successfully with difficulties similar to those which the Russians threw in their way in the course of last year.[56]

The Brock-Vansittart court martial on board the *Sybelle* was the fourth during Stirling's Far Eastern command, far fewer than the number he had had to attend when on the Malta station in the early 1840s, but still unfortunate. Lieutenant Brock had criticised his captain's actions in a letter the previous June,[57] when all officers and men had been under pressure in the hunt for Russians. Brock felt his criticisms were valid, and resented his subsequent treatment. But his peers found him guilty of insubordination. As his record was otherwise excellent, he was reprimanded rather than dismissed. When this news reached *The Times* in London, it was referred to as another of 'the inglorious results of Admiral Stirling's command',[58] again hurtful for his family.

The latter part of January was marked by official gun salutes and Stirling's preparations for a redeployment of his fleet. When the American Commissioner for Hong Kong, Dr Parker, inspected the US flagship *Vandalia* on the 23rd, Stirling also came on board from the *Winchester* to meet him, the two ships exchanging salutes. Preble, who was winding up affairs before returning to America, observed how 'tickled' the Commissioner was at these proceedings, whereas the day before, when boarding the US sloop *Macedonian*, Stirling had specifically requested not to be saluted. He knew saluting had its hazards, for on one of his farewell visits to the British ships in port, a young marine on post duty had 'shot one of his fingers off by accident'.[59]

Redeployment duties meant that much of the squadron was about to be scattered—the *Hornet*, to deliver provisions to the *Racehorse* in Foo-chow before proceeding to Shanghai; the *Bittern*, heading north to implement the convoy plan;[60] the *Encounter*, scheduled for Singapore; and the *Spartan*, to Whampoa for naval supplies. Thus, on 25 January, when Lieutenant-Colonel Graham asked that shipping be provided to take a detail of Royal Artillery (recently relieved) to Ceylon, and thence to England, Stirling had to answer that there simply was no ship-of-war or other government vessel at present available, and he had to accept a tender for the trader *Harriet Armitage* to act as a troop transport ship.[61]

Back in England, Stirling's request to relinquish his command had been received and accepted by the Admiralty Board.[62] A notice appeared in the Naval and Military Intelligence section of *The Times* on 15 February that:

> Rear Admiral Sir James Stirling, commanding the East India Station, is recalled from his command. It is stated that this step has been taken at the gallant officer's own solicitation.

This was seen by his Mangles brothers-in-law and the next day, among the Letters to the Editor section, the following appeared:

> Sir, It is stated in your paper of this morning, under the head of Naval and Military Intelligence, that 'Rear Admiral Sir James Stirling, commanding the East India Station, is recalled from his command'. As the expression used may lead to misapprehension…I beg to state that Sir James Stirling has not been 'recalled' but has resigned his command, a course which he had for some time contemplated in consequence of ill-health, under which he had been suffering for several months. I am, Sir, your most obedient servant, Ross D Mangles.[63]

A few days later *The Times* named Rear Admiral Sir Michael Seymour KCB, formerly second-in-command of the Baltic Fleet, as Stirling's successor in the East Indies. The new Commander-in-Chief's flagship would be HMS *Calcutta 84*, but Seymour was not to wait for her, instead proceeding 'to relieve Sir James by the overland route'.[64]

Confirmation of his request to resign did not reach Stirling until 30 March. The intervening weeks were filled with the minutiae of command administration, made harder by sultry weather, but at least alleviated on 9 March by the arrival of the mail steamer with Admiralty dispatches and private mail. If he had not learned already, Stirling would have heard then that a tentative date in June had been set for the wedding of his third daughter, Ellinor, to James Alexander Guthrie. It was a match of which James thoroughly approved, as Guthrie came from an old Scottish family with lands in Forfarshire, and commercial interests in merchanting and banking. The trading firm Chalmers & Guthrie, in which his prospective son-in-law worked, even had branches in Portsmouth.[65] Stirling hoped approval for his release from duty would arrive in the next mail so that he could still make it home in time for the wedding.

A little excitement arose around 23 March when Governor Bowring requested Stirling to seize two ships which he believed had violated the Chinese Passengers Act. One of the less reputable 'trades' which occurred along the Chinese coast involved the capture of coolie labourers who were sent to such destinations as California, Peru and the British plantation colonies. Bowring had complained about it in 1852, but had noted that the legal pretext of 'indentures' used by shippers prevented the Royal Navy from detaining coolie ships as slavers, though in human terms the difference was imperceptible.[66] Indeed, it was said that any naval officer attempting to stop a coolie ship ran the risk of a suit for damages. But in 1855 the crew of a British ship, *Inglewood*, had revolted against the traffic in very young girls and brought their plight to the attention of the British consul in Amoy.[67]

The Chinese Passengers Act was supposed to counter this type of activity. The two ships Stirling had been asked to investigate were the *Levant*, a Hawaiian ship carrying Chinese passengers, and a merchant ship, the *General Blanco*, so he ordered men from the *Winchester* to board each ship and turn any passengers over to the Queen's Proctor in Hong Kong.[68] Morally and professionally Stirling was quite correct in giving these orders, but, in complying with Bowring's request, he intervened in a power struggle between the keenly reformist Governor and the Lieutenant-Governor, Caine, who in April 1854 had been given most of the administrative power in Hong Kong. The idea in London had been to free Bowring to concentrate on revisions of the China Treaty, but Bowring was 'not the man to agree to remain aloof from Hong Kong affairs',[69] especially when he occupied Government House. The discord between the two men had come to a head just the previous month, February 1856, over the appointment of a temporary Colonial Chaplain, a matter Bowring felt was his to command. It was a small thing, but enough for Bowring to refer back to the Home Government as evidence of the anomaly of his position. In supporting Bowring over the order to seize suspect ships, Stirling had correctly guessed that London would back the Governor, and late in April 1856 Bowring was granted the full powers of his office.[70]

On 27 March the *Nankin* returned from a supply trip to Trincomalee, and on board was a young man of great interest to Stirling. It was Captain Charles Fremantle's nephew, Lieutenant Edmund Fremantle, who had been appointed to the *Spartan* under Sir William Hoste.[71] Stirling appears to have organised a transfer for the young man to the *Winchester* and was pleased to welcome him aboard the flagship two days later.[72] Then on the 30th the P&O mail steamer *Madras* arrived. Among its two dozen Admiralty dispatches was an auspicious one—No. 47—with the long-awaited approval of his request to be relieved. At last Stirling could leave Hong Kong.

But by this stage, too, Stirling had become aware of the criticisms of his treaty, despite the difficulties he had experienced in winning the not inconsiderable privileges it granted Britain. *The Times* had reflected this in its editorial covering the treaty on 23 January, copies of which probably arrived in Hong Kong with this mail. The editorial read:

The text of the convention between Japan and Great Britain is now before us, and, as might be expected, adds but little to our information with regard to this singular country, or the state of our own relations with the Japanese. The convention is similar to one that has already been signed between the United States and the Japanese Empire and represents nothing but a *minimum* [sic] which could be conceded under the immediate pressure of an armed force and the apprehension of a still more serious attack...[73]

For Stirling, who had explained the situation so many times, this was dispiriting. He was tired and longed for home, so immediately began preparations for departure. Final orders and farewells were sent to the senior naval officers at each of the treaty ports, and receptions were held to take leave of all the high-ranking officers with whom he had worked, including the commander of the 59th Regiment. A private farewell visit would have been paid to the Bowring family, for Stirling had become quite attached to them, though his relationship with Sir John had been more aloof. On 1 April Stirling advised Bowring officially of his departure, expressing his gratitude at the Governor's 'urbanity and readiness' in dealing with his various representations, and personally acknowledging his 'ability and experience in public affairs'.[74]

The two men had worked amicably on many issues, but there were others where they had differed considerably—notably Japan. On the same day that Stirling penned his letter of thanks, Bowring wrote to the Foreign Office begging to differ with Lord Clarendon's view that the Convention 'as it now stands' would be commercially beneficial.

No one appears at present to contemplate commercial operations with Japan, and I do not find that Sir James Stirling believes that the convention confers the right to trade. I understand it to be his opinion...that it is better nothing should be done for obtaining a commercial Treaty, and that it should be left to other powers to open the doors through which we may hereafter enter. I do not concur in the view that this is a becoming position for Great Britain to occupy in these regions.[75]

Bowring asked to be authorised to go to Japan himself, believing the Japanese might 'to some extent' be opened to commerce; but noted his 'paramount difficulty' would be with Clause 7 of the Treaty which stated: 'When this Convention shall be ratified no High officer coming to Japan shall alter it...'

Bowring also found other niggling shots to fire on the eve of the Admiral's departure. He took issue with Stirling's representation of Dutch privileges in Japan as 'unenviable by British subjects'; rather, he said, they amounted to a trade worth '5 millions of florins'. And he was annoyed at the dearth of naval ships available for diplomatic visits, particularly as the French and American consuls had access to several warships for this purpose. On a third front, he was annoyed at being bypassed in official correspondence over the ratification of the Treaty. Stirling had sent his own confidential November 1855 report direct to the Admiralty, and now Bowring somewhat petulantly asked him, in a short memorandum on 1 April, 'to be furnished with it, that I may be the better able to give effect to the instructions I have received'.[76] Stirling clearly wanted to consult with Admiralty officers before releasing his confidential dispatch, and at the time of his departure from Hong Kong the Governor still had not got his copy.

Just two days after receiving written permission to leave, Stirling commanded the Master of the *Winchester* to ready for sea. At noon on 2 April 1856 she weighed anchor and was towed by the *Barracouta* out of Victoria harbour.[77] On deck with Captain Currie, who had shared so many of his adventures beside him, Stirling watched the Hong Kong skyline fade into the distance. But he would not stay in the familiar surrounds of his flagship for long. Although the Admiralty had at first approved of Stirling's plan to take the *Winchester* to England, all this changed with Sir Michael Seymour's appointment. The latter's designated new flagship, the *Calcutta*, would take time to be fitted out and proceed to Hong Kong, so the *Winchester* had to remain as an interim base for the new Admiral.

Accordingly, on 5 April, when well clear of Hong Kong, Stirling's luggage was shifted to the *Encounter* for the voyage to Singapore. After a short formal farewell, his flag was lowered from the *Winchester* for the last time, and Stirling and his retinue were rowed to the waiting *Encounter*.[78] With her ability to use engines when the wind failed, the *Encounter* made excellent time and reached Singapore on 15 April. Five days later the mail steamer *Singapore* arrived bearing Sir Michael Seymour,[79] providing a chance for valuable discussions between the two men. On the 22nd the *Encounter*'s log recorded hauling down the flag of Rear Admiral Sir James Stirling for the last time at sunset (Admiral Sir Michael Seymour's flag was raised the following morning). Stirling left Singapore promptly, proceeding by steam packet and overland transport to Marseilles,[80] where he took a train to Calais for the Channel crossing, arriving in London in the second week of June 1856. He had been away for two years and just over three months.

When calling at the Admiralty to report his arrival, Stirling was alerted to the fact that, as a Senior Officer of Her Majesty's Navy, returning from active service abroad, he must pay his respects to the Queen at the next levee opportunity, which would be on 25 June. Ellinor had already applied for a special licence and confirmed that her wedding would be on the 24th, so with two important occasions on consecutive days, it promised to be a busy time for her father before he was free to really relax at Belmont.

30

A Welcome Retirement

1856–1860

STIRLING ARRIVED HOME to find Belmont in the midst of feverish preparations. Last-minute fittings involved not only dressmakers for the bride and her mother and sisters, but also tailors, as the boys were all home. Frederick had already arrived from China, Walter had sat and passed his second examinations for Sandhurst military academy on 17 January 1856, and was having a break before applying for an East Indian Army cadetship. Charles was back from Sebastapol where, as a Lieutenant in the Horse Brigade with the Royal Artillery, he had won a medal and clasp with a Turkish head. Andrew, the eldest, was probably there too, though no confirmation has been found. As for James, it was a case of repairing to his Portsmouth tailor, for not only had his size changed in the tropics, so had all naval uniforms in recent times. A new outfit was imperative, not just for the wedding but for his Court appearance the following day. The new blue and gold embroidered uniforms were described as very handsome, especially the sword, with its 'solid hilt, half basket guard, crown and anchor badge, and lion head backpiece'.[1]

On Tuesday 24 June 1856 Stirling proudly led his 18-year-old daughter Ellinor down the aisle of the twelfth-century stone church of St Thomas's at Bedhampton, Havant, and gave her hand to James Alexander Guthrie.[2] At 32, the groom was following the Stirling tradition of marrying much younger women. Stirling had no worries for his daughter's future, for he knew Guthrie was financially sound and, furthermore, he had bestowed a handsome marriage settlement.[3] At the conclusion of the ceremony the two fathers joined the bride and groom to act as witnesses in signing the register. David Charles Guthrie gave his occupation as Merchant whilst James signed as Admiral of the Red. The happy couple then left the church to be showered with rose petals by some of the villagers who had gathered outside. Afterwards, family and guests repaired to the waiting carriages for the short ride back to Belmont House where a reception had been prepared.

At the reception Stirling was able to brief his nephew-by-marriage, Lieutenant Arthur Onslow, on Court procedure, as he had been asked to present Onslow to Queen Victoria at St James' Palace the following day. Both Onslow and Stirling

Ellinor Stirling, married at the age of 18 to James Guthrie
at Bedhampton Church, Havant (below)

Portrait courtesy the Hon. Lavinia Fleming; church from P. Rogers, The Borough of Havant in Old Picture Postcards

were mentioned in the published list of those presented, some thirty in all.[4] For James, the chance to kiss his sovereign's hand was one he treasured, as he was a royalist through and through. But the adrenalin of anticipation dissipated when his turn was over, and he was swamped with fatigue. Around him was bright chatter, but he was so tired he could hardly raise a smile. On the following evening a grand Navy Club banquet was scheduled to honour the First Lord of the Admiralty, the Right Hon. Sir Charles Wood MP, presided over by Admiral Sir Thomas Cochrane. But even if he had intended to go to this dinner, Stirling had to make his apologies. He was just too tired. All he wanted was to return to the quiet of Belmont to begin his retirement.

The last six months of 1856 passed quietly for Stirling, who was in a state of convalescence. His strength had been sapped by the strains of the past year and he was thankful to sink into the comforts of home. Like many others who served in the tropics in that era, he evidently contracted malaria and now suffered the after-effects of multiple infections. Severe infection from the anopheles mosquito is known to lead to periodic bouts of fever, chills and jaundice lasting for years.[5] This could partially explain the sudden noticeable lack of written evidence about the affairs of this hitherto voluminous correspondent and extraordinarily active man. However, it is known from the Bedhampton Church Warden's accounts that, from his return from the Far East until 1859, Stirling lived predominantly at Belmont House, and paid regularly for his family pew at St Thomas's.[6]

A fortnight after the wedding, James' son Frederick Henry had notice of a new command. He had been on furlough since returning from China, but on 15 July 1856 was appointed commander of HMS *Wasp*, on which he would serve for the next thirty-one months.[7] James' reaction was typical of any proud father—though glad for his son, he was sorry to see him go, as they had shared much over the past two years. But the rest of the family claimed his attention as his strength returned. Ellen had collected various newspaper cuttings, relating not only to his time in China, but others that might interest him, including one of Governor Kennedy's arrival at Fremantle to take over the reins from Fitzgerald. This had featured in the *Illustrated London News* on 24 May, together with a picture of Perth from Mount Eliza[8] which the couple would have looked at in some amazement. Perth was clearly no metropolis, but its jetties, solid buildings and extent were so different from the precarious small village they had left twenty years earlier.

As Charles and Frederick Mangles had kept in touch with Western Australia during his absence, Stirling would quickly have gleaned the colony's latest news, including the beneficial effects of the convict inflow, particularly as so many of its native-born young men had left for the eastern gold rushes. James already knew of the downturn in fortunes of the Western Australian Company and its Australind venture, and was not surprised to hear of further problems. The company was now being asked to fulfil the location dues (improvements) of 1s 6d per acre, or face resumption. Paying the dues was impossible as it had lost almost all of its assets, so a member of its beleaguered English Board was writing to the Colonial Office to see whether a remission on the duties could be organised.[9] Pressed to rule on the matter, the Land and Emigration Board provided no answer, but simply asked to interview the writer,[10] explaining that delay would be no problem as resumptions were not due until the following May. Stirling must have been concerned about this issue, as he had sold land to the company and, together with his brothers-in-law, still held unimproved lots in the colony.

There was another 'Swan River' problem that concerned the Mangles brothers at this time which they no doubt discussed with Stirling. They had heard complaints about the lack of convict labour in farming districts and a reduction in Commissariat supply contracts which together were badly affecting farmers by hitting the market for their produce. To make matters worse, the Government had been over-ordering imported supplies for the public service, resulting in frequent auctions of superfluous stores, again dampening prices. Frederick outlined all of this in a letter to the Colonial Office, pointing out that it constituted 'a direct inter-ference with the legitimate trade of the colony'.[11] But, as had happened so often in Stirling's own dealings with them in the past, the Colonial Office reaction was stiff and defensive. They defined the complaint as simply one in which 'Western Australians object to allowing the Govt. to buy of any British producers but themselves…It seems…better to announce plainly that no such demands can ever be yielded to…' An annotation on Mangles' letter pointed out the benefits of the Home Government's 'rescue' of the colony by assenting to its petition to receive convicts, which meant the inhabitants had, 'for the first time in their history begun to prosper', but they 'should not be pampered'.[12] The drafted official reply stated that the Colonial Office could not support a system favouring Western Australian growers, nor 'in maintaining more convict depots than requisite, merely in order to give particular districts the profit of a large Government expenditure'.[13]

Events far removed from Western Australia also engrossed Stirling before the end of 1856—distant reminders of the skirmishes he had been involved in between the rebels and the Imperialists in Canton and Shanghai, with all their diplomatic repercussions. A furore had broken out in November following a stand-off between Hong Kong's Governor Bowring and Canton's Viceroy Yeo over disputed ownership of a ship, the *Arrow*. The commerce-minded Bowring, who was still demanding entry to Canton, was determined that British authority should not be undermined, and had endorsed a bombardment of the city by British naval forces under Admiral Seymour's command. The issue became the major topic of debate in Parliament in early 1857 with both sides of the House pouring scorn on Governor Bowring and Consul Parkes for disregarding government instructions. Gladstone even linked Bowring's actions to the 'pernicious, demoralizing…opium trade', but Palmerston stood by the Governor. He vilified Viceroy Yeo as 'one of the most savage barbarians that ever disgraced a nation', and stated further that his restrictions 'on our commerce…are one cause of that trade in opium…'[14] Once again Palmerston won the argument—and the subsequent election. But Admiral Seymour's acquiescence to Bowring's wishes to bombard Canton was in direct contrast to his predecessor. Stirling had run counter to Bowring on a number of occasions and been determined to prevent any escalation of tension, notably during hostilities in Shanghai. Nevertheless, Seymour's role in the *Arrow* incident was unquestioned and Sir Michael emerged from 'the hurly burly unbruised'.[15]

It is possible that Stirling was ill during the winter of 1856-57, for his signature was missing from a petition organised by the Mangles brothers, urging the British Government not to withdraw or downsize the convict establishment at Swan River. The petition was supported by many in London with connections to the colony,[16] but was received by Colonial Office staff on 12 January 1857 with some surprise, as they actually had no intention of ending the scheme.[17]

Family visits over Christmas-New Year kept Stirling in good spirits, and when he turned 67 on 28 January 1858 it was with some pleasure that he could reflect on his children's various positions. All his younger sons were doing well: Frederick was still in command of the *Wasp*, Charles was now First Captain with the Royal Artillery Depot Brigade and stationed in London, while Walter, the youngest, had just been accepted as a Cornet in the Bengal 2nd Light Cavalry and had sailed for India. Of the oldest boy, Andrew, there was little mention in any of the family papers, and a strange comment in Stirling's will, to the effect that Ellen could give him £80 a year '*if she thinks fit*',[18] suggests that somewhere along the line there had been a serious breach. Andrew served for a while in India and married a Sarah Reece, living in later life at Beaumaris, but there were no children and the date of the marriage is unknown.[19] Of Stirling's daughters, Mary was now 25 and her single state was a matter of concern to both parents. Ellinor was living in London and happily pregnant with the first grandchild, Anna was 17 and almost ready for her first season in society, while 15-year-old Dorothea and 12-year-old Georgina were still under the care of their governess.

On Ellen's side there was cause for celebration, for Charles Mangles had won the seat of Newport, Isle of Wight, in the March 1857 elections.[20] He thus joined his brother Ross in Parliament, as Ross Donnelly Mangles had held on to his Guildford seat, despite the swing in Government to the Conservatives. More celebrations were called for when, on 22 August 1857, James heard that he had been promoted, by seniority, from Rear Admiral to Vice Admiral.[21] This meant an increase in his half-pay pension and took him a step closer to full Admiral status, something to which he still aspired.

But any pleasure that Ellen and James derived from this promotion was tempered soon afterwards by concern for their youngest son's well-being, as news of the Cawnpore massacre in India began to filter into the papers. Their uneasiness, sadly, was justified, for unbeknown at the time Walter had been injured in the massacre of British soldiers and civilians at Cawnpore on 27 June and was to die as a result, aged only 20, on 27 November 1857.[22] His demise at the threshold of a promising career would have hurt Stirling badly and contributed to severe depression. In a bitter-sweet coincidence, his nephew Ross (Ross Donnelly Mangles' son), serving in the same arena, had won the Victoria Cross for outstanding bravery. The citation, gazetted in July 1859, described how the injured 'Mr Mangles, with a signal gallantry…carried for several miles, out of the action, a wounded soldier of her Majesty's 37th Regiment, after binding up his wounds under a murderous fire'.[23]

Nothing concrete is known of Stirling's activities from the end of 1857 until April 1858. He was still based at Belmont, and would have rejoiced to hear of the safe arrival of a second grandchild, Amelia Frances Guthrie, born in London in March. By April 1858 he was definitely in the city, for a letter from young Charles Stirling, written on 3 April, noted that 'Uncle James has taken a house in Harley St for some months'.[24] The Stirlings probably took the London rental for the season as Anna, now 18, was ready to be presented to the Queen and enter the marriage market. Brother Walter, now 78, who had moved with 59-year-old sister Agnes to 18 Curzon Street, just opposite Hyde Park Corner, was very concerned about family marriage prospects,[25] and most likely was involved in planning the season's activities. At 30 Portland Place, Marylebone, Ellinor Guthrie would also have been involved in the planning—especially the choice of attire for Anna's all-important presentation. There was a strict dress code for these events, the gown having to be of a pale colour but elaborately decorated with a long train. A headdress, usually of ostrich feathers, long gloves and a suitably decorated fan completed the outfit.[26] Anna would have been sponsored either by her mother, Lady Stirling, or someone else with entrée to the court. Presentations were generally held in the evening at either St James' or Kensington Palace, and on the appointed evening Anna and Ellen would have joined others waiting, sometimes for hours, until their name was called. Led by Ellen, Anna would have walked nervously towards the Queen, being careful not to trip over her train. After her mother's introduction, she would make her curtsey and then walk a yard or so backwards, as no one ever turned their back on the Queen. Fathers were usually not present at such events, but they would foot the substantial bills and see to it that their daughters were invited to all the major gatherings of the season, and generally hold a lavish entertainment themselves. Stirling would have been no exception.

During the day Stirling probably sought sanctuary in his club, the United Services Club, and here he no doubt heard through his various contacts that the Land and Emigration Office had at last given an answer to the issues raised by the WA Company and its supporters. Their major concern had been the 21-year improvement clause, for by purchasing Latour's land they had been expected to improve it by 1850 when Latour's 21-year period expired. They had asked for an extension and the Land and Emigration Commissioners believed they had just cause, concluding on 14 April 1858 that the company had the right to date the 21-year improvement period from November 1843, when the boundaries had been finalised, and that the Governor should be so informed.[27] Their judgment had been based on a very long report from Roe, the Western Australian Surveyor-General, dated 27 November 1857, a report which of necessity also attempted, fairly successfully, to sort out Stirling's Western Australian land holdings from 1828 onwards.[28]

Roe explained that Stirling's final land selections had been made in September 1837 and had included three locations in the Leschenault-Wellington area, which at that time had not been fully surveyed. Nevertheless:

> 13 Sep 1837 has been entered in the records of the Survey Office as the date on which the 21 years claimed for the performance of location duties were considered to commence on all the land comprised in the 3 first selections therein reported (61,284 acres)…

Further communications had led to a final adjustment of boundaries to most of the selections made in 1837, 'and for which he has since been granted full title', but they had excepted the selection on the eastern shore of Geographe Bay which overlapped the land previously assigned to Latour. Roe explained that he had not registered this selection, as Latour's land was expected to be resumed for non-performance of Location dues in 1840, and noted 'How nearly this view of the case was to being realised remains a matter of record by Mr Hutt's resumption of Col. Latour's land on 27 Apr 1840'. However, he added,

> as the whole was subsequently restored by the Secy of State and eventually granted in fee simple, Sir James' Selection No 3 which had then passed into the possession of the WA Company by purchase had necessarily to be revised…

He then referred to the 'voluminous correspondence' involved in that revision which 'terminated only on the 20th Nov. 1843' when Clifton received, on behalf of the WA Company, five separate locations totalling 61,284 acres, which was the amount they had bought from Stirling. These selections 'completed also Sir J S's claim to 100,000 acres'. Roe then set out the company's position as regards improvement:

Total selection by the WA Company in right of Sir Jas Stirling	61,284 acres
Amount of improvement effected thereon—£1,253 @ 1/6	16,464 acres
Remain to be improved	44,817 acres
acres @ 1/6	= £3,361.6.3

> …improvements to the value of £3,3616.3 would therefore be due upon the land selected by the Company before they would be entitled to claim it in fee simple…

Roe then stated that he felt the company had 'a claim to the indulgent consideration' of Government regarding improvements due because their land claim had only been finalised on 30 November 1843, and performance of improvements should only be reckoned from that date.[29] Hence the decision made by the Lands and Emigration Commissioners. But Roe's letter also commented that:

> For reasons not necessary to advert to, the Company subsequently reconveyed to Sir J. S. 12,800 acres of the location distinguished at No 50, and on Sir J's Agent in this Colony proving the performance duties upon it, the reconveyed land was granted to him in fee simple as Location 50A.[30]

So James now held all his Leschenault lands in fee simple. Title to Location 26 had been granted on 10 September 1841, that to Location 41 on 13 December 1842, Location 12 on 8 October 1851 and finally Location 50A in 1857, as certified above by Roe. Apparently Clifton believed that Stirling had gained title to 50A at the expense of the company, and had sent a written complaint to the Colonial Office. Roe, when asked for his opinion, noted on 29 June 1858, that

> its full title being acquired by location duties performed by Sir James's tenants and money [to the sum of £1,255[31]], and not at all I believe by any outlay or arrangement of the Company.[32]

The Mangles were probably aware of these proceedings, for Frederick Mangles had organised the improvements that had gained title to most of Stirling's Plantagenet lands.[33] Ross Donnelly Mangles had resigned his Guildford seat in June 1858 and was planning another visit to India, but Charles Mangles was still Member for Newport and in town for a good part of the year.[34] Here he could keep in touch both with Frederick, who was still running the now reduced shipping business, and his cousin James Mangles, the botanist who had visited James and Ellen in Western Australia.

In August 1858 it is likely that Stirling had a visit from an old friend, Sir Charles Howe Fremantle, who had recently been appointed Commander-in-Chief of the Channel Fleet, and given command of the *Renown 91*. As Rear Admiral of the Red, Fremantle had hoisted his flag on that ship at Spithead on 14 August, then gone on leave.[35] Living relatively close to Portsmouth made it possible for a number of naval friends to visit Stirling, who would thus have kept abreast of inside news. He would have been particularly interested to hear in subsequent months that the Foreign Office Envoy, Lord Elgin, had managed to forge another Anglo-Japanese Treaty in August 1858, providing for unsupervised trade and a British Residency in Japan.

Possibly on advice that he could benefit from a change of air, Stirling rented a house in Ryde, within Charles Mangles' constituency on the Isle of Wight, over the winter months of 1858–59. Stirling had long discussed with Charles, the first of the Mangles he had known, his dreams for Western Australia—in particular his hopes for a stronger Indian connection. Australind had been a failure, but various horse-breeding establishments to provide remounts for the Indian Army were now beginning to make money.[36] His early hopes that the colony would become a place of rest and recreation for British officers requiring leave, after long periods of service in the tropics, was once again aired. In January 1859 Charles put a proposal to the Colonial Office that they should 'establish in Western Australia a sanatorium for the reception of European soldiers who may lose their health in India',[37] but it was squashed on grounds that the War Office and India Department had not been interested when the matter had been raised previously.[38]

Now settled on the fashionable outskirts of Ryde, Stirling and his family were visited from 15 February to 15 March by Frederick, who had just completed his three-year command of the *Wasp*.[39] His father would have been pleased to see a letter of commendation that Frederick had received from the Admiralty Board 'for the very efficient state of the *Wasp*',[40] and probably commiserated over a subsequent Admiralty letter expressing dissatisfaction over 'unregulated punishments'.[41] Stirling senior had not always stuck exactly to the book, and knew how hard it was to walk the fine line between meting out sufficient punishment to command the respect and obedience of hundreds of men, but not enough to cause rebelliousness through grievances.

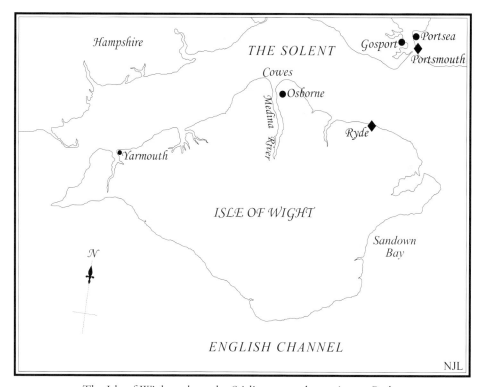

The Isle of Wight, where the Stirlings rented premises at Ryde,
not far from the Queen's summer residence at Osborne Castle

Whilst at Ryde, Stirling had rented his Belmont home to Mrs Augusta Wilder, who paid the parish fees in his absence.[42] The family loved their stay on the Isle of Wight, except for Dorothea, who at almost 18 wanted the same introduction to London society that her sister had experienced. Feeling better after the break, James appears to have given in to his daughter and returned to London for the season, possibly renting the same house in Harley Street that he had used before. He was certainly in London in June 1859 when, at St John's in Hampstead on the 16th, he stood in lieu of father-of-the-bride in giving away Catherine Ann Leake, when she married a Lee Steere. After the season and all the presentations the family returned to Belmont where they were listed in end-of-year church records.[43]

During the latter half of 1859 James heard that his brother Edward's estranged wife, Anna Isabella, had died in London. Edward had settled in Jersey after retiring from the East India service in 1846 with failing eyesight, and had made a disastrous marriage in 1850. He had been inveigled into it by 23-year-old Miss Anna Glascock, who believed him to be very wealthy. She had first tried to hoodwink her poor-sighted husband by taking her lover with them on honeymoon, and thereafter lived a shameless life, though attempting reconciliation when her funds ran low, until Edward was forced to take legal measures to stop her. The case became a *cause célèbre* in the Press and even made legal history when Anna filed for alimony whilst her estranged husband was in the midst of annulment proceedings.[44] The years of bitter public fighting had been most upsetting for the Stirling family, who set high values on honour, and news of her death would have been a relief to all. The only family member who had kept in touch with Edward was young Charles, James' nephew, who had visited his uncle on several occasions. He reported that Edward had kept his sanity throughout the ordeal by throwing himself into the construction of a large residence in the hills above St Helier, appropriately named 'Stirling Castle'. From the turreted roof Edward could just make out the harbour, whilst the interior had been deliberately built without doors to accommodate his near blindness. He was looked after by a loyal housekeeper, Miss Mertz, who was rumoured to have borne his child in 1854.[45] It was a sad life for a man who had been one of the first to explore the rough terrain of Afghanistan.

At the end of 1859 James had worries of his own. The financial drain of a London season, and the amount of money needed to fund the upkeep of the Belmont Estate, had strained his resources. Rent from the tenants of his farms was barely covering the cost of his stables and park maintenance, and there was no income from his Western Australian properties, all having gone into the necessary improvements. The small amount of extra money he had made in China was now exhausted and his half-pay, though adequate, was insufficient to meet all his outstanding expenses and repayments. Belmont had been mortgaged soon after purchase and in 1852 he had transferred the mortgage to his brothers-in-law, so that avenue of fund-raising was closed. There was no other option left, and on 10 April 1860 Stirling signed the Deeds of Conveyance to sell the Belmont estate to William

Pitt Morgan and others for £9,200.[46] This was £550 less than he had bought it for in 1846, and would have been disappointing as he had mortgages of £5,000 to Charles and Frederick Mangles. Nevertheless, the sale would leave him nearly a clear £4,000 which would pay for the lease of a suitable country house for many years to come.

While negotiating the sale of the house Stirling made several visits to London. He and his brothers-in-law had been instrumental in forming a new group, known as the Western Australian Association, to promote the affairs of the colony, and the inaugural meeting took place at the London Tavern on 13 February, with Stirling taking the chair. As well as the Mangles (Ross Donnelly, Charles and Frederick) the others present were H. Landor, F. Buckle, R. W. Habgood, W. Andrews, H. R. Greller, J. McDonald and J. W. McLaren.[47] A second meeting followed on 3 March, when members considered 'formation of a company which may assist the development of the...resources of the colony'.

Mr Andrews had already addressed the Mersey Dock Board regarding the remarkable properties of Western Australian mahogany (jarrah), and the meeting was told his information would be passed to their engineer.[48] A memorial was then drawn up and presented to the Colonial Office on 20 April with a rider to the effect that self-interest was not at stake, rather 'the general good of the Colony'.[49]

Broadly speaking the memorial, addressed to the Secretary of State for Colonies, the Duke of Northumberland, covered the issues of development of timber resources, the effects of lack of labour, and ways to achieve prosperity in Western Australia. In a specific comment on 'the maladministration of the convict system and the want of judicious application of its labour supply', it recalled that

Stirling was involved in suggesting reforms for the convict establishment at Fremantle, where the prison housing 870 inmates was completed in 1859

By permission of the National Library of Australia R734

Six thousand convicts have been received in Western Australia since June 1850, and…Convict labour has been almost exclusively devoted during that long period to erection of buildings for the convicts themselves, and of very handsome residences for the Officers connected with the Convict Department, the former of which are at present…only very partially occupied, some of them, not in use at all…

The memorial then listed deficiencies in the colony's development to date, particularly in communications. There was still no proper road linking the capital with Fremantle port, or Albany, and mail between Perth and King George's Sound often took seven days or more. One result was that 'Invalids in India [were deterred] from resorting to Western Australia…for the recovery of their health', so depriving the colony of another means towards progress and prosperity. Noting the importance of 'large and frequent intercourse with India', the memorial pointed out that the development of railway operations both there and in Ceylon had opened up a market for the hardy jarrah, but that this potential export trade was being inhibited by the

expensive, uncertain and defective character of the only available labour, namely that furnished by the hiring of Ticket of Leave and Conditional Pardon convicts… even the best of them are stated to work well only for a short time, gradually relapsing into an indifferent and listless mode of labour, from which the stimulus of liberal wages is found to be insufficient to rouse them…

The memorialists felt the only solution to the labour problem as it pertained to the timber trade lay either in taking probation prisoners on assignment, or importing coolies from China, in which latter case they expected serious objections might be raised. In favouring the former method, they went on to say:

Were the assignment of probation prisoners substituted for convicts on hire, there would be a double stimulus to exertion, (1) in the fear of being remanded to a prison, and (2) in the hope of earning by good conduct such remission of punishment, as would accelerate the arrival of the period at which a Ticket of Leave with freedom to work for wages would be attainable…

The memorial then pressed home the point that 'when cheap labour is once more placed at the command of the Colonists, a stimulus will be given to private enterprise'. Even the rich northern copper and lead mines would benefit, as 'tram roads' would help to bring their produce closer to coastal ports. Furthermore, surplus revenue should be used to overcome the lack of steam communication along the coast.

Concluding, the memorial remarked how Governor Fitzgerald 'did much for the improvement and development of the Colony more especially in reference to the erection of public buildings in Perth', while leaving it £14,000 in debt. Governor

Kennedy had paid off the debt, purportedly accruing 'a very considerable sum in the Colonial Chest', but had 'made no outlay, of any importance, for any public purpose'. The speedy liquidation of the debt and the accumulation of surplus funds demonstrated 'the strength and buoyancy of the resources of this young but rising Colony'; but now a reconsideration of the system of convict management was required to ensure rapid progress towards prosperity.[50]

Though not among the signatories, Stirling's influence is clearly behind the ideas expressed in this memorial. He had often mentioned the potential of the colony's timber, had been behind moves to encourage steam communication between the ports, and had vigorously promoted links with India. And all of these ideas were sound. Twenty years later Western Australia would begin to benefit from the timber trade proposed here,[51] but inadequate transport facilities did slow progress. Poor communication and transport between the main port of call for P&O mail vessels at King George's Sound and Perth restricted development until the end of the century, when major harbour works elevated Fremantle's status to principal port.

The memorialists' plea for a change in the convict system also had justification, but not the solution they proposed. Their request for a system of convict assignment would never have been countenanced after Bigge's report on its misusage in New South Wales,[52] and Chinese labour was an idea which had been around even before Stirling had left the colony, but never seriously entertained. However, when Western Australia had been constituted a penal settlement, colonists had asked for a better class of criminal, not the worst offenders. As a result, most of the first convict shipments brought men whose sentences would soon expire and thus entitle them to ticket-of-leave status (i.e. freedom to work privately under reporting constraints) within a year or so of arrival. And these early arrivals were, of necessity, fully occupied in building the prisons that would accommodate later transportees. Just as the memorial stated, colonists were indeed upset that there appeared to be so little public benefit from several years of penal status. But most of them, and indeed the memorialists themselves, appeared unaware that rectification of the situation could only occur if the type of criminal transported to Western Australia was changed. Convicts guilty of worse crimes, with commensurately longer sentences, would be eligible for labour on public projects for years before earning their ticket-of-leave.[53] In the event, pressure from the colony *did* lead to the change in the type of convict transported, and much more work of a public nature was performed by convict labour until convict transportation to Western Australia ceased in 1868.[54] But apart from this misapprehension, the memorialists were extremely perceptive in summing up the potential and needs of the colony. It is therefore interesting that their document received the following treatment from Colonial Office staff. The first annotation concluded:

> it is much more reasonable to suppose that the local Government and the Resident colonists are the fit judges of the order in which those wants demand attention,

than to assume that an Absentee Body like the Memorialists are to dictate the manner in which the resources of the colony are to be appropriated. GG [Gardiner] 4 May.

But another added:

The Gentlemen who have signed this Memorial have a large stake in the Colony, and we cannot be surprised that they should feel anxious about its languishing condition. As the Duke will probably grant the interview which they seek, I have thrown together a separate paper, on the chance of their being any use to His Grace…TFE [Elliot] 8 May.[55]

Elliot's 'thrown together' paper, in fact, contained some refreshingly perceptive insights, and an interesting conclusion. He noted:

In my opinion the causes of failure of Western Australia have been three: 1st the want of a good harbour on the Western Coast, 2nd the occurrence of a belt of bad land between the sea and the fertile country but 3rdly and chiefly the unfortunate impolicy of the Home Government in lavishing free grants to an indefinite extent upon the early settlers. They created a Society where all were to be Masters and none Servants, and they conferred moreover a monopoly of all the eligible land upon the first band of newcomers, so as to discourage to the present day any fresh accession of men of capital. The bitter experience is now beginning to be forgotten…but no one who has witnessed the history of this little Colony from its origin will ever doubt that sound principles cannot be violated with impunity.

Undeniably, Elliot stated, the large expenditure on the convict scheme had given 'an artificial stimulus', as evident in increased revenue and trade. But after large numbers in the initial three years, convict numbers had fallen—only 224 had been sent out in 1859. The real danger threatening the colonists, which he believed 'has hardly yet occurred to anybody', was

the constant decrease in the supply of Convicts from home…When the annual number of convicts available for transportation has been sinking from 500 to less than 300, it would seem probable that this Country will some day doubt whether the despatch of that number of men is worth an expenditure in the Colony of upwards of £50,000 a year, over and above the charge of transport and of Military Guards…TFE 8 May.[56]

Of course, his assumption that no one realised that ending convict transportation would hit the colony hard was clearly incorrect, for several rumours to this effect had galvanised the Mangles brothers and Stirling into action in the past.

The WA Association's meeting on 16 July 1860, again chaired by Stirling, discussed the poor state of roads in the colony, and it was pointed out that 'the passage overland between Perth, the Capital, and King George's Sound occupies 9 or 10 days'. As most ships unloaded at the Sound, this was a severe drawback. A new road was a priority. After much discussion, the meeting authorised Ross D. Mangles to address the home authorities, 'submitting that convicts with a longer servitude before them would be most welcomed by the colonists'.[57] This was the last meeting Stirling attended, and as the resulting change in the nature of convicts transported led to substantial improvements in public works, he had once again intervened to the benefit of Western Australia.

31

Final Years: an Enduring Legacy

By mid-year Stirling had made arrangements to move his family, comprising Ellen and their four unmarried daughters, back to Ryde. Just before they moved, it appears that James and Ellen attended the marriage on 19 July between Ross Donnelly Mangles' son Ross and Henrietta More-Molyneux, of Losely Park, a large estate outside Guildford and not far from Woodbridge. The couple were bound for India, so father Ross was determined to send them off in style. On this occasion the Stirlings met the bride's first cousin, Catherine Lowndes Stone, who would in future open new doors for Ellen and James.

In Ryde the Stirlings rented a house at 109 Spencer Road, not unlike the one they had had before. Part of the attraction of Ryde for Stirling, as a staunch royalist, was that it was only a few miles from Osborne House, where Queen Victoria spent much of her time in the summer. The house he chose was on the higher east side of the bustling little town, amongst luxuriant woodlands and commanding sea views.[1] It was only 4½ miles across the water from Spithead Channel, so there was daily shipping for Stirling to inspect by telescope, while Ellen and the girls would have enjoyed the attractions of shopping, in the elegant Royal Victoria Arcade and Union Street, and the classically built Assembly Rooms and markets. The long pier, first built in 1813, was being widened at this time to take trams and was a popular place for a stroll, as well as allowing direct access for ferries from the mainland. The mild climate, spaciousness and reputed health benefits of the town made it a haven for those in retirement, and the Stirlings would have found a number of acquaintances among existing residents.

In September 1860 the family had a visit from Walter, James' older brother, who was compiling the family history. (This was the basis for *The Stirlings of Cadder*, a major family resource.) A letter to him from another brother, Charles, illustrates the close connections of this large family.

> Dear Walter, I received the book two days ago & I should sooner have acknowledged its receipt…Our branches of the family are much beholden to you

for the great expense and trouble which you have had in compiling this work and you will leave a valuable as well as a curious document to hand down to future generations of Stirlings.

Charlotte attained her 60th birthday on Friday…I hope that you are enjoying the air of Ryde although the weather is certainly not pleasant for outside excursions. With kind love to yourself, Agnes and Lotty and also to James and his family. Believe me always yours affectionately…[2]

In November Ellen came into a small inheritance. Honouring their late father's wish, Frederick Mangles had decided to sell Down Farm and divide the result.[3] As the Mangles family was large, each individual's share was relatively small, but for Ellen it would have been welcome pin money. She could well have used some of it in preparation for two family weddings held at Stoke Church, Guildford, in January 1861. Her nephew, Henry Hughes Onslow, sister Caroline's eldest son, married on 8 January, and niece Mary Mangles, Ross Donnelly's second daughter, was married by the Bishop of London on the 23rd. For Ellen, the gathering of the clan at Woodbridge, the home she grew up in and loved, would have been a time of happiness. James' 70th birthday followed just a few days later, on 28 January, an occasion for further family togetherness.

In March 1861 the ten-year census had arrived again—for most families a sure reminder of the passing of time. James was back in Ryde to complete it, and record his household as comprising himself and Ellen, son Frederick Henry, 32, and three daughters, Mary, 28, Anna, 20 and Dorothea, 19, plus a live-in staff totally changed since the 1851 census: a housemaid, two lady's maids, kitchen maid, footman and butler.[4] No cook was listed—presumably she lived nearby and came daily. Stirling's youngest daughter Georgina, 16, was missing from the list, as she had spent census night visiting a friend and her widowed mother. Ellinor Guthrie, Stirling's second surviving daughter, was still living at 30 Portland Place, Marylebone, London, and the description of her six-servant household indicates a very comfortable lifestyle.[5] Statistics for the Guthrie family would soon change, for on 25 July 1861 Ellinor gave birth to the longed for boy, David Charles Stirling Guthrie, James' first grandson.

Early in 1862 James and Ellen decided to leave Ryde. They had lived there for the best part of three years and, while it suited their needs, it was doing little for the marriage prospects of their daughters. It was a time of change all round. Ross Donnelly Mangles was moving from Woodbridge to nearby but grander Stoke Park, which he was leasing from Lord Onslow. At the same time his son's wife's cousin, Catherine Lowndes Stone, was to marry a Thomas Norton of Anningsley Park, Chertsey, a comfortable gabled residence surrounded by sloping lawns. As the married couple planned to move into the Norton family home, Brightwell Park, the desirable Anningsley became available for lease to the Stirlings.

The peace and security of English country life at this time was in sharp contrast to America, now in the throes of a civil war calamitous to those in the cotton industry like Thomas Mayne Stirling, who was running the family cotton mill in Manchester. The Stirlings had maintained their American connections through the Willing and Lister families, and letters received at this time were passed around to all. As Francis Lister explained to James' brother Charles, the war had taken its toll even on civilian life in New England.

> I see no prospect of a speedy termination of our difficulties…The business of our City largely depends on the Southern trade which is all cut off…You can easily imagine the state of uncertainty and unhappiness into which we have been thrown.[6]

Despite the effect of the war on the cotton trade, James Stirling's sympathies would have lain with the North, for he was firmly against slavery. Soon after moving to Anningsley James' usually chatty letters took a sombre turn, as condolences had to be sent to his brother Charles at Muiravonside, whose wife Charlotte had died on 25 June, leaving seven, now adult, surviving children.[7]

In November 1862 came rousing news—at long last Stirling had been promoted to full Admiral, realising a long-held dream. A delighted Ellen would have fussed over alterations to his uniform, even if he would never wear it on active service again. But he might, she mused, be able to wear it to a daughter's wedding! Anna had been receiving letters and calls from a man of good family and Australian connections. Alexander Grant had gone out to South Australia in 1839–40 with a friend, Philip Butler, and had taken out a pastoral licence over a property subsequently called Coonatto. In a strange coincidence Butler had, in 1849, married Matilda Roe, daughter of Stirling's former Surveyor-General at Swan River, but after bearing eight children she had unfortunately died the previous year.[8] Alexander had returned to England to take up an inheritance, which involved changing his name to Grant-Thorold, and at the age of 43 had fallen in love with 23-year-old Anna, whom he had met in London.

Both Ellen and James were very pleased with the match and encouraged his visits to Anningsley. The wedding was set for 28 July 1863 at St John's Church in Paddington. At the request of the groom's family, who owned Cosgrove Hall in north Yorkshire, the service was conducted by His Grace the Archbishop of York, assisted by the bride's uncle, the Reverend Albert Mangles, the youngest of Ellen's brothers.[9] It was quite a society wedding and Admiral Stirling would have looked with pride at his family that day. Ellen, as always, was elegantly dressed and had seen to it that all her daughters were becomingly gowned. Even Ellinor was there with her husband, despite the fact she had borne her fifth child, Rose, only four months previously. To their parents' delight, sons Charles and Frederick also showed up— Charles taking time off from his Royal Artillery duties, Frederick on furlough after coast-guard duty on the *Hero*. It was a welcome chance afterwards for Frederick to spend some family time at Anningsley, for his next appointment, on the

James and Ellen's fourth daughter, Anna Hamilton
Courtesy Battye Library 225187P

Cumberland, did not come about until 8 September. Less than a month later he was promoted to Post Captain, and on 10 October transferred to the steamship *Tamar*.[10]

Meanwhile an interesting situation was developing at Anningsley. For some years Ellen and James had been concerned about their eldest daughter Mary. At 30 she had seen two of her younger sisters wed. She was not unattractive, and visitors invited to the house had been impressed by her quiet charm, but she had discouraged all advances—or so it seemed. A letter written by her Uncle Charles to Walter on 10 December 1863 noted otherwise:

> I was very glad, as we all were, to hear of Mary's intended marriage; for many reasons. It is a great comfort and particularly as it seems to afford James & Ellen so much pleasure. All the accounts you have of the gentleman seem to be much in his favour affording a prospect of happiness to Mary & satisfaction to all.[11]

Mary's beau was Victor Buckley, a diplomat in the Foreign Office whom she had likely known for some years.[12] James and Ellen thoroughly approved the match as Victor was the fifth son of General Edward Perry Buckley (who had served at

Waterloo and been MP for Salisbury), and Lady Catherine (daughter of the Earl of Radnor), and was some six years older than Mary. But overseas postings meant it would be a long engagement, for the two were not to marry until 1866.

New Year's Day 1864 became a dark day for the whole family. Eighty four-year-old Walter died in London—a terrible shock, as he had been active to the last, always interested in everyone's doings and ready with kindly advice in his frequent letters. The Family Bible entry, written by Charles, the next in line, recorded the death as follows:

> 1864 January 1st at his residence 18 Curzon St, Mayfair, my brother Walter Stirling of Drumpellier departed this life in his 84th year. Buried at Kensal Green Cemetery in the same vault with his brother William.

Walter's death shattered James, and forcibly brought home his own mortality. Within the week he had made out his own will. Essentially, he left everything he had to be managed for the benefit of his wife and children by four individuals: his youngest brother-in-law, the Reverend Albert Mangles; his son, Captain Frederick Henry Stirling RN; and his sons-in-law, James Alexander Guthrie and Alexander Grant-Thorold. The choice of Albert made sense, as he had not been involved in land deals and mortgages with Stirling, as the other Mangles brothers had, and he was not only Ellen's brother but also a man of the cloth to whom she could turn for comfort.

Details of the will, signed on 7 January 1864, included a legacy of £100 to be paid 'to my beloved wife Ellen Stirling as soon as possible after my death as well as all plate, china, linen, wines, books, furniture and all other household effects, carriages, horses, harness and all stable and outdoor effects'. The residuary estate, after payment of debts and funeral expenses, was to be managed by his named trustees who were to pay an income to Ellen:

> during her life, she bearing the cost of maintaining my three unmarried daughters Mary Stirling, Dorothea Stirling, and Georgina Janet Stirling as long as they shall remain unmarried, but also allowing during her life to my son Andrew Stirling (if she shall think fit) an annual sum not exceeding £80. If any of my unmarried daughters should marry or cease to reside with their mother, then during my wife's life the Trustees shall pay them an annuity of £100 for their sole and separate use.

He then made special reference to Ellinor:

> Upon the marriage of my daughter Ellinor Guthrie I entered a covenant with the Trustees of her settlement for the payment of £1,500 on the death of self and wife and now declare this sum shall be counted as part of her share of the residuary estate. My wife and I also appointed £3,500 to her Settlement—if that sum shall

be less than her one seventh share of the sum appointed to Frederick Henry Stirling, Mary Stirling, Charles Edward Stirling, Anna Hamilton Grant, Dorothea Stirling, and Georgina Janet Stirling, then the deficiency shall be made up to the said Ellinor Guthrie out of the shares of the other children.

This implied (although it was not said) that when Ellen died he wished the remaining estate to be divided equally among his children. He empowered his trustees to sell real estate and invest the money, but specified that such investment should be in:

> the public funds of Great Britain, or on mortgage in England or heritable estate in Scotland, or in Bank Stock, East India Stock or loan to the East India Government in Council, or stock, fully paid up shares, bonds or debentures issued by an incorporated company. If the Trustees wish to retire, others may be appointed. I appoint my wife sole guardian of my daughter Georgina Janet during her minority.[13]

The witnesses, Archer and James Richard Upton, of 20 Austin Friars, were the same lawyers that Walter had used in drafting his will, and Stirling probably met them while in London for the funeral.

The reading of Walter's will may have caused some surprise, for although he never married he left an annuity of £200 'to my daughter Harriet Lower'. Never mentioned in family letters, Harriet had apparently married William Humphrey Lower, a Colonel in the East India Company's service. The annuity was 'to be paid half-yearly at Christmas and Midsummer, for her own personal use and not to be disposed of to a third party'. All the rest of Walter's land and property, valued at some £60,000, went to his sister Agnes, who had lived with him through the years.[14] She must have known of the child, but it may well have been kept secret from others in the family who had lived far from London.

As Walter had no male issue, the Cadder title should have passed to John, the next in the male line. But as he had died in 1853, it passed to his eldest son. This was the Andrew who had died in Western Australia, so it went further down his line to Thomas Mayne Stirling, who was managing the Manchester mill. As Walter had owned other property in Scotland (where Thomas also held his father's estate at St Andrews), it is possible that Thomas assisted Agnes in having Walter's will registered in the Books of the Lords of Council and Session in Edinburgh, which was accomplished on 10 February 1864. It was finally proved in London on 2 March.[15]

When the flurry of activity engendered by Walter's death subsided, Stirling returned to Anningsley but remained very depressed. Occasional visits from his grandchildren lifted his spirits, for he loved children and playing small practical jokes. He probably teased little David Charles Guthrie, as the only boy among five sisters, for Ellinor had given birth to another girl, Georgina Lilias, the previous December.

Anna was not to have her first child until 1866, so Ellinor's children were the only grandchildren that James knew. Mary, Dorothea and Georgina, who were still living at home aged 33, 24 and 19 respectively, would also have enjoyed the children's visits, and no doubt stayed with their older sister in London from time to time.

Between bouts of depression James spent time in 1864 talking to a number of people about his affairs. He looked through all the documentation he had on his estates in Western Australia and undoubtedly contacted George Elliot, who was still overseeing his interests at Leschenault, though none of this correspondence survives. It must have galled him to be called on 12 July as witness before Chancery in yet another case brought by Latour seeking additional lands in WA. Stirling was asked to verify Latour's initial grants, as the Colonial Office claimed to have no records. To most queries he gave short, succinct answers, but claimed 'not to particularly remember' specific details, such as meeting Latour before departure.[16] The claim was eventually rejected, as Stirling had predicted. By the end of 1864 he was ready to contact his lawyers to set out in detail the disposal of his estate. It would have taken

Stirling, pictured here in later life, drew comfort from daughters Georgina,
Ellinor (standing) and Dorothea (seated right)

Courtesy Battye Library 67856P and 225186P (daughters)

them some time, as James had made many arrangements in the past concerning his Western Australian lands, but the entire complicated series of indentures, releases and conveyances were ready for signing on 10 January 1865. Set out as two memorials, the first stated:

> Indenture of lease and release between Sir James Stirling and Frederick Mangles (1) Charles Edward Mangles (2) Ross Donnelly Mangles (3) and Sarah Stockley widow, John Farnaby Cator and Ulysses Latreille (4) for the division of the land referred to *(hereunder)* into two lots one exclusively to Sir James and the other to the other parties…for the purpose of giving effect to a certain agreement dated 19 May 1852. Consideration £4,400.0.0 (1865)
>
> Part 1 *(to be divided)*
>
>   Leschenault Location No 26 containing 3,940 acres
>
>   Leschenault Location No 41 containing 16,610 acres
>
> Part 2 [Stirling only]
>
>   Garden Island containing 2,240 acres
>
>   4,000 acres on the left bank of the Swan adjoining Guildford
>
>   Albany Suburban Lot E1 containing 4 acres
>
>   Wellington Location 50A containing 12,800 acres
>
>   Plantagenet Location 12 containing 4,000 acres[17]

Essentially what James had done in this first (and very lengthy) memorial was to cancel a previous agreement made on 19 May 1852 whereby all his Western Australian estates had been held as tenants in common by five parties: himself, the three Mangles brothers independently, and a joint holding by Sarah Stockley, Cator and Latreille. Sarah's husband, William Stockley, had been party to an even earlier agreement, whilst Cator and Latreille were professionals to whom Stirling seems to have been indebted. At that stage 'each party held an undivided eighth part' and Stirling held 'four undivided eighth parts'. The others had already paid £2,000 of the promised £4,400 to Stirling, the remainder being due in 1862 but still not paid. Now that initial agreement was to be annulled, and his estate divided into two specified lots. Locations 26 and 41, excepting those parts already disposed of, were to go to the Mangles and others, when they paid James £1,800, while Stirling held the rest as specified.

On the same day, 10 January 1865, Stirling signed another memorial, this time involving his wife.

> Indenture of conveyance between Sir James Stirling (1)…Ellen Stirling (2) James Tennant Simpson (3) Frederick Mangles (4) Charles Edward Mangles (5) Ross Donnelly Mangles (6) and Sarah Stockley widow, John Farnaby Cator and Ulysses Latreille (7) for giving effect to an agreement for partition mentioned next above

Part 1

Leschenault Location 26 containing 3,940 acres

Part 2

439 acres part of Leschenault No 26

15 acres ditto

15 acres ditto

386 acres ditto

15 acres near the town of Bunbury

4½ acres part of Wellington Location 26

Part 3

Leschenault Location 41 containing 16,610 acres

Part 4

Part of Leschenault Location No 41 as per boundaries given in the Memorial [referring to stumps of trees and distances from rivers][18]

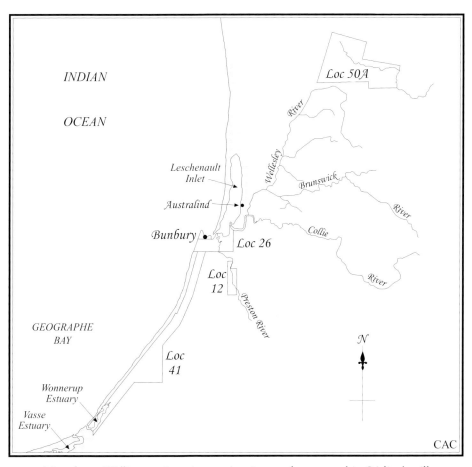

Map shows Wellington Locations 50A, 26, 41 and 12, named in Stirling's will

This second memorial is confusing, as he seems to divide Locations 26 and 41, already given to the parties mentioned in the first memorial, into four parts, excepting those small parts already disposed of (e.g. the Pensioner Guard cottage lands). This time James Tennant Simpson is added to the previous group because:

> …Ellen Stirling at the request and with the permission of the said Sir James Stirling did grant and release unto the said James Tennant Simpson and his heirs that piece or parcel of land situate and being in Leschenault in the district of Wellington in the Colony of Western Australia containing three thousand nine hundred and forty acres [margin—1st part of Schedule, part of location 26].

Ellen could have owed Simpson money and asked her brothers to settle this way, or it could have been a Mangles' obligation. There are no further clues, Part two, with all the smaller land lots, seems to have gone to Stockley, Cator and Latreille, while parts 3 and 4 (actually the same Location 41 and containing most of the land) went to the three Mangles brothers outright. Witnesses to both memorials included the butler at 18 Curzon Street and two of the clerks at F. Mangles and Co. The memorials were also registered in Perth at the Department of Land Administration by G. F. Stone, solicitor, on 13 and 18 December 1865.[19]

Signing the memorials left Stirling free to assign the rest of the land, categorised solely as his own in the first memorial, to the management of his executors. Apart from Locations 21 and 46, which went to the Mangles in the above memorials, Stirling had already assigned Plantagenet Location 33 on the Hay River to F. and C. E. Mangles whose names were on the title deed when granted in October 1843. The remaining land belonging to Stirling included Cockburn Location 9 (Garden Island), Swan Location 16 (Woodbridge), Albany suburban Lot E1, Wellington Location 50A (Korajakup),[20] Avon Location 3 (Beverley),[21] and Plantagenet Location 12 (the Moorilup allotment at the foot of the Stirling Range). The Arthur's Head land was not mentioned and seems to have remained with the Crown after Hutt's resumption. Although not originally named in Stirling's will as executors, Frederick and Charles Mangles ended up managing the remaining 23,044 acres of Stirling's original 100,000 acres for the family, as Frederick was mostly at sea, and the other named executors were unable to comply.[22]

As noted, the same lawyers in Austin Friars, London, who had drawn up Stirling's will the year before, drew up the 1865 memorials. The lawyers must have been just as surprised as Stirling to receive, only a week after the memorials were signed, a 'Deed Poll of Disclaimer' from the Reverend Albert Mangles. Albert had removed himself from the office of Trustee in Stirling's will, signing this document on 18 January 1865. No explanation was given for his action, but as Albert died later in 1865 he may well have been ill at the time and felt unable to cope. Stirling did not replace him.

By the end of January Stirling was feeling constantly tired and was having digestive difficulties. He had good days and bad days through February, but was losing weight and tiring easily. He most probably had cancer of the pancreas or liver, and by March had realised that he would not recover. It appears that at this stage he asked Ellen to take him back to Woodbridge, the Mangles' family home, where all his Western Australian adventures had begun. Woodbridge House was empty at this time and, with her brothers' ready consent, Ellen and the girls took the frail Stirling by carriage from Chertsey to Guildford. Here James spent his last days. Ellen's younger sister, the widowed Hamilla Preston, came to Woodbridge to help Ellen with the nursing and she was with James when he died on 22 April. The death certificate gave the cause of death as 'Jaundice of one month's standing'. Charles recorded the event in the Family Bible as follows:

> 1865 April 23rd my brother Admiral Sir James died at Woodbridge, Surrey in the 75th year of his age and was interred at Stoke Church.

The incorrect date in the Bible could be due to the time it took letters to reach Charles in Scotland, for the news could have been expressed in terms such as 'yesterday', rather than an exact date. Unfortunately very little was carried by the Press by way of an obituary, as Stirling's death coincided with the breaking news of Abraham Lincoln's assassination. But it was noted by the Admiralty, for on 26 April *The Times* carried the small notice:

The final resting place of James Stirling at Stoke Church, Guildford,
as shown above in 1869

Courtesy Guildford Museum and Lyn Clark

By the death of Admiral Sir James Stirling, Vice Admiral the Hon. Sir Frederick Grey KCB, a Lord Commissioner of the Admiralty becomes an Admiral; Rear Admiral Lord Clarence Paget MP, First Secretary at the Admiralty; and Captain Thomas Pickering Thompson obtains the ranks of Rear Admiral.[23]

Three days later the same notice was placed in the *Portsmouth Times and Naval Gazette* together with a lengthy obituary, which wrongly placed his death at Anningsley, not Woodbridge, and, in reference to his Governorship of Western Australia, carried the observation, 'his name will ever be identified with the establishment of that Colony'.[24] *The Gentleman's Magazine* carried a longer obituary, placing much more emphasis on his pedigree and naval career.[25] In Western Australia there was practically no response to the news: the *Perth Gazette*, which he had seen established and supported throughout his Governorship, carried no obituary at all, whilst the *Inquirer and Commercial News* of Wednesday 28 June 1865 simply stated:

> Admiral Sir James Stirling has just died at his residence, Anningsley, in Surrey. The deceased Admiral, who was born in 1791, entered the Navy at an early age, and continued in active service throughout the French war. For ten years he was Governor and Commander-in-Chief in Western Australia. The deceased officer was a Knight-Commander of the Redeemer of Greece.[26]

On 29 August a longer obituary appeared in the *Australian and New Zealand Gazette & Colonial Chronicle*, published weekly in London. This would have been submitted by those who knew more of his Western Australian connection (probably one of the Mangles), and spoke of the 'zeal and alacrity he always displayed in the execution of whatever services he was employed upon'.[27]

It was a career to be proud of and, in days when overseas service brought rich rewards, one which might have been expected to leave him a wealthy man. But when Stirling's estate was valued for probate, including the value of his Western Australian lands, it came to under £9,000.[28] James had lived comfortably, but never extravagantly, and this summation of his wealth was less than he had paid for Belmont in 1846, and far less than the £60,000 his older brother Walter, who had scarcely ever left London, bequeathed to sister Agnes. Part of the latter estate, of course, included Walter's interest in the Manchester mill, which John's son Thomas Mayne Stirling continued to manage until November 1865, when it was put up for sale. The value of the mill (after pulling down and removing steam engines) was given as £5,967 which, as Thomas told his aunt Agnes, 'valued the machinery and building too high and the land too low'.[29]

This sale severed James' family's connection with the textile trade, a connection which had run through four generations. Thomas Mayne Stirling remained in the merchanting field and became prosperous. His marriage to his cousin Anna

(Charles' daughter) cemented the family and ensured the continuation of the Cadder title which had meant so much to grandfather Andrew. The joining of the two cousins also perhaps accounts for the amount of family material which has been retained in that line, most recently by Margaret Lenfestey, although Frank Stirling from the same line now holds the Cadder title.

Ellen was only 57 when James died, but it had been such a long and close partnership the loss would have been extremely difficult. He had always been a larger-than-life figure to herself and the girls, and his death left a gaping hole. She was determined that his contribution to the country he had loved would not be forgotten, and carried this out by impressing on her family and extended family the role he had played in Australia and elsewhere. Stories of their time at Swan River, particularly the arrival of the *Parmelia*, were told and retold to grandchildren and all were made to feel proud of the man who had founded a British colony on the other side of the world. Perhaps because she had not been with James during his Far Eastern command, Ellen mentioned his remarkable achievement in forging the first British Treaty with Japan less frequently, and consequently this did not become part of the family lore. For Ellen it was enough that her husband was remembered as a remarkable man. She hoped that history would be kinder to James Stirling than the bureaucracy he had served so faithfully and for so long. Only she knew how truly his life had lived up to the words he had said before leaving Swan River: 'my study and my endeavour has been to be an honest man'.[30]

Ellen lived until 1874, outliving all James' remaining brothers and sisters. Charles Stirling died in August 1867, survived by two sons and three daughters; Anna Home died in June 1866, survived by a son; Agnes died unmarried in February 1873, and Edward Stirling died without legal issue at St Helier in December 1873. Of Ellen's own brothers, Frederick Mangles died in 1869, leaving three sons and three daughters, Charles in 1874, the same year as herself, leaving four sons and six daughters, and Ross Donnelly in 1877, also leaving four sons and six daughters. So old James Mangles' line continued.

One of Ellen's greatest sorrows must have been the lack of a male heir. She had borne James eleven children, five of them boys, but none had had male issue. Her first son Andrew (b 1824) had married but died aged 48 on the Isle of Anglesea, Beaumaris in August 1873, leaving no children. Frederick Henry (b 1829) was her pride and joy, as he followed in his father's footsteps in the navy. From 1873 to 1876 he was Naval ADC to Queen Victoria, promoted Rear Admiral in 1877 and in 1879 Commander-in-Chief of the Pacific Station, based in Sydney, until 1881. While in Sydney he married Helen (Nellie), daughter of the New South Wales Colonial Secretary, Sir Edward Deas Thompson.[31] They had one daughter, Olive (b 1880), who married a Norwegian diplomat, Sigurd Bentson, but had no children. It was Olive who donated her grandfather's cup, sword and snuff box to the Western Australian Museum in 1937. Vice-Admiral Frederick Henry Stirling died in Hove in 1885. Ellen's third son William (b 1831) had died in Western Australia as an infant, while Charles Edward (b 1834), after distinguished service at Sebastapol, pursued his army career, serving in India, Bermuda and Nova Scotia. Charles apparently married the sister of a deceased army colleague, Emily Teasdale,[32] and they had a daughter, Ada Jane, who was born in Norwood, England in 1866. According to family legend, Charles was then posted abroad and after a long absence Emily, presuming him dead, accepted a proposal from George Wratten, whom she married in 1870. They had another daughter, Kate, in 1871 and the family believe that Charles then reappeared, as Emily died of an overdose of sleeping pills six weeks after Kate's birth. George Wratten brought up Ada Stirling with his own daughter. Lieutenant-Colonel Charles Stirling died at Lucerne in 1895 with no further issue, but his sister Ellinor saw to it that Ada benefited from his estate.[33] Ellen and James' youngest son Walter (b 1837) had predeceased them, having died at Cawnpore in India at the age of 20.

So it was through his daughters that James would be remembered. And of the five daughters who survived to adulthood, all but one married well and produced numerous offspring. The eldest daughter Mary (b 1832), who married Victor Buckley in 1866, had four children: two boys and two girls, and in their line Edward Buckley is now regarded as the senior family descendant. Mary died in 1906. Ellinor (b 1838) who married James Alexander Guthrie in 1856, had nine children: six girls and three boys. Lavinia Fleming, who has done so much to assist the compilation of this book, is directly descended from Ellinor's sixth child, Georgina Lilias. James Guthrie died in January 1873 and six years later Ellinor married Forster Fitzgerald Arbuthnot, who also died before she did. Ellinor was a beautiful woman and a striking full-length portrait of her wearing a green dress was painted by Lord Leighton (1830–96) and now hangs in the Yale Centre of British Art.[34] Ellinor died in May 1911. The next daughter, Anna Hamilton (b 1840) had married Alexander Grant-Thorold in 1863 and had five children, two girls and three boys, all born before 1874 and so seen by their grandmother. Anna died in 1899. The daughter born in Lisbon, Dorothea, (b 1842) never married and died without issue in 1910. The youngest daughter, Georgina Janet (b 1845), married well, her first husband, in 1869, being Major General Sir Henry Tombs VC. They had a girl and a boy before Tombs died in 1874, the same year as Ellen. Three years later Georgina married another distinguished army man, General Sir Herbert Stewart, and they had three boys. Georgina died in 1910.

In her lifetime Ellen saw sixteen of her twenty-five grandchildren. In the 1871 census, Lady Stirling was living with daughter Dorothea at 19 Albert Mansions, Victoria Street, Westminster, not far from her sister-in-law Agnes at 18 Curzon Street and daughter Ellinor Guthrie at Portland Place. When Ellinor's first husband James Guthrie died, Ellen went to live with her, and she died there on 8 June 1874. Administration of her affairs, valued by probate at under £1,500, was granted to Charles and Dorothea, whom she had named next-of-kin, as Frederick Henry was then in Australia.[35] Ellen had expressed a wish to be buried at Stoke Church,

Guildford, with James, and the family carried out her wishes. The simple granite headstone, repaired and reinstated in Western Australia's sesquicentenary year 1979,[36] now stands in a place of honour between the Church and the Hall, which is called the 'The Stirling Centre'. The inscription on the stone reads:

Sacred

To the Memory of

Admiral Sir James Stirling

Who died at Woodbridge

In this Parish

On the 22nd day of April 1865

Aged 74 years

'I am the Resurrection and the Life'

Also

To the beloved memory of

Ellen, widow of

Admiral Sir James Stirling

Born 4th of September 1808

Died 8th of June 1874

'Thou wilt shew me the paths of life,

in thy presence is fullness of joy

at thy right hand there are pleasures for evermore.'

Psalm XVI v 11

Notes

OUP	Oxford University Press
P&O	Peninsular and Orient Steam Navigation Company
Preble's Diary	B. Szczesniak (ed.), *The Opening of Japan: A Diary of Discovery in the Far East 1853–1856 by Rear Admiral George Henry Preble U.S.N.* (University of Oklahoma Press, 1962)
PRO	Public Records Office, Kew, London
Stirlings of Cadder	T. W. Stirling, *The Stirlings of Cadder: An account of the Original Family of that Name and of The Family of The STIRLINGS OF DRUMPELLIER With which the Representation Of the Ancient House of Cadder now lies* (St Andrews University Press, 1933)
SDR	Survey Department Records (also SR), WA Archives
SRP	Swan River Papers—early CO material in WA Archives
UWA	University of Western Australia
UWAP	University of Western Australia Press
VDL	Van Diemen's Land, later Tasmania
WA	Western Australia
WAA	Western Australian Archives (now State Records Office of Western Australia)

NB Some abbreviated titles occur in endnote references to books and articles. See Select Bibliography for full publication details.

CHAPTER 1: THE FORMATIVE YEARS

1. See T. Stirling, *The Stirlings of Cadder*, and a more inaccurate account in *Minute Book of the Green Cloth 1809–1820*, p. 147, and also a genealogy of all Stirlings which disagrees with the Cadder Pedigree, in A. Stirling, *Gang Forward—A Stirling Notebook*.

2. 'Their family is beyond dispute the oldest in Glasgow; indeed except the High Kirk, it is the oldest thing in Glasgow', cited in *Old Country Houses of the Old Glasgow Gentry*, p. 84.

3. *The Stirlings of Cadder*, p. 109.

4. Drumpellier is now a golf course and its history was written up for the centenary in 1994. See P. Drummond, *Drumpellier Golf Course 1894–1994*, pp. 23 and 63.

5. Anne to Andrew Stirling, 14 Jan. 1778 (Lenfestey).

6. Sir Walter to Andrew, 13 June 1781 (Lenfestey).

7. ibid., 14 Oct. 1780 (Lenfestey).

8. See Stirling, *Gang Forward*, p. 96.

9. *Stirlings of Cadder*, p. 55.

10. *Glasgow Herald*, 2 Feb. 1880.

11. J. O. Mitchell, *Old Glasgow Essays*, p. 4.

12. G. Thomson, *The Monkland Canal*, pp. 6–12.

13. G. Hutton, *Monkland—The Canal that Made Money*, Introduction, and Allan Peden, *The Monklands*, p. 53.

14. Thomson, pp. 6–12.

15. James Stirling, on the *Brazen* at Sheerness, to Anne Stirling, York Hill, near Glasgow, 7 April 1813, WAA351A/MN590.

16. Sir Walter to Andrew Stirling, 13 June 1781 (Lenfestey).

17. Peden, p. 64.

18. Copy of letter from Andrew at Drumpellier to Mr Willing, 10 May 1783 (Lenfestey).

19. Dorothea's last wish was 'to clear up the unhappy breach which had embittered her life' by 'declaring her perfect innocence of the things laid to her charge with respect to her uncle's will'. Andrew Stirling to Mr Willing, 10 May 1783 (Lenfestey).

20. *Glasgow Herald*, 2 Feb. 1880. John held 26 shares and Andrew 20, but in 1790 Andrew gained another 45 shares to become the major shareholder.

21. *Glasgow Herald*, 2 Feb. 1880 and *Glasgow Past & Present*, vol. 1, p. 164.

22. John (b 1752, d 1811) married Janet Bogle and had two sons, William and George (the same cousin William Stirling who went with James to WA and died there in 1831). See *Minute Book of the Green Cloth 1809–1820*, p. 147.

23. James of Stair (b 1760) married Margaret Murdoch and died 1822, *Stirlings of Cadder*, p. 56.

24. Anne's second daughter, Mary, was born at Drumpellier Dec. 1783 but died three months later. Another Mary was born in London July 1785 but died there in October (Family Bible).

25. Thomson, pp. 6–12. By 1806 the Faskine lands, purchased for £5,500 in 1790, were providing an annual income of £3,030.

26. The canal was 4½ ft deep and 15 ft wide at the bottom and 30 ft at the surface, *Glasgow Past & Present*, vol. 1, p. 164.

27. The godmother was Andrew's sister Elizabeth who had married William Hamilton, son of the 4th Baronet of Airdrie (Family Tree).

28. Mitchell, p. 8.

29. See *London Directories* for 1792–93.

30. Letter from the Saltmarket Society to Andrew Stirling of Drumpellier, 21 Dec. 1792 (Lenfestey).

31. Anne to William Stirling, 10 June 1796 (Lenfestey).

32. ibid.

33. John Stirling, aged 11, on *Jason*, to brother Walter, 24 Surrey St, Strand, 31 Jan. 1797, with a note added by Charles Stirling, WAA449A/MN595.

34. See *The Britannic Magazine* 1794, details at <http://www.hillsdale.edu/dept/History/War/Navy3/1794-1June.htm>

35. Anne to William Stirling, 5 April 1798 (Lenfestey).

36. Mitchell, p. 8.

37. In early 1800 Andrew Stirling was listed in the *London Directories* as living at 24 Surrey St, Strand.

38. John Stirling, Newland College, Glasgow, to brother Walter, Bow Church Yard, 29 Oct. 1799, typescript WAA449A/MN595.

39. Thomson, pp. 6–12.

40. Dugald Bannatyne (Agnes' husband) to Anne Stirling at Bow Church Yard, London, 10 March 1802 (Lenfestey).

41. G. F. Barker/A. H. Stenning, *The Record of Old Westminsters.*

42. J. D. Carleton, *Westminster School: a History*, p. 48, pp. 50–1.

43. ibid., p. 40.

44. John Field, *The King's Nurseries*, p. 23.

45. ibid., p. 23.

46. ibid., p. 54.

47. ibid., p. 69. These were called Declams or Declamations.

48. Field, in ibid., 'Select List of old Westminsters', pp. 136–7.

49. Carleton, p. 44.

50. Barker/Stenning records 'James b1791, brother of Charles, in school lists 1801 and 1803. Left 1803, entered Royal Navy 12 Aug 1802 and brother Charles (4th son of Andrew Stirling of Drumpellier) b1789 at school under Vincent in school lists May and Oct 1803 left 1803.'

51. *Stirlings of Cadder*, p. 67.

52. JS Service Record, ADM107/41, Volumes of Lieutenants passing certificates f97.

53. JS Service Record. On 20 Jan. 1805 he had served one year and six days as a volunteer.

54. JS Service Record, ADM107/41 f97.

CHAPTER 2: NAVAL TRAINING

1. See *The Britannic Magazine* 1794, 'Glorious First of June 1794'.

2. JS Service Record, ADM107/41 f97.

3. Stuart Stirling, *Admiral Sir James Stirling 1791–1991 Founder and first Governor of Western Australia*, p. 3.

4. L. Stephen/S. Lee, *Dictionary of National Biography,* Admiral Sir Charles Stirling.

5. James Stirling, *Glory*, at sea, to John Stirling, Grosvenor Square, London, 18 Sept. 1805. Original WAA Acc 351A/MN590.

6. Anne at Drumpellier to John Stirling, aged 19, in London, 2 Dec. 1805 (Lenfestey).

7. See <http://broadside.napoleonic.wars.com/broadside5.html> re 'Pay and Prize money' and apportionment levels before and after 1808.

8. JS Service Record, ADM107/41 f97.

9. Jan Read, *The New Conquistadors*, p. 20.

10. J. D. Grainger, 'The Navy in the River Plate 1806–08', p. 287.

11. Admiral Charles Stirling's Journal, ADM50/50 and Charles Staples, 'Spanish Colonial Influence on Sir James Stirling', *JRWAHS*, vol. 10, part 6 (1994).

12. See note in *The Mariners Mirror* 82 (4), Nov. 1996, p. 466, Admiral Stirling at Rio de Janeiro 1806.

13. Admiral Charles Stirling's Journal, ADM50/50 and *Sampson,* Muster Book, ADM36/16934.

14. *The Mariners Mirror* 82 (4), Nov. 1996, pp. 466–7, details problems encountered, including five desertions.

15. Read, p. 22.

16. In the official record James left the *Sampson* on 7 Dec. 1806 and joined the *Diadem* the following day, but this appears to have been predated. JS Service Record, ADM107/41 f97.

17. Grainger, pp. 287–99.

18. Stephen/Lee, Admiral Sir Charles Stirling.

19. Postscript to June 1807 James Stirling, Montevideo, to John Stirling. Original WAA Acc 351A/MN590.

20. Whitelocke was later court-martialled and cashiered for being 'deficient in zeal, judgment and personal exertion'. See Stephen/Lee, Admiral Charles Stirling.

21. Read, p. 22.

22. John to William Stirling, still at Drumpellier, 2 July 1807 (Lenfestey).

23. The Seignority (or Superiority) in Scottish land law is separate from ownership of the property *per se.* Both are distinct tenements held heritably; the Drumpellier Superiority was sold and left the family in 2000.

24. John to William Stirling, still at Drumpellier, 2 July 1807 (Lenfestey).

25. James Stirling's Rio report, Aug. 1807, WAA449/12.

26. J. Marshall, *Royal Naval Biography*, vol. 1, part 2, Admiral Charles Stirling.

27. James Stirling, *Warspite* in the Downs, to John Stirling, Bow Church Yard, London, Nov. 1808, WAA351A/MN590.

28. Anne at Carleton Place to John Stirling in London, 11 Oct. 1808 (Lenfestey).

29. James Stirling, *Warspite* in the Downs, to John Stirling, Bow Church Yard, London, Dec. 1808, WAA351A/MN590.

30. Charles in London to John Stirling, Glasgow, 18 Feb. 1809 (Lenfestey).

31. Lieutenants examination papers, ADM6/107 and ADM107/41.

32. *Stirlings of Cadder*, p. 68.

33. Andrew in Glasgow to John Stirling at Bow Church Yard, 4 Oct. 1809 (Lenfestey).

34. Stephen/Lee, Admiral Sir Charles Stirling.

35. The larger *Hibernia* was probably needed for war service elsewhere.

36. Andrew in Glasgow to John Stirling at Bow Church Yard, 2 Dec. 1810 (Lenfestey).

37. *Stirlings of Cadder*, p. 68.

38. Richard Willing (cousin then aged 36) on board the *Bengal*, at anchor off Catigat, to John Stirling (future brother-in-law) in London, 24 Aug. 1811 (Lenfestey).

39. Marshall notes Admiral Sir Charles Stirling made C-in-C in Jamaica, Oct. 1811.

40. JS Service Record, ADM196/6 f235.

41. Commander, his posting was listed on 19 June 1812. JS Service Record, ADM196/6 f235 and ADM107/41 f97.

CHAPTER 3: FIRST COMMAND HMS *BRAZEN*

1.   JS Service Record, ADM196/6 f235.

2.   J. Colledge, *Ships of the Royal Navy.*

3.   *Brazen* Log, ADM51/2013, piece 31824.

4.   ibid.

5.   Captain James Stirling to Admiral Charles Stirling, report, 15 Nov. 1812, University of Hull Library, DDHO/7/93.

6.   Cockburn led attacks at Chesapeake Bay, Havre de Grace, Georgetown, Frederickstown and against Washington. See Marshall, *Royal Naval Biography*, vol. 1, part 2, Cockburn entry, pp. 518–23.

7.   ibid., and Stephen/Lee, *Dictionary of National Biography*, pp. 640–2.

8.   James Stirling, Portsmouth to John Stirling, Bow Church Yard, 11 Feb. 1813, WAA351A/MN590.

9.   William at Bow Church Yard to Anne Stirling in Glasgow, 22 Feb. 1813 (Lenfestey).

10. James Stirling, on the *Brazen* at Sheerness, to Anne Stirling at York Hill, near Glasgow, 7 April 1813, WAA351A/MN590.

11. ibid.

12. William at Bow Church Yard to Anne Stirling in Glasgow, 18 May 1813 (Lenfestey).

13. W. Schooling, *The Hudson's Bay Company 1670–1920*, pp. 87–8.

14. *Brazen* Log, ADM51/2013, piece 318, 24–25 June 1813.

15. ibid., ADM51/2014, from 25 June 1813 to 25 June 1814.

16. Governor MacDonnell, the first Governor of the region, held a joint appointment between the company and Lord Selkirk. Schooling, p. 89.

17. ibid.

18. ibid., chapter on Indians.

19. *Brazen* Log, ADM51/2013–14.

20. ibid., ADM51/2013.

21. William to Anne Stirling in Glasgow, 9 Sept. 1813 (Lenfestey).

22. Field, *The King's Nurseries*, 'Select List of Old Westminsters', pp. 136–7.

23. F. C. Danvers, *Memorials of Old Haileybury College*, has Edward there 1813–16.

24. Lord Kinnoull to Anne Stirling, Jan. 1814 (Lenfestey).

25. James Stirling at sea to John Stirling at Bow Church Yard, 10 April 1814, WAA351A/MN590.

26. Anna Stirling in Glasgow to brother John in London, 25 May 1814 (Lenfestey).

27. *The Times*, 2 May 1814.

28. Papers relating to Charles Stirling's court martial are extensive. See ADM1/5442.

29. Stephen/Lee, entry for Admiral Sir C. Stirling.

30. Anna Stirling in Glasgow to brother John in London, 25 May 1814 (Lenfestey).

31. Duckworth had taken part in the action on the 'Glorious First of June' and was thus somewhat of a hero to James.

32. *Encyclopedia Britannica* (1969), p. 809.

33. Bolivar was guest of a wealthy merchant, Mr Hyslop, in Jamaica. In ibid., p. 810.

34. See Read, *The New Conquistadors*, and Salvador de Madriarga, *Bolivar*. Bolivar's 'Jamaica letter' analysed why he failed to unite South America against the Spanish.

35. Read, p. 25.

36. Lt-Gen. Sir Harry Smith, *Autobiography*, G. C. Moore Smith (ed.), p. 251.

37. ibid., p. 257.

38. ibid.

39. A. Hasluck, *Portrait with Background*, pp. 11–12.

40. Anne Stirling (Bath?) to son John at Bow Church Yard, 17 Feb. 1815 (Lenfestey).

41. Mary Noel Stirling, Westhorp House, to brother John, c/- Messrs Willing, Philadelphia, 31 Aug. 1815 (Lenfestey).

42. J. Beeler, 'Fit for Service Abroad: Promotion, Retirement and Royal Navy Officers 1830–1890', pp. 300–01.

43. ADM37/5822, piece 51879, complement of the *Brazen*, and *Brazen's* Log, ADM51/2014, part 3.

44. Anne at Henley Park to William Stirling, 24 Feb. 1816 (Lenfestey).

45. Family Bible, 'My son Andrew Stirling died of a fever (Midshipman in the Royal Navy) on board HMS *Inconstant* Frigate (Com. Sir James Yeo) on 5 June 1816 on the coast of Africa'.

46. Brown, an ex-British sailor, had been made an Admiral of the South American Fleet after taking part in the recapture of Buenos Aires. See FO72/205 f65 and 69.

47. FO72/205 f81, testimony of William Brown.

48. The case went before the Vice Admiralty Court in Antigua on 14 Oct. 1816, FO72/205 f84.

49. Read, p. 38, and Brown's testimony to the Vice Admiralty Court, Antigua, 18 Oct. 1816, FO72/205 f81.

50. See *The Times*, 22 Jan. 1819, Admiralty Court, Thurs. 21 Jan., the ship *Hercules*.

51. Madriarga, p. 309.

52. ibid.

53. Stuart Stirling, a distant connection, has researched James' time in South America but, apart from his brief monograph cited below, wanted to use his material in another publication. His interpretation may be different.

54. James Stirling's report to Harvey, 12 Feb. 1817, FO72/205 f125.

55. A. C. Staples, 'Spanish Colonial Influence on Sir James Stirling', p. 599.

56. James Stirling's report to Harvey, 12 Feb. 1817, FO72/205 f125.

57. Madriarga, p. 296.

58. ibid., p. 299.

59. Read, *The New Conquistadors*, p. 79.

60. FO72/202 10 Dec. 1817, Barrow to Hamilton enclosing f169 27 Aug. 1817, 'Simon Bolivar Supreme Chief of the Republic of Venezuela etc to all who shall see these presents'.

61. Read, p. 27 and G. S. Graham/R. A. Humphries, *The Navy and South America*.

62. S. Stirling, *Admiral Sir James Stirling*, p. 4.

63. Report from Jamaica, 20 July 1817, Douglas to Foreign Office, FO72/207 f198.

64. Sir John Harvey (C-in-C Leeward Island), *Antelope*, Carlisle Bay, Barbados, to John Wilson Croker, Admiralty, 19 March 1818, no. 20 (Q30 rec. 4 May), ADM1/337.

65.   ADMI52/35.
66.   Quoted in *Stirlings of Cadder*, p. 83 (a letter held by the family but not located).
67.   *Navy Lists* 1819.

CHAPTER 4: MANGLES, MARRIAGE AND A NEW CHALLENGE

1.   E. Erskine to Anne Stirling, Henley Park, Guildford, 19 Oct. 1819 (Leeper).
2.   *Stirlings of Cadder,* Appendix 2, 'The service of 1818', p. 108ff.
3.   W. G. Stirling (cousin on father's side) took a first lease on Borthwood farm in 1803 for fourteen years, renewing it for a similar term in 1811 and 1821.
4.   See Robin McInnes, *The Garden Isle*, Introduction.
5.   See Staples, 'Spanish Colonial Influence on Sir James Stirling'. No evidence has been found to support such early diplomatic work.
6.   Marshall, *Naval Biography*, vol. 1, pp. 361–3.
7.   ibid., pp. 362–3, and *Sunday Times*, 8 May 1977.
8.   The Irby-Mangles book was reviewed in the *London Literary Gazette*, 1 Nov. 1823.
9.   See Charles Bateson, *The Convict Ships*, pp. 157 and 233. The *Guildford* and the *Surrey* between them did nine convict voyages between 1812 and 1822.
10.   R. P. & R. M. Mangles, *The Mangles Story*, Chap. 3.
11.   Family story and Lyn Clark, *Stoke next Guildford*, p. 58.
12.   Henley Park remained Stirling's base and postal address. See James Stirling, Henley Park, Guildford to John Barrow, 10 Jan. 1821, Admiralty ADM1/2549 CapS5.
13.   See *London Gazette*, 22 July 1819, and *Stirlings of Cadder*, p. 69.
14.   *Stirlings of Cadder*, p. 69.
15.   Andrew was born in Philadelphia on 31 July 1818, died in WA 1844.
16.   ADM12/28, 'Admirals unemployed' letter from Admiral Charles Stirling re favourable consideration of his sentence, 16 July 1821.
17.   ADM12/ADM1, Admiralty Board minute, 17 July 1821.
18.   *London Gazette*, 27 Oct. 1822.
19.   John Stirling at Manchester to wife Elizabeth at Bow Church Yard, 27 July 1822 (Lenfestey).
20.   *Mangles Story,* p. 17. Mother Mary from Woodbridge reports Stirling's offer to her brother, General Sir John Hughes at Mount Charles, Ayrshire, 26 Nov. 1822 (full letter courtesy Major Robin Mangles).
21.   See illustrations in Clark, p. 57.
22.   Family story courtesy Hon. L. Fleming.
23.   *Mangles Story*, p. 12. The crosses and band were from his father's arms and the leopards and fleurs-de-lis from his wife's family arms.
24.   Captain James Stirling, Pirbright near Guildford, to John William Croker, Admiralty, 3 Sept. 1823, ADM1/2251 CapS118.
25.   Marriage certificate at Stoke-next-Guildford. Marriage Register, reg. no. STK2/4, is clearly marked 4 Sept. which was Ellen's birthday.
26.   I have not seen the Mangles Bible; this is quoted from Malcolm Uren, who did see it, and cited it in *Land Looking West*, p. 19.
27.   *Mangles Story,* Chap. 3, p. 14. A letter to George Hughes from James Mangles sen., Woodbridge, 5 Dec. 1823, 'We are just now adding to our cottage, which when completed, will make us very comfortable'.

28. Captain James Stirling, Ryde, Isle of Wight, to John Barrow, 4 Oct. 1825, CapS204 (rec. 6 Oct. 1825), ADM1/2552 (reinstatement of half pay).

29. ibid.

30. *Stirlings of Cadder*, Appendix, p. 108ff.

31. Dr Thomas Young wrote to Stirling at Woodbridge with the decision on 8 Nov. 1824, *Board of Longitude Papers*, Royal Greenwich Observatory 14/8 f24–5 and 214, Cambridge University Library, Manuscript Room.

32. Stephen/Lee, *Dictionary of National Biography*, vol. iv, p. 196 under Robert Dundas. Note also that Cockburn was a Commissioner on the Board of Longitude, in Marshall, vol. 1, p. 518.

33. Captain James Stirling, Woodbridge near Guildford, to John Barrow, 25 Aug. 1825. ADM1/2552 CapS169 (battle stowage).

34. Captain Stirling to J. W. Croker, 20 Dec. 1825, ADM1/2552 CapS265.

35. Ceded on 17 March 1824, see J. M. R. Cameron, 'The Northern Settlements: Outposts of Empire', p. 275.

36. ibid., pp. 273–7.

37. John Barrow, Admiralty, to Wilmot Horton, Colonial Office, 30 April 1825, CO201/164 f46.

38. John Begbie, Secretary to the E. I. Trade Committee, to R. W. Hay, 18 March 1826, CO201/176 f324.

39. See Hay to Barrow, 6 April 1826, ADM1/4240 & *HRA* I xii, p. 224; also Hay to Begbie, 6 April 1826, *HRA* III v, p. 796, and Bathurst to Darling, 7 April 1826, *HRA* I xii p. 224 (ship-of-war to visit Melville Is.).

40. Admiralty Board minutes, 23 Jan. 1826, ADM3/217; also JS Service Record ADM196/6 '*Success* 2 years 1 month 5 days'.

41. See Uren, p. 19; R. T. Appleyard/T. Manford, *The Beginning*, p. 37; J. M. R. Cameron, *Ambition's Fire*, p. 13; P. Statham, 'Western Australia Becomes British', p. 125.

42. The HEI Company's involvement was complicated by Singapore. See J. M. R. Cameron, 'Traders, government officials and the occupation of Melville Island', pp. 88–99 for an accurate version, also Cameron, 'The Northern Settlements', pp. 279–91.

43. See *The East India Register and Directory* for the years 1823–27, and Charles Prinsep, *Record of Services of the Honourable East India Company's Civil Servants* which includes an alphabetical listing of all EIC Directors 1741–1858. There is no mention of James Mangles, though his son Ross Donnelly Mangles (godson of Admiral Ross Donnelly) is shown as a Director from 1847.

44. Horace Twiss, the son of James' sister's school mistress in Bath and an old acquaintance, was a clerk in the Admiralty Office at this time and provided an entrée to their thinking.

45. See Bateson and *Mangles Story*, p. 12.

46. Various letters in the *Melville Paper*, ML MSS1–67.

47. Stephen/Lee, *Dictionary of National Biography*, p. 641.

48. Marshall, entries for Cockburn and Charles Stirling.

49. See ibid., vol. 1, Cockburn entry, pp. 518-23, and Stephen/Lee, Cockburn entry, pp. 640–2.

50. Marshall, vol. 1, p. 528.

51. Leslie Marchant, *France Australe*, p. 230.

52. Circular letter to Governors, 18 Jan. 1826, CO324/145 f239.

53. Marchant, pp. 230–1.

54. George Harrison, Treasury, to Wilmot Horton, Colonial Office, 20 Feb. 1826, transmitting letter from Commissariat Clerk, Miller, Fort Dundas Melville Is., CO201/176 f28.

55. J. C. Herries, Treasury Chambers, to R. W. Hay, 22 July 1825, CO201/165 f295.

56. Colonial Office to Treasury, 23 May 1826, CO201/165 f295.

57. ADM51/3460 and ADM 52/4341.

58. Captain's Log, *Success*, ADM51/3460, and Master's Log, ADM52/4341.

59. Colledge, *Ships of the Royal Navy.*

60. *Navy Lists* 1826–27 and Marshall, vol. 1, entry for Carnac and Preston.

61. See list of the ship's complement in Captain James Stirling, HMS *Success*, Simon's Bay, to John Wilson Croker, 8 Sept. 1826, CapS182 (rec. 30 Nov. 1826), ADM1/2553.

62. It was not until July that it was official, see *London Gazette*, 28 July 1826.

63. James Stirling to brother Walter, Bow Church Yard, 19 Feb. 1826, WAA Acc 351A/MN590.

64. C. Longe, Manchester, to Anne Stirling, 21 Feb. 1826 (Lenfestey).

65. King was made Captain in 1830. He was born in Australia in 1791 but eleven months later than Stirling.

66. King left May 1826, see *ADB* vol. 2, p. 62.

67. J. S. Battye, *Western Australia: a History,* p. 54.

68. Battye, citing King, *ibid.,* p. 55, and Appleyard/Manford, p. 29.

69. *Sydney Gazette,* 10 June 1826, 4 Nov. 1826 and 11 Nov. 1826. *Mary Hope* reached Milford on 27 May; Brisbane reached London 5 June after a brief trip to Scotland.

70. M. S. Riviere, *The Governor's Noble Guest: Hyacinthe de Bougainville's account of Port Jackson 1825,* pp. 129 and 270.

71. Riviere, p. 270.

72. *Success* Log, ADM51/3460.

CHAPTER 5: SECOND COMMAND HMS *SUCCESS*

1. See John Begbie, Secretary to the E. I. Trade Committee, to R. W. Hay, Colonial Office, 18 March 1826, CO201/176 f324; *HRA* I xii, p. 224.

2. *Success* Log, ADM51/3460.

3. Captain J. Stirling, HMS *Success*, Simon's Bay, to J. W. Croker, 8 Sep 1826, CapS182 (rec. 30 Nov. 1826), ADM1/2553. NB, Admiral Lord de James Saumarez, 70, had been C-in-C at Plymouth, and why he was travelling to the Cape is unknown. His portrait hung in James' United Service Club.

4. *Success* Log, ADM51/3460.

5. In the *Discovery,* with *Chatham* as escort, Vancouver arrived in KGS 26 Sept., left 11 Oct. 1791, *ADB* vol. 2, p. 551.

6. The whole story of early exploration, including Vlamingh's voyage, is well told in Appleyard/Manford, *The Beginning*, Chaps 1 & 3, especially pp. 78–9.

7. *Sydney Gazette*, 29 Nov. 1826.

8. *Success* Log, ADM51/3460.

9. Sir James Brisbane was a cousin of the recently departed Governor, Sir Thomas Brisbane.

10. I. H. Nicholson, *Shipping Arrivals and Departures Sydney 1826–1840*, p. 14. The *Volage* actually arrived two days earlier.

11. Rear Admiral Gage, C-in-C Eastern Station, *Boadicea*, Trincomalee, to J. W. Croker, 15 Aug. 1826, S89 (rec. 18 Dec. 1826), ADM1/192 f297.

12. *Sydney Gazette*, 2 Dec. 1826.

13. Governor Darling, NSW, to R. W. Hay, 9 Oct. 1826 (duplicate), CO323/146 f220.

14. John Barrow, Admiralty to Hay, 13 Feb. 1826, CO 201/175 f11.

15. Bathurst to Darling, 1 and 11 March 1826, *HRA* I xii, p. 218ff.

16. Darling, NSW, confidential, to Earl Bathurst, 24 Nov. 1826 (rec. 7 June 1827), CO323/228 f228. Also *HRA* I xii, p. 701.

17. Instructions to Lockyer, 24 Nov. 1826, *HRA* I xii, p. 701.

18. These reasons are amplified in Statham, 'Western Australia Becomes British', pp. 121–2. See also C. M. H. Clark, *A History of Australia*, vol. 2, pp. 71–5.

19. Sir James Brisbane, *Warspite*, Port Jackson, to J. W. Croker, 5 Dec. 1826, ADM1/193 f316 (rec. 15 Nov. 1827), S96.

20. H. Rosenman (ed.), *An account of two voyages…by Capt. Jules Dumont D'Urville*, vol. 1, p. 69.

21. See Marchant, *France Australe*, pp. 286–7.

22. Appleyard/Manford, pp. 100–01.

23. C. Cornell (trans.), *The Journal of…Nicolas Baudin*, p. 503.

24. This scenario has been constructed around the fact that Stirling paid relatively little attention in his 1827 reports to the area of the river below Heirisson Islands compared to the detailed descriptions of the upper reaches.

25. Marchant, p. 253.

26. *HRA* III vi, pp. 641–3 and 645–9. See also G. Graham, *Great Britain and the Indian Ocean*, pp. 244–5.

27. Darling per *Corsair* to Bathurst, 4 Dec. 1826 (rec. June 1827), *HRA* I xii, p. 729.

28. Sir James Brisbane, *Warspite*, Port Jackson, to J. W. Croker, 5 Dec. 1826, S96 (rec. 15 Nov. 1827), ADM1/193 f316.

29. Captain Stirling, HMS *Success*, to Darling, 8 Dec. 1826, *HRA* I xii, p. 775.

30. Captain Stirling, 14 Dec. 1826, HMS *Success*, Sydney, to Darling, *HRA* I xii, p. 777.

31. ibid.

32. Darling, NSW, to R. W. Hay, 9 Oct. 1826, CO323/146 f220.

33. Darling to Bathurst, 18 Dec. 1826 (rec. 7 June 1827), *HRA* I xii, p. 773.

34. *Sydney Gazette*, 23 Dec. 1826.

35. Captain J. Stirling, HMS *Success*, Sydney Cove, to J. W. Croker, Admiralty, 20 Dec. 1826 (rec. 8 July 1827), CapS144, ADM1/2554.

36. Captain J. Stirling, HMS *Success*, Madras Roads, to Croker, 31 Aug. 1827 (rec. 6 Aug. 1828), CapS172, ADM 1/2556.

37. *Sydney Gazette*, 23 Dec. 1826.

38. *Sydney Gazette*, 20 Dec. 1826. Note they refer to Yonge as Young. Heathcote also must have been taken on in Sydney during this reshuffle.

39. Despite considerable research, the reason for Stirling's choice of Peter Belches is unknown.

40. *Sydney Gazette*, 27 Dec. 1826.

41. James Stirling, HMS *Success*, Sydney Cove, to Croker, 11 Jan. 1827 (rec. 23 June 1827), CapS154, ADM 1/2554.

42. A cutter is a single-masted 28 to 32 ft long boat often used in inland and coastal exploration; a pinnace is a sturdier masted boat used in the open sea; a gig is a long, narrow row boat for six oarsmen in a line.

43. *ADB*, vol. 1, Frazer entry, pp. 416–7.

44. *ADB*, vol. 1, Garling entry, p. 427. Examples of his NSW works are in the Dixson and Mitchell libraries, and Royal Yacht Squadron.

45. *Success* Log, ADM51/3460. On 31 Jan. 1827 *Success* shifted to berth between Bruni Island and Pierson's Point in the d'Entrecasteaux Channel 'off Kelly's Farm'.

46. Mrs Macleay to her son William, Feb/Mar?? 1827, *Macleay Correspondence*, Linnean Society, London, AJCP M596–7.

47. ibid. The Sir Walter mentioned was Stirling's uncle, the banker.

48. *Hobart Town Gazette*, 10 Feb. 1827.

49. Report to Admiralty enclosed in Captain J. Stirling, HMS *Success*, Madras Roads, to J. W. Croker, 31 Aug. 1827, CapS172, ADM 1/2556.

50. Report to Colonial Office in Gov. Darling to Bathurst, 21 April 1827 (rec. 2 Oct. 1827), CO201/182 f208, *HRA* I xiii, p. 264.

CHAPTER 6: SWAN RIVER EXPLORED

1. Report to Colonial Office, 21 April 1827, Governor Darling, Sydney Dispatch 56 per *Australia* to Bathurst (rec. 2 Oct. 1827), CO201/182 f208, *HRA* I xiii, p. 264 and ff. enclosure, Captain Stirling to Gov. Darling, 18 April 1827 (encl. no. 1).

2. Report to Admiralty, 31 Aug. 1827, Captain J. Stirling, HMS *Success*, Madras Roads, to J. W. Croker (rec. 6 Aug 1828), CapS172, ADM1/2556.

3. The 'Narrative of Operations' contained 6,412 words, 46 of the total 117 paragraphs in the report to Darling.

4. 'Observations and Capabilities' took 5,681 words excluding Frazer, the botanist's report of 2,380 words which was appended to the report to Darling, but included within the Admiralty report.

5. The Admiralty report was 9,439 words in all—the 'Narrative' of day-to-day activities was cut to 870 words.

6. See Robin McInnes, *The Garden Isle*, Introduction.

7. Remarks Book of HMS *Success* 1826, Hydrography Office, Taunton, Misc. Papers, vol. 107.

8. Barbara Chapman, *The Colonial Eye*, p. 76.

9. See notes by Mary Eagle in the catalogue to accompany the Heytesbury Gallery exhibition of paintings from the Holmes à Court collection in Jane Clark (ed.), *Exploration and Transformation*.

10. *Success* Log, ADM51/3460. Note inconsistency; Stirling says he sent Belches in the gig and returned in the cutter, but the log records the gig returning with Stirling.

11. The garden was planted at 'Woodmans cove' (named after the purser of *Success*) which is no longer marked on maps of Garden Island. The name was transferred by Fremantle to a point on the mainland opposite the northern end of the island.

12. Report to Admiralty, 31 Aug. 1827 (rec. 6 Aug 1828), CapS172, ADM 1/2556.

13. George Seddon, ABC Radio, 'Ockham's Razor', transcript, 7 Sept. 1997.

14. Cameron, *Ambition's Fire*, pp. 19–20.

15. See Battye, *Western Australia*, pp. 64–9; Cameron, pp. 29–30; Appleyard/Manford, *The Beginning*, pp. 46–55.
16. Marnie Basset, *The Hentys*, p. 85.
17. Governor Darling to R. W. Hay, 14 May 1827, *HRA* I xiii, p. 303.
18. Letter to J. W. Croker, encl. 1, ADM1/2556.
19. See Lockyer's report, *HRA* III vi, p. 504, pp. 604–06.
20. *Success* Log, ADM51/3460.

CHAPTER 7: MELVILLE ISLAND AND HOME

1. Captain J. Stirling, HMS *Success*, Sydney, to Governor Darling, 18 April 1827, *HRA* III vi, pp. 551–84.
2. For reference to quote, see Cameron, *Ambition's Fire,* p. 28; Appleyard/Manford, *The Beginning,* p. 51 etc.
3. Captain James Stirling to Governor Darling, 18 April 1827, *HRA* III vi, pp. 551–84.
4. I am indebted to Prof. Brian Bosworth (Classics, UWA) for the reference to Virgil's *Aeneid* 3.163 and 1.530. The point was also made by William Lines in *An All Consuming Passion*, p. 77.
5. Darling, Sydney, Dispatch 56 per *Australia* to Bathurst, 21 April 1827 (rec. 2 Oct. 1827), CO201/182, *HRA* I xiii, p. 264.
6. The Garlings are not listed in Darling's enclosures but were mentioned in the Admiralty correspondence.
7. *Sydney Gazette*, 24 April 1827.
8. ibid., 30 April 1827.
9. *The Monitor*, Shipping Intelligence, 20 April 1827.
10. *Success* Log, ADM51/3460.
11. Darling to R. W. Hay, 14 May 1827, *HRA* I xiii, p. 303.
12. Captain James Stirling to Lord Bathurst, 15 May 1827, *HRA* I xiii, p. 307.
13. Note that Darling was a military man and at this time there was some antipathy between the services. Most early Governors had been naval men.
14. Darling, Government House, Sydney, to Hay, 15 May 1827, CO201/182, *HRA* I xiii, p. 306.
15. ML Register, 11 (AO7/462, reel 2549), entry 99, 'Sir James Stirling Knt of Western Australia, 2,560 acres in Parish of Torrens, co of Bathurst…Being the land promised to the said Sir James Stirling…and of which he was authorised to take possession on the 19 Apr 1828 as a reserve being also the land inserted as No 49 in Government Notice of 15 August 1826. Date of Order 17 May 1827.'
16. *Sydney Gazette*, 3 May 1827.
17. Darling, Government House, Sydney, to Lord Bathurst, 21 May 1827, CO201/182 (rec. 2 Oct. 1827). Marked for Admiralty, to whom copy was sent 20 Jan. 1828 (ans. 8 Feb. 1828), *HRA* I xiii, p. 315.
18. ibid.
19. Captain James Stirling, HMS *Success*, Madras Roads, to J. W. Croker, 31 Aug. 1827, CapS172 ADM1/2556.
20. ibid.
21. ibid., 'Report of the Proceedings of His Majesty's Ship *Success* while forming a new Settlement on the North Coast of New Holland'.

22.   Stirling to Croker, 31 Aug. 1827.

23.   Remarks Book of HMS *Success*, Captain J. Stirling by R. D. Milroy, Master, 1826, Hydrography Office, extract from Misc. Papers, vol. 7.

24.   John Barrow, Admiralty, to Under-Secretary Stanley, Colonial Office, 9 Jan. 1828 (rec. 9 Jan.), CO201/195 f10, *HRA* III v, p. 811.

25.   Cameron, 'The Northern Settlements', pp. 278–9.

26.   Enclosure no. 4, 'Report on Raffles Bay and Neighbourhood in June–July 1827' in Stirling to J. W. Croker, 31 Aug. 1827, CapS172 ADM1/2556.

27.   John Barrow, Admiralty, to Under-Secretary Stanley, Colonial Office, 9 Jan. 1828 (rec. 9 Jan.), CO201/195 f10, *HRA* III v, p. 811.

28.   See shipping movements from Raffles Bay and Melville Island. I am indebted to Dr J. M. R. Cameron for this information.

29.   The settlement established at Port Essington in 1837, and named Victoria, was to prove no more successful than Raffles Bay, being abandoned in 1849.

30.   Stirling to Croker, 31 Aug. 1827, CapS172 ADM1/2556.

31.   ADM1/193 f152, S55. Rear Admiral W. H. Gage, C-in-C, *Java* at Malacca, to J. W. Croker, 1 Oct. 1827 (rec. 6 Aug. 1828), 'Hearing from Captain James Stirling of His Majesty's Ship *Success* that he had a favourable opportunity before he joined my flag, of communicating to you for their Lordships duplicates of the Reports which he had prepared for me under the date of 27th August last'. Filed in March but held over pending a covering letter until 6 Aug. 1828.

32.   *Success* Log, ADM51/3460; also the Master's Log AJCP, microfilm 6307.

33.   *Success* Log, ADM51/3460.

34.   ADM1/193 f107 (rec. 29 April, stamped 5 May 1829), S53, Rear Admiral Gage, C-in-C, *Java* at Prince of Wales Island, to J. W. Croker, 14 Nov. 1828.

35.   *Success* Log, ADM 51/3460.

36.   These items were enclosed in James Stirling to Croker, 28 July 1828, 'Memos given under my hand on board HMS *Java* in Trincomalee Harbour this 21st day of February 1828. William Martin, Surgeon.'

37.   James Stirling to brother John at St Andrews, 4 Aug. 1828 (Lenfestey).

38.   Memo from Surgeon Martin, *Java* in Trincomalee Harbour, 21 Feb. 1828, encl. in James Stirling to Croker, 28 July 1828.

39.   This was an unusual step and it meant that Stirling had to find (and later claim back) the first-class fare on the *Henry Porcher* of £150.

40.   *Morning Chronicle*, Shipping Intelligence, 10 July 1828.

41.   Anne Stirling to son John at St Andrews, 9 July 1828 (Lenfestey).

CHAPTER 8: ASSAULT ON DOWNING STREET

1.   Captain James Stirling, 22 Norfolk St, to J. W. Croker, Admiralty, 28 Jan. 1828 (rec. 2 Aug.), CapS167 ADM1/2556.

2.   Colonial Office memorandum, Huskisson to Hay, 24 Dec. 1827, CO201/182 f206.

3.   Under-Secretary Stanley, Downing St, to Captain Stirling, 29 Nov. 1827, *HRA* III vi, p. 584.

4.   William Huskisson, Downing St, to Governor Darling, 28 Jan. 1828, *HRA* I xiii, p. 739.

5. William Sacheverell Coke, Sydney Barracks to father, 10 Feb. 1828, *Brickhill Hall Collection,* Derby Record Office, AJCP reel M793, 'They talk of sending a strong detachment to Swan River, it is in Lat 32 I believe, the climate is beautiful, and the Land of the very best quality, and will soon be able to be thrown open to Settlers'.

6. J. Darl, East India House, to Thomas Peregrine Courtenay, 6 Mar. 1828. Enclosed in India Board to Colonial Office, 1 Aug. 1828, CO18/1 f126.

7. Uren, *Land Looking West,* title to Chap. 6.

8. Captain J. Stirling, 18 Baker St, to R. W. Hay, Colonial Office, 30 July 1828, *HRA* III vi, pp. 585–6.

9. See Jonathan Lee, 'Edward Stirling of Stirling Castle,' p. 1.

10. *Mangles Story,* Chap. 4.

11. Hay, Colonial Office, to John Barrow, Admiralty, 13 Oct. 1828, C0202/19 f2.

12. Barrow, Admiralty, private to Horton, Colonial Office, 15 Oct. 1827, CO201/185 f23.

13. Barrow to Hay, 23 May 1828, CO201/195 f40.

14. Barrow, private to Horace Twiss, 2 Aug. 1828, CO18/1 f96.

15. J. S. Roe to brother William, Newbury Rectory, Berkshire, 4 Aug. 1828. Cited in J. L. Burton Jackson, *Not An Idle Man,* p. 35.

16. James Stirling, Lansdown House, Southampton, to brother John, St Andrews, 4 Aug. 1828. Original ML A4144, typescript WAA Acc 449A/MN595.

17. Darl, East India House, to Courtney, 1 Aug. 1828. Enclosed in India Board to the Colonial Office, CO 18/1 f126.

18. James to John Stirling, 23 Aug. 1828, WAA Acc 449A/MN595.

19. Thomas Moody, 23 Bolton St, to Hay, Colonial Office, 6 Aug. 1828, CO323/155 f187.

20. James to John Stirling, 23 Aug. 1828, WAA Acc 449A/MN595.

21. Captain J. Stirling and Major T. Moody, 21 Aug. 1828, *HRA* III vi, pp. 586–7.

22. Moody to Wilmot Horton, 23 Aug. 1828, *Catton Papers,* D3155/2849.

23. See A. M. Lambert, *The Making of the Dutch Landscape,* p. 244.

24. James to John Stirling, 23 Aug. 1828, WAA449A/MN595.

25. See P. A. Pemberton, 'The London Connection: The formation and early years of the Australian Agricultural Company 1824–1834'.

26. Anne Stirling, Henley Park, to son John, St Andrews, 9 July 1828 (Lenfestey).

27. James to John Stirling, 23 Aug. 1828, WAA449A/MN595.

28. James to John Stirling, 11 Oct. 1828, ML A4144, WAA Acc 449A/MN595.

29. Anne Stirling to John at St Andrews, 7 Oct. 1828 (Lenfestey) also refers to James and wife staying at Henley Park.

30. James Stirling, Henley Park to John Stirling, St Andrews, Scotland, 11 Oct. 1828, ML A4144, WAA Acc 449A/MN595.

31. Murray's speech in the House of Commons cited in Battye, *Western Australia,* p. 70.

32. See J. M. R. Cameron, 'The Foundation of Western Australia Reconsidered'.

33. R. W. Hay, Deal Castle, to John Barrow, Admiralty, 3 Oct. 1828, CO324/86 f69.

34. Barrow to Hay, 4 Oct. 1828, CO323/152 f216.

35. See Cameron, *Ambition's Fire* , Chap. 5, p. 71.

36. See for example Bandock, 20 Oct. 1828, CO18/2, f7; Goodman 21 Oct. 1828, CO18/2 f86.

37. Alexandra Hasluck, *Thomas Peel of Swan River,* pp. 9–10.

38. *ibid.,* p. 10.

39. See letter from James to John Stirling, 23 Aug. 1828, WAA449A/MN595.

40. For MacQueen's experience in NSW, see R. Roxburgh, 'Thomas Potter Macqueen of Segenhoe, NSW'; E. W. Dunlop, 'Thomas Potter Macqueen,' pp. 195–6; and W. A. Wood, *Dawn in the Valley: A Story of Settlement in the Hunter Valley to 1833.*

41. This ruling had been introduced in 1817, and applied to the AA Co. in 1824 but had been modified in 1826 to 1 acre for every 3 shillings. See *HRA* I xii, pp. 377–8.

42. Edward W. H. Schenley, T. P. Macqueen to Sir George Murray, CO18/1 f83; *HRA* III, vi, pp. 588–90.

43. Thomas Peel, 106 Pall Mall, to Twiss, Colonial Office, 6 Nov. 1828, CO18/1 f81 and Hasluck, p. 21.

44. The original is missing but referred to in John Barrow, Admiralty, to Under-Secretary Twiss, 7 Nov. 1828, CO18/1 f98, *HRA* III vi, p. 587. The Colonial Office asked for a ship to be despatched from the Cape of Good Hope, which the Admiralty changed, eventually commanding *Challenger* under Captain Fremantle to depart from the India Station. *Challenger* had been commissioned around 10 Nov. in Portsmouth with Capt. Fremantle, Lts Mowatt, Henry and Pakenham, and Surgeon Street. *Morning Chronicle*, 10 Nov. 1828.

45. Battye, p. 71.

46. John Barrow, Admiralty, to Under-Secretary Twiss, 13 Nov. 1828, CO18/1 f100, *HRA* III vi, p. 588.

47. *HRA* III vi, p. 589, and E. S. Whitely, *The Military Establishment in Western Australia 1829–1863,* Chap. 1.

48. Barrow to Twiss, 13 Nov. 1828, CO18/1 f100 and *HRA* III vi, p. 588.

49. e.g. Latour, 17 Nov. 1828, CO323/155 f180.

50. Referred to in Hay to Treasury, 30 Dec. 1828, T1/3426 Long Bundle, WA.

51. *Morning Chronicle*, 10 Nov. 1828.

52. Colonial Office to Treasury, 30 Dec. 1828, T1/3426 Long Bundle, WA.

53. Peel to Twiss, 2 Dec. 1828, CO18/1, *HRA* III vi, pp. 591–2.

54. James Stirling to brother John, 5 Dec. 1828, ML A4144, WAA Acc 449A/MN595.

55. Horace Twiss was the nephew of Mrs Siddons and cousin of Fanny Kemble; see also Hasluck, p. 26.

56. Thomas Peel, 8 St James' Square, to Horace Twiss, 2 Dec. 1828, CO18/1, *HRA* III vi, pp. 591–2.

57. James Stirling, 6 Cannon Row, to John Stirling, St Andrews, 5 Dec. 1828, ML A4144, WAA Acc 449A/MN595.

58. R. W. Hay, Colonial Office, to Thomas Peel, Vincent, Macqueen and Schenley, 6 Dec. 1828, *HRA* III vi, pp. 593+, CO18/1 f89.

59. ibid.

60. Enclosed in Hay to Thomas Peel, Vincent, Macqueen and Schenley, 6 Dec. 1828, *HRA* III vi, pp. 593+, CO18/1 f89.

61. Vincent, Peel and Schenley, 8 St James' Square, to Hay, Colonial Office, 18 Dec. 1828, *HRA* III vi, p. 596, CO18/1 f91.

62. Memo (Hay?) Colonial Office, CO18/1 f94 (on letter 6 Dec.).

63. James Stirling, London, to Hay, 26 Dec. 1828, *HRA* III vi, p. 598.

64. Hay to Stirling, 1 Jan. 1828 (as cited in JS's 'Title' to WA Company in Clifton Letterbooks, WAA698A).

65. James to John Stirling, 5 Dec. 1828, ML A4144, WAA Acc 449A/MN595.

66. Captain J. Stirling, Cannon Row, to Hay, 26 Dec. 1828, *HRA* III vi, p. 598.

67. Lord FitzRoy, Somerset Horse Guards, to Under-Secretary Twiss, *HRA* III vi, p. 597.
68. Hay to Drummond, 29 Dec. 1828, CO324/86 f82.
69. James to John Stirling, 15 Dec. 1828, ML A4144, WAA Acc 449A/MN595.
70. Sir George Murray, Dispatch 1, to Captain Stirling, 30 Dec. 1828, *HRA* III vi, pp. 600+ (Instructions as Lieutenant Governor).
71. Captain J. Stirling, London to J. W. Croker, 31 Dec. 1828 (rec. 3 Jan), CapS3, 71–29, ADM1/2557.
72. Captain J. Stirling, London, to R. W. Hay, 31 Dec. 1828, *HRA* III vi, p. 602.
73. Dates of appointment and salaries are also given in the *Murray Papers,* National Library of Scotland, MS 46.8.11, f102. This includes also the Chaplain, J. B. Wittenoom, appt. 23 Jan. 1829 on salary of £250.
74. R. W. Hay to G. R. Dawson, Treasury, CO18/1 X/N 02169.

CHAPTER 9: PREPARATIONS AND THE *PARMELIA*

1. Jonathan Lee, 'Edward Stirling of Stirling Castle', and J. L. Lee, *The Journals of Edward Stirling in Persia and Afghanistan 1828–29.*
2. Anne Stirling to son John, 5 Jan. 1829 (Lenfestey).
3. John Stirling to R. W. Hay, 10 Jan. 1829, CO18/4 f366, and ditto 24 Jan. 1829, CO18/4 f368.
4. Hay, Downing St, to John Stirling, 39 Duke St, 14 Jan. 1829, CO397/1 f51 (refusal was based on the intended vs actual importation).
5. Regulations 13 Jan. 1829, *HRA* III vi, p. 606ff.
6. Uren, *Land Looking West*, p. 67.
7. John Stirling, 39 Duke St, to Hay, 24 Jan. 1829, CO18/4 f368.
8. Hay, Downing St, to John Stirling, 31 Jan. 1829, CO397/1 f86.
9. J. Stewart, Treasury Chambers, to Hay, 11 Dec. 1828, *HRA* III vi, p. 595.
10. James Stirling, private, to Horace Twiss, 16 Jan. 1829, CO18/3 f7.
11. *The Times*, 17 Jan. 1828.
12. H. Twiss to T. Peel, 21 Jan. 1829, CO324/86, and Twiss to Sir F. Vincent, Messrs Peel and Schenley, 21 Jan. 1829, *HRA* III vi, pp. 608–9, CO397/1 f69.
13. Thomas Peel to Hay, 21 Jan. 1829, CO323/157 f295.
14. E. W. H. Schenley, 8 St James' Square, to Thomas Peel, 23 Jan. 1829 (encl. in Peel to Twiss, 28 Jan. 1828), *HRA* III vi, p. 611.
15. Hay to Schenley, 6 Jan. 1829, CO397 f36.
16. ibid., 11 Jan. 1829, CO397/1 f45.
17. Thomas Peel to Twiss, 28 Jan. 1829, *HRA* III vi, pp. 610–11.
18. Levey's story is told in J. S. Levi/G. F. Bergman, *Australian Genesis*, Chap. 8.
19. Twiss to Peel and Stirling, 29 Jan. 1829, cited in Hasluck, *Thomas Peel,* pp. 35–6.
20. Colonial Office to Latour, 29 Jan. 1829, CO326, vol. 151, see L.
21. See P. Statham, 'Peter Augustus Latour: Absentee Investor Extraordinaire', p. 226.
22. This was the *Calista*—detailed lists of Latour's property and values are filed in the *Clifton Records*, WAA 698A, reel 4, series 5, item no. 5.
23. J. Lachlan, Great Aile Street, to Captain Stirling, 23 Dec. 1828, *HRA* III vi, p. 597.
24. J. S. Roe to father, cited in Burton Jackson, *Not an Idle Man*, p. 42.
25. Navy Office to Captain Stirling, 15 Jan. 1828, WASR49, Col. Sec. In 1/8.

26. ibid., 23 Jan. 1829, WASR49 Col. Sec. In 1/15. 1829.

27. *Morning Chronicle*, Shipping Intelligence, 28 Jan. 1829.

28. Roe to father, 3 Feb. 1829, cited in Uren, p. 70.

29. R. W. Hay, Downing St, to John Barrow, Admiralty, 27 Dec. 1828, CO324/86 f9, and enclosure, Admiral Sir H. Blackwood, Admiralty House, Rochester, to Hay, Colonial Office, 2 Jan. 1829.

30. Navy Office to Captain Stirling, 24 Jan. 1829, WASR49, Col. Sec. In 1/20.

31. Hay to Stirling, and Navy Office to Stirling, 28 Jan. 1829, WASR49, Col. Sec. In 1/30.

32. Navy Office to Colonial Office, 5 Feb. 1830 (re paying for Stirling's passage, viz. 10 adults £99, 1 child £4 19s, 25 tons of housing stuffs…£123 15s), CO18/7 f201.

33. For his story, see Rica Erickson, *The Drummonds of Hawthornden*.

34. Appointed early in 1829, see Hay to Captain Stirling, 5 Jan. 1829, CO397/1 f32.

35. Requisition for books, for the Use of the Settlement on Swan River, 23 Jan. 1829, CO18/3 f9 (in JS's handwriting with insertions by Horace Twiss).

36. James Stirling, Cannon Row, to Twiss, 14 Jan. 1829, CO18/3 f11.

37. Twiss to Stirling, 29 Jan. 1829, annotation to CO18/3 f11.

38. *Morning Chronicle*, 29 Jan. 1829.

39. See *HRA* I xii, p. 113, 'clauses in the royal instructions to Governor Darling, respecting the division of the territory, grants of land and clergy reserves, excepting those parts which related to convicts and the formation of a church corporation'.

40. *Morning Chronicle*, under Shipping Intelligence, 3 Feb. 1829.

41. Lt Gov. James Stirling, *Parmelia*, Spithead, to Horace Twiss, 5 Feb. 1829, CO18/3 f17 (not in JS's hand, but signed).

42. Stirling to Twiss, 5 Feb. 1829, CO18/3 f17, 'The only Artificers who have been found willing to pass from His Majesty's Dockyard here to that in the New Settlement, are those named in the margin'.

43. ibid.

44. Log of HMS *Sulphur*, ADM51/3471, 25 Nov. 1828 – May 1829, entry 8–9 Feb.

45. Uren, *Land Looking West*, quoting Roe, p. 71.

46. Navy Office to Captain Stirling, 28 Jan.1829, WASR49, Col. Sec. In 1/23.

47. Cameron, *Ambition's Fire*, title of Chap. 4, but used previously by many whom he cites in this chapter.

48. *Colonial Times,* 16 July 1830.

49. e.g. *The Times*, 17 Jan. 1829, advertised the *Norfolk* and the *Hope* as bound for the new settlement.

50. *Quarterly Review*, vol. 39, April 1829, p. 318.

51. Cameron, Chap. 5, esp. p. 76.

52. Uren, p. 81.

53. This child was often called Henry or Harry in his youth but took his first name when he later joined the navy. To avoid confusion, both will be used.

54. Log of HMS *Sulphur*, ADM51/3471, 25 Nov. 1828 – May 1829, entry 9 March.

55. *The Times,* 26 May 1829.

56. Charles Stirling at Summer Place, Manchester, to brother John at St Andrews, 29 May 1829 (Lenfestey).

57. William Stirling, Manchester, to brother John, St Andrews, 12 July 1829 (Lenfestey).

58. Lt Gov. Stirling, Cape Town, 29 April 1829, private to H. Twiss (rec. 4 July), CO18/3 f21.

59. James Stirling, Cape Town, to John Stirling, 25 April 1829. Original ML A4144, typescript WAA Acc 449A/MN595 25/2/02.

60. Captain Dance, Cape Town, to J. Stirling, 29 April 1829, WASR49, Col. Sec. In 1/32.

61. Lt Gov. Stirling, Cape Town, 29 April 1829, private to Horace Twiss (rec. 4 July), CO18/3 f21, 'total cost £41.15.3'.

62. William Lines, *An All Consuming Passion*, p. 91.

63. Captain James Stirling, Cape of Good Hope, to Gov. Arthur, 20 April 1829, *Arthur Papers*, ML A2209 f335.

64. Alexander Collie to his brother, 9 June 1829 from HMS *Sulphur*, *Collie Letters*, WAA, 'My Dear George, The speculations ran high at the Cape that a French expedition which touched there in January last had taken previous possession of Swan River, and this idea seemed to gain credit among us as we advanced'. See also R. W. Hay, 5 May 1829, private and confidential to Lord Stuart de Rothesay, 'The Report of the French Government having dispatched some Vessels of War to make an Establishment on the Coast of New Holland is again revived, as the last news from the Cape of Good Hope announced that a Settlement has been formed by them at Shark's Bay, which is the most western Part of that Great Island, & rather nearer than is agreeable to our new Colony at Swan River...', CO324/86 f98.

65. Fremantle *Letters*, p. 23.

66. Initially orders had gone to HMS *Tweed* (7 Nov. 1828) but this was countermanded by Barrow in favour of *Challenger*, 2 Dec. 1828; latter left 25 Dec. 1828, Fremantle *Letters*, p. 22.

67. Lt Gov. Stirling, Cape Town, private to H. Twiss, 29 April 1829 (rec. 4 July), CO18/3 f21.

68. Instructions to the Surveyor-General were dated 12 March, and to the Colonial Secretary 16 March, on which day he also set out the composition and duties of the Board of Audit that was to evaluate each settler's application for land.

69. Journal of Events connected with the Public Service (f39) enclosed in 10 Sept. 1829 Lt Gov. Stirling, Perth, WA to Sir G. Murray, *HRA* III vi, p. 614 Swan River (rec. 27 Jan. 1830), CO18/3 f33.

70. Fremantle *Diary*, 26 April – 3 May.

71. James Stirling, WA, to brother Walter, 7 Sept. 1829, original ML A4144; WAA Acc 449A/MN595. (A brief extract of this letter appeared in the *Maidstone Gazette*, 2 Feb. 1830.)

72. James Stirling, WA, to Commodore (illegible), 7 Sept. 1829 (copy), in *Letters to Hooker*, vol. 1 f127, Royal Botanic Gardens, Kew, AJCP M731, frame 292.

73. Fremantle *Letters*, 8 Oct. 1829 from Trincomalee, p. 24.

74. Fremantle *Diary*, 4 June, p. 60.

75. Fremantle *Letters*, 8 Oct. 1829, pp. 24–5.

76. Fremantle *Diary*, 7 June, p. 61.

77. ibid., 10, 11 June, pp. 62–3.

78. The well on this site still remains today.

79. Fremantle *Letters* , 8 Oct. 1829, p. 25 and Stirling's Journal of Events, CO18/3 f33.

80. Fremantle *Diary*, p. 61.

81. Lt Gov. Stirling, Perth, to Sir George Murray, 10 Sept. 1829, *HRA* III vi, p. 614 (rec. 27 Jan. 1830), CO18/3 f33, schedule (f35).

82. Lt Gov. Stirling, Perth, to Sir George Murray, 10 Sept. 1829, CO18/3 f33 encl. no 2. The proclamation was 936 words long.

83. Fremantle *Diary*, 25 May, p. 53.

84. Navy Office, 15 May 1829, CO18/3 f188.

85. Navy Office, 11 Mar. 1829, CO18/3 f184.

86. *Hampshire Telegraph*, Portsmouth, 31 Jan. 1829.

87. R. W. Hay, Downing St, private to Captain Stirling, 11 Mar. 1829, CO324/86 f93.

88. Hay, Downing St, private to Captain Stirling, 16 April 1829, CO324/86 f96; re Mr Bland, rec. by Lord Belgrave, 22 April 1829, CO324/86 f97 re Mr Edward Waterton, rec. by Mr Bedingfield of the Royal Institution (was his nephew), 23 April 1829, CO324/86 f97; re Mr John Kellam, rec. by Mr Eden, 16 May 1829, CO324/86 f100; re Mr Neil Talbot, rec. by Lady Glengall, 21 May 1829, R. W. Hay, CO324/86 f101; re Mr Woodward, rec. by Mr Wilmot Horton.

89. Peel cartoons, see Hasluck, p. 52.

CHAPTER 10: SWAN RIVER COLONY FIRST SIX MONTHS

1. Fremantle *Diary*, 9 June 1829, p. 62.

2. Murray to Stirling, 30 Dec. 1828, *HRA* III vi, pp. 600ff.

3. Fremantle *Diary*, 12 Aug. 1829, p. 68.

4. Stirling, KGS, private, to R. W. Hay, 7 Jan. 1832, (rec. 27 Aug. 1832), CO18/10 f15.

5. James Stirling, WA, to brother Walter, 7 Sept. 1829. Original ML A4144; typescript WAA Acc 449A/MN595. A brief extract of this letter appeared in the *Maidstone Gazette,* 2 Feb. 1830.

6. Bryan, 'Cygnet', *Swan River Booklets*, no. 4, 'The Story of the Birth of Perth', p. 11.

7. Alexander Collie to his brother, from HM Sloop *Sulphur*, Cockburn Sound, 14 July 1829, Collie *Letters*, WAA 332.

8. Captain Luscombe to Lt Gov. J. Stirling, 16 July 1829, WASR49, Col. Sec. In 1/97, reg. as B83.

9. Captain Fremantle to Lt Gov. J. Stirling, 17 July 1829, WASR49, Col. Sec. In 1/107, reg. as B87.

10. Fremantle *Diary*, 5 Aug. 1829, p. 67.

11. ibid., 7 July to 5 Aug., pp. 65–7.

12. James Stirling, WA, to Commodore (illegible), 7 Sept. 1829 (copy), in *Letters to Hooker*, vol. 1, f127, Royal Botanic Gardens, Kew, AJCP M731, frame 292.

13. Government Notice, 27 July 1829 (and Bryan no. 4, p. 13).

14. Fremantle *Diary*, 12 Aug. 1829, p. 67.

15. ibid., p. 66.

16. The box, with inscription, is in the Perth Museum. A note attached reads 'Queen Mary found this box in an antique shop in London and presented it to the people of Perth'.

17. Fremantle *Diary,* pp. 67–8, and Bryan no. 4, p. 14.

18. William Leake, Oxford St, to Twiss, 4 Feb. 1830, CO18/7 f322.

19. James Stirling, WA, to Walter, 7 Sept. 1829. Original ML A4144, typescript WAA Acc 449A/MN595.

20. James Stirling to Commodore (illegible), 7 Sept. 1829. *Letters to Hooker*, vol. 1 f127, Royal Botanic Gardens, Kew, AJCP M731, frame 292.

21. Alexander Collie to his brother, dated 9 June 1829 but continued to 21 Aug., *Collie Letters*, WAA 332A.

22. *Challenger* was prevented by bad weather from making it into the open sea until 28 Aug. 1829, Fremantle *Letters*, p. 26.

23. Lt Gov. Stirling, Garden Island, private, to Horace Twiss 25 Aug. 1829 (rec. 10 Jan. 1830), CO18/3 f23.

24. James Stirling, WA, to Walter, 7 Sept. 1829. Original ML A4144, typescript WAA Acc 449A/MN595.

25. Collie to his brother, 7 Sept. 1829, *Collie Letters*, WAA 332.

26. Govt. Notice re Crown Land, 'additional permanent liabilities of all grants', 12 Aug. 1829, WASR 50/1, 1/22.

27. William Stirling, Counsel and Audit Board no. 13 to Col. Sec. Brown, 4 Sept. 1829, WASR49 Col. Sec. In 2/23, reg. as A153. No. 1 transmits report on valuation of the property imported by G Leake…£1,116 10s 4d.

28. Lt Gov. Stirling, Perth, to Sir George Murray, 10 Sept. 1829, *HRA* III vi, p. 614, CO18/3 f33 (rec. 27 Jan. 1830).

29. Edward Pomeroy Barrett Lennard (b 1799) was the brother-in-law of Stirling's first cousin, Dorothy Ann Stirling, who had married John Barrett Lennard in 1819 (Family Tree). Edward arrived, single, on the *Marquis of Anglesea*, 23 Aug. 1829. See Michael Bourke, *On the Swan: A History of the Swan District Western Australia*, p. 39. Barrett Lennard was entitled to 13,200 acres and was allocated 2,906 acres on the Swan, which he called St Lennards. See P. Statham, *Dictionary of Western Australians*, vol. 1, pp. 200–1.

30. Quoted in D. Barrett-Lennard, *Edward Pomeroy Barrett Lennard*, pp. 3–4.

31. William Stirling, writing for Sir James Home re valuation of land, 22 Sept. 1829, WASR49 Col. Sec. In 2/55, no. 13: £200 (2,666 acres).

32. See Nathanial Ogle, *The Colony of Western Australia*, Appendix no. XIV, rural grants allocated, taken from official documents.

33. ibid.

34. Captain Fremantle to J. Stirling, 25 Aug. 1829, WASR49 Col. Sec. In 2/7, reg. as A131.

35. Ogle, p. 182.

36. Documentation for this example is contained in P. Statham, 'Economic Development of Swan River Colony 1829–1850', p. 108.

37. John Lord, Supercargo, *Euphemia*, Gage's Road, to Col. Sec. Brown, 10 Oct. 1829, WASR49 Col. Sec. In 2/101.

38. J. Reveley, Civil Engineer's Office, to Brown, 7 Oct. 1829, WASR49 Col. Sec. In 2/95.

39. See Bruce Devenish, *Man of Energy and Compassion…Henry Trigg, Swan River Pioneer and Church Founder*.

40. William Stirling to Col. Sec. Brown, 30 Oct. 1829, WASR49 Col. Sec. In 2/184.

41. For detail see Statham, 'Peter Augustus Latour', p. 226ff.

42. Lt Gov. Stirling, Perth, to Sir George Murray, 20 Jan. 1830 (rec. 14 Jun 1830), CO18/7 f32, *HRA* III vi, pp. 615–40.

43. ibid.

44. *Collie Letters*, 9 Nov. 1829, WAA332A.

45. Hasluck, *Thomas Peel*, pp. 72–3.

46. *Colonial Times*, Hobart, 2 April 1830 and Hasluck, pp. 73–4.

47. See Hasluck, p. 75.

48. Apart from the *Parmelia* (55 passengers) there was the *Calista, Marquis of Anglesea, St Leonard, Lotus, Caroline Atwick* and *Gilmore*.

49. *Collie Letters*, 9 Nov. 1829, WAA332A.

50. T. B. Wilson, *Narrative of a Voyage Around the World*, p. 207.

51. ibid., p. 220.

52. ibid., pp. 193–5.

53. Lt Gov. Stirling to Sir George Murray, 30 Jan. 1830, *HRA* III vi, pp. 615–40.

54. See A. R. (Don) Pashley, *Policing Our State 1829–1945*, p. 6.

55. Rev. Thomas Hobbes Scott arrived on HMS *Success* from Sydney. See C. Hawtry, *The Availing Struggle,* p. 19. The town of Kelmscott was named in his honour. See WASR 50/1 2/223, 30 June 1830.

56. Wilson, p. 222.

57. Letter from James to Walter, 7 Sept. 1829, 'weight on my shoulders too heavy'. Original ML A4144, typescript WAA Acc 449A/MN595.

58. Lt Gov. Stirling to Murray, 30 Jan. 1830, *HRA* III vi, pp. 615–40.

59. Erickson, *The Drummonds of Hawthornden*, p. 9.

60. Lt Gov. Stirling to Murray, 30 Jan. 1830, *HRA* III vi, pp. 615–40.

61. Sylvia J. Hallam, 'Population and resource usage on the Western Littoral', pp. 16–36; Appleyard/Manford, *The Beginning*, p. 104.

CHAPTER 11: UNCERTAIN PROSPECTS

1. James Stirling, Perth, to Sec. of State, 17 Jan. 1830 (rec. 14 June 1830), CO18/7 f3.

2. Lt Gov. Stirling, Perth, to Sir George Murray, 20 Jan. 1830 (rec. 14 June 1830), CO18/7 f32, *HRA* III vi, pp. 615–40.

3. See E. M. Russell, 'Early Lawyers of Western Australia'.

4. Frank Crowley, 'Master and Servant in WA 1829–1851', p. 96.

5. Wages and Conditions: Govt Notice 25 March 1830. WAA/CSF 2/85ff.

6. Crowley, p. 100.

7. Stirling, Perth, to Sir George Murray, 20 Jan. 1830, CO18/7 f32, *HRA* III vi, pp. 615–40.

8. Stirling, WA, private, to Twiss, 26 Jan. 1830, CO18/7 f68.

9. ibid.

10. Stirling, private, to Twiss, 26 Jan. 1830, CO18/7 f68. See also Hay to Stewart, Treasury, 5 Aug. 1830 where he writes, 'George Murray is of the opinion that the able manner in which Captain Stirling has executed the task with which he was entrusted, entitles him to the favourable consideration of the Government and that the time has arrived when by the terms of the original agreement, an adequate salary ought to be assigned to him…' T1/3426 Long Bundle, WA.

11. Stirling to Sir George Murray, 20 Jan. 1830, CO18/7 f32.

12. Stirling, private, to Twiss, 26 Jan. 1830, CO18/7 f68.

13. Stirling to Sir George Murray, 20 Jan. 1830, CO18/7 f32, *HRA* III vi, pp. 615–40.

14. ibid. Annotation CO18/3, f86, 'Extracts sent to Victualling Office, the Treasury & Commander in Chief, 10 July 1830'.

15. Stirling to Sir George Murray, 20 Jan. 1830, CO18/3 f86.

16. Uren, *Land Looking West*, title of Chap. XVIII.

17. *Bell's Messenger*, London, 31 Jan. 1830.

18. Sir Francis Freeling, Sec. General, Post Office, to Henry Goulburn, 26 Jan. 1830, CO18/7 f258. Enclosed extract of a letter from Messrs Solomon & Co. at St Helena, 27 Nov. 1829.

See also Cameron, *Ambition's Fire,* pp. 88–9. Cameron was the first to unravel the way the news reached England, and his book details the distortion process.

19. See Solomon & Co., St Helena, to Sir Francis Freeling, 27 Nov. 1829, in Freeling to Goulburn, 25 Jan. 1830, CO18/7 f258.

20. Captain Bayly, 15 Feb. 1830. See *Bayly's Journal,* p. 126.

21. The Swan River Job letter (written Swan River 10 Sept. 1829) was published in the *Morning Journal,* 28 Jan. 1830 and *Morning Herald,* 29 Jan. 1830.

22. *Courier,* 27 Jan. 1830.

23. Solomon Levey, 1 Eagle Place, Piccadilly, to Sir George Murray, 26 Jan. 1830, CO18/7 f320.

24. William Leake, Oxford St, to Twiss, 4 Feb. 1830, CO18/7 f322.

25. *Globe,* 27 Jan. 1830; *Morning Chronicle,* 28 Jan. 1830.

26. James Mangles, Woodbridge Cottage, Guildford, to Twiss, 16 Feb. 1830, CO18/7 f325.

27. James Stirling to Colonial Office, 18 Oct. 1830, CO18/7 (printed parliamentary version).

28. *Bayly's Journal,* 17 Feb. 1830, p. 127.

29. ibid., pp. 127–8.

30. ibid., p. 135.

31. ibid., 12 March 1830, p. 135.

32. Govt Notice, 25 March 1830, and Uren, pp. 163–4.

33. *Leicester Journal,* 24 Sept. 1830.

34. James Henty to his father, William Henty, encl. in Wm Henty, West Tarring near Worthing, to Lord Howick, 30 Dec. 1830. CO18/7 f302 contains two letters, one 20 March and the other 1 May 1830.

35. James Henty, WA, 1 May 1830 (rec. 23 Dec. 1830), CO18/7 f302.

36. Alexandra Hasluck, *Portrait with Background*, p. 68.

37. Mary Morgan to her brother, 4 Jan. 1831, *Morgan Letters*, WAA147.

38. *Diary of Mary Ann Friend.*

39. WASR, Col. Sec. Out, Govt Notice (2–107), 12 April 1830.

40. Henry King, aged 7, drowned in the Swan River on 15 April 1830.

41. WASR, Col. Sec. Out, Govt Notice (2–95), 29 March 1830.

42. *Diary of Anne Whatley,* p. 25.

43. See Henty to Worthing, 1 May 1830 (rec. 23 Dec.), 'The Natives are not very numerous. We may have seen in all between this & Port Vasse 200. They are very ignorant & on the whole harmless. I would not however trust them too far. We are never allowed to see the Women or young Children scarcely one has been seen, and that by accident.' CO18/7 f302.

44. See the seminal work of Sylvia Hallam, *Fire and Hearth.*

45. Stirling assumed from the start the Government would provide for the sick, unlike Sydney where, following British Poor Law Practice, this service was refused. See G. C. Bolton and P. Joske, *History of Perth Hospital*, pp. 2–3.

46. *General Report on The Progress, Condition, and Prospects of His Majesty's Colony in Western Australia up to 31 March 1831* (hereafter *General Report 1831*), CO18/7 f14.

47. In March the Harbour Master had been sent to Cape Leeuwin to look for the ship *Cumberland*, reported wrecked in the vicinity, and had reported favourably on his return. See *General Report 1831,* CO 18/7 f14.

48. Thomas Turner, *Turners of Augusta,* letter of 28 Aug. 1830.

49. Turner, p. 77.

50. The story of Georgiana Molloy is given in Hasluck, *Portrait with Background.*

51. F. C. Irwin to Stirling, 18 May 1830, CO18/7 f169.

52. Hasluck, *Thomas Peel*, pp. 101–05.

53. Morgan's letter of 14 July 1830 is quoted in Hasluck, *Thomas Peel*, p. 101.

54. ibid., p. 102.

55. ibid., p. 102 and CSR7/15.

56. Enclosure B, no. 2, in James Stirling to Colonial Office, 18 Oct. 1830 (rec. 15 Feb. 1831), CO18/7 f104 (printed parliamentary version includes report on diseases at the Clarence).

57. Supposed to be 18 Oct. 1830, Uren, p. 131.

58. *General Report 1831*, CO18/7 f14.

59. ibid.

60. *Sydney Gazette*, 24 July 1830.

61. *General Report 1831*, CO18/7 f14.

62. *Diary of Anne Whatley*, CO18.

63. *General Report 1831*, CO18/7 f14.

64. See E. S. Whitely, 'A Short History of the British Regiments in Western Australia 1826–1863'.

65. James Stirling to Colonial Office, 18 Oct. 1830, CO18/7 f104.

66. Collie to brother George, 16 Aug. 1830, *Collie Letters*, WAA332A.

67. ibid.

68. *General Report 1831*, CO18/7 f14.

69. At least two large families on the *Hooghly* were bound for Hobart. See *Bayly's Journal* and Statham, 'Economic Development', Appendix 3.6.

70. Letter from George Dunnage re poll tax, CSR Swan River, vol. 12, also WASR Col. Sec. Out, Govt Notice (2–21), permission to replace fee.

71. CSO vols. 4–8 (Jan. to Aug. 1830) contain many applications for 'permission to leave'.

72. *Diary of Anne Whatley*', p. 44.

73. *Collie Letters*, 3 Oct. 1830, WAA332A.

74. *General Report 1831*, CO18/7 f14.

75. See Rica Erickson, *Old Toodyay and Newcastle*, p. 25, 'Governor Stirling selected land along a pool of permanent water, next to the Toodyay townsite, later known as "Deepdale" Location 13'.

76. *Collie Letters*, 3 Oct. 1830, WAA332A.

77. CO18/9 f5 and *General Report*, 31 March 1831, CO18/7 f14.

78. See G. F. Moore, *Diary of Ten Years of an Early Settler in Western Australia*.

79. Original Moore *Letters*, 20 Nov. 1830, WAA406A.

80. ibid., mid-Dec. 1830, WAA406A.

81. Moore *Diary*, p. 28.

82. Turner, p. 91.

83. Stirling to Murray, 18 Oct 1830, CO18/7 (printed parliamentary version).

CHAPTER 12: A DISMAL YEAR

1. Colonel J. Hanson, a visitor from India, Sept. 1831. See booklet *Woodbridge, Guildford, Western Australia* by the National Trust of WA.

2. J. Stirling to Rear Admiral Owen, C-in-C, Eastern Station, 10 Jan. 1831, WASR Col. Sec. Out, vol. 3, f101.

3. Robert Menli Lyon arrived per *Marquis of Anglesea* aged 40 from Invernesshire with assets to entitle him to 3,813 acres. Granted Swan River Loc. 4 (later transferred to Shaw). Statham, *Dictionary*, p. 210.

4. R. M. Lyon, Fremantle, to Sec. of State, 11 Feb. 1831, CO18/9 f315.

5. Moore *Letters*, 26 March 1831, WAA 1075A.

6. Lyon to Sec. of State, 11 Feb. 1831, CO18/9 f315.

7. See Darling to Colonial Office, 31 Jan. 1831, no. 13, CO201/220, *HRA* I xvi, p. 55ff.

8. Govt Notice, *The Western Australian Chronicle and Perth Gazette*, 12 March 1831, CO18/9 f94.

9. Donald Garden, *Albany: A Panorama of the Sound*, p. 35.

10. J. Stirling, Perth, to John Stirling, St Andrews, Scotland, 2 April 1831. Original ML A4144, typescript WAA Acc 449A/MN595.

11. 'A note by William', 25 May 1830 (Lenfestey).

12. *Fremantle Observer*, 25 April 1831.

13. Report of Captain Bannister's overland journey to KGS, dated 5 Feb. 1831, in J. Cross, *Journals of Several Expeditions made in Western Australia during the years 1829–1832*, p. 108.

14. Collie *Letters*, 12 March 1831, WAA332A.

15. R. W. Hay, private, to Captain Stirling, 8 June 1830, CO324/86 f144.

16. *General Report 1831*, CO18/7 f14.

17. ibid.

18. J. Stirling, Perth, to John Stirling, St Andrews, 2 April 1831. Original ML A4144, typescript WAA Acc 449A/MN595.

19. J. Stirling, WA, to Governor Arthur, 12 April 1831, *Arthur Papers*, ML A2209, f347.

20. *General Report 1831*, CO18/7 f14.

21. James Mangles, Commander RN, 15 Surrey St, Strand, to John Barrow, Admiralty, 7 Dec. 1830, ADM 1/2206, 'Being about to proceed to the Swan River in order to explore that Country…I have to request their Lordships will be pleased to grant me two years' leave of absence for that purpose'.

22. Anglican Burial Register, Registrar Births Deaths and Marriages 1831, William Stirling, aged 32, buried 16 April, William Stirling, infant 3 months, buried 2 May 1831.

23. Hawtry, *The Availing Struggle*, p. 20.

24. Moore *Diary*, 22 June 1831, p. 45.

25. Moore *Letters*, 26 March 1831, WAA406A.

26. J. Stirling, Perth, Dispatch no. 7 to Viscount Goderich, 17 June 1831 (rec. 7 Dec. 1831), CO18/9 f96.

27. James Mangles to Howick, Colonial Office, 21 June 1831, CO18/9 f338.

28. J. Stirling, WA, private, to R. W. Hay, 14 March 1831 (rec. 16 Aug. 1831), CO18/9 f86.

29. Moore *Letters*, 3 July 1831, WAA406A.

30. William Lane Milligan was the replacement surgeon of the 63rd Regiment (after Daly's death) who arrived with his wife and family on the *Wanstead* in Jan. 1830. Dr Charles Simmons was then Colonial Surgeon, and after Milligan's arrival Stirling sent Simmons south to Augusta where he remained until January 1831. He was not well thereafter and died 21 Oct. 1831. It was Milligan who opened the first tent hospital in June 1830, looking after both military and civil officers and families, and private patients as well. Stirling transferred a Swan River grant opposite Woodbridge (RS Loc. 01), which had been assigned originally to William Stirling, to Milligan in April 1831. See J. Brine, *Looking for Milligan*, Chap. 4.

31. Moore *Letters*, 25 Aug. 1831.

32. Moore *Diary*, p. 65.

33. John Okey Davis to his cousin, Mrs Maria Hepburn, Southwark, 20 Jan. 1832, WAA H5/8.

34. Collie, KGS, to his brother, 4 Aug. 1831, *Collie Letters*, WAA332A.

35. Moore *Letters*, 15 Oct. 1831.

36. William Stirling had been Fremantle's agent and with his death there was no one to oversee improvements on Fremantle's grant.

37. James Henty to Stirling, Aug. 1830 in Marnie Bassett, *The Hentys*, p. 141ff.

38. ibid., p. 141.

39. ibid., p. 144.

40. ibid., p. 142.

41. See Ogle, *The Colony of Western Australia,* p. 216.

42. Bassett, p. 144.

43. ibid., p. 191.

44. A letter from VDL written 16 June 1832 says that they were on salt provisions for the whole three years at Swan River, *Dyer Letters*, WAA1598A.

45. Moore *Letters*, 21 Oct. 1831.

46. J. Stirling, KGS, to Lord Goderich, 30 Nov. 1831 (rec. 22 June 1832), CO18/9 f100.

47. Stirling to Colonial Office, 7 Jan 1832 for discharge, CO18/10 f5; Collie *Letters* re appointment 3 Oct. 1830 and 12 March 1831, WAA332A.

48. *Collie Letters,* dated 30 Oct. but runs on to end Nov. 1831, WAA332A.

49. *Morgan Letters*, 8 March 1832, *SRP,* vol. 14, p. 35.

50. Garden, pp. 41–5. These included 18-year-old John Henty, Digby Geake, John Morley and George Cheyne.

51. See Garden, pp. 17 and 39.

52. Their fourth child and first daughter, Mary, was conceived during this all too short summer period.

53. Stirling, KGS, to J. S. Roe, 16 Dec. 1831, WASR SDUR/S1/142A.

54. Stirling, KGS, to Roe, 23 Jan. 1832, WASR SDUR/S2/143.

55. For the full Commission, see Ogle, Appendix no. 1, p. 299.

56. Battye, *Western Australia,* pp. 109–10.

57. Elliot, Admiralty, to Howick, Colonial Office, 3 Oct. 1831 (rec. 10 Oct.), CO18/9 f111.

58. Lt Gov. Stirling, KGS, private, to R. W. Hay, 5 Jan. 1832, CO18/10 f15.

59. ibid.

60. Lt Gov. Stirling, KGS, Dispatch no. 9, to Lord Goderich, 7 Jan. 1832 (rec. 27 Aug. 1832), CO18/10 f5.

61. 'Minutes of the Executive Council of Western Australia from the 6 Feb. [its commencement] to June 1832', CO 20/1, minutes 11 Feb. 1832.

62. Currie and his wife Jane had taken a grant on what is now Matilda Bay—named after Matilda Roe, wife of the Surveyor-General.

63. Executive Council minutes, 11 Feb. 1832, CO 20/1.

64. Stirling, KGS, no. 9, to Goderich, 7 Jan. 1832, CO18/10 f5 (annotated: 24 Nov. Extract for Treasury).

65. ibid.

66. ibid.

CHAPTER 13: A TURNING POINT

1. Lt Gov. Stirling, no. 10, Perth, to Goderich, 14 Feb. 1832 (rec. 27 Aug. 1832), CO18/10 f24.

2. John Okey Davis, Canning River, to his cousin Mrs Hepburn, 20 Jan. 1832, WAA H5/80. John Okey Davis (b 1777) arrived on the *Lotus* 6 Oct. 1829 with wife Frances b 1783 and seven children. He selected 7,026 acres in the Canning region on 14 Nov. 1829 and started to distil perfume from flowers in addition to farming. Wife Frances died March 1835 and he died a year later, the estate passing to his son John.

3. Stirling, no. 13, to Goderich, 28 June 1832 (rec. 1 Dec. 1832), CO 18/10 f56.

4. Stirling to Hay, 1 March 1833, CO18/12 f66.

5. L. A. Whitfeld, *Founders of Law in Australia*, p. 89.

6. Exec. Council minutes, 6 Feb. 1832, CO20/1.

7. Stirling to Hay, 1 March 1833, CO18/12 f66.

8. Exec. Council minutes, 14 Feb. 1832. Overall expenditure was some £665 higher than the parliamentary estimates, but Stirling reported that where the estimates had included £871 9s 9d for work by artisans, only some £305 had been spent, leaving an overall increase of only £98 10s 9d.

9. *Collie Letter*, 5 May 1832, WAA332A.

10. Stirling, no. 10 to Goderich, 14 Feb.1832, CO18/10 f24.

11. Comptroller's Office, 6 Nov. 1832, T1/3426 Long Bundle, WA.

12. Memorial from Swan River, CO18/10 f23.

13. Stirling, no. 10 to Goderich, 14 Feb. 1832, CO18/10 f24.

14. J. Okey Davis to cousin, dated 20 Jan. 1832 but posted end Feb. or later, WAAH5/80.

15. ibid.

16. Moore *Diary*, p. 103.

17. ibid., p. 109.

18. J. Morgan to Hay, 8 March 1832, *SRP*, vol. 14, pp. 34–6.

19. Stirling, KGS, private, to Hay, 7 Jan. 1832 (rec. 27 Aug. 1832), CO18/10 f15.

20. Morgan to Hay, 8 March 1832, *SRP*, vol. 14, pp. 36–63.

21. Stirling had written an earlier dispatch re Peter Brown's reply to a complaint of unpaid debt. This was entirely separate to his £1 note issue in 1833 and only important in that Stirling stated his total confidence in 'Mr Brown's punctuality and integrity'. Stirling to Howick, 30 March 1832, CO18/10 f34.

22. Stirling, no. 12 to Goderich, 2 April 1832 (rec. 11 Sept. 1832, C18/10 f42.

23. Exec. Council minutes, 14 Feb. 1832.

24. Stirling, no. 11 to Goderich, 2 April 1832 (rec. 11 Sept. 1832), CO18/10 f40.

25. ibid., and Stirling, no. 12, to Goderich, 2 April 1832, C18/10 f42.

26. See E. G. Wakefield, *England and America*, vol. II, and R. C. Mills, *The Colonization of Australia*, p. 73.

27. Stirling, nos 11 and 12 to Goderich, 2 April 1832, CO18/10 f40 and 42.

28. This was a precursor to the Arrowsmith 1833 map of WA.

29. Much of the information contained in Wakefield's book *England and America* appears to stem from this dispatch.

30. Stirling, no. 12 to Goderich, 2 April 1832, C18/10 f42.

31. 1832 census, Colonial Office 18/10, pp. 112–56. Interpreted by Ian Berryman in *A Colony Detailed*.

32. Stirling, no. 12, to Goderich, 2 April 1832, C18/10 f42.
33. Exec. Council minutes, 20 March 1832.
34. ibid.
35. Exec. Council minutes, 27 March 1832.
36. Stirling, private, to Hay, 26 June 1832, CO18/10 f 54.
37. Exec. Council minutes, 6 March 1832.
38. There is no direct evidence that this was Stirling's idea, but there is ample proof that the plan was implemented. See Morgan to Hay, 4 May 1833, *SRP*, vol. 16, p. 67, Moore *Diary*, p. 180, and individual letters filed in CSR vols. 10 to 19.
39. Fifteen shillings per bushel was the price offered for wheat produced in 1831 when the few successful farmers had been getting between 12 and 23 bushels to the acre. See Cameron, *Ambition's Fire*, pp. 125–6.
40. Public Notice, WASR50, CSO vol. 6/75.
41. Exec. Council minutes, 22 June 1832 (NB incorrectly dated 22 May).
42. Exec. Council minutes, 29 June 1832.
43. Stirling, HMS *Sulphur* at sea, to Goderich, 20 Sept. 1832, CO18/10 f218.
44. Petition re taxes, 13 July 1832, CSR vol. 25/163. See also Lamb *et al* to Sec. of State, 26 July 1832, CO18/11 f248.
45. Exec. Council minutes, 22 and 29 June 1832.
46. Stirling, no. 13 to Goderich, 28 June 1832 (rec. 1 Dec. 1832), CO18/10 f56.
47. A useful table setting out major public works in WA 1826 to 1846 may be found in R. G. Hartley, *Industry and Infrastructure in Western Australia 1829–1940*, pp. 9–12.
48. Report on Public Works and Buildings, March 1832, CO18/10 f97.
49. Stirling, no. 14 to Goderich, 28 June 1832 (rec. 1 Dec. 1832), CO18/10 f74.
50. Stirling, private, to Hay, 26 June 1832 (rec. 16 Nov.), CO18/10 f54.
51. *Collie Letters* and *Morgan Letters* re the lady, and Stirling to Gov. Arthur, 10 Aug. 1832, that leave had been approved, *Arthur Papers* ML A2209 f351.
52. Stirling to Arthur, 10 Aug. 1832, *Arthur Papers* ML A2209 f351.
53. Paraphrased from responses in Exec. Council minutes, 29 June 1832.
54. Exec. Council minutes, 30 June 1832.
55. Public Notice, 2 July 1832, WASR 50, Col. Sec. Index of Letters out, vol. 6/75.
56. Moore *Diary*, p. 121.
57. Stirling to Goderich, 20 Sept. 1832, CO 10/10, encl. no. 3, f226.
58. ibid., encl. no. 4, f228.
59. ibid., encl. no. 5, f230.
60. Collie to brother George, 28 July 1832, *Collie Letters*, WAA332A.
61. Stirling to J. S. Roe, 14 July 1832, WASR SDUR/S2/169.
62. ibid.
63. Latour's agent had submitted a claim for 113,000 acres, based on property introduced on the *Calista* and the ill-fated *Marquis of Anglesea*. The claim was approved by the Board of Audit and he was granted 10,000 acres in the Perth region and 103,000 at Leschenault on the north side of Geographe Bay in April 1830.
64. Memorandum for Mr Roe, 14 July 1832, WARS/S2/170.
65. See for example Burton Jackson, *Frowning Fortunes*, p. 31.
66. Peter John Boyce, 'The role of the Governor in the Crown Colony of Western Australia 1829–1890'.

67. See letter from brother John to William Stirling dated Manchester 9 Nov. 1831 (Lenfestey).

68. James Stirling to Surveyor-General Roe, 21 July 1832, WARS SDUR/H1/103 (covering sheet: James Stirling Esq Agent for Sir James Hume, transferring to Richard Lewis, 2666 acres on Swan. 21 July 1832. Sanctioned). Lewis had arrived on the *Calista* and had been appointed Superintendent of Fremantle gaol in 1831, but was among those suspended early in 1832.

69. Stirling to Capt. W. T. Dance, 18 July 1832, CO 18/12 f102.

70. Exec. Council minutes, 30 July 1832.

71. Dance to Lt Gov. Stirling, 25 July 1832, encl. no. 4, CO18/12 f110 & 112.

72. Stirling to Dance, 26 July 1832, CO18/12 f114.

73. Stirling to Hay, 18 June 1833, CO 8/12 f98.

74. Extracts from notes made by Capt. Stirling, CO18/12 f102.

75. Enclosure no. 5, Stirling to Dance, 26 July 1832, CO18/12 f114.

76. Exec. Council minutes, 17 Aug. 1832.

77. Richard Morrell to John and Charles Wilson, 8 Aug. 1832, *Morrell Letter* WAA 62A (original plus Fremantle sketch in Art Gallery of Western Australia).

78. *Morrell Letter*, WAA62A

79. Petition re HMS *Sulphur*, July 1832, *SRP.*

80. Stirling, HMS *Sulphur* at sea, to Goderich, 20 Sept. 1832 (rec. 11 Dec. 1832), CO18/10 f218.

81. Stirling (CGH) to Capt. Dance, 30 Sept. 1832, CO18/12 f120.

82. Dance, HMS *Sulphur* (CGH), to J. Stirling, 1 Oct. 1832, CO18/12 f122.

83. Stirling, Simon's Bay, to Dance, HMS *Sulphur*, 4 Oct. 1832, CO18/12 f124.

84. Dance, Simon's Bay, to Stirling, 5 Oct. 1832, CO18/12 f126.

85. Log and proceedings of HMS *Sulphur*, ADM51/3471.

86. See Stirling to Hay, 22 Dec. 1832, CO18/10, f242–251.

CHAPTER 14: THE INTERIM RETURN

1. James Stirling, United Services Club, Pall Mall, to John Stirling, St Andrews, 23 Dec. 1832. Original ML A4144, WAA Acc 449A/MN595 (also Lenfestey).

2. Stated as his address in James to John at St Andrews, 23 Dec. 1832.

3. ibid.

4. Edward Merrell, 13 Clements Lane, Lombard St, to Mr Hay, Colonial Office, 15 Sept. 1832, CO18/11 f155.

5. James to John, 23 Dec. 1832 (Lenfestey).

6. Hay to Lord Goderich (internal), 24 Dec. 1832, CO20/13 f31.

7. Walter Stirling in London to William, 27 Dec. 1832 (Lenfestey).

8. Dorothea to John Stirling, Summer Place, Manchester, 4 Jan. 1833 (Lenfestey).

9. See Henry Amswick, St John's Wood, to Hay, 20 Nov. 1832, CO18/11 f87.

10. *Collie Letters*, 31 May 1833 WAA332A, 'We are anxious about a Governor; you will have heard before this who is to be appointed and what encouragement and assistance is to be afforded by the Mother Country'.

11. James Stirling to Hay, 5 Jan. 1833, CO18/12 f3.

12. J. Stirling, London to Hay, 7 Jan. 1833 (rec. 7 Jan.), CO18/12 f12.

13. Hay to J. Stewart, Treasury Chambers, 8 Jan. 1833, CO397/3.
14. ibid., 12 Jan. 1833, CO397/3.
15. Stewart, Treasury, to Hay, 25 Jan. 1833, CO18/13 f33.
16. J. Stirling, London, to Hay, 8 Jan. 1833, CO18/12 f14.
17. Colonial Boatbuilder, see CapS36 ADM 1/2560, 18 March 1833.
18. Lt Peter Belches RN, Ship Tavern, Charing Cross, to R. W. Hay, 5 Nov. 1833 (rec. 7 Nov.), CO18/13 f187.
19. J. Stirling, London, to Hay, 28 Feb. 1833, CO18/12 f58.
20. M. J. Currie, 14 Great Cumberland Place, to Viscount Goderich, 12 Jan. 1833, CO18/13 f192.
21. Minute attached to memorandum, CO18/13 f192.
22. Hay to James Stirling, Guildford, 23 Jan. 1833, CO397/2.
23. Colonial Office dispatch to Stirling, 2 Jan. 1833, WAA Acc 391.
24. J. Stirling to Hay, 11 Jan. 1833, CO18/12 f18.
25. Snelling and Barron, 'The Colonial Office and its permanent officials 1801–1914'.
26. J. Stirling, London, to Lord Goderich, 5 Feb. 1833, CO18/12 f28.
27. ibid.
28. Lord Goderich to Capt. Stirling, 8 March 1833, CO 397/2.
29. This was a precursor to the Glenelg Regulations applied in the colonies in 1837.
30. Lord Goderich to Capt. Stirling, 8 March 1833, CO397/2.
31. ibid.
32. See Lord FitzRoy Somerset, Horse Guards, to Hay, 9 July 1832, CO18/11 f18. This refers to a letter from Stirling stating that the original 63rd detachment was undermanned due to the large number of women allowed to accompany them, and requesting a larger force.
33. Lord Goderich to Stirling, 8 March 1833, CO397/2.
34. See Pike (ed.), *ADB,* Gouger entry, pp. 461–2.
35. Robert Gouger & Co., 148 Leadenhall St, to Lord Goderich, 9 Feb. 1833, CO18/13 f239.
36. Memorial from Friends, 18 May 1833. Signatories: Richard Hinds, 13 Henrietta St, Brunswick Square (son in the colony); Thomas Bland, 43 Bedford Row (brother ditto); Edward T. Richardson, 60 Lincolns Inn Fields (cousin ditto); Henry Manning, 251 High Holborn (brother ditto); Samuel Bickley, at Lloyds (son ditto); Thomas Habgood, 16 Hatton Gardens (two sons in the colony), CO18/13 f182.
37. T. Bland, 43 Bedford Row, to Hon. E. G. Stanley, Colonial Office, 28 May 1833. CO318/13 f181.
38. Wakefield, *England and America.*
39. Hay to Robert L. Calvert, Mill Hill, 22 Feb. 1833, CO397/3.
40. *Perth Gazette,* 27 July 1833.
41. H. L. Wickham, Downing Street, to Hay, CO323/171 f544.
42. Sir Richard Spencer, Lyme Regis, Dorset, to J. Barrow, Admiralty, 9 Nov. 1829, CapS197, ADM1/2557.
43. Spencer, 22 Arundel St, Strand, to Hay, 1 March 1833, CO18/13 f376.
44. Hay to Spencer, 11 March 1833, CO397/3.
45. Spencer, Salopian Coffee Lounge, Charing Cross, to Hay, 14 March 1833, CO18/13 f378.
46. Spencer, Lyme Regis, Dorset, to Hay, 25 March 1833, CO18/13 f382.
47. Hay to Sir Herbert Taylor, 29 March 1833, CO324/93 f295.

48. Sir Herbert Taylor, Windsor Castle, to Hay, 31 March 1833, CO323/171 f497.

49. As first Earl of Ripon, he is best remembered in Australia through the Ripon (Land) Regulations—see Devereux W. Jones, *Prosperity Robinson: The life of Viscount Goderich 1782–1859.*

50. See *London Gazette*, 31 May 1833, order from the Lord Chamberlain's office.

51. *The Times* and *Morning Chronicle*, 4 April 1833.

52. The *London Gazette*, 4 April 1833.

53. ibid., 3 April 1833.

54. Geoffrey Blackburn, *The Children's Friend Society*, pp. 1–2.

55. ibid., p. 3.

56. ibid., p. 19.

57. Family lore. The smaller of the two sideboards in the dining room at Government House, Perth is thought to be one of these pieces.

58. James Stirling, London, to R. W. Hay, 6 May 1833, CO18/12 f84.

59. Sir George Murray, 5 Belgrave Sq., to Hay, 8 May 1833, CO323/171 f178, 'I have always considered Capt. Stirling to be an honourable and an intelligent man, but before replying to the enclosed, I should like to know whether the same opinion is entertained respecting him at the Colonial Office. G Murray.' (9 May, answered that Sir J Stirling was looked upon favourably by the Department.)

60. James Stirling, London, to Hay, 6 May 1833, CO18/12 f84 (annotated 7 May: 'half allowance may be granted to take Governor out in merchant ship'. Treasury written to 9 May).

61. *The Mangles Story*, Chap. 4.

62. Frank Broeze, 'British Intercontinental Shipping and Australia', p. 199.

63. Announced in the *Perth Gazette*, 28 June 1834.

64. J. Stirling, Guildford, to Hay, 22 May 1833, CO18/12 f88.

65. ibid.

66. W. T. Dance, late Commander of HMS *Sulphur*, 13 Caroline Place, Regent's Park, to R. W. Hay, 4 June 1833, CO20/13 f222.

67. Dance, 6 Woodland Place, Lisson Grove, London, to J. Stirling, ?? Mar. 1833 ('not dated, postmark 14 March 1833', copy).

68. J. Stirling, London, to Dance, 18 March 1833 (copy), encl. no. 15, CO18/12 f132.

69. Dance, 6 Woodlands Place, Lisson Grove, to the Under Secretary of State, 9 Feb. 1833, CO20/13 f216 (9 March, copy to Admiralty).

70. J. Stirling, London, to Hay, 18 June 1833, CO18/12 f98.

71. Horace Twiss, 5 Park Place, to Hay, 29 June 1833, CO18/13 f424.

72. J. Stirling, London, to Hay, 28 June 1833, CO18/12 f140.

73. ibid., 22 June 1833, CO18/12 f134.

74. ibid., 28 June 1833, CO18/12 f140.

75. *The Times*, 23 June 1833.

76. The cup now resides in the Western Australian Museum, having been presented to the State in 1925 by the Grant-Thorold family, descendants of Stirling's daughter Anna. Subscribers to the cup were *(committee starred)*: Bland Dr Grasham; Bland Rev. W. H.; *Bland Thomas; *Bickley Samuel; *Bishop George; Brockman Rev. Thomas; Brockman Rev. J. D.; Brockman C.; Brockman R.; Bussell Mrs; Carter Miss; Calvert Will; Camfield ?; Christ J. G.; *Cross Joseph; Davy ?; Dutherraw ?; Green ?; *Gouger Robert; *Habgood Thomas; Habgood Thomas jun.; Hardey William sen.; Hardy ??;

*Hinds Richard; Horne Edward; Hutt William MP; Kelham William; Levey S.; Levi Isaac; *Manning J.; Moore Joseph; Murray Sir George Bart; *Richardson Edward T.; Rice J. Howard; Samson Lewis; Sears Thomas; Stone John; Taylor Patrick; *Turner George; Wake R.; Whatley Joseph; Whatley Richard; Waylin Robert; Weir Edwin; Webber Robert; Wittenoom Charles Dirk; Willis J. S.; Yates ?.

77. *Perth Gazette*, 26 April 1834 (taken from the *Observer*).
78. J. Stewart, Treasury, to R. W. Hay, Colonial Office, 27 May 1833, CO18/13 f74.
79. Stirling, Guildford, to Hay, 6 Aug. 1833, CO18/13 f150.
80. ibid.
81. J. Stirling, London, to Hay, 26 Sept. 1833, CO18/13 f158.
82. E. G. Stanley, no. 3, to Sir James Stirling, 28 July 1833, CO397/2.
83. J. Stewart, Treasury, to Hay, 13 Sept. 1833, CO18/13 f133.
84. J. Stirling, London, to John Stirling, St Andrews, 27 Sept. 1833, original WAA Acc 351A/MN590.
85. This legend is linked to the first expedition in 1829 (see *The Colonisation of Western Australia by Settlers from Worplesdon and Pirbright in 1829*, BL Acc PR11980), but there is no evidence to support a group of Stirling acquaintances and friends emigrating at that time. It does, however, appear to fit the facts surrounding this second mission.
86. J. Stirling, Duke Street, St James, to Hon. Capt. C. B. Elliot, Sec. Admiralty, 5 Nov. 1833, CapS ADM/2560.
87. J. Stirling, London, to William Stirling, Moseley Street, Manchester, 13 Sept. 1833, WAA Acc 351A/MN590.
88. Agnes at Manchester to John at St Andrews, 20 Jan. 1834 (Lenfestey).
89. There is some confusion regarding Charles Edward's date of birth. His American descendants believe it was 17 January, the English relatives have 24 January, which would seem to fit with Agnes' letter of 20 Jan. 1834.
90. Agnes to John, 20 Jan. 1834 (Lenfestey).
91. Halsey left Henley Park after Anna's death, at first leasing then finally selling it. He married again soon afterwards, leaving Mary's children with the Stirlings.
92. J. Stirling, Portsmouth, to Hay, 9 Feb. 1834 (rec.19 Feb.), CO18/14 f37 (annotated: 'Capt. Irwin to call Tuesday').
93. The details of Daniel and the 21st Regiment can be found in G. Blackburn, *Conquest and Settlement: The 21st Regiment in Western Australia 1833–1840*.
94. Daniel's oaths of office noted in Exec. Council minutes, 14 Sept. 1833.
95. Irwin to Stanley, 19 Feb. 1834 (rec. 3 March), CO18/12 f362.
96. Stanley to Hay (internal), 19 Nov. 1833, CO397/2, 'I must lament that the same judicious course [of imprisonment and release] was not followed after the capture of one of the offenders'.
97. Moore *Diary*, p. 193.
98. ibid., 15 Aug. 1833, p. 206.
99. See Lord FitzRoy Somerset, Horse Guards, to Hay, 9 July 1832, CO18/11 f18 re Stirling's letter.
100. All details in Irwin to Somerset, 12 Feb. 1834, enclosed in Somerset to Colonial Office, 20 Feb. 1834, CO18/14 f221.
101. Hay to Sir Francis Freeling, PMG Portsmouth, 19 Nov. 1833, CO397/3.
102. J. Stirling, Portsmouth, to Hay, 9 Feb. 1834, CO18/14 f37.

CHAPTER 15: A HOUSE AND A BATTLE

1. James Stirling, KGS, to Gov. Arthur, 24 June 1834, *Arthur Papers*, ML A2209, f363. He told Arthur it lasted 32 weeks.
2. Blackburn, *The Children's Friend Society*, cites Mary Bussell's *Diary*, p. 19.
3. *Perth Gazette*, 23 Aug. 1834.
4. Garden, *Albany*, p. 50.
5. See Statham, 'The Economic Development of Swan River Colony,' Appendices 3.7 and 3.9.
6. J. Stirling, KGS, private, to Hay, 23 June 1834 (rec. 5 Jan. 1835), CO18/14 f39.
7. J. Stirling, London, to Arthur, 11 Nov. 1833, *Arthur Papers*, ML A2209, f359.
8. J. Stirling, KGS, to Arthur, 24 June 1834, *Arthur Papers*, ML A2209, f363.
9. Arthur, Hobart, to Gov. Bourke, 10 July 1834, *Bourke Papers*, ML A1926, CY980.
10. *Perth Gazette*, 16 May 1835 (and earlier).
11. J. Stirling, KGS, to Sir R. Spencer, Govt Resident, Albany, 28 June 1834, WARS SDUR/S3/244A.
12. See Survey Dept Registers, WAA Acc 1803, item 1, Plantagenet.
13. *Perth Gazette,* editorial, 23 Aug. 1834.
14. *Perth Gazette*, 'Fremantle address', 23 Aug. 1834.
15. ibid.,'Reply to the Fremantle address'.
16. E. G. Shann, *Cattle Chosen*, pp. 36–7.
17. Shann states in a footnote p. 38 that the wreck when found had already been plundered and the Bussell silver not recovered.
18. *Perth Gazette*, 6 Sept. 1834.
19. Exec. Council minutes, 22 Aug. 1834.
20. *Perth Gazette*, 16 May 1835. Meares then sold the horse to a NSW buyer, but it died in transit.
21. Reported *Perth Gazette*, 30 Aug. 1834.
22. *Perth Gazette,* reply to the Guildford address, 30 Aug. 1834.
23. ibid.
24. Burton Jackson, *Not an Idle Man*, p. 74.
25. Exec. Council minutes, 30 Aug. 1834.
26. See 'Proclamation' in the *Perth Gazette*, 6 Sept. 1834.
27. Exec. Council minutes, 30 Aug. 1834.
28. Erickson, *The Drummonds of Hawthornden*, p. 13, citing Australian Letters 1834–51 vol. LXXIII, no. 106 from Kew Royal Botanical Gardens Library.
29. Exec. Council minutes, 30 Aug. 1834.
30. ibid.
31. Attached Paper to the Exec. Council minutes of 30 Aug. 1834.
32. Erickson, p. 13, citing WAACSO33, 1834/216.
33. ibid.
34. Erickson, p. 14, citing Kew Gardens Library, vol. LXXIII, no. 106, AJCP M732.
35. See J. Stirling, no. 2, to Hay, 14 Sept. 1834 (rec. 2 Feb. 1835), CO18/14 f43. Moore refused the initially offered £200 but took £300.
36. Exec. Council minutes, 2 Sept. 1834.
37. See J. Stirling, no. 6, to Hay, 18 Sept. 1834 (rec. 2 Feb. 1835), CO18/14 f79 re. Govt House.
38. *Perth Gazette*, 20 Sept. 1834.

39. ibid., 6 Sept. 1834.
40. *Trigg Letters,* WAA1584A.
41. *Perth Gazette,* Govt Notice and report, 13 Sept. 1834.
42. Hasluck, *Thomas Peel*, p. 48.
43. *Perth Gazette*, 13 Sept. 1834.
44. Exec. Council minutes, 30 Sept. 1834.
45. *Perth Gazette,* report on Leg. Council meetings, 27 Sept. 1834.
46. Hasluck, p. 150.
47. *Perth Gazette*, Letter to the Editor from Seymour G. Meares, 10 July 1868.
48. J. Stirling, no. 14, to Stanley, 1 Nov. 1834 (rec. 28 May 1835), CO18/14 f134.
49. Mrs Peel and two children had arrived on the *Quebec Trader* in April 1834.
50. *Perth Gazette*, 6 Sept. 1834.
51. Moore *Diary*, pp. 231, 232 and 234.
52. See *Perth Gazette*, 18 Oct. 1834.
53. Moore *Diary*, p. 234.
54. ibid., p. 235.
55. *Perth Gazette*, 16 Oct. 1834.
56. ibid.
57. *Perth Gazette*, editorial, 16 Oct. 1834.
58. J. Stirling, no. 14, to Stanley, 1 Nov. 1834, CO18/14 f134.
59. See Blackburn, *Conquest and Settlement*, p. 51.
60. *Perth Gazette,* 25 Oct. 1834.
61. ibid.
62. Hasluck, p. 154.
63. There is also an account by William Burgess, who was not present but spoke to many who were, in the *Perth Gazette*, 3 July 1868.
64. Early settlers referred to the Swan River tribe and the Guildford tribe, the Murray men and the Mountain men. With the exception of the latter they appear to be talking about tribes people collectively known since the 1950s as 'Nyungars'.
65. Natalie Contos and Theo A. Kearing, *Pinjarra Massacre: Site Research and Development Project.*
66. This historiography is traced in P. Statham, 'James Stirling and Pinjarra: A battle in more ways than one', *Studies in Western Australian History.*
67. See H. Reynolds, *The other side of the Frontier, With the White People, Why weren't we told?,* and *An Indelible Stain.*
68. See Battye, *Western Australia,* p. 133; Daisy Bates' 1926 'Causes and Consequences of the Battle of Pinjarra' in P. Bridge (ed.), *Aboriginal Perth: Bibbulman Biographies & Legends by Daisy Bates*; Paul Hasluck, *Black Australians A Survey of Native Policy in Western Australia 1829–97,* pp. 183–91; Uren, *Land Looking West,* pp. 226–31; Frank Crowley, *Australia's Western Third,* p. 30; Hasluck, *Thomas Peel,* pp. 152–60; C. T. Stannage, *The People of Perth,* p. 42; Ronald Richards, *The Murray District of Western Australia—A History,* Chaps 5 & 6.
69. Neville Green, *Aborigines and White Settlers in the 19th Century*; Chap. 3 of C. T. Stannage, *A New History of Western Australia*; and his own book, *Broken Spears: Aboriginals and Europeans in the Southwest of Australia.*
70. J. Stirling, no. 14, to Stanley, 1 Nov. 1834 (rec. 28 May 1835), CO18/14 f134.
71. J. S. Roe's Registered Fieldbook no. 3, 28 Oct. 1834.

72. ibid.

73. J. Stirling to Stanley, 26 Nov. 1834, CO18/14 f149.

74. Contos/Kearing, *Pinjarra Massacre*, p. 41.

75. ibid., p. 42.

76. ibid.

77. *Macquarie Dictionary*, 1981.

78. Contos/Kearing, p. 1.

79. *Perth Gazette*, 8 Nov. 1834, p. 1.

80. ibid., 25 April 1835. See also the *West Australian*, 25 Aug. 1999.

81. Contos/Kearing, p. 34.

82. ibid., part 2, titled 'In Search of Sites', looks at information concerning the actual site of the massacre and then at the results of various archaeological surveys.

83. Sylvia Hallam and Louis Tilbrook, *Aborigines of the South-West Region*, Introduction; and Louis Tilbrook, *Nyungar Tradition*, pp. 7–8.

84. *Perth Gazette*, Letter to Editor by Seymour Meares, 10 July 1868.

85. Blackburn, *Conquest and Settlement*. Blackburn is an expert in the use of antique firearms and has carefully researched the nature of guns used at the time; see ftn. 25 to Chap. 5, pp. 69–70 which includes an analysis of the guns introduced by Stirling in 1834.

86. Blackburn, p. 57.

87. J. Stirling, Perth, to Gov. Arthur, 29 Dec. 1834, *Arthur Papers*, A2209, f371.

88. *Perth Gazette,* 1 Nov. 1834.

89. ibid.

90. Moore *Diary*, 3 Nov. 1834.

91. *Perth Gazette*, 22 Nov. 1834.

92. Daisy Bates on Pinjarra in the *Western Mail*, 5 Aug. 1926.

93. Later found to be caused by poisoning from eating *Oxylobium*, a native shrub.

94. Moore *Diary*, p. 245.

95. *Perth Gazette*, 15 Nov. 1834.

96. He confirmed this in writing to Roe on 17 Nov. See WAA SDUR/3/286.

97. Stirling would have met Macleay in 1827 as he had been Secretary to Gov. Darling. See entry in *ADB* vol. 2, p. 177.

98. J. Stirling, WA, to Hon. Alexander Macleay, Sydney, 2 Dec. 1834, *Macleay Correspondence*.

99. Moore *Diary*, p. 239.

100. Exec. Council minutes, 16 Nov. 1834.

101. Leg. Council meeting, 26 Sept. 1834. The bill was read for the third time.

102. Stirling to Macleay, Sydney, 2 Dec. 1834, *Macleay Correspondence*.

103. *Perth Gazette*, 8 Nov. 1834.

104. Stirling, no. 21, to Stanley, 3 Dec. 1834 (rec. 28 May 1835), CO18/14 f197 encloses a petition to the Secretary of State from certain persons settled at KGS.

105. *Perth Gazette*, 13 Dec. 1834, 'False and Malicious Statements relative to this colony' in Gouger's article on the proposed colony of South Australia.

106. Hasluck, *Thomas Peel*, pp. 158–9.

107. Moore *Diary*, p. 252.

CHAPTER 16: A MORE STABLE STATE

1. J. Stirling, no. 24 to Spring-Rice, 1 Jan. 1835 (rec. 20 Jun.), CO18/15 f3 (annotated: 'Copy sent to Treasury 11 Sep 1835').

2. Draft reply, 16 May 1837, appended to 1 Jan. 1835, JS no. 24 to Spring-Rice (rec. 20 Jun.), CO18/15 f3.

3. J. Stirling, no. 25 to Hay, 1 Jan. 1835 (duplicate), CO18/15 f14.

4. J. Stirling, no. 26 to Spring-Rice, 2 Jan. 1835 (rec. 20 June), CO18/15 f18 (Quarantine Regulations) in JS no. 27 to Hay, 2 Jan. 1835, CO18/15 f20. Debts due to the Crown by Mr Brown in JS no. 28 to Spring-Rice, 3 Jan. 1835 (rec. 20 June), CO18/15 f28.

5. *Perth Gazette,* 31 Jan. 1835.

6. Turner, *Turners of Augusta,* p. 116.

7. Garden, *Albany,* p. 60.

8. ibid., p. 61.

9. Moore *Diary,* p. 254.

10. The meeting on 16 Feb. was fully reported in the *Perth Gazette,* 21 Feb. 1835.

11. P. Statham, *The Tanner Letters,* p. xvi.

12. *Perth Gazette,* 21 Feb. 1835. Committee comprised W. Andrews, W. Trimmer, D. Thompson, M. McDermott, W. Burgess, J. Hardey, M. Clarkson, A. Waylen, W. Samson, T. Walters, G. Leake, T. Yule, W. Brockman, J. Phillips, Major Nairn, H. Trigg, S. Knight and J. Morrell.

13. J. Stirling, unofficial, to Hay, 10 March 1835 (rec. 26 Aug.), CO18/15 f43.

14. Moore *Diary,* p. 255.

15. A memorial had been sent to all colonies in Nov. 1824 giving details of the uniforms to be worn by all colonial officers—it was blue with red facings and Stirling wished it adopted by his councillors, CO854/1.

16. J. Stirling, no. 35 to Hay, 13 Mar. 1835 (rec. 19 Oct.), CO18/15 f47 (annotated: 'Wants enclosure. 29 Feb. Copy to Treasury letter to Treasury of 10 Oct. 1836').

17. Draft letter to A. Y. Spearman, Treasury, Downing St, Sept 1836, appended to JS no. 35 to Hay, 13 March 1835 (rec. 19 Oct.), CO18/15 f47.

18. J. Stirling, WA, to Alexander Macleay, 21 March 1835, *Macleay Correspondence.*

19. He eventually sold his stallion 'Grey Leg' for £300 to Captain Meares who did send him to Sydney. See *Perth Gazette,* 3 Oct. 1835.

20. Moore *Diary* pp. 258–9.

21. *Perth Gazette,* 4 April 1835, report of Leg. Council proceedings.

22. ibid., 5 April 1835, Governor's Address.

23. J. Stirling, no. 79, to Aberdeen, 15 Oct. 1835 (rec. 8 June), CO18/15 f352.

24. *Perth Gazette,* 8 Aug. 1835.

25. Exec. Council minutes, 11 April 1835. Stirling, Daniel, Brown and Roe.

26. Exec. Council minutes, 16 April 1835, and adjourned meeting 21 April.

27. Enclosure to JS no. 45 to Spring-Rice, 7 May 1835 (rec. 28 Jan. 1836), CO18/15 f159.

28. *Perth Gazette,* 5 April 1835, cricket match.

29. J. Stirling, no. 49 to Aberdeen, 6 July 1835 (rec. 28 Jan.), CO18/15 f239.

30. Impey to Colonial Office, CO18/16 f529, and memorial, CO18/16 f542.

31. Walter Stirling, London, to brother John, St Andrews, 30 March 1836, WAA Acc 449A/MN595.

32. J. Stirling, WA, to Gov. Arthur, 19 Sept. 1835, *Arthur Papers,* ML A2209, f375.

33. *Perth Gazette*, 8 Aug. 1835.
34. Gingling was a popular game played at English county fairs when blindfolded competitors tried to catch a bellringing leader. In the Foundation Day version at Swan River they also pushed wheelbarrows.
35. *Perth Gazette,* 6 June 1835.
36. Exec. Council minutes, 7 June 1835. Stirling, Brown, Roe and Moore.
37. McKail only went as far as Albany where he went into business. T. Austen, *A Cry in the Wind: Conflict in Western Australia 1829–1929,* p. 23.
38. Exec. Council minutes, 18 Aug. 1834, and Austen, p. 23.
39. Exec. Council minutes, 28 Aug. 1835.
40. Ogle, *The Colony of Western Australia*, Appendix on land allocations.
41. Moore *Diary*, 10 Oct 1835, p. 280.
42. James Stirling to brother John, St Andrews, Scotland, 6 Aug. 1835. Original ML A4144, typescript WAA Acc 449A/MN595.
43. *Perth Gazette,* 17 Oct. 1835.
44. J. Stirling to Hay, 14 Aug. 1835 (rec. 11 Feb.), CO18/15 f319.
45. *Perth Gazette,* 12 Dec. 1835.
46. Moore *Diary*, p. 280.
47. J. Stirling, no. 84 to Glenelg, 19 Dec. 1835 (rec. 8 June), CO18/15 f431.
48. *Perth Gazette,* 7 Nov. 1835.
49. ibid., 26 Dec. 1835.
50. Garden, *Albany*, p. 63.
51. *Perth Gazette,* 12 Dec. 1835.
52. J. Stirling to Roe, 8 Dec. 1835, WASR SDUR/S3/262.
53. *Perth Gazette,* 28 Nov. 1835.
54. ibid., 26 Dec. 1835.
55. Statham, Jan. 1835, pp. 115–17.
56. *Perth Gazette,* 28 Nov. 1835.
57. J. Stirling to Irwin, 22 Dec. 1835, extracts from CO18/17 f239.
58. Dorothea to John Stirling at St Andrews, 1 Jan. 1835 (Lenfestey).
59. Walter Stirling, London, to brother John, St Andrews, 30 March 1836, WAA Acc 449A/MN595.
60. Statement of Expenditures and receipts connected with the Administration of the Govt of WA between 11 Sept. 1828 and 30 June 1837 (Stirling's own A/c).
61. Walter Stirling, London, to John, St Andrews, 30 March 1836, WAA Acc 449A/MN595 —comment from Mrs Donaldson.
62. *Perth Gazette,* 16 Jan. 1836.
63. These figures were cited again in J. Stirling, no. 127 to Glenelg, 12 July 1836 (rec. 16 Jan. 1837), CO18/16 f239.
64. J. Stirling, no. 97 to Hay, 21 Jan. 1836 (rec. 8 June), CO18/16 f72.
65. Annotation to 21 Jan. 1836, J. Stirling no. 97 to Hay (rec. 8 June), CO18/16 f72.
66. J. Stirling, no. 101 to Hay, 19 Feb. 1835 (rec. 17 Nov.), CO18/16 f108.
67. Annotation to 19 Feb. 1835, J. Stirling no. 101 to Hay, CO18/16 f108.
68. J. Stirling, no. 96 to Glenelg, 20 Jan. 1836 (rec. 8 June), CO18/16 f27.
69. J. Stirling, no. 104 to Glenelg, 20 Feb. 1836 (rec. 17 Nov.), CO18/16 f122.
70. Annotation to 20 Feb. 1836, JS no. 104 to Glenelg, CO18/16 f122.
71. WAS SDUR/S3/263, 2 Feb. 1836.

72. *Perth Gazette*, 20 Feb. 1836.
73. ibid., 19 Mar. 1836.
74. ibid., 9 April 1836.

CHAPTER 17: DISSENSION AND EXPLORATION

1. *Perth Gazette,* 26 March 1836.
2. ibid.
3. *Perth Gazette,* 16 April 1836.
4. J. Stirling, no. 44 to Spring-Rice, April 1835 (rec. 28 Jan), CO18/15 f124 and Stirling no. 79 to Aberdeen, 15 Oct. 1835 (rec. 8 June), CO18/15 f352.
5. Stirling's estimates for 1836, CO18/16 f347.
6. £479. This was made up of £383 for horses, the rest for a Superintendent of Police.
7. *Perth Gazette*, 23 April 1836. Councillors' total expenditure estimate (which also included certain salaries) was £4,175, some £481 less than the Governor's.
8. Moore *Diary*, p. 300.
9. *Perth Gazette*, 21 May 1836. Mrs Roe had given birth to a son the previous month.
10. *Perth Gazette*, 26 April 1836. Arrived on the *Maria* from Launceston and Port Phillip.
11. *Perth Gazette,* 18 June 1836.
12. Exec. Council minutes, 30 June 1836. Gov., Commdt, Col. Sec., AG and SG.
13. Lt H. W. Bunbury, *Early Days in WA*, letter dated York, 10 July 1836, p. 27.
14. Bunbury, p. 30.
15. Lord Hill, Horse Guards, to Stanley, 11 March 1834, CO18/14, f233, and Irwin to George Grey, 14 Nov. 1836, CO18/17 f237.
16. Stirling, Swan River, to Capt. F. C. Irwin, c/-Messrs Mangles, Austin Friars, London, 1 April 1836, *Irwin Letters*, BL Private Archives Stack ACC910A.
17. Lord Hill, Horse Guards, to Glenelg, 9 June 1836, CO 18/17 f7.
18. Stirling, no. 127, to Glenelg, 12 July 1836 (rec. 16 Jan), CO18/16 f239 (ans. 7 March 1837).
19. ibid.
20. Draft reply appended to Stirling, no. 127 to Glenelg, 12 July 1836, CO18/16 f239.
21. W. Tanner at Calne to Glenelg, 25 May 1836, CO18/17 f320.
22. Stirling, no. 128, to Glenelg, 13 July 1836 (rec. 16 Jan. 1837), CO18/16 f261 (ans. 7 March 1837).
23. *Perth Gazette*, 4 June 1836.
24. ibid., 21 May 1836.
25. Extract from a dispatch dated 23 July 1835 in *Perth Gazette*, 30 July 1836.
26. *Perth Gazette*, 30 July 1836.
27. W. Nairn Clark to Sec. of State, 11 July 1836, re. new bill, 6th William IV no. 1, allowing admission to certain legal practitioners, AJCP36.
28. Annotation on Stirling no. 134 to Glenelg, 13 July 1836, CO18/16 f422.
29. Stirling no. 137 to Glenelg, 26 Aug. 1836 (rec. 25 April), CO18/16 f445.
30. Although Treasury Bills paid no interest, they were not subject to discount and were exchangeable anywhere in the British Empire, and accepted by most ship captains, so they were usually sought after by importers.
31. Annotation to Stirling no. 137 to Glenelg, 26 Aug. 1836, CO18/16 f445.
32. Henry Reynolds, *This Whispering in our Hearts,* p. 84.

33. Moore *Diary*, p. 303.

34. Stirling no. 139 to Glenelg, 26 Aug. 1836 (rec. 25 April), CO18/16 f455.

35. Reynolds, p. 86.

36. Biblical quotation from Joshua 24:27.

37. *Perth Gazette*, 8 Sept. 1836.

38. Stirling no. 125 to Glenelg, 5 July 1836 (rec. 16 Jan.), CO18/16 f230 (land returns for the quarter to June 1836).

39. Stirling no. 143 to Glenelg, 29 Aug. 1836 (rec. 25 April), CO18/16 f509.

40. Annotations to Stirling no. 143 to Glenelg, 29 Aug. 1836, CO18/16 f509.

41. *Swan River Guardian*, 29 Dec. 1836.

42. Stirling no. 144 to Glenelg, 29 Aug. 1836, CO18/16 f518.

43. Irwin to Glenelg, 27 May 1835 (rec. 2 June), CO18/15 f531.

44. Stirling may also have discussed the idea of northern settlement with George W. S. Earle who arrived in the colony in 1830 and went to Augusta (leaving in 1832 for Port Essington, and thereafter to champion similar ideas)

45. Stirling no. 144 to Glenelg, 29 Aug. 1836, CO18/16 f518 (f523 draft reply May 1837).

46. F. C. Irwin, *The State & Position of Western Australia*, Chap. 7.

47. *Perth Gazette,* 14 Jan. 1837.

48. D. R. Hainsworth, *The Sydney Traders,* Chaps 9 and 10.

49. *Perth Gazette*, 27 Aug. 1837.

50. J. Stirling no. 153 to Glenelg, 3 Nov. 1836 (rec. 25 April), CO18/16 f548.

51. Annotation to J. Stirling no. 153 to Glenelg, 3 Nov.1836, CO18/16 f548.

52. *Perth Gazette*, 17 Sept. 1836.

53. As reported in the Exec. Council minutes, 13 Sept. 1836.

54. See A. G. L. Shaw, 'The Founding of Melbourne', pp. 208–12.

55. Exec. Council minutes, 13 Sept. 1836.

56. *Perth Gazette,* 1 Oct. 1836.

57. ibid., 29 Oct. 1836.

58. ibid., 21 Jan. 1837, sketch of the year 1836.

59. ibid., 20 Oct. 1836.

60. ibid*.,* 10 Nov. 1836.

61. ibid*.,* 3 Nov. 1836.

62. ibid*.,* 1 Dec. 1836.

63. Exec. Council minutes, 11 Nov. 1836. Gov., Commdt and Col. Sec.

64. Stirling no. 160 to Glenelg, 16 Nov. 1836 (rec. 20 April), CO18/16 f621.

65. Stirling to Surveyor-General Roe, 23 Dec. 1836, WAA SR SDUR/S3/273.

66. Exec. Council minutes, 24 Dec. 1836.

67. *Perth Gazette*, 3 Dec. 1836.

68. ibid., 10 Dec. 1836.

69. Stirling no. 177 to Glenelg, 13 Feb. 1837 (rec. 2 Oct.), CO18/18 f21.

70. Net loss of 25. See Stannage (ed.), *A New History of Western Australia,* p. 189.

71. See annotation to Stirling no. 177 to Glenelg, 13 Feb. 1837, CO18/18 f21.

72. Stirling no. 177 to Glenelg, 13 Feb. 1837, CO18/18 f21.

CHAPTER 18: SIGNS OF PROSPERITY

1. Issued 30 Dec. 1836, printed in the *Swan River Guardian*, 5 Jan. 1837.
2. *Perth Gazette*, 21 Jan. 1837.
3. Exec. Council minutes, 13 Jan. 1837, CO20/2.
4. Exec. Council minutes, 3 Feb. 1837. Gov., Commdt, Col. Sec., SG, AG.
5. *Swan River Guardian*, 16 Feb. 1837.
6. Pike (ed.), *ADB* vol. 1, entry for Darling, pp. 285-6.
7. J. Stirling no. 181 to Glenelg, 15 March 1837 (rec. 23 Oct.), CO18/18 f53.
8. Stirling no. 186 to Glenelg, 18 March 1837 (rec. 23 Oct.), CO18/18 f106.
9. Stirling no. 187 to Glenelg, 19 March 1837 (rec. 23 Oct.), CO18/18 f122.
10. Stirling no. 185 to Glenelg, 17 March 1837 (rec. 23 Oct.), CO18/18 f102.
11. Dispatch no. 17 dated 15 Aug. 1837.
12. Stirling no. 192 to Glenelg, 26 March 1837 (rec. 23 Oct.), CO18/18 f145.
13. Memo attached to Stirling no. 192 to Glenelg, 26 March 1837, CO18/18 f151, 'You had offered him the vacancy of Asst. Civil Architect in Mauritius, but he doubted his ability to fill it as he has not had an education as an architect, having only been employed in surveying. GG'. 25 Nov. 'Yes, appoint Ommanney'.
14. Prospectus in the *Perth Gazette,* 21 Jan. 1837.
15. *Perth Gazette*, Sketch of Occurrences in 1837, 3 Feb. 1838.
16. *Perth Gazette*, 21 Jan. 1837.
17. Exec. Council minutes, 27 March 1837. Gov., Commdt, Col. Sec., SG, AG.
18. Two such instances are given in the *Perth Gazette,* 1 April 1837.
19. Neither Reveley's nor Kingsford's water had proved effective, see *Perth Gazette*, 28 April 1837, and P. M. Hasluck, 'Early Mills of Perth'.
20. *Perth Gazette*, 17 Feb. 1838.
21. Exec. Council minutes, 10 May 1837.
22. *Perth Gazette,* 22 April 1837.
23. Exec. Council minutes, 27 March 1837. Gov., Commdt, Col. Sec., SG, AG.
24. *Perth Gazette,* 29 April 1837.
25. ibid., report 6 May 1837.
26. Moore *Diary*, 6 May, p. 307 and Exec. Council minutes, 10 May 1837.
27. Exec. Council minutes, 10 May 1837. Gov., Commdt, Col. Sec., SG, AG.
28. See W. McNair/H. Rumley, *Pioneer Aboriginal Mission: The work of Wesleyan Missionary John Smithies*, and E. J. Storman, *The Salvado Memoirs*.
29. Ruth Johnson, *The Tranby Hardys*.
30. Exec. Council minutes, 19 May 1837. Gov., Commdt, Col. Sec., SG, AG.
31. *Perth Gazette*, 26 May 1837.
32. Moore *Diary*, late May, pp. 309–10.
33. *Swan River Guardian*, 15 June 1837.
34. *Perth Gazette,* 10 June 1837.
35. Exec. Council minutes, 6 June 1837. Gov., Commdt, Col. Sec., SG, AG.
36. Stirling no. 198 to Glenelg, 15 June 1837 (rec. 20 March), CO18/18 f178 (copies to Board of Admiralty, 28 Mar 1838. extract for Ship Owners' Society).
37. See annotations to Stirling no. 198 to Glenelg, 15 June 1837, CO18/18 f178.
38. CO18/18 f190 and 191.
39. *Perth Gazette*, 10 June 1837.

40. ibid.
41. Exec. Council minutes, 22 June 1837. Gov., Commdt, Col. Sec., SG, AG.
42. Exec. Council minutes, 22 June 1837.
43. *Perth Gazette*, editorial, 24 June 1837.
44. *Perth Gazette*, transcript of Leg. Council meeting, 1 July 1837.
45. *Perth Gazette*, editorial, 24 June 1837.
46. Moore *Diary*, just before 18 June 1837, p. 314.
47. ibid., p. 314.
48. *Perth Gazette,* Shipping Intelligence, 8 July 1837.
49. Moore *Diary*, pp. 316–17.
50. *Swan River Guardian,* 6 July 1837.
51. *Government Gazette,* 22 June 1839. See also P. Joske, C. Jeffrey & L. Hoffman, *Rottnest Island, A Documentary History*, p. 29.
52. Exec. Council minutes, 11 July 1837. Gov., Commdt, Col. Sec., AG.
53. Exec. Council minutes, 14 July 1837. Gov., Commdt, Col. Sec., SG, AG.
54. *Perth Gazette*, 15 July 1837.
55. ibid., editorial on natives, 12 Aug. 1837.
56. ibid., 29 July 1837.
57. ibid., 22 July 1837. Govt Notice dated 21 July 1837.
58. *Perth Gazette,* editorial, 22 July 1837.
59. *Swan River Guardian,* 27 July 1837.
60. *Perth Gazette,* 12 Aug. 1837.
61. *Swan River Guardian*, 3 Aug. 1837.
62. *Perth Gazette*, 5 Aug. 1837.
63. *Swan River Guardian,* 21 Sept. 1837.
64. Exec. Council minutes, 17 Aug. 1837.
65. ibid.
66. *Perth Gazette*, 19 Aug. 1837.
67. ibid., 12 Aug. 1837.
68. ibid., 27 Aug. 1837.
69. ibid., 26 Aug. 1837.

CHAPTER 19: GLENELG REGULATIONS

1. Exec. Council minutes, 1 Sep 1837, CO20/2. Gov., Commdt, Col. Sec., SG, AG.
2. Exec. Council minutes, 11 Sep 1837.
3. ibid.
4. Irwin was one of the founders of the Western Australian Association in London whose chairman was Mr Charles Mangles.
5. The *Swan River Guardian,* 14 Sept 1837, maintained that the Surveyor-General, the Commissary, the Colonial Surgeon, Mr Lamb, Captain Bannister, Mr Spofforth and Mr Trimmer were not present.
6. *Perth Gazette*, 9 Sept. 1837.
7. ibid.
8. *Swan River Guardian*, 14 Sept. 1837.

9.   *Perth Gazette*, 9 Sept. 1837.

10. ibid.

11. *Swan River Guardian,* 14 Sept. 1837.

12. *Perth Gazette,* 2 Sept. 1837.

13. Exec. Council minutes, 8 Sept. 1837.

14. ibid.

15. Old regulations published in *Government Gazette,* 12 Sept., and *Perth Gazette,* 16 Sept. 1837.

16. *Perth Gazette,* 30 Sept. 1837, extract from the *Government Gazette* and editorial.

17. Stirling to Surveyor-General Roe, 13 Sept. 1837, WAAMN1294 Acc 698A and 4165A.

18. Surveyor-General Roe to Stirling, 17 Sept. 1837, WAAMN1294 Acc 698A and 4165A.

19. Stirling no. 209 to Glenelg, 2 Oct. 1837 (rec. 20 March), CO18/18 f256.

20. Draft reply appended to Stirling no. 209 to Glenelg, 2 Oct. 1837, CO18/18 f256-8.

21. Sir R. Spencer, Albany, to Glenelg, 10 Nov. 1837 (rec. 23 May), CO18/19 f295 (annotated: 'Answered 30 May 1838').

22. Stirling no. 212 to Glenelg, 6 Oct. 1837 (rec. 7 June), CO18/18 f278.

23. Statham, 'The Economic Development of Swan River Colony 1829-1850', effect of the Glenelg regulations, pp. 217 and 219.

24. Stirling no. 212 to Glenelg, 6 Oct. 1837, CO18/18 f278.

25. *Perth Gazette,* 7 Oct. 1837.

26. Stirling no. 216 to Glenelg, 12 Oct. 1837 (rec. 4 June), CO18/18.

27. Stirling to Glenelg, 12 Oct. 1837, CO18/18 (annotation f306 memo on 1094).

28. *Perth Gazette*, 21 Oct 1837.

29. ibid., 18 Nov. 1837.

30. *Swan River Guardian*, 29 June 1837.

31. Stirling no. 222 to Glenelg, 3 Nov. 1837 (rec. 7 June), CO18/18 f320.

32. Annotation to Stirling no. 222 to Glenelg, 3 Nov. 1837, CO18/18 f320, f322.

33. *Perth Gazette*, 11 Nov. 1837.

34. See J. L. Stokes, *Discoveries in Australia…HMS Beagle 1837–43*, p. 49ff.

35. He had visited KGS in 1836 on his return trip to England. See Patrick Armstrong, *Charles Darwin in Western Australia.*

36. Stokes, p. 51.

37. Proclamation dated 18 Nov. 1837 in the *Perth Gazette*, 25 Nov. 1837.

38. *Perth Gazette*, 18 Nov. 1837.

39. ibid., 25 Nov. 1837 and *Swan River Guardian,* 21 Dec. 1837.

40. Moore *Diary*, 9 Dec. 1837, p. 333.

41. *Perth Gazette*, 2 Dec. 1837.

42. ibid., 23 Dec. 1837.

43. ibid., 2 Dec. 1837, cites *Hampshire Telegraph,* 15 July 1837 as source.

44. *Perth Gazette*, 23 Dec. 1837.

45. J. Backhouse, *A Visit to the Australian Colonies,* p. 530.

46. *Perth Gazette*, 23 Dec. 1837.

47. Stirling no. 233 to Glenelg, 29 Dec. 1837 (rec. 8 June), CO18/18 f575. Acknowledges Dispatch 61, 19 June 1837.

48. Stirling no. 233 to Glenelg, 29 Dec. 1837, CO18/18 f575.

49. *Perth Gazette,* 8 Sept. 1837.

50. Backhouse, p. 532.

51. *Perth Gazette,* 6 Jan. 1838.

52. ibid., 20 Jan. 1838.

53. ibid.

54. ibid.

55. See Shann, *Cattle Chosen,* Chap. vii.

56. Shann, Chap. vii, p. 107, Bessie Bussell's diary, 19 July 1837, 'Three women, one man and one boy are known to be dead but more are supposed to be dying'; also p. 111, Charles Bussell, the affair 'did not, however meet with the entire approbation of the Government'.

57. *Perth Gazette,* 20 Jan. 1838.

58. Battye, *Western Australia,* p. 397, and Statham, *Dictionary,* p. 293.

59. Exec. Council minutes, 26 Jan. 1838. Gov., Commdt, Col. Sec., SG and AG.

CHAPTER 20: PENULTIMATE CONCERNS

1. J. Stirling no. 10 to Glenelg, 1 Feb. 1838 (rec. 18 June), CO18/20 f61–63.

2. Net immigration had been +1 in 1837 and there were only 788 adult males, a figure that would drop to 622 in 1839. See Statham, Ph.D thesis, Appended Tables, p. 229.

3. Stirling no. 10 to Glenelg, 1 Feb. 1838, CO18/20 f61 and f63.

4. *Perth Gazette,* 27 Jan. 1838.

5. ibid., 3 Feb. 1838.

6. ibid., editorial, 10 Feb. 1838.

7. ibid., 7 April 1838.

8. Clark did return some months later but eventually left permanently for Tasmania where he died in 1854. Pike (ed.), *ADB,* vol 1, p. 227.

9. Memorandum (459) 16 March 1838, Land of Sir James Stirling in WA, WASR SDO/1/f314.

10. Stirling to Surveyor-General Roe, 14 March 1838 (no. 3373), WASR SDUR/S3/284.

11. *Perth Gazette,* 24 March 1838.

12. Moore *Diary,* p. 340.

13. *Perth Gazette,* 14 April 1838.

14. Exec. Council minutes, 20 April 1838. Gov., Commdt, Col. Sec., SG, AG.

15. Exec. Council minutes, 18 April 1838. Gov., Commdt, Col. Sec., SG, AG.

16. Exec. Council minutes, 20 April 1838.

17. *Perth Gazette,* 5 May 1838.

18. ibid., 28 April 1838.

19. ibid., 12 May 1838.

20. The two exceptions 'of an unexpected description' were a disallowed claim on the parliamentary grant, and funding for the new church.

21. *Perth Gazette,* 19 May 1838.

22. ibid., 9 June 1838.

23. ibid.

24. *Perth Gazette,* 2 June 1838.

25. Moore *Diary,* 3 June, p. 350.

26. Moore *Diary,* 7 June, p. 351.

27. *Perth Gazette,* 9 June 1838, 'A considerable time was spent by them…following a labyrinth of rivers which brought them back to their starting place, with one of their party, Mr Grey, seriously wounded…We must observe that if [their expenditure] had

been placed at the disposal of Sir James Stirling for a similar purpose far more satisfactory results might have been realised'.

28. *Perth Gazette*, 9 June 1838.
29. Exec. Council minutes, 14 June 1838. Gov., Commdt, SG and AG.
30. R. Thomson to Gov. Stirling, 18 June 1838, CSO 62/679.
31. Joske et. al., *Rottnest Island*, p. 25.
32. *Perth Gazette,* 25 Aug. 1838, and also Welsh to Col. Sec., 27 Aug. 1838, CSO 62/229.
33. Moore *Diary*, 26 Aug., p. 359.
34. Exec. Council minutes, 15 June 1838. If Thomson wanted the whole compensation in land, he would get a remission ticket for two square miles or 1,280 acres.
35. *Perth Gazette,* 16 June 1838.
36. Stirling no. 18 to Glenelg, 18 June 1838 (rec. 1 Dec.), CO18/20 f90.
37. Annotation to Stirling no. 18 to Glenelg, 18 June 1838, CO18/20 f90
38. Stirling no. 19 to Glenelg, 19 June 1838 (rec. 16 Feb. 1839), CO18/20 f94.
39. Moore *Diary*, 16 July p 354.
40. *Perth Gazette*, 14 July 1838.
41. Memorandum by Sir James Stirling to Surveyor-General Roe (3377), 19 July 1838, WASR /S3/287 (annotated: 'Sir James Stirling: Selection of 4,000 acres of land, in lieu of same quantity originally selected on west side, Geographe Bay. 2,000 acres on Preston River assigned 23 July 1840').
42. Exec. Council minutes, 31 July 1838. Gov., Commdt, Col. Sec., SG and AG.
43. *Perth Gazette,* 28 July 1838.
44. Exec. Council minutes, 3 Aug. 1838. Gov., Commdt, Col. Sec., SG and AG.
45. This would have been either Mary or Sarah Maria, the two eldest daughters of Thomas Helms. Statham, *Dictionary*, p. 152.
46. Exec. Council minutes, 3 Aug. 1838. Gov., Commdt, Col. Sec., SG and AG.
47. Moore *Diary*, p. 358, and *Perth Gazette*, 4 Aug. 1838.
48. Stirling to Surveyor-General Roe (3380), 13 Aug. 1838, WASR SDUR/S3/288.
49. Exec. Council minutes, 15 and 16 Aug. 1838. Gov., Commdt, Col. Sec., SG and AG.
50. *Perth Gazette,* 25 Aug. 1838.
51. Dr James Crichton and wife arrived on the *Joshua Carroll* from London, 2 Nov. 1836.
52. Bolton/Joske, *History of Perth Hospital*, pp. 7–8.
53. *Perth Gazette*, 15 Sept. 1838.
54. Bolton/Joske, p. 8.
55. B. C. Cohan, *A History of Medicine in Western Australia*. Dr Harrison was the only surviving private practitioner and he was at KGS. A number of private medical men arrived between 1839 and 1843.
56. Exec. Council minutes, 22 Aug. 1838. Gov., Commdt, Col. Sec., SG and AG.
57. ibid.
58. See Crowley, 'Master and Servant in WA', pp. 96–7, and Proclamation, 17 Nov. 1829 and 26 March 1830, WAA/CSF 1b/217ff 2/82–85.
59. Stirling no. 28 to Glenelg, 1 Sept. 1838, CO18/20 f156.
60. George Elliot was the son of Matilda Elliot née Halsey, elder sister of William Halsey and therefore a nephew to James' sister Mary. (George Elliot's mother Matilda died June 1828 and Mary Halsey in 1834.)
61. Moore *Diary*, 3 Sept. 1838.
62. *Perth Gazette*, 8 Sept. 1838.

63. ibid.
64. The strength of the military at this time numbered some 118 men, plus 19 women and 50 children. See Statham Ph.D thesis, Appendix 3.9, The Military Establishment in Western Australia 1829–1850.
65. *Perth Gazette*, 15 Sept. 1838.
66. Workforce occupational breakdown in *Perth Gazette*, 2 June 1838.
67. *Perth Gazette,* 15 Sept. 1838.
68. Exec. Council minutes, 20 Sept. 1838.
69. *Perth Gazette*, 22 Sept. 1838.
70. Moore *Diary*, p. 362.
71. Stirling no. 32 to Glenelg, 30 Sept. 1838 (rec. 8 Feb.), CO18/20 f230.
72. ibid.
73. Annotation to Stirling to Glenelg, 30 Sept. 1838, CO18/20 draft reply f 234.
74. Stirling no. 33 duplicate to Glenelg, 30 Sept. 1838, CO18/20 f238.
75. Stirling no. 33 to Glenelg, 30 Sept. 1838, CO18/20 f238 (annotated: 'copy to Admiralty 20 June 1839').
76. ibid.
77. The report and f234, Stirling's lengthy commentary, was eventually tabled in the British Parliamentary Papers.
78. Grey's annotation to Stirling no. 33 to Glenelg, 30 Sept. 1838, CO18/20 f243, plus memo on f245 (praise of Stirling's statistics).
79. Henry Labouchere replaced Grey on 23 Feb. 1839.
80. *Perth Gazette,* 13 Oct. 1838.
81. ibid., 13, 20 and 27 Oct. 1838.
82. ibid., 13 Oct. 1838.
83. Wakefield's *England and America* had been widely read in the colony and his criticisms of Swan River in that publication bitterly resented.
84. Moore *Diary*, 11 Oct., p. 362.
85. Memo by Surveyor-General Roe c. 10 Oct. 1838, WASR SDUR/S3/289.
86. Erickson, *Old Toodyay and Newcastle,* p. 25.
87. The grant was left to William's sisters Isabella Stirling, Margaret Stewart Stirling and Elizabeth Agnes Stirling, see WAA Cons 1800, memorial vol. 2 no. 111, 1 March 1841, Deed Poll 15 June 1840.
88. Oct. 1838 (WASR CSR vol. 63 no. 78) memorial to Gov. Stirling published *Perth Gazette*, 13 Oct. 1838. Thirty-two signatures including L. Samson, G. F. Moore, J. S. Roe, J. Chipper, H. W. Reveley, A. H. Stone, Peter Brown, C. McFaull, W. Armstrong, J. B. Wittenoom, G. Shenton, H. Trigg, R. Habgood, W. B. Andrews, G. Leake etc.
89. Exec. Council minutes, 17 Oct. 1838. Gov., Commdt, Col. Sec, SG and AG
90. ibid.
91. *Perth Gazette,* 20 Oct. 1838.
92. Stirling no. 41 to Glenelg, 3 Dec. 1838 (rec. 22 April), CO18/20 f317 (annotated: 'copy to Board of Trade; Shipowners Society; Western Australian Association 7 May 1839').
93. Blue books and Statham, Ph.D Appendices.
94. Stirling no. 41 to Glenelg, 3 Dec. 1838, CO18/20 f317.
95. *Perth Gazette,* 10 Nov. 1838.
96. She had even promised to deliver Georgiana Molloy's boxes of seeds and plants. See Hasluck, *Portrait with Background,* p. 179.

CHAPTER 21: A YEAR OF TRANSITION

1. Moore *Diary*, p. 365.
2. *Perth Gazette*, 8 Dec. 1838.
3. ibid., 3 Nov. 1838.
4. Moore *Diary*, p. 364.
5. *Perth Gazette*, 3 Nov. 1838.
6. Stirling no. 37 to Glenelg, 30 Nov. 1838 (rec. 22 April), CO18/20 f287.
7. *Perth Gazette*, 3 Nov. 1838 gives details of Brockman's failed speculation in India.
8. *Perth Gazette*, 17 Nov. 1838.
9. The Viveashes were relatives of the Tanners. See Statham, *The Tanner Letters*, Introduction, and P. Cowan, *A Faithful Picture: the letters of Eliza and Thomas Brown*, Introduction.
10. *Perth Gazette*, 8 Dec. 1838.
11. ibid., 15 Dec. 1838.
12. Moore *Diary*, pp. 368–9.
13. ibid., p. 369.
14. Exec. Council minutes, 24 Dec. 1838. Gov., Commdt, Col. Sec., SG, AG.
15. ibid., 31 Dec. 1838.
16. ibid.
17. Exec. Council minutes, 31 Dec. 1838. Gov., Commdt, Col. Sec., SG, AG.
18. Stirling no. 46 to Glenelg, 31 Dec. 1838 (rec. 1 June), CO18/20 f349.
19. *Perth Gazette*, 5 Jan. 1839.
20. ibid.
21. Moore *Diary*, p. 372.
22. ibid.
23. *Perth Gazette*, 5 Jan. 1839.
24. Conveyed personally by Stirling to the Colonial Office.
25. Passenger list from *South African Commercial Advertiser*, 2 March 1839, and details from Statham, *Dictionary of Western Australians*.
26. Statham, *Dictionary*.
27. *South African Commercial Advertiser*, 2 March 1839, announced that on 24 Feb. the *Champion*, Captain Dring, had arrived in Simon's Bay.
28. Sir James Stirling, CGH, to Glenelg, 1 March 1839 (rec. 1 June), CO18/24 f401.
29. Annotation to Stirling to Glenelg, 1 March 1839, CO18/24 f401.
30. Colonial Office to Stirling, 13 Aug. 1839, CO18/24 f409.
31. *Perth Gazette*, 17 Aug. 1839. The name of the ship and dates for leaving the Cape or arriving in England are unknown.
32. *Mangles Story*, p. 14, and memorial in Wyke Church. James Mangles died 25 Sept. 1838.
33. Frederick Mangles to cousin, 31 May 1839. See *Mangles Story*, pp. 17–18.
34. *The Times*, 31 May 1839.
35. J. Stirling, 39 Duke St, to Stephen, 31 May 1839 (rec. 1 June), CO18/24 f411.
36. Baring, Treasury, to James Stephen, 3 June 1839 (rec. 4 June), CO18/24 f86, 'Did his return take place under circumstances as would entitle him to the payment of passage allowance at public expense?' (Annotated: '4 June. answer in the affirmative. JS. done 10 June').

37. Thomas Bannister, Trafalgar Square, to Lord Normanby, 4 June 1839 (rec. 5 June), CO18/24 f166 (annotated: 'Copy to Sir J Stirling, 22 Aug. Ans. 20 June').

38. Colonel P. A. Latour, 38 Harley St, Cavendish Square, to Labouchere, Colonial Office, 8 June 1839 (rec. 10 June), CO18/24 f327.

39. ibid.

40. Note on Colonial Office file, 11 June 1839, CO18/23 f431.

41. Sir James Stirling, 39 Duke St, St James, to Labouchere, 22 June 1839 (rec. 24 June), CO18/24 f428 (annotated: '25 June. See Note of this date on No. 1246').

42. Draft letter from Labouchere to Colonel Latour, 3 July 1839, CO18/24 f331.

43. Stirling, 39 Duke St, to Lord Normanby, 30 June 1839 (rec. 1 July), CO18/24 f437.

44. ibid. Annotated 1 and 6 July 1839.

45. Draft note re Sir James Stirling, 5 July 1839, CO18/24 f439 (annotated: 'Sir Jas Stirling's claims to Land. No copy').

46. William Hutt, 51 Conduit St, to Labouchere, Colonial Office, 6 July 1839, CO18/24 f235 (annotated: 'Copy to Governor 5 Oct. Referred to Mr Elliot 10 July with Proposals').

47. ibid.

48. Lord John Russell, Colonial Office, to Hutt, 19 Mar. 1840, WA inward dispatches.

49. See Statham, Ph.D thesis, p. 264 (Land Surrenders 1840).

50. *Inquirer*, 12 May 1841.

51. James Stirling, Woodbridge, Guildford to Labouchere, Colonial Office, 17 July 1839 (rec. 19 July), CO18/24 f 449 (annotated: 'Copy to Treasury 27 Nov 39').

52. Stirling, Woodbridge, to Labouchere, 26 July 1839 (rec. 27 July), CO18/24 f33. (Ans. 29 Aug 1839. Copy to Treasury, 27 Nov 1839.)

53. J. Knight to Labouchere, 14 Aug. 1839 (rec. 16 Aug.), CO18/24 f255.

54. Draft reply to Sir James Stirling, 29 Aug. 1839, CO18/24, f399 (stamped 'Forwarded Mr Gairdner 7th; Mr Stephen 7th, Marquis of Normanby 27th Aug.').

55. ibid.

56. J. Knight to Lord John Russell, 9 Sept. 1839 (rec. 13 Sept.), CO18/24 f261 & f265.

57. Sir James Stirling, Woodbridge, to Russell, 25 Sept. 1839 (rec. 28 Sept.), CO18/24 f461.

58. ibid.

59. J. Stirling, London, to Russell, 2 Oct. 1839 (rec. 7 Oct.), CO18/24 f473.

60. Note on WA, CO18/23, c f477.

61. J. Stirling, London, to Rt Hon. Richard M. O'Ferrall, Secretary, Admiralty, 24 Oct. 1839 (rec. 2 Nov.), CapS463 ADM1/2567.

CHAPTER 22: THE AUSTRALIND VENTURE

1. J. Knight to R. Vernon Smith, Colonial Office, 1 Jan. 1840, CO18/26 f233 & f333.

2. Knight to Vernon Smith, 16 Jan. 1840 (rec. 7 Jan.), CO18/26 f238 (sic 338), and Knight to Vernon Smith, 25 Jan. 1840 (rec. 27 Jan.), CO18/26 f243 (sic 343).

3. Garden, *Albany*, p. 67.

4. James Stirling, 34 Harley St, to Lord John Russell, Colonial Office, 3 Feb. 1840, CO18/26 f203 (sic 403). Annotated: 'Ansd. 13 Feb. 1840'.

5. Statham, *Dictionary of Western Australians*, p. 316, and Pike (ed.), *ADB* vol. 2, p. 465.

6. George Russo, *A Friend Indeed: Louisa Clifton of Australind WA*, p. 52.

7. WA Company Board minutes, 9 March 1840. BL Acc 336A/33, minutes of Board of Directors, 9 March – 27 Oct 1840.

8. Stirling, 34 Harley St, to Vernon Smith, 20 March 1840 (rec. 21 May), CO18/26 f206 (sic 406). Annotated: '21 March letter to Treasury'.

9. Vernon Smith to James Stirling, 25 March 1840, CO397/4 f364.

10. Vernon Smith to Knight, 4 April 1840, CO397/4 f365, draft CO18/26 f40.

11. C. E. Trevelyan, Treasury, to James Stephen, Colonial Office, 23 April 1840 (rec. 23 April), CO18/26 f49, and Vernon Smith to James Stirling, 30 April 1840, CO397/4 f369, draft at CO18/26 f30.

12. Stirling, 34 Harley St, to Lord John Russell, 7 May 1840, CO18/26 f209 (sic 409). Annotated: '15 May and 15 June copy to Treasury'.

13. ibid.

14. Vernon Smith to Stirling, 15 May 1840, CO397/4 f375 draft, CO18/26 f211 (sic 411).

15. Chairman, William Hutt MP; Deputy-Chairman, John Chapman; Directors, Thomas H. Brooking, Captain Sweeny RN, Edward Gibbon Wakefield, Henry Buckle, Charles Enderby, Jacob Montefiore, James Irving, George Robert Smith MP; Secretary, Thomas John Buckle; Solicitors, Messrs Few, Hamilton & Few; Bankers, Messrs Wright & Co., Smith, Payne & Co.; Chief Commissioner (WA), M. Waller Clifton Esq. FRS.

16. Marshall Waller Clifton, Series I, Journals A1, Foundation of the Company in 1841, BL MN1294 Acc 4165A (hereafter *Clifton Papers* 4165A).

17. *Clifton Papers*, 4165A.

18. Peter Burroughs, *Britain and Australia 1831–1855*, p. 352.

19. Stirling, 34 Harley St, to Lord John Russell, 3 June 1840 (rec. 6 June), CO18/26 f228 (sic 428).

20. Walter Stirling, Manchester, to his niece Dorothea, 16 June 1840 (Lenfestey).

21. James Stirling, London, to John Stirling, St Andrews, 27 Aug. 1840, original WAA Acc 351A/MN590.

22. Russo, p. 84.

23. Anna's exact birth date cannot be found. The 1841 census states she was born in London and she was baptised at Stoke Church, Guildford, on 29 Sept. 1840.

24. Vernon Smith to Stirling, 17 Aug. 1840, CO18/26 f393, draft at CO18/26 f112.

25. Stirling, 34 Harley St, to Vernon Smith, 19 Aug. 1840, CO18/26 f230 (sic 430).

26. Vernon Smith to Stirling, 29 Aug. 1840, CO397/6 f1, draft at CO18/26 f231 (sic 431).

27. Memo 18 Sept. 1840 from Sir James Stephen to Lord John Russell, *Russell Papers*, PRO30/24/4C f87, see also Gov. Gipps to Colonial Office, 25 March 1840 (rec. 17 Aug.), CO209/6 f66, (reporting that Hobson, NZ, had suffered partial paralysis).

28. James Stirling to John Stirling, 16 Oct. 1840, original WAA Acc 351A/MN590.

29. Russo, from Clifton's diary, p. 106.

30. ibid.

31. Letter of 21 Sept. to Vernon Smith enclosed in C. E. Trevelyan, Treasury, to James Stephen, 24 Nov. 1840, CO18/26 f142.

32. ibid.

33. Stirling's letter of 21 Sept. 1840 is out of order in the Colonial Office papers, has no forwarding note, and is enclosed with the reply written in November. See above.

34. Stoke Church baptismal records.

35. *Perth Gazette,* 2 May 1840.

36. Vernon Smith to E? Prothero, 26 Sept. 1840, CO397/6 f14.

37. Memo by James Stephen, 14 Oct. 1840, CO18/26, f204.

38. 15 Oct. 1840 Hutt: memo for Lord John Russell, CO18/26 f156.

39. Annotation to memo by James Stephen, 15 Oct. 1840, CO18/26 f204.

40. Colonial Office minute, 16 Oct. 1840, CO18/26 f212.

41. ibid.

42. See Charles Staples, *They Made their Destiny*, p. 56.

43. The Arrowsmith River does not appear on maps—Gantheaume Bay is just above Kalbarri.

44. J. Buckton, Western Australian Company, 6 Adelphi Terrace, to Lord John Russell, 20 Oct. 1840 (rec. 21 Oct.), CO18/26 f160 (annotated: '22 Dec. copy to Land Board').

45. Vernon Smith to Buckton, 21 Oct. 1840, CO397/6 f20, draft at CO18/26 f162.

46. WA Co. Board Minutes, 9 March 1840, BL Acc 336A/33, minutes of meetings of the Board of Directors, 22 Oct 1840–9 Feb 1841.

47. Buckton, Western Australia House, 6 Adelphi Terrace, to Lord John Russell, 23 Oct. 1840 (rec. 24 Oct.), CO18/26 f171.

48. Buckton to Vernon Smith, 4 Nov. 1840 (rec. 5 Nov.), CO18/26 f177.

49. WA Co. Board minutes, 12 Nov. 1840, *Clifton Papers*, 4165A.

50. ibid.

51. ibid.

52. Captain's Log, HMS *Indus*, ADM51/3616.

53. Marshall Waller Clifton was born 1787, arrived March 1841 with wife Elinor and eleven of his fourteen children. See Statham, *Dictionary*, p. 60.

54. See M. Burgess, 'The Australind Settlement', in the 1926 *Report of the Meeting of the Australian Association for the Advancement of Science*, pp. 484–5; also Peter Burroughs, *Britain and Australia*, pp. 349–50.

55. Russo cites Louisa Clifton's diary, p. 127.

56. ibid., p. 149.

57. See law case in the *Inquirer*, Mangles vs Scott, 7 Aug. 1878.

58. See Wellington Locations ACC1803, item 1, and maps 1893 S22 45/16 298C.

CHAPTER 23: THIRD COMMAND HMS *INDUS*

1. M. E. Chamberlain, *Pax Britannica British Foreign Policy 1789–1914*, p. 75.

2. J. Clarke, *British Diplomacy and Foreign Policy 1782–1865*, pp. 197–207.

3. C. J. Bartlett, *Great Britain and Sea Power 1815–1853*, p. 3.

4. Concern about the trend to larger ships in foreign navies led the government to make provision in the estimates for 1840 for the construction of several larger (first- and second-rated) ships. Bartlett, p. 136.

5. HMS *Indus* Description Book, 1840–44, ADM38/8364.

6. Captain's Log, HMS *Indus*, 2 Nov. 1840 to 1844, ADM51/3616.

7. Captain James Stirling RN, HMS *Indus,* Portsmouth, to Lord John Russell, 18 Jan. 1841 (rec. 20 Jan.), CO18/30 f271B.

8. J. Vernon Smith, Colonial Office, to Stirling, ? 1841, CO 397/6 f46, draft CO18/30 f275.

9. Captain's Log of HMS *Indus*, ADM51/3616.

10. ibid.

11. James Stirling, United Services Club, to Russell, 7 May 1841 (rec. 8 May), CO18/30 f283.

12. Entries in Pike (ed.), *ADB 1788–1850*, reveal that of the early Australian governors, Phillip had no criticism and no pension but became an Admiral of the Blue. Hunter was recalled to face criticism, but eventually given a pension of £300. Brisbane left under a cloud and was made a GCB in 1837, more for his services to astronomy. Darling was made a GCH in 1835 after being cleared by a Select Committee of Enquiry. Macquarie was criticised deeply by Bigge but finally granted a pension of £1,000 in 1824—though he did not live to receive it. Arthur was recalled in Jan. 1836 amid intense criticism of his land deals and treatment of Aborigines, but was cleared to be made a KH and sent as Lt Gov. to Canada.

13. Stirling, London, to J. Stephen, Colonial Office, 7 May 1841 (rec. 8 May), CO18/30 f231.

14. Vernon Smith to Stirling, 2 May 1841, CO397/6 f76, draft CO18/30 f285.

15. HMS *Indus* Description Book, ADM38/8364.

16. Stirling, Portsmouth, to Russell, 5 July 1841 (rec.7 July), CO18/30 f287.

17. Stirling, Portsmouth, to Russell, 22 July 1841 (rec. 23 July), CO18/30 f291.

18. Vernon Smith to Stirling, 9 Aug. 1841, CO397/6 f95, draft CO18/30 f293.

19. Journal of Rear Admiral Sir J. Ommanney, C-in-C Mediterranean, 12 Sept. 1841 (hereafter *Ommanney's Journal*), ADM50/205.

20. Convention of the Straits: France joined the Quadruple Alliance with regard to Turkey (agreeing that Mehemet Ali could retain Egypt as a hereditary possession, and Southern Syria for life, as long as he surrendered Northern Syria to Turkey and gave up Crete).

21. Clarke, p. 207.

22. *Ommanney's Journal*, 23 Sept. 1841, ADM50/205.

23. Harold Acton, *The Last of the Bourbons of Naples,* pp. 137–8.

24. Partly due to Palmerston's replacement as Foreign Sec. by Aberdeen from July 1841 elections.

25. James Stirling, HMS *Indus*, Malta, to Lord Stanley, 20 Oct. 1841 (rec. Nov 10), CO18/30 f295.

26. G. W. Hope, Colonial Office, to Stirling, 23 Nov. 1841, CO397/6 f122, draft CO18/30 f301.

27. Edith Slatter, *Xanthus: Travels of Discovery in Turkey*, p. 6.

28. Vice Admiral Owen, HMS *Queen*, Malta, no. 146, confidential to Henry Herbert MP, Admiralty, 8 March 1841. Enclosed 2 (copy) Owen, HMS *Queen* at Malta, no. 281, confidential to Captain Sir James Stirling, HMS *Indus*, 1 March 1844, ADM1/5540.

29. Owen, HMS *Queen* at Malta, no. 295, confidential to Captain Sir James Stirling, HMS *Indus*, 5 Mar 1844 (rec. 6 Apr 1844), ADM1/5540, N219.

30. Maria di Gloria was daughter of absentee Portuguese King Dom Pedro, who was living in Brazil.

31. Commander Coffin to R. M. O'Ferrall, Admiralty, 10 June 1843, FO63/537.

32. Admiralty to Foreign Office, 3 Jan. 1842, FO63/558, encl. Captain and Senior Officer, James Stirling, HMS *Indus* in the Tagus, to the Hon. Sidney Herbert MP, Admiralty, 31 Jan. 1842, FO63/558.

33. Baptismal record at St George's Church. No exact date of birth for this child, but the 1851 census cites January in Lisbon.

34. James Stirling, HMS *Indus*, in the Tagus, to Lord Stanley, 17 Jan. 1842 (rec. 25 Jan.), CO18/33 f407.

35. *Murray Papers,* National Library of Scotland, MS 46.9.13, pp. 78–9.

36. G. W. Hope to Stirling, 9 Feb. 1842, CO397/6 f145, draft CO18/33 f409.

37. Stirling on the *Indus* in the Tagus to Sidney Herbert, Foreign Office, 7 Feb. 1842, FO63/558 f51361, also 13 Feb.1842, Admiralty to Foreign Office, FO63/558.

38. Foreign office to Admiralty, 12 Feb. 1842, draft letter, FO63/558.

39. Admiralty to Foreign Office, 21 Feb. 1842, FO63/588, enclosing report from James Stirling, Captain and Senior Officer, HMS *Indus* in the Tagus, to the Hon. Sidney Herbert MP, Admiralty, 14 Feb. 1842.

40. Captain's Log, HMS *Indus*, ADM 51/3616.

41. WA Co. to Captain Sir James Stirling RN, HMS *Indus*, Mediterranean, 26 Jan. 1842, BL Acc 336A/329; Colonial Letter Book (London) 12 May 1840 – 10 May 1861, p. 136.

42. WA Co. to Captain Sir James Stirling RN, HMS *Indus*, Mediterranean, 25 Feb. 1842. BL Acc 336A/329; Colonial Letter Book, p. 140.

43. James Stirling, HMS *Indus* on the Tagus, to Lord Stanley MP, 9 May 1842 (rec. 16 May), CO18/33 f411.

44. See, for example, Few, Hamilton & Few to Colonial Office, 9 March 1842, CO18/33 f317; G. W. Hope, Colonial Office, to Few, Hamilton & Few, Henrietta St, Covent Garden, 23 March 1842, CO397/6 f157 (draft reply CO18/33 f319); Few, Hamilton & Few to Hope, 24 March 1842 (rec. 26 March), CO18/33 f321.

45. Journal of Vice Admiral Owen (hereafter *Owen's Journal*), 13 and 14 Aug. 1842 Inwards, ADM50/212.

46. 'Journal of the proceedings of Vice Admiral Sir Edward Owen, Commander in Chief on the Mediterranean Station 15 Oct 1841 to 29 Sep 1845'), Admiralty no. 266 noted in Inwards, 1 Oct. 1842, ADM50/212.

47. G. W. Hope to Stirling, 6 June 1842, CO397/6 f175, draft CO18/33 f421.

48. FO195/199 draft letter from Canning to Admiral Owen, 27 Nov. 1842.

49. Slatter, pp. 58–9.

50. ibid., p. 60.

51. ibid.

52. Stirling, HMS *Indus*, Smyrna, to Canning, 27 Dec. 1842, FO195/199.

53. ibid., 28 Dec. 1842.

54. Owen, HMS *Queen* at Malta, to Canning, 21 Jan. 1843, FO195/199.

55. Captain's Log, HMS *Indus*, 26 Jan. 1843, ADM51/3616.

56. Stirling, HMS *Indus* at Athens, 1 Feb. 1843 (rec. 18 March), CO18/36 f365.

57. Annotation to 1 Feb. 1843 J. Stirling, *Indus* at Athens (rec. 18 March), CO18/36 f365.

58. *Owen's Journal*, 1 March 1843 Outwards, ADM50/212.

59. R. Seton Watson, *Britain in Europe 1789–1914*, p. 235.

60. Stirling on the *Indus*, Piraeus, to John Stirling, Cornbrook Bank, Manchester, 10 Feb. 1843, original WAA Acc 351A/MN590.

61. Stirling, HMS *Indus*, Athens, to Stanley, 3 March 1843 (rec. 24 March), CO18/36 f374.

62. CO18/36 f376.

63. CO18/36 f370 draft reply, 30 March 1843.

64. Captain's Log, HMS *Indus*, April–May 1843, ADM51/3616.

65. Acton, p. 157.

66. *Owen's Journal*, 15 Aug. 1843 Outwards, ADM50/212.

67. ibid., 27 Aug. 1843 Outwards.

68. *Owen's Journal*, 5 Sept. 1843 Inwards, ADM50/212.

69. ibid., 23 Sept. 1843 Inwards.

70. Slatter, p. 201.

71. Douglas Dakin, *The Unification of Greece 1770–1923*, p. 76.

72. Watson, pp. 234–5.

73. Vice Admiral Owen, HMS *Formidable* at Malta, no. 312 to Sidney Herbert MP, Secretary of the Admiralty, 25 May 1844 (rec. 13 July), ADM1/5540 N410.

74. *Owen's Journal*, 29 Nov. 1843 Outward, 'to J. Stirling, no. 1692, enclosing gold medal', ADM50/212.

75. Information about the Order of the Redeemer was supplied by the Ministry of Foreign Affairs Protocol Department and the Embassy of Greece, Canberra, and thanks to Adam Adaminides for confirming Stirling's receipt of this award. The award was made on 11 May 1844.

76. Lord Aberdeen, Foreign Office, no. 49, to Sir Edmund Lyons, Athens, 2 July 1844, FO286/102.

77. Enclosure no. 5. Owen, HMS *Queen* at Malta, confidential, to HE Sir Edmund Lyons, HM Minister at Athens, 5 March 1844, ADM1/5540 N219 (rec. 6 April 1844).

78. Captain's Log, HMS *Indus*, 4 April 1844, ADM51/3616.

79. ibid.

CHAPTER 24: A GENTLEMAN'S ESTATE

1. Messrs Baxendale, Tatham, Upton & Johnson, 7 Great Winchester St, to Lord Stanley, 27 June 1844 (rec. 23 June), CO18/38, f198.

2. G. W. Hope, Colonial Office, to Baxendale & Co., CO397/6 f305.

3. Daniel Scott, 33 Mark Lane, to Colonial Office, 19 July 1844 (rec. 20 July), CO18/38 f305.

4. Enclosed in Daniel Scott, 33 Mark Lane, to Colonial Office, 19 July 1844, CO18/38 f305.

5. A. Hillman, 'Plan of Arthur's Head, showing the improvements made by Fremantle Whaling Company, 1838'. Map: Fremantle 19c (author's possession).

6. Daniel Scott to Colonial Office, 19 July 1844, CO18/38 f310, memorandum, 17 Oct. 1844 (annotated).

7. James Stephen, Colonial Office, to Daniel Scott, 2 Nov. 1844, CO397/6 f326.

8. Sir Charles Napier had purchased Quallets Grove (later Merchistoun Hall) near Horndean, some 4 miles direct from Belmont. His cousin, General Sir Charles Napier, settled at Oaklands in Bedhampton. I am grateful to John Pile for this and other information which has stemmed from his research into the history of the Belmont Estate. See 'A brief History of Belmont Park and its people' (1998) in the Havant Museum and soon to be published.

9. Pile, p. 11.

10. ibid., p. 8.

11. James Stirling to John Stirling, Sept. 1844, original WAA Acc 351A/MN590.

12. Petition dated 12 Dec. 1844 (rec. 17 Dec.), CO18/38, f265.

13. Draft reply, 30 Dec. 1844, CO18/38 f268.

14. White's 'Dictionary of Hampshire and the Isle of Wight', 1859, Hampshire County Council, pp. 360–1.

15. Prospectus for the sale of Belmont in 1911, courtesy John Pile and Havant Museum.

16. James Stirling, Belmont, to Walter Stirling, May 1845, original WAA Acc 351A/MN590.

17. Mrs Boyd was Andrew's housekeeper and had been mentioned in a letter from James to his family, 2 April 1831, so was an old retainer.

18. *Perth Gazette,* 9 Nov. 1844.

19. ibid.

20. Andrew's death certificate is Guildford 142 of 1844, Registrar's Office, Perth.

21. Apparently icterus (jaundice) can be caused by the germ leptospirosis which is carried by animals, including horses, and can be caught through contact with their urine or tissue—a tenuous link.

22. James Stirling, Belmont, to John Stirling, 15 May 1845, original WAA Acc 351A/MN590. (NB, handwriting looks like '5' but content makes it clear it was 15 May.)

23. Baxendale & Co. to Lord Stanley, 14 Jan. 1845, CO18/41 f190.

24. Hope to Baxendale & Co., 31 Jan. 1845, CO397/6 f343.

25. James Stirling, United Services Club, to James Stephen, 'unofficial', 31 Jan. 1845 (rec. 1 Feb.), CO18/41 f255.

26. Annotation on Stirling to Stephen, 'unofficial', 31 Jan. 1845, CO18/41 f255.

27. Alfred Waylen, 5 Mark Lane, to James Stephen, 5 Feb. 1845 (rec. 7 Feb.), CO18/41 f279.

28. Hope to Alfred Waylen, 13 Feb. 1845, CO397/6 f349.

29. Waylen to Lord Stanley, 21 Feb. 1845 (rec. 24 Feb.), CO18/41 f283, encl. f285 (copy) J. Stirling to A. Waylen of the Fremantle Whaling Company.

30. Hope to Waylen, 28 Feb. 1845, CO397/6 f351.

31. Waylen to Hope, 4 March 1845 (rec. 6 March), CO18/41 f291 (annotated: 'answered & copy to the Land Board, 14 March').

32. Baxendale & Co. to Lord Stanley, 10 March 1845 (rec. 12 March), CO18/41 f204.

33. ibid.

34. Annotations to Baxendale & Co. to Lord Stanley, 10 March 1845, CO18/41 f204.

35. Waylen to Lord Stanley, 17 March 1845 (rec. 19 March), CO18/41 f295 (annotated: 'copy to Land Board 27th March. 12 June further letter').

36. Hope to Waylen, 27 March 1845, CO397/6 f359.

37. Baxendale & Co. to Lord Stanley, 21 May 1845 (rec. 22 May), CO18/41 f209.

38. Hope to Baxendale & Co., 31 May 1845, CO396/6 f373.

39. Land Commissioners to James Stephen, 4 June 1845 (rec. 5 June), CO18/41 f102.

40. Annotation to Land Commissioners to Stephen, 4 June 1845, CO18/41 f102.

41. Colonel P. A. Latour, United Services Club, to Stanley, 12 Aug. 1845 (rec. 15 Aug.), CO18/41 f242.

42. Hope to Latour, 21 Aug. 1845, CO397/8 f3.

43. Stirling, Havant, to Lord Stanley, 13 Dec. 1845 (rec. 15 Dec.), CO18/41 f261.

44. Annotation to Stirling to Stanley, 13 Dec. 1845, CO18/41 f261.

45. Surveyor-General Roe to Colonial Secretary, 27 Nov. 1857, WASR SDO/2 ff 278-82.

46. See WASR SDO3 f 442, Surveyor-General's minute, 6 June 1863.

47. Few, Hamilton & Few, Covent Gardens, to T. J. Buckle, Adelphi Tce, 28 Aug. 1840, BL Acc 336A/63/3. WA Company: Letters addressed to the Secretary 1840–71.

48. Burroughs, *Britain and Australia,* p. 353, and A. J. Barker and M. Laurie, *Excellent Connections*, p. 21, and Staples, *They made their Destiny*, p. 145ff.

49. Deed of Sale dated 23 April 1846 at Portsmouth Archives, 115A/1/34.

50. Mortgage papers, Portsmouth Archives, 115A/1/34.

51. *Illustrated London News*, 21 Feb. 1846—a copy of the picture and article can be seen in the vestry of the old St Mary's to this day.

52. See correspondence, Latour to Gladstone, 23 March 1846, CO18/43, and reply 9 June Latour to Gladstone 10 June, and reply 17 June 1846.

53. Frank Broeze, *Mr Brooks and the Australian Trade,* p. 183.

54. Roger Morriss, *Cockburn and the British Navy in Transition*, p. 242.

55. This meant that promotion was still very difficult and even Cockburn had to admit that connections, aristocratic, naval or political, were still of value to those seeking appointments. See Morriss, p. 268.

56. Morriss, p. 237.

57. Bartlett, *Great Britain and Sea Power 1815–1853,* pp. 183–5.

58. ibid., pp. 229-30.

59. ibid., p. 231.

60. Morriss, pp. 276-7.

61. Princess Louisa Fernanda, sister of Isabella II of Spain, had married the Duc de Montpensier, youngest son of King Louis Phillippe, in October—contrary to an undertaking to Lord Aberdeen in 1843.

62. Bartlett, p. 188.

63. H. N. Williams, *The life and letters of Admiral Sir Charles Napier,* p. 220.

64. See Stirling's Service Record, ADM107/41, and Log of HMS *Howe*, ADM53/2694-6.

65. HMS *Howe* Log, 4 May – 1 Nov. 1847, ADM53/2694.

66. Details from Stephen/Lee, *The Dictionary of National Biography.*

67. There was Mr Thomas Baring MP for Huntington 1844–73 and financier, who was connected to Stirling through his brother John's wife's family; Mr John Bright, ex-MP, a friend of Cobden's and founding member of the Anti-Corn Law League; Sir George Clerk, ex-Lord of the Admiralty and MP 1811–1852; Sir Howard Douglas, ex-Colonial Governor (New Brunswick and Ionian Islands), author of works on military fortifications and gunnery; Mr T. Hume, possibly related to the radical reformist and MP, Joseph Hume; Mr John Liddell (later Sir), Inspector of Fleets and Hospitals; Mr George Lyall, MP for the City of London 1833–35 and 1841–47, Chairman of the East India Company from 1841; Mr McCarthy, whose background has not been traced; Mr Thomas Alexander Mitchell, Chairman of the Chartered Bank of India, Australia and China, and MP for Bridport from 1841 until his death; Mr John Lewis Ricardo, son of the famous economist David Ricardo and avid free trader, MP for Stoke-on-Trent 1841–1862; Mr William Thompson, Alderman of the City of London, Chairman of Lloyds and Master of the Ironworkers Company; and finally, although not named in the official list of committeemen but certainly asking questions, Mr Villiers, ex-Colonial Office, MP and Chair of the Reform Club Committee.

68. Sixteen closely typed pages in *British Parliamentary Papers.*

69. Morriss, p. 261.

70. ibid.

71. ibid., pp. 253–5.

72. Broeze, p. 183.

CHAPTER 25: FOURTH COMMAND HMS *HOWE*

1. The Builder's Measure was adopted in 1773 to gauge the tonnage of a ship and was measured as length minus half beam, × beam × half beam divided by 94. The *Indus* had been a two-decker, 2098 BM.

2. Log of HMS *Howe*, 4 May – 1 Nov 1847, ADM53/2694.

3. Williams, *Admiral Sir Charles Napier*, p. 220.

4. Log of HMS *Howe*, entry 2 and 4 Aug. 1847, ADM53/2694.

5. 'Journal of the proceedings of Rear Admiral Sir Charles Napier KCB commanding the Squadron of Evolution 27 July 1847 to 9 Apr 1849' (hereafter *Napier's Journal*), 21 Aug. 1847, ADM50/251.

6. ibid., 27 July 1847–9 April 1849.

7. *The Times*, 'Embarkation of the Queen Dowager', 9 Sept. 1847.

8. *Lisbon 1997 Guidebook*; some interpretations call it 'Arabo-Gothic' or 'the Portuguese Balmoral'.

9. Queen Adelaide, Lisbon to Queen Victoria, 29 Oct. 1847, Royal Archives at Windsor, Vic Y2/128.

10. Sir H. Seymour, Lisbon, no. 411, to Lord Palmerston, 27 Oct. 1847, FO63/657.

11. Log of HMS *Howe*, 27 Oct. 1847, ADM53/2694.

12. The fine gold-plated dress sword and scabbard was one of several made in 1847 by Wilkinson's Prosser (maker to Her Majesty, of Charing Cross, London) and taken with the Queen Dowager for presentations.

13. Stirling's snuff box is now at the WA Museum (item CH3.210), presented by Mr and Mrs Bentson (Stirling's granddaughter) in 1950, and transferred in 1953 from Art Gallery to Museum. Snuff box 5.2 cm × 3.8 cm. Blue glass set in the front with initials.

14. Queen Adelaide, Bay of Funchal, to Queen Victoria, 1 Nov. 1847, RA Vic Y2/129.

15. *Napier's Journal*, 10 Nov. 1847, ADM50/251.

16. ibid., 29 Feb. 1848.

17. ADM50/235 'Journal of the proceedings of Vice Admiral Sir William Parker GCB C-in-C of the Mediterranean Station 1845–48' (hereafter *Parker's Journal*), 17 March, Palermo—from ADM 112 (9th), 'Captain Sir James Stirling of HMS *Howe* a Naval ADC to the Queen'.

18. Napier's son was in command of one of these ships, the steamer *Avenger*, and died in a storm on the way. See Williams, pp. 225–6.

19. J. Stirling, HMS *Howe*, Portsmouth, to Lord Grey, 13 May 1848, CO18/49 f272.

20. Brian H. Fletcher, *Ralph Darling A Governor Maligned*, pp. 334–5.

21. B. Hawes, Colonial Office, to Sir James Stirling, 20 May 1848, CO397/8 f227.

22. *Parker's Journal*, ADM50/235.

23. See Paul Kennedy, *The Rise and Fall of British Naval Mastery*, pp. 196–9.

24. Log of HMS *Howe*, 28 June 1848, ADM53/2696.

25. He remained with the *St Vincent* till April 1849. See ADM196/1 f578.

26. See Service Record, ADM196/1, parts 3 & 4 f578.

27. *Parker's Journal*, 29 July 1848, ADM50/235.

28. ibid., 31 Dec. 1848.

29. ibid., 10 Feb. 1849, Naples.

30. ibid., 26 Sept. 1849.

31. Canning, Therapia, no. 324, to Palmerston, 2 Nov. 1848, FO78/781.

32. Log of HMS *Howe*, 28 Oct. 1849 – 27 April 1850, entry 1 Nov. 1849, ADM53/2699.

33. *Parker's Journal*, 4 and 6 Nov. 1849, ADM50/235.

34. ibid., 8 Nov. 1849.

35. ibid., Dec. 1849.

36. Log of HMS *Howe*, 15–18 Dec. 1849, ADM53/2699.

37. ibid., 18 Dec. 1849.

38. ibid., 28 Dec. 1849.

39. *Parker's Journal,* entry 3 Jan. 1850, ADM50/235.

40. This became known as the Don Pacifico Affair. 'Don Pacifico, a Portuguese Jew with a technical claim to British citizenship, lost property in anti-Semitic riots in Athens in 1847. He appealed to Palmerston for help, Palmerston wanted an excuse for a show-down with the Greeks who had defaulted on the 1831 loan.' M. E. Chamberlain, *Pax Britannica: British Foreign Policy 1789–1914,* p. 98.

41. FO 566/212 Greece 1850–54, 1 Feb. 1–19 3, Letter from King Otho to Lyons, 18 Jan. 1850.

42. *Parker's Journal*, entry 18 Feb. 1850, ADM50/235.

43. ibid., 27 and 29 Jan. 1850.

44. Admiral Parker, *Queen,* in Salamis Bay, no. 36, to Admiralty, 8 Feb. 1850, ADM1/5603, N68.

45. *Parker's Journal,* entry 10 Feb. 1850, ADM50/235,

46. A. W. Ward and G. P. Gooch, *Cambridge History of Foreign Policy 1783–1919,* vol. 2, p. 598.

47. *Parker's Journal*, 20 April 1850, ADM50/235.

48. ibid., 27 and 29 April 1850.

49. ibid., 10 Feb. 1850.

50. JS Service Record, ADM196/6.

CHAPTER 26: BELMONT AND FAMILY TRIBULATIONS

1. See portrait/photo taken when in his 60s.

2. Address etc., given in the 1851 census.

3. Walter had also kept in touch with the Halseys, their deceased sister Mary's children, and both Ellen and James would have been pleased to know they were well provided for— Anna Halsey (aged 26 in 1850) married Henry Ralph Ricardo in July 1851; Henry Halsey (aged 25 in 1850), nothing known; Mary (aged 24 in 1850) married Rev. Robert Wedgewood 1847; Dorothea (aged 20 in 1850) married Rev. William Spicer 1849; William Stirling (aged 19 in 1850) career in HEICS; Agnes (17 in 1850) married Hugh Tennant (date u/n).

4. P. N. Rogers, *The Borough of Havant in Old Picture Postcards,* plate 15, 'The Station completed in 1847'.

5. 1851 census, Preston Household at Borde Hill, Cuckfield, Sussex, HO107/1642 f209.

6. Ward/Gooch, *The Cambridge History of Foreign Policy,* p. 599.

7. ibid., p. 599, esp. ftn 2.

8. P. Statham, 'Origins and Achievements: Convicts and the Western Australian Economy', *Westerly,* Sept. 1985.

9. CO18/52 f600 dated Oct. 1849.

10. See correspondence between Lord Grey and Earl Grey, Oct. 1849, CO397/8 ff338–59, and the *Inquirer* (WA) supplement, 12 June 1850.

11. This is based on his subsequently expressed views.

12. Blue Books for Western Australia and census taken 10 Oct. 1848.

13. Statham, *Dictionary of Western Australians,* p. 239.

14. Lewis brothers, Western Australia Bank Agency Office, 1 Church Ct, Clement's Lane, to Hawes, Colonial Office, 15 April 1850, CO18/57 f200.

15. Charles Bateson, *The Convict Ships*, entry on the Mangles.

16. In 1857 brother Charles stood successfully for Newport, Isle of Wight, which he represented for two years. *Mangles Story*, Chap. 5.

17. Called Broun in his latter years, Peter Nicholas Brown had arrived in the *Parmelia* with his family in 1829 and had died 5 Dec. 1846. During Stirling's absence in 1833, Broun had issued £1 notes to relieve the critical shortage of liquidity, but as a result became indebted to the government (est. in 1844 to be some £1,245) and forced to auction his property. See S. Butlin, *Foundations of Australia's Monetary System*, pp. 383–4. His early death (or suicide) was ascribed to his involvement in this matter, see C. Bryan and F. Bray, 'Peter Nicholas Brown'.

18. See extensive correspondence in CO2125 WA and CO18/70.

19. Though listed in the Kensal Green cemetery records, the Stirling vault could not be found on a recent visit, though there are several large vaults covered with vegetation in the vicinity of the designated plot.

20. 1851 census, Belmont House, Havant, Parish of Bedhampton, HO107/1656, lists James Stirling, 60, Head, Retired Captain RN Half Pay, Farmer of 50 acres employing 4 Agricultural Labourers, born Scotland; Ellen, 44, Wife, born Guildford Surrey; Ellinor, 12, daughter, scholar, born Australia; Anna, 10, daughter, scholar, born London; Dorothea, 9, daughter, scholar, born Lisbon, British Subject; Georgina, 6, daughter, scholar, born Havant HAM; Elizabeth Blackwell, 29, Governess, Unm., Instructress, born Holstein; George Parker, 23, Visitor, Unm., Commander Half Pay RN, born Chester CHS; Justine Mucherd, 24, Servant, Unm., Lady's maid, born Paris France; Sarah Williams, 24, Servant, Unm., Cook, born Pembrokeshire; Hannah Peters, 23, Servant, Unm., Housemaid, born Midhurst Sussex; Charity Harland, 11 (sic), Servant, Unm., Housemaid, born Brighton Sussex; James Afflick, 20, Servant, Unm., Groom, Born Compton Surrey.

21. 6 April 1851 memorial to Earl Grey, 6 April 1851 (rec. 7 April), CO18/64 f191.

22. Marginal note on draft reply, Colonial Office to Lewis brothers, 14 April 1851, CO18/64 f193.

23. ibid.

24. Catalogue of the 1851 Exhibition, NLA, shows an exhibit by W. Stirling and Sons, Glasgow, manufacturers, 'Specimens of Turkey red dying and printing on cotton Fabrics', *Official and descriptive Catalogue of the Great Exhibition of the works and industry of all the Nations*, Class 18, Item 56'. These Stirlings were James' father's brother's family.

25. *Official and descriptive Catalogue*, NLA.

26. Later Service Record, ADM193/37 f1282.

27. Letter asking for appointment, 30 July 1851, ADM. AU (Admiral Unemployed).

28. Frederick to Cousin George Hughes, Aug. 1851, in *Mangles Story*, Chap. 5, p. 249.

29. Appointed 17 Jan. 1852 (Service Record).

30. *The Times*, 14 Feb. 1852.

31. *The Times*, Naval Intelligence, 14 Feb. 1852.

32. ibid., 16 Feb. 1852.

33. *London Gazette,* 20 Feb. 1852, and *The Times*, 21 Feb. 1852.

34. *The Times*, 16 March 1852, 'At Borde Hill Sussex, on the 13th inst. aged 78, Mary, widow of the late James Mangles Esq. of Woodbridge, Surrey, formerly MP for Guildford'. Mary's final request gave the family some difficulty, for Mary had never accepted her husband's desire to be buried in the chapel he had prepared at Wanborough, as it had

never been consecrated. The chapel was part of the remains of St Bartholomew's Church, disused from 1674 to 1861. Mary made it clear that she wanted him to be re-interred with her in the new church at St Mark's.

35. St Mark's, Wyke, Normandy, in the Parish of Ash, was built in 1847.

36. The first reads: 'Sacred to the memory of James Mangles Esquire of Woodbridge in the county of Surrey who died the 25th day of September MDCCCXXXVIII. During three sessions he represented the Borough of Guildford in Parliament. Active benevolence, liberality without ostentation and strict integrity were the distinguishing features of his character, his widow and his children have the deepest cause to deplore his death, but their hope and consolation is that he sleeps in Jesus.' The other: 'Sacred to the memory of Mary, widow of the late James Mangles Esquire of Woodbridge, departed this life on the 13th of March MDCCCLIII. She lived and died a humble believer in the Lord Jesus Christ, proving by the cheerfulness of her spirit and by the happiness which she diffused, that the ways of true religion are ways of pleasantness and all her paths are peace.'

37. Related by Ellen's great-great-granddaughter, Lavina Fleming.

38. For the history of this group see F. H. Broomhall, *The Veterans: A History of the Enrolled Pensioner Force in Western Australia 1850-1880.*

39. Rt Hon. W. Beresford, War Office, to Sir J. Pakington, Colonial Office, 13 March 1852 (rec. Mar 15), CO18/70 f171.

40. Annotation to Beresford, to Pakington, 13 March 1852, CO18/70 f171.

41. Colonial Office draft reply to War Office, 26 May 1852, CO18/70 f175.

42. Mentioned in WAA Memorial vol. 6, no. 1946, reg. 13 Dec. 1865.

43. Of Charles and Charlotte's children, Andrew and Charles were in the navy, but still at home in 1852–53 were Charlotte 19, William 16, about to join the Royal Artillery, Anna 14, Francis 12 and Agnes 9 (Family Tree).

44. Caroline (Mangles) Onslow married Thomas Burton Jones, of Twyning Park, near Tewkesbury, on 17 Feb. 1853. She had two sons from the previous marriage—Henry who had taken the name Hughes-Onslow in 1840 on the death of (and an inheritance from) a maternal uncle, and Charles, who had married an Onslow cousin in 1852 (Family Tree).

45. Death certificate states 'Died on 9th May 1853 Agnes Stirling aged 17 of 14 Marine Parade in Brighton, of a heart condition of many years standing. Present at the death, Mary Gibbs of 2 High St, Brighton. Reg. on 12 May.'

46. Colonial Land and Emigration Commissioners to T. F. Elliot, Colonial Office, 13 June 1853 (rec.18 June), CO18/77 f326.

47. Annotation to Commissioners, to Elliot, 13 June 1853, CO18/77 f326.

48. No record of these dealings has been found. Garden Island passed wholly into Government hands in the 20th century through the 'Transfer Act'. See WASD Acc 1800 item 1, f77, Cockburn Sound Loc. 9.

49. These letters form the basis of the Lenfestey collection, Margaret Lenfestey being a direct descendant of John Stirling.

50. See *St Andrews Cathedral*, Official Guide Book: Historic Scotland 1993.

51. Sir George Bonham to Lord John Russell, 22 March 1853, cited in G. Graham, *The China Station*, p. 276.

52. ADM2/1611, 9 May 1853 (no. 53); Graham, p. 277.

53. *The Times*, 28 Dec. 1853.

54. Details in Graham, *The China Station*, p. 278, and Graham, *Great Britain and the Indian Ocean*, pp. 415–17 and 421. Pellew was beached, not dismissed, becoming a full Admiral

in 1858. The simplified reason for his dismissal was that he had inflicted unauthorised corporal punishment upon six seamen.

55. Graham, *The China Station*, p. 278.

56. Grace Fox, *British Admirals and Chinese Pirates 1832–1869*, p. 60.

57. Admiralty to Inglefield, 3 Aug. 1846, ADM13/3, cited in Fox, pp. 53–4.

58. Jack Beeching, *The Chinese Opium Wars*, p. 164.

59. A Rear Admiral hoisted his flag, a long, thin pennant of the appropriate colour (blue, white or red, indicating ascending seniority) on the mizzen mast, a Vice Admiral on the foremast, and a full Admiral on the main mast. The ships in his squadron would fly the same coloured ensign on their jackstaff (at the stern).

60. ADM50/278, part 1, East India Station, 'Journal of the Proceedings of Rear Admiral Sir J. Stirling Commander in Chief from the 19th Jan. to the 30th June 1854' (hereafter *Stirling's Journal*).

61. *Stirling's Journal*, entry 20 Feb. 1854, ADM 50/278.

62. 'An Act For Encouraging the Capture or Destruction of Piratical Ships and Vessels', 1825.

63. Amended by the 'Head of Money Act', 1850, and the 'Naval Prize Act', 1854. See Beeching, p. 169.

64. ibid., p. 172.

65. *Stirling's Journal*, entry 24 Feb. 1854, ADM 50/278.

CHAPTER 27: FIFTH COMMAND HMS *WINCHESTER*

1. Not to be confused with the *Sybelle* sent out later; *Sibella* was smaller and retired soon thereafter.

2. J. Stirling, no. 280, *Barracouta*, Singapore, to ADM, 30 April 1854 (rec. 19 June 1854), S123 ADM1/5629 f55.

3. ibid.

4. *Stirling's Journal*, entries for 24 Feb. – 5 April 1854, ADM50/278.

5. J. Stirling, *Barracouta* at Singapore, no. 26, 29 April 1854 (rec. 13 June 1854), ADM1/5629 S133.6 52.26 x–14 85 f100, encl. 8. J. Stirling, *Barracouta*, Singapore, to Captain G. O'Callaghan, 20 April 1854.

6. Graham, *The China Station*, p. 279.

7. Stirling to Admiralty, 13 July 1854, cited in Graham, p. 279.

8. Graham, p. 281.

9. Douglas Hurd, *The Arrow War: An Anglo-Chinese Confusion*, p. 22.

10. *Stirling's Journal*, entry 11 May 1854, ADM50/278.

11. T. D. Manning & C. F. Walker, *British Warship Names*.

12. Complement of the *Winchester*: 450 men—32 officers, 51 petty officers, 250 seamen, 67 boys 1st and 2nd Class, and 70 marines, *Winchester* Log, April 1854 – Mar 1855, ADM53/5633.

13. *Navy Lists*, *Winchester*, March 1854. Whether this Nelson was related to the hero of Trafalgar is not known.

14. J. Stirling, HMS *Winchester* at sea, no. 36, 24° 3' N 119° 9' E (Formosa Straits?), to Admiralty, 31 May 1854 (rec. 7 Sept.), ADM1/5632.

15. ADM1/5629 S64 circular no. 66, Admiralty, 18 July 1850.

16. Stirling, HMS *Winchester* at sea, to Admiralty, 31 May 1854, ADM1/5632.

17. John died 5 Nov. 1854 at Battle of Inkerman, Crimea, aged 18.

18. Stirling, HMS *Winchester* at sea, to Admiralty, 31 May 1854, ADM1/5632.

19. Graham, p. 288, and Stirling's Maritime Policy document, below.

20. General Order no. 13, *Stirling's Journal*, entry 9 June 1854, ADM50/278.

21. J. Stirling to the Admiralty, no. 41, 'On the present state of Shanghai', 19 June 1854, FO17/223 f245 ff.

22. ibid.

23. *Stirling's Journal*, entry 12 June 1854, ADM50/278.

24. J. Stirling, *Encounter* at Shanghai, no. 44, June 1854 (rec. Sept. 25), ADM1 S164 f128, 52.25 x-26.

25. Wilson replaced Fitzgerald and Stirling Wainwright. Lts Nelson and Bushnell remained but all other Lts were replaced, the Chaplain, Instructor and the Surgeon, Robert Clark, remained. See *Navy Lists* 1854.

26. ADM1/5657 encl. 2/, 'Diary of Events kept by Capt. MJ Currie RN, in Correspondence pertinent to the Negotiation of the Convention with Japan' (hereafter *Currie's Diary*), entry for 6 Sept. 1854.

27. J. Stirling, private, *Winchester* at Hong Kong, to the Rt Hon. Sir James R. G. Graham Bt GCB, Admiralty, 27 Oct. 1854, ADM1/5657 S10.

28. J. Tronson, 'Personal Narrative of a voyage in HMS *Barracouta*', cited in Hugh Cortazzi, *Victorians in Japan* pp. 4–5.

29. Recorded in his journal after the expedition when ready to return to his place of employment, *Stirling's Journal*, entry 16 Nov. 1854, ADM50/278.

30. Rear Admiral James Stirling to the Governor of Nagasaki, 7 Sept. 1854, *British Parliamentary Papers 1856* (2077) LXI, 215, 'Correspondence respecting the late negotiation with Japan Presented to both Houses of Parliament 1856', (hereafter *B.P.P. Convention*), encl. no. 2 in Letter 1.

31. It was restated in *Stirling's Journal*, entry 7 Sept. 1854, ADM50/278.

32. Tronson, cited in Cortazzi, p. 6.

33. Enclosure no. 3, 9 Sept. 1854 in *B.P.P. Convention* 1856 (2077) LX1.215.

34. Enclosure no. 27, *Currie's Diary* 1854, ADM1/5657–76075.

35. Enclosure no. 4, 27 Sept. in *B.P.P. Convention* (2077) LX1.215.

36. Enclosure no. 5, 28 Sept. 1854 in *B.P.P. Convention* (2077) LX1.215.

37. Cortazzi, Introduction, p. x.

38. Enclosure no. 5, 28 Sept. 1854 in *B.P.P. Convention* (2077) LX1.215.

39. Enclosure no. 27, *Currie's Diary* 1854, p. 22, ADM1/5657–76075.

40. Tronson, cited in Cortazzi, p. 7.

41. Enclosure no. 27, *Currie's Diary* 1854, p. 25, ADM1/5657–76075.

42. Tronson, cited in Cortazzi, p. 7.

43. Enclosure no. 27, *Currie's Diary* 1854, pp. 26–28, ADM1/5657–76075.

44. *Stirling's Journal*, part 3, entry 5, Oct., ADM 50/278.

45. Appendix no. 3 to *Currie's Diary* 1854, ADM1/5657–76075, encl. no. 27, p. 43.

46. Enclosure no. 6, 9 Oct. 1854, in *B.P.P. Convention* (2077) LX1.215.

47. See 'Exposition of the Articles' in *B.P.P. Convention* (2014) LX1.207.

48. *The Illustrated London News*, 28 April 1855, p. 414.

49. See the 'Convention and Explanations' in *B.P.P. Convention* (2014) LX1.207.

50. Enclosure no. 9 in *B.P.P. Convention* (2077) LX1.215.

51. Tronson, cited in Cortazzi, p. 8.

52. Enclosure no. 10 in *B.P.P. Convention* (2077) LXI.215. See also *Stirling's Journal*, ADM 50/278, part 3, entry 17 Oct., 'to Mezi-ro-Chek-no-kami—the Governor General of Nagasaki'.

53. Enclosure no. 12 in *B.P.P. Convention* (2077) LXI.215.

54. ibid., encl. no. 11.

55. ibid., encl. no. 14.

56. *Currie's Diary* 1854, encl. no. 27, p. 42, ADM1/5657–76075.

57. *Stirling's Journal*, part 3, entry 20 Oct. 1854, ADM 50/278.

58. Enclosure no. 1, *B.P.P. Convention* (2077) LXI.215. See also ADM50/278 (no. 71).

59. FO 26 Dec. 1854 encl. no. 2 in *B.P.P. Convention* (2077) LXI.215.

60. J. Stirling, private, *Winchester* at Hong Kong, to Rt Hon. Sir James R. G. Graham Bt GCB, 27 Oct. 1854, ADM1/5657 S10.

61. *Stirling's Journal*, part 3, entry 27 Oct. 1854, ADM 50/278.

62. *The Overland Register*, 28 Oct. 1854, ADM1/5620 f194.

CHAPTER 28: PIRATES, REBELS AND RUSSIANS

1. Cited in Graham, *The China Station*, p. 284.

2. FO Stirling to Bowring, 16 Nov. 1855, encl. in no. 1 Bowring to Clarendon, 20 Nov 1855 (no. 370), and Graham, p. 284 ftn 21.

3. J. Stirling to Admiralty, *Winchester* at Hong Kong, 25 Nov. 1854, FO17/238 f152–4.

4. ibid.

5. B. Szczesniak (ed.), *The Opening of Japan: A Diary of Discovery in the Far East 1853–1856 by Rear Admiral George Henry Preble U.S.N.*, pp. 262–6 (hereafter *Preble's Diary*).

6. FO17/238 f152–4.

7. *Preble's Diary*, pp. 262–6.

8. ADM1/5657–76075 sub-enclosure in encl. no. 3, J. Stirling to ADM 3 Nov. 1854.

9. ADM 1/5657–76075 J. Stirling to ADM 3 Nov. 1854.

10. FO 17/224 Clarendon to Bowring, 24 Jan. 1855.

11. *Stirling's Journal*, part 3, entry 19 Nov. 1854, ADM50/278.

12. *Preble's Diary*, p. 279.

13. Beeching, *The Chinese Opium Wars*, p. 181.

14. ibid., p. 201.

15. *Stirling's Journal*, part 3, entries for 11–14 Dec. 1854, ADM 50/278.

16. ibid., entry 22 Dec. 1854.

17. ADM1/5657–75075, 22 Dec. 1854, sub-enclosure in encl. no. 1 in East India Station letter no. 10 of 1855.

18. R. E. J. Eitel, *Europe in China: The History of Hong Kong*, p. 304.

19. JS, *Winchester* at Hong Kong, no. 10, 14 Jan. 1855 (rec. 8 March), 'On the present state of affairs at Canton', ADM1/5618 S39.

20. *Stirling's Journal*, part 3, entry 30 Dec. 1854, ADM 50/278.

21. ibid., part 4, entry 2 Jan. 1855.

22. Enclosure no. 2, JS to the Chief of the Insurgent Force in Blenheim Reach, Whampoa, 2 Jan. 1855 (encl. in ADM1 S39, J. Stirling, *Winchester* at Hong Kong, no. 10, 14 Jan. 1855).

23. Enclosure no. 3, Chumninlung, Chief of the Rebel Forces, to JS, 3 Jan. 1855 (encl. in ADM1 S39, J. Stirling, *Winchester* at Hong Kong, no. 10, 14 Jan. 1855).

24. Beeching, p. 203.

25. J. Stirling to Admiralty, 13 Jan. 1855, ADM1/5657 S38.

26. Text has been derived from JS to Admiralty 13 Jan. 1855, ADM1/5657 S38, and JS to Admiralty, 14 Feb. 1855 FO 17/239 f80–87, and from annotations to FO/ADM correspondence. See FO17/238 f167 FO to Admiralty, 29 Jan. 1855, FO17/238 f254 FO to Admiralty, 19 Feb. 1855.

27. J. Stirling to Admiralty, 14 Feb. 1855, FO17/239 f80–87.

28. ibid.

29. Admiralty to J. Stirling, 28 March 1855, FO17/238 f35.

30. Beeching, p. 202.

31. J. Stirling, no. 18, *Winchester* at Hong Kong, 15 Feb. 1855, ADM 1 S58.

32. Eitel, p. 304.

33. Beeching, p. 202.

34. Enclosure no. 2, J. Stirling to the Chief of the Insurgent Force in Blenheim Reach, Whampoa, 2 Jan. 1855, encl. in ADM1 S39, JS, *Winchester* at HK, no. 10, 14 Jan. 1855.

35. *Stirling's Journal,* part 4, entry 9 Feb. 1855 noting dispatch from Commander C. Frederick, HMS *Pacific,* dated 22 Nov. 1854, ADM 50/278.

36. A. J. Barker, *The Vainglorious War 1854–56,* p. 274.

37. ADM1/5632 draft Admiralty order, 4 Dec. 1854.

38. Draft order to Rear Admiral Stirling, 4 Dec 1854, confidential, ADM1/5632.

39. Draft Admiralty order, 20 Jan. 1855, ADM1/5632.

40. Rear Admiral Stirling, *Winchester* in Hong Kong, to Rear Admiral La Guerre, 6 March 1855, ADM1/5632.

41. *Stirling's Journal,* entry 7 March, ADM 50/278.

42. Rear Admiral Stirling, no. 30, *Winchester* at Hong Kong to Admiralty, 15 March 1855 (rec. 10 May 1854), ADM1/5632.

43. Graham, pp. 295–7.

44. Rear Admiral Stirling, Dispatch 43 to Admiralty, 15 April 1855, encl. 3, ADM1/5632.

45. *Stirling's Journal*, part 5, entry 12 April, ADM 50/278.

46. Stirling, Dispatch 43 to Admiralty, 15 April 1855, encl. 4, ADM1/5632.

47. G. A. Lensen, *The Russian Push toward Japan,* p. 334.

48. Enclosure no. 2 in Dispatch 43 to the Admiralty, ADM1/5632.

49. Lensen, p. 334.

50. ibid., p. 337.

51. ibid., p. 340.

52. ADM 50/278 *Stirling's Journal,* there is a gap between 30 April and 3 May (latter entry is at sea).

53. Rear Admiral Stirling, Dispatch 43 to Admiralty, 15 April 1855, ADM1/563.

54. J. Stirling, no. 49, *Winchester* at Hong Kong, 28 April 1855, ADM 1/5632.

55. *Stirling's Journal*, entry 11 April, ADM 50/278.

56. ADM 1 S99, 'Purchase of *Tartar* for Tender to Flag Ship. 91–6 50–6 to Thomas Phinn, Admiralty, 7 Sept. 1855'. (*Tartar* of 171 tons, Master Robert D. Guthries, built at West Cowes in the Isle of Wight in 1853.)

57. *Stirling's Journal*, entry 26 April 1855, ADM 50/278.

58. ibid., entry 10 May 1855.

59. ibid., entry 17 May 1855.

60. Cortazzi, p. 33.

61. *Illustrated London News*, 6 Oct. 1855, vol. 27, p. 403.

62. Graham, p. 292.

63. *Illustrated London News*, 6 Oct. 1855, vol. 27, p. 403.

64. Elliot on *Sybelle* in the Gulf of Tartary, Lat. 49° 46', Long. 141° 33', encl. 2 in no. 11 of 1855 from J. Stirling, ADM1/5657.

65. *Stirling's Journal*, entry 30 May 1855, ADM 50/278.

66. ADM1/5657 encl. no. 3: Elliot, *Sybelle* in the Gulf of Tartary, 7 June 1855, in J. Stirling no. 55, 2July 1855.

67. *Illustrated London News*, 6 Oct. 1855, vol. 27, p. 403.

68. *Stirling's Journal*, part 5, entry 7 June 1855, ADM 50/278.

69. Jonquiere Bay Lat. 50° 54', Long. 142° 07'.

70. *Stirling's Journal*, entry 26 June 1855, ADM 50/278.

71. *Illustrated London News*, 20 Oct. 1855, vol. 27, p. 462.

72. *Stirling's Journal*, entry 27, June 1855, ADM 50/278.

73. Especially without the steamers, which probably towed the Russians out.

74. J. Stirling no. 11, *Winchester*, Hong Kong, to Sec. Admiralty, 13 Feb. 1856 (rec. 2 April), S64 ADM1/5672 (in reply to Mr Phinn's Dispatch no. 238 of 8 Dec. 1855).

75. Annotated memo on 13 Feb. 1856, J. Stirling no. 11, to ADM S64 ADM1/5672.

76. *Stirling's Journal*, entry 29 June 1855, ADM 50/278.

77. *Illustrated London News*, 6 Oct. 1855, vol. 27, p. 403.

78. P. Kennedy, *The Rise and Fall of British Naval Mastery*, p. 205.

79. Extract of a dispatch from Elliot on *Sybelle*, Sept. 1854, ADM1/5657 f76.

80. *Stirling's Journal*, entries 1–7 July 1855, ADM50/278.

81. ibid., entry 7 July 1855.

82. ibid., entry 12 July 1855.

83. *Illustrated London News*, 20 Oct. 1855, p. 463.

84. Tronson, cited in Cortazzi, p. 37.

85. *Stirling's Journal*, entry 17 July 1855, ADM50/278.

86. ibid., entry 20 July 1855.

87. ibid., entry 20 & 22 July 1855.

88. G. A. Lensen, *The Russian Push toward Japan*, 1 Aug., p. 341.

89. *Stirling's Journal*, entry 15 Aug. 1855, ADM50/278.

90. Memoir by Sir J. Stirling on the Maritime Policy of England in the Eastern Seas, encl. in Stirling to Wood (AD), Hong Kong, 15 Nov. 1855, ADM1/5660, read by Lord Palmerston 3 March 1856.

91. Memoir by Sir J. Stirling, 15 Nov. 1855, ADM1/5660.

CHAPTER 29: FROM TREATY RATIFICATION TO RESIGNATION

1. *Stirling's Journal*, entry 28 Sept. 1855, ADM50/278.

2. ibid., entry 29 Sept. 1855.

3. FO17/223 minute f317 and letter of 26 Dec. 1854.

4. FO17/223 minute f317.

5. FO17/238 f89 11 Jan. 1855.

6.   FO17/223 minute f317.

7.   *B.P.P.* 1856 (2077) LXI, 215 encl. in no. 3.

8.   FO17/238 to Admiralty, 25 Jan. 1855, (137).

9.   *B.P.P.* 1856 (2077) LXI, 215 encl. no. 4, Hammond, Foreign Office, to Hamilton, Sec. Admiralty.

10. *B.P.P.* 1856 (2077) LXI, 215 encl. no. 5, Admiralty to Hammond, 27 Jan. 1855.

11. ibid.

12. *B.P.P.* 1856 (2077) LXI, 215 encl. no. 2, Foreign Office to Admiralty, 26 Dec.

13. *B.P.P.* 1856 (2077) LXI, 215 encl. no. 6, Admiralty to Hammond, 9 Feb. 1855.

14. *B.P.P.* 1856 (2077) LXI, 215 encl. no. 7, Hammond to Admiralty, 22 May 1855.

15. *Stirling's Journal*, entry 29 Sept. 1855, ADM50/278.

16. ibid., entry 1 Oct. 1855.

17. ibid.

18. Seymour, *Winchester* at sea, 22 Sept. 1856 (visited Nagasaki 3 Sept. with *Pique* and *Barracouta*), ADM1/5672 S174.

19. *Stirling's Journal*, entry 8 Oct. 1855, ADM50/278.

20. *Illustrated London News*, 26 Jan. 1856, p. 86, vol. 28, 84–86, letter from one of the officers on the *Winchester*, Nagasaki, 10 Oct. 1855.

21. *B.P.P.* (2077) LXI. 215 encl. 8 in no. 8, minute verifying the Exchange of Ratifications. The signatories were James Stirling—*Rear Admiral*, F. W. Nicholson *Capt.* HMS *Pique*, W. Hoste *Capt.* HMS *Spartan,* Thomas Wilson *Capt.* HMS *Winchester*, M. J. Currie *Capt. RN & Secretary to C-in-C*, F. H. Stirling *Commander* HMS *Winchester*, A. Bland *Lieut* HMS *Pique*, Ed. Nares *Flag Lieut.* HMS *Winchester*, Arthur Morrell *Lieut.* HMS *Spartan*, J. H. Bushnell *Lieut* HMS *Winchester*, Francis H. May *Master* HMS *Winchester*, Geo. L. Carr *Master* HMS *Pique*, P. L. Penrose *Capt. Royal Marines* HMS *Winchester*, Thos. Davis *Chaplain* HMS *Pique*, R. Whitmore Clarke *Staff Surgeon* HMS *Winchester*, Thos. Nelson *Surgeon* HMS *Pique*, Thos. Russell Pickthorne *Surgeon* HMS *Spartan*, J. B. Hay *Paymaster* HMS *Pique*, Beresford Scott *Paymaster* HMS *Winchester*, Edw. Grant Stokes *First Lieut. Royal Marines* HMS *Spartan*, B. Colley *Asst. Paymaster & Secretary's clerk* HMS *Winchester*.

22. *Illustrated London News*, 26 Jan. 1856, p. 86.

23. *Stirling's Journal*, entry 15 Oct. 1855, ADM50/278.

24. J. Stirling, *Winchester*, Hong Kong, no. 78 to Sec. Admiralty, 8 Nov. 1855 (rec. 2 Jan 1856), ADM1/5672 S16.

25. *Stirling's Journal*, entry 10 Oct. 1855, ADM50/278.

26. ibid., entry 14 Oct. 1855.

27. ibid., entry 16 Oct. 1855.

28. ibid., entry 20 Oct. 1855.

29. ibid.

30. FO/255 f3 from Admiralty, encl. J. Stirling to Admiralty 15 Nov. 1855, 'On the suppression of piracy and State of affairs in Shanghai'.

31. J. Stirling, *Winchester*, Hong Kong, no. 86, to Sec. Admiralty, 11 Nov. 1855 (rec. 2 Jan 1856) 'On the disposal of Russian Prisoners', ADM1/5672 S17.

32. *Stirling's Journal*, entry 2 Dec. 1855 incoming mail, ADM50/278.

33. Annotation to 11 Nov. 1855 J. Stirling to Sec. of the Admiralty, 'On the disposal of Russian Prisoners'.

34. *Preble's Diary*, pp. 262–6.

35. *Stirling's Journal*, entry 15 Nov. 1855, ADM50/278.

36. No copy of this letter of resignation has been found, but the timing of subsequent events makes this the most likely time it was sent.

37. *Preble's Diary*, 19 Nov., Hong Kong.

38. ibid., p. 382, 25 Nov., Hong Kong.

39. *Stirling's Journal*, entry 28 Nov. 1855, ADM50/278.

40. *Preble's Diary*, 1 Dec. 1855, p. 383.

41. W. Allen, 'The Unnecessary War', in *Milestones in History*, vol. 9, Chap. 1, p. 19.

42. *Preble's Diary*, 3 Dec., p. 384, 'Sir James Stirling received news by mail of his promotion, and hoisted his flag as Rear Admiral of the Red RN'.

43. ibid., 15 Dec. 1855, pp. 386–7.

44. ibid., 18 Dec. 1855, p. 387.

45. J. Stirling, *Winchester*, Hong Kong, no. 101, to Sec. of the Admiralty, 11 Dec. 1855 (rec. 4 Feb. 1856), ADM1/5672 S22.

46. JS, *Winchester*, Hong Kong, no. 101 to Sec. of the Admiralty, 11 Dec. 1855 (rec. 4 Feb. 1856), ADM1/5672 S22 cover sheet.

47. *Preble's Diary*, pp. 389–40.

48. Stirling to Bowring, 16 Nov. 1855, encl. in Bowring to Clarendon, 20 Nov. 1855 (no. 370), FO17/235.

49. A view expressed officially too, see note from Admiralty, 9 Oct. 1855, FO17/241 China domestic f25.

50. *Hong Kong Gazette*, first week of Jan. 1856, FO17/244.

51. JS, *Pique*, Hong Kong, no. 6, to Sec. Admiralty, 14 Jan. 1856 (rec. 7 March), ADM1/5672 S16.

52. J. Stirling, *Winchester*, Hong Kong, to Admiralty, 9 Nov. 1855.

53. Dated 2 and 22 Sept. 1855, these reports were printed in the *London Gazette*, 11 Jan. 1856.

54. Noted in J. Stirling, *Winchester*, Hong Kong, to Admiralty, 9 Nov. 1855.

55. W. A. Fellowes, HMSS *Rattler*, Hong Kong, to JS, 6 Aug. 1855, printed in the *London Gazette*, 11 Jan. 1856.

56. *The Times,* editorial, 13 Jan. 1856.

57. *Stirling's Journal*, entry 6 July 1855, ADM50/278.

58. *The Times,* 28 Feb. 1856, Naval Intelligence.

59. *Preble's Diary*, 25 Jan., p. 399.

60. *Stirling's Journal*, entry 23 Jan. 1856, ADM50/278.

61. ibid., entries 25–6 Jan., 9 Feb. 1856.

62. Stirling's letter of retirement, delivered by his son, has not been found. However, Stirling informed Bowring of it 1 April 1856, and stated that the dispatch relieving him of his command was dated 9 Feb. 1856. See JS to Bowring, FO17/246 China Bowring f93t.

63. *The Times,* 16 Feb. 1856, Letter to the Editor.

64. *The Times,* 19 Feb. 1856, Naval Intelligence.

65. Some of this comes from the marriage certificate and some from the 1861 census, RG9/70 p. 9.

66. Beeching, *The Chinese Opium Wars*, p. 175.

67. Beeching, p. 177.

68. *Stirling's Journal*, entries 20, 22, 24, 27 March 1856, ADM50/278.

69. G. B. Endacott, *A History of Hong Kong*, p. 89.

70. Endacott, p. 90.

71. Ann Parry, *The Admirals Fremantle 1788–1920,* part II, Edmund Robert Fremantle Service Record, p. 199.

72.   *Winchester* Log, entry 29 March 1856, ADM53/5635.

73.   *The Times,* editorial, 23 Jan. 1856.

74.   J. Stirling to John Bowring, *Winchester,* 1 April 1856, FO17/246 f93.

75.   FO17/246 f109ff Bowring to Clarendon.

76.   FO17/246 f114ff Bowring to Stirling, 1 April 1856.

77.   *Winchester* Log, entry 2 April 1856, ADM53/5635.

78.   *Winchester* Log, entry 5 April 1856, states the retinue consisted of 'Sir James Stirling, Captain Currie, Lt Stirling, Mr Arnold—Secretary's Clerk, Mr Harney—ditto, William Rogers—Admiral's domestic, Jas. Lunn—ditto, H. V. Higgins—Secretary's servant, also Lt Fremantle and Mr Mayen—Acting 2nd Master, ADM53/5635.

79.   *Encounter* Log, entry 20 April 1856, ADM53/5963.

80.   *Allen's India Mail,* 3 June 1856, vol. IX, Jan.–Dec. 1856.

CHAPTER 30: A WELCOME RETIREMENT

1.   *Illustrated London News,* 24 May 1856.

2.   *Portsmouth Times and Naval Gazette,* 2 Aug. 1856. Marriages 'On the 24th ult at Bedhampton, James Alexander, eldest son of David Charles Guthrie esq. of Portland Place to Ellinor, second living daughter of Rear Admiral Sir James Stirling of Belmont, Hants'.

3.   James Stirling's will (Somerset House) stated 'upon the marriage of my daughter Ellinor Guthrie I entered a covenant with the Trustees…(and) appointed £3,500 to her Settlement'.

4.   *Portsmouth Times and Naval Gazette,* 28 June 1856.

5.   Liver damage and jaundice are two of the outcomes of untreated malaria. See Berkow and Fletcher, 16th. ed., *Merk Manual of Diagnosis and Therapy,* pp. 229–30.

6.   Portsmouth Record Office, CHU26/2A/3, Bedhampton Rate Book and Church Warden's Accounts 1829–1888.

7.   See F. H. Stirling's Service Record ADM196/1, part 3, f578.

8.   *Illustrated London News,* 24 May 1856, p. 573.

9.   John Chapman, Deputy Chairman, WA Co., 2 Leadenhall St, to Labouchere, Colonial Office, 11 Jul. 1856 (rec. Jul. 14.), CO18/97 f181.

10.   Thos Murdoch, Emigration Office, Park St, Westminster, to Mr Gairdner, Colonial Office, 12 Aug. 1856, CO18/97 f186.

11.   Frederick Mangles, 17 Gracechurch St, London, to Labouchere, 1 Oct. 1856 (rec. 2 Oct.), CO18/97 f652.

12.   Annotation: F. Mangles to Colonial Office, 1 Oct. 1856 (rec. 2 Oct.), CO18/97 f652.

13.   Draft reply to Frederick Mangles, 13 Oct. 1856, CO18/97 f654.

14.   Beeching, *The Chinese Opium Wars* p. 231.

15.   Beeching, p. 229.

16.   CO18/102 f386 (Misc. Offices), 12 Jan. 1857…'Memorial in favour of making the Colony a Penal Settlement'.

17.   Annotation on the above, 'This memorial, delivered by a deputation today, is important as a declaration of the sentiments of representatives of the principal interests of the Colony. It might perhaps be communicated to the Governor, with some intimation that the capabilities of Western Australia for the reception of convicts are not overlooked by HMG. T. Elliot 31 Jan.'

18.   Will of Sir James Stirling proved London, Dec. 1865 (Somerset House).

19. Andrew Stirling's will (1 Avenue House), *Administration*, 28 April 1876. Andrew Stirling, late of Beaumaris in the County of Angelsey, Gentleman who died 21 August 1873...without child or father and intestate, (probate granted to) Charles Edward Stirling...Lawful Brother of the said deceased, he having been first sworn duly to administer Sarah Reece Stirling the lawful Widow...Under £1,000. No leaseholds.

20. *Mangles Story*, Chap. 4.

21. J. Stirling's Senior Service Record, ADM196/37f1282.

22. There is some dispute as to the actual date of death; family papers give it as June, this from service record. He was the only one in his regiment (9th Bengal Cavalry) to have died at that time and there was no stated cause.

23. *London Gazette*, 8 July 1859. The Military Museum, London has a portrait of Ross Mangles in action.

24. Charles Stirling, 14 Portland Terrace, to Uncle Walter, 3 April 1858 (Lenfestey).

25. Charles Stirling, Southsea, to Walter Stirling, 21 April 1858, (Lenfestey).

26. See *Kensington Palace: The official Guidebook*, The Royal Ceremonial Dress Collection pp. 46–7.

27. Emigration Office to H. Merivale, Colonial Office, April 1858 (rec. 14 April), CO18/107 f85.

28. Encl. Emigration Office to Merivale, Colonial Office, in April 1858, CO18/107 f85.

29. Emigration Office to Merivale, April 1858, CO18/107 f85.

30. Surveyor-General to Colonial Secretary, 27 Nov., BL WASR SDO/2/ ff 278–282.

31. ibid.

32. Surveyor-General (1113) to Col. Sec., 29 June 1858, WASR SDO/2/ ff 306–309.

33. Fred Mangles' name is on the title to Plantagenet 33 when granted in 1843. See title deed no. 390, vol. XXIII 181 (984).

34. Charles Mangles maintained a house at 165 Gresham St, near Old Broad, London, *London Directories.*

35. *Portsmouth Times and Naval Gazette*, 18 Aug. 1858.

36. Battye, *Western Australia*, Appendix 2, Value of Horses Exported from the Colony in 1858 reached £14,035 (previous average just over £1,700).

37. Charles E. Mangles, West India Mail Office, to Sir Edward Bulwer Lytton, Colonial Office, 28 Jan. 1859 (rec. 29 Jan.), CO18/113 f153.

38. Annotations: Charles Mangles to Bulwer Lytton, 28 Jan. 1859, CO18/113 f153.

39. Frederick's Service Record, ADM196/37(2).

40. ibid., letter 10 March 1858.

41. ibid., 12 Jan. 1859.

42. Portsmouth Record Office, CHU26/2A/3 (Bedhampton), Rate Book and Church Warden's Accounts 1829–1888.

43. Portsmouth Record Office (Bedhampton), Rate Book 1829–1888.

44. See J. Lee, 'Edward Stirling of Stirling Castle' and J. L. Lee, *The Journals of Edward Stirling in Persia and Afghanistan 1828-29.*

45. Sophie Mertz died aged 10 in 1864, see above.

46. Title deeds to the Belmont Estate, and all related mortgage documents are in the Portsmouth Record Office. The 'others' in the sale document included Edward and Charles Snell, who were there in the 1861 census. See also a monograph by John Pile, 'The History of the Belmont Estate', Havant Museum.

47. *Australian and New Zealand Gazette & Colonial Chronicle*, London, 25 Feb. 1860.

48. ibid., 3 and 17 March 1860.

49. Alexander Andrews, Hon. Sec., WA Association, 2 Church Court, Clements Lane, City (EC) to Colonial Office, 20 April 1860 (rec. 3 May), CO18/116 f199.

50. Andrews to Colonial Office, 20 April 1860 (rec. 3 May), CO18/116 f199. Memorial signed by John Chapman, Ross D. Mangles, Henry R. Greillat, W. Jackson & Co., F. Buckle, John Weston, Robert W. Habgood, Sam'l Lorelick?, F. Boucher, Alexander Andrews, Fred'k Mangles, William Andrews, Henry A. Lawford, Mark O'Shann.

51. See, for example, V. G. Fall, *The Sea and the Forest A History of the Port of Rockingham Western Australia*, p. 102f.

52. The Bigge Report on the State of NSW 1822, CO 201/36-113. See also the annotation, A. Andrews to Colonial Office, including memorial, on 20 April 1860 (rec. 3 May), CO18/116 f203 & ff which stated, 'Assignment has for obvious reason always been the favourite system with Settlers, but it was condemned on account of its inconsistency with good discipline. It created a sort of white slavery, accompanied by all the inequalities of that condition and also by various sources of corruption.'

53. For further detail see Louise Bavin, 'Punishment, Prisons and Reform: Incarceration in Western Australia in the Nineteenth Century'; Pamela Statham, 'Origins and Achievements: Convicts and the Western Australian Economy'; Sandra Taylor, 'Who were the Convicts?'; J. E. Thomas/A. Stewart, *Imprisonment in Western Australia Evolution, Theory and Practice*, Chap. 2.

54. Taylor, 'Who were the Convicts?'.

55. Annotation: A. Andrews to Colonial Office, including memorial, 20 April 1860 (rec. 3 May), CO18/116 f203 & ff.

56. 'State and Prospects of Western Australia', 8 May 1860, CO18/116 f210.

57. *Australian and New Zealand Gazette & Colonial Chronicle*, London, 21 July 1860.

CHAPTER 31: FINAL YEARS

1. This and the following come from a brief history written by Nick Burton for the Ryde 1907 map series of Old Ordinance Survey Maps UK 1999.

2. Charles Stirling, Buckridge, to Walter Stirling, 2 Sept. 1860, (Lenfestey).

3. Frederick to cousin George Hughes, Nov. 1860, in *Mangles Story*, Chap. 4.

4. Ryde RG9/ 657-9 Census March 1861, 'James Stirling, Head, 70, Rear Admiral half pay, b. Lanark Scotland, Ellen Stirling, wife, 53, b. Stoke, Guildford, Frederick , Unm. son, 32, Post Captain RN half pay, b. at sea, Mary, Unm. daughter, 28, b. at sea, Anna, Unm. daughter, 20, b. London, Dorothea, Unm. daughter, 19, b. Lisbon, Ellen Edwards, Unm., 25, Housemaid, b. Seale, Hester Sadler, Unm., 23, Lady's maid, b. Cheltenham, Elizabeth Markham, Unm., 24, Lady's maid, b. Wantage, Emily Edwards, Unm., 24, kitchen maid, b. Surrey Tongham, Frederick Self, Unm., 17, Footman, b. Long Parish Hamps, John Gingall, Unm., 34, Butler, b. Castle Combe Wiltshire, James Dennett, Unm., 20, Coachman, b. Charing Kent.

5. RG9/70–9, 30 Portland Place, Marylebone, March 1861.

6. Francis Lister, Alverthorpe, to Mr Stirling (John's son Thomas), 919 Walnut St, Philadelphia, 20 May 1862, ans. 1 Aug 1862 (Lenfestey).

7. Charles Stirling (1789–1867) m. (1827) Charlotte Stirling (1800–1862) issue Andrew (1829–1909), Charles (1830–1915), Charlotte (1833–1885), William (1834–1906), Anne (m. Thomas Mayne Stirling, John's son) (1837–1926), Francis (1839–1880), Walter (1841–1853), Agnes (1842–1927)—Stirling family tree.

8. Matilda had died in 1862 after bearing eight children. See Burton Jackson, *Not an Idle Man,* p. 173, and Elizabeth Hutchinson, *The Butler Family.*

9. Marriage registration certificate, Anna Hamilton Stirling to Alexander Grant Thorald.

10. F. H. Stirling's Service Record, ADM196/1 (parts 3 & 4) f578.

11. Charles Stirling, Muiravonside, to his brother Walter, 10 Dec. 1863 (Lenfestey).

12. Based on the will of Victor Buckey 'of Foreign Office', d. 10 June 1882 at 28 Stanhope Gardens, South Kensington.

13. Memorial vol. 6 no. 1983, 7 Jan. 1864, reg. 19 Feb. 1866.

14. English Probate Index (Somerset House), Stirling Walter (under £60,000) of Drumpellier, formerly 18 Upper Baker St but late of 18 Curzon St, Mayfair. d. 1 Jan. 1864. Agnes Stirling, of 18 Curzon St, sister and sole executor.

15. English Probate Index (Somerset House), 2 March 1864.

16. CO18/134 f245 ff.

17. Memorial vol. 6, no. 1946, 10 Jan. 1865, reg. 17 Dec. 1865.

18. Memorial vol. 6, no. 1947, 10 Jan. 1865, reg. 18 Dec. 1865.

19. State Records Office of Western Australia Ref: Cons 1800/6, Memorial 1946 and 1947. Memorial received from George Frederick Stone, 1946 reg. 13 Dec. 1865, Perth, and no. 1947 on 18 Dec. 1865.

20. See Staples, 'The Harvey', *Historical studies of Australia and New Zealand*, vol. 4, May 1951, no. 16, p. 318.

21. Beverley Loc. 3 is the only location the author has been unable to trace completely.

22. Frederick Mangles was named on title deeds as owning 'as Executor' in the late 1860s Plantagenet Loc. 12, see WAA Cons 1803 Mem. vol. VI 433(2907) and Avon Loc. 3, WAA Cons. 1803 Mem. vol. VII 924(204).

23. *The Times,* 26 April 1865.

24. *Portsmouth Times and Naval Gazette*, 29 April 1865.

25. *The Gentleman's Magazine*, no. 63 New Series 1865, p. 801.

26. *The Inquirer and Commercial News*, 28 June 1865, p. 3.

27. *Australian and New Zealand Gazette & Colonial Chronicle*, London, 29 April 1865.

28. English Probate Index, Somerset House.

29. Thomas Mayne Stirling to Aunt Agnes, Manchester, 17 Nov. 1865 (Lenfestey).

30. *Perth Gazette,* 9 Sept. 1837 (Irwin's welcome home dinner).

31. See the *Inquirer*, 3 Sept. 1874, and the *Sydney Empire,* 16 July 1874, for descriptions of the 15 July wedding which was a high society affair.

32. No trace of this marriage has been found, but understandable if overseas. For Charles' military details, see War Office Misc/655/Records. D. Emily used her maiden name when she married George Haggard Wratton. Ada Stirling married Herbert Teare in 1896 and died in Cleveland, Ohio in 1942. Interestingly, she inherited property in Florida from Charles Stirling.

33. Information from descendant Clayton H. Zeidler, of Ohio, grandson of Ada Teare née Stirling.

34. This painting was purchased by the Yale Centre of British Art and went on tour, including Australia. See also booklet *Torosay Castle and Gardens* by Christopher James, Ellinor's great-great-grandson, who has a copy of the portrait.

35. English Probate lists, Ellen Stirling, proven June 1874.

36. The story of its restoration is told in A. E. Williams, *Western Australia: A Potted History*, p. 79.

Select Bibliography

PRIMARY SOURCES

PRIVATE LETTERS

Privately held letters in manuscript

Lenfestey Collection: This collection of Stirling letters, dating from the 1740s to the 1890s, was passed down by James Stirling's brother John's family and was in the keeping of direct descendant Margaret Lenfestey. I have used only a portion of the handwritten letters, which will be left in typescript as the Lenfestey-Stirling Letter Collection at various libraries. The whole collection of originals is now deposited in St Andrews University Library as the *Stirling of Cadder Papers* Acc ms 38526.

Leeper letters: A few fragments of manuscript letters are held by another descendant of the same line, Marion Leeper. These will be incorporated in the typescript of the Lenfestey-Stirling Collection.

Stirling letters held in Australia

Some original handwritten letters (and typescripts) are held in WA and NSW, courtesy of a donation by descendant Olive Benson in the 1930s. Most of these are also in the Lenfestey Collection and any missing will be incorporated in the typescript mentioned above.

Battye Library section of the Alexander Library, Perth, WAA Acc 351A/MN590, 449A/MN595.

Mitchell Library, Sydney, A4144.

OFFICIAL CORRESPONDENCE AT THE PUBLIC RECORD OFFICE, KEW

Admiralty files (ADM)

James Stirling's service record.

ADM107/41, ADM 193/37 f282 and ADM 196/6 f235. Service record of son F. H. Stirling, ADM 196/1 f578 & ADM 196/37.

Ships' Logs.

Log of HMS *Moselle* 1811–12 ADM51/2572.

Log of HMS *Brazen* 1812–18 ADM51/2013–4.

Complement of HMS *Brazen* 1812 ADM37/5822, piece 51879.

Log of HMS *Success* 1826–28, Captain's Log ADM51/3460 & Master's Log ADM52/4341 (AJCP Microfilm 5754).

Log of HMS *Sulphur* 1828–34 ADM51/3471.

Log of HMS *Indus* 1841–43 ADM51/3616.

Description book of HMS *Indus* ADM38/8364.
Log of HMS *Howe* 1847–1850 ADM53/2694–9.
Log of HMS *Winchester* 1854–56 ADM53/5633–5.

Journals of Admirals in command in the Mediterranean during Stirling's command of HMS Indus and HMS Howe.
Journal of the proceedings of Admiral Owen ADM 50/212 (1844).
Journal of the proceedings of Vice Admiral Sir William Parker GCB, ADM50/235 (1848).
Journal of Rear Admiral Sir J. Ommanney KCG, ADM50/205 (1841–42).
Journal of Rear Admiral Charles Napier ADM 50/251.

Stirling's Journal as C–in–C China Station 1854–56 ADM50/278.

Correspondence to and from the Admiralty.
ADM1/193 Admirals' Dispatches East Indies.
ADM1/5620–5660 China Station.
ADM1/5657–76075 Enclosure no. 27, *Currie's Diary* 1854.
ADM1/2554 Cap S—Letters to and from Stirling.

Foreign Office files (FO)
FO17/233–256 China Domestic.
FO63 Lisbon 1842–47.
FO72/202–207 West Indies, South America and the *Hercules* affair (205).
FO78 Turkey 1842.
FO195 Turkey Embassy and Smyrna Consul 1840s.
FO286 Greece 1840s.
FO566 Portugal, Sicily and Spain 1840s.

Colonial Office files (CO)
Available in Australia on Australian Joint Copying Project (AJCP) reels and some also in *Historical Records of Australia*, Series I and III, various vols.
CO18 Western Australia, original correspondence. From piece 1 (reel 292) 1828 to piece 32 (reel 432) Dec. 1842.
CO20 Sessional Papers, WA Executive and Legislative Council. From piece 1 (reel 1117) 1832 to piece 3 (reel 1118) 1841.
CO22 WA Miscellanea, Blue Books. From piece 10 (reel 1123) 1834 to piece 16 (reel 1203) 1839; see especially piece 14 (reel 1203) which contains the 1837 Report.
CO201 New South Wales Original Correspondence.
CO202 New South Wales Entry Books of Correspondence.
CO397 WA Entry books of Correspondence. From piece 1 (reel 303) to piece 13 (reel 777) 1853–54.

Treasury files (T)
Treasury T1/3426 Long Bundle—Western Australia.

OFFICIAL CORRESPONDENCE IN WESTERN AUSTRALIAN ARCHIVES

WA Colonial Secretary, Inwards Correspondence 1829–34 (includes Govt Notices in early period) WASR49.

WA Colonial Secretary, Index of letters forwarded 1829–1837 WASR 50.

Swan River Papers (transcripts of early CO correspondence) vols 1–16.

Survey Dept Records (WASR) SDUR/S1–3, SDUR/M1–3, SDO/3.

Register of Memorials, and Index to Memorials (Memorials WAS 417 = CONS 1800 and 5713).

See also:

Census of 1837, Battye Library Acc36A.

Pamphlet (no author) entitled *The Colonisation of Western Australia by Settlers from Worplesdon and Pirbright in 1829*), Battye Library Acc PR11980.

STIRLING'S MAJOR REPORTS (VARIOUS SOURCES)

1807 Rio Janeiro Report, Aug. WAA449/12.

1812 Florida Report, Captain James Stirling to Admiral Charles Stirling, 1 Nov. 1812 (University of Hull Library DDHO/7/93).

1817 South American (Revolutionaries) Report, Stirling on board the *Brazen* to Rear Admiral John Harvey, Commanding Officer of the West Indies Station, 12 Feb. 1817.

1827 Report to Admiralty on Swan River and Raffles Bay, 31 Aug. 1827, Captain James Stirling, HMS *Success*, Madras Roads, to John Wilson Croker (rec. 6 Aug. 1828), annotated CapS172, ADM 1/2556.

1827 Report on Swan River to Darling (and Colonial Office), Captain James Stirling, HMS *Success*, Sydney, to Governor Darling 18 April 1827, *HRA* III vi, p. 551ff.

1836 Report on settlement of North West Australia, J. Stirling no. 144 to Glenelg, 29 Aug. 1826, duplicate (rec. 25 April), CO18/16 f518.

1854 Report 'On the present state of Shanghai', 19 June 1854, FO17/223 f245.

1855 Memoir on the Maritime Policy of England in the Eastern Seas, J. Stirling to the Parliamentary Secretary of the Admiralty Board, Charles Wood, 15 Nov. 1855, ADM1/5660.

COLLECTIONS OF PAPERS

Arthur Papers, Mitchell Library ML A2209.

Bourke Papers, Mitchell Library ML A1926, CY980.

Clifton Papers, Letterbooks of M. W. Clifton, WA Archives A698A.

Collie Letters, WA Archives WAA332A.

Hooker Letters, vol. 1 f127, Royal Botanic Gardens, Kew, AJCP M731, frame 292.

Macleay Correspondence, Linnean Society, London, AJCP M596–7.

Miscellaneous Papers at the Hydrography Office, Taunton 1827–1834.

Moore Family Records, Alexander Library, Perth, WA Archives Acc 1075A.

Morgan Letters, Alexander Library, Perth, WA Archives Acc 1075A 147A.

Murray Papers, National Library of Scotland, MS 46.9.13 pp. 78–9.

Portsmouth Record Office, CHU26/2A/3, Bedhampton Rate Book and Church Warden's Accounts 1829–1888.

Portsmouth Record Office, Archives 115A/1/34, Deed of Sale of Belmont.

Royal Archives at Windsor, 1847 Correspondence, Vic Y2/129, RA Vic Y2/128, RA Vic Y2/131, RA Vic Y2/134.

Russell Papers, Public Record Office, Kew, PRO 30/24/4C.

Western Australia Company Board Minutes, Alexander Library, Perth, Battye Library section, WA Acc 336A/33, and WAA Acc 336A/329, Colonial Letter Book (London) 1840–1861.

UK CENSUSES (FAMILY HISTORY CENTRE, LONDON)

1841 HO107/1080 *Parish of Ash,* Henley Park; *Parish of Ash with Normandy*, Pirbright Lodge; *Parish of Stoke*, Woodbridge.

1851 HO107/1594 (1–215) *Parish of Pirbright*, Pirbright Lodge; (215–553) *Parish of Stoke*, Woodbridge House; HO107/1656 *Parish of Bedhampton*, Belmont House.

1861 RG9/657 9, Ryde.

CONTEMPORARY NEWSPAPERS & JOURNALS (SELECTED YEARS)

UK

Edinburgh Review 1802–1829.

Glasgow Herald 1815–1830.

Hampshire Telegraph 1828–30.

Imperial Review 1819+.

John Bull 1820+.

Journal of the Royal Geographic Society 1826–1830.

London Gazette 1820–1865.

Maidstone Gazette 1828–30.

Morning Chronicle 1828–30.

Morning Review 1828–30.

Portsmouth Times and Naval Gazette 1827–1860.

Quarterly Review 1829–30.

The Athenaeum 1828–1840.

The Gentleman's Magazine 1785–1865.

The Illustrated London News 1845–65.

The Mirror of Literature, Amusement and Instruction XIII (1829).

The Observer 1827–30.

The Times 1820–1865.

Australia

Australian and New Zealand Gazette & Colonial Chronicle 1845–1865.

Colonial Times 1830s.

Hobart Town Gazette 1827–1834.

Swan River Guardian 1835–1838.

Sydney Gazette 1826–1834.

The (Hobart Town) Courier 1827–1834.

The Inquirer 1840–1860.

The Monitor 1829–30.

The Perth Gazette and Western Australian Journal 1833–1865.

WA Government Gazette 1835–1850.

Others
Hong Kong Gazette.
The Overland Register.
Allen's India Mail.
South African Commercial Advertiser.

CHURCH RECORDS

Old Monklands Parish Register, Scotland. List of children of Andrew Stirling of Drumpellier
    and Anna Stirling born and baptised by Rev. John Bower. (Old Parochial Registers,
    Latter Day Saints microfilm, call no. 1066602, frame 214.)
St George's Anglican Church, Lisbon for Dorothea's baptism.
St John's, Stoke-next-Guildford, Memorial to James and Ellen Stirling.
St Mark's, Wyke, Normandy, in the Parish of Ash, for James and Mary Mangles' Memorials.
St Mary the Virgin, Pirbright, Harmondsworth, Middlesex (from microfiche) for Sir Walter
    Stirling of Faskine and Vice Admiral Charles Stirling.
St Thomas's Bedhampton, Havant for Ellinor's wedding, and Rate Book and Church Warden's
    Accounts 1829–1888 (Portsmouth Archives).

CONTEMPORARY DIRECTORIES (SELECTED YEARS)

London Directories, Guildhall, London, private and business, 1803–1875.
Navy Lists 1803–1856.
Army Lists 1820–1850.
Bourke's Peerage (1923 ed.).
Barnes Directory 1825.
Slater's Directory 1845–1894.
Slater's Directory of Lancashire 1848.

SECONDARY SOURCES

Appleyard, R. T. and Manford, T., *The Beginning: European Discovery and early settlement of
    Swan River Western Australia*, UWAP, 1979.
Armstrong, Patrick, *Charles Darwin in Western Australia*, UWAP, 1985.
Austen, T., *A Cry in the Wind: Conflict in Western Australia 1829–1929*, Darlington Publishing
    Group, Perth, 1998.
Backhouse, J., *A Visit to the Australian Colonies*, London, 1843.
Barker, A. J., *The Vainglorious War 1854–56*, Weidenfield & Nicholson, 1970.
Barker, A. J., & Laurie, M., *Excellent Connections*, City of Bunbury, 1992.
Barker, G. F., & Stenning, A. H., *The Record of Old Westminsters: A Biographical list of all those
    who are known to have been educated at Westminster School from earliest times to 1927*,
    2 vols & supplement, 1928.
Barrett-Lennard, D., *Edward Pomeroy Barrett Lennard,* 1985.
Bartlett, C. J., *Great Britain and Sea Power 1815–1853*, Clarendon Press, Oxford, 1923.
Bassett, Marnie, *The Hentys*, MUP, 1954.

Bateson, Charles, *The Convict Ships 1787–1868,* Brown & Sons, Glasgow, 1959, 2nd ed., Sydney, 1974.

Battye, J. S., *Western Australia: A History from its Discovery to the Inauguration of the Commonwealth*, Oxford, 1924, facsimile ed. UWAP, 1978.

Bavin, Louise, 'Punishment, Prisons and Reform: Incarceration in Western Australia in the Nineteenth Century', in Fox, C. (ed.), *Historical Refractions: Studies in Western Australian History*, vol. 14, 1993.

Beeching, Jack, *The Chinese Opium Wars,* Hutchinson, London.

Beeler, J., 'Fit for Service abroad: Promotion, Retirement and Royal Navy Officers 1830–1890', *The Mariners Mirror*, vol. 81, no. 3, Aug. 1995.

Berryman, Ian, *A Colony Detailed*, Creative Research, Perth, 1979.

Blackburn, Geoffrey, *Conquest and Settlement: The 21st Regiment in Western Australia 1833–1840*, Hesperian Press, Perth, 1999.

—— *The Children's Friend Society*, Access Press, Perth, 1993.

Bolton, G., & Joske, P., *History of Perth Hospital*, UWAP for Royal Perth Hospital, 1982.

Bourke, Michael, *On the Swan: A History of the Swan District Western Australia*, UWAP, 1987.

Boyce, Peter John, 'The role of the Governor in the Crown Colony of Western Australia 1829–1890', MA thesis, UWA, 1961.

Bridge, Peter (ed.), *Aboriginal Perth: Bibbulman Biographies & Legends by Daisy Bates*, Hesperian Press, Perth, 1992.

Brine, John (ed.), *Looking for Milligan*, Perth, 1991.

British Parliamentary Papers (2077) LXI, 215, correspondence respecting the late negotiation with Japan presented to both Houses of Parliament, 1856.

Broeze, Frank, 'British Intercontinental Shipping and Australia', *Journal of Transport History*, vol. IV, no. 4, Sept. 1978.

—— *Mr Brooks and the Australian Trade—Imperial Business in the Nineteenth Century,* MUP, 1993.

—— *Island Nation: A History of Australians and the Sea*, Allen & Unwin, 1998.

Broomhall, F. H., *The Veterans: A History of the Enrolled Pensioner Force in Western Australia 1850–1880*, Hesperian Press, Perth, 1985.

Bryan C., & Bray, F., 'Peter Nicholas Brown', *JRWAHS*, vol. 2, part XVIII, 1935.

Bunbury, Lt H. W., *Early Days in Western Australia*, OUP, 1930.

Burgess, M., 'The Australind Settlement' in the 1926 Report of the Meeting of the Australian Association for the Advancement of Science, vol. XVII.

Burroughs, Peter, *Britain and Australia 1831–1855*, Clarendon Press, Oxford, 1967.

Burton Jackson, J. L., *Not an Idle Man: A Biography of John Septimus Roe*, Fremantle Arts Centre Press, 1982.

—— *Frowning Fortunes The Story of Thomas Bannister and the Williams District*, Hesperian Press, Perth, 1993.

Butlin, S., *Foundations of Australia's Monetary System*, Sydney University Press, 1953.

Cameron, James M. R., 'The Foundation of Western Australia Reconsidered', *Studies in Western Australian History*, no. 3, Nov. 1978.

—— 'Sir James Stirling, The Founder', in Hunt, Lyal (ed.), *Westralian Portraits*, UWAP Sesquicentenary Series, 1979.

—— *Ambition's Fire: The Agricultural Colonization of Pre-convict Western Australia*, UWAP, 1981.

—— 'Traders, government officials and the occupation of Melville Island', *Great Circle,* vol. 7 (2), 1985.

—— 'The Northern Settlements: Outposts of Empire', in Statham (ed.), *Origins of Australia's Capital Cities,* CUP, 1989.

—— 'Bushmanship: The explorers' silent partner', *Australian Geographer,* vol. 30, no 3, 1999.

—— 'George Fletcher Moore', *Studies in Western Australian History,* vol. 20, 2000, pp. 21–34.

Canning, George, 1770–1827, *Corrected report of the speech of the right Honourable George Canning in the House of Commons, 25th April, 1822,* Hatchard & Son, London, 1822.

Carleton, J. D., *Westminster School: a History,* Hart-Davis, London, 1965.

Chamberlain, M. E., *Pax Britannica: British Foreign Policy 1789–1914,* Longmans Studies in Modern History Series.

Chapman, Barbara, *The Colonial Eye,* Art Gallery of Western Australia, 1979.

Clark, C. M. H., *A History of Australia,* MUP, 1968.

Clark, Jane (ed.), *Exploration and Transformation,* Heytesbury Pty Ltd, 2000.

Clark, Lyn, *Stoke next Guildford,* Phillimore, West Sussex, 1999.

Cohan, B. C., *A History of Medicine in Western Australia,* Paterson Brokensha, Perth, 1965.

Colledge, J., *Ships of the Royal Navy: A complete Record of all fighting ships of the Royal Navy from the 15th century to the present,* Naval Institute Press, n.d.

Contos, Natalie, & Kearing, Theo, *Pinjarra Massacre Site Research and Development Project,* Murray Districts Aboriginal Association, 1998.

Cornell, C. (trans.), *The Journal of Post Captain Nicolas Baudin,* Adelaide, 1974.

Cortazzi, Hugh, *Victorians in Japan: In and around the Treaty Ports,* The Athalone Press, London, 1987.

Costin, W., *Great Britain and China 1833–1860,* Clarendon Press, Oxford, 1937.

Cottesloe, C. B., *Diary and Letters of Admiral Sir C. H. Fremantle Relating to the Founding of the Colony of Western Australia,* Fremantle Arts Centre Press, 1979.

Cowan, P., *A Faithful Picture: the letters of Eliza and Thomas Brown at York in the Swan River Colony 1841–1852,* Fremantle Arts Centre Press, 1977.

Cross, J., *Journals of Several Expeditions made in Western Australia during the years 1829–1832,* London, 1833.

Crowley, F., 'Master and Servant in WA 1829–1851', *JRWAHS,* vol. IV, part V, Perth, 1953.

—— *Australia's Western Third,* Macmillan, 1960.

Cullity, Thomas Brendon, *Vasse: An Account of the Disappearance of Thomas Timothee Vasse,* Dept of Lands Administration, Perth, 1992.

'Cygnet', Bryan, C., *Swan River Booklets,* especially no. 4, 'The Birth of Perth', Paterson Brokensha, Perth, 1935.

Dakin, Douglas, *The Unification of Greece 1770–1923,* Ernest Benn Ltd, London, 1972.

Danvers, F. C., *Memorials of Old Haileybury College,* London, 1894.

Devenish, Bruce, *Man of Energy and Compassion—The Life, Letters and Times of Henry Trigg, Swan River Pioneer and Church Founder,* Wongaburra, Perth, 1996.

Diary of Anne Whatley, WAA 326A & *JRWAHS,* vol. VIII & new series vol. 6, Feb. 1945.

Diary of Mary Ann Friend, JRWAHS, vol. IX, 1931.

Drummond, Peter, *Drumpellier Golf Course 1894–1994,* printed privately in Glasgow, 1994.

Eitel, R. E. J., *Europe in China: The History of Hong Kong,* Luzac & Co., London, 1895.

Endacott, G. B., *A History of Hong Kong,* London University Press, 1958.

Erickson, Rica, *The Drummonds of Hawthornden,* Lamb Paterson, Perth, 1969.

—— *Old Toodyay and Newcastle,* Toodyay Shire Council, 1974.

—— *The Dempsters*, UWAP, 1978.

Ewers, J. K., *The Western Gateway: A History of Fremantle* (rev. ed.), UWAP, 1971.

Fall, V. G., *The Sea and the Forest A History of the Port of Rockingham Western Australia*, UWAP, 1972.

Field, John, *The King's Nurseries: The story of Westminster School*, James & James, London, 1987.

Fletcher, Brian H., *Ralph Darling A Governor Maligned*, OUP, Melbourne, 1984.

—— *Colonial Australia Before 1850*, Nelson, Melbourne, 1976.

Fox, C. (ed.), *Historical Refractions: Studies in Western Australian History*, vol. 14, 1993.

Fox, Grace, *British Admirals and Chinese Pirates 1832–1869*, Kegan Paul, London, 1940.

Garden, Donald, *Albany: A Panorama of the Sound*, Nelson, 1977.

Glasgow Past and Present, 2 vols, Glasgow, 1884.

Graham, G. S., & Humphries, R. A., *The Navy and South America*, Spottiswood Ballantyne for the Navy Records Society, 1962.

Graham, Gerald, *Great Britain and the Indian Ocean*, OUP, 1967.

—— *The China Station—War and Diplomacy 1830–1860*, Clarendon Press, Oxford, 1978.

Grainger, J. D., 'The Navy in the River Plate 1806–8', *The Mariners Mirror*, vol. 81, no. 3, Aug. 1995.

Green, Neville, 'Aborigines and white settlers in the 19th Century', Chap. 3 in Stannage, C. T., *A New History of Western Australia*, UWAP, 1981.

—— *Broken Spears: Aboriginals and Europeans in the Southwest of Australia*, Focus Education, Perth, 1984.

Grey, George, *Expeditions in Western Australia 1837–1839*, 2 vols, facsimile of 1841 ed., Hesperian Press, Perth, 1983.

Hainsworth, D. R., *The Sydney Traders*, Cassell Australia, 1971.

Hallam, Sylvia, *Fire and Hearth*, Australian Institute of Aboriginal Studies, Canberra, 1975.

—— 'Population and resource usage on the Western Littoral', ANZAAS 1977 Section 25 A, vol. 2.

Hallam, Sylvia, & Tilbrook, Louis, *Aborigines of the South-West Region*, vol. VIII, *Dictionary of Western Australians*, UWAP, 1990.

Hartley, R. G., *Industry and Infrastructure in Western Australia 1829–1940*, Heritage Council of WA, 1995.

Hasluck, Alexandra, *Thomas Peel of Swan River*, OUP, 1965.

—— *Portrait with Background*, OUP, 1955, reprinted by Fremantle Arts Centre Press, 1990.

Hasluck, P. M., 'Early Mills of Perth', *JRWAHS*, vol. 1, part VIII, 1930.

—— *Black Australians: A Survey of Native Policy in Western Australia 1829–1897*, MUP, 1942.

Hawtry, C. L. M., *The Availing Struggle*, The Anglican Book Depot & Paterson Press, 1946.

Heal, Lilian, *Jane Dodds 1788–1844: A Swan River Pioneer*, Sydney, 1988.

Hurd, Douglas, *The Arrow War—an Anglo-Chinese Confusion 1856–1860*, Collins, London, 1967.

Hutchinson, Elizabeth, *The Butler Family*, 1996.

Hutton, Guthrie, *Monkland—The Canal that Made Money*, Lanarkshire Heritage Series, UK, 1993.

Irwin, F. C., *The State & Position of Western Australia*, London, 1835.

Johnson, Ruth, *W. L. Brockman—A Portrait*, Darelle Publications, Perth, 1982.

—— *The Tranby Hardys*, Parmelia Publishing Co., Perth, 1988.

Jones, W. Devereu, *Prosperity Robinson; the life of Viscount Goderich 1782–1859*.

Joske, P., Jeffrey, C., & Hoffman, L., *Rottnest Island: A Documentary History*, UWA, 1995.

Lambert, A. M., *The Making of the Dutch Landscape*, London, 1885.

Lee, J. L., *The Journals of Edward Stirling in Persia and Afghanistan 1828–29*, published Naples, 1991 assisted by the British Institute of Persian Studies and the Instituto Universitario Orientale, Naples.

Lee, Jonathon, 'Edward Stirling of Stirling Castle', in *Societe Jersiaise Annual Bulletin*, 1991.

Lensen, G. A., *The Russian Push toward Japan*, Princeton University Press, 1959.

Levi, J. S., & Bergman, G. F., *Australian Genesis: Jewish Convicts and Settlers 1788–1850*, Rigby, 1974.

Madriarga, Salvador de, *Bolivar*, Hollis & Carter, London, 1952.

Mangles, Ross Patrick & Robert Miller, *The Mangles Story*, unpublished m/s Guildford Muniment Room P249–12189, now in the Surrey Record Office, Woking.

Manning, T. D., & Walker, C. F., *British Warship Names,* Putman, 1959.

Marchant, Leslie, *France Australe,* Artlook Books, Perth, 1982.

Marshall, John, *Royal Naval Biography*, 2 vols, London, 1823.

McInnes, Robin, *The Garden Isle: Landscape paintings of the Isle of Wight 1790–1920*, Crossprint, Newport, Isle of Wight, 1990.

McNair, W., & Rumley, H., *Pioneer Aboriginal Mission The work of Wesleyan Missionary John Smithies in the Swan River Colony 1840–1855,* UWAP, 1981.

Merk Manual of Diagnosis and Therapy, Merk Research Lab., Rahway, New Jersey, 1992.

Mills, R. C., *The Colonization of Australia,* Dawsons of Pall Mall, 1968.

Minute Book of the Green Cloth 1809–1820, privately printed Glasgow, MDCCCXCI.

Mitchell, J. O., *Old Glasgow Essays*, Maclehose, publisher to the University of Glasgow, 1905.

Moore, G. F., *Diary of Ten Years of an Early Settler in Western Australia*, facsimile ed., UWAP, 1978.

Moore Smith, G. C. (ed.), *Autobiography* of Lt Gen. Sir Harry Smith, 2 vols, London, 1902.

Morriss, Roger, *Cockburn and the British Navy in Transition*, University of South Carolina Press, 1997.

Nicholson, I. H., *Shipping Arrivals and Departures Sydney 1826–1840*, Roebuck Books, Sydney, 1963.

Official and descriptive Catalogue of the Great Exhibition of the works and industry of all the Nations, copy, National Library of Australia.

Ogle, Nathanial, *The Colony of Western Australia—A Manual for Emigrants,* London, 1839 and facsimile, Ferguson, Sydney, 1977.

Old Country Houses of the Old Glasgow Gentry, Glasgow, 1878.

Palmer, A. (ed.), *Milestones of History*, vol. 8, 'Age of Optimism', Weidenfeld & Nicholson, New York, 1974.

Parry, Ann, *The Admirals Fremantle 1788–1920*, Chatto & Windus, London, 1971.

Pashley, A. R. (Don), *Policing Our State 1829–1945*, Optima Press, Perth, 2000.

Peden, Allan, *The Monklands—an Illustrated Architectural Guide*, Pillans & Wilson, Edinburgh, 1992.

Pemberton, P. A., 'The London Connection: The formation and early years of the Australian Agricultural Company 1824–1834', Ph.D. thesis, ANU, 1992.

Pike, Douglas (ed.), *Australian Dictionary of Biography 1788–1850*, 2 vols, MUP, 1967.

Pile, John, 'A Brief History of Belmont Park and its People', m/s, Havant Museum, 1998.

Preble's Diary—see Szczesniak.

Prinsep, C., *Record of Services of the Honourable East India Company's Civil Servant*, London, 1885.

Read, Jan, *The New Conquistador,* Evans Bros, London, 1980.

Reece, R., & Pascoe, R., *A Place of Consequence: A Pictorial History of Fremantle*, Fremantle Arts Centre Press, 1983.

Reynolds, Henry, *This Whispering in our Hearts*, Allen & Unwin, 1998.

Richards, Ronald, *The Murray District of Western Australia—A History*, Shire of Murray, Perth, 1978.

Riviere, M. S., *The Governor's Noble Guest: Hyacinthe de Bougainville's account of Port Jackson 1825*, MUP, 1999.

Rogers, P. N., *The Borough of Havant in Old Picture Postcards*, European Library, 1985.

Rosenman, H. (ed.), *An account of two voyages to the South Seas by Capt. Jules Dumont D'Urville,* University of Hawaii Press, 1987.

Roxburgh, R., 'Thomas Potter Macqueen of Segenhoe, NSW', *JRAHS*, 58 (2), 1972.

Russell, E. M., 'Early Lawyers of Western Australia', *JRWAHS*, vol. IV, part 3, 1951.

Russo, George, *A Friend Indeed—Louisa Clifton of Australind WA*, Vanguard Press, Perth, 1995.

Schooling, W., *The Hudson's Bay Company 1670–1920*, London, 1920.

Shann, E., *Cattle Chosen*, 1926, facsimile ed., UWAP, 1978.

Shaw, A. G. L., *Sir George Arthur 1784–1854,* MUP, 1980.

—— 'The Founding of Melbourne', Chap. X in Statham, *Origins of Australia's Capital Cities*, CUP, 1989.

Snelling & Barron, 'The Colonial Office and its permanent officials 1801–1914', in Sutherland, G. (ed.), *Studies in the Growth of Nineteenth Century Government,* 1972.

Stannage, C. T., *The People of Perth,* Perth City Council, 1979.

—— (ed.), *A New History of Western Australia*, UWAP, 1981.

—— (ed.), *Convictism in Western Australia: Studies in Western Australian History*, vol. IV, 1981.

Staples, A. C., 'The Harvey', Historical Studies of Australia and New Zealand, vol. 4, no. 16, May 1951.

—— *They made their Destiny*, Shire of Harvey, 1979.

—— 'Spanish Colonial Influence on Sir James Stirling', *Early Days,* vol. 10, part 6, 1994.

Statham, P., 'The Economic Development of Swan River Colony 1829–1850', Ph.D. thesis, UWA, 1980.

—— 'Why Convicts?', in Stannage, C. T., *Convictism in Western Australia: Studies in Western Australian History,* vol. IV, 1981.

—— (comp.), *Dictionary of Western Australians 1829–1850*, vol. 1, UWAP, 1981.

—— *The Tanner Letters: A Pioneer Saga of Swan River and Tasmania 1831–45*, UWAP, 1981.

—— 'Origins and Achievements: Convicts and the Western Australian Economy', *Westerly*, vol. 30, no. 3, Sept. 1985.

—— 'Peter Augustus Latour Absentee Investor Extraordinaire', *JRAHS*, vol. 72, part 3, Dec. 1986.

—— (ed.), *The Origins of Australia's Capital Cities*, CUP, 1989.

Statham, P., & Erickson, R., *A life on the Ocean Wave: Voyages to Australia, India and the Pacific from the Journals of Captain George Bayly*, Miegunyah Press/MUP, 1998.

Stephen, L., & Lee, S., *The Dictionary of National Biography from earliest times to 1900*, OUP, 1917.

Stevenson, John, '1851 Queen Victoria's Crystal Palace', in Palmer, A. (ed.), *Milestones of History,* vol. 8, 'Age of Optimism', Weidenfeld & Nicholson, New York, 1974.

Stirling, A., *Gang Forward: A Stirling Notebook*, Hawthorn Press, Melbourne, 1972.

Stirling, Stuart, 'Admiral Sir James Stirling: The Chronicle of a Naval Career', Monograph, Battye Library AcQB/STI.

Stirling, T. W., *The Stirlings of Cadder: An account of the Original Family of that Name and of The Family of the STIRLINGS OF DRUMPELLIER With which the Representation Of the Ancient House of Cadder now lies*, St Andrews University Press, 1933.

Stokes, J. L., *Discoveries in Australia…during the voyage of HMS Beagle 1837–43,* London, 1846.

Storman, E. J., *The Salvado Memoirs*, UWAP, 1977.

Sutherland, G. (ed.), *Studies in the Growth of Nineteenth Century Government*, 1972.

Szczesniak, B. (ed.), *The Opening of Japan: A Diary of Discovery in the Far East 1853–1856 by Rear Admiral George Henry Preble U.S.N.*, University of Oklahoma Press, 1962.

Taylor, Sandra, 'Who were the Convicts?', in Stannage, C. T., *Convictism in Western Australia: Studies in Western Australian History*, vol. IV, 1981.

Thomas, J. E., & Stewart, A., *Imprisonment in Western Australia Evolution, Theory and Practice*, UWAP, 1978.

Thomson, G., *The Monkland Canal: A sketch of the Early History*, Monklands Library Services, c. 1945.

Tilbrook, Louis, *Nyungar Tradition: Glimpses of Aborigines of South-Western Australia 1829–1914*, UWAP, 1983.

Turner, T., *Turners of Augusta*, Paterson Brokensha, Perth, 1956.

Uren, Malcolm, *Land Looking West The Story of Governor James Stirling in Western Australia*, OUP, 1948.

Wakefield, E. G., *England and America: A Comparison of the Social and Political State of both Nations*, Richard Bentley, London, 1833.

Ward, A. W., & Gooch, G. P., *The Cambridge History of Foreign Policy 1783–1919*, CUP, 1923.

West, D. A. P., *The Settlement on the Sound: Discovery and Settlement of the Albany Region 1791–1831*, WA Museum, 1996 reprint of 1976 ed.

White's *Dictionary of Hampshire and the Isle of Wight*, Hampshire County Council, 1859.

Whitely, E. S., 'The Military Establishment in Western Australia 1829–1863', unpublished M/S, Battye Library, Perth Q355–009.

Whitely, E. S. & C. G. S., 'A Short History of the British Regiments in Western Australia 1826–1863', *Sabrateche: Journal of Military History*, Jan. 1961.

Whitfeld, L. A., *Founders of Law in Australia,* Butterworths, 1971.

Williams, A. E., *Western Australia a Potted History,* Perth, 1979.

Williams, H. Noel, *The life and letters of Admiral Sir Charles Napier*, London, 1917.

Wilson, T. B., *Voyage round the World,* London, 1835, Dawsons Pall Mall, reprint, 1968.

Wood, W. A., *Dawn in the Valley: A Story of Settlement in the Hunter Valley to 1833*, 1972.

Index

Illustrative material is indicated with **bold** page numbers. A number prefixed with **C** indicates a colour plate that follows the page number shown.